Lecture Notes in Artificial Intelligence   6098

Edited by R. Goebel, J. Siekmann, and W. Wahlster

Subseries of Lecture Notes in Computer Science

Nicolás García-Pedrajas
Francisco Herrera   Colin Fyfe
José Manuel Benítez   Moonis Ali (Eds.)

Trends in Applied Intelligent Systems

23rd International Conference
on Industrial Engineering and Other Applications
of Applied Intelligent Systems, IEA/AIE 2010
Cordoba, Spain, June 1-4, 2010
Proceedings, Part III

 Springer

Series Editors

Randy Goebel, University of Alberta, Edmonton, Canada
Jörg Siekmann, University of Saarland, Saarbrücken, Germany
Wolfgang Wahlster, DFKI and University of Saarland, Saarbrücken, Germany

Volume Editors

Nicolás García-Pedrajas
University of Cordoba, Dept. of Computing and Numerical Analysis
Campus Universitario de Rabanales, Einstein Building, 14071 Cordoba, Spain
E-mail: npedrajas@uco.es

Francisco Herrera
José Manuel Benítez
University of Granada, Dept. of Computer Science and Artificial Intelligence
ETS de Ingenierias Informática y de Telecomunicación, 18071 Granada, Spain
E-mail: {herrera,j.m.benitez}@decsai.ugr.es

Colin Fyfe
University of the West of Scotland, School of Computing
Paisley, PA1 2BE, UK
E-mail: colin.fyfe@uws.ac.uk

Moonis Ali
Texas State University-San Marcos, Department of Computer Science
601 University Drive, San Marcos, TX 78666-4616, USA
E-mail: ma04@txstate.edu

Library of Congress Control Number: 2010926289

CR Subject Classification (1998): I.2, H.3, F.1, H.4, I.4, I.5

LNCS Sublibrary: SL 7 – Artificial Intelligence

ISSN   0302-9743
ISBN-10   3-642-13032-1 Springer Berlin Heidelberg New York
ISBN-13   978-3-642-13032-8 Springer Berlin Heidelberg New York

springer.com

© Springer-Verlag Berlin Heidelberg 2010

Typesetting: Camera-ready by author, data conversion by Scientific Publishing Services, Chennai, India
Printed on acid-free paper   06/3180

Preface

The need for intelligent systems technology in solving real-life problems has been consistently growing. In order to address this need, researchers in the field have been developing methodologies and tools to develop intelligent systems for solving complex problems. The International Society of Applied Intelligence (ISAI) through its annual IEA/AIE conferences provides a forum for international scientific and industrial community in the field of Applied Artificial Intelligence to interactively participate in developing intelligent systems, which are needed to solve twenty first century's ever growing problems in almost every field.

The 23rd International Conference on Industrial, Engineering and Other Applications of Applied Intelligence Systems (IEA/AIE-2010) held in Córdoba, Spain, followed IEA/AIE tradition of providing an international scientific forum for researchers in the field of applied artificial intelligence. The presentations of the invited speakers and authors mainly focused on developing and studying new methods to cope with the problems posed by real-life applications of artificial intelligence. Papers presented in the twenty third conference in the series covered theories as well as applications of intelligent systems in solving complex real-life problems.

We received 297 papers for the main track, selecting 119 of them with the highest quality standards. Each paper was revised by at least three members of the Program Committee. The papers in the proceedings cover a wide number of topics including: applications to robotics, business and financial markets, bioinformatics and biomedicine, applications of agent-based systems, computer vision, control, simulation and modeling, data mining, decision support systems, evolutionary computation and its applications, fuzzy systems and their applications, heuristic optimization methods and swarm intelligence, intelligent agent-based systems, internet applications, knowledge management and knowledge based systems, machine learning, neural network applications, optimization and heuristic search, and other real-life applications.

The main track was complemented with 13 special sessions whose topics included soft computing in information access systems on the web, data preprocessing in data mining, engineering knowledge and semantic systems, applied intelligent systems for future classrooms, soft computing methods for environmental and industrial applications, soft computing in computer vision and image processing, distributed problem solving with artificial intelligence techniques, ensemble learning, interactive and cognitive environments, context information in intelligent systems, data analysis, optimization and visualization for bioinformatics and neuroscience, industrial applications of data mining and semantic and linguistic visual information.

Together, these papers highlight new trends and frontiers of applied artificial intelligence and show how new research could lead to new and innovative applications. They also show that new trends are appearing to cope with the increasingly difficult new challenges that are faced by artificial intelligence. We hope you will find them interesting and useful for your own research.

The conference also invited five outstanding scholars to give plenary keynotes speeches. They were Nitesh Chawla, from the University of Notre Dame, USA, Óscar Cordón from the European Center for Soft Computing, Spain, Ludmila Kuncheva, from the University of Bangor, UK, José Luis Verdegay, from the University of Granada, Spain, and Pierre Rouzè, from Ghent University, Belgium.

We would like to express our thanks to the members of the Program Committee and all the reviewers of the special sessions for their hard work. This work is central to the success of any conference.

The conference was organized by the Research Group on Computational Intelligence and Bioinformatics of the University of Córdoba jointly with the Soft Computing and Intelligent Information Systems Research Group of the University of Granada in cooperation with the International Society of Applied Intelligence (ISAI).

We would like to thank all members of the organization for their unselfish efforts to make the conference a success. We also would like to thank the University of Córdoba and its Polytechnic School for their support. We would like to thank Springer for their help in publishing the proceedings. We would like to thank our main sponsors, ISAI, as well as our other sponsors: Association for the Advancement of Artificial Intelligence (AAAI), Association for Computing Machinery (ACM/SIGART), Canadian Artificial Intelligence Association (CA-IAC), European Neural Network Society (ENNS), International Neural Network Society (INNS), Japanese Society for Artificial Intelligence (JSAI), Taiwanese Association for Artificial Intelligence (TAAI), Taiwanese Association for Consumer Electronics (TACE), and Texas State University-San Marcos.

We would like to thank the invited speakers for their interesting and informative talks of a world-class standard. We cordially thank all authors for their valuable contributions as well as the other participants in this conference. The conference would not have been possible without their support.

Thanks are also due to the many experts who contributed to making the event a success.

March 2009

Nicolás García-Pedrajas
Francisco Herrera
Colin Fyfe
José Manuel Benítez
Moonis Ali

Conference Organization

General Chair

Moonis Ali

Texas State University, San Marcos, Texas, USA

Program Chairs

Colin Fyfe

University of the West of Scotland, UK

Nicolás García-Pedrajas

University of Córdoba, Spain

Francisco Herrera

University of Granada, Spain

Local Organizing Chair

César García-Osorio

University of Burgos, Spain

Special Session Chairs

José Manuel Benítez

University of Granada, Spain

Evelio González-González

University of La Laguna, Spain

Publicity Chair

Rafael Alcalá

University of Granada, Spain

Organizing Committee

Cecilio Angulo-Bahón	Technical University of Catalonia
Bonifacio Castaño-Martin	University of Alcalá
Antonio Fernández-Caballero	University of Castilla-La Mancha
Rafael del Castillo-Gomariz	University of Córdoba
Gonzalo Cerruela-García	University of Córdoba
Salvador García	University of Jaén
César García-Osorio	University of Burgos, Spain
Aida de Haro-García	University of Córdoba
Domingo Ortiz-Boyer	University of Córdoba
Jesús Maudes-Raedo	University of Burgos
Carlos Pardo-Aguilar	University of Burgos
Javier Pérez-Rodríguez	University of Córdoba
Juan Antonio Romero del Castillo	University of Córdoba
Miguel Ángel Salido	Technical University of Valencia

Special Sessions

1. Soft Computing in Information Access Systems on the Web
   Enrique Herrera-Viedma, Antonio G. López-Herrera, Eduardo Peis and
   Carlos Porcel
2. Data Preprocessing in Data Mining
   Jose A. Gámez and José M. Puerta
3. Engineering Knowledge and Semantic Systems (IWEKSS)
   Jason J. Jung and Dariusz Król
4. Applied Intelligent Systems for Future Classroom
   Jia-Ling Koh
5. Soft-Computing Methods for Environmental and Industrial Applications
   Juan M. Corchado, Emilio S. Corchado and Dante I. Tapia
6. Soft Computing in Computer Vision/Image Processing
   Edurne Barrenechea, Humberto Bustince, Pedro Couto and
   Pedro Melo-Pinto
7. Distributed Problem Solving with Artificial Intelligence Techniques
   Miguel Á. Salido and Adriana Giret
8. Ensemble Learning: Methods and Applications
   Juan J. Rodríguez and César García-Osorio
9. Interactive and Cognitive Environments
   Cecilio Angulo and Juan Antonio-Ortega
10. Context Information in Intelligent Systems
    José Manuel Molina López and Miguel Ángel Patricio
11. New Frontiers in Data Analysis, Optimization and Visualization for
    Bioinfomatics and Neuroscience
    Fazel Famili, José M. Peña, Víctor Robles and Ángel Merchán
12. Industrial Applications of Data Mining: New Paradigms for New Challenges
    Cèsar Ferri Ramírez, José Hernández Orallo and María José Ramírez
    Quintana
13. Semantic and Linguistic Visual Information: Applications
    Jesús Chamorro-Martínez and Daniel Sánchez

Invited Speakers

Nitesh Chawla	University of Notre Dame, USA
Óscar Cordón	European Center for Soft Computing, Spain
Ludmila Kuncheva	University of Bangor, UK
José Luis Verdegay	University of Granada, Spain
Pierre Rouzè	Ghent University, Belgium

Program Committee

Acosta Sánchez, L., Spain
Aguilar, J., Spain
Ajith, A., Norway
Alba, E., Spain
Bae, Y., South Korea
Bahamonde, A., Spain
Becerra-Alonso, D., Spain
Barbakh, W., Palestine
Belli, F., Germany
Bello, R., Cuba
Benavides Cuéllar, C., Spain
Bernadó-Mansilla, E., Spain
Borzemski, L., Poland
Bosse, T., The Netherlands
Brézillon, P., France
Bugarín, A. J., Spain
Bull, L., UK
Bustince, H., Spain
Caballero, Y., Cuba
Carse, B., UK
Carvalho, J. P. B., Portugal
Casillas, J., Spain
Castillo, Ò., Mexico
Chan, C. W., Hong Kong
Chan, Ch.-Ch., USA
Chang, Ch.-I., USA
Charles, D., UK
Chen, Sh.-M., Taiwan
Chien, B.-Ch., Taiwan
Chou, J.-H., Taiwan
Chung, P. W. H., UK
Coelho, A. L. V., Brazil
Corchado, E., Spain
Corchado, J. M., Spain
Cordón, Ó., Spain
Cornelis, C., Belgium
Cotta, C., Spain
Da Costa, J. M., Portugal
Dapoigny, R., France
De Baets, B., Belgium
De Carvalho, A., Brazil
De Melo, P. J., Portugal
Del Jesús, M. J., Spain

Dreyfus, G., France
Esposito, F., Italy
Fatima, S., UK
Fernández, F., Spain
Ferri, F., Spain
Ferri, C., Spain
Gámez, J. A., Spain
García, S., Spain
Giráldez, R., Spain
Girolami, M., UK
Gomide, F., Brazil
Guesgen, H. W., New Zealand
Gutiérrez, P. A., Spain
Hagras, H., UK
Hendtlass, T., Australia
Herrera-Viedma, E., Spain
Hirota, K., Japan
Hong, T.-P., Taiwan
Hoogendoorn, M., The Netherlands
Huang, Y.-P., Taiwan
Hüllermeier, E., Germany
Hung, Ch.-Ch., USA
Hwang, G.-J., Taiwan
Ishibuchi, H., Japan
Ito, T., Japan
Jacquenet, F., France
Kinoshita, T., Japan
Klawonn, F., Germany
Kumar, A. N., USA
Kumova, B. Í., Turkey
Larrañaga, P., Spain
Lee, Sh.-J., Taiwan
Lin, T. Y., USA
Llanes, O., Cuba
Loia, V., Italy
López Ibáñez, B., Spain
Lozano, J. A., Spain
Lozano, M., Spain
Ludermir, T. B., Brazil
Madani, K., France
Mahanti, P., Canada
Mansour, N., Lebanon
Marcelloni, F., Italy

Marichal Plasencia, N., Spain
Martínez, L., Spain
Matthews, M. M., USA
Mehrotra, K. G., USA
Meléndez, J., Spain
Mizoguchi, R., Japan
Molina, J. M., Spain
Monostori, L., Hungary
Murphey, Y. L., USA
Nedjah, N., Brazil
Nguyen, N. T., Poland
Ohsawa, Y., Japan
Okuno, H. G, Japan
Olivas, J. Á., Spain
Pan, J.-Sh., Taiwan
Pedrycz, W., Canada
Pelta, D., Spain
Peña, J. M., Spain
Peregrín, A., Spain
Pereira de Souto, M. C., Brazil
Prade, H., France
R-Moreno, M. D., Spain
Raj Mohan, M., India
Ramaswamy, S., USA
Rayward-Smith, V. J., UK
Rivera, A. J., Spain
Rodríguez, J. J., Spain
Rojas, I., Spain
Romero Zaliz, R., Spain

Sadok, D. F. H., Brazil
Sainz-Palmero, G., Spain
Sánchez, D., Spain
Sánchez-Marré, M., Spain
Schetinin, V., UK
Selim, H., Turkey
Shpitalni, M., Israel
Soomro, S., Austria
Stützle, T., Germany
Sun, J., UK
Suzuki, K., Japan
Tamir, D., USA
Tan, A.-H., Singapore
Tereshko, V., UK
Thulasiram, R. K., Canada
Tseng, L.-Y., Taiwan
Tseng, V. SH.-M., Taiwan
Valente de Oliveira, J., Portugal
Valtorta, M., USA
Vancza, J., Hungary
Viharos, Z. J., Hungary
Wang, L., Singapore
Yang, Ch., Canada
Yang, D.-L., Taiwan
Yang, Y., China
Yin, H., UK
Zhang, Q., UK

Special Session Reviewers

Adeodato, P.
Alonso, C.
Alonso, J.
Alonso, R.S.
Alonso, S.
Álvarez, L.
Anguita, D.
Aranda-Corral, G. A.
Argente, E.
Arroyo Castillo, Á.
Bajo, J.
Barber, F.
Baruque, B.

Berlanga, A.
Bermejo, P.
Bielza, C.
Boström, H.
Bustamante, A.
Cabestany, J.
Cabrerizo, F.
Cao, L.
Carrasco, R.
Carrascosa, C.
Casacuberta, F.
Castanedo, F.
Catala, A.

Cavallaro, A.
Chang, C.
Chen, B.
Chen, L.
Chiang, C.
Cilla, R.
Corral, G.
Costa, J. A.
Damas, S.
De Bra, P.
De la Cal, E.
De la Ossa, L.
De Paz, J. F.

Del Valle, C.
Dorronsoro, J.
Duro, R.
Escalera, S.
Escot, D.
Esteva, M.
Euzenat, J.
Fang, C.
Fauteux, F.
Fernández Caballero, A.
Fernández-Luna, J.
Fernández-Olivares, J.
Fernández, J.
Flach, P.
Flores, J.
Frías-Martínez, E.
García Varea, I.
García, J.
Gasca, R.
Godoy, D.
Gómez-Verdejo, V.
Gómez-Vilda, P.
González-Abril, L.
González, S.
Graña, M.
Guadarrama, S.
Guerra, L.
Han, Y.
Herrero, A.
Herrero, P.
Hou, W.
Iñesta, J. M.
Jatowt, A.
Julián, V.
Jurado, A.
Kang, S.

Kokol, P.
Ku, W.
Kuncheva, L.
Lachice, N.
Latorre, A.
Lorkiewicz, W.
Luis, Á.
Malutan, R.
Martín-Bautista, J.
Martínez, A.
Martínez-Madrid, N.
Mateo, J.
Medina, J.
Menasalvas, E.
Micó, L.
Montes, J.
Morales, J.
Morente, F.
Muelas, S.
Nebot, A.
Olivares, J.
Peis, E.
Petrakieva, L.
Phan, S.
Porcel, C.
Poyatos, D.
Prados Suárez, B.
Pujol, O.
Rauterberg, M.
Regazzoni, C.
Ribeiro, B.
Rinner, B.
Rodríguez Aguilar, J.
Rodríguez, A.
Rodríguez, L.
Rodríguez, S.

Romero, F. P.
Ruíz, R.
Rumí, R.
Salmerón, A.
Sánchez, J.
Santana, R.
Schmid, U.
Sedano, J.
Seepold, R.
Serrano-Guerrero, J.
Sevillano, X.
Shan, M.
Simic, D.
Soares, C.
Soto Hidalgo, J.
Stiglic, G.
Stoermer, H.
Tapia, E.
Tchagang, A.
Tortorella, F.
Valentini, G.
Van den Poel, D.
Varela, R.
Vela, C.
Velasco, F.
Vellido, A.
Ventura, S.
Victor, P.
Villar, J.
Wozniak, M.
Zafra, A.
Zhang, Ch.
Zhang, M.-L.

Additional Reviewers

Al-Shukri, S.
Appice, A.
Aziz, A.
Barrenechea, E.
Carmona-Poyato, Á.
Ceci, M.

Chamorro-Martínez, J.
Chen, N.
Chen, W.
Coheur, L.
Couto, P.
D'Amato, C.

Di Mauro, N.
Fanizzi, N.
Fernández, A.
Galar, M.
García, Ó.
Gaspar-Cunha, A.

Table of Contents – Part III

Neural Network Applications

New Frontiers in Data Analysis, Optimization and Visualization for Bioinfomatics and Neuroscience

Optimization and Heuristic Search

Real Life Applications

Semantic and Linguistic Visual Information: Applications

Soft Computing in Computer Vision/Image Processing

Soft Computing in Information Access Systems on the Web

Soft Computing Methods for Environmental and Industrial Applications

Generalized Logistic Regression Models Using Neural Network Basis Functions Applied to the Detection of Banking Crises

P.A. Gutierrez[1], S. Salcedo-Sanz[2], M.J. Segovia-Vargas[3], A. Sanchis[4],
J.A. Portilla-Figueras[2], F. Fernández-Navarro[1], and C. Hervás-Martínez[1]

[1] Universidad de Córdoba, Córdoba, Spain
pagutierrez@uco.es
[2] Universidad Complutense de Madrid, Madrid, Spain
sancho.salcedo@uah.es
[3] Universidad de Alcalá, Alcalá de Henares, Madrid, Spain
[4] Bank of Spain, Madrid, Spain

Abstract. The financial system plays a crucial role in economic development. Financial crises are recurrent phenomena in modern financial systems. The literature offers several definitions of financial instability, but it is well known that a financial crisis with a banking crisis is the most common example of financial instability. In this paper we introduce a novel model for detection and prediction of crises, based on the hybridization of a standard logistic regression with Product Unit (PU) neural networks and Radial Basis Function (RBF) networks. These hybrid approaches are described in the paper, and applied to the detection and prediction of banking crises by using a large database of countries in the period 1981 to 1999. The proposed techniques are shown to perform better than other existing statistical and artificial intelligence methods for this problem.

1 Introduction

The recent financial collapse has stressed the crucial role of the financial system to guarantee economic development. The financial system is the responsible for the allocation of resources over time and among different alternatives of investment, by pricing the postposition of consumption (free risk rate) and pricing the risk (risk premium). In the last twenty years at least ten countries have experienced the simultaneous onset of banking and currency crisis, with contractions in Gross Domestic Product of between 5% and 12% in the first year of the crisis, and negative or only slightly positive growth for several years thereafter [1]. This emphasizes the fact that preserving financial stability is one of the main goals for policy makers from the beginning of the monetary systems. It is the especial role that banks play in the financial system and their specificities as money issuers that explain why a great number of financial crises have had the banking sector as protagonist.

N. García-Pedrajas et al. (Eds.): IEA/AIE 2010, Part III, LNAI 6098, pp. 1–10, 2010.

Several previous works have analyzed different episodes of banking crisis occurred. Most of these works consist of case studies, many of them applying econometric analysis of different situations. For example in [2] an econometric model is used to predict bank failures using Mexican data for the period 1991-95. In a more recent work [3], the behavior of a number of macroeconomic variables in the months before and after a banking crisis is analyzed. Thus, the authors try to identify variables that act as "early warning signals" for crises. Other studies apply classical statistical techniques such as discriminant, logit or probit analysis [4,5]. However, although the obtained results have been satisfactory, all these techniques present the drawback that they make some assumptions about the model or the data distribution that are not usually satisfied. So in order to avoid these disadvantages of statistical methods, it has been recently suggested in the economic field the use of Soft-computing techniques, mainly neural networks or evolutionary computation algorithms.

In recent years, neural networks have been successfully applied to bankruptcy prediction [6,7]. In the majority of cases, multilayer perceptrons (MLPs) have been applied [8], due to its simple architecture yet powerful problem-solving ability. However, alternatives to MLP have arisen in the last few years, which has not been fully tested in bankruptcy. Product Unit Neural Network (PUNN) models are an alternative to MLPs and are based on multiplicative neurons instead of additive ones. They correspond to a special class of feed-forward neural network introduced by Durbin and Rumelhart [9]. Networks that make use of Product Units (PUs) have the added advantage of increased information capacity [9]. Another interesting alternative to MLPs are Radial Basis Function Neural Networks (RBFNNs). RBFNNs can be considered a local approximation procedure, and the improvement in both its approximation ability as well as in the construction of its architecture has been note-worthy [10]. RBFNNs have been used in the most varied domains, from function approximation to pattern classification, time series prediction, data mining, signals processing, and non-linear system modeling and control, but again there are very few works testing this model in bankruptcy or crisis prediction.

In this paper we consider the hybridization of these novel networks (PUs and RBFs) with a standard logistic regression to improve the performance of the classifiers in the problem of bank crises prediction. Logistic Regression (LR) has become a widely used and accepted method of analysis of binary or multi-class outcome variables as it is flexible and it can predict the probability for the state of a dichotomous variable (in our case, the probability of crisis) based on the predictor variables (macroeconomic variables in this case). The hybridization of LR and PUNNs or RBFNNs is done following the model of classifier construction given in [11], where Evolutionary Algorithms (EAs) are used to obtain the best structure of the classifiers. In this paper we show that the hybrid models involving LR, PUNNs and RBFNNs outperforms several other existing classification techniques in the problem of banking crises prediction, and they are therefore a very interesting tool to take into account in this field.

The structure of the rest of the paper is as follows: section 2 describes in detail the hybrid models (LR-PUNNs and LR-RBFNNs) proposed in this paper. Section 3 presents the experimental section of the paper, in which we test the good performance of the proposed approaches in a Financial Crisis Database, formed by a sample of data of 79 countries in the period 1981-1999. The results are also discussed in this section. Finally, the paper is closed with some remarks and conclusions in section 4.

2 Description of the Hybrid Methodologies Proposed

The hybrid models we analyze in this paper for the prediction of banking crises are Generalized Logistic Regression models based on the hybridization of the standard linear model and non-linear terms. These non-linear models are constructed with basis functions obtained from Evolutionary Product Unit Neural Networks (EPUNNs) and Evolutionary Radial Basis Function Neural Networks (ERBFNNs). In this section, we describe the main characteristics of the binary LR approach and the hybrid models considered. Note that a complete description of the EPUNNs and ERBFNNs is not carried out due to space reasons (the reader can check the references [11,12,13] for a complete description of the models and the EA used to optimize these models).

2.1 Binary Logistic Regression (LR)

Typically, in supervised classification, a set of n_T training samples $(x_1, y_1), \ldots,$ (x_{n_T}, y_{n_T}) is given. The inputs x_i (i.e. the set of macroeconomic and financial variables) form a feature space $\mathbf{X}$, and the output y_i (i.e. the bankrupt class) has a class label c, which belongs to a finite set $\mathbf{C}$. A classification rule is designed based on the training data, so that, given a new input x_i with the corresponding values for the macroeconomic variables, a class c from $\mathbf{C}$ with the smallest probability of error is assigned to it.

In this paper the situation considered is the following: a binary outcome variable y (bankrupt or non-bankrupt) is observed together with a vector $\mathbf{x}_i = (1, x_{i1}, x_{i2}, \ldots, x_{ik})$ of covariates for each of the n_T training samples (assuming that the vector of inputs includes the constant term 1 to accommodate the intercept). The two-class is coded via a 0/1 response y_i, where $y_i = 1$ for a bankrupt sample and $y_i = 0$ for non-bankrupt samples. Let p be the conditional probability associated with the first class. Logistic Regression (LR) [14] is a widely used statistical modeling technique in which the probability p of the dichotomous outcome event is related to a set of explanatory variables x in the form:

$$\text{logit}(p) = \ln\left(\frac{p}{1-p}\right) = f_{\text{LR}}(x, \beta) = \beta^T x \tag{1}$$

where $\beta = (\beta_0, \beta_1, \ldots, \beta_k)$ is the vector of the coefficients of the model, β^T is the transpose vector and $f_{\text{LR}}(x, \beta)$ is the linear function of the LR model. We refer to $p/(1 - p)$ as odds-ratio and to the expression (1) as the log-odds or logit transformation. A simple calculation in (1) shows that the probability of occurrence of an event as a function of the covariates is non-linear and is given by:

$$p(\mathbf{x}; \boldsymbol{\beta}) = \frac{e^{\boldsymbol{\beta}^T \mathbf{x}}}{1 + e^{\boldsymbol{\beta}^T \mathbf{x}}} \quad . \tag{2}$$

The complementary event probability can therefore be obtained as $(1 - p(\mathbf{x}; \boldsymbol{\beta}))$. Once the conditional probability function defined in (2) is known, the Bayesian (optimal) decision rule can be constructed:

$$r(\mathbf{x}) = \text{sign} \left\{ \ln \left(\frac{p(\mathbf{x}; \boldsymbol{\beta})}{1 - p(\mathbf{x}; \boldsymbol{\beta})} \right) \right\} \quad .$$

Given the set of macroeconomic variables $\mathbf{x}$ for a specific bank, the probability p that the bank belongs to the first class can be determined from (2). Similar to the maximum-likelihood classification, these class probabilities for each new bank may be outputted to produce a soft classification. The results from this paper advocate the utility of the LR as a potential approach for the soft classification similar to other recent approaches such as the MLP neural networks or the decision tree regression. A hard classification can be produced by assigning the class having a maximum probability (in our case, as a binary outcome variable is considered, we can simply check if the probability p is greater or lower than the value 0.5). Observe that LR not only constructs a decision rule but it also finds a function that for any input vector defines the probability p that the vector $\mathbf{x}$ belongs to the first class.

Let $D = \{(\mathbf{x}_l, y_l); 1 \leq l \leq n_T\}$ be the training data set. Here it is assumed that the training sample is a realization of a set of independent and identically distributed random variables. The unknown regression coefficients β_i, which have to be estimated from the data, are directly interpretable as log-odds ratios or, in term of $\exp(\beta_i)$, as odds ratios. The log-likelihood used as the error function is:

$$l(\boldsymbol{\beta}) = \sum_{l=1}^{n_T} y_l \log p(\mathbf{x}_l; \boldsymbol{\beta}) + (1 - y_l) \log(1 - p(\mathbf{x}; \boldsymbol{\beta})) \quad . \tag{3}$$

The estimation of the coefficient vector $\boldsymbol{\beta}$ is usually carried out by means of an iterative procedure like the Newton-Raphson algorithm or the Iteratively Re-weighted Least Squares (IRLS) [15].

2.2 Logistic Regression Using Initial Covariates and Product Units (LRIPU) and Radial Basis Functions (LRIRBF)

These two hybrid methods consider evolutionary optimization to obtain a PUNN or a RBFNN structure and input-to-hidden layer weights accurate enough. When these are obtained, a multilogistic regression maximum likelihood (ML) optimization is applied over the basis functions (PUs or RBFs) of the NN selected, considering also the initial covariates **x** of the problem. So their generic expression is given by:

$$f(\mathbf{x}, \boldsymbol{\theta}) = \alpha_0 + \sum_{i=1}^{k} \alpha_i x_i + \sum_{j=1}^{m} \beta_j B_j(\mathbf{x}, \mathbf{w}_j) \tag{4}$$

where $\boldsymbol{\theta} = (\boldsymbol{\alpha}, \mathbf{W})$, $\boldsymbol{\alpha} = (\alpha_0, \alpha_1, \ldots, \alpha_k, \beta_1, \ldots, \beta_m)$ and $\mathbf{W} = (\mathbf{w}_1, \mathbf{w}_2, \ldots, \mathbf{w}_m)$, with $\mathbf{w}_j = (w_{j1}, w_{j2}, \ldots, w_{jk})$, $w_{ji} \in R$. The coefficients $\mathbf{W}$ are given by the EA, they not being adjusted by the ML method (the reader can check the references [11,12,13] for a complete description of this EA). The ML method only optimizes the linear part of the model, i.e. the $\boldsymbol{\alpha}$ coefficients.

The ML algorithm considered is the SimpleLogistic algorithm [16], which incrementally constructs the model and applies cross-validation, resulting in an automatic covariate selection. We obtain then two different hybrid methods: SimpleLogistic Regression using Initial Covariates and PUs (LRIPU) and SimpleLogistic Regression using Initial Covariates and RBFs (LRIRBF).

3   Computational Experiments and Results

In this section, we describe first the Database used to evaluate the performance of our hybrid approaches. Several existing algorithms for comparison purposes are described in subsection 3.1. Finally, the main results obtained with the proposed techniques are presented in subsection 3.2 and subsection 3.3 includes some discussion about these results.

The Financial Crisis Database used in this study is formed by a sample of 79 countries in the period 1981-1999 (annual data). The binary dependent variable is:

- Systemic and non-systemic banking crises dummy: equals one during episodes identified as in [17]. They present information on 117 systemic banking crises (defined as much or all of bank capital being exhausted) that have occurred since the late 1970s in 93 countries and 51 smaller non-systemic banking crises in 45 countries during that period. The information on crises is cross-checked with that of [5] and with International Monetary Fund staff reports and financial news.

The independent variables are the following: Monetary policy strategies, Central Bank Independence, Inflation, Real Interest Rate, Net Capital Flows to GDP, Real GDP per capita in 1995 US dollars, Real GDP growth, World Real GDP growth, Domestic Credit growth, Bank Cash to total assets, Bank Foreign Liabilities to Foreign Assets and Previous crises. More information about these variables can be obtained in [18].

3.1   Alternative Statistical and Artificial Intelligence Methods Used for Comparison Purposes

Different state-of-the-art statistical and artificial intelligence algorithms have been implemented for comparison purposes. Specifically, the results of the following algorithms have been compared with the soft-computing techniques presented in this paper:

1. The Logistic Model Tree (LMT) [16] classifier.
2. The C4.5 classification tree inducer [19].
3. The k Nearest Neighbor (k-NN) classifier.
4. The Support Vector Machine (SVM) classifier [15] with RBF kernels and using the Sequential Minimal Optimization (SMO) algorithm.
5. A Gaussian Radial Basis Function Network (RBFNet) [20], deriving the centers and width of hidden units using k-means, and combining the outputs obtained from the hidden layer using logistic regression.
6. The Multilayer Perceptron (MLP) neural network [8], trained with a simple BackPropagation (BP) algorithm.
7. The Naive Bayes standard learning algorithm (NaiveBayes) [21].
8. The Rough Set methodology for classification [22].

These algorithm have been selected for comparison since they are some of the best performing algorithms of recent literature on classification problems. Many of these approaches have also been tested before in bankruptcy detection problem. For the LRIPU and LRIRBF methods, the experimental design was conducted using a 10-fold cross-validation procedure, with 10 repetitions per each fold. For the other methods, the results have been obtained performing 10 times a 10-fold cross validation, because all are deterministic methods, i.e. they are not based in random values and return the same result for each execution. The comparison measure is the accuracy on the generalization set or Correctly Classified Rate (CCR_G).

3.2 Results

In this section we compare the proposed LRIPU and LRIRBF methods with the alternative artificial intelligence methods summarized above. Table 1 shows the results obtained with all these different techniques, and the result obtained by the LRIPU and LRIRBF networks. Note that the LRIPU obtains the best result in terms of CCR_G over all techniques compared. The difference in CCR_G is really significant with respect to techniques such as Naive Bayes learning, SVM/SMO, MLP, RBFNet or the k-NN approach. Other techniques obtain closer results in terms of CCR_G, note that the Rough Set approach is the second best technique over all the compared approaches, obtaining a result slightly better than the LRIRBF, and slightly worse than the LRIPU algorithm. The LRIRBF is the third best algorithm after LRIPU and Rough Set methodology.

In order to determine if there are significant differences in the mean results obtained, an ANOVA statistical study has also been carried out. A preliminary F-test has been applied for assessing if there are significant differences between the mean CCR_G corresponding to the distinct methodologies, obtaining a p-value of 0.001 lower than the critical value $\alpha = 0.05$, what means that there are significant differences between the mean obtained by the methods compared. Then a multiple comparison test has been applied to rank the different methods, previously

Table 1. Statistical results (Mean and Standard Deviation, SD) of the CCR_G of the hybrid methods proposed compared to those obtained using different statistical and artificial intelligence methods and ranking of the different methods based on the Tamhane test. The best quantitative result method is represented in bold face.

Method	CCR_G Mean $\pm$ SD
LMT	76.09 ± 5.23
C4.5	76.35 ± 5.38
k-NN	74.17 ± 5.29
SVM/SMO	70.29 ± 2.34
SLogistic	76.49 ± 4.66
RBFNet	70.27 ± 4.38
MLP	74.58 ± 5.52
MLogistic	76.30 ± 4.84
NaiveBayes	69.16 ± 2.23
Rought sets	77.0 ± 3.42
LRIRBF	76.88 ± 3.03
LRIPU	$\mathbf{77.17 \pm 3.59}$

Ranking
$$\mu_{\text{LRIPU*}} \geq \mu_{\text{RoughSets}} \geq \mu_{\text{LRIRBF}} \geq$$
$$\geq \mu_{\text{SLogistic}} \geq \mu_{\text{C4.5}} \geq \mu_{\text{MLogistic}} \geq$$
$$\geq \mu_{\text{LMT}} \geq \mu_{\text{MLP}} > \mu_{\text{SMO}};$$
$$\mu_{\text{SMO}} \geq \mu_{\text{RBFNet}} \geq \mu_{\text{NaiveBayes}};$$
$$\mu_{\text{MLogistic}} > \mu_{\text{MLP}}$$

evaluating whether the equality of variances can be assumed using the Levene's test. This equality can not be assumed (p-value > 0.05 for all methods), so the multiple comparison test of Tamhane is applied. The last row of Table 1 includes the final ranking obtained by this test, where $\mu_A \geq \mu_B$ is used for indicating that methodology A yields better results than methodology B, but the differences are not significant, and $\mu_A > \mu_B$ is used for indicating that methodology A yields better results than methodology B with significant differences in mean. From the observation of this ranking, it can be concluded that the LRIPU* obtain higher mean accuracy but non significant differences when compared to Rough set, SLogistic, C4.5, MLogistic, LMT and MLP methods and the differences favouring LRIPU* are significant when compared to the other methods.

In general, these results show that the proposed hybrid approaches based on LR and PU or RBF networks are robust approaches to tackle the prediction of banking crises, and obtain better results than the majority of the existing alternative methods.

3.3 Discussion

This section include some discussion about the models obtained. The economical interpretation of the model is based on the output of the LRIPU, shown in Table 2. In this table, the best model obtained by using the LRIPU methodology

Table 2. Probability expression of the best LRIPU model, CCR_G value and testing confusion matrix associated to this model

Best LRIPU Crisis Probability model

$$p_{Crisis} = 1 - \frac{e^{f(\mathbf{x},\boldsymbol{\theta})}}{1+e^{f(\mathbf{x},\boldsymbol{\theta})}}$$

$$f(\mathbf{x},\boldsymbol{\theta}) = -2.63 + 1.47PU_1 + 1.63PU_2 + 3.73PU_3$$

$$PU_1 = x_4^{0.64} \ x_{10}^{-1.04} \ x_{13}^{1.83} \ x_{16}^{-1.68} \ x_{17}^{0.28} \ x_{18}^{-0.41} \ x_{19}^{1.06} \ x_{21}^{-0.35} \ x_{22}^{-3.16}$$

$$PU_2 = x_5^{0.42} \ x_{10}^{1.31} \ x_{12}^{2.35} \ x_{15}^{-3.53}$$

$$PU_3 = x_2^{1.33} \ x_5^{-3.75} \ x_9^{-2.42} \ x_{10}^{-4.41} \ x_{11}^{-2.25} \ x_{22}^{-4.28}$$

$x_2 \leftarrow$ (exchange = CB); $x_4 \leftarrow$ (exchange = MF); $x_5 \leftarrow$ (exchange = PC)

$x_9 \leftarrow$ (monpolicy = 3); $x_{10} \leftarrow$ (cbanIndep); $x_{11} \leftarrow$ $realIntRat$;

$x_{12} \leftarrow$ (domCredGrowth); $x_{13} \leftarrow$ (bankCashRev); $x_{15} \leftarrow$ (gdpGrowth);

$x_{16} \leftarrow$ (inflation); $x_{17} \leftarrow$ (netKFlows); $x_{18} \leftarrow$ (gdpPerHead);

$x_{19} \leftarrow$ (previousCrisis = 0); $x_{21} \leftarrow$ (previousCrisis = 2);

$x_{22} \leftarrow$ (previousCrisis = 3);

$CCR_G = 86.54\%$

Test Confusion Matrix

	Predicted	
Target	0	1
0	35	1
1	6	10

is presented. This model includes 3 PU basis functions and 23 coefficients. At the bottom of the table, the corresponding confussion matrix for the generalization set is included, where it can be observed that only 7 banks are incorrectly classified. This is the model that shows the best performance in terms of classification. In this model is possible to see that the most important set of variables is represented by the PU3 node, followed by the other two nodes with a similar explicatory power. We focus the discussion then on the PU3 node: it shows that the combination of a currency regime close to a pegged regime instead of a currency board regime, a long lasting crisis (the country is on crisis for more than three years), a flexible monetary policy (in which objective function does not enter monetary aggregates neither inflation targets), an independent central bank, and high real interest rates positively contribute to an increment of the probability of being in crisis next year. The length of the crisis has a positive contribution in terms of the likelihood to remain in crisis, as expected. Indeed, each additional year in crisis affects more than proportionally consumer and investors confidence in absence of policies (or a positive external shock) that helps to recover it. Regarding the currency policy, the currency regime could be used to recover the confidence in the economy through stabilizing the level of prices by borrowing credibility from other countries with more stable economies. The success of this strategy will depend on the credibility in maintaining the commitments that each regime implies. The currency board regime appears as superior in terms of getting out of the crisis as a pegged regime. Both regimes reduce the level of autonomy of the national policies, but the former is more much restrictive than the later. Therefore it seems that the pegged regime is not a commitment strong enough to anchor agent's expectations because they still leave some room for policy maker's discretion. In addition, a flexible design of the monetary policy does not help to make this commitment credible. The design of the monetary policy needs to be perfectly aligned with the currency regime in order for the framework to be consistent. Otherwise the currency commitment would become unsustainable. This is why the independence of the central bank is not a good feature and does not appear in this node. The stabilization policy does not depend on internal monetary policy objectives but on currency policy objectives. Therefore, a dependent central bank likely does not interfere with the currency objectives that need mainly a strong political support. Finally, in this situation, the higher the interest rates, the more likely we are in crisis in the next period, because is more difficult to finance any project.

4 Conclusions

In this paper we have applied several hybrid algorithms mixing Logistic Regression with Product Unit neural networks (PUNNs) or Radial Basis Function networks (RBFNNs) for detecting and predicting banking crises. Both hybrid approaches consist of the evolutionary training of a PUNN or a RBFNN using an evolutionary programming approach. These hybrid models have been shown to be very strong in the problem of bank crisis prediction. In this paper we have tested these hybrid approaches in a Financial Crisis Database, formed by macroeconomic variables of 79 countries in the period 1981-1999, and the corresponding crisis/non-crisis decision variable. The results obtained have proven the good performance of the proposed approaches, that improve the results of other existing statistical and artificial intelligence techniques in the problem.

Acknowledgement

This work has been partially supported by Universidad de Alcalá and Comunidad de Madrid under grant number CCG07-UAH/AMB-3993, by the TIN 2008-06681-C06-03 project of the Spanish Inter-Ministerial Commission of Science and Technology (MICYT), FEDER funds and by the P08-TIC-3745 project of the "Junta de Andalucía" (Spain).

References

1. Hanson, J.: Postcrisis challenges and risks in East Asia and Latin America. In: Caprio, et al. (eds.) Financial Crisis (2006)
2. González-Hermosillo, B.: Banking sector fragility and systemic sources of fragility. International Monetary Fund, working paper 12 (1996)
3. Kaminsky, G., Reinhart, C.: The twin crises: the causes of banking and balance-of-payments problems. American Economic Review 89(3), 473–500 (1999)
4. Pasiouras, F., Tanna, S.: The prediction of bank acquisition targets with discriminant and logit analyses: Methodological issues and empirical evidence. Research in International Business and Finance 24(1), 39–61 (2009)

5. Doma, I., Martínez-Peria, M.S.: Banking crises and exchange rate regimes: is there a link? The World Bank, working paper 2489 (2000)
6. Falavigna, G.: An analysis of the key-variables of default risk using complex systems. International Journal of Business Performance Management 10(2-3), 202–230 (2008)
7. Charalambous, C., Charitou, A., Kaourou, F.: Comparative Analysis of Artificial Neural Network Models: Application in Bankruptcy Prediction. Annals of Operations Research 99(1-4), 403–425 (2000)
8. Bishop, C.M.: Neural networks for pattern recognition. Oxford University Press, Oxford (1995)
9. Durbin, R., Rumelhart, D.: Products Units: A computationally powerful and biologically plausible extension to backpropagation networks. Neural Computation 1(1), 133–142 (1989)
10. Bishop, C.M.: Improving the generalization properties of radial basis function neural networks. Neural Computation 3(4), 579–581 (1991)
11. Hervás-Martínez, C., Martínez-Estudillo, F.J., Carbonero-Ruz, M.: Multilogistic Regression by means of Evolutionary Product-Unit Neural Networks. Neural Networks 21(7), 951–961 (2008)
12. Gutiérrez, P.A., Hervás-Martínez, C., Carbonero, M., Fernández, J.C.: Combined Projection and Kernel Basis Functions for Classification in Evolutionary Neural Networks. Neurocomputing 72(13-15), 2731–2742 (2009)
13. Martínez-Estudillo, A.C., Martínez-Estudillo, F.J., Hervás-Martínez, C., García-Pedrajas, N.: Evolutionary product unit based neural networks for regression. Neural Networks 19(4), 477–486 (2006)
14. Hosmer, D., Lemeshow, S.: Applied logistic regression. Wiley Interscience, Hoboken (2000)
15. Hastie, T., Tibshirani, R., Friedman, J.: The Elements of Statistical Learning. Springer, Heidelberg (2001)
16. Landwehr, N., Hall, M., Frank, E.: Logistic Model Trees. Machine Learning 59(1-2), 161–205 (2005)
17. Caprio, G., Klingebiel, D.: Episodes of systemic and borderline financial crises, dataset mimeo. The World Bank (2003)
18. Sanchis, A., Segovia-Vargas, M.J., Gil, J.A., Heras, A., Villar, J.L.: Rough Sets and the role of the monetary policy in financial stability (macroeconomic problem) and the prediction of insolvency in insurance sector (microeconomic problem). European Journal of Operational Research 181(3), 1554–1573 (2007)
19. Quinlan, J.R.: C4.5: Programs for Machine Learning. Morgan Kaufmann, San Francisco (1993)
20. Nabney, I.T.: Efficient Training of RBF Networks for Classification. International Journal of Neural Systems 14(3), 201–208 (2004)
21. Duda, R.O., Hart, P.E., Stork, D.G.: Pattern Classification, 2nd edn. Wiley Interscience, Hoboken (2000)
22. Slowinski, R., Zopounidis, C.: Application of the rough set approach to evaluatio of bankruptcy risk. International Journal of Intelligent Systems in Accounting, Finance and Management 4(1), 27–41 (1995)

Design and Evaluation of Neural Networks for an Embedded Application

Paolo Motto Ros* and Eros Pasero**

INFN Gruppo V, sezione di Torino
Laboratorio di Neuronica, Dipartimento di Elettronica, Politecnico di Torino,
Corso Duca degli Abruzzi 24, 10129 Torino, Italy
paolo.mottoros@polito.it, eros.pasero@polito.it

Abstract. In this study we compare different training strategies and configurations of Artificial Neural Networks (ANNs) designed for a real application, a mobile reader device for blind people. They are used to recognize characters found in input images; since the application has a real-time behaviour, we have improved the already implemented ANN subsystem rather than looking for new and more complex solutions.

The main idea has been to setup a pool of configurations and then to select the best one through a rigorous test. All the results have been computed on both the development platform and the target one, considering implementation issues. This method has led to improve the performances of the classifier maintaining the same complexity as the starting one.

1 Introduction

This study is a part of an Italian national project, named Stiper2 (STImolazione PERcettiva, funded by INFN and developed by Dipartimento di Elettronica del Politecnico di Torino and Istituto Superiore di Sanità di Roma), whose aim is to develop a set of aids for blind people in everyday life. One of the first designed prototype is a mobile device able to read printed text in a real-time way. Targeting at the mobile world means to use low-power hardware solutions, and hence usually with reduced computational resources. It is clear that the recognition subsystem, based on ANNs (Artificial Neural Networks), is the most computational power demanding part of the overall application; we have measured that, even with optimizations enabled, it takes the 57% of the overall processing time (on average). Actually it is still an acceptable value, but it should not increase.

The separation between the main application and the particular ANN architecture, once defined its inputs/outputs, has enabled us to quickly setup a first working prototype and only afterwards to focus the attention on how to improve its performances. Such basic implementation has been already discussed

---

* Research associate at Politecnico di Torino, INFN associate (INFN Gruppo V sezione di Torino).
** Professor at Politecnico di Torino, INFN associate (INFN Gruppo V sezione di Torino).

N. García-Pedrajas et al. (Eds.): IEA/AIE 2010, Part III, LNAI 6098, pp. 11–20, 2010.

in [6]. One network for each symbol to be recognized has been trained and then a winner-takes-all approach has been used to identify the correct result. In such preliminary study, we have preferred not to use fully connected ANNs, both to avoid overfitting issues and to keep low the overall system complexity. This, for the ANN approach, can be roughly estimated as the amount of connections, since the multiplication is the most expensive arithmetic operation[1]. For these reasons we have decided not to change the network architecture (even if we designed a new topology with roughly the same size). We preferred to focus the attention on selecting new performance evaluation parameters for ANNs (Sect. 3), investigating the behaviour on specific subsets of the data set (Sect. 4), improving the training process (Sect. 5) and in the end considering the peculiarities of the target device (Sect. 6). The proposed classifier has been chosen among the others through a set of rigorous tests in order to find the best one (Sect. 7).

2   Method

The solution proposed in [6] has been used as the starting point: although it worked properly, it was also clear that the whole performances should have been improved. Such comparison has been made by evaluating only the MSE (Mean Squared Error); the configuration tested, and hence the explored solutions, were few. We will talk about "configurations of ANNs" since not only the topology plays an important role, but also how the training is performed. The set of all its parameters, the type of input data and the layout, all make what we call a configuration. Anyway, all the solutions can be grouped in families, depending on the different topologies. They are beta, beta-h64 (derived from [6][2]) and the new 2Dn and 2Dp ones. These last ones, which should take advantage of the bidimensional nature of the input data, have been served as the base for most of the work discussed here.

It is very difficult to evaluate *a priori* which parameter could lead, taken alone, to better performances without any doubt, because it interacts with all the others. The idea is to further analyze the results and to find some hints on how to train different ANNs, in order to have a set of configurations from which to choose the best one. As already pointed out in [4], there is no scientific algorithm that gives as result the optimal ANN. It is more an iterative process based on a trial and error approach, but we can identify some guidelines on how to design new configurations. We will follow the Occam's razor principle, which states, once satisfied the requirements and achieved the goal, to prefer the simplest solution.

An automatic build system has been developed to train and evaluate the proposed ANNs. This means that all the tests discussed here have been performed on all the configurations, but in order to show how and why new ways have

---

[1] The activation functions could be more expensive, but in our implementation they are approximated by a piecewise linear function.

[2] For practical reasons, the configurations discussed in the previous cited work have been renamed, so the 16x16 prefix has become beta and 8x8 has turned into alpha.

been investigated, only the interesting subsets of data (and not from all the configurations) will be presented. Almost all the results have been obtained with the training and validation set defined in [6], i.e. with the 90% of the whole set (composed by more than 10000 samples) used for the training and the remaining 10% for the validation. It is not the best solution, but it is a good starting point; in Sect. 7 we will revise this choice.

3   Evaluation Parameters

The sole parameter used in [6] to evaluate different configurations has been the MSE. This is the most used measure, but in practice it is more suited to regression tests, where functions are approximated, while in our case we classify a data set. The outputs are ideally of boolean type, because they are the result of the comparison between the ANN outputs and some reference values (the thresholds used in the winner-takes-all approach). In synthesis, we are not so much interested in estimating the distance of the proposed model from the desired results, but rather to know how many samples in the validation set make the model fail, i.e. to have an answer to how many errors we had.

An answer can be the *BitFail* parameter. This is a simple true/false property of the ANN that, given an input, states whether the error of the output is above a certain threshold, called *BitFail limit* or $BitFail_{lim}$; it corresponds to what in literature is called the 0/1 loss function [10]. Hence it is possible to obtain the *rate of wrong outputs*, by running the network over a set of samples and counting when such condition is verified. This should give a better idea about the classification performances of the tested configuration, although it does not take into consideration how the ANN results are combined together in the final decision algorithm (this is true also for the MSE).

Table 1. Comparison of the BitFail (along with the MSE) parameter for the already designed ANN configurations

Name	Input type	Total neurons	Total connections	BitFail	MSE
beta	16x16-n	291	833	0.004973	0.000599
beta-h64	16x16-n	323	897	0.005595	0.000493
2Dn	16x16-n	388	1025	0.007413	0.000687
2Dp	16x16-p	388	1025	0.007425	0.001209

The BitFail can be used as the training goal, in order to create ANNs good enough to classify the desired data, rather than to output accurate values. In Table 1 we can see the BitFail (along with the MSE) results for the configurations used as the starting point for this work[3]. Anyway, choosing the right

---

[3] These results, along with the ones in similar tables, have been collected by running all the networks on all the data set. This means that we have about 85 * 10000 values to compute the MSE/BitFail.

configuration only considering such information is premature, since we have neither an insight of the behaviour on the validation set nor any clear idea about the generalization ability of the overall classifier: further analysis are needed.

4   Behaviour on Specific Data Subsets

Using the main application in preliminary tests, it was observed that almost all the fails of the character recognition subsystem were due to the low output of the corresponding network. Considering only the results about the MSE and BitFail presented above, it should be quite surprising. Trying to exploit this phenomenon, two types of measure have been defined: the *intra-class* MSE/BitFail ($MSE_{IC}/BitFail_{IC}$) and the *extra-class* MSE/BitFail ($MSE_{EC}/BitFail_{EC}$)[4]. The former is the MSE/BitFail reported by a network over the validation examples that it should recognize, i.e. the positive set; the latter is the error in all the other cases (the ones that it should reject), i.e. the negative set.

For the configurations examined until now, we have observed (some of these results are presented, along with the ones of the next section, in Table 2) a maximum BitFail ratio of about 70, but, for other configurations, it has been up to 182. This is due to the large disproportion between the positive and the negative set. Each network is trained with its own right input set, against all the other 84 subsets[5], composing the negative set (the one-against-all approach [11]). Thus, if we look at the variety of the samples used in the training, we can see that the positive set is roughly $\frac{1}{85}$ of the whole set. It is clear that, since the parameter that drives the learning is an average of the results, the final ANNs will be more suited to reject input patterns than to accept the right ones. This also explains the trend found when investigating their behaviour in the final application: as pointed out previously, whenever there is recognition fail, it is due to low network outputs rather than too many high ones.

5   Training Strategies

As examined above, the training process is a crucial aspect to obtain networks able to give good results, so we have to modify it in order to counterbalance the disproportion in the data set. This is a well-known problem that can be tackled in numerous ways (see [2]), anyway, for practical reasons, we preferred to quickly setup a basic but effective system with the option to improve it later. The idea is to increase the positive training set, for example allowing the training algorithm to automatically replicate such data a prefixed number of times or in an automatic way. The first way is conceptually similar to give a *weight* to each

---

[4] We will refer to the *global* MSE/BitFail as the MSE/BitFail mentioned until now, i.e. the ones on the entire validation set, in order to distinguish them from these new definitions.

[5] The whole classifier is composed by 85 networks.

sample in the training set, while the second one tries to train the corresponding ANN through a set equally divided into positive and negative samples. This second option is derived from the consideration that the number of samples is not the same for each class, and it could be interesting to set the "multiplier parameter" automatically, on a network by network basis.

Table 2. Results obtained with the replication of the positive set during the training

Name	Positive set multiplier	Stop criterion	$\frac{BitFail_{IC}}{BitFail_{EC}}$	BitFail	$\frac{BitFail_{IC}}{BitFail_{EC}}$
2Dn-xa-10k	auto	Err	4.25	0.019132	7.43
2Dn-x85-10k	85	Err	4.26	0.020421	3.32
2Dn-x100-10k	100	Err	4.79	0.023967	7.52
2Dn-xa-bf1-10k	auto	BitFail	4.99	0.016461	7.56
2Dn-x50-10k	50	Err	6.01	0.018326	6.94
2Dn-x10-10k	10	Err	12.30	0.018280	19.65
2Dn	—	Err	40.47	0.007413	174.98
beta	—	Err	42.92	0.004973	11.66
2Dp	—	Err	50.32	0.007425	141.36
beta-h64	—	Err	69.31	0.005595	177.68

Some results are reported in Table 2, compared to the previous best ones. As expected, in general, multiplying the positive training set leads to better results, because the ratio between the intra-class and extra-class BitFail decreases by an order of magnitude. This is true only up to a certain amount, since it seems that using too high multipliers could be counter-effective (see 2Dn-x100-10k). The automatic way of equalizing the training set is not always so effective, although it offers a general improvement and the best configuration in this experiment uses this option. The BitFail criterion as the stop condition does not lead to better results than using the MSE (see 2Dn-xa-10k and 2Dn-xa-bf1-10k, which only differ in the stop criterion), but it still offers an opportunity to create different configurations.

As a final remark we can state that, generally speaking, using the technique of replicating part of the training set, leads to a worse global MSE and BitFail. Given that the idea is to mainly focus on the positive outputs, the learning process will take "less care" of the results on the other input data. Despite this, looking for example at the two best configurations (2Dn-xa-10k and 2Dn-x85-10k) respect to the "original" one (2Dn), we can see that we have obtained an improvement of one order of magnitude on the intra/extra class BitFail ratio, compared with a worsening of the global BitFail by a factor of 2.4–3.3. We have verified that MSE exhibit the same behaviour. This should not be seen as a problem, since the algorithm used to choose the winner ANN is based on thresholds that are some orders of magnitude greater than the MSE. Anyway the purpose of this system is the classification task and not a regression analysis, for which the global MSE could be the most important performance measure. The same reasoning can be applied to the BitFail parameter: in these tests the limit used was $BitFail_{lim} = 0.05$, which is significantly smaller than the afore mentioned thresholds. This does not mean that such information are useless, but they have to be used in the right way, i.e. simply considered as a term of comparison to understand how to design new and possibly better classifiers, leaving the task of determining their real performances to a final comparison, examined in Sect. 7.

6   Results on the Target Platform

All the studies about the ANNs made until now have been done on the development platform, which is a common PC and hence with at our disposal all the desired resources, including the possibility of using the floating-point arithmetic without incurring in any penalty. However, on the target platform there is a 32 bit system-on-a-chip for mobile appliances and hence without the FPU (for obvious reasons). So it is better to switch to the fixed-point arithmetic: we have measured that the recognition subsystem was more than four times faster.

The ability of fixed-point networks to satisfy the goal and the related minimum required precision is a long-standing issue in the neural network field, both addressed in theoretical studies (see [1]) and tested in practical problems (e.g. [3]). Anyway, as long as 32 bit data type provides good results we will not try to further optimize the involved algorithms. There are two ways to obtain fixed-point ANNs: the first one is to design a learning algorithm, possibly derived from the classical ones, that specifically uses this arithmetic (as done in [3]); the second one still relies a standard training process, with floating-point numbers, and then converts the resulting ANNs to the desired type. This is a pretty straightforward step, and in our case it is directly handled by the library used for the whole neural network subsystem. Nevertheless it is better to check again their behaviour with this arithmetic, in order to confirm the performances and the validity of the new training strategies.

All the other processing routines have been extensively validated with custom test tools, but it is not possible to use the same approach for the classifier component. It is very difficult to directly compare, sample by sample, the internal behaviour of ANNs with the two types of arithmetic and to demand to have always the same identical results. Our goal is the classification of feature vectors obtained from the character images, and as long as we will have the same system performances, we will not take care of these intermediate discrepancies. Running all the configurations in fixed-point mode, we have seen that, generally speaking, duplicating the positive set during the training will give better results. Anyway, both the global MSE and BitFail for each configuration is slightly increased, thus would be interesting to further investigate the phenomenon by examining the conversion of a floating-point ANN into a fixed-point one.

The library used for the ANNs (the FANN library, see [7] for further details) has an automatic algorithm that, given a network, decides the best format to represent the weights. This choice is made considering the greatest number that could be computed, deduced from the weight values and avoiding to incur into an overflow. Therefore the place of the decimal point depends upon each ANN, and it is (in general) not the same for all the networks belonging to the same configuration. A higher value for the decimal point of course means a greater precision, since it represents the numbers of bits used for the fractional part. In practice, a value greater than 6 should be sufficient to achieve good results (as reported in the documentation [7] provided with the ANN library), but it is better to check it anyway. According to [3], there should not be any significant performance loss if using more than 8 bits to represent the weights, and in our case all the numbers are represented by 32 bit words. In order to better understand the differences about the execution of the ANNs with the two approaches, it is useful to highlight the average decimal point used for each configuration, along with the MSE and the BitFail (defined analogously to the one previously used) obtained from the comparison of the outputs in the two ways. To further exploit whether switching away from the floating-point arithmetic could lead to worse or better results, the ratio between the global MSE in fixed-point mode end the one in floating-point mode are reported, and the same for the BitFail performance value, of course. These results, for the configuration already introduced are reported in Table 3 (the minimum and maximum decimal point are omitted here, for brevity reasons).

Table 3. Results of the comparison of the floating-point mode and the fixed-point one

Name	MSE	BitFail	Average dec. point	$\frac{MSE_{fxp}}{MSE_{fp}}$	$\frac{BitFail_{fxp}}{BitFail_{fp}}$
beta-h64	0.000036	0.009819	10.0	1.18	1.03
2Dp	0.000542	0.023552	7.7	1.31	1.12
2Dn-xa-10k	0.001666	0.055117	9.6	1.26	0.92
2Dn	0.003125	0.026016	8.1	5.61	1.52
2Dn-x50-10k	0.005290	0.108415	9.4	2.77	1.11
2Dn-x100-10k	0.005376	0.108611	9.4	0.70	0.67
2Dn-x85-10k	0.006873	0.104777	9.4	4.55	1.19
2Dn-x10-10k	0.007990	0.105905	8.9	3.50	1.31
2Dn-xa-bf1-10k	0.012345	0.064338	9.3	1.36	1.02

From the data of the Table 3 it is possible to state that the difference between a direct comparison of the two modes is not so great, but looking at how the global MSE changes, this seems to be more affected than the BitFail by the numeric conversion. This operation can be seen, from the mathematical standpoint, as an introduction of some sort of noise, and thus it directly affects the MSE. Conversely, if we still consider the BitFail (proportional to the amount of outcomes significantly different from the desired values), its effect is not so relevant. We have to remember that, for the classification task, it could be better to look at how the BitFail changes, and this, in some cases, it is even smaller. These results are important, since they lead to the conclusion that converting the ANNs should not worsen so much the system performances.

7 Classifier Selection

All the considerations made in the previous sections were geared towards the design of new ANN configurations among which to choose the best one, since it is not possible to state *a priori* which change improves the results.

After having done all those variants on the same new network topology, the natural question is whether these efforts are still useful to improve other ANNs. For example we can re-consider networks based on the previous topologies, exhibiting better performances in a "classical" training (i.e. trained with the MSE as the goal and without a partial replication of the training set). Following this methodology, we have defined an overall amount of 36 different configurations, even if, for brevity reasons, only some of them have been presented here.

In particular, these ideas have been applied to the `beta-h64` base configuration which, in the previous work [6], has been chosen as the best one. The Table 4 shows that the answer to the question is positive (`2Dn-x85-10k`, the best of the 2Dn family, has been included for direct comparison purposes). Also with this configuration we have the same trends found for the 2Dn and 2Dp families, although now replicating the positive set 100 times seems to give better results.

Table 4. Results improvement obtained from the `beta-h64` base configuration (fixed-point mode)

Name	Positive set multiplier	Stop criterion	$\frac{BitFail_{IC}}{BitFail_{EC}}$	MSE	BitFail
beta-h64-x100-10k	100	Err	7.65	0.001444	0.020421
beta-h64-x85-10k	85	Err	8.13	0.001363	0.019558
beta-h64-xa-bf1-10k	auto	BitFail	9.81	0.000881	0.011891
2Dn-x85-10k	85	Err	9.83	0.007479	0.024289
beta-h64-x50-10k	50	Err	11.92	0.001075	0.016864
beta-h64-x85-bf2-10k	85	BitFail	13.60	0.000536	0.005618
beta-h64-x10-10k	10	Err	23.80	0.000845	0.014861
beta-h64-10k	—	Err	54.19	0.001330	0.014033
beta-h64	—	Err	110.44	0.000561	0.005756

Everything presented until now does not clearly show which solution could be the best one, and so a final test is required. Those information only give an idea of an "average behaviour" of the ANNs for each configuration, but they do not consider the algorithm used to choose the winner (and hence the symbol recognized) inside the set. The only substantially interesting test is a classification one, with the option of making distinction between the wrong classifications and the so called "unknown" ones (in order to increase the reliability of the results).

From this classification test, we obtained a solution, `beta-h64-x85-bf2`, able to correctly recognize the 97.1% of the validation set, with only a 0.40% of wrong results and a 2.5% of "unknown" results (the least ones among all the configurations). It is important to note that both the replication of the positive set (by a factor of 85) and the BitFail as the training goal have been useful

Table 5. Final classification results (%) of the best configurations (running in fixed-point mode) with the stratified two-fold cross-validation (the confidence level is 99%)

Name	Correct results	Confidence interval	Wrong results	No results
beta-h64-x85-bf2-10k	94.7208	94.1189–95.2641	0.9929	4.2863
beta-h64-x50-10k	92.7055	92.012–93.3432	1.4746	5.8199
beta-h64-x85-10k	92.5875	91.8891–93.2301	1.4845	5.928
beta-h64-x100-10k	92.5186	91.8175–93.1642	1.5434	5.9379
beta-h64-xa-bf1-10k	92.499	91.7971–93.1454	1.2977	6.2033
beta-h64-x10-10k	92.0763	91.3575–92.7401	1.2977	6.626
beta-h64-x85-bf2-1k	91.3685	90.6228–92.0601	1.6418	6.9898
beta-h64	90.1494	89.3607–90.8857	0.757	9.0936

to achieve such results. According to this test, at a first glance we could be sure to have found the almost ideal classifier for our purposes. But besides the numerical results, we have also to consider how they have been obtained and their accuracy. The most simple way to evaluate the generalization properties is the *holdout* method, which is the one used up until now, with the results on the validation set as an estimate of them. It is well known that, with this method, the main issue is how to properly split the whole data set [9], establishing the right proportions. In this respect there is no best choice, thus we have to make some trades-off: with the actual division (90% training, 10% validation) we have privileged the learning process, in order to be sure to have well trained ANNs. On the other hand, the need for an accurate estimate of the generalization properties would suggest to reverse the proportions. We repeated all the trainings and evaluations according to such scenario, and the correct recognition rate of the best configuration (always `beta-h64-x85-bf2-10k`) dropped to 79%. This could be due to a low generalization capability, but since the same trend is verified across all the solutions, we could also hypothesize that it is because of the small training set. As already pointed out in [4], the training set should be made larger as long as the ANNs get more complex, and, in our case, having only the 10% could be insufficient. In the end, the problem is the holdout method itself, which is inadequate for our purposes; the alternatives [9] are the k-*cross-validation* [8] and the *bootstrap* method. In [5] those two techniques have been compared: the first one has in general a slightly higher variance, while the second one has a low variance but an extremely large bias in some cases. It is also reported that stratification helps to obtain even better results in cross-validation, and the suggested method is thus the stratification ten-fold cross-validation.

For this project, a custom software, able to train and evaluate the ANN configurations, through both the holdout and the stratified cross-validation[6], has been developed. According to this setup, we obtained the results shown in Table 5 (we computed also the confidence interval, for more information, see [5,9]) The

---

[6] For practical reasons, actually the k-cross-validation is limited to $k = 2$, nevertheless it still gives a good estimate about the generalization properties.

best solution is again `beta-h64-x85-bf2-10k` which has the highest percentage of correct recognition (about 95%), the second lowest error rate (1%) and the lowest amount of no output at all (about 4%). Even if these results seem worse than the previous ones, they are much more reliable and accurate, because of the stratified cross-validation.

8 Conclusion

In conclusion, we have studied and designed the classifier based on ANNs that, is the core of the character recognition subsystem of an embedded appliance. We optimized the training process, leading to have a system characterized by an accuracy of about 95%, with only a 1% of possible wrong results. It has been chosen among a pool of 36 different configurations, and the performances have been measured through the stratified two-fold cross-validation, which is one of the most accurate way of computing those results. The proposed solution has been tested with the fixed-point arithmetic, which is the one that will be used in the final application, thus taking into account almost every practical aspect.

References

1. Draghici, S.: On the capabilities of neural networks using limited precision weights. Neural Netw. 15(3), 395–414 (2002)
2. He, H., Garcia, E.A.: Learning from imbalanced data. IEEE Trans. on Knowl. and Data Eng. 21(9), 1263–1284 (2009)
3. Holt, J., Baker, T.: Back propagation simulations using limited precision calculations. In: IJCNN-91-Seattle International Joint Conference on Neural Networks, July 1991, vol. 2, pp. 121–126 (1991)
4. Kavzoglu, T.: Determining optimum structure for artificial neural networks. In: Proceedings of the 24 th Annual Technical Conference and Exhibition of the Remote Sensing Society, pp. 675–682 (1999)
5. Kohavi, R.: A study of cross-validation and bootstrap for accuracy estimation and model selection. In: International Joint Conference on Artificial intelligence (IJCAI), pp. 1137–1143. Morgan Kaufmann, San Francisco (1995)
6. Motto Ros, P., Pasero, E.: Artificial neural networks for real time reader devices. In: International Joint Conference on Neural Networks, IJCNN 2007, August 2007, pp. 2442–2447 (2007)
7. Nissen, S.: Implementation of a fast artificial neural network (FANN). Tech. rep., Department of Computer Science, University of Copenaghen (DIKU) (October 2003), http://leenissen.dk/fann/
8. Schaffer, C.: Technical note: Selecting a classification method by cross-validation. Mach. Learn. 13(1), 135–143 (1993)
9. Tan, P.N., Steinbach, M., Kumar, V.: Introduction to Data Mining. Pearson Education, US (2006)
10. Vapnik, V.N.: An overview of statistical learning theory. IEEE Transactions on Neural Networks 10(5), 988–999 (1999)
11. Webb, A.R.: Statistical Pattern Recognition, 2nd edn. John Wiley and Sons Ltd., Chichester (2002)

Component Stress Evaluation in an Electrical Power Distribution System Using Neural Networks

Miguel A. Sanz-Bobi[1], Rodrigo J.A. Vieira[1], Chiara Brighenti[1], Rafael Palacios[1], Guillermo Nicolau[2], Pere Ferrarons[2], and Petronio Vieira[3]

[1] Comillas Pontifical University, Instituto de Investigación Tecnológica,
Alberto Aguilera, 23,
28015 Madrid, Spain
[2] Endesa Distribución, Avinguda Parallel 51,
Barcelona, Spain
[3] Federal University of Pará,
Augusto Corrêa, 1, ZIP 66.075-900,
Belém / Pará – Brazil
masanz@upcomillas.es

Abstract. This paper presents a procedure that permits a qualitative evaluation of the stress in components of an electric power distribution system. The core of this procedure is the development of a set of models based on neural networks that are able to represent and to predict the normal behavior expected of the components under different working conditions. The paper includes the application to the characterization of the thermal behavior of power transformers and the operation time of circuit breakers.

Keywords: diagnosis, multi-layer perceptron, normal behavior models, self-organised map, anomaly detection, component stress.

1 Introduction

The knowledge of the health condition of an industrial asset is very important in order to apply the resources required to its maintenance, keeping its value and useful life-cycle as much as possible [1], [2]. Several maintenance strategies have been proposed with this objective, for example [3], [4] and [5]. Also, different artificial intelligent techniques have contributed to the detection and diagnosis of failures in many industrial sectors such as the electrical sector, and many contributions have been published about this. A small sample of references using artificial neural networks for condition monitoring of electrical components are the following: [6], [7], [8] and [9]. This paper is based on previous investigations by authors in the fields of diagnosis and maintenance [10], [11] and includes a new concept concerning stress estimation for a component using neural networks. This concept can help with the difficult process of decision taking in the asset management context. This paper describes the application of this new methodology to key components of an electrical power distribution system such as power transformers and circuit breakers. The paper is organized as follows: first, there is a definition of normal behavior model of a component based on

N. García-Pedrajas et al. (Eds.): IEA/AIE 2010, Part III, LNAI 6098, pp. 21–30, 2010.

the characterization of the information collected from its operation through the use of multi-layer perceptrons. The next section presents how to use the normal behavior models in the detection of anomalies and evaluation of the stress in power transformers. Finally, a set of self-organized maps are used to model the normal behavior of circuit breakers.

2 Normal Behavior Models

When a component is performing the function for which it was designed under healthy conditions, the ageing effect is usually the cause of failures. However in addition to this effect, sometimes a component is stressed due to hard working conditions or to extreme environmental conditions or, to a combination of both. When a component has been stressed, there is a higher probability or risk of an undesirable failure. For this reason it is important to characterize which is the normal behavior expected for a component when it is performing its function under several typical working conditions, because any deviation with respect to this behavior could alert about the presence of a possible failure. The sooner this is detected, the sooner it could be possible to mitigate the effect of a failure. This section describes the process followed for the development of that which the authors have called "normal behavior models" of components belonging to an electrical power distribution system.

These models are able to characterize the typical dynamical evolution of variables when the component is working under different operating conditions without symptoms of failure or without stress that could cause a failure mode. These models are able to predict the evolution of a variable using the information corresponding to other variables related with it and for this reason they can be used for the detection of anomalies.

In order to detect as soon as possible an anomaly that can cause some stress in a component, it is recommended to use information collected in real-time about the evolution of the main variables that can characterize the performance of a component. In particular, the models developed are based on information collected in real-time from a set of power transformers in an electrical substation in northeastern Spain. A set of sensors were installed in the power transformers in order to mainly monitor their thermal behavior. The models developed use multi-layer perceptrons [12] to learn the typical thermal behavior of the power transformers studied.

Fig. 1 shows the flow of information used to detect anomalies in the thermal normal behavior expected for the monitored power transformers. The outputs of the normal behavior models correspond to key variables for the detection of failure modes.

Once a normal behavior model has been elaborated, it can be used in real time with the values of the variables required. The prediction will correspond to the expected value for normal behavior under the current working condition. Any incipient failure will produce a deviation between the expected value and the real value measured of the monitored variable and it will cause stress in the component for one or several failure modes.

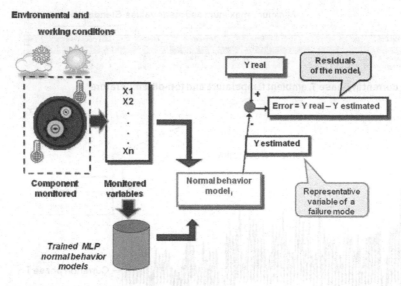

Fig. 1. Flow of information for the detection of anomalies or deviations with respect to the normal behavior expected

The development of the normal behavior models consists of the following main steps:

- Analysis of the information or time series [13] collected in order to observe the possible relationships among the measured variables;
- Characteristics of the failure modes that could be detected;
- Formulation of models by training several options of multilayer perceptrons;
- Validation of models.

As an example of the procedure followed for the development of normal behavior models, the case of the normal behavior model for the prediction of the top-oil temperature will be described. This model is able to predict the oil temperature on top of the power transformer using information from two input variables: the current which is circulating through one of its phases and the ambient temperature of the power transformer. This process will be described in the following paragraphs.

First, it is necessary to select, from all the data available, those periods of time where the performance of the component has been considered to be normal by operation and maintenance staff. Also, the data selected must cover a wide and typical range of working conditions of the component. Fig. 2 presents the evolution of three variables that can be related. The variables represented are the top oil temperature inside the power transformer, the current circulating through one of the three phases and the ambient temperature outside the transformer. Previously, the currents circulating through the three phases of the power transformer were checked and all of them had the same profile and values. The equilibrium of currents suggests the use of any one of them as an indication of the working load of the power transformer. The ambient temperature can be used to complete the working condition of the transformer.

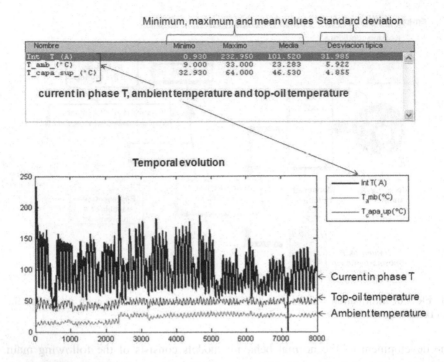

Fig. 2. Main characteristics of the variables to be used in a model of normal behavior for the top-oil temperature of the power transformer. (time axis in 15 min units).

Both variables, current and ambient temperature, could explain the value of the top oil temperature and this could be done using a normal behavior model. The period of time represented includes data from the four different seasons of the year.

In order to create the normal behavior models for the characterization of the thermal condition of the power transformer, a software tool was developed in MATLAB able to train different architectures of multi-layers perceptrons [6], [8] at the same time. These architectures are based on a unique hidden layer with variable numbers of neurons with sigmoid activation functions. The output layer uses linear activation functions. The training algorithm used is the Levenberg-Marquardt backpropagation. Fig. 3 shows the results obtained after training three different numbers of neurons in the hidden layer. Any of the options offered can be selected in order to analyze the main features of the normal behavior model.

The option chosen to be the possible normal behavior model can be analyzed through different characteristics that the application offers in order to confirm its quality. These characteristics are, for example, the error histogram, the approximation obtained, the autocorrelation of residuals, and the sensibility of the inputs for the prediction of the outputs. The model can include the consideration that the best relationship between an input and an output could be observed after some delay.

Once the normal behavior model has been obtained, it can be used for the detection of possible anomalies with respect to the behavior expected. Fig. 4 shows the use of the top-oil normal behavior model of a power transformer with new data collected and

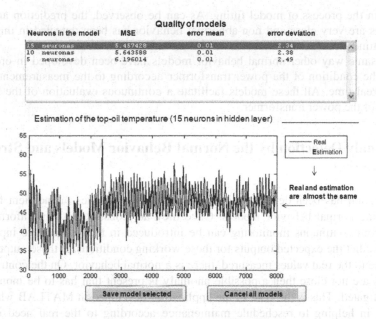

Fig. 3. Testing of three MLP with a different number of neurons in the hidden layer to model the normal behavior of the top-oil temperature. (time axis in 15 min units).

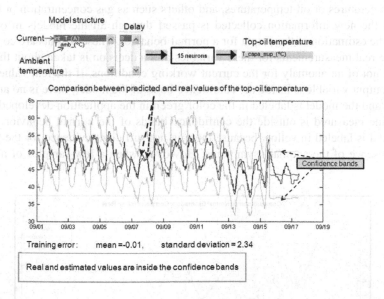

Fig. 4. Using the normal behavior model of the top-oil temperature of a power transformer for detection of anomalies

not used in the process of model fitting. As can be observed, the prediction and the real values are very close and non-abnormal behavior has been detected in this new period of time.

In the same way other normal behavior models have been developed in order to evaluate the condition of the power transformer according to the measurements collected in real time. All these models facilitate a continuous evaluation of the health condition of the power transformer.

3   Anomaly Detection by the Normal Behavior Models and Stress Evaluation

An application has been developed in order to detect anomalies or incipient failure modes using normal behavior models. Once they are constructed, new information coming from continuous monitoring can be introduced in their respective inputs in order to predict the expected outputs for these working conditions. If these outputs are fairly close to the real values measured, there is a normal behavior. On the contrary, if the values are not close then a possible anomaly is present that has to be monitored and investigated. This is the core of the application developed in MATLAB which is important in helping to reschedule maintenance according to the real need of the components monitored and their life.

The current application uses 12 models of normal behavior in order to characterize significant variables for the thermal aspect of the transformer monitored such as hotspot temperatures or oil temperatures, and others such as gas concentration or humidity. All the new information collected is passed through all the models in order to obtain the estimation of the output for a normal behavior. These outputs are compared with the real measurements for these variables and a decision is taken about the presence or not of an anomaly for the current working conditions. If the real value of the model output variable is inside the confidence band of the model, there is no anomaly present and the model is labeled in the color green in the application developed. If the real value measured is outside the confidence bands of the normal behavior model, the model is labeled in yellow because there is not sufficient evidence for the permanent presence of the anomaly symptoms. However, when a few samples of a model

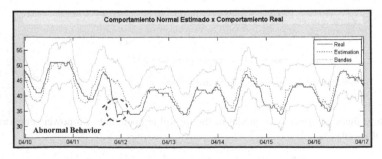

Fig. 5. Detection of anomalies

are continuously labeled in yellow, it changes to red and the presence of an abnormal behavior is confirmed. Fig 5 shows an example of abnormal behavior detected. Since any abnormal behavior is likely to evolve into a failure mode if no actions are taken, this is a key point in a predictive maintenance strategy and in making a decision to perform some maintenance action.

Fig. 6 shows the main window of the application developed for anomaly detection. The information on the left column corresponds to the normal behavior models monitored. The right column shows the outputs of the models. The thin column in the middle includes a color flag for each model according to the codification previously mentioned (green, yellow or red).

Another important window of this application, the status window, also is presented in Fig. 6. The information presented in this window is more detailed than that presented in the main window. It includes a schematic representation of the transformer being monitored and when clicking on the name of the variable it is possible to observe in a graph the real and estimated values of a normal behavior model and its confidence bands, like in Fig. 4 and 5. Also, at the bottom of the window there appears a chronological sequence of events related to the anomaly detection process.

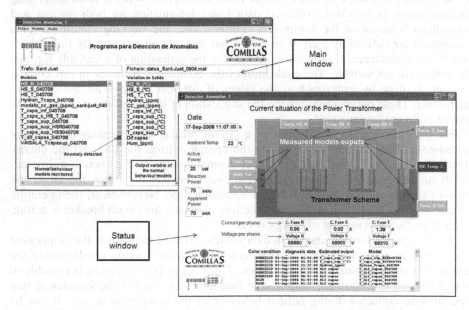

Fig. 6. Detection of anomalies. Window with general and detailed information.

Once the detection of anomalies has been evaluated, the stress can be assessed as a sum of the deviations between normal behavior and the real value of the variable monitored. Fig 7 shows the deviations and the stress component observed in April by the top oil temperature model.

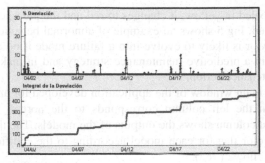

Fig. 7. Deviation between the normal and real behavior and stress component

4 Detection of Anomalous Behavior in Circuit Breakers by Self-organised Maps

This section presents the use of self-organized maps [12] for classifying working conditions of an electrical component in order to detect anomalies.

When monitoring the life of an electrical component it is not always possible to know whether it is working under normal conditions or not. When a sufficiently long monitorization is provided, collected data gives information on both normal and anomalous behavior of the component. Furthermore, the working conditions of a component are defined by a set of variables that may not all be mutually linked by a functional dependence. In this case, models for the estimation of a variable through the others are not suitable. The evaluation of the component behavior in this context can only be done by analyzing how the values of different variables are associated to each other. These observations lead to the suggestion of using self-organized maps to handle collected information.

For example, working conditions of a circuit breaker that operates on different transmission lines may be described by the operation time, the line and the energy interrupted and the I2t for the case. Under normal conditions the operation time depends on energy and the current which the circuit breaker is cutting; the larger the power that it is cutting, the larger be the operation time. Nevertheless, the operation time may vary as well depending upon the line on which the circuit breaker is acting, even when the same amount of energy is cut.

A self-organized map trained with data values collected throughout the component life is able to group together data that represent similar working conditions of the component while separating different ones. Once the map is trained, it is possible to assign to each neuron of the map a state that indicates whether the samples in that neuron were collected during normal behavior of the component or not. It can be observed that monitoring the life of an electrical component would provide many more data relative to normal behavior than to anomalies. Therefore a criterion for defining the state of a neuron is to evaluate the number of samples assigned to it with respect to the total number of collected data. If a high number of samples is associated to a neuron, that means it is representative of a set of normal working conditions; otherwise, if a few samples are assigned to a neuron, this means that those data were collected during anomalous behavior because they do not correspond to a typical condition. Neurons can then be divided into three groups: those describing normal

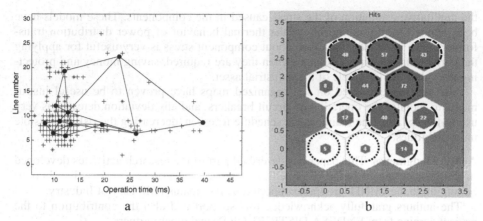

Fig. 8. a. Training data set (+), testing data set (*) and map neurons (o). b. Distribution of the data samples on the map. Qualitative state assignation: normal behavior neurons (-), uncertain behavior neurons (--) and anomalous behavior neurons (··).

behavior, those describing anomalous behavior and those within the two that correspond to an uncertain behavior.

Once the map is validated, every new collected data set can be used to evaluate the component behavior with the map, by simply observing to which neuron data are assigned. Alarm and warning signals can be set to indicate when new data fall into a neuron of which the state is of anomalous and uncertain behavior, respectively.

A software application using Matlab has been developed to provide for data analysis and map training and testing. This analysis has been done for a circuit breaker in an electrical substation in northeastern Spain, as an example. Available data measured by sensors are the operation time and the lines on which the component is acting at each sample time. In this case, a 4 by 3 map is trained in a batch unsupervised mode with 600 iterations. Fig. 8.a shows how neurons are put in order in the data space. Notice that most of the data fall in the area with operation time within 7 ms and 13 ms and line value within 5 and 12. These can be considered as normal working conditions. More in detail, Fig. 8.b shows the number of samples in each neuron of the map; the upper-right part of the map shows grouping data of normal behavior while on the bottom-left the few data are collected corresponding to data points having large operation times or large line values.

As more data becomes available, a new map can be trained in order to be able to classify more working conditions.

5 Conclusions

This paper has described a procedure to evaluate the stress of components belonging to an electric power distribution system. This is based on models that characterize the normal behavior expected according to real data collected during the typical operation of these components. The models used are multilayer perceptrons and self-organized maps. The first ones permit the detection of possible anomalies as soon as possible based on the normal behavior expected for variables representative of failure modes, and also, using the deviations in respect to the normal behavior observed, they permit the qualitative evaluation of the stress caused in the components. These models have been applied to the monitoring of the thermal behavior of power distribution transformers. The knowledge obtained about component stress is very useful for applying the correct maintenance resources when they are required, saving money and protecting the value and life-cycle of the industrial asset.

Also the models based on self-organized maps have proven to be useful instruments to monitor the operation of circuit breakers, and any deviation detected is very useful for updating the maintenance schedule foreseen, decreasing the risk of possible unavailabilities.

Acknowledgments. This paper has described part of the research activities developed in the project named DENISE (Intelligent, secure and efficient energy distribution) belonging to the CENIT program supported by the Spanish Ministry of Industry.

The authors gratefully acknowledge this support and also the contribution to the project coming from ENDESA DISTRIBUCIÓN and other partners.

References

1. Schneider, J., Gaul, A., Neumann, C., Hogräfer, J., Wellssow, W., Schwan, M., Schnettler, A.: Asset management techniques. Electrical Power and Energy Systems 28(9) (2006)
2. Tor, O., Shahidephpour, M.: Power distribution asset management. IEEE Power Engineering Society General Meeting (June 2006)
3. Tavner, P.J.: Review of condition monitoring of rotating electrical machines. IET Electric Power Applications 2(4), 215–246 (2008)
4. Denny Chelladurai, E., Santosh Kumar, A., Yadav, M., Venkatasami, A.: Design review as a diagnostic tool for power transformers — A case study. In: International Conference on Condition Monitoring and Diagnosis, April 2008, pp. 989–992 (2008)
5. Abu-Elanien, A.E.B., Salama, M.M.A.: Asset management techniques for transformers. Electric Power Systems Research (2009), doi:10.1016/j.epsr.2009.10.008
6. Tian, Z.: An artificial neural network approach for remaining useful life prediction of equipments subject to condition monitoring. In: 8th International Conference on Reliability, Maintainability and Safety, July 2009, pp. 143–148 (2009)
7. Gebraeel, N., Lawley, M.A.: A neural network degradation model for computing and updating residual life distributions. IEEE Transactions on Automation Science and Engineering 5, 154–163 (2008)
8. Wu, S., Gebraeel, N., Lawley, M.A.: A Neural Network Integrated Decision Support System for Condition-Based Optimal Predictive Maintenance Policy. IEEE Transactions on Systems, Man and Cybernetics 37(2), 226–236 (2007)
9. Lee, J.P., Ji, P.S., Lim, J.Y., Kim, S.S., Ozdemir, A., Singh, C.: Diagnosis of power transformers using modified self organizing map. IEEE Power Engineering Society General Meeting 2, 1869–1874 (2005)
10. Arranz, A.L., Cruz, A., Sanz-Bobi, M.A., Ruíz, P., Coutiño, J.: DADICC: Intelligent system for anomaly detection in a combined cycle gas turbine plant. Expert Systems with Applications 34(4), 2267–2277 (2008)
11. García, M.C., Sanz-Bobi, M.A., del Pico, J.: SIMAP: Intelligent System for Predictive Maintenance: Application to the health condition monitoring of a windturbine gearbox. Computers in Industry 57(6), 552–568 (2006)
12. Bishop, C.M.: Pattern Recognition and Machine Learning. Springer, Heidelberg (2006)
13. Box, G.P., Jenkins, G.M., Reinsel, G.C.: Time Series Analysis. Forecasting and Control, 4th edn. Wiley, Chichester (July 2008)

Combining Adaptive with Artificial Intelligence and Nonlinear Methods for Fault Tolerant Control

Adriana Vargas-Martínez and Luis E. Garza-Castañón

Instituto Tecnológico y de Estudios Superiores de Monterrey (ITESM)
Ave. Eugenio Garza Sada 2501 Sur Col. Tecnológico
64849 Monterrey, Nuevo León, México
{A00777924,legarza}@itesm.mx

Abstract. In this article different schemes for Fault Tolerant Control (FTC) based on Adaptive Control, Artificial Intelligence (AI) and Robust Control are proposed. These schemes includes a Model Reference Adaptive Controller with a Neural Network and a PID controller optimized by a Genetic Algorithm (MRAC-PID-NN), a Model Reference Adaptive Controller with a Sliding Mode Control (MRAC-SMC) and a classical Model Reference Adaptive Controller (MRAC). In order to compare the performance of these schemes, an Industrial Heat Exchanger was used as test bed in which two different types of faults (abrupt and gradual) with different magnitudes (10% and 20%) were simulated. The simulation results showed that the use of AI methods improves the FTC schemes, developing a robust control system against sensor faults and a wider threshold to accommodate actuator faults in comparison with the two other schemes.

Keywords: Artificial Intelligence, Fault Tolerant Control, Model Reference Adaptive Control, Neural Network, PID, Sliding Mode Control.

1 Introduction

Global markets have increased the demand for more and better products, which requires higher levels of plant availability and systems reliability. This issue has allowed that engineers and scientists give more attention to the design of methods and systems that can handle certain types of faults (i.e. Fault Tolerant Systems). On the other hand, global crisis creates more competition between industries and production losses and lack of presence in the markets are not an option. In addition, modern systems and challenging operating conditions increase the possibility of system failures which can cause loss of human lives and equipments. In all these environments the use of automation and intelligent systems is fundamental to minimize the impact of faults. For the above reasons, Fault Tolerant Control methods have been proposed, in which the most important benefit is that the plant continues operating in spite of a fault, no matter if the process has certain degradation in its performance. This strategy prevents that a fault develops into a more serious failure. Although, most of the FTC methods that have been developed are based on classical control theory [1], the use of Artificial Intelligence in FTC has emerged recently [2]. Classical AI approaches such

N. García-Pedrajas et al. (Eds.): IEA/AIE 2010, Part III, LNAI 6098, pp. 31–41, 2010.

as Neural Networks (NN), Fuzzy Logic (FL), Neuro-Fuzzy (NN-FL) and Genetic Algorithms (GA) offer an advantage over traditional methods used by the control community such as state observers, statistical analysis, parameter estimation, parity relations and residual generation [3], [4]. The reason is that AI approaches can reproduce the behavior of nonlinear dynamical systems with models extracted from data. Also, there are many learning processes in AI that improve the FTC performance. This is a very important issue in FTC applications on automated processes, where information is easily available, or processes where accurate mathematical models are hard to obtain.

In last year's, NNs have been applied in FTC because they arc helpful to identify, detect and accommodate system faults. The application of NNs to FTC can be divided in three groups. The first group includes NNs used as fault detectors by estimating changes in process models dynamics [5]. The second group includes NNs used as controllers [6]; and the third group integrates NNs which performs both functions: fault detection, and control [7], [8]. Recently, Genetic Algorithms (GA) have been applied in fault tolerant control as a strategy to optimize and supervise the controlled system in order to accommodate system failures. Additionally, the combination of nonlinear control techniques (Sliding Mode Control) with adaptive control (MRAC) is helpful in tracking problems and can create a more robust system [9]. Therefore, it could be helpful in the development of FTC systems.

In this research different approaches for FTC based on Adaptive and Nonlinear Control are proposed. The first method is a combination of a Model Reference Adaptive Controller, a Neural Network controller and a PID controller whose parameters were optimized by a Genetic Algorithm (MRAC-NN-PID), the second method incorporates a Model Reference Adaptive Controller and a Sliding Mode Control system (MRAC-SMC). The third method is a classical MRAC controller (MRAC). Results showed that the MRAC-NN-PID had a better performance than the MRAC-SMC and the classical MRAC approach.

2 Background

2.1 Model Reference Adaptive Control

The MRAC implements a closed loop controller that involves the parameters that should be optimized, in order to modify the system response to achieve the desired final value. The adaptation mechanism adjusts the controller parameters to match the process output with the reference model output. The reference model is specified as the ideal model behavior that the system is expected to follow. The mathematical procedure to design the MRAC system is the following. First, equation (1) should be transformed in order to include the Process Model and the Reference Model with their respective inputs [10]:

$$e = y_{process} - y_{reference} = \text{Process} * u - \text{Reference Model} * u_c . \tag{1}$$

where e, $y_{process}$, $y_{reference}$, u and u_c represent the error, process output, reference output, process input and controller input, respectively.

To reduce the error, a cost function was used, in the form of:

$$J(\theta) = {}^1\!/_2 \, e^2(\theta) . \tag{2}$$

where θ is the adaptive parameter inside the controller. In our case, the implemented MRAC scheme for the Heat Exchanger process has two adaptation parameters: adaptive feedfoward gain (θ_1) and adaptive feedback gain (θ_2). These parameters will be updated to follow the reference model. Then, the input is rewritten in terms of the adaptive feedforward (θ_1) and adaptive feedback (θ_2) gain:

$$u = \theta_1 u_c - \theta_2 y_{process} . \tag{3}$$

Equation (3) was defined to derive an equation for the Process output ($y_{process}$):

$$y_{process} = Process * u = \left(\frac{b_r}{s^2 + a_{1r}s + a_{0r}}\right)\left(\theta_1 u_c - \theta_2 y_{process}\right) = \left(\frac{b_r \theta_1}{s^2 + a_{1r}s + a_{0r} + b_r \theta_2}\right) u_c . \tag{4}$$

Using equation (4), the error can be redefined as:

$$e = \left(\frac{b_r \theta_1}{s^2 + a_{1r}s + a_{0r} + b_r \theta_2}\right) u_c - (\text{Reference Model} * u_c) . \tag{5}$$

Therefore, equation (2) can be minimized if the parameters θ change in the negative direction of the gradient J, this is called the gradient descent method and is represented by:

$$d\theta/dt = -\gamma \, \partial J/\partial \theta = -\gamma \, \partial e/\partial \theta \, e . \tag{6}$$

where γ is the parameter to adjust and represent the speed of learning. The above equation is known as the MIT rule and determines how the parameter θ will be updated to reduce the error [11]. The error partial derivatives with respect to the adaptive feedforward (θ_1) and adaptive feedback (θ_2) gain are specified as:

$$\partial e/\partial \theta_1 = \left(\frac{b_r}{s^2 + a_{1r}s + a_{0r} + b_r \theta_2}\right) u_c \quad \text{and} \quad \partial e/\partial \theta_2 = \left(\frac{b_r^2 \theta_1}{(s^2 + a_{1r}s + a_{0r} + b_r \theta_2)^2}\right) u_c = -\left(\frac{b_r \theta_1}{s^2 + a_{1r}s + a_{0r} + b_r \theta_2}\right) y_{process} . \tag{7}$$

Consequently, the Process characteristic equation can be transformed into equation (8), because the MRAC system purpose is to approximate the Process Model with the Reference Model.

$$s^2 + a_{1r}s + a_{0r} + b_r \theta_2 \approx s^2 + a_{1r}s + a_{0r} . \tag{8}$$

Finally, with equation (11) defined, the error partial derivatives are transformed; and employing the MIT rule, the update rules for the adaptive feedforward (θ_1) and adaptive feedback (θ_2) gain are written. This is shown in equations (9) and (10).

$$\partial e/\partial \theta_1 = \left(\frac{a_{1r}s + a_{0r}}{s^2 + a_{1r}s + a_{0r}}\right) u_c \rightarrow d\theta_1/dt = -\gamma \, \partial e/\partial \theta_1 \, e = -\gamma \left(\frac{a_{1r}s + a_{0r}}{s^2 + a_{1r}s + a_{0r}} u_c\right) e . \tag{9}$$

$$\partial e/\partial \theta_2 = -\left(\frac{a_{1r}s + a_{0r}}{s^2 + a_{1r}s + a_{0r}}\right) y_{process} \rightarrow d\theta_2/dt = -\gamma \, \partial e/\partial \theta_2 \, e = \gamma \left(\frac{a_{1r}s + a_{0r}}{s^2 + a_{1r}s + a_{0r}} y_{process}\right) e . \tag{10}$$

2.2 Neural Networks

NNs are mathematical models that try to mimic the biological nervous system. An artificial neuron have multiple input signals $x_1, x_2, \ldots, x_n$ entering the neuron using connection links with specific weights $w_1, w_2, \ldots, w_n$, and also have a firing threshold b, an activation function f and an output of the neuron that is represented by $y = f(\sum_{i=1}^{n} w_i x_i - b)$. The firing threshold b or bias can be represented as another weight by placing an extra input node x_0 that takes a value of 1 and has a $w_0 = -b$ [12] (see **Figure 1**).

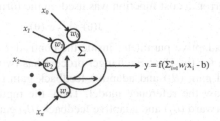

Fig. 1. Artificial Neural Network

A neural network with more than one input layer of neurons, a middle layer called the hidden layer and an output layer is named a multi-layer neural network. Also, a NN can have a feedback or a feed-forward structure. In the feedback structure the information can move back and forward. In the feed-forward structure, the information moves only forward from the input nodes through the outputs nodes with no cycles in the network. The NN need to be trained from examples, in a process called supervised learning. Once a successfully training is done, the neural network is ready if and only if the networks reproduce the desired outputs from the given inputs. The most common methodology for this kind of learning is the backpropagation algorithm, where the weights of the neural network are determined by using iteration until the output of the network is the same as the desired output.

To create and train the Neural Network controller, the original process inputs were introduced as well as the desired outputs. In our proposal, the created NN is a two-layer feed forward neural network with 20 sigmoid hidden neurons and a linear output neuron. To train the network, the Levenberg-Maquard backpropagation algorithm was used. This training algorithm is a combination of Gauss-Newton and gradient descent methods which integrates the benefits of the global and local convergence properties from the gradient descent and Gauss-Newton methods, respectively.

2.3 Genetics Algorithms

GA are searching and optimizing algorithms motivated by natural selection evolution and natural genetics [13]. The simplest GA follows the next steps: Generate a random initial population of chromosomes (potential solutions), calculate the fitness of every chromosome in the population, apply selection, crossover and mutation and replace the actual population with the new population until the required solution is achieved. The main advantages of GA are: powerful computational effect, robustness, fault tolerance, fast convergence to a global optimal, capability of searching in complex landscape where the fitness function is discontinuous, can be combined with traditional optimization techniques (Tabu search) and have the ability to solve problem without needing human experts [13].

In our experiments, the parameters for the PID controller were obtained by using a Genetic Algorithm Pattern Search to track the desired system trajectory. The desired parameters for the system were first established as the model reference desired trajectory (no faults in the system) and then the Genetic Algorithm obtained the best parameter optimization.

2.4 Sliding Mode Control

The sliding mode controller is a technique in which the states of the systems reach a sliding surface (denoted by s) and are maintained there by a shifting law design in order to stabilize the system using a state feedback control law [14]. In order to develop the procedure to design this controller, first the original transfer function is decomposed in to a cascade system, and the following equations are obtained:

$$\dot{x}_1 = -\alpha_1 x_1 - \alpha_2 x_2 + u, \quad \dot{x}_2 = x_1 \quad \text{and} \quad y = \alpha_3 x_2 \tag{11}$$

Where α_1, α_2, and α_3 are constants, x_2 is equal to the system output, $\dot{x}_2$ is the derivative of x_2 and $\dot{x}_1$ is the derivative of x_1. With the above variables defined, the following equations can be established:

$$\dot{x}_1 = f(x) + g(x)u \quad \text{and} \quad \dot{x}_2 = x_1 . \tag{12}$$

Where: $f(x)$ and $g(x)$ are nonlinear functions, $g(x) > 0$, $f(x)$ and $g(x)$ need not to be continuous and x_2 is stable if:

$$\dot{x}_2 = -ax_2, \ a > 0 . \tag{13}$$

On the other hand, if:

$$s = x_1 + ax_2 \ \rightarrow \ \dot{x}_2 = x_1 = -ax_2 + s . \tag{14}$$

Then, the time derivate of s is:

$$\dot{s} = \dot{x}_1 + a\dot{x}_2 = f(x) + g(x)u + ax_1 . \tag{15}$$

Therefore, the Lyapunov candidate function is:

$$V = \frac{1}{2} s^2 . \tag{16}$$

Where:

$$\dot{V} = \dot{s}s = [f(x) + g(x)u + ax_1] . \tag{17}$$

$\dot{V}$ is negative definite if

$$f(x) + g(x)u + ax_2 \begin{cases} <0 \text{ for } s>0 \\ =0 \text{ for } s=0 \\ >0 \text{ for } s<0 \end{cases} . \tag{18}$$

The stability is ensured if

$$u \begin{cases} <\beta(x) \text{ for } s>0 \\ =\beta(x) \text{ for } s=0 \\ >\beta(x) \text{ for } s<0 \end{cases} \quad \text{and} \quad \beta(x) = -\frac{f(x) + ax_1}{g(x)} \tag{19}$$

Finally, the control law that will be used is:

$$u = \beta(x) - K\text{sign}(s) . \tag{20}$$

where $K > 0$.

3 Proposed Scheme

Three different FTC schemas were proposed: MRAC, MRAC-SMC and MRAC-PID-NN (see **Figure 2**). To test the proposed approaches, an industrial heat exchanger was used (shown in **Figure 3** and **Table 1**). This process is a shell and tube industrial heat exchanger with two inputs: water and steam flows controlled by pneumatic valves (FSV$_1$ and FSV$_2$, respectively), the water flows inside the tubes at room temperature and the steam flows through the tube walls in order to transfer heat to the water. In addition the industrial heat exchanger has one output, in which the water temperature is measured by a thermistor (TT$_2$). Variations in water and steam flows are determined by flow transmitters (FT$_1$ and FT$_2$, respectively). To develop the continuous model of the Heat Exchanger process, an identification experiment was performed, where a Pseudo Random Binary Sequence (PRBS) was applied to water and steam valves, and variations in water temperature were recorded. With the data obtained in the PRBS test, the identification was achieved and the following model with an 87% of accuracy was obtained:

$$G_p = G_{steam} + (-G_{water}) = \frac{0.00002}{s^2 + 0.004299s + 0.00002} + \frac{-0.000013}{s^2 + 0.007815s + 0.00008}. \tag{21}$$

$$T(s) = \frac{0.00002}{s^2 + 0.004299s + 0.00002} F_{steam}(s) - \frac{0.000013}{s^2 + 0.007815s + 0.00008} F_{water}(s). \tag{22}$$

where G_p represents the Process Model, G_{steam} and G_{water} describes the steam and water model of the industrial heat exchanger, respectively. $T(s)$ describes the Water Temperature at the exit and $F_{steam}(s)$ and $F_{water}(s)$ represent the steam and water flow, respectively.

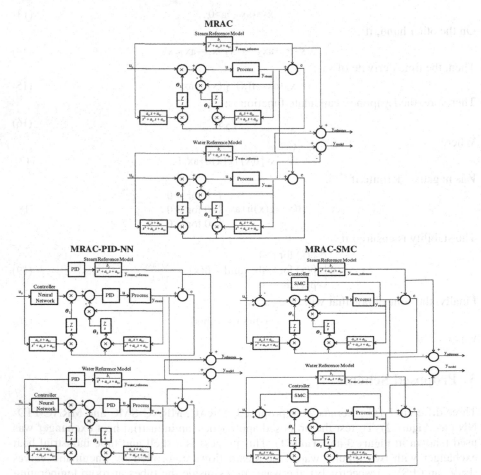

Fig. 2. Different proposed schemes: MRAC (upper figure), MRAC-PID-NN (lower left corner) and MRAC-SMC (lower right corner)

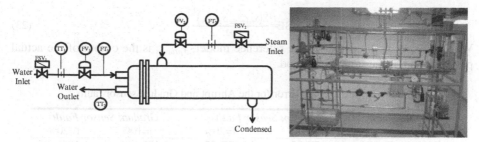

Fig. 3. Industrial Heat Exchanger used in the experiments

Table 1. Industrial Heat Exchanger Sensors/Transmitters Description

Tag Name	Description
FSV_1	Solenoid valve in the water inlet
TT_1	Temperature transmitter of the water inlet
FV_1	Pneumatic control valve in the water inlet
FT_1	Flow transmitter in the water inlet
TT_2	Temperature transmitter of the water outlet
FV_2	Pneumatic control valve in the steam inlet
FT_2	Flow transmitter of the steam inlet
FSV_2	Solenoid valve in the steam inlet

4 Experiments and Results

In these experiments two different types of faults were simulated in the implemented schemes: abrupt faults and gradual faults (also called *soft faults*). In the abrupt faults case, the whole magnitude of the fault is developed in one moment of time and was simulated with a step function. Instead, gradual faults are developed during a period of time and are implemented with a ramp function. Both types of faults, abrupt and gradual, are applied in sensors (feedback), in which the properties of the process are not affected, but the sensor readings are mistaken. And also, are implemented in actuators (process entry) in which the process properties are not affected either, but the process behavior can change or can be interrupted.

The above types of faults were tested in the following schemes: MRAC-PID-NN, MRAC-SMC and classical MRAC. In order to the compare the different system structures, several different experiments with different faults sizes were simulated. In each experiment a fault was introduced at time 5000 seconds. The fault size is in terms of percentage deviation from de normal operational value, f=fault. Therefore, three different results can be obtained: robust (no changes occur in the system after the fault), fault tolerant (the system tolerates and accommodates the fault) and system degradation (the system does not tolerate the fault). For the gradual faults the slope was of 10% deviation from the normal operational value per second but had a saturation block stopping this percentage at the values indicated in the different figure rows of **Figure 4** and **Figure 5** (for the purpose of this paper two different fault sizes are tested f=10% and f=20%).

In addition, the Mean Square Error (MSE) was calculated for all the experiments, the results are showed in **Table 2**, **Table 3** for sensor and actuator faults, respectively.

$$MSE = \frac{\Sigma\left(y_{reference} - y_{process}\right)^2}{n-2}. \tag{23}$$

Where $y_{reference}$ is the output of the reference model, $y_{process}$ is the output of the actual process and n is the sampling period.

Table 2. Mean Square Error for the Abrupt and Gradual sensor faults

Approaches	Abrupt Sensor Faults		Gradual Sensor Faults	
	f= 10%	f=20%	f=10%	f=20%
MRAC-PID-NN	1.107E-05	1.107E-05	1.107E-05	1.107E-05
MRAC-SMC	3.915E-06	3.915E-06	3.922E-06	3.922E-06
MRAC	0.0037909	1.7679362	0.0037909	1.7678667

Table 3. Mean Square Error for the Abrupt and Gradual actuator faults

Approaches	Abrupt Actuator Faults		Gradual Actuator Faults	
	f= 10%	f=20%	f=10%	f=20%
MRAC-PID-NN	1.107E-05	1.107E-05	1.107E-05	1.107E-05
MRAC-SMC	0.0012004	0.0038321	0.0012012	0.0038347
MRAC	0.1445393	0.0016271	0.1445286	0.0016268

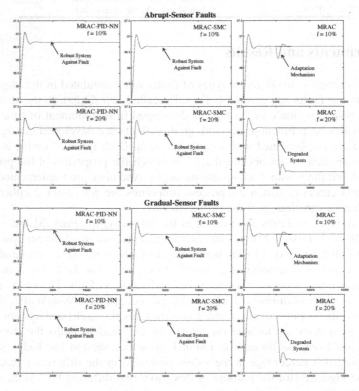

Fig. 4. Abrupt-sensor faults results and Gradual-sensor faults for fault magnitudes of 10% and 20% (the fault was introduced at 5000 secs)

In **Figure 4** is it observed that for abrupt-sensor fault case, the best schemes are the MRAC-PID-NN and the MRAC-SMC because they are robust against faults of 10% and 20% of deviation, the same happened for the gradual-sensor faults. On the other hand for the MRAC scheme, the system is fault tolerant to faults of 10% of deviation and is degraded for fault of 20% of deviation. This also occurred in the MRAC for gradual-sensor faults. These results are corroborated with the MSE of **Table 2**.

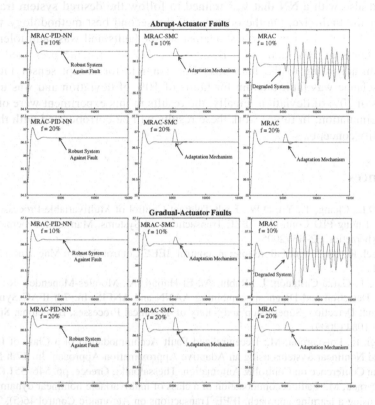

Fig. 5. Abrupt-actuator faults and Gradual-actuator faults results, for fault magnitudes of 10% and 20% (the fault was introduced at 5000 secs)

In **Figure 5** is it observed that for abrupt-actuator fault case, the best scheme is the MRAC-PID-NN because is robust against faults of 10% and 20% of deviation, the same happened for the gradual-actuator faults. The second best scheme is the MRAC-SMC approach, because this scheme is fault tolerant to faults of 10% and 20% of deviation, this results also applied for the gradual-actuator faults. Finally the MRAC scheme for faults of 10% has certain degradation after the occurrence of the fault; and for faults of 20% of deviation the MRAC scheme is fault tolerant. Furthermore, the results of **Figure 5** are confirmed with the MSE of **Table 3**.

5 Conclusions

The MRAC-PID-NN methodology showed the best results because was robust against sensor and actuator faults (f=10% and 20%) with almost a 0% error between the reference model and the process model no matter the size of fault; this method resulted the best scheme because is a combination of two type of controllers, one is the PID optimized by the GA with the best parameters to handle the fault, and also with a NN that was trained to follow the desired system trajectory no matter the fault size. On the other hand, the second best methodology was the MRAC-SMC because it was robust against sensor faults and was fault tolerant for actuator faults of 10% and 20%. Besides, the MRAC scheme presented certain affectation according to the fault size. For example for abrupt sensor faults the MRAC scheme was fault tolerant for faults of 10% of deviation and was unstable for faults of 20% of deviation. Finally, the results in this experiment were obtained through simulation. In future work these results will be corroborated with theoretical stability concepts.

References

1. Yu, D.L., Chang, T., Yu, D.W.: Fault Tolerant Control of Multivariable Processes Using Auto-Tuning PID Controller. IEEE Transactions on Systems, Man, and Cybernetics-Part B: Cybernetics, 32–43 (2005)
2. Stengel, R.: Intelligent failure-tolerant control. IEEE Control System Magazine 11, 14–23 (1991)
3. Nieto, J., Garza-Castañón, L., Rabhi, A., El Hajjaji, A., Morales-Menendez, R.: Vehicle Fault Detection and Diagnosis combining AANN and ANFIS. In: 7th IFAC Symposium on Fault Detection, Supervision and Safety of Technical Processes, Barcelona, Spain, pp. 1079–1084 (2009)
4. Panagi, P., Polycarpou, M.: Decentralized Fault Accommodation of a Class of Interconnected Nonlinear Systems using an Adaptive Approximation Approach. In: 17th Mediterranean Conference on Control & Automation, Thessaloniki, Greece, pp. 546–551 (2009)
5. Polycarpou, M.: Fault accommodation of a class of multivariable nonlinear dynamical systems using a learning approach. IEEE Transactions on Automatic Control 46(5), 736–742 (2001)
6. Pashilkar, A., Sundararajan, N., Saratchandran, P.: A Fault-tolerant Neural Aided Controller for Aircraft Auto-landing. Aerospace Science and Technology 10, 49–61 (2006)
7. Perhinschi, M., Napolitano, M., Campa, G., Fravolini, M., Seanor, B.: Integration of Sensor and Actuator Failure Detection, Identification, and Accommodation Schemes within Fault Tolerant Control Laws. Control and Intelligent Systems 35(4), 309–318 (2007)
8. Patan, K., Korbicz, J.: Fault detection and accommodation by means of neural networks. Application to the boiler unit. In: 7th IFAC Symposium on Fault Detection, Supervision and Safety of Technical Processes, Barcelona, Spain, pp. 119–124 (2009)
9. Lian, J., Zhao, J., Dimirovski, G.: Model Reference Adaptive Integral Sliding Mode Control for Switched Delay Systems. International Journal of Innovative Computing, Information and Control, 2025–2032 (2008)

10. Nagrath, J.: Control Systems Engineering. Anshan Ltd, Indian Institute of Technology, Delhi (2006)
11. Whitaker, H., Yamron, J., Kezer, A.: Design of Model Reference Adaptive Control Systems for Aircraft, Report R-164. Instrumentation Laboratory. MIT Press, Cambridge (1958)
12. Nguyen, H., Nadipuren, P., Walker, C., Walker, E.: A First Course in Fuzzy and Neural Control. CRC Press Company, United States (2002)
13. Mitchell, M.: An introduction to genetic algorithms. MIT Press, Massachusetts (1996)
14. Khalil, H.: Nonlinear Systems. Prentice Hall, United States (2002)

Recognition and Generation of Sentences through Self-organizing Linguistic Hierarchy Using MTRNN

Wataru Hinoshita[1], Hiroaki Arie[2], Jun Tani[2],
Tetsuya Ogata[1], and Hiroshi G. Okuno[1]

[1] Graduate School of Informatics, Kyoto Univ.
Engineering Building #10, Sakyo, Kyoto, 606-8501, Japan
[2] Brain Science Institute, RIKEN
2-1 Hirosawa, Wako-shi, Saitama, 351-0198, Japan

Abstract. We show that a Multiple Timescale Recurrent Neural Network (MTRNN) can acquire the capabilities of recognizing and generating sentences by self-organizing a hierarchical linguistic structure. There have been many studies aimed at finding whether a neural system such as the brain can acquire languages without innate linguistic faculties. These studies have found that some kinds of recurrent neural networks could learn grammar. However, these models could not acquire the capability of deterministically generating various sentences, which is an essential part of language functions. In addition, the existing models require a word set in advance to learn the grammar. Learning languages without previous knowledge about words requires the capability of hierarchical composition such as characters to words and words to sentences, which is the essence of the rich expressiveness of languages. In our experiment, we trained our model to learn language using only a sentence set without any previous knowledge about words or grammar. Our experimental results demonstrated that the model could acquire the capabilities of recognizing and deterministically generating grammatical sentences even if they were not learned. The analysis of neural activations in our model revealed that the MTRNN had self-organized the linguistic structure hierarchically by taking advantage of differences in the time scale among its neurons, more concretely, neurons that change the fastest represented "characters," those that change more slowly represented "words," and those that change the slowest represented "sentences."

1 Introduction

The question of whether a neural system such as the brain can acquire a creative command of languages without innate linguistic capabilities has been the object of discussion for many years. Chomsky [1] claimed that there should be an innate faculty for language in the human brain because of the "poverty of the stimulus" argument. This argument is that the linguistic stimuli that a child can experience in reality are not enough in either quantity or quality for him or her to

N. García-Pedrajas et al. (Eds.): IEA/AIE 2010, Part III, LNAI 6098, pp. 42–51, 2010.

induce general rules of the language from these. Linguists who support nativism emphasize the fact that children can learn to recognize and generate diverse new grammatical sentences using only limited linguistic stimuli, which include virtually no evidence of what is ungrammatical. However, the recent progress made in analyzing dynamical systems and chaos [2] has revealed that diverse complex patterns can emerge from a few input patterns. Thus, the controversy between nativists and experientialists about language acquisition is not over.

Many studies have aimed at revealing whether neural systems can acquire languages using neural network models [2,3,4,5,6,7,8]. Pollac [2] showed the phase transition of non-linear dynamical systems can lead to generative capacity of language using his higher-order-recurrent neural network, but his model required both positive and negative examples of language to learn the rules. Elman [3,4,5] proposed the Simple Recurrent Network (SRN) and showed that it could self-organize grammar using only a sentence set. However, this model could not deterministically generate sentences, but could predict the possibilities of the next word from those that had been input up to that step. Sugita and Tani [9] and Ogata et al. [10] used an RNN model with Parametric Bias (RNNPB) [11] for language learning. These models could learn multiple sequences and deterministically generate them by changing the parametric bias. However, they dealt with simple sentences composed of two or three words, because the models had difficulty learning long complex sequences. Thus, the question as to whether a neural system can acquire generative capacity from a sentence set still remains unanswered. This question is crucial to the problem of language acquisition because generative capacity is an essential part of human language functions.

Existing RNN models for language acquisition such as SRN and RNNPB require a predetermined word set to learn the grammar [3,4,5,6]. Learning languages without such previous knowledge requires the capability to hierarchically compose characters into words, and words into sentences. This capability is essential for dealing with the diversity of expressions in language. Thus, it is also important to find whether a neural system can acquire such hierarchical structures.

We discovered that a Multiple Timescale Recurrent Neural Network (MTRNN) [12] can acquire the capabilities of recognizing and generating sentences even if they are not learned through the self-organization of the linguistic hierarchical structure. We trained an MTRNN using only a sentence set without any previous knowledge about the lexicon or grammar.

2   Language Learning Model

Our language learning model is based on an MTRNN, an extended RNN model proposed by Yamashita and Tani [12]. An MTRNN deals with sequences by calculating the next state $S(t + 1)$ from the current state $S(t)$ and the contextual information stored in their neurons. The model is composed of several neuron groups, each with an associated time constant. If the neurons have a larger time constant, their states change more slowly. The time scale difference causes the information to be hierarchically coded. An MTRNN can deterministically generate sequences depending on the initial states of certain context nodes. Moreover, given a sequence, the model can calculate the initial states from which it generates the target sequence. Therefore, this model can be used as the recognizer and generator of the sequences. The initial state space is self-organized based on the dynamical structure among the training sequences. Thus, the model deals with even unknown sequences by generalizing the training sequences.

Figure 1 shows an overview of our language learning model that has three neuron groups, which are input-output (IO), Fast Context (Cf), and Slow Context (Cs) groups, in increasing order of time constant (τ). The IO has 30 nodes and each of them corresponds to one of the characters from the 26 letters in the alphabet ('a' to 'z') and four other symbols (space, period, comma, and question mark). Cf has 40 nodes and Cs has 11. We choose six neurons from Cs to be used as the Controlling Slow Context (Csc), whose initial states determine the sequence. In our model, a sentence is represented as a sequence of IO activations corresponding to the characters. The model learns to predict the next IO activation from the activations up to that point. Therefore, we only need to use a set of sentences to train our model. Figure 2 shows an example of the training sequence for this model.

The activation value of the i-th neuron at step t ($y_{t,i}$) is calculated as follows.

$$
y_{t,i} = \begin{cases} \dfrac{\exp(u_{t,i} + b_i)}{\displaystyle\sum_{j \in I_{IO}} \exp(u_{t,j} + b_j)} & \cdots (i \in I_{IO}) \\[4ex] \dfrac{1}{1 + \exp(-(u_{t,i} + b_i))} & \cdots (i \notin I_{IO}) \end{cases} \tag{1}
$$

$$
u_{t,i} = \begin{cases} 0 & \cdots (t = 0 \wedge i \notin I_{Csc}) \\ Csc_{0,i} & \cdots (t = 0 \wedge i \in I_{Csc}) \\ \left(1 - \dfrac{1}{\tau_i}\right) u_{t-1,i} + \dfrac{1}{\tau_i}\left[\displaystyle\sum_{j \in I_{all}} w_{ij} x_{t,j}\right] & \cdots \text{(otherwise)} \end{cases} \tag{2}
$$

$$
x_{t,j} = y_{t-1,j} \qquad \cdots (t \geq 1) \tag{3}
$$

$I_{IO}, I_{Cf}, I_{Cs}, I_{Csc}$: neuron index set of each group ($I_{Csc} \subset I_{Cs}$)

I_{all} : $I_{IO} \cup I_{Cf} \cup I_{Cs}$

$u_{t,i}$: internal state of i-th neuron at step t

b_i : bias of i-th neuron

$Csc_{0,i}$: initial state that controls MTRNN

τ_i : time constant of i-th neuron

w_{ij} : connection weight from j-th neuron to i-th neuron

$w_{ij} = 0 \cdots (i \in I_{IO} \wedge j \in I_{Cs}) \vee (i \in I_{Cs} \wedge j \in I_{IO})$

$x_{j,t}$: input from j-th neuron at step t

The connection weights (w_{ij}), biases (b_i), and initial states ($Ccs_{0,i}$) are updated using the Back Propagation Through Time (BPTT) algorithm [13] as follows.

$$w_{ij}^{(n+1)} = w_{ij}^{(n)} \quad -\eta \frac{\partial E}{\partial w_{ij}} \quad = w_{ij}^{(n)} \quad -\frac{\eta}{\tau_i} \sum_t x_{t,j} \frac{\partial E}{\partial u_{t,i}} \tag{4}$$

$$b_i^{(n+1)} = b_i^{(n)} \quad -\beta \frac{\partial E}{\partial b_i} \quad = b_i^{(n)} \quad -\beta \sum_t \frac{\partial E}{\partial u_{t,i}} \tag{5}$$

$$Ccs_{0,i}^{(n+1)} = Ccs_{0,i}^{(n)} - \alpha \frac{\partial E}{\partial Ccs_{0,i}} = Ccs_{0,i}^{(n)} - \alpha \frac{\partial E}{\partial u_{0,i}} \qquad \cdots (i \in I_{Csc}) \tag{6}$$

$$E = \sum_t \sum_{i \in I_{IO}} y_{t,i}^* \cdot \log\left(\frac{y_{t,i}^*}{y_{t,i}}\right) \tag{7}$$

$$\frac{\partial E}{\partial u_{t,i}} = \begin{cases} y_{t,i} - y_{t,i}^* + (1 - \dfrac{1}{\tau_i})\dfrac{\partial E}{\partial u_{t+1,i}} & \cdots (i \in I_{IO}) \\ y_{t,i}(1 - y_{t,i}) \displaystyle\sum_{k \in I_{all}} \dfrac{w_{ki}}{\tau_k} \dfrac{\partial E}{\partial u_{t+1,k}} + (1 - \dfrac{1}{\tau_i})\dfrac{\partial E}{\partial u_{t+1,i}} & \cdots (otherwise) \end{cases} \tag{8}$$

n : number of iterations in updating process

E : prediction error

$y_{t,i}^*$: value of current training sequence for i-th neuron at step t

η, β, α : learning rate constant

When using the BPTT algorithm, the input values ($x_{t,j}$) of IO are calculated along with the feedback from the training sequence using the following equation instead of (3).

$$x_{t,j} = (1 - r) \times y_{t-1,j} + r \times y_{t-1,j}^* \qquad \cdots (t \geq 1 \wedge j \in I_{IO}) \tag{9}$$
$$r \ : \ \text{feedback rate } (0 \leq r \leq 1)$$

The initial Csc states determine the MTRNN's behavior. Thus, we define a set of initial states (Csc_0) as follows.

$$Csc_0 = \{(i, Ccs_{0,i}) | i \in I_{Csc}\} \tag{10}$$

Csc_0 is independently prepared for each training sequence while the network weights (connection weights and biases) are shared by all the sequences. The initial state space is self-organized based on the dynamical structure among the training sequences through a process where the network weights and Csc_0 are simultaneously updated.

To recognize a sequence, the Csc_0 representing the target sequence is calculated using the BPTT with fixed network weights from (6). In this recognition phase, the input values of IO are calculated by using (9) if the value of the target sequence is given, otherwise they are calculated by using (3). Thus, the MTRNN can recognize sequences even if only partial information is given.

A sequence is generated by recursively executing a forward calculation ((1), (2), and (3)) using a Csc_0 that represents the target sequence.

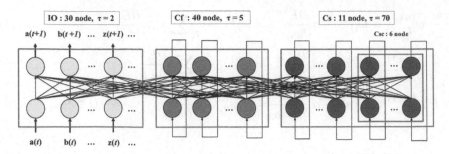

Fig. 1. Overview of Language Learning MTRNN: $a(t)$ is activation value of neuron corresponding to 'a'. The others $(b(t), ..., z(t), ...)$ are defined in the same way. The sentences are represented by successive activations of IO neurons.

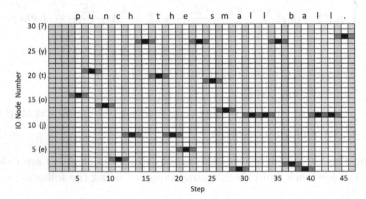

Fig. 2. Example of training sequence: "punch the small ball"

3   Language Learning Experiment

We trained the MTRNN to learn language using only a sentence set, without any previous knowledge about the words or grammar, but only the character set with each character corresponding to one of the IO neurons. This experiment was aimed at finding whether the MTRNN could learn to recognize and generate sentences even if they were not included in the training sentences. If the model could acquire the necessary capabilities, the linguistic structure would have been self-organized by MTRNN from the sentence set.

In this experiment, we used a very small language set to make it possible to analyze the linguistic structure self-organized in the MTRNN. Our language set contained 17 words in seven categories (Table 1) and a regular grammar that consisted of nine rules (Table 2). (It was designed for robot tasks.)

3.1   Experimental Procedure

1. Derive 100 different sentences from the regular grammar.
2. Train the MTRNN using the first 80 sentences.

Table 1. Lexicon

Category	Nonterminal symbol	Words
Verb (intransitive)	V_I	jump, run, walk
Verb (transitive)	V_T	kick, punch, touch
Noun	N	ball, box
Article	ART	a, the
Adverb	ADV	quickly, slowly
Adjective (size)	ADJ_S	big, small
Adjective (color)	ADJ_C	blue, red, yellow

Table 2. Grammar

S → V_I
S → V_I ADV
S → V_T NP
S → V_T NP ADV
NP → ART N
NP → ART ADJ N
ADJ → ADJ_S
ADJ → ADJ_C
ADJ → ADJ_S ADJ_C

3. Test the trained MTRNN's capabilities using both the 80 sentences and the remaining 20 sentences. The testing procedure was involved three steps.
   (i) Recognition: Calculate Csc_0 from a sentence.
   (ii) Generation : Generate a sentence from the Ccs_0 gained in (i).
   (iii) Comparison: Compare the original and generated sentence.
4. Test the MTRNN using another 20 sentences that are ungrammatical as a control experiment.

The calculation of Csc_0 by the BPTT from (6) sometimes falls to a local minimum in the recognition phase. Therefore, we calculate it 20 times while changing the initial value in the updating process ($Ccs_{0,i}^{(0)}$), and choose the result with the lowest error E (cf. (7)).

3.2   Results

We found that our model could correctly generate 98 of 100 grammatical sentences. To correctly generate a sentence, a stable trajectory representing the sentence should be formed in the dynamical system of the MTRNN and its Csc_0 should be properly embedded into the initial state space. We have listed the sentences that the model failed to generate in Table 3.

We also found that the generated sentences did not match the originals for all of the 20 ungrammatical sentences in the control experiment. This is because the recognition error (E (cf. (7)) in the recognition phase) did not adequately decrease. Indeed, the average recognition error for the 20 ungrammatical sentences was about 22 times that of the 20 unknown grammatical sentences.

These results revealed that our model self-organized the linguistic structure using only the sentence set.

Table 3. Failed sentences

Sentence number	Original sentence	Generated sentence
082 (not learned)	"kick a big yellow box."	"kick a sillylllow box."
100 (not learned)	"jump quickly."	"jump slowloxl"

4   Analysis

We claim that our model hierarchically self-organized a linguistic structure, more precisely that IO neuron activation represents the "characters," Cf represents the "words," and Cs represents the "sentences." We illustrate the basis of this argument in this section by analyzing our model.

We analyzed the neural activation patterns when the MTRNN generated sentences to reveal the linguistic structures self-organized in the MTRNN. We used principle component analysis (PCA) in our analysis. We have given some examples of the transitions of Cf neural activation in Fig. 3, and those of Cs in Fig. 4. The three activation patterns in these figures correspond to the sentences, "walk slowly.," "punch the yellow box slowly.," and "kick a small yellow ball.." We have summarized the results of the analysis for each neuron group below.

IO : Each IO neuron corresponds to a character. Thus, their activation patterns obviously represent the sequences of the "characters."

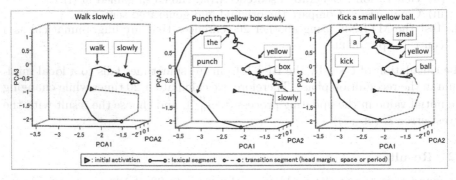

Fig. 3. Transitions of Cf activation : dimensions are reduced from 40 to 3 by PCA (the total contribution rate is 86%). The same words are represented as the same trajectories, and the words in the same categories are represented in similar ways.

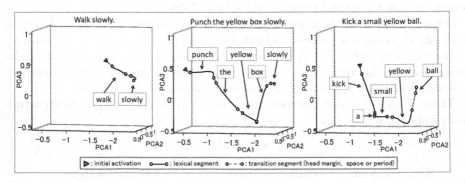

Fig. 4. Transitions of Cs activation : dimensions are reduced from 11 to 3 by PCA (the total contribution rate is 95%). In different sentences, even the same words are represented in different ways.

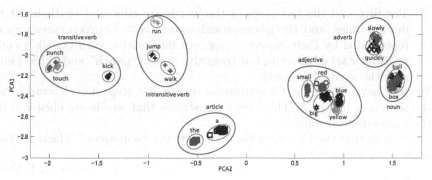

Fig. 5. Cf activation in first step of each word: words are clustered based on their categories

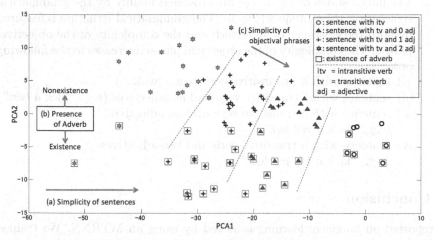

Fig. 6. Initial state of Cs (Csc_0): dimensions are reduced from 6 to 2 by PCA (total contribution rate is 90%). The sentences are clustered based on their grammatical structure. (a) The value of PCA1 seems to be negatively correlated with the number of words in sentences, i.e., the complexity of sentences. (b) There seems to be a PCA2 threshold that separates whether a sentence has an adverb or not. (c) Focusing on the number of words in an objectival phrase, there seems to be an axis correlated with it.

Cf : We claim that Cf activation represents the "words" including their grammatical information. Our claim is based on the following facts, which are found in Fig. 3.

1. The correspondence between characters and activations disappeared. This can easily be confirmed since the activation patterns are different even if the characters are the same.
2. The same words are represented by the same trajectories (e.g., "yellow" in the center and to the right of the figure).
3. The words in the same category are represented in a similar way (e.g., "punch" in the center of the figure and "kick" to the right of the figure).

4. The first and the last steps of the words are clustered by their grammatical roles, and the grammatical associativity between categories is represented by their closeness (e.g., an intransitive verb ("walk") ends near the start of adverbs, but transitive verbs ("punch" and "kick") end near the start of articles).

We also have shown the Cf activations in the first step of each word in all the sentences in Fig. 5. This clearly illustrates that words are clustered by their grammatical roles.

Cs : We claim that the Cs activation represents the "sentences." These are two main bases for our claim.

1. The correspondence between words and activations disappeared. Even the same words in different sentences are represented in different ways in Fig. 4 (e.g., "yellow" in the center and to the right of the figure).

2. The initial states of Cs (Csc_0) are clustered mainly by the grammatical structure of the sentences (Fig. 6). The grammatical structure is featured by both the existence of an adverb and the complexity of the objectival phrase. The complexity of the objectival phrase increases in the following order.

   (i) sentence with a intransitive verb (e.g., "walk.")

   (ii) sentence with a transitive verb and no adjectives (e.g., "kick *a box.*")

   (iii) sentence with a transitive verb and an adjective
   (e.g., "kick *a red box.*")

   (iv) sentence with a transitive verb and two adjectives
   (e.g., "kick *a big red box.*")

5   Conclusion

We reported on language learning achieved by using an MTRNN. We trained the model to learn language using only a sentence set without any previous knowledge about the words or grammar, but only about the character set. As a result of our experiment, we found that the model could acquire capabilities of recognizing and generating sentences even if they were not learned. Therefore, we found that our model could self-organize linguistic structures by generalizing a sentence set. To discover this structure, we analyzed the neural activation patterns in each neuron group. As a result of the analysis, we found that our model hierarchically self-organized language taking advantage of the difference in time scales among neuron groups. More precisely, the IO neurons represented the "characters," the Cf neurons represented the "words," and the Cs neurons represented the "sentences." The alternative view was that the network weights of IO coded the sequence of characters for each word, and those of the Cf coded the grammars as the associativity between words, and those of the Cs coded the separate sentences themselves. The model recognizes and generates sentences through the interaction between these three levels.

We proved in an experiment that a neural system such as a MTRNN can self-organize the hierarchical structure of language (e.g., characters → words → sentences) by generalizing a sentence set, and it can recognize and generate new sentences using the structure. This implies that the requirements for language acquisition are not innate faculties of a language, but appropriate architectures of a neural system (e.g., differences in the time scale). Of course, this is not direct evidence for experientialism in language acquisition, but important knowledge supporting that theory.

In future work, we intend to deal with language acquisition from the viewpoint of the interaction between linguistic cognition and other types of cognition (this viewpoint is that of cognitive linguists). Specifically, we are going to connect the language MTRNN with another MTRNN for the sensori-motor flow of a robot. We expect the robot to acquire language grounded on its sensori-motor cognition using the dynamical interaction between the two MTRNNs.

Acknowledgement. This research was partially supported by a Grant-in-Aid for Scientific Research (B) 21300076, Scientific Research (S) 19100003, Creative Scientific Research 19GS0208, and Global COE.

References

1. Chomsky, N.: Barrier. MIT Press, Cambridge (1986)
2. Pollack, J.B.: The induction of dynamical recognizers. Machine Learning 7(2-3), 227–252 (1991)
3. Elman, J.L.: Finding structure in time. Cognitive Science 14, 179–211 (1990)
4. Elman, J.L.: Distributed representations, simple recurrent networks, and grammatical structure. Machine Learning 7(2-3), 195–225 (1991)
5. Elman, J.L.: Language as a dynamical system. In: Port, R., van Gelder, T. (eds.) Mind as Motion: Explorations in the Dynamics of Cognition, pp. 195–223. MIT Press, Cambridge (1995)
6. Weckerly, J., Elman, J.L.: A pdp approach to processing center-embedded sentences. In: Fourteenth Annual Conference of the Cognitive Science Society, vol. 14, pp. 414–419. Routledge, New York (1992)
7. Cleeremans, A., Servan-Schreiber, D., McClelland, J.L.: Finite state automata and simple recurrent networks. Neural Computation 1(3), 372–381 (1989)
8. Giles, C.L., Miller, C.B., Chen, D., Chen, H.H., Sun, G.Z., Lee, Y.C.: Learning and extracting finite state automata with second-order recurrent neural networks. Neural Computation 4(3), 393–405 (1992)
9. Sugita, Y., Tani, J.: Learning semantic combinatoriality from the interaction between linguistic and behavioral processes. Adaptive Behavior 13(1), 33–52 (2005)
10. Ogata, T., Murase, M., Tani, J., Komatani, K., Okuno, H.G.: Two-way translation of compound sentences and arm motions by recurrent neural networks. In: IEEE/RSJ International Conference on Intelligent Robots and Systems (IROS 2007), pp. 1858–1863 (2007)
11. Tani, J., Ito, M.: Self-organization of behavioral primitives as multiple attractor dynamics: A robot experiment. IEEE Trans. on Systems, Man, and Cybernetics Part A: Systems and Humans 33(4), 481–488 (2003)
12. Yamashita, Y., Tani, J.: Emergence of functional hierarchy in a multiple timescale neural network model: a humanoid robot experiment. PLoS Comput. Biol. 4 (2008)
13. Rumelhart, D.E., Hinton, G.E., Williams, R.J.: 8. In: Learning internal representations by error propagation, pp. 318–362. MIT Press, Cambridge (1986)

Neural Dynamic Matrix Control Algorithm with Disturbance Compensation

Maciej Ławryńczuk

Institute of Control and Computation Engineering, Warsaw University of Technology
ul. Nowowiejska 15/19, 00-665 Warsaw, Poland, Tel.: +48 22 234-76-73
M.Lawrynczuk@ia.pw.edu.pl

Abstract. This paper is concerned with a nonlinear Dynamic Matrix Control (DMC) algorithm in which measured disturbances are compensated. Neural networks are used to calculate on-line step response coefficients for the current operating point. Such models are obtained easily off-line, no recurrent training is necessary. The algorithm is computationally efficient since the optimal future control policy is determined on-line from an easy to solve quadratic programming problem and the model is not linearised on-line. It is shown that when applied to a significantly nonlinear process the algorithm offers good control accuracy (both trajectory tracking and disturbance compensation tasks are considered).

Keywords: Process control, Dynamic Matrix Control, neural networks, optimisation, quadratic programming.

1 Introduction

Model Predictive Control (MPC) algorithms [6,12] have been successfully used for years in numerous fields, not only in chemical, food and motor industries, but also in medicine and aerospace [11]. It is because they take into account constraints imposed on process inputs (manipulated variables) and outputs (controlled variables), which determine quality, economic efficiency and safety. Moreover, MPC techniques are very efficient in multivariable process control.

A great number of nonlinear MPC algorithms have been developed [4,7,8,12]. Although different nonlinear models can be used, artificial neural networks [5,9,10,12,13] are frequently applied. It is because neural models have excellent approximation abilities, a small number of parameters and a simple structure. Usually, the neural model is successively linearised on-line around the current operating point and the obtained linear approximation of the nonlinear model is next used for prediction and optimisation of the future control policy. Thanks to linearisation, during on-line control a numerically efficient quadratic programming approach is used, the necessity of nonlinear optimisation is avoided.

Irrespective of developments in nonlinear MPC, Dynamic Matrix Control (DMC) [2] algorithm is used in the majority of applications [1,11,12]. It is because the algorithm uses step response models. Such models can be obtained

N. García-Pedrajas et al. (Eds.): IEA/AIE 2010, Part III, LNAI 6098, pp. 52–61, 2010.

easily, which is very important in the industry. To find a model, it is only necessary to record the output response of the process to a step excitation signal, no
complicated model identification algorithms are used. In many applications accuracy of the classical DMC algorithm is very good. On the other hand, properties
of many technological processes are in fact nonlinear. Moreover, in advanced
control systems significant set-point changes may be enforced by the economic
set-point optimisation layer [12]. In such cases the classical DMC algorithm based
on linear step response models may be insufficiently accurate, even unstable.

This paper presents a nonlinear DMC algorithm with compensation of measured disturbances. It uses a nonlinear step response model of the process in
which step response coefficients are calculated on-line by two neural networks.
Such a model can be obtained in a straightforward way off-line, no recurrent
training is necessary. The algorithm is computationally efficient since the future
control policy is calculated on-line from a quadratic programming problem, no
linearisation is necessary.

2   Model Predictive Control Algorithms

In MPC algorithms [6,12] at each consecutive sampling instant k, $k = 0, 1, \ldots,$
a set of future control increments is calculated

$$\triangle \boldsymbol{u}(k) = [\triangle u(k|k) \ \triangle u(k+1|k) \ldots \triangle u(k+N_u - 1|k)]^{\mathrm{T}} \qquad (1)$$

It is assumed that $\triangle u(k+p|k) = 0$ for $p \geq N_u$, where N_u is the control horizon.
The objective of MPC is to minimise differences between the reference trajectory
$y^{\mathrm{ref}}(k+p|k)$ and predicted outputs values $\hat{y}(k+p|k)$ over the prediction horizon
$N \geq N_u$, i.e. for $p = 1, \ldots, N$. For optimisation of the future control policy (1)
the following quadratic cost function is usually used

$$J(k) = \sum_{p=1}^{N} (y^{\mathrm{ref}}(k+p|k) - \hat{y}(k+p|k))^2 + \sum_{p=0}^{N_u-1} \lambda_p (\triangle u(k+p|k))^2 \qquad (2)$$

where $\lambda_p > 0$ are weighting coefficients. Only the first element of the determined
sequence is actually applied to the process, i.e. $u(k) = \triangle u(k|k) + u(k-1)$. At
the next sampling instant, $k+1$, the prediction is shifted one step forward and
the whole procedure is repeated.

Usually, constraints must be imposed on input and output variables. In such a
case future control increments are found on-line from the following optimisation
problem (for simplicity of presentation hard output constraints [6,12] are used)

$$\min_{\triangle u(k|k),\ldots,\triangle u(k+N_u-1|k)} \{J(k)\}$$

subject to

$$u^{\min} \leq u(k+p|k) \leq u^{\max}, \quad p = 0, \ldots, N_u - 1 \qquad (3)$$

$$-\triangle u^{\max} \leq \triangle u(k+p|k) \leq \triangle u^{\max}, \quad p = 0, \ldots, N_u - 1$$

$$y^{\min} \leq \hat{y}(k+p|k) \leq y^{\max}, \quad p = 1, \ldots, N$$

where $u^{\min}$, $u^{\max}$, $\triangle u^{\max}$, $y^{\min}$, $y^{\max}$ define constraints.

Predictions $\hat{y}(k + p|k)$ of the output over the prediction horizon, i.e. for $p = 1, \ldots, N$, are calculated from a model of the process. In the classical DMC algorithm the process is modelled by the discrete step response model which shows reaction of the process output to a step excitation input signal (usually a unit step). The output of the classical linear step response model is [12]

$$y(k) = y(0) + \sum_{j=1}^{k} s_j \triangle u(k - j) \tag{4}$$

Real numbers $s_1, s_2, s_3, \ldots$ are step response coefficients of the model. Provided that the process is stable, after a step change in the input the output stabilises at a certain value s_∞, i.e. $\lim_{k \to \infty} s_k = s_\infty$. Hence, the model needs only a finite number of step response coefficients: $s_1, s_2, s_3, \ldots, s_D$, where D is the horizon of process dynamics.

3   Neural Dynamic Matrix Control

3.1   Step Response Neural Models

In nonlinear MPC algorithms input-output or state-space models are usually used [12]. Frequently, they are realised by neural networks or fuzzy systems. Training of such models is significantly more difficult than obtaining linear step response models used in the classical DMC algorithm.

In the considered nonlinear DMC algorithm properties of the process are described by a step response neural model. Instead of constant step response coefficients $s_1, s_2, s_3, \ldots, s_D$, time-varying coefficients $s_1(k), s_2(k), s_3(k), \ldots, s_D(k)$ are used. Their values depend on the current operating point of the process. Analogously to (4), one has

$$y(k) = y(0) + \sum_{j=1}^{k} s_j(k) \triangle u(k - j) \tag{5}$$

It is assumed that the process is affected by a measured disturbance h which is measured. Hence, the model must also take into account this disturbance. The disturbance model is comprised of coefficients $s_1^{\mathrm{h}}(k), s_2^{\mathrm{h}}(k), s_3^{\mathrm{h}}(k), \ldots, s_{D^{\mathrm{h}}}^{\mathrm{h}}(k)$ (disturbance step response coefficients) whose values also depend on the current operating conditions (D^{h} is the horizon of disturbance dynamics). Taking into account the input of the process and the measured disturbance, the output of the nonlinear step response model is

$$y(k) = y(0) + \sum_{j=1}^{k} s_j(k) \triangle u(k - j) + z(0) + \sum_{j=1}^{k} s_j^{\mathrm{h}}(k) \triangle h(k - j) \tag{6}$$

Step response coefficients depend on the current operating point which is determined by most recent values of process signals, i.e. by the value of the input variable at the previous sampling instant and the value of disturbance and output variables at the current sampling instants

$$s_p(k) = f_p(u(k-1), h(k), y(k)) \tag{7}$$

where $p = 1, \ldots, D$, functions $f_p \colon \mathbb{R}^3 \to \mathbb{R}^D$ are realised by the first neural network. Analogously, disturbance step response coefficients also depend on the operating point

$$s_p^{\mathrm{h}}(k) = f_p^{\mathrm{h}}(u(k-1), h(k), y(k)) \tag{8}$$

where $p = 1, \ldots, D^{\mathrm{h}}$, functions $f_p^{\mathrm{h}} \colon \mathbb{R}^3 \to \mathbb{R}^{D^{\mathrm{h}}}$ are realised by the second neural network.

It is assumed that Multi Layer Perceptron (MLP) neural networks [3] are used to calculate step response coefficients and disturbance step response coefficients for the current operating point. Both networks have 3 input nodes, one hidden layer and D (the first network) or D^{h} (the second network) linear outputs. Consecutive outputs of the first neural network are

$$s_p(k) = w_{p,0}^2 + \sum_{i=1}^{K} w_{p,i}^2 \varphi(w_{i,0}^1 + w_{i,1}^1 u(k-1) + w_{i,2}^1 h(k) + w_{i,3}^1 y(k)) \tag{9}$$

where $\varphi \colon \mathbb{R} \to \mathbb{R}$ is the nonlinear transfer function (e.g. hyperbolic tangent) used in the hidden layer of the network. The number of hidden nodes is K, weights are denoted by $w_{i,j}^1$, $i = 1, \ldots, K$, $j = 0, 1, 2, 3$, and $w_{i,j}^2$, $i = 0, \ldots, D$, $j = 0, \ldots, K$, for the first and the second layer, respectively. Consecutive outputs of the second neural network are

$$s_p^{\mathrm{h}}(k) = w_{p,0}^{\mathrm{h},2} + \sum_{i=1}^{K^{\mathrm{h}}} w_{p,i}^{\mathrm{h},2} \varphi(w_{i,0}^{\mathrm{h},1} + w_{i,1}^{\mathrm{h},1} u(k-1) + w_{i,2}^{\mathrm{h},1} h(k) + w_{i,3}^{\mathrm{h},1} y(k)) \tag{10}$$

where the number of hidden nodes is K^{h}, weights are denoted by $w_{i,j}^{\mathrm{h},1}$, $i = 1, \ldots, K^{\mathrm{h}}$, $j = 0, 1, 2, 3$, and $w_{i,j}^{\mathrm{h},2}$, $i = 0, \ldots, D^{\mathrm{h}}$, $j = 0, \ldots, K^{\mathrm{h}}$, for the first and the second layer, respectively.

For model identification at first step responses obtained for different operating conditions must be recorded. They show reaction of the process output to step input and disturbance signals. Next, neural networks are trained off-line to find relations (7) and (8) between the current operating point (determined by signals $u(k-1), h(k), y(k)$) and step response coefficients $s_1(k), \ldots, s_D(k)$ and $s_1^{\mathrm{h}}(k), \ldots, s_D^{\mathrm{h}}(k)$. Because in (6) it is assumed that a unit step is used as the excitation signal at the sampling instant $k = 0$, obtained step response coefficients should be scaled

$$s_p = \frac{y(p) - y(0)}{\delta u}, \qquad s_p^{\mathrm{h}} = \frac{y(p) - y(0)}{\delta h} \tag{11}$$

where the initial value of the output signal is denoted by $y(0)$, excitation increments of input and disturbance signals are δu, δh, respectively.

3.2 Optimisation of the Control Policy

In the discussed nonlinear DMC algorithm the future control policy is calculated from an easy to solve quadratic programming problem, but in contrast to MPC algorithms based on nonlinear input-output models or state-space models linearisation is not necessary. The general prediction equation is [6,12]

$$\hat{y}(k + p|k) = y(k + p|k) + d(k) \tag{12}$$

for $p = 1, \ldots, N$. Quantities $y(k + p|k)$ are calculated from the step response neural model. The unmeasured disturbance $d(k)$ is assumed to be constant over the prediction horizon. It is estimated from

$$d(k) = y(k) - y(k|k - 1) \tag{13}$$

where $y(k)$ is a real (measured) value while $y(k|k - 1)$ is calculated from the model. The step response neural model (6) used for the sampling instant $k + p$ gives

$$y(k + p) = y(0) + \sum_{j=1}^{k+p} s_j(k)\triangle u(k - j + p) + \sum_{j=1}^{k+p} s_j^{h}(k)\triangle h(k - j + p) \tag{14}$$

Prediction for the sampling instant $k + p$ calculated at the current instant k is

$$\hat{y}(k + p|k) = y(0) + \sum_{j=1}^{p} s_j(k)\triangle u(k - j + p|k) + \sum_{j=p+1}^{k+p} s_j(k)\triangle u(k - j + p) \tag{15}$$

$$+ z(0) + \sum_{j=1}^{p} s_j^{h}(k)\triangle z(k - j + p|k) + \sum_{j=p+1}^{k+p} s_j^{h}(k)\triangle z(k - j + p) + d(k)$$

where

$$d(k) = y(k) - \left(y(0) + \sum_{j=1}^{k} s_j(k)\triangle u(k - j) + z(0) + \sum_{j=1}^{k} s_j^{h}(k)\triangle h(k - j) \right) \tag{16}$$

Using (15), (16), remembering that $s_p(k) = s_D(k)$ for $p > D$, $s_p^{h}(k) = s_{D^h}^{h}(k)$ for $p > D^h$ and after some transformations one obtains predictions

$$\hat{y}(k + p|k) = \sum_{j=1}^{p} s_j(k)\triangle u(k - j + p|k) \tag{17}$$

$$+ y(k) + \sum_{j=1}^{D-1} (s_{j+p}(k) - s_j(k))\triangle u(k - j)$$

$$+ \sum_{j=1}^{p-1} s_j^{h}(k)\triangle h(k - j + p|k)$$

$$+ s_p^{h}(k)\triangle h(k) + \sum_{j=1}^{D^h - 1} (s_{j+p}^{h}(k) - s_j^{h}(k))\triangle u(k - j)$$

If predictions of the future disturbance h are not known in advance, it is assumed that it is constant over the prediction horizon, i.e. increments $\triangle h(k-j+p|k) = 0$. Obtained predictions (17) can be expressed in the following compact form

$$\hat{\boldsymbol{y}}(k) = \underbrace{\boldsymbol{G}(k)\triangle\boldsymbol{u}(k)}_{\text{future}} + \underbrace{\boldsymbol{y}(k) + \boldsymbol{G}^{\mathrm{P}}(k)\triangle\boldsymbol{u}^{\mathrm{P}}(k) + \boldsymbol{G}^{\mathrm{h}}(k)\triangle\boldsymbol{h}(k)}_{\text{past}} \qquad (18)$$

where $\hat{\boldsymbol{y}}(k) = [\hat{y}(k+1|k)\ldots\hat{y}(k+N|k)]^{\mathrm{T}}$, $\boldsymbol{y}(k) = [y(k)\ldots y(k)]^{\mathrm{T}}$ are vectors of length N, $\triangle\boldsymbol{u}^{\mathrm{P}}(k) = [\triangle u(k-1)\ldots\triangle u(k-(D-1))]^{\mathrm{T}}$ is a vector of length $D-1$, $\triangle\boldsymbol{h}(k) = [\triangle h(k)\ldots\triangle h(k-(D^{\mathrm{h}}-1))]^{\mathrm{T}}$ is a vector of length $D^{\mathrm{h}}-1$, matrices

$$\boldsymbol{G}(k) = \begin{bmatrix} s_1(k) & 0 & \cdots & 0 \\ s_2(k) & s_1(k) & \cdots & 0 \\ \vdots & \vdots & \ddots & \vdots \\ s_N(k) & s_{N-1}(k) & \cdots & s_{N-N_u+1}(k) \end{bmatrix} \qquad (19)$$

$$\boldsymbol{G}^{\mathrm{P}}(k) = \begin{bmatrix} s_2(k)-s_1(k) & s_3(k)-s_2(k) & \cdots & s_D(k)-s_{D-1}(k) \\ s_3(k)-s_1(k) & s_4(k)-s_2(k) & \cdots & s_{D+1}(k)-s_{D-1}(k) \\ \vdots & \vdots & \ddots & \vdots \\ s_{N+1}(k)-s_1(k) & s_{N+2}(k)-s_2(k) & \cdots & s_{N+D-1}(k)-s_{D-1}(k) \end{bmatrix} \qquad (20)$$

$$\boldsymbol{G}^{\mathrm{h}}(k) = \begin{bmatrix} s_1^{\mathrm{h}}(k) & s_2^{\mathrm{h}}(k)-s_1^{\mathrm{h}}(k) & s_3^{\mathrm{h}}(k)-s_2^{\mathrm{h}}(k) & \cdots & s_{D^{\mathrm{h}}}^{\mathrm{h}}(k)-s_{D^{\mathrm{h}}-1}^{\mathrm{h}}(k) \\ s_2^{\mathrm{h}}(k) & s_3^{\mathrm{h}}(k)-s_1^{\mathrm{h}}(k) & s_4^{\mathrm{h}}(k)-s_2^{\mathrm{h}}(k) & \cdots & s_{D^{\mathrm{h}}+1}^{\mathrm{h}}(k)-s_{D^{\mathrm{h}}-1}^{\mathrm{h}}(k) \\ \vdots & \vdots & \vdots & \ddots & \vdots \\ s_N^{\mathrm{h}}(k) & s_{N+1}^{\mathrm{h}}(k)-s_1^{\mathrm{h}}(k) & s_{N+2}^{\mathrm{h}}(k)-s_2^{\mathrm{h}}(k) & \cdots & s_{N+D^{\mathrm{h}}-1}^{\mathrm{h}}(k)-s_{D^{\mathrm{h}}-1}^{\mathrm{h}}(k) \end{bmatrix} \qquad (21)$$

are of dimensionality $N \times N_{\mathrm{u}}$, $N \times (D-1)$ and $N \times D^{\mathrm{h}}$, respectively.

Thanks to using the prediction equation (18), the optimisation problem (3) becomes the following quadratic programming task

$$\min_{\triangle\boldsymbol{u}(k)} \left\{ \left\| \boldsymbol{y}^{\mathrm{ref}}(k) - \boldsymbol{G}(k)\triangle\boldsymbol{u}(k) - \boldsymbol{y}(k) - \boldsymbol{G}^{\mathrm{P}}(k)\triangle\boldsymbol{u}^{\mathrm{P}}(k) - \boldsymbol{G}^{\mathrm{h}}(k)\triangle\boldsymbol{h}(k) \right\|^2 \right.$$
$$\left. + \|\triangle\boldsymbol{u}(k)\|_{\boldsymbol{\Lambda}}^2 \right\}$$

subject to $\qquad (22)$

$$\boldsymbol{u}^{\min} \le \boldsymbol{J}\triangle\boldsymbol{u}(k) + \boldsymbol{u}(k-1) \le \boldsymbol{u}^{\max}$$
$$-\triangle\boldsymbol{u}^{\max} \le \triangle\boldsymbol{u}(k) \le \triangle\boldsymbol{u}^{\max}$$
$$\boldsymbol{y}^{\min} \le \boldsymbol{G}(k)\triangle\boldsymbol{u}(k) + \boldsymbol{y}(k) + \boldsymbol{G}^{\mathrm{P}}(k)\triangle\boldsymbol{u}^{\mathrm{P}}(k) + \boldsymbol{G}^{\mathrm{h}}(k)\triangle\boldsymbol{h}(k) \le \boldsymbol{y}^{\max}$$

where $\boldsymbol{y}^{\mathrm{ref}}(k) = [y^{\mathrm{ref}}(k+1|k)\ldots y^{\mathrm{ref}}(k+N|k)]^{\mathrm{T}}$, $\boldsymbol{y}^{\min} = [y^{\min}\ldots y^{\min}]^{\mathrm{T}}$, $\boldsymbol{y}^{\max} = [y^{\max}\ldots y^{\max}]^{\mathrm{T}}$ are vectors of length N, $\boldsymbol{u}^{\min} = [u^{\min}\ldots u^{\min}]^{\mathrm{T}}$, $\boldsymbol{u}^{\max} = [u^{\max}\ldots u^{\max}]^{\mathrm{T}}$, $\triangle\boldsymbol{u}^{\max} = [\triangle u^{\max}\ldots\triangle u^{\max}]^{\mathrm{T}}$, $\boldsymbol{u}(k-1) = [u(k-1)\ldots u(k-1)]^{\mathrm{T}}$, are vectors of length N_{u}, $\boldsymbol{\Lambda} = \mathrm{diag}(\lambda_0,\ldots,\lambda_{N_{\mathrm{u}}-1})$, $\boldsymbol{J}$ is the all ones lower triangular matrix of dimensionality $N_{\mathrm{u}} \times N_{\mathrm{u}}$. To cope with infeasibility problems, output constraints should be softened [6,12].

At each sampling instant k of the nonlinear DMC algorithm the following steps are repeated:

1. For the current operating point of the process calculate step response coefficients $s_1(k), \ldots, s_D(k)$ and disturbance coefficients $s_1^h(k), \ldots, s_{D^h}^h(k)$ using neural models (9) and (10).
2. Solve the quadratic programming task (22) to find the control policy $\triangle u(k)$.
3. Implement the first element of the obtained vector $u(k) = \triangle u(k|k) + u(k-1)$.
4. Set $k := k + 1$, go to step 1.

4 Simulation Results

The process under consideration is the free-radical polymerisation of methyl methacrylate with azo-bis-isobutyronitrile as initiator and toluene as solvent taking place in a jacketed continuous stirred tank reactor [7]. The output $NAMW$ (Number Average Molecular Weight) is controlled by manipulating the inlet initiator flow rate F_I. The flow rate F of the monomer is the measured disturbance.

The fundamental model is used as the real process during simulations. At first, the model is simulated open-loop in order to obtain step response coefficients for different operating points. The range of operation is determined by constraints imposed on the manipulated variable: $F_I^{min} = 0.003$, $F_I^{max} = 0.06$ and by the range of the measured disturbance: $F^{min} = 0.5$, $F^{max} = 2$. Horizons of dynamics are $D = D^h = 50$, the sampling time is 1.8 min. Excitation steps are $\delta u = 0.0001$

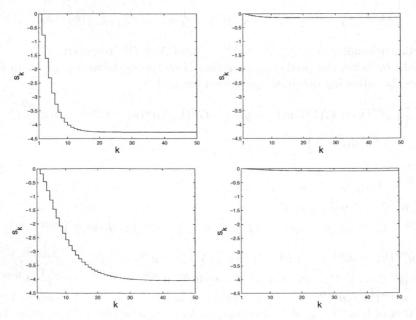

Fig. 1. Scaled step responses s_k for four different operating points: $\mathbf{P}_1$ (*bottom left*), $\mathbf{P}_2$ (*bottom right*), $\mathbf{P}_3$ (*top left*), $\mathbf{P}_4$ (*top right*); the same y-axis is used

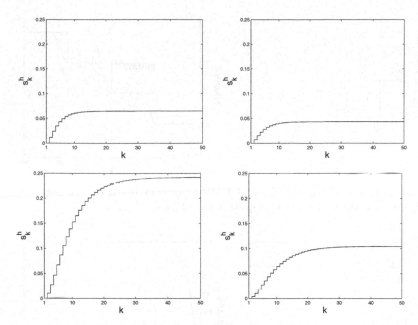

Fig. 2. Scaled disturbance step responses s_k^h for four different operating points: $\mathbf{P}_1$ (*bottom left*), $\mathbf{P}_2$ (*bottom right*), $\mathbf{P}_3$ (*top left*), $\mathbf{P}_4$ (*top right*); the same y-axis is used

and $\delta h = 0.001$. Step responses are scaled using (11). Step responses for 900 different operating conditions are recorded. Fig. 1 shows scaled step responses s_k for four different operating points: $\mathbf{P}_1$: $F_I = F_I^{\min}$, $F = F^{\min}$, $\mathbf{P}_2$: $F_I = F_I^{\max}$, $F = F^{\min}$, $\mathbf{P}_3$: $F_I = F_I^{\min}$, $F = F^{\max}$, $\mathbf{P}_4$: $F_I = F_I^{\max}$, $F = F^{\max}$. Fig. 2 shows scaled disturbance step responses s_k^h. Due to nonlinearity of the process, obtained responses strongly depend on the operating point.

A great number of different step response neural models have been obtained (with different number of hidden nodes). Finally, step response models with $K = K^h = 5$ hidden nodes are chosen.

At first trajectory tracking is assessed. Two algorithms are compared: the classical DMC algorithm based on a constant linear model (from the nominal operating point $NAMW = 20000$) and the neural DMC approach. Tuning parameters of both algorithms are the same: $N = 10$, $N_u = 3$, $D = D^h = 50$, $\lambda_p = 0.2$. Fig. 3 simulation results. Due to nonlinearities of the process, the classical DMC algorithm is unstable while the neural one is stable and precise.

Fig. 4 demonstrates disturbance compensation of the neural DMC algorithm in two versions: with measured disturbance compensation and without compensation. The output reference is constant $NAMW^{\text{ref}} = 25000$, at the beginning of the experiment ($k = 1$) the disturbance changes from $F = 1$ to $F = 1.75$. Thanks to taking into account the disturbance in the model (6), its influence is compensated efficiently. Table 1 shows accuracy of the neural DMC algorithm without and with disturbance compensation for different operating points. In all cases the algorithm with disturbance compensation performs significantly better.

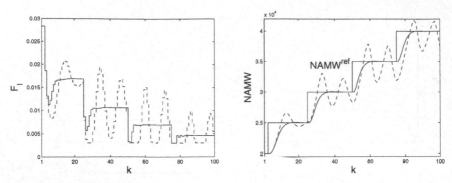

Fig. 3. Trajectory tracking: the classical DMC algorithm based on the linear model (*dashed line*) and the neural DMC algorithm (*solid line*)

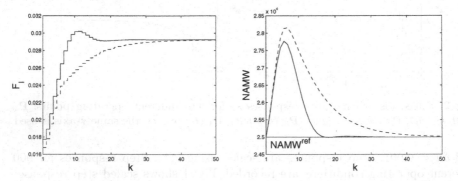

Fig. 4. Disturbance compensation for the operating point $NAMW = 25000$: the neural DMC algorithm with measured disturbance compensation (*solid line*) and the same algorithm without compensation (*dashed line*)

Table 1. Accuracy of the neural DMC algorithm in terms of the SSE performance index (Sum of Squared Errors between the reference and the actual output value)

Operating point	Neural DMC	Neural DMC with disturbance compensation
$NAMW = 20000$	$9.1045 \cdot 10^7$	$4.6203 \cdot 10^7$
$NAMW = 25000$	$8.3261 \cdot 10^7$	$4.1972 \cdot 10^7$
$NAMW = 30000$	$7.2334 \cdot 10^7$	$3.5316 \cdot 10^7$
$NAMW = 35000$	$6.5324 \cdot 10^7$	$2.9012 \cdot 10^7$
$NAMW = 40000$	$6.0530 \cdot 10^7$	$2.4986 \cdot 10^7$

5   Conclusions

In the neural DMC algorithm the step response neural model is used to calculate on-line step response coefficients for the current operating point. The algorithm is computationally efficient, the control policy is found from a quadratic programming problem. When applied to the nonlinear chemical reactor the classical DMC algorithm is unstable whereas the neural DMC algorithm results in good control. Compensation of the measured disturbance significantly improves control.

When compared to input-output or state-space neural models, the neural step response neural model has a few advantages. It can be obtained easily. Because output predictions do not depend on previous predictions, for model training no complicated recurrent algorithms must be used and the prediction error is not propagated. Finally, in comparison with other neural MPC approaches [5,12], algorithm implementation is simpler, because the model is not linearised on-line.

Acknowledgement. The work presented in this paper was supported by Polish national budget funds for science for years 2009-2011.

References

1. Blevins, T.L., Mcmillan, G.K., Wojsznis, M.W.: Advanced control unleashed. ISA (2003)
2. Cutler, C.R., Ramaker, B.L.: Dynamic matrix control – a computer control algorithm. In: Proceedings of the Joint Automatic Control Conference, San Francisco, USA (1979)
3. Haykin, S.: Neural networks – a comprehensive foundation. Prentice Hall, Englewood Cliffs (1999)
4. Henson, M.A.: Nonlinear model predictive control: current status and future directions. Computers and Chemical Engineering 23, 187–202 (1998)
5. Ławryńczuk, M.: A family of model predictive control algorithms with artificial neural networks. International Journal of Applied Mathematics and Computer Science 17, 217–232 (2007)
6. Maciejowski, J.M.: Predictive control with constraints. Prentice Hall, Englewood Cliffs (2002)
7. Maner, B.R., Doyle, F.J., Ogunnaike, B.A., Pearson, R.K.: Nonlinear model predictive control of a simulated multivariable polymerization reactor using second-order Volterra models. Automatica 32, 1285–1301 (1996)
8. Marusak, P.: Advantages of an easy to design fuzzy predictive algorithm in control systems of nonlinear chemical reactors. Applied Soft Computing 9, 1111–1125 (2009)
9. Nørgaard, M., Ravn, O., Poulsen, N.K., Hansen, L.K.: Neural networks for modelling and control of dynamic systems. Springer, London (2000)
10. Peng, H., Yang, Z.J., Gui, W., Wu, M., Shioya, H., Nakano, K.: Nonlinear system modeling and robust predictive control based on RBF-ARX model. Engineering Applications of Artificial Intelligence 20, 1–9 (2007)
11. Qin, S.J., Badgwell, T.A.: A survey of industrial model predictive control technology. Control Engineering Practice 11, 733–764 (2003)
12. Tatjewski, P.: Advanced control of industrial processes, structures and algorithms. Springer, London (2007)
13. Zamarreño, J.M., Vega, P., Garcia, L.D., Francisco, M.: State-space neural network for modelling, prediction and control. Control Engineering Practice 8, 1063–1075 (2000)

The Fuzzy Gene Filter: An Adaptive Fuzzy Inference System for Expression Array Feature Selection

Meir Perez[1], David M. Rubin[2], Tshilidzi Marwala[1], Lesley E. Scott[3], Jonathan Featherston[4], and Wendy Stevens[4]

[1] Department of Electrical and Electronic Engineering Technology,
University of Johannesburg, South Africa
mperez@uj.ac.za
[2] School of Electrical and Information Engineering,
University of the Witwatersrand, Johannesburg, South Africa
[3] Department of Molecular Medicine and Haematology,
University of the Witwatersrand, Johannesburg, South Africa
[4] The National Health Laboratory Service, Johannesburg, South Africa

Abstract. The identification of class differentiating genes is central to microarray data classification. Genes are ranked in order of differential expression and the optimal top ranking genes are selected as features for classification. In this paper, a new approach to gene ranking, based on a fuzzy inference system - the Fuzzy Gene Filter - is presented and compared to classical ranking approaches (the t-test, Wilcoxon test and ROC analysis). Two performance metrics are used; maximum Separability Index and highest cross-validation accuracy. The techniques were implemented on two publically available data-sets. The Fuzzy Gene Filter outperformed the other techniques both with regards to maximum Separability Index, as well as highest cross-validation accuracy. For the prostate data-set it a attained a Leave-one-out cross-validation accuracy of 96.1% and for the lymphoma data-set, 100%. The Fuzzy Gene Filter cross-validation accuracies were also higher than those recorded in previous publications which used the same data-sets. The Fuzzy Gene Filter's success is ascribed to its incorporation of both parametric and non-parametric data features and its ability to be optimised to suit the specific data-set under analysis.

1 Introduction

The microarray has allowed for high throughput analysis of genetic expression. Microarrays are used to quantify tissue mRNA content, allowing one to identify over or under expressed genes [1]. A microarray consists of a thousands of oligonucleotide probe-sets bound on a chip substrate [1] and, for a given tissue sample, generates an expression value for each gene represented on the chip. Microarray data can be used to identify malfunction in genetic expression and can also be used to develop diagnostic and prognostic classifiers [2].

N. García-Pedrajas et al. (Eds.): IEA/AIE 2010, Part III, LNAI 6098, pp. 62–71, 2010.

One of the most important aspects of microarray data analysis is the identification of class-differentiating genes. If good features are used for classification then even the most simple classifier can achieve high accuracies [3]. For the classification of microarray data, the features are the expression values of genes which demonstrate significant variation between samples of different types. These genes are identified by first ranking the genes in order of differential expression, followed by a cross-validation scheme, which is used to identify the optimal number of top ranking genes required for classifier training and testing [2].

Presented in this paper is a novel approach to microarray gene expression feature ranking, based on an adaptive Fuzzy Inference System, entitled the Fuzzy Gene Filter (FGF) [4]. The FGF is extended to include both parametric and non-parametric inputs. A Genetic Algorithm (GA) is also incorporated in order to identify optimal parameters for the fuzzy membership function. The FGF is tested using two publicly available data-sets and the results are compared to those of classical feature ranking techniques, as well to results previously obtained using the same data-sets. The techniques are compared using two criteria: maximum class separability and cross-validation accuracy.

2   Gene Ranking

The FGF is compared to the t-test, the Wilcoxon test and the ROC (Receiver Operating Characteristics) curve technique (for details on ROC analysis applied to microarray feature selection see Hiroshi et.al [5]).

2.1   Classical Gene Ranking Techniques

The most primitive gene ranking criteria is fold change. If a particular gene, on average, is under-expressed for one class of samples and is over-expressed for another class then it is identified as being a class differentiating gene. The problem with fold change is that it does not take into account the variance of a particular gene within a class, thus leading to more appropriate parametric ranking techniques, such as the t-test.

The two-sample t-test is a parametric hypothesis test which examines whether two data-sets were sampled from the same distribution [6]. In the context of gene ranking, the smaller the p-value generated from the test, the better the gene's class differentiating ability. It is assumed that, for a particular gene, the expression values across two classes are of an unequal sample size and have an unequal variance [6]. Hence an unpaired t-test is generally implemented on expression array data. Small intra-class standard deviations and a large inter-class mean difference result in a small t-statistic, indicative of a good class differentiating gene.

The Wilcoxon test is a non-parametric hypothesis test which sums the ranks of samples of a particular class and based on the rank sum, determines a p-value [6]. For a particular gene, the samples are ranked in order of increasing intensity value. The rank values of the samples from each class are then summed. If the sum of ranks are similar then the gene does not differentiate between samples of

Fig. 1. FGF System Overview

different classes and hence will have a high p-value. If the rank sums are different then gene is differentially expressed.

2.2 Fuzzy Gene Filter

The FGF [4] is a rule based gene ranking technique based on a Fuzzy Inference System.

A Fuzzy inference System is a robust decisive tool which mimics the way human beings make decisions based on imprecise data [7]. At the core Fuzzy Inference is fuzzy set theory. Fuzzy set theory, as opposed to classic set theory, assigns each variable value a degree of membership: whereas boolean logic only deals with binary membership, fuzzy logic can assign a single point to multiple groups with varying degrees of membership.

The motivation behind using fuzzy logic for gene ranking lies in its ability to tolerate imprecise data. Fuzzy logic is suitable for microarray data analysis due to its inherent imprecision - expression variation of biological replicates is inevitable. Also, due to its heuristic nature, diverse biological and statistical expert knowledge can be incorporated when ranking genes.

A schematic overview of the FGF is presented in figure 1. The FGF is based on a Mamdani fuzzy inference architecture (due to it's intuitive implementation [7]) and consists of five components: Input layer, input fuzzy membership functions, rule block, output fuzzy membership functions and output layer.

Input Layer: The purpose of the input layer is to extract the relevant features which are used for gene ranking. Whereas classical approaches are either parametric or non-parametric, the FGF employs both elements when ranking genes. For each gene, three statistical features are extracted from the data: fold change, intra-class variability (parametric) and the sum of ranks (non-parametric).

The fold change, for each gene, is simply the absolute value of the log_2 ratio of the mean intensity values for the two classes. The absolute value is considered since a 2 fold change (a log_2 ratio fold change value of 1) is the same as a 1/2 fold change (a log_2 ratio fold change value of -1), the only difference being whether the gene is over of under expressed. This simplifies the FGF since only two fold change membership functions need to be considered.

Intra-class variability is calculated using the denominator of the two sample unpaired t-test [6]. The sum of ranks is calculated as described in section 2.1. Since both low and high rank sums are indicative of differential expression, the mean rank sum is subtracted from each rank sum value and the absolute value

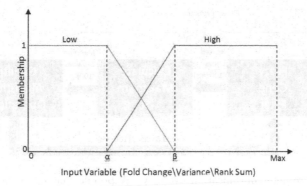

Fig. 2. Input fuzzy membership functions

is taken. This simplifies the FGF since only two rank sum membership functions are considered (large and small), as opposed to three (large medium and small).

Input Fuzzy Membership Functions: The fuzzification of microarray data variables arises naturally from the subjective nature of the assignment of biologically relevant cut-off values. For example, the assignment of a biologically significant fold change cut-off is dependent on the biological question being asked and could vary between experiments [8] (the use of the universal 2 fold change cut-off has been critisised [8]). Fuzzy set theory allows one to take this subjectivity into account by eliminating the need to assign a crisp cut-off value. Instead, a region which allows for fold change values to be considered as being both small and large, with varying degrees, is introduced.

The input fuzzy membership functions depict the various fuzzy sets to which each input can belong. For example, a gene can have a high or low fold change between samples from two different conditions. Hence two input membership functions are allocated to the fold change input variable, namely high and low, as depicted in figure 2 [4]. There are three regions depicted in figure 2:

- The region between 0 and α, where a fold change value is defined as 100% low.
- The region from β upwards defines fold change values which are 100% high.
- The region between α and β where fold change values can belong to both low and high fuzzy sets with various degrees of membership - the fuzzy region.

Fuzzy Parameter Optimisation Identifying optimal values for α and β, is crucial when ranking genes. Just as the assignment of a fold change cut-off value differs from data-set to data-set, so too does the fuzzy fold change region. Hence the optimal α and β values, for each specific data-set, need to be determined. A genetic algorithm (GA) is employed to identify these values. GA has been extensively applied to fuzzy control system optimisation [9,10], whereby fuzzy parameters are optimised for a specific task. In this context, they are optimised to identify the gene-set which results in the maximum inter-class separability.

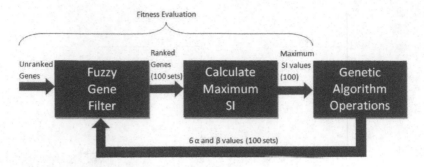

Fig. 3. FGF Parameter optimisation overview. A population of 100 potential fuzzy parameter-sets are iteratively guided towards identifying the optimal set.

GA is a population based stochastic optimisation technique, inspired by biological evolution [11]. A population of individuals is initialised. An individual is defined as a potential solution the function being optimised. Each individual consists of a combination of genes. A gene in this context is defined as an α or β value. Since there are three inputs, each having two membership functions, each individual comprises six genes. α and β values are bounded decimal numbers which have the following constraints:

- $\alpha < \beta$
- $\beta < Max$
- $\alpha > 0$.

Where Max is the largest fold change value present in the data-set.

After initialisation, the population undergoes iterations, or generations, of mating and mutation. Mating entails 'crossing over' or sharing the genes of two individuals to produce offspring, resulting in a new generation of potential solutions. Mutation entails modifying the genes of a randomly selected individual, preventing the algorithm from premature convergence (converging to a local optimum). The population is maintained at a fix size, where an elite count is used to determine how many of the fittest individuals survive to the next generation.

The GA is guided by a fitness function. The fitness function indicates the proximity of an individual to the optimum or to grade individuals. It is used when selecting individuals for mating and mutation. As with biological evolution, selection for mating favors fitter individuals.

The fitness function used here is the Separability Index (SI) [12,13]. SI quantifies the extent of separation between data points from different classes, given a particular set of features. SI is discussed in detail in section 3.1. Genes are ranked by the FGF using specific α and β values. The fitness value is simply the maximum SI value attained when examining the SI values associated with each top ranking gene-set (the top 2 genes, the top 3 genes the top 4 genes etc.). For more information, see section 3.1. An overview of the fuzzy parameter optimisation scheme is depicted in figure 3.

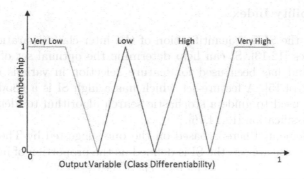

Fig. 4. Output fuzzy membership functions

Fuzzy Rule Block and Output Fuzzy Membership Functions: The rule block relates the input fuzzy variables to the output fuzzy variables, using a set of expert knowledge based linguistic expressions. In this application, expert knowledge is extracted from the underlying statistics (both parametric and non-parametric) as described in section 2.1. For example, if a gene has low intra-class variance, a high fold change and a high rank sum then the gene is deemed to display good class differentiability and is hence assigned to the *very high* output fuzzy membership function. On the other hand, if the gene has high intra-class standard deviations, a low fold change and a low rank sum then the gene displays poor class differentiability and is assigned to the *very low* output fuzzy membership function. If two of the three criteria for good class differentiability are met the gene is assigned to the *high* output fuzzy membership function. If only one criteria is met, then it is assigned to the *low* output membership function.

Input fuzzy membership functions (antecedents) are combined using a min/ max fuzzy operator: a fuzzy OR operation selects the minimum membership of the three fuzzy inputs while a fuzzy AND operation selects the maximum.

The output fuzzy membership functions (figure 4) depict the various degrees of class differentiability exhibited by the gene, based on the input features: very low, low, high and very high class differentiability. These membership functions are chosen due to the fact that there are three inputs, each having two membership functions. The fuzzy outputs are clipped and aggregated by applying the fuzzy OR operation. A crisp output is attained via centroid de-fuzzification, producing the degree of class differentiability exhibited by the gene. Class differentiability is expressed as a number from 0 to 1, 0 being the worst class differentiability, 1 being the best class differentiability. The FGF is used to rank all the genes present in the data. The genes are then ranked in order of class differentiability.

3 Comparative Metrics

The techniques discussed above are compared to one another using two metrics: maximum SI and cross-validation accuracy.

3.1   Separability Index

As mentioned, the SI is a quantification of the inter-class separation, based on a set of features [12,13]. SI can help determine the optimal set of features for classification and has been used for feature selection in various classification application [12,14,15]. A feature-set which has a high SI is a good feature-set. SI can also be used to guide a stochastic search algorithm to identify optimal features for classification [12,14,16].

The SI implemented here is based on the one suggested by Thornton et. al. [13]. For a given feature-set, the SI is defined as the proportion of instances with nearest neighbours belonging to its own class (nearest hits).

In the context of microarray gene selection, SI indicates the extent that a particular gene-set differentiates between groups of samples with different diagnoses. SI has been used to identify the optimal cut-off for gene selection [15]. SI can also be used as a metric to compare gene-sets produced by different feature selection techniques.

Once the genes have been ranked, a SI vector is generated, where each entry in the SI vector indicates the SI of the corresponding number of top ranking genes. For example, the 10th entry indicated the SI of the top 10 ranking genes. The maximum SI value in the SI vector is then identified, indicating the optimal number of top ranking genes to be used for classification. The ranking technique with the highest SI is deemed the best. If two techniques have the same maximum SI value then the one with the fewer number of top ranking genes is deemed better since less redundant genes are included in the feature space.

3.2   Cross-Validation

Since SI is also used to optimise the FGF, it is necessary to implement a non-bias alternate comparison metric for the various gene ranking techniques: cross-validation. A classifier is iteratively re-trained and tested, incrementing the number of top ranking genes used until the gene-set which results in highest classification accuracy is identified. This gene-set is then selected as the classifier input space.

It is also necessary to identify the optimal classifier parameters, for each gene-set being tested. Hence, a nested stratified Leave-one-out cross-validation (LOOCV) scheme is implemented [2]. The scheme consists of an inner loop and an outer loop. The inner loop identifies the optimal parameter values for the classifier (using a 10 fold cross-validation scheme [2]). The outer loop calculates the LOOCV accuracy for the gene-set being tested.

This approach is also used since it is similar to the one used by the original authors of the test data-sets (see section 4), where a K Nearest Neighbour (KNN) classifier was used to diagnose prostate cancer [17] and differentiate between Diffuse Large B-cell Lymphoma and Follicular Lymphoma [18]. Hence, a KNN classifier is also used here to allow for comparison. It is also similar to the scheme used by Statnikov et.al. [2] who used the same data-sets (amongst others) to compare various classifier architectures.

4   Implementation

All techniques were implemented in MATLAB R2008a on an Intel Core 2 Duo 2.2GHz, 4GB RAM, PC. The Bioinformatics toolbox was used to implement the t-test, the Wilcoxen test and the ROC test. The Fuzzy logic toolbox was used to implement the FGF. SI and cross-validation were coded in MATLAB.

The techniques were compared using two publically available data-sets. The first comprises 50 healthy and 52 cancerous prostate samples [17,2]. The second comprises 58 Diffuse Large B-Cell Lymphoma samples and 19 Follicular Lymphoma samples [18,2]. The prostate data-set was generated using the Affymetrix HG-U95 Gene Chip [17] and comprises 10509 gene expression values per sample. The lymphoma data-set was generated using the HU6800 oligonucleotide array [18] and comprises 54070 gene expression values per sample.

Background correction was done using the Affymetrix MAS 5.0 algorithm [2]. In addition, quantile normalisation with a median polish was also implemented.

5   Results

Table 1 and table 2 summarise the performance of the various ranking techniques on the prostate and lymphoma data-sets respectively. Maximum SI and highest cross-validation accuracy are both obtained using the same number of top ranking genes.

As summarised in table 1 and table 2, the FGF outperformed the other approaches, both with regards to maximum SI, as well as highest cross-validation accuracy. The FGF's performance is ascribed to the fact that it incorporates multiple features of the data when ranking genes.

Furthermore, the FGF parameters are optimised to the specific data-set being analysed: the optimised fuzzy parameters for the prostate data-set are different to those of the lymphoma data-set. For example, the FGF α and β values for the fold change membership functions, optimised for the prostate data-set, are 0.0862 and 0.7787. In contrast, the FGF α and β values, optimised for the lymphoma data-set, are 0.1098 and 0.5378.

The fold change fuzzy region for the the lymphoma data-set is smaller than the prostate's. A small fuzzy region indicates less ambiguity in defining a gene as having a high or low fold change. Reduced ambiguity is a result of a clear distinction between genes which have a high fold change and genes which do not. A data-set which contains genes with high fold change values indicates that the data is highly class-separable. Thus, the lymphoma data is more class-separable than the prostate data. This is due to the fact that the two types of

Table 1. Performance summary on the prostate data-set

Technique	T-test	Wilcoxon	ROC	FGF
Maximum SI	0.91	0.92	0.90	0.96
Cross-validation Accuracy	93.1%	94.1%	93.1%	96.1%
Optimal number of top-ranking genes	3	15	6	9

Table 2. Performance summary on the Lymphoma data-set

Technique	T-test	Wilcoxon	ROC	FGF
Maximum SI	0.97	0.95	0.96	1
Cross-validation Accuracy	97.4%	94.8%	98.7%	100%
Optimal number of top-ranking genes	6	4	2	13

samples being compared in the lymphoma data-set originate from different cell lines (B-cell vs. follicular) whereas the prostate samples all have the same cell lineage (the only difference being whether a sample is cancerous or healthy). Hence, differential expression between samples from the prostate data-set is less pronounced than those from the lymphoma data-set. This is also seen in the fact that the maximum SI obtained from the prostate data-set (0.96) is less than the SI obtained from the lymphoma data-set (1).

The prostate data-set was originally used by Singh et. al. [17] to develop a classifier for prostate cancer diagnosis. The maximum cross-validation accuracy reported in the original paper was 86% using a 16 gene model (genes were ranked using a signal to noise ranking scheme [17]). Statnikov et. al. reported an accuracy of 92% on the same data-set [2]. All the techniques presented here outperformed both studies with the FGF attaining an accuracy of 96.1%.

The lymphoma data-set was originally used by Shipp et. al. [18]. The accuracy reported in the original paper was 77% using weighted voting classification technique. Statnikov et. al. reported an accuracy of 97.5% on the same data-set [2]. The FGF outperformed both studies, attaining an accuracy of 100%.

6   Conclusion

The development of a novel approach to expression array data feature selection, the FGF, has been presented. The FGF considers both parametric and non-parametric data features when ranking genes. The FGF also incorporates a GA for fuzzy parameter optimisation. The FGF was compared to standard statistical parametric and non-parametric gene ranking techniques (the t-test, Wilcoxon test and ROC analysis) using two performance metrics: maximum SI and highest cross-validation accuracy. The techniques were implemented on two publically available data-sets. The FGF outperformed the other techniques both with regards to maximum SI, as well as highest cross-validation accuracy. For the prostate data-set it a attained a LOOCV accuracy of 96.1% and for the lymphoma data-set, 100%. The FGF's success is ascribed to it's ability to incorporate both parametric as well as non-parametric data features when ranking genes as well as its ability to adapt to the specific data-set being analysed.

References

1. Coleman, W.B., Tsongalis, G.J.: Molecular Diagnostics For the Clinical Laboratorian, 2nd edn. Humana Press, New Jersey (2006)
2. Statnikov, A., Aliferis, C.F., Tsamardinos, I., Hardin, D., Levy, S.: A comprehensive evaluation of multi-category classification methods for microarray gene expression cancer diagnosis. Bioinformatics 25(5), 631–643 (2005)
3. Bishop, C.M.: Pattern Recognition and Machine Learning. Springer, Cambridge (2006)
4. Perez, M., Rubin, D.M., Scott, L.E., Marwala, T., Stevens, W.: A hybrid fuzzy-svm classifier, applied to gene expression profiling for automated leukaemia diagnosis. In: Proceedings of the IEEE 25th Convention of Electrical and Electronics Engineers in Israel, Eilat, Israel, pp. 41–45 (2008)
5. Mamitsuka, H.: Selecting features in microarray classification using roc curves. Pattern Recognition 39(12), 2393–2404 (2006)
6. Huber, W., von Heydebreck, A., Sltmann, H., Poustka, A., Vingron, M.: Variance stabilization applied to microarray data calibration and to the quantification of differential expression. Bioinformatics 18, 96–104 (2002)
7. Dubois, D., Prade, H.: Fuzzy Sets and Systems: Theory and Applications. Academic Press, New York (1980)
8. Mariani, T., Budhraja, V., Mecham, B.H., Gu, C., Watson, M.A., Sadovsky, Y.: A variable fold change threshold determines significance for expression microarrays. FASEB 17, 321–323 (2003)
9. Herrera, F., Lozano, M., Verdegay, J.L.: Tuning fuzzy logic controllers by genetic algorithms. International Journal of Approximate Reasoning (12), 299–315 (1995)
10. Homaifar, A., McCormick, E.: Simultaneous design of membership functions and rule sets for fuzzy controllers using genetic algorithms. IEEE Transactions on Fuzzy Systems 3(2), 299–315 (1995)
11. Goldberg, D.: Genetic algorithms in search, optimization and machine learning. Addison-Wesley, Reading (1989)
12. Mthembu, L., Marwala, T.: A note on the separability index. Technical report, University of the Witwatersrand, Johannesburg, School of Electrical and Information Engineering (2007)
13. Thornton, C.: Truth from Trash: How Learning Makes Sense. MIT Press, Cambridge (2002)
14. Gidudu, A., Heinz, A.: Comparison of feature selection techniques for svm classification. In: Proceedings of the 10th International Symposium of Physical Measurements and Signatures in Remote Sensing, vol. (11) (2005)
15. Perez, M., Featherston, J., Rubin, D.M., Marwala, T., Scott, L.E., Stevens, W.: Differentially expressed gene identification based on separability index. In: Proceedings of the Eighth International Conference on Machine Learning and Applications, pp. 429–434 (2009)
16. Perez, M., Rubin, D.M., Marwala, T., Scott, L.E., Featherston, J., Stevens, W.: A population-based incremental learning approach to microarray gene expression feature selection. In: Proceedings of the Eighth International Conference on Machine Learning and Applications (2009)
17. Singh, D., et al.: Gene expression correlates of clinical prostate cancer behavior. Cancer Cell, 203–209 (2002)
18. Shipp, M.A., et al.: Diffuse large b-cell lymphoma outcome prediction by gene expression profiling and supervised machine learning. Nature Medicine (8), 68–74 (2002)

Intelligent Network Management for Healthcare Monitoring

Karla Felix Navarro, Elaine Lawrence, and John Debenham

FEIT, University of Technology, Sydney, Australia
elaine@it.uts.edu.au

Abstract. Intelligent network management models monitor personal health parameters rather than computer network modalities. We describe a multi-agent system for managing safety critical processes to work in conjunction with the remote monitoring capabilities of the systems.

Keywords: Network, management, agents, healthcare, monitoring.

1 Introduction

We have developed a series of Wireless Sensor Network (WSN) health monitoring prototypes, under the generic name of *ReMoteCare* that can be adapted for healthcare monitoring, both at a patients home and in a care facility. The research demonstrates that accepted and proven network management techniques may be applied to the development of wireless sensor network personal healthcare applications for such monitoring. This paper describes a laboratory prototype in the ReMoteCare project, as well as the functional aspects relevant to the building and testing of the evolving systems. The work strengthened the areas that were exposed through the prototyping phases to either improve the effectiveness in the functioning of the system or to enhance its usability. A key component here is a robust multi-agent system to manage the safety-critical, possibly life-dependent, processes. This multi-agent system is developed on top of the Network Management (NM) Open System Interconnection (OSI) Functional model and by adapting the Two-Tier, Three-Tier and Agent Server NM Organisational models which all together form the theoretical underpinning of this work. The OSI Functional model was used to form the basis of the ReMoteCare health monitoring systems by adapting its fault, performance and security management functional branches for the transportation and monitoring of medical data. To aid to the readability of this paper the 'ReMoteCare project' will be used to refer to each and all of the different developed systems [1], [2], [3]. The paper is set out as follows: Section 2 provides an overview of the ReMoteCare system and describes the Multi-agent developments for safety critical processes. In Section 3 we outline the Network Management and Wireless Sensor Network application development followed by Section 4 which is a description of the applicability of Network management tools and models to healthcare monitoring. Section 5 illustrates event correlation techniques and we conclude in Section 6 and point to further research opportunities.

N. García-Pedrajas et al. (Eds.): IEA/AIE 2010, Part III, LNAI 6098, pp. 72–81, 2010.
© Springer-Verlag Berlin Heidelberg 2010

Fig. 1. Overview of the ReMoteCare system

2   The Multi-agent System for Safety Critical Processes

The ReMoteCare project is an enhancement by the University of Technology in Sydney (UTS) of Harvards CodeBlue project. It is a software platform using a wireless sensor network to gather medical data in pre- and in-hospital emergency care, disaster response, and stroke patient rehabilitation scenarios [1]. This generic ReMoteCare architecture allows automatic wireless monitoring and tracking of patients and medical staff. By combining different services and protocols while interconnected to many different devices (such as laptops, wireless sensors, location beacons, and 3G mobile phones), ReMoteCare acts as an integrated care-management system.

Wireless devices, called 'motes' are small, wireless, low-powered devices that are also low in computational capacity (see #1 in Fig. 2(a)). Attached to these motes are different sensors such as an electrocardiogram (ECG) for capturing the heart rate or a pulse oximeter (see #2 in Fig. 2(a)) to check the oxygen saturation in the blood [3]. Data gathered by the motes is processed in a way to minimize radio traffic and is sent via their radio devices to an access point (called Stargate, see #3 in Fig. 2(a)) which will forward it to the server (see #4 in Fig. 2(a)). Processing on the motes is quite limited and they contain no intelligence — they communicate, possibly indirectly, with the Stargate access points using a protocol with persistent transmission until a confirmation is received for each message sent. This in effect passes the responsibility from the motes to the Stargates that each host an agent in the multi-agent system — see Fig. 1. All healthcare workers must carry 3G mobile phones that display their immediate work schedule. This schedule is modified when a signal from a mote is given a sufficiently high priority and the phones emit a warning signal.

ReMoteCare extended CodeBlue by a video surveillance feature in the access points [1]. The video functionality enables the Stargate to monitor the area of its radio range. In case of an emergency the personnel in a nursing home for instance, can get a better impression of the scene. The video stream is provided by the Stargate on a HTTP socket so that any TCP/IP device can get access

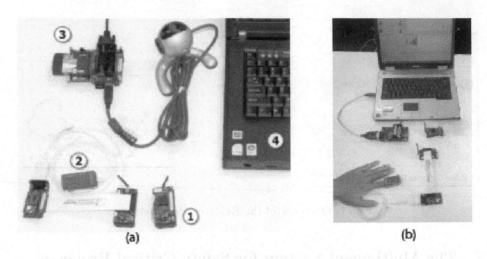

Fig. 2. The principal components

to it. A Simple Network Management Proxy (SNMP) serves as an universal interface for vital sign data [2].

The ReMoteCare safety-critical application requires failure-proof management of the processes that is achieved[1] by treating all processes as 'goal-driven processes'. A *goal-driven process* has a process goal, and can be associated with a — possibly conditional — sequence of sub-goals such that achievement of this sequence "always" achieves the process goal. Goal-driven processes are unlike 'production workflow' in that tasks may fail to achieve their goal, and the reason for failure may lie outside the understanding of the system. For example, if John's blood pressure drops suddenly then this is communicated to John's Stargate where a plan is activated with the goal "A doctor has attended to John's blood pressure." — this plan remains active until the goal is achieved by what ever means the plans stipulate.

Goal-driven processes may be modelled as *state and activity charts* [4]. The primitives of that model are *activities* and *states*. An activity chart specifies the data flow between activities. An *activity chart* is a directed graph in which the arcs are annotated with data items. A *state chart* is a representation of a finite state machine in which the transitions are annotated with event-condition-action rules. Each event on a state chart is associated with a goal to achieve that event, and so a state chart may be converted to a plan whose nodes are labelled with such goals. To represent goal-driven processes, a form of plan is used (see Fig. 2) that can manage failure.

The Plans — Proactive Reasoning. The form of plan is slightly more elaborate than the form of agent plan described in [5] where plans are built from

---

[1] No system is 100% failure-proof. The system described will only fail if there is a total system failure that we assume will come to the attention of the medical staff.

single-entry, triple-exit blocks. Those three exits represent success, failure and abort. Powerful though that approach is, it is inappropriate for process management where whether a plan has executed successfully is not necessarily related to whether that plan's goal has been achieved.

A necessary sub-goal in every high-level plan body is a sub-goal called the success condition. The *success condition* is a procedure whose goal is to determine whether the plan's goal has been achieved. The success condition is the final sub-goal on every path through a plan. The success condition is a procedure; the execution of that procedure may succeed (✓), fail (✗) or abort (**A**). If the execution of the success condition fails then the overall success of the plan is unknown (?). So the four possible plan exits resulting from an attempt to execute a plan are as shown in Fig. 2.

A plan body is represented as a directed AND/OR graph, or state-transition diagram, in which some of the nodes are labelled with sub-goals. The plan body may contain the usual conditional constructs such as **if... then**, and iteration constructs such as **while... do....** The diagram of a plan body has one start state (activation condition [ac],

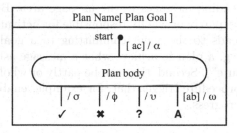

Fig. 3. The Stargate agent plan

and activation action a), and stop states either labelled as success states "✓" (success action σ), fail states "✗" (fail action ϕ), unknown states" ?" (unknown action ν) or abort states "**A**" (abort condition [ac], and abort action ω).

Reactive Reasoning. Reactive reasoning plays two roles: first, if a plan is aborted then its abort action is activated; second, if a procedure trigger fires then its procedure is activated — this includes hard wired procedure triggers that deal with urgent messages (e.g. "John's heart rate is 30 beats per minute.").

Reactive reasoning is achieved by rules of the form:
if < trigger state > **and** < belief state > **then** < action > **and** < trigger state >
where the < trigger state > is a device to determine whether the trigger is active or not, and < belief state > is something that the agent may believe; < action > may be simply to transfer some value to a partly executed plan, or may be to abort a plan and decommit a goal.

Each plan contains an optional abort condition [ab] as shown in Fig. 2. These abort conditions are realised as procedural abort triggers that may be activated whilst their plan is active.

The Agent Architecture. The ReMoteCare architecture proposes one agent for each (human) user; the patient's agents reside on a Stargate . The healthcare worker's agents reside on a server and interact with the user using a robust communication protocol with the user's 3G mobile phone that contains the scheduled commitments of the user and provides panels and buttons for inputting information.

The conceptual architecture of these agents belongs to a well-documented class of the three-layer, BDI agent architectures [6]. One member of this class is the InteRRaP architecture [7], which has its origins in the work of [5]. The Re-MoteCare conceptual architecture differs slightly from the InteRRaP conceptual architecture. It consists of a two-pass, three-layer BDI architecture together with a message area. A *message manager* manages the message area. Access to the message area is available to other agents in the system who may post messages there and, if they wish, may remove messages that they have posted. The message area is rather like a person's office "in-tray" into which agents may place documents, and from which they may remove those documents if they wish. The agent's world beliefs are derived either from reading messages received from a user, or from reading the documents involved in a process instance, or from reading messages in the message area. Beliefs play two roles. First, they may be partly or wholly responsible for activating a local or cooperative trigger that leads to the agent committing to a goal, and may thus initiate an intention (eg. a plan to achieve what a message asks, such as "Check John's blood pressure"). Second, they can be partly or wholly responsible for activating a reactive procedure trigger that, for example, enables the execution of an active plan to progress.

3   The NM-WSN Application Development Overview

The development of the ReMoteCare systems followed two major stages. The first stage investigated and correlated the two focal areas of research of the project, namely WSN based personal healthcare applications and network management systems. This stage comprised the corresponding literature reviews of these two key areas of knowledge and the identification of the intersecting general application requirements and functional principles between them. The systems development methodology was applied at this stage for systems requirement identification, including the interfacing features of the system. Important elements were encountered in this crucial stage such as the mapping of healthcare WSN application requirements to the potential alternative solutions that network management systems had to offer. The intersecting requirement commonalities across areas were identified.

4   The Three-Tier NM Organisational Model

The Three-Tier Organisational model contains three elements, the manager, the agent and an intermediate entity that can act as a manager to manage the agent below or as an agent to send information to the manager entity on top. In this model, there are two databases; one that belongs to the manager and the second one to the intermediate agent/manager.

In the health monitoring system the managed objects are the deployed Wireless Sensor nodes located on either the human body or in the environment.

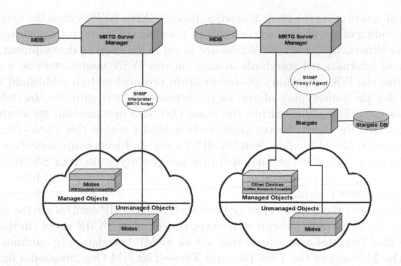

Fig. 4. Adapted Two-Tier and Three-Tier NM Organisational Models to the Stargate ReMoteCare and Medical ReMoteCare Systems

Instead of merely polling information regarding the management of such networked nodes, we used this model for the organisation and polling of the collected health/sensor data nodes in the prototyped Personal Health Care Monitoring system . Most of the wireless sensor nodes utilised for this work are MICA2 and MicaZ Motes, tiny sensors developed by Berkeley. Due to some inherent characteristics of most current wireless sensor network technologies, some important changes in this proposed model were made. For instance, in order to overcome the limitations of the sensor nodes to communicate through the NM standard communication protocols such as Simple Network Management Protocol (SNMP) [8] the researchers wrote a script based on the Agent Server Organisation model structure on the first three health monitoring systems to inject the collected data on behalf of the absent mote-SNMP-agent into the selected NM managing systems. The use of a tailored SNMP proxy agent to communicate to the managed devices was subsequently used in the ReMoteCare system [1], [2], [3].

SNMP is a device independent standard to manage devices in a network which allows multiple managers to talk to multiple devices (agents) . Network devices can be monitored by querying them over SNMP. Those devices will then answer to the queries with the appropriate answer [1]. SNMP uses the management information term to refer to the operational parameters provided by SNMP-capable devices. The definition of Managed Objects shown in Two-Tier and Three-Tier Organisational models in Figure 4 can be broken down into three attributes, the Name or Object Identifier (OID) that uniquely defines a managed object, the Type and syntax that uses a subset of Abstract Syntax Notation One (ASN.1) to specify the representation and transmission of the data between managers and agents within an SNMP platform independent context, and at last, the Encoding which is a single instance of a managed object encoded into a string of octets using the Basic Encoding Rules (BER). BER defines the encoding and decoding of the objects so they can be transmitted over a transport medium such as Ethernet [8]. Because WSNs are at an early stage of development with a lack of international standards among various WSN manufacturers, we had to utilize the WS proprietary communication protocol and an additional agent entity for the prototyping of the early systems and experiments. In order to address these limitations within the same OSI/ISO organisation structure, we incorporated the Agent Server Organisation Model within the Three-Tier NM Organisation Model to allow Non-SNMP Managed objects communication with the Manager. However the final ReMoteCare prototype used an SNMP proxy agent. Management proxies [9] are entities that provide management information on behalf of other entities.

In the case of the ReMoteCare systems such Non-SNMP entities are the motes, and the Agent entity is either a script-type object or an SNMP agent (in the case of the final ReMoteCare system) that act as SNMP translators to communicate with the Manager of the Two-Tier and Three-Tier NM Organisational models; such an adaptation is shown in Figure 4. An important variation in the adapted Three-Tier NM Organisation model (right diagram on Figure 4) is the database structure of the middle management or agent entity. This database is native to the WSN Stargate middle management entity, and not of an SNMP management information nature as in the original Three-Tier NM Organisational model. This maintains simplicity in the ReMoteCare systems communication with the SNMP Proxy / Agent entity by allowing the use of one SNMP proxy agent per NM Manager. The adaptation of the Three-Tier NM Organisation model allowed us to reduce the memory and processing power used by the sensor nodes from buffering. This adaptation was required because the motes have limited storage and processing capabilities. Furthermore this model also allows for a distributed environment with more than one Manager or Middle Manager/Agent entities without adding any processing burden to the sensor nodes from redundant continuous polling.

Network Management Functional Model. The Network Management Functional Model is the primary means for understanding the major functions of network management systems. These five conceptual areas are extended with an explanation of their functionality in a generic WSN Application for Personal Health Care purposes. We concentrated on Performance and Fault management for the building of the prototypes. The main objective of fault management is to detect, isolate, log, notify users and, whenever possible, to automatically correct abnormal network operations to keep the network running effectively. In the ReMoteCare health scenario if the system or a carer detects that that temperature of the patient is steadily rising, an alarm sounds to alert the medical staff to this problem so that action can be taken immediately.

The objective of *performance management* is to measure and make available various aspects of network performance so that it can be maintained to an acceptable level. For the purposes of this research Performance Management variables were for monitoring and measuring variables that can be indicative of the status or evolution of a specific health condition or illness over time. In the first three systems we monitored and measured environmental variables such as light and room temperature, adding medical sensors, namely Pulse Oximeters, in the last developed Medical ReMoteCare.The ReMoteCare project collected and measured health indicative variables of interest to the medical practitioner or caregiver. Management entities, such as health providers and caregivers, are able to continually monitor performance variables. When a performance threshold is exceeded, an alert is generated and sent to the Stargate where a goal is triggered as described in Section 2. One example would be for a patient suffering from heat stroke — if the surrounding environmental temperature increased dramatically such a person would be placed in danger so an alarm would sound in the care givers room to alert the healthcare giver. In the same manner, proactive performance management in a Personal Health Care System allow doctors or carers to predict and avoid undesirable health conditions in patients by analysing previous personalised statistical data, either from its management database with previous historical measurements, or by accessing and comparing existing external knowledge base systems from reliable medical sources. This aspect of the ReMoteCare systems made the system context aware.

The objectives of a *security management* subsystem are to control access to network resources to ensure that sensitive information cannot be accessed by those without appropriate authorisation. Security management subsystems perform several functions that need to be applied in a WSN Personal Healthcare monitoring system. Security issues could prove potentially disastrous in a medical or healthcare setting where privacy must be protected. Security measurements were incrementally added in the various series of ReMoteCare systems. When accessing the monitored data via the handheld device, or remotely through the use of the web interface, the ReMoteCare systems includes an authenticating method for users. Furthermore the Medical MoteCare prototype incorporated the use of version 3 SNMP security features such as the authentication and encryption to the secure polling of the data thorough the LAN and WAN networks. The use of the security management subsystem of Network management tools should assist in securing the vital medical information that is being monitored by the ReMoteCare system. However, the security setup for the series of health monitoring systems would be considered insufficiently robust for a health monitoring environment and will require further development.

The goal of *configuration management* is to monitor network and system configuration information so that the effects on network operation of various versions of hardware and software elements can be tracked and managed. The area of configuration management in the adapted model is intended to keep track and associate health records and relevant personal information with each monitored patient or user. Configuration management subsystems store this information in a database for easy access, so then when an alarm is triggered this database can be searched to aid the caregiver or medical practitioner to access in a timely manner the personal health records of the patient in question. We used the Multi Router Traffic Grapher [10] an open source Network management tool for configuration management for the MoteCare, Mobile MoteCare and Stargate MoteCare systems. The choice of MRTG as an open source tool was made for the following reasons:

- compression of the data with an effective algorithm to define trends via averaging
- it was freely available from the web;
- it had been used effectively by Network managers for over a decade and therefore was essentially an effective NM tool as a result of this continual testing and updating by the inventor and a global team of network managers who contributed to its robust and stable operation;
- it was able to provide essential functions by gathering data and visualising and consolidating the collected data for the testing of the prototypes.

5   Event Correlation Techniques

Other network management techniques that could be usefully employed in a health monitoring system include Event Correlation Techniques. Event correlation techniques are mainly utilised in Fault Management and Performance management subsystems to identify the presence of undesirable behaviours by correlating events, messages or alarms and prioritising them ([11], [12]).Event correlation techniques embedded in various network management tools allow for the development of personalised applications, specific to certain health conditions. Current techniques such as Rule-based reasoning (RBR), Code-based reasoning (CBR) and Case-based reasoning [13] are utilised to add intelligence to Network Management Systems (NMS) and tools by correlating events and prioritising them based on thresholds for labelling, various algorithms and hierarchical structures associated with them. For instance if some "events" in the system are triggered at the same time, e.g. temperature of the person and temperature of the environment, the system will check correlation and prioritise in order to trigger an alarm/message/action. Fault management is the most relevant functional area for a Personal Health Care monitoring system, as it is the functional subsystem that can not only detect undesirable symptoms in the monitored patient, but it could alert the nurse, medical practitioner or relatives in case of an emergency event. It could even be automated to set up alarms or trigger the calling of an ambulance or even dialling emergency numbers in extreme cases.

6   Conclusion and Future Plans

This paper explained the role of Network Management Models and Techniques and their applicability to the development of a WSN Personal Healthcare application. Network Management concepts and techniques including the ISO OSI Model as well as Network Management architectures were explained. The emphasis is on Fault and Performance Management. We outlined how an adapted

Network management architecture and tools such as MRTG are used to provide the first three MoteCare applications with the basic infrastructure for data collection, storing, formatting, and accessing of bio and environmental signals in almost real time. The ReMoteCare systems also apply NMS compression techniques of the stored information up to two years of historical data. It also offers a feasible method for publishing in a website in a graphical form health and environment parameters through a user friendly web interface. In the Medical ReMoteCare health monitoring application the author used pulse oximeters for measuring heart rate and blood oxygen levels, an SNMP proxy and a variety of modified proprietary NM tools. Furthermore we have shown how multi-agent systems can assist safety critical processes. Our future work will concentrate on further enhancements to our multi-agent systems. We thank all the members of the mHealth laboratory at UTS who helped us with our work on this ongoing project.

References

1. Fischer, M., Lim, Y.Y., Lawrence, E., Ganguli, L.K., Kargl, F.: ReMoteCare: Health Monitoring with Streaming Video. In: IEEE 7th International Conference on mBusiness, Barcelona, Spain (2008)
2. Felix Navarro, K., Lawrence, E., Lim, B.: A distributed personal healthcare monitoring system', the international conference on ehealth. In: IEEE Telemedicine and Social Medicine, eTELEMED 2009, Cancun, Mexico (2009)
3. Felix Navarro, K., Lawrence, E., Lubrin, E.: A network management approach to wireless sensor networks in personal healthcare environments. In: The Fifth IASTED International Conference on Communication Systems and Networks CSN 2006, Palma de Mallorca, Spain (2006)
4. Muth, P., Wodtke, D., Weisenfels, J., Dittrich, A.K., Weikum, G.: From centralized workflow specification to distributed workflow execution. Journal of Intelligent Information Systems (JIIS) 10, 159–184 (1998)
5. Rao, A., Georgeff, M.: BDI-agents: from theory to practice. In: First International Conference on Multi-Agent Systems (ICMAS 1995), San Francisco, USA, pp. 312–319 (1995)
6. Wooldridge, M.: Multiagent Systems. Wiley, Chichester (2002)
7. Müller, J.P.: The Design of Intelligent Agents. Springer, Heidelberg (1996)
8. Mauro, D., Schmidt, K.: Essential SNMP. O'Reilly, Sebastopol (2005)
9. Cisco: Network management basics (2006),
   http://www.cisco.com/univercd/cc/td/doc/cisintwk/ito_doc/nmbasics.html
10. http://oss.oetiker.ch/mrtg/ (2009)
11. http://platformx.sourceforge.net (2009)
12. Tyffanny, M.: A survey of event correlation techiques and related topics,
    http://www.tiffman.com/netman/netman.pdf
13. Subramanian, M.: Network Management: Principles and Practice. Addison Wesley, Reading (2000)

S.cerevisiae Complex Function Prediction with Modular Multi-Relational Framework

Beatriz García Jiménez, Agapito Ledezma, and Araceli Sanchis

Universidad Carlos III de Madrid
Av.Universidad 30, 28911, Leganés, Madrid, Spain
beatrizg@inf.uc3m.es

Abstract. Gene functions is an essential knowledge for understanding how metabolism works and designing treatments for solving malfunctions. The Modular Multi-Relational Framework (MMRF) is able to predict gene group functions. Since genes working together, it is focused on group functions rather than isolated gene functions. The approach of MMRF is flexible in several aspects, such as the kind of groups, the integration of different data sources, the organism and the knowledge representation. Besides, this framework takes advantages of the intrinsic relational structure of biological data, giving an easily biological interpretable and unique relational decision tree predicting N functions at once.

This research work presents a group function prediction of *S.cerevisiae* (i.e.Yeast) genes grouped by protein complexes using MMRF. The results show that the predictions are restricted by the shortage of examples per class. Also, they assert that the knowledge representation is very determinant to exploit the available relational information richness, and therefore, to improve both the quantitative results and their biological interpretability.

Keywords: Relational Data Mining architecture, Gene function, Biological data integration, Machine Learning, Gene networks.

1 Introduction

Functional genomic is an open problem in molecular biology. Knowing the functions of the genes it is necessary to understand how the organism tasks are distributed, and which gene/s is/are involved in each biological process. Then, if we are faced with a possible malfunction in the metabolism, we will have to locate the problem at molecular level. This knowledge is essential to design a solving treatment to the corresponding disease.

Nowadays, we still do not have this complete functional genomic knowledge. There are many distributed fragments of gene annotation, from multiple researching studies: wet or in-silico, in wide sense or specialized, in a particular area or function. But uncertainty, changeable, incomplete and unreliable annotations suggest us to develop new techniques to improve this essential gene function knowledge.

N. García-Pedrajas et al. (Eds.): IEA/AIE 2010, Part III, LNAI 6098, pp. 82–91, 2010.

Going beyond in functional genomic, actually an isolated gene is not responsible for a specific function, but each function is carried out by a group of genes. Every biological process can be reached due to the collaboration of all genes in the group. Without some of these genes, the biological result would be different, unfinished or non-existent. Thus, a gene annotation might differ depending on the gene groups in which it works. For example, when a gene A works in a group $G1$ with genes B and C, the gene A function ($F1$) will be different from the gene A function ($F2$) in group $G2$ consisting of genes A, D, E and H. So, functional genomic should be understood as gene *group* function instead gene function; that is, functions are related to a gene group, not to an individual gene.

Given a gene group, if individual gene function are calculated and after the simple union of these functions are considered as the functions of this group, some drawbacks are ignored; mainly, lack of precision (i.e. a false positive increase) and lack of sensitivity (i.e. a false negative increase). First, a gene can get involved in several functions, although all these functions are not carried out with the same gene group. So, the union of all individual gene functions turns out an over-assignation of group functionality. It means that there are functions that are carried out by a gene of the current group but only working in a different group, with other genes.

Second, related to lack of sensitivity, the union of individual gene functions produces also an under-assignation of functionality. In other words, there would probably have joint properties (knowledge shared by several genes) without which it is imposible to assign a specific function to a gene group, even less to an individual gene. Consequently, it is neccesary to support the functional annotation with knowledge about relations among genes.

The wide range of kinds of gene relations in molecular biology results in multiple criteria to make groups of genes: the same regulation network, protein complex, pathway, or protein interaction network [11,18]; genes with similar patterns in expression profiles from DNA arrays [7,14]; genes with certain level of sequence similarity, with the same cellular location, protein family, functional annotation [20] or with common phenotypical data (for instance, pathology or tissue), and so on.

There are several methods to build gene groups through biological networks [16], through Gene Ontology functional annotation [20] or from other sources [9], and some techniques to determine if a gene group is statistically significant [19,22]. However, they are not focused on assigning function to gene groups, as our approach does.

In order to get a suitable gene group functional annotation, different kind of available data sources should be integrated, including both individual gene features (mainly come from gene sequences) and data from several relations among genes (from a group or from whichever gene relation). The huge quantity of these biological data requires the use of computational methods to manage this task. Since the experimental techniques are costly in resources and time, the function prediction methods have shown an useful alternative in the last years [15]. Some interesting approach working with gene groups and functions have been developed, where different data sources are combined [1], but without taking into account the advantages of Multi-Relational Data Mining (MRDM).

We think that MRDM [6] is more suitable for solving the gene group function prediction problem than traditional propositional Data Mining (DM) [6]. In biological domain, there are many relational information, due to the intrinsic structure of the molecules, the importance of the similarity among different species (i.e. homology associations), and even more the relations among genes in groups, which are essential in this domain. Additional advantages of MRDM over the propositional DM approach are: (a)a decrease in the number of redundant features and missing values (very common facts in biological domains); (b)a better representation of real world problems, without losing the semantic after a proposionalization process; (c)an improved storage and management of the data, organised in modules or tables, according to the relations; (d)an easier representation of structured information, such as networks or graphs in interaction networks, pathways or semi-structured data from text mining results.

MRDM have been successfully applied to individual gene function prediction [4,24]. Other similar biological domains have been faced with relational techniques also: protein-protein interaction prediction [23] and a work with gene groups although only related with microarrays [21].

Uncertainty and unknown information in biology always make difficult the bioinformatics problems. Gene group function annotation is even a harder domain, mainly due to the high variability in its context. First, it varies because there is a frequently changeable environment, caused by the improvement in the high-throughput experimental technologies that produces a huge quantity of data that is constantly renewed, and not neccesary compatible with the old ones. Second, it varies according the bio-expert interest, who alters the selection of the grouping criterion and the kind of input/output data. So, particular and very specific systems are not good solutions for this problem.

This paper proposes a modular framework which is adaptable to be applied to any different gene group function prediction problems. Functional annotation of *S.cerevisiae* genes grouped by complexes is a real open problem dealt with this new multi-relational and flexible approach.

This paper is organised as follows: Section 2 explains the application of the Modular Multi-Relational Framework in yeast genome. Section 3 presents and analyses the application results. Finally, in Section 4, conclusions and future work are summarized.

2   Modular Multi-Relational Framework Applied to Yeast Complex Function Prediction

Modular Multi-Relational Framework (MMRF) [8] is a new approach for solving the domain of *Gene Group Function Prediction*, facing the problem from a relational and flexible point of view.

MMRF is designed by modules for managing the high variability which this biological domain entails; changing independently data, criteria and methodology.

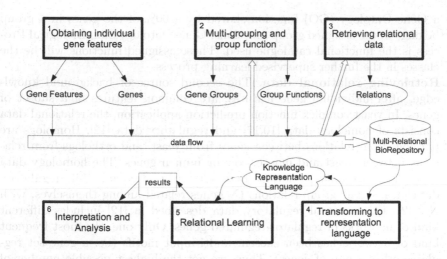

Fig. 1. The schema of the proposed Modular Multi-Relational Framework (MMRF). The rectangles represent modules and the ellipses represent data.

MMRF uses a multi-relational approach (in representation and learning) for fitting the intrinsic relational structure of gene grouping data, and for integrating different data sources.

MMRF is splitted into six modules (see Figure 1) covering all involved domain tasks (grouping, representing and learning). Each module consists of one or several abstract tasks [8] which must be individually instantiated in a particular application of the framework.

The MMRF application described in this work predicts the function of gene groups in *S.cerevisiae* (i.e.Yeast), where genes are grouped by protein complexes. The instantiation of all the framework modules in this application are described below, that is, the definition of the particular value for the tasks in each MMRF module. The specific results and analysis appear in the Section 3.

1. **Obtaining individual gene features.** In this application, the individual features for yeast organism are retrieved from Ensembl project [10], through the BioMart tool [17]. Most of them are extracted from gene and protein sequences. Some examples are the gene length, the chromosome name, the gene biotype, the protein family domain, if it is or not a coiled-coil domain, etc.
2. **Multi-Grouping and group function.** This module includes two main activities. (a) Making gene groups, according to a specific criterion. Several of these criteria are listed above (Section 1). In this application, the genes are grouped by protein complexes. They are extracted from high-throughput experimental data from the detailed Krogan et.al. study [11]. These 547 protein complexes are inferred from protein-protein interaction data, after applying a Markov clustering algorithm [11]. The 2,375 interaction pairs are identified by two different mass spectrometry methods, in order to increase the data reliability. (b) Assigning functions to each group. In this initial application,

a Gene Ontology (GO) function shared by a 60% of the genes in a group belongs to the assigned group functions. Gene Ontology Slim:Biological Process is the functional catalogue used. These assigned functions will be the classes in the further supervised learning process.

3. **Retrieving relational data.** The second source of background knowledge, after individual gene features, are common features of a subset of genes. In yeast complex function prediction application, the relational data consists of homology data [10,17] and regulatory data [12]. Homologs are paralogs from relations between genes from yeast, and orthologs from relations between yeast and mouse, cow or human genes. The homology data represents only binary relations between a pair of genes, while regulatory data means gene group relations (N genes related among themselves, with N>=2). Experimental regulatory data described in [12] includes different kind of networks of regulator-regulated genes. Only one, the most frequent kind of network, has been chosen: multi-input motifs (i.e. a gene set regulates other group of genes). Thus, we get the highest possible number of instances for the learning task, but avoiding to mix different sources. It means 257 gene group relations, and besides 826 regulator-regulated group binary relations.

4. **Transforming to representation language.** The knowledge representation language is defined as first-order logic predicates [13], in a prolog syntax, involving all the collected data described above (see Figure 2).

```
gene_in_group(groupID,geneID).        cds_length(geneID,length).
group_function(groupID,goID).          paralog(geneID,geneID,identity,coverage).
gene(geneID,chrom,length,strand).      ortholog(geneID,geneID,identity,id2,type).
pfam_domain(geneID,pfamID).            ortholog_signal_domain(geneID).
transmembrane_domain(geneID).          gene_in_coregulated(coregGroupID,geneID).
ncoils_domain(geneID).                 regulator(coregGroupID,geneID).
...
```

Fig. 2. Fragment of the knowledge representation language in gene group function prediction domain

5. **Relational Learning.** Using the previously defined logic predicates, we apply the machine learning algorithm TILDE, Top-down induction of logical decision trees [2], implemented in the ACE tool. It is a classical Quinlan decision tree adapted to a relational approach, through first-order logic. This tree has logic clauses in nodes instead of attribute-value comparisons. Before applying TILDE, we carried out a data pre-process, inspired by other works [3,24], in order to get a multi-class and multi-label learning in an unique classifier. Briefly, each gene group is represented by a Boolean vector of classes, and a regression prediction is applied to each possible class, at the same time. It is neccesary because a group of genes (example) can have more than one function assigned (class). This fact is very important in this domain, since it increases its complexity and makes difficult its resolution.

6. **Interpretation and Analysis.** A biological interpretation aproximation of the relational tree appears in the next section. Since the positive predictions are the most interesting in this domain and the highly-skewed data set, Precision-Recall curves (PRC) are the measure more suitable for leading the computational analysis of the learning results [5].

3 Results and Discussion

3.1 Experimental Design

The goal of this section is to show how MMRF is applied to a real gene function context, and what results it brings out. The relational system learns from 208,098 logic predicates, where different kind of them are included. In particular, 7,124 gene, 20,989 ortholog, 11,412 interpro_ domain or 2,246 gene_in_coregulated predicates. The initial number of groups retrieved from [11] is 547. In that set, on average, there are 4.9 genes per group, ranged from 2 to 54 genes, being most of the groups small. Besides, the set has on average 2.7 functions per group, ranged from 1 to 10 functional annotations in the same group.

The number of groups in the dataset is reduced after filtering those gene groups without any GOSlim function assignation and following the 60% of shared functions criterion (task 2.b). The final number of groups depends on the required minimum **number of examples per class**. According to that parameter, three different datasets (a, b and c) are defined. These datasets mainly differ in the number of classes (functions) and the number of examples (groups):

a) *At least 1 group per function (≥ 1):* This dataset has 40 different classes in 360 examples (on average, 24 positives and 336 negatives per class).
b) *At least 10 groups per function (≥ 10):* This dataset has 24 different classes in 357 examples (on average, 37 positives and 320 negatives per class).
c) *At least 50 groups per function (≥ 50):* This dataset has 8 different classes in 280 examples (on average, 57 positives and 223 negatives per class).

These 3 datasets have been defined because the original one is very skewed through the number of examples available for predicting each class. The values goes from 1 to 68 examples per class, underlining a 40% with less than 10 examples per class and a 62.5% with less than 25 examples per class. The effect of this fact is evaluated in the experiments in the next section.

Moreover, there is one more difference in the experiments done, related to the **relational knowledge** used in the learning process: *(1)binary relations* (i.e. homology data) or *(2)binary and group relations* (that means to add regulator and gene_in_coregulated predicates). This separation let us to analyse the influence of group relations in the learning process.

The next section shows the results for the 6 configurations we have considered (2 relations subsets x 3 datasets). The remainder background knowledge (i.e. logic predicates) and learning parameters are the same for all the configurations.

A comparison with other techniques (relational or not) applied to the same problem can not be included because it is not known any study which predicts function directly for groups, as we do.

3.2   Results and Analysis

The results shown in Table 1 and Figure 3 come from 10 folds cross validation experiments. Table 1 shows several quantitative measures which evaluate different aspects of the relational learning process, from the solution size (two first rows) to the prediction goodness (two last rows). In addition, Precision-Recall curves appear in Figure 3 for some configurations. All of them are the average results about overall classes in a specific configuration. Although several individual classes in the same configuration have its Precision-Recall curve higher than this average curve (see Figure 3, "individual class 2.c" line).

Table 1. Quantitative results from yeast complex function prediction with MMRF. AU(PRC): Area Under Precision-Recall Curve.

	Relational knowledge					
	1) only binary			2) binary+group		
	No. examples per class					
	≥1	≥10	≥50	≥1	≥10	≥50
Tree nodes:	32.6	33.9	28.5	34.8	32.1	29.9
Tree literals:	89.3	93.3	72.1	94.3	66.3	75.3
Correlation:	0.009	0.015	0.056	0.008	0.031	0.049
AU(PRC):	0.120	0.134	0.230	0.116	0.144	0.226
	1.a	1.b	1.c	2.a	2.b	2.c

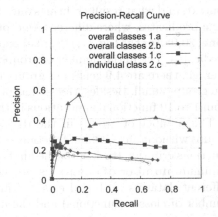

Fig. 3. Precision-Recall curves from yeast complex function prediction with MMRF, in different configurations

Analysing the obtained results, we can conclude that the quantitative measures are not very high, although they are closer to the results in similar biological domain. For example, our preliminary AU(PRC)s are not very distant from the maximum of 0.3 reached in individual gene function prediction with relational data mining [24].

Furthermore, Table 1 and Figure 3 point out that the predictions improve from "a" to "b", and from "b" to "c" configurations. It means that the results are better when the number of examples per class is higher. Although it also implies that the set of predicted classes is smaller. Therefore, improving the results implies to search alternative ways in order to increase the number of groups. For example, looking for experimental data producing a higher number of gene groups, mixing data from several experimental studies, modifying the grouping criterion to another which gives more groups, or even joining groups coming from different grouping criteria.

The remaining analysis proposed in Section 3.1 is about the different relational knowledge used in the learning process, i.e. configuration 1 vs 2. Looking at Table 1 and the decision trees in different configurations (very similar to the tree shown in Figure 4), we realise that the numeric results barely change from configurations 1 to 2. Moreover, the new regulatory predicates hardly ever appear in the decision tree nodes in configurations 2. Hence, it does not matter if we add more relational information, even more enriching one (group relations is better than only binary relations), because the learning process does not take advantage of it. At least, with the current defined knowledge representation.

Additional experiments have been carried out, in order to try to solve the low quantitative results, mainly modifying the grouping criterion in module 2, from protein complexes to coregulated genes or both criteria together. In these additional experiments the flexibility of the framework is checked, because only swapping gene_in_group and gene_in_coregulated predicates a new framework application is defined: *co-regulated gene function prediction*. So, now the grouping criterion (module 2.a) is co-regulated genes and relational background knowledge (module 3) includes protein complex relations. In this dataset, only 56 examples appear for predicting 30 differents classes, versus 360 examples for 40 classes in the previous application. All classes have less than 10 examples for learning. Consequently, the output predictor will not be generic, but very dependent on these few examples. Since the results depend very much on the specific MMRF application, we must take care of its design.

Other experiments consist of increasing the number of groups and examples per class by joining groups coming from different grouping criteria, particularly protein complexes and co-regulated genes criteria. Thus, we define easily other new application. Here, the number of groups increases from 360 to 415, with at least one assigned GO function. However, the results are practically the same as Table 1 shows, since groups from complexes are much more abundant than from co-regulation, so the latter are covered by the former. This is the bad consequence of mixing data for increasing the number of examples. Therefore, with these two modifications, it is checked as a tricky domain.

```
1: class(-A,-B,-C,-D,-E,-F,-G,-H,-I)
2: [0.186507936507937] 252.0
3: gene_in_group(A,-J),gene(J,-K,-L,-M),ncoils_domain(J) ?
4: +--yes: [0.12258064516129] 155.0
5: |        paralog(J,-N,-O,-P),O>=23 ?
6: |        +--yes: [0.15714285,0.37142857,0.17142857,0.07142857,
7: |                0.25714285,0.18571428,0.1,        0.37142857]
8: |                70.0
9: |                [0.04381267,0.05816884,0.04537138,0.03100409,
10:|                0.05261569,0.04681516,0.03611575,0.058168843]
11:|        +--no:  [0.141176470588235] 85.0
12:|                ortholog(J,-Q,-R,-S,-T),R>=22 ?
13:|                ...
```

Fig. 4. Fragment of the relation decision tree in configuration '1.c'

Finally, a biological interpretation (module 6) of a relational decision tree MMRF output is described. The tree in the Figure 4 means that given a gene J belonging to the group A, if gene J had a coiled-coil domain and a paralog relationship with gene N with an identity $\geq 23\%$, then the eigth regression values in lines 6 and 7 determine the functions assigned (among B to I) to group A. For example, with a threshold of 0.35, the functions $C=GO:0006350$ and $I=GO:00050709$ would be predicted to the group A. The line 8 in Figure 4 tells how many examples satisfy these conditions, and line 9 and 10 show the error measured in the regression process. The tree goes on checking if other logic predicates are true in the knowledge base.

4   Conclusions and Further Work

In this work, a variation of gene function prediction domain is tackled: gene *group* function prediction. The Modular Multi-Relational Framework (modular for flexibility and Multi-Relational due to the structured data) is proposed to solve this new domain. It is applied to a specific real problem, the yeast complex function prediction. Preliminary quantitative results are around low levels, although not very distant from typical ones in related domains. However, it seems clear that the prediction is very restricted by the high number of functions (i.e. classes) and mainly by the few groups per function. It means that when the latter number increases (and consequently the former decreases), the predictions improve. In addition, it is concluded that the group relational data is not exploited with the current knowledge representation.

Thus, an important improvement in this research would be to modify the knowledge representation (module 4) so that the learning process can take advantage of the fundamental information existing in bio-relational data. As further work related to the skewed classes, we could explore different alternatives in order to increase the number of groups in yeast, analysing their influence in the prediction results. Another proposal is to include new grouping criteria, with several goals; such as, to apply the system to multi-grouping scenarios, to define new framework applications changing the instantiation of module 2 (for example, pathways function prediction or co-expressed gene function prediction), and to increase the number of groups too. Other closer idea is to add new relational information (module 3), integrating more data sources. Also, the functional catalogue could be changed to other less generic than Gene Ontology.

However, it might occur that the collected data and similar one does not contain enough knowledge to face the problem of predicting group functions directly. Maybe the next step should be to slightly change the approach, splitting the prediction process in two phases. First, predicting individual gene function with Relational Data Mining (whose viability has been checked in closer domain [4,24]), although increasing the relevance of gene group membership, as background knowledge. Second, predicting group functions, through the inferred individual function from the first phase.

Finally, probably the most relevant improvement is to change the objective organism from yeast to human. It implies more interesting gene groups and more useful annotations (for instance, related to some disease). Thus, this framework could be applied to predict results so relevant as the unknown function of human gene groups.

Acknowledgments. This research work has been supported by CICYT, TRA 2007-67374-C02-02 project and by the expert biological knowledge of the Structural Computational Biology Group in Spanish National Cancer Research

Centre (CNIO). The authors would like to thank members of TILDE tool developer group in K.U.Leuven for providing their help and many useful suggestions.

References

1. Al-Shahrour, F., et al.: Fatigo+: a functional profiling tool for genomic data. Nucl. Acids Res. 35, 91–96 (2007)
2. Blockeel, H., De Raedt, L.: Top-down induction of logical decision trees. Artificial Intelligence 101(1-2), 285–297 (1998)
3. Blockeel, H., et al.: Decision trees for hierarchical multilabel classification: A case study in functional genomics. In: Fürnkranz, J., Scheffer, T., Spiliopoulou, M. (eds.) PKDD 2006. LNCS (LNAI), vol. 4213, pp. 18–29. Springer, Heidelberg (2006)
4. Clare, A.: Machine learning and data mining for yeast functional genomics. PhD thesis, University of Wales, Aberystwyth (2003)
5. Davis, J., Goadrich, M.: The relationship between precision-recall and roc curves. In: ICML, pp. 233–240. ACM, New York (2006)
6. Dzeroski, S., Lavrac, N.: Relational Data Mining. Springer, Heidelberg (2001)
7. Edgar, R., et al.: Gene Expression Omnibus: NCBI gene expression and hybridization array data repository. Nucl. Acids Res. 30(1), 207–210 (2002)
8. Garcia, B., et al.: Modular multi-relational framework for gene group function prediction. In: ILP (2009)
9. Glez-Pena, D., et al.: WhichGenes: a web-based tool for gathering, building, storing and exporting gene sets with application in gene set enrichment analysis. Nucl. Acids Res. 37, 329–334 (2009)
10. Hubbard, T., et al.: Ensembl 2009. Nucl. Acids Res. 37, 690–697 (2009)
11. Krogan, N., et al.: Global landscape of protein complexes in the yeast saccharomyces cerevisiae. Nature 440(7084), 637–643 (2006)
12. Lee, T., et al.: Transcriptional regulatory networks in saccharomyces cerevisiae. Science 298, 799–804 (2002)
13. Lloyd, J.W.: Foundations of logic programming. Springer, New York (1987)
14. Parkinson, H., et al.: Array express update–from an archive of functional genomics experiments to the atlas of gene expression. Nucl. Acids Res. 37, 868–872 (2009)
15. Pavlidis, P., et al.: Learning gene functional classifications from multiple data types. Journal of computational biology 9(2), 401–411 (2002)
16. Sharan, R., et al.: Network-based prediction of protein function. Mol. Syst. Biol. 3 (2007)
17. Smedley, D., et al.: Biomart-biological queries made easy. BMC Genomics 10 (2009)
18. Stark, C., et al.: Biogrid: a general repository for interaction datasets. Nucl. Acids Res. 34, 535–539 (2006)
19. Subramanian, A., et al.: Gene set enrichment analysis: A knowledge-based approach for interpreting genome-wide expression profiles. PNAS 102, 15545–15550 (2005)
20. Tang, Z., et al.: Prediction of co-regulated gene groups through gene ontology. In: IEEE CIBCB 2007, pp. 178–184 (2007)
21. Trajkovski, I., et al.: Learning relational descriptions of differentially expressed gene groups. IEEE Transactions on Systems, Man, and Cybernetics 38(1), 16–25 (2008)
22. Trajkovski, I., et al.: Segs: Search for enriched gene sets in microarray data. Journal of Biomedical Informatics 41(4), 588–601 (2008)
23. Tran, T., et al.: Using inductive logic programming for predicting protein-protein interactions from multiple genomic data. In: Jorge, A.M., Torgo, L., Brazdil, P.B., Camacho, R., Gama, J. (eds.) PKDD 2005. LNCS (LNAI), vol. 3721, pp. 321–330. Springer, Heidelberg (2005)
24. Vens, C., et al.: Decision trees for hierarchical multi-label classification. Machine Learning 73(2), 185–214 (2008)

Integrative Data Mining in Functional Genomics of *Brassica napus* and *Arabidopsis thaliana*

Youlian Pan[1], Alain Tchagang[1], Hugo Bérubé[1], Sieu Phan[1], Heather Shearer[2],
Ziying Liu[1], Pierre Fobert[2], and Fazel Famili[1]

[1] Knowledge Discovery Group, Institute for Information Technology, NRC,
1200 Montreal Road, Ottawa, Ontario, K1A 0R6, Canada
[2] Seed Systems, Plant Biotechnology Institute, NRC, 110 Gymnasium Place, Saskatoon,
SK S7N 0W9
{youlian.pan,alain.tchagang,hugo.berube,sieu.phan,
heather.shearer,ziying.liu,pierre.fobert,
fazel.famili}@nrc-cnrc.gc.ca

Abstract. Vast amount of data in various forms have been accumulated through many years of functional genomic research throughout the world. It is a challenge to discover and disseminate knowledge hidden in these data. Many computational methods have been developed to solve this problem. Taking analysis of the microarray data as an example, we spent the past decade developing many data mining strategies and software tools. It appears still insufficient to cover all sources of data. In this paper, we summarize our experiences in mining microarray data by using two plant species, *Brassica napus* and *Arabidopsis thaliana*, as examples. We present several successful stories and also a few lessons learnt. The domain problems that we dealt with were the transcriptional regulation in seed development and during defense response against pathogen infection.

Keywords: Integrative data mining, microarray, transcription regulation, seed development, plant defense.

1 Introduction

Knowledge discovery from various sources, such as biological experiments and clinical or field trial information, is a complex and challenging task. This requires an in-depth understanding of the domain and development of appropriate strategies for data preprocessing and subsequent analysis. High throughput determination of gene expression profiles has been prevalent in the past decades, particularly with the advent of microarray technology. This has motivated researchers to utilize tools, techniques, and algorithms developed through many years of data mining and knowledge discovery research, to search for useful patterns in the gene expression data. This is exemplified by the abundance of computerized data analysis tools that have become available to perform clustering, pattern recognition, and motif identification in gene's promoters. One of the greatest challenges is to understand how the expression pattern of thousands of genes in a living organism is regulated and related to one another. Two

N. García-Pedrajas et al. (Eds.): IEA/AIE 2010, Part III, LNAI 6098, pp. 92–101, 2010.
© Springer-Verlag Berlin Heidelberg 2010

examples of these are: (*i*) the discovery of relationships between genes and their expression profiles over a time-series, such as genes' progressive responses to drug treatment over time or stages during embryonic development, and (*ii*) genes' responses at one discrete time point to various treatments, to knock-out or knock-down of certain transcription factors.

Generally, no single data analysis method is able to be successfully applied to all different datasets. Often, researchers have to select methods or develop a new algorithm based on a particular dataset. Microarray gene expression data is subject to multiple sources of noise [1]. To cope with such instability in the data, many normalization techniques have been developed, but these techniques can only ease rather than solve the problems completely. As a consequence, the confidence in knowledge derived from the data by a single analysis tool is dependent on the extent of noise and bias. One of the important questions in data mining is how to understand the scope and minimize the impact of such noise and bias within the data.

Our research team is currently working on knowledge discovery from plant genomes, specifically *Brassica napus*, the canola oil producer, and *Arabidopsis thaliana*, a small model plant, with regard to seed development and defense mechanism against pathogen infection, respectively. The data were produced by using various microarray platforms. Thus the data have different degrees of complexity. We have used several integrative approaches to mine these data. In order to facilitate efficient knowledge discovery through incremental learning, we are developing a knowledge base in the area. This paper is to present some successful stories and lessons learnt from our data mining investigations.

In the following sections, we present the two biological problems as examples of our current research. We first describe the problems and our solutions. Then, we present result highlighting the benefit of integrative approaches. This is followed by a brief feature description of the knowledge base. We conclude with a discussion.

2 The Biological Problems and Solutions

2.1 Endosperm of *Brassica napus*

This problem was to identify highly expressed genes and understand the mechanism behind the changes of gene expression in the endosperm during embryogenesis of *B. napus* seeds. Three embryogenesis stages were considered in this study: globular, heart, and cotyledon. The microarray experiment was done in dual channel array representing two different developmental stages, i.e. heart vs. globular, cotyledon vs. globular, or cotyledon vs. heart. Paralleled with the microarray data, there were also EST (expressed sequence tag) data. Details are available in [2].

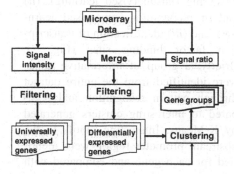

Fig. 1. *Brassica* microarray data mining procedure

Our approach was first to identify a group of significantly and differentially expressed genes. There are two aspects in the domain question: *1*) to find significantly expressed genes *a*) in some stages but not necessarily in other stages, and *b*) across all stages; *2*) to group differentially expressed genes based on their patterns of variations [3]. Unlike the traditional approach of analyzing the ratio data only, our approach was to consider both signal ratio data and signal intensity data from each channel in parallel as detailed in Fig. 1.

2.2 Defense Response in *Arabidopsis thaliana*

The goal of this research was to identify transcriptional regulation of plant defense responses against pathogen infection, using data generated by microarray. The data analysis addressed two main variables: the effect of salicylic acid (SA), a key elicitor of pathogen-induced Systematic Acquire Resistance (SAR) in plants, and the effect of mutations in transcription factors central to the response to SA. These transcription factors included the NPR1 (Non-expressor of Pathogenesis Related gene 1) gene and TGA family genes. In *Arabidopsis*, the NPR1 gene is essential for SA-mediated SAR [4], through its interaction with TGA family of DNA-binding bZIP transcription factors [5-9]. Seven (TGA1-TGA7) of the ten TGA factors in *Arabidopsis* have been characterized to interact with NPR1 [10-12]. These seven TGAs can be divided into three groups based on sequence homology [13]. Group I consists of TGA1 and TGA4; Group II TGA2, TGA5 and TGA6; and group III TGA3 and TGA7. In this research, we used four genotypes: Columbia wild type plant and three sets of mutants (*npr1-3*, a group I TGA factor mutant, *tga1 tga4*, and a group II TGA factor mutant, *tga2 tga5 tga6*). SA was sprayed on each plant to mimic pathogen infection and to induce changes in the expression of genes involved in SAR. Samples were taken 0, 1, and 8 hours afterward.

This research was performed in two phases. In the first phase, SA was applied on two genotypes, the wild type and the mutant *npr1-3*. We used an approach that consisted of several iterations of integration of three components: (*i*) clustering (unsupervised learning), (*ii*) pattern recognition (supervised learning), and (*iii*) identification of transcription factor binding sites (Fig. 2). Briefly, a group of informative genes were identified from the entire dataset through pattern recognition and compared to interesting clusters generated by K-Means. Interesting motifs in the upstream promoter region were identified for each gene and compared with other genes in the same cluster. A combination of results of informative genes,

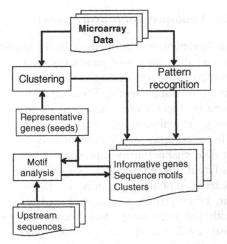

Fig. 2. *Arabidopsis* microarray data mining process – phase I

gene expression profiles and motif information constituted a representative gene for each interesting cluster, which were used as seeds for subsequent re-clustering through K-Means to determine more refined clusters [14].

In the second phase, SA was applied to all four genotypes. The knowledge discovery was done by using integration of an expanded version of frequent itemset mining approach (EFIM) [15] and an order preserving three-dimensional-clustering approach (OPTricluster) [16]. The EFIM looked after differential expression at each time point, whereas OPTricluster dealt with temporal profiles of gene expression.

The EFIM approach begins with a discretization of gene expression matrix into three distinct values (-1, 0, 1) representing down-regulation, no significant difference, and up-regulation, respectively, based on a predefined threshold value, and relative to a baseline, which is the wild type in our study. The algorithm consists of matrix decomposition and All-1 sub-matrix identification; detailed description is available in [15].

The OPTricluster approach is a combination of order preserving pattern feature [17] with clustering. It first discretizes a gene expression profile by ranking expression value at all time points based on a predefined threshold value disregarding up or down regulation. The number of discretization values is $\leq T$, where $T =$ number of time points, depending on the threshold and the variability of the expression profile. This approach identifies similarities and differences in terms of gene expression profiles between the wild type and the mutant sets. In other words, it identifies groups of genes that have the same sequential variation patterns unique in one genotype plants or others and may be the same between two, three or across all four genotypes [16].

3 Results

3.1 Endosperm of *Brassica napus*

The detailed result of this research has been recently published in [2, 3]. Here we highlight relationship of two key transcription factors that might shine some light in cascading of transcription regulation of seed development and fatty acid metabolism. Leafy cotyledon1 (LEC1) is a key regulator of fatty acid biosynthesis in *Arabidopsis* [18]. The function of LEC1 is partially dependent on WRINKLED1 (WRI1) and other two transcription factors (ABI3 and FUS3) in regulating fatty acid biosynthesis [19]. In our work, the expression profiles of LEC1 and WRI1 are identical based solely on the log ratio values (Fig. 3A), which lead us to a conclusion that the LEC1 and WRI1 co-regulate the FA metabolism in *B napus*. While looking into the expression intensity of the two TFs, we found that there was a difference of about one order of magnitude between them (Fig. 3B). This result was consistent with the number of ESTs, 56 and 8 found for LEC1 and WRI1, respectively [3]. When the expression of LEC1 was moderate at the globular stage, the expression of WRI1 was very low. When expression of LEC1 became more significant at later stages, expression of WRI1 increased markedly. This observation allows us to deduce that high expression of LEC1 probably enhances the expression of WRI1 in *B napus*, whether directly or indirectly through another transcription factor. A recent study revealed that LEC2 directly regulated WRI1 [20]. However, over-expression of LEC1 does not directly affect the level of LEC2 [18]. Therefore, we can conclude that both LEC1 and LEC2 are the upstream regulators to WRI1 (Fig. 4). This result is similar to what is found in *Arabidopsis* [18]. However, this cascading relationship between the two transcription factors would not be possibly revealed without considering the signal intensity data.

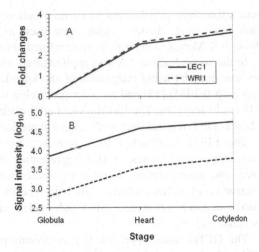

Fig. 3. Gene expression of the two transcription factors, LEC1 and WRI1

3.2 Defense Response in *Arabidopsis thaliana*

The details of phase one work have been published in [14]. Here we provide a highlight of this phase. Through several iterations of semi-supervised clustering, we were able to identify and confirm 24 genes that were differentially expressed, 12 up-regulated and 12 down-regulated, in mutant *npr1* as compared to the wild type following SA treatment. Using the pattern recognition approach, we were able to identify 15 highly informative genes, the majority (8) of which were in the down-regulated cluster described above and highly enriched with ASF-1 motif (TGACG [21]) and W box (TTGAC [22]) in their promoters. The TGA factors binds to ASF-1 motif and WRKY transcription factors, which are dependent on NPR1 [23], bind to W box. This consistent with the fact that NPR1 indirectly regulates the target genes of both TGA factors and WRKY factors.

In the second phase, we first identified 3945 significantly expressed genes through preprocessing. We used both EFIM and OPTricluster to analyze this set of genes with a threshold of 0.5 fold changes. Using the EFIM approach we identified genes that were up- or down-regulated at a discrete time point in mutant alone, and those collectively affected by two or all three mutants based on differential expression of mutants over the wild type [15]. For example, the Venn diagram in Fig. 5 shows 8 hours after application of SA, 57 and 16 genes are up and

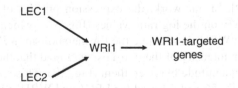

Fig. 4. Schematic transcriptional relationship between the transcription factors

down regulated, respectively, in all three mutants in this study. Similarly, 11 and 9 genes are exclusively up and down regulated, respectively, in both mutants of TGA factors. But 742 and 711 genes are uniquely up and down regulated, respectively, in *npr1-3*.

Through the order preserving clustering approach [16], we were able to identify genes that were *not* affected by one or more mutations (Fig. 6) across the time series. For example, 15.92% genes are independent of any genotypes in this study (W_P_T1_T2); 30.37% genes are independent of mutation of TGA factors (W_T1_T2). From the difference between these two numbers, we were able to derive 14.45% genes that are affected by mutant *npr1-3*, i.e. regulated by NPR1.

After integration of these two sets of analyses, we will be able to pin-point cer-

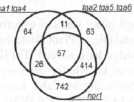

Up-regulated

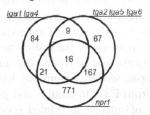

Down-regulated

Fig. 5. The Venn diagram of 8th hour after SA treatment on *Arabidopsis thaliana* showing the number of genes that are affected by the mutations

tain group of genes that are regulated by one transcription factor or co-regulated by more transcription factors at one specific time point, or across the entire time series, and therefore infer the dynamic regulatory behavior of these transcription factors during SAR in *A. thaliana*. More post processing is in progress. Additionally, we are applying the same integrative approach to seed developments and its association with fatty acid metabolism in *B. napus*. Preliminary results indicate this approach is promising and has a broad application.

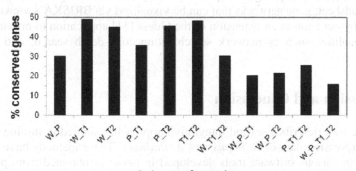

Fig. 6. Summary result of the order preserving clustering approach. W = wild type, P = *npr1*, T1 = *tga1 tga4*, T2 = *tga2 tga5 tga6*. W_P_T1_T2 = genes whose expression profile conserved across all genotypes, i.e. independent of any mutations.

4 Result Integration into the Knowledge Base

Through many years of experimentation, vast amount of data have been accumulated and available at Plant Biotechnology Institute, NRC. Currently, we are developing a knowledge base named BRISKA (*Brassica* Seed Knowledge Application) [24] that integrates knowledge discovered through our many years of data mining processes with publically available knowledge in literature and public databases, such as GO [25], KEGG [26], TRASFAC [27], etc. The objective of this knowledge base is to support subsequent integrated reasoning in new knowledge discovery processes. Our ultimate goal is to build a robust virtual seed system through incremental learning.

Currently, a prototype of the knowledge base has been developed. It contains various tools and results of analysis from both public and private sources. BRISKA integrates microarray data alongside sequence-based data, such as ESTs and promoter sequences, and provides data analysis results generated by using different tools. For example, sequence similarity has been done on all sequence-based data to allow linkage from EST, to contigs and genes while also proposing possible orthologs for any gene of interest in related species. The schema used in BRISKA is based on the Chado [28] model and, through its ontology-driven design, supports complex representation of biological knowledge such as clusters of co-expressed genes, gene regulatory network modules, and expression plots. Public microarray experiment data have been acquired from Gene Expression Omnibus (GEO) and selected by the relevance to our actual research interests. Genes, ESTs, and contigs are from the TAIR database [29] while information on transcription factors and their binding sites is mostly from PlantTFDB [30]. Annotation information such as gene ontology, KEGG identifiers has also been added. Private data are mostly acquired from the Plant Biotechnology Institute and consist mainly of EST and microarray gene expression data.

An interactive web-based interface along with visualization tools have been developed to provide intuitive access to the knowledge base. An analysis explorer tool grants user access to their data, analyses results along with the protocol used to generate the results. For example, gene expression analysis results are provided in an interactive spreadsheet; gene networks that can be visualized via BRISKA's viewer, which were built by our team as an extension of the Guess [31] application to provide multiple functionalities such as network search, connection-depth search, and network manipulation.

5 Discussion and Conclusion

In this paper, we described several integrative approaches applied in mining microarray gene expression data of *B. napus* and *A. thaliana*. These methods have been incorporated in various software tools developed in-house or obtained from publically available resources. It is important first to investigate the data structure, their associated features and attributes, the noise content and the associated strategy to minimize its impact, and the domain problems. Once this basic information is known, one can then look into the tools needed to address these sets of problems.

In the *B. napus* endosperm work, we investigated both the signal intensity and the differential expression between different stages of embryogenesis. The conventional approach of analyzing the dual channel microarray data by looking into only the ratio data between the channels would miss the cascading relationship between the two transcription factors, LEC1 and WRI1. This research also alerts us that it is important to identify the characteristics of data. For example, the ratio data in the dual array experiment is derived from two signal intensities. In this case, the signal intensities are the primary data, while the ratio is derived data. Two ratios of the same value do not imply that the primary data, from which they are derived, are the same or similar. There could be a big difference between the two sets of primary data. Yet, some ratio data in a specific region of their parental primary data could be misleading [3]. This fact has been neglected in many of the dual channel array data analysis performed earlier.

In the first phase of *Arabidopsis* work, we integrated the unsupervised and supervised learning approaches with sequence motif search and identified a group of genes that were closely related with the transcription factor NPR1. Microarray data usually contains much noise [1]. A cross checking of results by various methods are necessary to ensure quality of the results. Our final results from the three sets of analyses support each other and increase our confidence. In the second phase of this work, we integrate results generated through EFIM, which identifies differential expression of the mutants at a given time point, and OPTricluster, which mines the sequential ranking pattern in the expression profile. The former identifies the static nature and the later illustrates the functionally dynamics nature of the gene expression data matrix.

Each step of knowledge discovery enriches our knowledge base, as we see in our *Brassica* Seed Knowledge Base that we are developing. The discovered knowledge will incrementally enhance the subsequent knowledge discovery process. For such reason, many bioinformatics knowledge bases, such as gene ontology [25], KEGG pathway [26], etc. became available. Our objective is to structure all forms of discovered and validated knowledge in order to provide means to augment our capability in subsequent knowledge discovery.

Through worldwide genomic research effort of the past decade, large amount of data in various forms have been accumulated. It is a challenge to integrate information in many different forms (e.g. ESTs, SNPs, small RNAs, microarray, protein-protein interactions and metabolomics data) and from various platforms (for example the microarray data could be from Affymetrix, Agilent chips, or in house chips) and to extract knowledge from this vast information pool. Our group has developed various data mining strategies, algorithms and tools based on our expertise in data mining and machine learning in order to effectively discover new knowledge from this vast information pool. This knowledge will be validated through literature search, local and public knowledge bases search, and follow-up wet lab experimentation. Finally, the knowledge can be presented as gene-gene associations, gene-metabolites associations, metabolic pathways, gene networks and various forms of predictive or descriptive models. These forms of knowledge presentation will be facilitated and interconnected through our BRISKA knowledge base. Our ultimate goal is to provide biologists an integrative and interactive environment to visualize seed development and fatty acid metabolism of *B. napus* and related species and to further conduct experiments in perturbing/modifying genetic parameters in a virtual world to improve canola oil production, seed yield and seedling vigour.

Acknowledgments. The data for *Brassica* endosperm work were from Jitao Zou's lab at Plant Biotechnology Institute, NRC and is available at Gene Expression Omnibus (GEO, GPL8090). This work is co-funded by Genomics and Health Initiative, Plant Biotechnology Institute, and Institute for Information Technology, National Research Council Canada.

References

1. Churchill, G.A.: Fundamentals of experimental design for cDNA microarrays. Nat. Genet. 32, 490–495 (2002)
2. Huang, Y., Chen, L., Wang, L., Phan, S., Liu, Z., Vijayan, K., Wan, L., Ross, A., Datla, R., Pan, Y., Zou, J.: Probing endosperm gene expression landscape in Brassica napus. BMC Genomics 10, 256 (2009)
3. Pan, Y., Zou, J., Huang, Y., Liu, Z., Phan, S., Famili, F.A.: Goal driven analysis of cDNA microarray data. In: IEEE Symposium on Computational Intelligence in Bioinformatics and Computational Biology (CIBCB 2009), pp. 186–192. IEEE Press, New York (2009)
4. Delaney, T.P., Friedrich, L., Ryals, J.A.: Arabidopsis signal transduction mutant defective in chemically and biologically induced disease resistance. Proc. Natl. Acad. Sci. 92, 6602–6606 (1995)
5. Zhang, Y., Fan, W., Kinkema, M., Li, X., Dong, X.: Interaction of NPR1 with basic leucine zipper protein transcription factors that bind sequences required for salicylic acid induction of the PR-1 gene. Proc. Natl. Acad. Sci. 96, 6523–6528 (1999)
6. Després, C., DeLong, C., Glaze, S., Liu, E., Fobert, P.R.: The *Arabidopsis* NPR1/NIM1 protein enhances the DNA binding activity of a subgroup of the TGA family of bZIP transcription factors. Plant Cell 12, 279–290 (2000)
7. Kinkema, K., Fan, W., Dong, X.: Nuclear localization of NPR1 is required for activation of PR gene expression. Plant Cell 12, 2339–2350 (2000)
8. Subramaniam, R., Desveaux, D., Spickler, C., Michnick, S.W., Brisson, N.: Direct visualization of protein interactions in plant cells. Nat. Biotech. 19, 769–772 (2001)
9. Johnson, C., Boden, E., Arias, J.: Salicylic acid and NPR1 induce the recruitment of transactivating TGA factors to a defense gene promoter in *Arabidopsis*. Plant Cell 15, 1846–1858 (2003)
10. Kesarwani, M., Yoo, J., Dong, X.: Genetic Interactions of TGA transcription factors in the regulation of pathogenesis- related genes and disease resistance in *Arabidopsis thaliana*. Plant Physiol. 44, 336–346 (2007)
11. Jakoby, M., Weisshaar, B., Droge-Laser, W., Vicente-Carbajosa, J., Tiedemann, J., Kroj, T., Parcy, F.: bZIP transcription factors in *Arabidopsis*. Trends Plant Sci. 7, 106–111 (2002)
12. Dong, X.: NPR1, all things considered. Curr. Opin. Plant Biol. 7, 547–552 (2004)
13. Xiang, C., Miao, Z., Lam, E.: DNA-binding properties, genomic organization and expression pattern of TGA6, a new member of the TGA family of bZIP transcription factors in *Arabidopsis thaliana*. Plant Mol. Biol. 34, 403–415 (1997)
14. Pan, Y., Pylatuik, J.D., Ouyang, J., Famili, A., Fobert, P.R.: Discovery of functional genes for systemic acquired resistance in *Arabidopsis thaliana* through integrated data mining. J. Bioinfo. Comput. Biol. 2, 639–655 (2004)
15. Tchagang, A.B., Shearer, H., Phan, S., Bérubé, H., Famili, F.A., Fobert, P., Pan, Y.: Towards a temporal modeling of the genetic network controlling systemic acquired resistance in *Arabidopsis thaliana*. In: IEEE Symposium on Computational Intelligence in Bioinformatics and Computational Biology (CIBCB 2010), Montreal, Canada, May 2-5 (2010)

16. Tchagang, A.B., Phan, S., Famili, F.A., Pan, Y.: OPTricluster: The Order Preserving Triclustering Algorithm. Technical Report, Knowledge Discovery Group, Institute for Information Technology, National Research Council Canada (2008)

17. Phan, S., Famili, F., Tang, Z., Pan, Y., Liu, Z., Ouyang, J., Lenferink, A., O'Connor, M.: A novel pattern based clustering methodology for time-series microarray data. Intern. J. Comput. Math. 84, 585–597 (2007)

18. Mu, J., Tan, H., Zheng, Q., Fu, F., Liang, Y., Zhang, J., Yang, X., Wang, T., Chong, K., Wang, X.-J., Zuo, J.: LEAFY COTYLEDON1 is a key regulator of fatty acid biosynthesis in *Arabidopsis*. Plant Physiology 148, 1042–1054 (2008)

19. Maeo, K., Tokuda, T., Ayame, A., Mitsui, N., Kawai, T., Tsukagoshi, H., Ishiguro, S., Nakamura, K.: An AP2-type transcription factor, WRINKLED1, of *Arabidopsis thaliana* binds to the AW-box sequence conserved among proximal upstream regions of genes involved in fatty acid synthesis. Plant J. 60, 476–487 (2009)

20. Baud, S., Mendoza, M.S., To, A., Harscoet, E., Lepiniec, L., Dubreucq, B.: WRINKLED1 specifies the regulatory action of LEAFY COTYLEDON2 towards fatty acid metabolism during seed maturation in *Arabidopsis*. Plant J. 50, 825–838 (2007)

21. Lebel, E., Heifetz, P., Thorne, L., Uknes, S., Ryals, J., Ward, E.: Functional analysis of regulatory sequences controlling PR-1 gene expression in *Arabidopsis*. Plant J. 16, 223–233 (1998)

22. Eulgem, T., Rushton, P.J., Robatzek, S., Somssich, I.E.: The WRKY super-family of plant transcription factors. Trends Plant Sci. 5, 199–205 (2000)

23. Yu, D., Chen, C., Chen, Z.: Evidence for an important role of WRKY DNA binding proteins in the regulation of NPR1 gene expression. Plant Cell 13, 1527–1539 (2001)

24. Bérubé, H., Tchagang, A., Wang, Y., Liu, Z., Phan, S., Famili, F., Pan, Y.: BRISKA: brassica seed knowledge application. In: Poster at 17th International Conference on Intelligent Systems in Molecular Biology, Stockholm (2009)

25. The Gene Ontology Consortium: Gene ontology: tool for the unification of biology. Nat. Genet. 25, 25–29 (2000)

26. Okuda, S., Yamada, T., Hamajima, M., Itoh, M., Katayama, T., Bork, P., Goto, S., Kanehisa, M.: KEGG Atlas mapping for global analysis of metabolic pathways. Nucleic Acids Res. 36, W423–W426 (2008)

27. Matys, V., Kel-Margoulis, O.V., Fricke, E., et al.: TRANSFAC and its module TRANSCompel: transcriptional gene regulation in eukaryotes. Nucleic Acids Res. 34, D108–D110 (2006)

28. Mungall, C.J., Emmert, D.B.: The FlyBase Consortium: A Chado case study: an ontology-based modular schema for representing genome-associated biological information. Bioinformatics 23, i337–i346 (2007)

29. The Arabidopsis Information Resource (TAIR), http://www.arabidopsis.org/

30. Guo, A.Y., Chen, X., Gao, G., Zhang, H., Zhu, Q.H., Liu, X.C., Zhong, Y.F., Gu, X., He, K., Luo, J.: PlantTFDB: a comprehensive plant transcription factor database. Nucleic Acids Res. 36, D966–D969 (2008)

31. Adar, E.: GUESS: a language and interface for graph exploration. In: CHI 2006. ACM, New York (2006)

Data Integration and Knowledge Discovery in Life Sciences

Fazel Famili, Sieu Phan, Francois Fauteux,
Ziying Liu, and Youlian Pan

Knowledge Discovery Group, Institute for Information Technology,
National Research Council Canada, 1200 Montreal Road, Ottawa, Ontario, K1A 0R6, Canada
{Fazel.Famili,Sieu.Phan,Francois.Fauteux,Ziying.Liu,
Youlian.Pan}@nrc-cnrc.gc.ca

Abstract. Recent advances in various forms of omics technologies have generated huge amount of data. To fully exploit these data sets that in many cases are publicly available, robust computational methodologies need to be developed to deal with the storage, integration, analysis, visualization, and dissemination of these data. In this paper, we describe some of our research activities in data integration leading to novel knowledge discovery in life sciences. Our multi-strategy approach with integration of prior knowledge facilitates a novel means to identify informative genes that could have been missed by the commonly used methods. Our transcriptomics-proteomics integrative framework serves as a means to enhance the confidence of and also to complement transcriptomics discovery. Our new research direction in integrative data analysis of omics data is targeted to identify molecular associations to disease and therapeutic response signatures. The ultimate goal of this research is to facilitate the development of clinical test-kits for early detection, accurate diagnosis/prognosis of disease, and better personalized therapeutic management.

Keywords: Data integration, Knowledge Discovery, Integrated Omics.

1 Introduction

"Omics" refers to the unified study of complex biological systems characterized by high-throughput data generation and analysis [1]. Bioinformatics methods for data storage, dissemination, analysis, and visualization have been developed in response to the substantial challenges posed by the quantity, diversity and complexity of omics data. In parallel, there has been an explosion of online databases and tools for genome annotation and for the analysis of molecular sequences, profiles, interactions, and structures [2, 3]. The next major challenge is to develop computational methods and models to integrate these abundant and heterogeneous data for investigating, and ultimately deciphering complex phenotypes.

DNA sequencing methods and technologies have evolved at a fast pace since the release of the first genome sequence of a free-living organism in the mid 90's [4]. There are currently over 350 eukaryotic genome sequencing projects [5]. Full genome sequencing has been completed in several organisms, including animal, plant, fungus

N. García-Pedrajas et al. (Eds.): IEA/AIE 2010, Part III, LNAI 6098, pp. 102–111, 2010.

and protist species. Genome annotation is a good example of the integration of multiple computational and experimental data sources [6]. In the human genome, the ENCyclopedia Of DNA Elements (ENCODE) aims to provide additional resolution, and to identify all functional elements, including all protein-coding and non-coding genes, cis-regulatory elements and sequences mediating chromosome dynamics [7].

Transcriptomics is also an advanced and relatively mature area, for which consensus data analysis methods are emerging [8]. Recent and versatile technologies, including high-density whole-genome oligonucleotide arrays [9] and massively parallel sequencing platforms [10] will likely improve the reliability and depth of genomic, epigenomic and transcriptomic analyses.

Notwithstanding the innovative aspects of technologies and sophisticated computational methods developed, each omics approach has some inherent limits. Ostrowski and Wyrwicz [11] mention that the input data for integration must: i) be complete, ii) be reliable and iii) correlate with the biological effect under investigation.

Although providing a reasonably exhaustive coverage of expressed genes, transcriptome analysis is not particularly reliable, and findings often need to be confirmed by additional experimental validation, e.g. using reverse transcription polymerase chain reaction (RT-PCR). Another common, legitimate concern with transcriptome analysis is that levels of mRNAs do not necessarily correlate with the abundance of matching gene product(s), and may only reveal gene regulation at the level of transcription. Proteomics, on the other hand, provides a more accurate picture of the abundance of the final gene products, but current methods, even with the latest high resolution technologies [12], are still associated with relatively low sensitivity in protein identification, and dubious reproducibility [13]. The analysis of transcriptomic and proteomic data is an example where data integration has the potential of improving individual omics approaches and overcoming their limitations [14].

Omics data that can eventually be integrated for the comprehensive elucidation of complex phenotypes include functional gene annotations, gene expression profiles, proteomic profiles, DNA polymorphisms, DNA copy number variations, epigenetic modifications, etc.

In the Knowledge Discovery Group at the Institute for Information Technology of the National Research Council Canada, one of our goals is to develop methods and tools for the integration of omics data. We aim to develop general methods with applications in diverse fields, e.g. the identification of biomarkers and targets in human cancer and the identification of genes associated with quantitative traits to be used in selection and engineering of crop plants. In this paper, different projects from our group are reviewed and approaches are illustrated with applications on biological data.

2 Integrative Approach to Informative Gene Identification from Gene Expression Data

2.1 A Multi-strategy Approach with Integration of Prior Knowledge

Owing to its relatively low cost and maturity, microarray has been the most commonly used technology in functional genomics. One of the fundamental tasks in microarray data analyses is the identification of differentially-expressed genes between two or more experimental conditions (*e.g.* disease vs. healthy). Several statistical methods have been used in the field to identify differentially expressed genes. Since different methods generate different lists of genes, it is difficult to determine the most reliable gene list and the most appropriate method. To retain the best outcomes of each individual method and to complement the overall result with those that can be missed using only one individual method, we have developed a multi-strategy approach [15] that takes advantage of prior knowledge such as GO (Gene Ontology [30]) annotation, gene-pathway and gene-transcription-factor associations.

Fig. 1 is an overview of the proposed multi-strategy approach with prior knowledge integration. Microarray data are first passed through a basic data preprocessing stage (background correction, normalization, data filtering, and missing value handling). The next step is to apply different experimental methods to obtain lists of differentially expressed genes. We then establish a confidence measure to select a set of genes to form the *core* of our final selection. The remaining genes in the lists form the *peripheral* set which is subject to exclusion or inclusion into the final selection by similarity searches between the *peripheral* and the *core* lists. The similarity searches are based on prior knowledge such as *i*) biological pathways (based *e.g.* on the KEGG, Kyoto Encyclopedia of Genes and Genomes, database [29]) or *ii*) biological function or process (based on GO annotations) or *iii*) regulation by similar mechanisms (based on common transcription factors).

Depending on the context, there is a variety of ways to define the confidence measure to form the *core* and *peripheral* sets of genes. A unanimous voting scheme could define a simple confidence measure, under which the *core* consists of genes that are identified by all methods that were applied. Another, less stringent voting scheme is to define the *core* as the genes that are selected by more than one method.

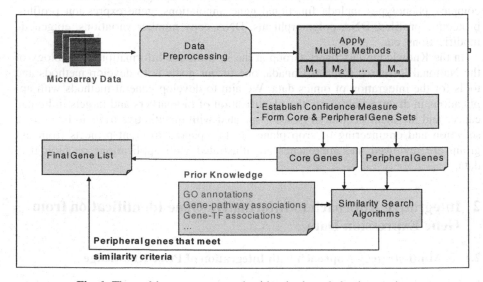

Fig. 1. The multi-strategy approach with prior knowledge integration

In this section we describe the application of the proposed methodology to identify defense response genes in plants [16]. When a plant is infected by a biotrophic pathogen, the concentration of salicylic acid (SA) rises dramatically and massive changes in patterns of gene expression occur. The accumulation of SA is needed to trigger different signaling events, which can also be triggered by exogenous spraying of SA on the plants, even in the absence of pathogen. To help establish the role of various transcription factors involved in disease resistance [17, 18] and the regulation of defense genes, a set of microarray experiments were conducted using four genotypes of *Arabidopsis thaliana*: Columbia wild-type Col-0, mutant *npr1*, double mutant in all Group I TGA factors, *tga1 tga4*, and triple mutant in all Group II TGA factors, *tga2 tga5 tga6*. Triplicate samples were collected before, 1 and 8 hours after SA treatment. Affymetrix *Arabidopsis* ATH1 (20K probe sets) microarray platform was used in this study. A total of 36 arrays were hybridized (Fig. 2).

Wild-type (Col-0)			Mutant *npr1*			Mutant *tga1-4*			Mutant *tga2-5-6*		
0H	1H	8H	0H	1H	8H	0H	1H	8H	0H	1H	8H
rep1	rep1	rep1	rep1	rep1	rep1	rep1	rep1	rep1	rep1	rep1	rep1
rep2	rep2	rep2	rep2	rep2	rep2	rep2	rep2	rep2	rep2	rep2	rep2
rep3	rep3	rep3	rep3	rep3	rep3	rep3	rep3	rep3	rep3	rep3	rep3

Fig. 2. 36 Affymetrix ATH1 (20K probe sets) microarrays

To identify SA-induced genes we identify the differentially-expressed genes for the following 7 pairs of conditions

- wild-type @ 8h vs. wild-type @ 0h
- npr1 @ 8h   vs. wild-type @ 0h
- tga1-4 @ 8h   vs. wild-type @ 0h
- tga2-5-6@ 8h   vs. wild-type @ 0h
- npr1 @ 8h   vs. wild-type @ 8h
- tga1-4 @ 8h   vs. wild-type @ 8h
- tga2-5-6@ 8h   vs. wild-type @ 8h

The background subtracted data were processed through global quantile normalization across 36 arrays and filtering. The final list contains 10256 genes. The following is the detail of applying the multi-strategy methodology:

- Four methods were used:
  - M1: t-test with fold-change set to 2 and p-value 5%
  - M2: SAM with fold-change set to 2 and FDR 5%
  - M3: Rank-Products (RP) with FRD set to 5%
  - M4: fold-change with threshold set at 1.5
- Confidence measure: majority voting model, i.e., genes that were identified by more than one method.

- Gene recruitment mechanisms (similarity search):
  - o Genes in the *peripheral* set that participate in the same biological pathway as some in the *core* set
  - o Genes in the *peripheral* set that have similar promoter characteristics as some in the *core* set.

The methodology identified a list of 2303 *core* genes and a list of 3522 *peripheral* genes. Through the similarity search with the aid of prior knowledge, we were able to identify an additional 408 genes from KEGG pathway search, and 198 genes from transcription factor binding site search. The recruitment algorithms uncovered many important SA mediated and other defence genes that could have been missed if single analysis method were used (a partial list is shown in Table 1).

Table 1. The prior knowledge search algorithms recruited additional important SA mediated and other defence genes (notes: TF: Transcription-Factor, PWY: Pathway)

Recruited genes	SA mediated response	Defence response	Immune response	External stimulated response
At3g46590	TF			
At3g11820	PWY	PWY	PWY	PWY
At4g11820	PWY	PWY		PWY
At3g52400	PWY	PWY	PWY	PWY
At1g74840	TF			
At5g67300	TF			
At4g31550		TF		
At3g63180		TF		
At5g46450		TF		
At4g19510		TF		
At3g14595		TF		
...				
...				

2.2 Transcriptomics and Proteomics Integration: A Framework Using Global Proteomic Discovery to Complement Transcriptomics Discovery

The transcriptome data generated by microarray or other means can only provide a snapshot of genes involved in a physiological state or a cellular phenotype at mRNA level. Advances in proteomics have allowed high-throughput profiling of expressed proteins to elucidate the intricate protein-protein interactions and various biological systems dealing with the downstream products of gene translation and post-translational modification. Genome-wide analysis at the protein level is a more direct reflection of gene expression. The consistency between proteomics and transcriptomics can increase our confidence in identification of biomarkers; differences can also reveal additional post-transcriptional regulatory or recover the missed genes by other reasons to complement transcriptomics discovery. In this section we exploit

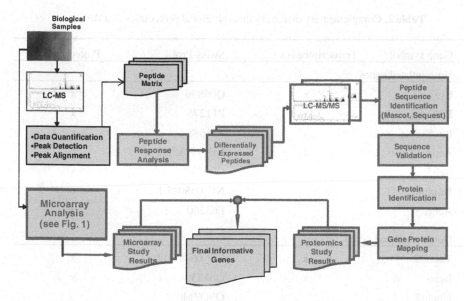

Fig. 3. A transcriptomics and proteomics complementary discovery framework

proteomics and transcriptomics in parallel. We developed a framework using global proteomics discovery, as shown in Figure 3, to enhance the confidence in transcriptomics analysis and to complement the discovery with genes that could have been missed for various reasons such as chemical contamination on the arrays, analysis threshold settings, or genes that were not spotted on the original platform.

In the following, we describe an application of the above framework to an experiment to identify EMT-related (Epitherial-to-Mesenchymal Transition) breast cancer biomarkers. The microarray experiments were performed by Biotechnology Research Institute, NRC. This dataset was generated by exposing JM01 mouse cell line [19] to a treatment with the Transforming Growth Factor (TGF-β) for 24 hours. TGF-β induces an Epithelial-to-Mesenchymal Transition in these cells, a phenomenon characterized by significant morphology and motility changes, which are thought to be critical for tumour progression. The transcriptome changes after 24 hours in TGF-β treated vs. non-treated control cells were monitored using Agilent 41K mouse genome array (four technical replicates). The microarray analysis was done using a multi-strategy approach as described in [15]. The proteomics experiments were performed by Institute for Biological Sciences, NRC [20]. The global proteomics discovered 13 proteins, which are induced by TGF-β, and are mapped to the corresponding transcriptomics results. As shown in Table 2, the discovery of this group of genes (Clu, Fn, Itga5, Acpp, Itgb5, Itga6, and Tacstd2) by transcriptomics approach were also confirmed by the proteomics approach. The proteomics approach identified additional genes (Actg1, Hnrnpu, Ubqln2, Pttg1ip, Ldlr and Itgb4) that were missed from the transcriptomics approach.

Table 2. Complementary discovery through global proteomics in JM01 data

Gene symbol	Transcriptomics	Swiss-Prot	Proteomics
Up-regulated genes			
Clu	x	Q06890	x
Fn1	x	P11276	x
Itga5	x	P11688	x
Acpp	x	NP_997551.1	x
Itgb5	x	O70309	x
Hnrnpu		NP_058085.1	x
Actg1		P63260	x
Down-regulated genes			
Tacstd2	x	NP_064431.2	x
Itga6	x	Q61739	x
Ubqln2		Q9QZM0	x
Pttg1ip		Q8R143	x
Ldlr		P35951	x
Itgb4		NP_598424.2	x

3 Integrative Data Analysis for Gene Set Biomarker and Disease Target Discovery

Complex human diseases occur as a result of multiple genetic alterations and combinations of environmental factors. The integrative analysis of multiple omics data sources is a promising strategy for deciphering the molecular basis of disease and for the discovery of robust molecular signatures for disease diagnosis/prognosis [11]. Oncology is the field of research where biomarker discovery is most advanced. Various types of biomarkers have been identified for use in prognostic and eventually provide patients with personalized treatment [21, 22]. Emerging themes in cancer research include *i*) the exploitation of panels of biomarkers for successful translation of discoveries into clinical applications [23] and *ii*) the understanding of cancer at the pathway-level [24]. We believe that there is a considerable potential for disease target discovery and biomarker identification in shifting from single gene to metabolic pathway (or other functional gene set) analysis of omics data. Moreover, having identified disease targets in their biological context may be useful in further steps of the commercialization process.

Gene Set Analysis (GSA) approaches intend to identify differentially expressed sets of functionally related genes [25]. Most GSA methods start with a list of differentially expressed genes, and use contingency statistics to determine if the proportion of genes from a given set is surprisingly high [26]. Gene Set Enrichment Analysis is a popular alternative [27]. It tests whether the rank of genes ordered according to P-values differs from a uniform distribution. Goeman and Bühlmann recently reviewed existing GSA methods, and strongly recommended the use of self-contained methods [28]. We are currently developing and testing statistical methods for GSA analysis of cancer expression profiles. The Kyoto Encyclopedia of Genes and Genomes (KEGG) [29] and the Gene Ontology (GO) [30] are used to group genes into sets, and differential expression is assessed for gene sets rather than individual genes. Future developments will include integration of pathway and ontology knowledge in combination with transcriptomics and proteomics analysis of tumor samples.

4 Conclusion

One of the major challenges in dealing with today's omics data is its proper integration through which various forms of useful knowledge can be discovered and validated. In this paper we discussed our attempts in integrating omics data and introduced case studies in which various forms of omics data have been used to complement each other for knowledge discovery and validation. Among methods developed, a novel multi-strategy approach showed some interesting results in the analysis of transcriptomics and proteomics data, which also includes biological experimental validation. Until now, all of our integrated case studies have resulted in interesting discoveries, among which are cases where using a single form of biological data would have resulted in missing some valuable information. This is evident from our transcriptomics/proteomics integration example explained in this paper. Our ultimate goal is to develop platforms that facilitate development of clinical test kits that are based on multiple sources of omics data.

Acknowledgments. The experiments on the effect of salicylic acid on *Arabidopsis thaliana* were conducted by Fobert's Lab at the Plant Biotechnology Institute, NRC. The microarray experiments for JM01 cell lines were conducted by O'Connor-McCourt's Lab at the Biotechnology Research Institute, NRC. The proteomics experiments (mass-spectrometry) for the JM01 were performed by Kelly's Lab at the Institute for Biological Sciences, NRC. We thank them for sharing the data.

References

1. Joyce, A.R., Palsson, B.O.: The model organism as a system: integrating 'omics' data sets. Nat. Rev. Mol. Cell Biol. 7, 198–210 (2006)
2. Baxevanis, A.D.: The importance of biological databases in biological discovery. Curr. Protoc. Bioinformatics Chapter 1: Unit 1.1 (2009)
3. Galperin, M.Y., Cochrane, G.R.: Nucleic acids research annual database issue and the nar online molecular biology database collection in 2009. Nucleic Acids Res. 37, D1–D4 (2009)
4. Fleischmann, R.D., Adams, M.D., et al.: Whole-genome random sequencing and assembly of Haemophilus influenzae Rd. Science 269, 496–512 (1995)

5. National Center for Biotechnology Information (NCBI): Genome sequencing projects statistics, http://www.ncbi.nlm.nih.gov (retrieved December 6, 2009)
6. Brent, M.R.: Steady progress and recent breakthroughs in the accuracy of automated genome annotation. Nat. Rev. Genet. 9, 62–73 (2008)
7. ENCODE Project Consortium: The ENCODE (ENCyclopedia Of DNA Elements) Project. Science 306, 636–640 (2004)
8. Allison, D.B., Cui, X., et al.: Microarray data analysis: from disarray to consolidation and consensus. Nat. Rev. Genet. 7, 55–65 (2006)
9. Mockler, T.C., Chan, S., et al.: Applications of DNA tiling arrays for whole-genome analysis. Genomics 85, 1–15 (2005)
10. Shendure, J., Ji, H.: Next-generation DNA sequencing. Nat. Biotechnol. 26, 1135–1145 (2008)
11. Ostrowski, J., Wyrwicz, L.S.: Integrating genomics, proteomics and bioinformatics in translational studies of molecular medicine. Expert. Rev. Mol. Diagn. 9, 623–630 (2009)
12. Hu, Q., Noll, R.J., et al.: The Orbitrap: a new mass spectrometer. J. Mass. Spectrom. 40, 430–443 (2005)
13. Lubec, G., Afjehi-Sadat, L.: Limitations and pitfalls in protein identification by mass spectrometry. Chem. Rev. 107, 3568–3584 (2007)
14. Nie, L., Wu, G., et al.: Integrative analysis of transcriptomic and proteomic data: challenges, solutions and applications. Crit. Rev. Biotechnol. 27, 63–75 (2007)
15. Liu, Z., Phan, S., Famili, F., Pan, Y., Lenferink, A., Cantin, C., Collins, C., O'Connor-McCourt, M.: A multi-strategy approach to informative genes identification from gene expression data. J. Bioinfo. Comput. Biol (2010) (in press)
16. Phan, S., Shearer, H., Tchagang, A., Liu, Z., Famili, F., Fobert, F., Pan, Y.: Arabidopsis thaliana defense gene response under pathogen challenge. In: The 9th GHI-AGM, Montreal, June 8-10 (2009)
17. Subramanian, A., Tamayo, P., et al.: Gene set enrichment analysis: a knowledge-based approach for interpreting genome-wide expression profiles. Proc. Natl. Acad. Sci. 102, 15545–15550 (2005)
18. Goeman, J.J., Buhlmann, P.: Analyzing gene expression data in terms of gene sets: methodological issues. Bioinformatics 23, 980–987 (2007)
19. Ogata, H., Goto, S., et al.: KEGG: Kyoto Encyclopedia of Genes and Genomes. Nucleic Acids Res. 27, 29–34 (1999)
20. Ashburner, M., Ball, C.A., et al.: Gene ontology: tool for the unification of biology. The Gene Ontology Consortium. Nat. Genet. 25, 25–29 (2000)
21. Fobert, P., Després, C.: Redox control of systemic acquired resistance. Curr. Op. Plant Biol. 8, 378–382 (2005)
22. Kesarwani, M., Yoo, J., Dong, X.: Genetic Interactions of TGA transcription factors in the regulation of pathogenesis-related genes and disease resistance in Arabidopsis. Plant Physiol. 14, 336–346 (2007)
23. Lenferink, A.E.G., Magoon, J., Cantin, C., O'Connor-McCourt, M.D.: Investigation of three new mouse mammary tumor cell lines as models for transforming growth factor (TGF)-β and Neu pathway signaling studies: identification of a novel model for TGF-β-induced epithelial-to-mesenchymal transition. Breast Cancer Res. 6, 514–530 (2004)
24. Hill, J.J., Tremblay, T.L., Cantin, C., O'Connor-McCourt, M.D., Kelly, J.F., Lenferink, A.E.G.: Glycoproteomic analysis of two mouse mammary cell lines during transforming growth factor (TGF)-β induced epithelial to mesenchymal transition. Proteome Science 7(2) (2009)

25. Tainsky, M.A.: Genomic and proteomic biomarkers for cancer: a multitude of opportunities. Biochim. Biophys. Acta 1796, 176–193 (2009)
26. Chin, L., Gray, J.W.: Translating insights from the cancer genome into clinical practice. Nature 452, 553–563 (2008)
27. Ross, J.S.: Multigene classifiers, prognostic factors, and predictors of breast cancer clinical outcome. Adv. Anat. Pathol. 16, 204–215 (2009)
28. The Cancer Genome Atlas Research Network: Comprehensive genomic characterization defines human glioblastoma genes and core pathways. Nature 455, 1061–1068 (2008)
29. Dinu, I., Potter, J.D., et al.: Gene-set analysis and reduction. Brief Bioinform. 10, 24–34 (2009)
30. Khatri, P., Draghici, S.: Ontological analysis of gene expression data: current tools, limitations, and open problems. Bioinformatics 21, 3587–3595 (2005)

Computer Assisted Identification, Segmentation and Quantification of Synapses in the Cerebral Cortex

Juan Morales[1,5], Lidia Alonso-Nanclares[2,3], José-Rodrigo Rodríguez[2,3],
Ángel Merchán-Pérez[2,4], Javier DeFelipe[2,3], and Ángel Rodríguez[1]

[1] Departamento de Tecnología Fotónica,
Universidad Politécnica de Madrid (UPM), Madrid, Spain
juan.morales@upm.es, arodri@ti.upm.es
[2] Laboratorio de Circuitos Corticales, Centro de Tecnología Biomédica,
Universidad Politécnica de Madrid (UPM), Madrid, Spain
{aidil,rodrigo,defelipe}@cajal.csic.es, amerchan@med.ucm.es
[3] Instituto Cajal, CSIC, Madrid, Spain
[4] Departamento de Arquitectura y Tecnología de Sistemas Informáticos,
Universidad Politécnica de Madrid (UPM), Madrid, Spain
[5] CesViMa, Universidad Politécnica de Madrid (UPM), Madrid, Spain

Abstract. Synapses are key elements in the organization of nervous circuits. Obtaining serial images from large samples of nervous tissue in an automated manner is now possible through combined focused ion beam milling and scanning electron microscopy. However, the identification, 3D reconstruction and quantification of synapses within these samples are labor intensive procedures that require continuous user intervention. We have developed a software tool to automatically perform the segmentation of synapses in a reconstructed 3D volume of the cerebral cortex, thereby greatly facilitating and accelerating these processes. The tool is interactive, allowing the user to supervise the segmentation process, to modify the appropriate parameters and to validate the results. It is also modular to enable new functions to be implemented as needed. We have also ensured it has a user friendly interface and that it is portable, making it accessible to a wide range of potential users.

1 Introduction

The exchange of information between neurons mainly takes place through highly specialized structures known as chemical synapses. These synapses communicate through a chemical substance, a neurotransmitter, that is released by the presynaptic axon terminal and that interacts with specific receptors on the postsynaptic membrane. Under the electron microscope, dark densities on the cytoplasmic sides of both the pre- and postsynaptic membranes are evident. These synaptic membrane densities, together with the space that separates them, the synaptic cleft, form the synaptic junction (Fig. 1). Presynaptic axon terminals are also characterized by the presence of synaptic vesicles that contain the neurotransmitter and that accumulate close to the presynaptic density [1,2,3].

In the cerebral cortex, two main types of synapses are recognized, asymmetric (or type I) and symmetric (or type II) [3,4,5], which can be distinguished morphologically

N. García-Pedrajas et al. (Eds.): IEA/AIE 2010, Part III, LNAI 6098, pp. 112–118, 2010.

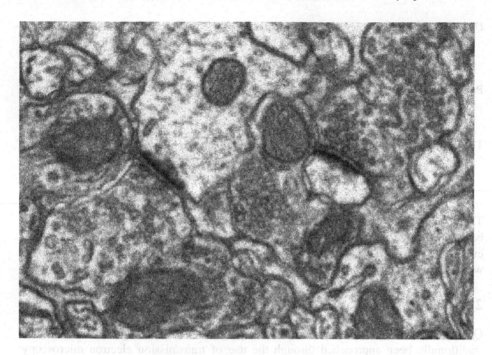

Fig. 1. Image captured by Focused Ion Beam milling and Scanning Electron Microscopy (FIB/SEM) showing two asymmetric synapses in the cerebral cortex

by the presence of a prominent or thin post-synaptic density in asymmetric or symmetric synapses, respectively. This classification is functionally relevant since asymmetric synapses are considered to be excitatory while symmetric synapses are inhibitory. Moreover, asymmetric synapses are much more abundant (75-95% of all neocortical synapses) than symmetric synapses (5-25%; for reviews, see [6,7,8,9]).

Synapses are key elements in the functional organization of neuronal circuits and thus, understanding their location, size and the proportion of the two different morphological types is extraordinarily important. The tool we have developed automatically performs the segmentation and 3D reconstruction of synapses in the cerebral cortex, helping the user to examine large tissue volumes and to interactively validate the results provided by the software.

The main principles for designing the tool can be briefly summarized as follows:

Interactivity: the experts must supervise the segmentation and reconstruction steps in order to validate the structures extracted. The scale of the available data varies between $10,000\times$ and $30,000\times$ magnification. Such a large variation demands user intervention to set the parameters of the corresponding scale. Furthermore, user interaction demands a very efficient response of the system, even when dealing with large 3D volumes.

Modularity: the experts are always working at the limits of the available data acquisition technology, which means that the tool must be very flexible to be able to implement and introduce new functions into the system.

Usability: taking into account the background of the potential users, the interface must be as user friendly as possible in order to minimize the learning curve of the tool, avoiding the potential discouragement of new users when faced with a very complex system.

Portability: considering the wide range of potential users, the technology used for the development of the tool must be robust and stable in numerous set-ups, operating systems and system architectures.

The main functionality of the system include the following tasks:

- 3D Volume navigation for exploring the contents of the stack.
- 3D Synapse segmentation.
- 3D Synapse reconstruction.

The rest of the paper contains a brief background in Section 2 which introduces some basic concepts related with the system described. Then Section 3 describes and discusses the proposed system, and finally Section 4 includes the conclusions and future work.

2 Background

Quantification of synapses under different experimental or pathological conditions has traditionally been approached through the use of transmission electron microscopy (TEM) and stereological methods. However, TEM is very limited when the intention is to study large tissue volumes and to perform 3D reconstruction, as it becomes technically difficult and extremely time consuming when dealing with long series of ultrathin sections.

It has recently been shown that the combined use of focused ion beam milling and scanning electron microscopy (FIB/SEM) overcomes most of the difficulties and artifacts inherent to TEM [10]. However, while this new technology automates the process of obtaining serial sections and the image acquisition, the quantification and reconstruction of synapses is still labor-intensive and requires continuous user intervention. Although software tools for the 3D reconstruction of synapses are available of synapses [11], they are mainly based on the manual tracing of the contours of the contours of the structures of interest.

3 System Description

We have developed a tool to perform three tasks that experts require to analyze long series of sections (up to 700) obtained by FIB/SEM:

- Free navigation inside the reconstructed volume to explore all the features and elements present in the stack of images.
- Assisted synapse segmentation, spreading a seed fixed by the user with a mouse click over the set of voxels that belong to the synapse considered.
- Automatic 3D synapse reconstruction from the segmented voxels.

We will describe each one of these tasks in more detail below, together with some features of the implementation.

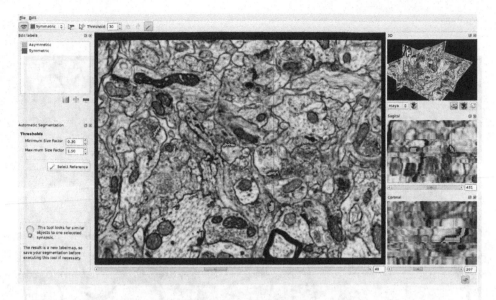

Fig. 2. Snapshot of the system interface

3.1 3D Navigation

The GUI is organized as a set of widgets that the user can select, move, raise or hide at his/her convenience (see Figure 2 for a snapshot of the system interface). We have implemented widgets for input/output operations, to manage several views of the data set, to set the segmentation parameters, and to manage the segmented or reconstructed synapses.

After loading the stack, the user can select which is the best view for his/her purpose from the views of the available XY, YZ and XZ projection planes and then, the volume can be positioned in the orientation required to optimize the visualization of the neural structures. Moving around the volume is performed by shifting the sliders associated to each visualization window or by enabling the mouse controls over each slice for zooming, making affine transformations and changing the active slice. All these resources allow a very fluid and flexible navigation.

3.2 3D Synapse Segmentation

We have adopted synaptic membrane densities as counting units for synapses [12]. When the synaptic cleft is visible (i.e.; when the plane of the section is perpendicular to that of the synaptic junction), both densities are considered as a single unit.

Once the user has recognized a synapse, he or she just clicks on the mouse within the region of the synapse and its volume is extracted using heuristics based on three features: gray levels, connectivity and size. Threshold segmentation from the selected voxels value is interactively adjusted with a specific widget that enables the gray level and the size threshold intervals to be adapted to the focus of attention, if necessary.

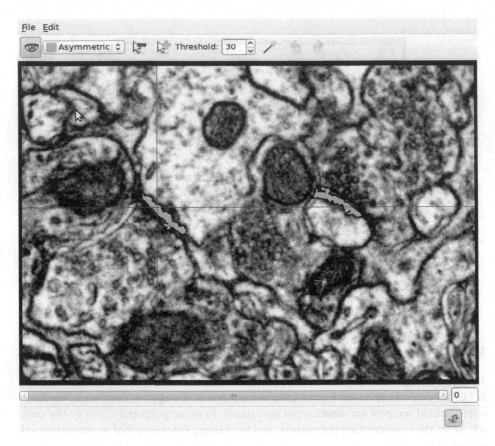

Fig. 3. Result of the segmentation of the two asymmetric synapses identified in Fig. 1

In Figure 3, the results of the segmentation obtained over one slice of the stack are shown, where two synapses have been identified by the user at that moment. Color labels are used to better identify and classify the volume extracted.

If the result of the segmentation is not satisfactory, the user may discard the "incorrect" synapses at any moment by activating the delete control. In addition, the user can use a "magic wand" to automatically segment the whole volume in one go. Unfortunately, a global threshold value cannot normally be applied to obtain results that do not require user intervention as described above.

3.3   3D Synapse Reconstruction

The final stage of the workflow is to extract the segmented regions. Once the user is satisfied with the results obtained in the segmentation stage, the geometry of each segmented synapse is collected in a data structure that can be saved in a file for later edition or visualization (see Figure 4 for the result of the 3D synapse reconstruction for the whole stack).

Fig. 4. 3D Reconstruction of the synapses found in the stack

Overlapping the raw data and the reconstructed synapses allows the user to compare the boundaries of both data sets: original and synthetic. Thus, if there are significant mismatches, the user can recover the workflow for that specific case at any of the previous stages.

3.4   Implementation Description

We followed a similar development methodology to *scrum* because the principles proposed in this method were very much like the environment we faced [13]. This methodology enables software to be developed rapidly on the basis of small sprints, the result of each representing a further improvement in the tool. In our case, each stage of the workflow was the result of the corresponding sprint and new improvements will be introduced in the near future.

Another issue taken into consideration was to ensure the portability of the tool across a wide range of systems. We chose a set of stable and widely tested free distribution tools that made this objective easier. Thus, we chose Python vs. 2.6 and C++ as the programming languages, ITK vs. 3.16 as the image processing library and VTK vs. 5.4 as the visualization library.

Accordingly, we have already successfully installed the tool on several systems with Linux and Windows, and it is expected that it should also migrate to Mac OS with no problems.

4   Conclusions and Future Work

The tool greatly accelerates the process of identifying, quantifying and reconstructing synapses in large tissue volumes obtained from FIB/SEM samples. Most asymmetric synapses are readily segmented without any user intervention. The user has only to delete the non-synaptic membranes or other dark densities that commonly arise from mitochondria. These "false positive" objects are reduced to a minimum by selecting an adequate size threshold. Moreover, "false negative" objects, that is true synapses that are not automatically identified by the tool, are easily and quickly identified by the user.

The main problem to be solved in the future is that of symmetric synapses. They are poorly identified automatically because the postsynaptic density is much less prominent than in asymmetric synapses, and it is often hard to distinguish them from the surrounding non-synaptic membranes. Other identification criteria, such as the presence of synaptic vesicles close to the presynaptic density, may help to overcome this difficulty in the future.

Acknowledgements

This work has been partially funded by the the the Spanish Ministry of Science and Innovation (Cajal Blue Brain Project and grant TIN2007-67188).

References

1. Colonnier, M.: The Electron-Microscopic Analysis of the Neuronal Organization of the Cerebral Cortex. In: Schmitt, F.O., Worden, F.G., Adelman, G., Dennis, S.G. (eds.) The Organization of the Cerebral Cortex, pp. 125–152. MIT Press, Cambridge (1981)
2. Peters, A., Palay, S.L., Webster, H.: The Fine Structure of the Nervous System. Neurons and their Supporting Cells. Oxford University Press, New York (1991)
3. Peters, A., Palay, S.L.: The Morphology of Synapses. J. of Neurocytol. 25, 687–700 (1996)
4. Gray, E.G.: Axo-Somatic and Axo-Dendritic Synapses of the Cerebral Cortex: An Electron Microscopic Study. J. Anat. 93, 420–433 (1959)
5. Colonnier, M.: Synaptic Patterns on Different Cell Types in the Different Laminae of the Cat Visual Cortex. An Electron Microscope Study. Brain Res. 9, 268–287 (1968)
6. Houser, C.R., Vaughn, J.E., Hendry, S.H., Jones, E.G., Peters, A.: GABA Neurons in the Cerebral Cortex. In: Jones, E.G., Peters, A. (eds.) Functional Properties of Cortical Cells, vol. 2, pp. 63–89. Plenum Press, New York (1984)
7. White, E.L.: Cortical Circuits: Synaptic Organization of the Cerebral Cortex. In: Structure, Function and Theory. Birkhäuser, New York (1989)
8. DeFelipe, J., Fariñas, I.: The Pyramidal Neuron of the Cerebral Cortex: Morphological and Chemical Characteristics of the Synaptic Inputs. Prog. Neurobiol. 39, 563–607 (1992)
9. DeFelipe, J., Alonso-Nanclares, L., Arellano, J.: Microstructure of the Neocortex: Comparative Aspects. J. of Neurocytol. 31, 299–316 (2002)
10. Merchán-Pérez, A., Rodríguez, J.R., Alonso-Nanclares, L., Schertel, A., DeFelipe, J.: Counting synapses using FIB/SEM microscopy: a true revolution for ultrastructural volume reconstruction. Frontiers in Neuroanatomy 3(18), 1–14 (2009)
11. Fiala, J.C.: Reconstruct: A Free Editor for Serial Section Microscopy. J. of Mircosc. 218, 52–61 (2005)
12. Mayhew, T.M.: How to count synapses unbiasedly and efficiently at the ultrastructural level: proposal for a standard sampling and counting protocol. J. of Neurocytol. 25, 793–804 (1996)
13. Rising, L., Janoff, N.S.: The Scrum Software Development Process for Small Teams. IEEE Softw. 17(4), 26–32 (2000)

Association Rules to Identify Receptor and Ligand Structures through Named Entities Recognition

A.T. Winck, K.S. Machado, D.D. Ruiz, and V.L. Strube de Lima

Pontifícia Universidade Católica do Rio Grande do Sul, Brazil
{ana.winck,karina.machado,duncan.ruiz,vera.strube}@pucrs.br

Abstract. One of the challenges in natural language processing (NLP) is to semantically treat documents. Such process is tailored to specific domains, where bioinformatics appears as a promising interest area. We focus this work on the rational drug design process, in trying to help the identification of new target proteins (receptors) and drug candidate compounds (ligands) in scientific documents. Our approach is to handle such structures as named entities (NE) in the text. We propose the recognition of these NE by analyzing their context. In doing so, considering an annotated corpus on the RDD domain, we present models generated by association rules mining that indicate which terms relevant to the context point out the presence of a receptor or ligand in a sentence.

Keywords: Named Entity, Association Rules, Receptor and Ligand.

1 Introduction

The increasing amount of textual documents containing information to be used for natural language processing (NLP) has been the main motivation for using text mining. Currently, 80% of the available information is within textual documents [1]. With the emergent interest in semantically processing applied domain corpora such as biomedicine and bioinformatics, knowledge representation in these domains appears as a contemporary field of study.

One area of research in bioinformatics is the rational drug design (RDD), where knowledge about protein and ligand structures is critical for a more efficient new drug development. A possible approach to identify the receptors and ligands that were already reported is to look for their presence in scientific papers. One interesting approach strategy is to handle such structures as named entities (NE), which are referred terms in a given context, through Named Entities Recognition (NER) techniques. In this work, we assume as NE all those terms that can be classified as receptors or ligands.

The main goal of the work described here is to develop a methodology to be adopted to NER on receptor and ligand structures domain, considering the context of terms around NEs. Hence, we propose a 3-step process. In the first step, a corpus of domain documents is built and annotated. The second one

N. García-Pedrajas et al. (Eds.): IEA/AIE 2010, Part III, LNAI 6098, pp. 119–128, 2010.

consists on preparing the annotated corpus and submitting them to association rules mining, to identify NE patterns. The third one makes use of the generated patterns, applying them to a test set and, at last, analyzing their effectiveness.

2   Contextualization

The interest in applying NLP to bioinformatics corpora has grown up in the last years, mainly because the increasing number of documents in this area, together with the importance of making use of the information contained in those documents in future research decisions, considering time and costs.

Corpora of the bioinformatics and biomedicine domain have particular characteristics and in this case NER can be applied to identify the whole events of specific blocks, usually proper names, as people, companies, genes and drugs [2].

We find in the literature different NER techniques applied to bioinformatics, in gene classification [3][4], chemical compounds identification [5], clinical documents [6], drug properties identification [7], and the recognition of genes and protein names [8]. Application of NER to bioinformatics makes use of different approaches. Among them we can mention the use of dictionaries that contain terms to be classified as NE, the mapping of lexical or morphologic characteristics and the analysis of the context around an NE [9].

Mansouri et al. [10] reviewed and tested different approaches to NER mentioning association rule mining. Although other machine learning techniques, such as Support Vector Machines (SVM) and K-Nearest Neighbors (KNN) appear in NER research, some works make use of association rules [11][12][13]. In this paper we propose to recognize NE through association rules by associative classification [14].

2.1   RDD Characteristics

Receptors are proteins that recognize and bind a compound. Ligands are small molecules with biological activities able to inhibit the target protein activity [15]. Researches dealing with RDD generally have a target biological molecule (receptor) and look for potential compounds able to inhibit such receptor. Identifying which receptor and ligand structures are being used to a given disease and to make use of the information obtained from the literature, comes up as an approach that may contribute to this process.

However, in RDD scientific papers, those terms appear in different ways. To identify and to classify such terms are not trivial tasks. Repositories of these substances is quickly increasing. In this case, to maintain a dictionary, as proposed above, is an expensive computational activity. Besides, names of receptors and ligands are not described in the same lexical structure, and it becomes impracticable to identify terms with specific characteristics that classify them. For instance, the Interleukin receptor can be described with different manners (eg. Interleukin; Interleukin 2; Interleukin-2; IL; IL-2; IL2; IL 2). If we consider the last 4 terms (a two letter uppercase and a number format) we can imagine that this is a good kind of identification. However, there is a structure called CD28 (that is represented by the same format of IL2) which is a ligand.

We know, by means of corpus observation, that both receptor and ligand names use to appear with terms that can suggest the class to which they belong. For instance, a receptor is a *protein* that has some molecular *activity* that *induces* some biochemical *effect*. A ligand, however, in the molecular *docking* can *associate* with a receptor and present a good *bind*, which is noticed through its *interaction* and potency to *inhibit* the target protein.

In the previous paragraph we deliberately used some expressions in italics. These are examples of terms that may indicate the presence of a given NE. However if such terms are isolated, maybe these characteristics are not effective. To discover some association rules between terms may be a promising manner to identify and to classify receptor and ligand structures, by their context, in biomedical literature.

To achieve our goals, we propose a 3-step process: data collection, data mining and application. The data collection step starts with a RDD context corpus building. This corpus is annotated in order to identify and classify the entities as well as the words relevant to the context. Having the annotated corpus in hand, the data mining step is started. This step applies preprocessing techniques to the annotated corpus so that such corpus can be read by association rule algorithms to produce models which indicate when a given entity can be identified. Such models are post-processed making them shorter and more accurate. Having these post-processed models, the application step is then initiated and the models are applied to a test set, so that they are evaluated and, finally, the results are produced, that is, the NE on the texts are recognized.

3 Data Collection

As a data collection, in our data collection step, we used the GENIA[1] corpus version 3.02. This corpus is composed by 2,000 documents (titles and abstracts) of areas of biomedicine. Initially we selected only the documents that had chances to be related to the RDD domain. The criterion was based on 5 previously selected keywords: if at least one of them appears in a document, it has chances to refer to some receptor or ligand structure. Appling such criterion we selected 798 documents. Table 1 shows the keywords we used, the number of documents selected by the correspondent keywords and the total frequency of each. The selection step used not only the listed words but also their stemming, so that the morphological variants of words having the same stem were removed.

This selected document set has to be annotated, such that specific terms and their context are visible from the application. One important aspect is that we did not find any annotated corpus on the RDD domain. In this sense, we manually annotated the selected corpus, according to a context-based knowledge. Manual annotation here is a preliminary task, and we are taking it as a lesson learned to future automated annotation.

---

[1] http://www-tsujii.is.s.u-tokyo.ac.jp/~genia

Table 1. Keywords initial document selection

Keywords	Documents	Frequency
Docking	8	12
Drug	46	57
Ligand	97	136
Receptor	615	1376
Target	154	193

3.1 Annotation

Considering that our proposal to identify receptor and ligand structures through NER uses the context around the entity, the annotation here has two main objectives: identify which terms are entities and assigning a class to each of them (where the classes can be receptors or ligands) and mapping the context of each entity, which means to identify which terms near an entity can refer to it, especially considering those terms belonging to the same sentence where an entity appears. In fact, we choose to consider all terms of a sentence, due to the difficulty in delimiting the best window for each entity.

We got to 106 manually annotated documents, from the 798 selected ones. To each entity we assigned its correspondent class. In order to identify an entity, its context has to be considered: all the terms around the entity are analyzed considering the presence of this NE. To exemplify, Table 2 illustrates an annotated sentence where each line shows a term of the sentence and its respective annotation. The NE E1A is a receptor. Terms annotated with 0 are not relevant to the context and, terms with 1 are relevant. We also removed, from the sentence, words having little information value (known as stopwords).

Table 2. Example of an annotated sentence

Term	Annotating
Stably	0
transfected	1
target	1
cells	0
exhibited	0
cytolytic	0
susceptibility	0
despite	0
expression	0
equivalent	0
levels	0
E1A	RECEPTOR
proteins	1
Ad-infected	0
targets	1

The context identification depends on the success cases, that is, cases in which the term is relevant. We recovered the annotated relevant terms (those ones where annotation is 1). From the 106 annotated documents, there were 946 occurrences of receptors and 459 occurrences of ligands.

4 Data Mining

The models here aim at quickly identifying which terms have chance to be receptors or ligands, among all the ones in the document. So, we aim at building models that indicate if a given sentence has some NE, specifying this entity class. To perform this task we applied association rule mining to the training set.

Han et al. [2] indicate that mining algorithms, such as association-based classification, have been used for text classification research. Such algorithm aims at finding strong associations between frequent itemsets implying in a class attribute. We hope that the produced models indicate either the presence of a term or a combination of terms in a sentence. To predict if such sentence contains an entity, we believe that association rules are the most promising mining task to be applied. In doing so, the preprocessing of documents must follow an adequate approach to be supported by this kind of algorithm.

4.1 Preprocessing

With the annotated terms and entities in hand, we defined the preprocessed data, with 87 attributes. The number of instances is equivalent to the number of events. The 86 first attributes represent the terms considered to be relevant to the context and the last one indicates the class of the entity in each event. It is worth mentioning that such 86 terms are our annotated terms after stemming. Each cell indicates the presence or absence of the attribute (term) in the sentence in which the NE was retrieved. If the term is present, the cell is filled with "1", else with "?". Table 3 illustrates the input file, exemplifying the presence of four entities and the presence or absence of the terms.

Table 3. Preprocessed data

Term 1	Term 2	Term 3	...	Term 86	Class
1	?	?	...	1	Receptor
?	?	?	...	1	Ligand
?	1	?	...	?	Receptor
?	?	?	...	?	Receptor

Note that each instance is related to an occurrence of a given entity in the sentence, considering all its relevant terms. In this sense, sequential and equal records may appear, as well as records with different classes but with the same annotated terms. This happens because in a given sentence, more than one event of the same entity class may appear. To exemplify, Table 4 shows part of an annotated sentence (without stopwords) where there are 3 events of entities of type receptor and 1 entity of type ligand. Such sentence produces 4 records, being 3 of receptor and 1 of ligand. The final prepared file has a total of 1405 records, being 946 of entities of type receptor and 459 of entities of type ligand.

4.2 Mining

The algorithm chosen was classification-based association rules, or Associative classification. An association rule is the implication in the form $x \rightarrow y$. In association rules have basically two measures: support and confidence.

Table 4. Example of sentence with different events of entities

Term	Annotation
ROIs	0
required	0
CD28	RECEPTOR
mediate	1
active	1
NF-kappa	LIGAND
B	0
CD28	RECEPTOR
response	1
complex	1
IL-2	RECEPTOR
Expression	1

Associative classification aims at finding strong associations among frequent itemsets resulting in a class attribute. In the domain being explored, we believe that this technique is able to (a) discover association between terms that imply a given entity (class attribute); (b) through the confidence value, define if the presence of a term is significant or not; (c) work well even with missing values; and (d) implicitly apply feature selection, considering that the generated rules take into account the values of minimum support and confidence.

We applied the Apriori Algorithm [16] as a classification association enabling the option to generate in the right side, only values of the class attribute. Although there are specific algoritms to classification association, as Predictive Apriori [14] we selected the Apriori due to the fact that: a) the obtained rules for both algorithms were very similar; b) the Apriori performance was better; and c) we are interested in individual support and confidence values, and the Predictive Apriori returns a delta from these values.

We chose to perform 7 different experiments. For all of them we requested to be produced up to a thousand of rules, where the support attribute was defined as 0.005 and the confidence attribute was defined between 0.4 and 1.0. Table 5 illustrates a summary of the produced models with the values of support and confidence, and the number of rules required and produced. It is important to mention that, for the domain of this work, the value of support may be less important that the value of confidence. That is, once we have a wide training set, the frequency of a rule may not be significant, but how frequent is the rule against the frequency of its left-side itemset.

4.3   Post-processing

To verify the effectiveness of the produced rules, we submitted them through a post-processing stage. The goal of this step is to eliminate redundant rules, reaching sharpener and more effective models. The steps listed in the sequence were also applied to each of the seven generated models (Table 5).

At first, these rules have been alphabetically sorted in order to identify those more comprehensive rules. That is, we eliminated all specialized rules that are contained in a more general rule. Figure 1(a) shows part of the fifth model rules

Table 5. Summary of the Apriori algorithm execution

Model	Support	Confidence	Requested rules	Produced rules
1	0.005	1.0	1,000	482
2	0.005	0.9	1,000	526
3	0.005	0.8	1,000	644
4	0.005	0.7	1,000	745
5	0.005	0.6	1,000	870
6	0.005	0.5	1,000	973
7	0.005	0.4	1,000	1,000

(a)	(b)
742. Complex → Receptor conf:(0.7)	616. Treatment → Receptor conf:(0.8)
466. Complex, Domain → Receptor conf:(1)	510. Altered, Treatment → Receptor conf:(0.91)
473. Complex, Domain, Protein → Receptor conf:(1)	763. Expression, Treatment → Receptor conf:(0.69)
693. Complex, Complex, Formation → Receptor conf:(0.75)	524. Receptor, Treatment → Receptor conf:(0.9)
448. Complex, Formation, Protein → Receptor conf:(1)	458. Acts, Altered, Effect, Treatment → Receptor conf:(1)
474. Complex, Formation, Transcript → Receptor conf:(1)	
704. Complex, Induce → Receptor conf:(0.74)	
631. Complex, Induce, Site → Receptor conf:(0.8)	
530. Complex, Protein → Receptor conf:(0.89)	
475. Complex, Protein, Site → Receptor conf:(1)	
731. Complex, Receptor → Receptor conf:(0.71)	
503. Complex, Response → Receptor conf:(0.92)	
588. Complex, Site → Receptor conf:(0.83)	
706. Complex, Stimulate → Receptor conf:(0.67)	

Fig. 1. Part of the fifth model for removing specialized rules

alphabetically ordered, being the rule followed by its confidence. This figure illustrates the generalization and specialization of the term "Complex". Note that the more general rule (742) is an implication of this term in the entity "Receptor". The other rules are implications of this combined with other terms in the entity "Receptor". In this sense, once the rule 742 covers other ones presented in the model, we eliminate those more specialized.

To improve the removal of more specialized rules, we identified how many terms were present in each rule. To illustrate, Figure 1(b) shows the rule 616 from the fifth model. This rule is made only by the term "Treatment" involving the entity "Receptor". This rule is contained in rules 510, 763, 524 and 458 (all of them contain the term "Treatment") therefore, they are excluded.

Conducting an initial assessment of the models, we noticed that lower confidence in the term, more general are the rules, although the number of terms grows when confidence decreases. To see which models were more effective it is necessary to evaluate them in the application set.

5   Application and Results

In order to test the produced and post-processed models we applied them to real and reliable bases. We selected 15 articles [2] easy for the specialist to infer all

[2] PUBMed IDs: 14693546, 11322792, 11735121, 10869170, 15908576, 7886450, 17716292, 10869356, 18094751, 16323864, 16647717, 14623976, 12164478, 16161997 and 16906155.

entities present in their abstracts. Table 6 presents a summary of abstracts used for application, showing the total number of entities of each file and how many of them are related to each class.

Table 6. Summary of the used documents in the application

	# abstract														
	1	2	3	4	5	6	7	8	9	10	11	12	13	14	15
Entities	16	5	4	20	11	8	4	13	21	9	16	17	3	2	7
Receptor	8	2	2	10	5	3	3	1	11	2	7	8	1	2	3
Ligand	8	3	2	10	6	5	1	12	10	7	9	9	2	0	4

The seven models previously inferred were evaluated on the application set by precision, recall and f-score, according to formulas proposed by Han et al. [2]. Both precision and recall are considered in calculating f-score. Figure 2 shows three graphics that represent each evaluated measure.

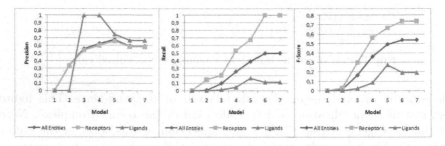

Fig. 2. Models evaluation

The f-score shows that, the lower the confidence value of the model is, the better the hit rate in the document analyzed will be. This hit rate, however, has stabilized when the confidence was set to 0.4. We can also note that for the confidence value of 100% it was not possible to hit any entity. We believe that this is due to the fact that models with low confidence value produce more general rules. Besides, we can see that in the three graphics the ligand behavior is different. In our test set there were more receptors than ligands entities, while in the application set the number of ligands was bigger. In doing so, the models were prone to identify receptors instead of ligands. Finally, although our intention was to produce the most accurate rules, we believe that the difference between receptors and ligands in our results is possibly related to the small number of files used for training.

6   Conclusions and Future Work

To treat documents at the semantic level is still one of the challenges of NLP. RDD are characterized in bioinformatics by looking for the best fit of a candidate drug compound (ligand) in a protein (receptor). Our approach to identify promising structures is looking for such structures in literature. To assist in this quest, this work proposes to deal with such structures as NE, introducing a strategy to recognize them through the context of the sentence in which they are found. We presented a process composed of 3 main steps: data collection, mining and application.

A data collection was built using the base GENIA, selecting only those documents related to the context of receptor and ligand structures. These documents were manually annotated, to identify the entities they mention. For the context identification we brought terms of sentences that were relevant to the identification of these entities. We obtained 106 annotated documents, and 946 instances of entities of type receptor and 459 occurrences of entities of type ligand. Such annotation has undergone a process of preparation such that it could be mined. The preprocessing had the goal of identifying all the terms relevant to the context and associating them with a given entity. These files were mined with association rules mining, identifying terms and relationships among them that can predict a given entity. The models were post-processed looking for making them more streamlined and comprehensive. These models were applied to a real base of documents, containing 15 articles. Among the experiments performed, the best of them presented an approximated f-score of 0.5 for the identification of entities in documents. Applying the measure individually, the best f-score was about 0.70 for receptors and about 0.27 for ligands.

As future work we intend to improve the annotation step so that it can indicate more accurately whether an entity is present, producing more consistent and complete corpus; improve a preprocessing that allows us to use classification algorithms; perform experiments with a wider range of confidence values to identify the best result, and also vary the value of support to identify different relationships among the terms; and apply statistical tests on the obtained results to identify relationships and significances.

Acknowledgments. This work was supported with grants from MCT/CNPq (14/2008). ATW is supported by CT-INFO/CNPq (17/2007) PhD scholarship. KSM is supported by a CAPES PhD scholarship. The research on NLP techniques was possible through the FAROL project, grant CAPES #35/05-0.

References

1. Tan, P.-N., Steinbach, M., Kumar, V.: Introduction to Data Mining. Addison-Wesley, Boston (2006)
2. Han, J., Kamber, M.: Data Mining: Concepts and Techniques. Morgan Kaufmann, San Francisco (2006)
3. Tsuruoka, Y., Tsujii, J., Ananiadou, S.: Accelerating the Annotation of Sparse Named Entities by Dynamic Sentence Selection. BMC Bioinformatics 9, S8 (2008)
4. Wong, W., Martinez, D., Cavedon, L.: Extraction of Named Entities From Tables in Gene Mutation Literature. In: BioNLP 2009: Workshop on Current Trends in Biomedical Natural Language Processing, pp. 46–54. Association for Computational Linguistics, Boulder (2009)

5. Corbett, P., Copestake, A.: Cascaded Classifiers for Confidence-based Chemical Named Entity Recognition. BMC Bioinformatics 9, S4 (2008)
6. Li, D., Kipper-Schuler, K., Savova, G.: Conditional Random Fields and Support Vector Machines for Disorder Named Entity Recognition in Clinical Texts. In: BioNLP 2008: Workshop on Current Trends in Biomedical Natural Language Processing, pp. 94–95. Association for Computational Linguistics, Columbus (2008)
7. Kolarik, C., Hofmann-Apitius, M., Zimmermann, M., Fluck, J.: Identification of New Drug Classification Terms in Textual Resources. Bioinformatics 23, 264–272 (2007)
8. Starlinger, J., Leitner, F., Valencia, A., Leser, U.: SOA-Based Integration of Text Mining Services. In: SERVICES 2009: Congress on Services - I, pp. 99–106. IEEE Computer Society, Los Angeles (2009)
9. Ananiadou, S., Kell, D., Tsujii, J.: Text Mining and its Potential Applications in Systems Biology. Trends in Biotechnology 24, 571–579 (2006)
10. Mansouri, A., Affendey, L.S., Mamat, A.: Named Entity Recognition Approaches. International Journal of Computer Science and Network Security 8, 339–344 (2008)
11. Budi, I., Bressan, S.: Association Rules Mining for Name Entity Recognition. In: Fourth International Conference on Web Information Systems Engineering (WISE 2003), pp. 325–328. IEEE Computer Society, Roma (2003)
12. Li, S., Janneck, C.D., Belapurkar, A.D., Ganiz, M.C., Yang, X., Dilsizian, M., Wu, T., Bright, J.M., Pottenger, W.M.: Mining Higher-Order Association Rules from Distributed Named Entity Databases. In: IEEE International Conference on Intelligence and Security Informatics, pp. 236–246. IEEE Computer Society, New Brunswick (2007)
13. Mendes, A., Antunes, C.: Pattern Mining with Natural Language Processing: An Exploratory Approach. In: Perner, P. (ed.) MLDM 2009. LNCS, vol. 5632, pp. 266–279. Springer, Heidelberg (2009)
14. Scheffer, T.: Finding Association Rules That Trade Support Optimally Against Confidence. Intelligent Data Analysis 9(4), 381–395 (2005)
15. Lesk, A.: Introduction to Bioinformatics. Oxford University Press, New York (2002)
16. Agrawal, R., Srikant, R.: Fast Algorithms for Mining Association Rules in Large Databases. In: VLDB 1994, Proceedings of 20th International Conference on Very Large Data Bases, pp. 487–499. Morgan Kaufmann Publishers Inc., Santiago de Chile (1994)

A Model for Generating Synthetic Dendrites of Cortical Neurons

Jaime Fernández[1], Laura Fernández[1], Ruth Benavides-Piccione[2,3],
Inmaculada Ballesteros-Yañez[4], Javier DeFelipe[2,3], and José-María Peña[1]

[1] Departamento de Arquitectura y Tecnología de Sistemas Informáticos,
Universidad Politécnica de Madrid, Madrid, Spain
[2] Laboratorio de Circuitos Corticales (Centro de Tecnología Biomédica),
Universidad Politécnica de Madrid, Madrid, Spain
[3] Instituto Cajal, Consejo Superior de Investigaciones Científicas, Madrid, Spain
[4] Facultad de Químicas, Universidad de Castilla-La Mancha, Ciudad Real, Spain

Abstract. One of the main challenges in neuroscience is to define the
detailed structural design of the nervous system. This challenge is one of
the first steps towards understanding how neural circuits contribute to
the functional organization of the nervous system. In the cerebral cortex
pyramidal neurons are key elements in brain function as they represent
the most abundant cortical neuronal type and the main source of cortical excitatory synapses. Therefore, many researchers are interested in
the analysis of the microanatomy of pyramidal cells since it constitutes
an excellent tool for better understanding cortical processing of information. Computational models of neuronal networks based on real cortical
circuits have become useful tools for studying certain aspects of the functional organization of the neocortex. Neuronal morphologies (morphological models) represent key features in these functional models. For these
purposes, synthetic or virtual dendritic trees can be generated through a
morphological model of a given neuronal type based on real morphometric parameters obtained from intracellularly-filled single neurons. This
paper presents a new method to construct virtual dendrites by means of
sampling a branching model that represents the dendritic morphology.
This method has been contrasted using complete basal dendrites from
374 layer II/III pyramidal neurons of the mouse neocortex.

Keywords: Bioinformatics, Machine Learning, Neurosciencie,
Microstructure Neuronal Morphology.

1 Introduction

Over the years, neuroscience has evolved considerably thanks to the use of a great
variety of in-vivo and in-vitro approaches. However, the study of the nervous
system is still subject to several major limitations which comes from three major
factors: (i) large number of elements (ii) the existence of an intricate web of
interactions between these elements, and (iii) limited knowledge of the functional
significance of these interactions.

N. García-Pedrajas et al. (Eds.): IEA/AIE 2010, Part III, LNAI 6098, pp. 129–138, 2010.
© Springer-Verlag Berlin Heidelberg 2010

To overcome some of these limitations, simulation and modeling mechanisms are proposed to manage the inherent complexity of the nervous system. These mechanisms take profit of the development of new tools integrated with laboratory research using experimental approaches.

In general, neurons adopt a considerable variety of shapes and sizes, as well as different patterns of dendritic and axonal arborizations. In particular, cortical pyramidal neurons consist of a typically pyramid cell body that gives rise to an apical and basal dendritic arbor. Their axons leave the region of origin, in which the cell body is located, and are therefore also called projection neurons.

One of the main challenges in neuroscience is to define the detailed structural design of the nervous system. This challenge is one of the first steps towards understanding how neural circuits contribute to the functional organization of the nervous system. In particular, the neocortex is the choice of numerous theoreticians and experimentalists because of its direct involvement in many aspects of mammalian behavior. In the neocortex, pyramidal neurons are key elements in its functional organization as they represent the most abundant cortical neuronal type (70-85%) and the main source of cortical excitatory synapses. They constitute the vast majority of projection neurons and are commonly subdivided according to their projection site and the pattern of their terminal axonal arborization (for reviews see [1], [2], [3], [4], [5], [6], [7], [8], [9]). Moreover, all dendritic surfaces of pyramidal cells are covered by spines, except the proximal segments arising directly from the cell soma which are spine-free. These dendritic spines constitute the major postsynaptic elements of excitatory synapses. Thus, dendritic spine are considered to be fundamental for memory, learning and cognition ([10], [11], [12], [13]). There is a spatial segregation of different inputs in different regions of the dendritic tree that can be divided into two major compartments: the apical dendrite with its collateral branches and dendritic tuft, and the basal dendrites. The basal dendrites form about 90% of the dendritic length of any cortical pyramidal neuron ([14]). Consequently, the basal dendritic arbor represents the major source of synaptic inputs to pyramidal neurons.

As a result, many researchers are interested in the analysis of the microanatomy of pyramidal cells since it constitutes an excellent tool for better understanding cortical processing of information. Computational models of neuronal networks based on real cortical circuits have become useful tools for studying certain aspects of the functional organization of the neocortex ([15]). A powerful method to examine developmental mechanisms and structure-function relationships of neuronal morphological parameters is computational modeling of neuronal morphology (e.g., [16]). For these purposes, synthetic or virtual dendritic trees can be generated through a morphological model of a given neuronal type based on real morphometric parameters obtained from intracellularly-filled single neurons.

This paper presents a new method to construct virtual dendrites by means of sampling a branching model that represents the dendritic morphology. This method has been contrasted using complete basal dendrites from 374 layer II/III pyramidal neurons of the mouse neocortex.

The rest of the paper is organized as follows: In Section 2 the main concepts about the morphology of pyramidal cells are briefly presented. Section 3 introduces the methodology to create the morphology model and the use of this model to create virtual dendrites. In Section 4 experimental results are reported. Finally, Section 5 discuses the results and future work.

2   Dendritic Morphologies of Pyramidal Cells

A remarkable characteristic of pyramidal cells is the great variations in their microanatomy, since significant differences between pyramidal cells in different cortical layers and areas and between species exist regarding the pattern of dendritic arborisation and in the number and density of dendritic spines (e.g., [14], [17], [18], [19], [20], reviewed in [21], [22]). This is an important issue in terms of function, since the morphology of the dendritic tree is related to the processing of synaptic inputs. For example, the structure of the dendritic tree itself affects the process of integration, while its size influences topographic sampling map and the mixing of inputs ([23],[24], for a recent work see [25]).

In general, a major limitation in analyzing the morphology of the neurons is that it is necessary to use relatively thin tissue slices to visualize labeled neurons, frequently in the order of a few microns, in contrast to the hundreds of microns or even millimeters over which neuronal processes may expand. Thus, labeled processes are frequently incomplete because during the slicing procedures of the tissue some parts of the neuron morphology are missing in a variable degree depending on the thickness of the sections and the relative localization of the labeled neuron within the slice. Currently, this problem can only be overcome by using serial sections to reconstruct the cell in 3D. However, neuronal processes are not always easy to trace and they may be lost in the background noise at times ([26]). Together, these obstacles make it very laborious and time-consuming to obtain meaningful measurements from neurons. Virtual neurons may also help to validate and develop algorithmic methods for repairing ([27]), using different sampling protocols. The advantage to obtain such a repair method is that pyramidal neurons might be examined in coronal sections to include both the apical and basal dendritic systems, though incomplete the repair methods might help to generate a complete picture of the pyramidal cell morphology.

Fortunately, the basal dendritic arbors of pyramidal cells can be fully reconstructed in single sections. Furthermore these sections are made in the horizontal plane and with a sufficient thickness as to include the whole dendritic tree (e.g., [17]). Thus, we have used data from fully reconstructed basal dendrites as they are particularly valuable to validate and develop methods to create virtual neurons.

3   Methodological Approach

Dendrites are complex tree-like 3D structures defined by many morphometric parameters. As a preliminary step towards the creation of virtual dendrites, this paper proposes a method to define the branching scheme of the dendrites. Instead of considering the 3D structure of the dendrite, the branching scheme represents some topological aspects, such as the number of branches and the symmetry of these branches, together with some aggregated morphometric parameters, such as the length of the dendrite (and branches) the distance to the cell soma and the tortuosity.

The method presented in this paper has two main components: (i) a procedure to construct a *branching model* and (ii) a *dendrite sampler* to use the model to produce virtual dendrites.

The construction of the model is an off-line process applied on the experimental data extracted from real-neurons. How this model is constructed is fully explained in Section 3.2. Nevertheless, it is easier to understand the objective of this model if the *dendrite sampler* (that uses this model) is first presented.

3.1   Dendrite Sampler

The *dendrite sampler* implements an algorithm to create virtual dendrites by means of sampling a *branching model*. The virtual dendrites created by this algorithm should be biologically feasible in terms of morphological aspects and statistically analogous to real dendrites obtained by experimental methods.

The *dendrite sampler* operates at the level of *segment*. A segment is the portion of a dendrite between two consecutive branch bifurcations, or between the soma and the first bifurcation of the dendrite. A segment has a given pathlength (the length of the corresponding portion of the dendrite, named segment pathlength). The pathlength is also computed between the end of the segment and the cell soma. Another parameter is the euclidean distance between the end of

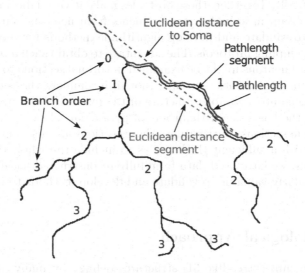

Fig. 1. Dendrite attributes

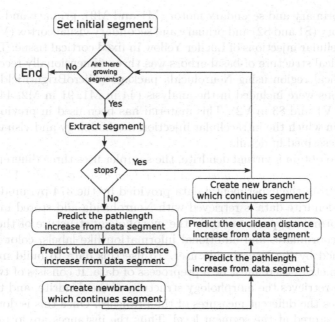

Fig. 2. Sampler flow diagram

the segment and the soma, as well as the euclidean distance between the beginning and the end of the segment. The ratio between this last euclidean distance and the pathlength is called tortuosity. Most of the attributes have been extracted from the literature ([28], [29], [30]) and there is a graphical explanation in Figure 1.

The dendrite sampler tries to simulate the growth of a real dendrite, it creates the branches in a breadth-first order. In Figure 2 there is a flow diagram to explain the procedure. There is a set of segments, called *growing segments*, which are in development stage. The sampler extracts the shortest (minimum global pathlength) one and uses the *termination model* to predict if the branch finishes at this position. If not, the segment has to bifurcate. The bifurcation is performed sampling a pathlength and a euclidean distance for each of the branches (using the *pathlength model* and the *euclidean distance model*). Then, both branches are included in the set of *growing segments*. The process is repeated iteratively until there are no growing branches in the set.

3.2   Model Construction

In the present study we have used homogeneous collections of complete basal dendritic arbors to generate synthetic dendritic morphologies using machine learning methods based in stochastic algorithms. In particular, the whole basal dendritic arbor of layer II/III pyramidal neurons was examined. In this experiment, these cells were obtained from 6 different cytoarquitectonic cortical areas of the mouse neocortex: primary and secondary motor (M1 and M2), primary and secondary somatosensory (S1 and S2) and primary and secondary visual cortex (V1 and V2) using intracellular injections of Lucifer Yellow in fixed cortical tissue. Thereafter, the geometrical structure of basal arbors was three-dimensionally reconstructed in each cortical region using Neurolucida package (MicroBrightField). A total of 374 neurons were included in the analysis (44 in M1, 91 in M2, 44 in S1, 71 in S2, 41 in V1 and 83 in V2). This material has been used in previous studies ([19], [20]) in which the intracellular injection methodology and visualization of neurons is described in detail.

In order to obtain a virtual dendrite, the sampler uses three different models: *termination model*, *pathlength model* and *euclidean distance model*. These models are induced from the experimental data provided by the 374 pyramidal cells.

The real dendrite data is retrieved with Neurolucida and stored in ASC format. This format supports basically the morphology structure of the dendrite with space coordinates and additional information like labels, color and other items specified by the Neurolucida user. To use this data to build models and extract the metrics there must be a preprocess of data. It consists of two phases, the first one retrieves the morphology structure of the dendrite, and the second one calculates the different measures of the branches. Once this is done, the information is stored at the segment level. Thus the instances are formed by the data of two consecutive segments, the attributes of the first one, and the finish value, pathlength increment and euclidean distance increment of the second segment. For example, if a segment A bifurcates into two children segments B and C, the following two instances will be created (A,B) and (A,C). These instances are used by *pathlength model* and *euclidean distance model*. The *termination model* uses a different dataset containing whole branches (from soma to the end of the branch). This data set records the pathlength and euclidean distance of the branches.

To maintain the quality of the data, there is a filter which excludes from the datasets those dendrites that are too small to exists in a real neuron. These are dendrites with only one branch or one bifurcation. The models are built with Weka from the final dataset and then provided to the sampler for generating the virtual dendrites.

The *termination model* uses a normal distribution of the dendrite pathlength estimated from the experimental data. The sample mean and variance are computed via maximum likelihood (using Bessel correction for the variance). The corresponding model, for each candidate branch, provides a probability to finish at the current pathlength. Then, a binomial distribution is sampled with probability p equals to the probability computed before. This binomial distribution indicates if the branch finishes or not.

The *pathlength model* is computed by sampling a normal distribution, but in this case the parameters are predicted using a regression model from the data. This regression model approximates the mean value of the increment pathlength using the rest of the information of the previous segment (branch order, previous segment pathlength, previous euclidean distance to soma, ...). The predicted value is considered the mean value of the normal distribution, for the variance the standard mean square error (MSE) is used.

The *euclidean distance model* is created using a very similar process. The main difference is that the model computes the euclidean distance increment. To construct this model the pathlength of the current segment (already sampled) is included.

4   Experimental Results

To validate the procedure several morphometric parameters have been used. These measure the whole dendrites, not segments: *Total length* (pathlength segment of each of the branches of the dendrite), *Number of branches* (number of branches in the dendritic tree), and *Maximum euclidean distance* (The euclidean distance reached by the most distant terminal of the branches of the dendrite).

These morphometric parameters have been extensively used in the literature, as they provide important information to construct functional models ([16], [13]).

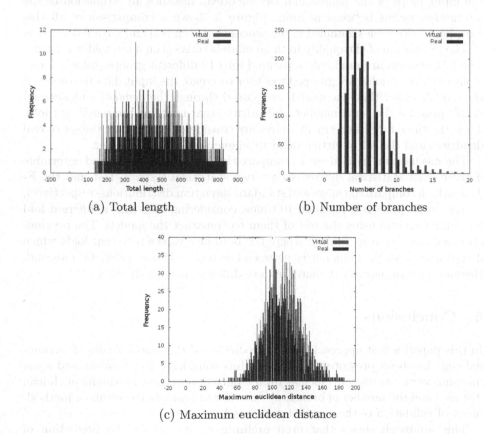

(a) Total length

(b) Number of branches

(c) Maximum euclidean distance

Fig. 3. Morphometrics comparison between all the real and virtual dendrites used

Table 1. Morphometrics p-values of T-Test and F-Test. Bold face indicates distributions with no significant statistical differences.

fold	Total length		Max. euclidean distance		Number of branches	
	T-Test	F-Test	T-Test	F-Test	T-Test	F-Test
0	**0,41919188**	**0,36478547**	0,02830407	**0,13246995**	0,00000289	0,00247477
1	**0,11765158**	**0,49714120**	0,05487532	0,07755403	0,00000022	0,00000577
2	**0,66068776**	0,00005603	**0,99464954**	0,01051810	0,00000259	0,00060837
3	**0,12481806**	0,00132655	**0,46224339**	**0,15136875**	0,00000039	0,00748735
4	**0,33458759**	**0,29449791**	**0,21931231**	**0,15544413**	0,00000055	0,00465168
5	**0,40131150**	**0,45813770**	**0,61319364**	**0,22591712**	0,00000188	0,00002223
6	**0,94251514**	**0,38969360**	0,04513971	**0,66399835**	0,00010505	0,00121797
7	0,00026773	**0,51401748**	0,00011822	**0,49456661**	0,00000000	0,00035040
8	0,02489360	**0,88807141**	0,02408693	**0,36758700**	0,00000026	0,00133224
9	0,00006949	**0,13280718**	0,00488902	**0,45006132**	0,00000000	0,00000558

The length and number of branches provide information of the complexity of the input maps of the neuron and the euclidean distance an estimation of the interaction radius between neurons. Figure 3 shown a comparison of all this morphometrics values obtained in the process between real and virtual dendrites.

The evaluation of the quality in these models consists on a ten-fold validation. The 374 neurons are randomly separated into 10 different groups (folds). Then, 9 out of these 10 folds are grouped together to create the input data to construct the models. After that, the models are passed through the *dendrite sampler* and it will produce the same number of dendrites that contains the remaining fold. Then the three morphometric measures are considered to compare the set of real dendrites and the set of virtual dendrites generated by the sampler.

The mechanisms carried out to compare the different measures and determine if there exist statistical differences are two statistical tests: T-Test and the F-Test, which compare the mean and standard deviation distributions, respectively.

The entire process is repeated 10 times, considering each time a different fold for validation and using the rest of them to construct the models. The p-values obtained are shown in Table 1, where the bold face values represent folds which do not have statistical differences between the real and virtual distributions and, therefore, we cannot assert than they are different from each other.

5   Conclusions

In this paper, a first approach on the prediction of the morphologies of pyramidal cells has been presented. This study has considered 374 neurons and some morphometric parameters (such as total length of branches, maximum euclidean distance and the number of branches). In order to evaluate the results a methodology of validation of the sampled data has been presented.

This approach shows that even preliminary studies on the prediction of neuronal morphologies can obtain promising good results for some of the morphometric parameters. The total pathlength for a given dendrite branch is easily predicted by the distribution of pathlengths in a homogeneous data set.

As the prediction for the total pathlength is well-adjusted the other two models have to compensate each other. The pathlength of the segment is not so precise and probably longer than expected, which reduces the number of branches required to reach the expected pathlength of the entire branch.

In the near future, more effort will be addressed to refine the segment pathlength model to improve the overall sampling procedure, by additionally analyzing the cells grouping them per cortical areas. As an open issue, the model will provide 3D structures of dendrites and will include other morphological elements.

The expectation of using this model in functional studies of cortical circuits is also clear. Besides the application to construct computational models, these virtual neurons have a short-term practical application to develop repair algorithm methods in order to reconstruct the missing portions of the labeled neurons ([27]). Such a repair method would allow to generate a complete picture of the pyramidal cell morphology in coronal sections, in which both basal and apical arbors are partially included within the sections.

Acknowledgements

The authors would like to thank the Cajal Blue Brain Project and the Blue Brain Project (EPFL), the technical expertise and assistance provided by CeSViMa and the Spanish Supercomputing Network. This work was supported by the Spanish Ministry of Science under TIN2007 - 67148, SAF2009 - 09394 grants and the Cajal Blue Brain Project.

References

1. Jones, E.: Anatomy of cerebral cortex: columnar input-output organization. Cerebral Cortex, 199–235 (1981)
2. Jones, E.: The columnar basis of cortical circuitry. In: Willis, W.D. (ed.) The clinical neurosciences, pp. 357–383 (1983)
3. Jones, E.: Laminar distribution of cortical efferent cells. Cerebral Cortex 1, 524–553 (1984)
4. Feldman, M.: Morphology of the neocortical pyramidal neuron. Cerebral cortex, 123–200 (1984)
5. Lund, J.: Anatomical organization of macaque monkey striate visual cortex. Ann. Rev. Neurosci. 11, 253–258 (1988)
6. White, E.L.: Cortical Circuits: Synaptic Organization of the Cerebral Cortex. In: Structure, Function and Theory. Birkhauser, Boston (1989)
7. Felleman, D., Van Essen, D.: Distributed hierarchical processing in the primate cerebral cortex. Cereb. Cortex 1, 1–47 (1991)
8. DeFelipe, J., Farinas, I.: The pyramidal neuron of the cerebral cortex: morphological and chemical characteristics of the synaptic inputs. Prog. Neurobiol. 39, 563–607 (1992)
9. Lund, J., Yoshioka, T., Levitt, J.: Substrates for interlaminar connections in area V1 of the macaque monkey cerebral cortex. Cerebral cortex 10, 37–60 (1994)

10. Elston, G.: Cortex, cognition and the cell: new insights into the pyramidal neuron and prefrontal function. Cereb. Cortex 13, 1124–1138 (2003)
11. Yuste, R., Bonhoeffer, T.: Genesis of dendritic spines: insights from ultrastructural and imaging studies. Nat. Rev. Neurosci. 5, 24–34 (2004)
12. Lamprecht, R., LeDoux, J.: Structural plasticity and memory. Nat. Rev. Neurosci. 5, 45–54 (2004)
13. Spruston, N.: Pyramidal neurons: dendritic structure and synaptic integration. Nat. Rev. Neurosci. 9, 206–221 (2008)
14. Larkman, A.: Dendritic morphology of pyramidal neurones of the visual cortex of the rat: I. Branching patterns. J. Comp. Neurol., 307–319 (1991)
15. Markram, H.: The blue brain project. Nat. Rev. Neurosci. 7, 153–160 (2006)
16. Donohue, D., Ascoli, G.: A comparative computer simulation of dendritic morphology. PLoS Comput. Biol. 4(5), e1000089 (2008)
17. Elston, G., Rosa, M.: The occipito-parietal pathway of the macaque monkey: comparison of pyramidal cell morphology in layer III of functionally related cortical visual areas. Cereb. Cortex 7, 432–452 (1997)
18. Jacobs, B., Schall, M., Prather, M., Kapler, E., Driscoll, L., Baca, S., Jacobs, J., Ford, K., Wainwright, M., Treml, M.: Regional dendritic and spine variation in human cerebral cortex: a quantitative golgi study. Cereb. Cortex 11, 558–571 (2001)
19. Benavides-Piccione, R., Hamzei-Sichani, F., Ballesteros-Yañez, I., DeFelipe, J., Yuste, R.: Dendritic size of pyramidal neurons differs among mouse cortical regions. Cerebral Cortex 16, 990–1001 (2006)
20. Ballesteros-Yañez, I., Benavides-Piccione, R., Bourgeois, J., Changeux, J., DeFelipe, J.: Topological reorganization of dendritic arbors of cortical pyramidal neurons in mice lacking high-affinity nicotine receptors (submitted 2010)
21. Jacobs, B., Scheibel, A.: Regional dendritic variation in primate cortical pyramidal cells. In: Schz, A., Miller, R. (eds.) Cortical areas: unity and diversity, pp. 111–131. Oxford University Press, Oxford (2002)
22. Elston, G.: Specializations in pyramidal cell structure during primate evolution. Evolution of nervous systems (2007)
23. Koch, C., Segev, I.: The role of single neurons in information processing. Nat. Neurosci. 3, 1171–1177 (2000)
24. Poirazi, P., Mel, B.: Impact of active dendrites and structural plasticity on the memory capacity of neural tissue. Neuron 29, 779–796 (2001)
25. Wen, Q., Stepanyants, A., Elston, G., Grosberg, A., Chklovskii, D.: Maximization of the connectivity repertoire as a statistical principle governing the shapes of dendritic arbors. Proc. Natl. Acad. Sci. 106, 12536–12541 (2009)
26. DeFelipe, J.: The neuroanatomist's dream, the problems and solutions, and the ultimate aim. Front Neurosci. 2, 10–12 (2008)
27. Anwar, H., Riachi, I., Hilland, S., Schurmann, F., Markam, H.: An approach to capturing neuron morphological diversity. Computational modeling methods for neuroscientists (2009)
28. Donohue, D.E., Ascoli, G.: A comparative computer simulation of dendritic morphology. PLoS Computational Biology 4, e1000089 (2008)
29. Uylings, H.B.M., Pelt, J.V.: Measures for quantifying dendritic arborizations. Brain Research 13, 397–414 (2002)
30. Van Pelt, J., Schierwagen, A.: Morphological analysis and modeling of neuronal dendrites. Mathematical Biosciences 188, 147–155 (2004)

A New Incremental Growing Neural Gas Algorithm Based on Clusters Labeling Maximization: Application to Clustering of Heterogeneous Textual Data

Jean-Charles Lamirel[1], Zied Boulila[1], Maha Ghribi[2], and Pascal Cuxac[2]

[1] INRIA team TALARIS-LORIA
[2] SRDI-INIST-CNRS
jean-charles.lamirel@loria.fr

Abstract. Neural clustering algorithms show high performance in the usual context of the analysis of homogeneous textual dataset. This is especially true for the recent adaptive versions of these algorithms, like the incremental neural gas algorithm (IGNG). Nevertheless, this paper highlights clearly the drastic decrease of performance of these algorithms, as well as the one of more classical algorithms, when a heterogeneous textual dataset is considered as an input. A new incremental growing neural gas algorithm exploiting knowledge issued from clusters current labeling in an incremental way is proposed as an alternative to the original distance based algorithm. This solution leads to obtain very significant increase of performance for the clustering of heterogeneous textual data. Moreover, it provides a real incremental character to the proposed algorithm.

1 Introduction

The neural clustering methods share the principle of taking into account relations of neighborhood between clusters, either they are preset (fixed topology), like the "self-Organizing Maps" (SOM) [9], or dynamic (free topology), like static "Neural Gas" (NG) [12] or "Growing Neural Gas" (GNG) [5]. As compared to usual clustering methods, like K-means, this strategy makes them less sensitive to the initial conditions, which represents an important asset within the framework of data analysis of highly multidimensional and sparse data, like textual data.

The architecture form of the SOM network is based on the understanding that the representation of data features might take the form of a self-organizing feature map which is geometrically organized as a grid. A mapping from a high-dimensional data space onto a two dimensional grid of neurons is thus defined. The SOM algorithm is presented in details in [9]. It consists of two basic procedures: (1) selecting a winning neuron on the grid and (2) updating weights of the winning neuron and of its neighboring neurons. One the main advantage of the SOM is that it combines in a single framework a clustering process with a complementary process of clustering results projection. However, special care must be taken of a well-known problem related to the SOM trained structure, namely the border effect. It means that units on edges of the network do not stretch out as much as they should towards the outliers

N. García-Pedrajas et al. (Eds.): IEA/AIE 2010, Part III, LNAI 6098, pp. 139–148, 2010.

data [9]. Last but not least, the SOM neurons do not necessarily get close to the structure of the data because of the fixed topological structure of the grid.

In the NG algorithm [12], the weights of the neurons are adapted without any fixed topological arrangement within the neural network. Instead of this, the NG algorithm utilizes a neighborhood ranking process of the neuron weights for a given input data. The weight changes are not determined by the relative distances between the neuron within a topologically pre-structured lattice, but by the relative distance between the neurons within the input space. Indeed, thanks to the loss of topographic constraints as compared to SOM, NG tends to better represent the structure of the data, yielding theoretically to better classification results. Nevertheless, one of the main drawbacks of the NG algorithm is that the number of neurons, materializing the final number of clusters, represents a fixed parameter.

The GNG algorithm [5] solves the static character of the NG algorithm by bringing out the concept of evolving network. Hence, in this approach the number of neurons is adapted during the learning phase according to the characteristics of the data distribution. Indeed, GNG gives the possibility of removing and creating neurons and connections between these latter. The suppression process relies on the notion of maximal age, or maturity, of a connection. On the other hand, the creation of the neurons is made only periodically (each T iteration or time period) between the two neighbor neurons that cumulated the most important error for representing the data. Different stopping criteria can be used such as the maximal number of neurons or the minimal change between the reference vectors of the neurons between two time periods. However, these criteria might not be systematically satisfied especially with complex or sparse multidimensional data. This is a major disadvantage of the GNG method.

The IGNG algorithm has been proposed by Prudent and Ennaji [15]. It represents an adaptation of the GNG algorithm that relaxes the constraint of periodical evolution of the network. Hence, in this algorithm a new neuron is created each time the distance of the current input data to the existing neuron is greater than a prefixed threshold σ. The σ value is a global parameter that corresponds to the average distance of the data to the center of the dataset. Moreover, each new neuron goes through an embryo phase during which it cannot be suppressed, even if it has lost all its neighborhood connections. Prudent and Ennaji have proven that the IGNG method produces better results than the existing neural methods on standard test distributions. However, the fact that the σ parameter must be computed prior to the learning and globally depends on the dataset is not in favor of the incremental character of the method, even if this capability has been defended by its authors.

The main goal of the I^2GNG method [7] is to solve the weakness of IGNG algorithm in term of incremental behavior. For that purpose, the I^2GNG algorithm makes use of a variable value of the threshold σ that is computed at each learning step and that depends on each neuron (i.e. each cluster). The data are dynamically associated to the neurons during learning. Hence, at time t, the threshold σ of each neuron corresponds to the average distance of its reference vector to its currently associated data. The I^2GNG algorithm has been successfully tested for the unsupervised classification of invoice documents. However, the major drawback of this algorithm is the initialization problem. Hence, a default threshold value must be set at the creation of each new neuron and no straightforward solutions have been proposed up to now by the authors to correctly manage this problem.

Our former remarks tipped the balance in the favor of the use of the upcoming IGNG algorithm for general clustering tasks. However, a clearer comparison of the behavior of the neural clustering algorithms using a common basis and especially a test of the quality of their results on complex data like heterogeneous textual data might be useful to bring more light on their effective quality and defects. Generic clustering quality measures and cluster labeling techniques that are independent of the clustering method are presented to this purpose in section 2. Section 3 proposes a comparison of the behavior of the neural clustering methods using the proposed measures. Both homogeneous and heterogeneous data are considered for experiments and the Walktrap non neural clustering method is also considered for serving as an external reference in our comparison. On the basis of the results in section 3, we propose in section 4 several ameliorations of the IGNG algorithm and an amelioration of the I^2GNG one. We especially show in section that the incremental exploitation of cluster labels maximization can act as a similarity measure and thus be substituted to the classical use of distance in the IGNG context.

2 Clustering Quality Evaluation and Cluster Labeling

As soon as anyone aims at comparing clustering methods, he will be faced with the problem of selecting reliable clustering quality measures. It has been shown in [8] and in [10] that the inertia measures or their adaptations [2] [3], which are based on cluster profiles, are often strongly biased and highly dependent on the clustering method. Accordingly, they cannot be used for comparing different methods. Our own approach takes its inspiration from the behavior of both symbolic classifiers and information retrieval (IR) systems with the advantage to be independent of the clustering methods and of their operating mode.

The **Recall** and **Precision** measures that we introduce hereafter evaluate the quality of a clustering method in an unsupervised way[1] by measuring the relevance of the cluster content in terms of shared properties. In our further descriptions, the cluster content is supposed to be represented by the documents associated with this latter after the clustering process and the indexes (i.e. the properties) of the documents are supposed to be weighted by values within the range [0,1].

Let us consider a set of clusters C resulting from a clustering method applied on a set of documents D, the local *Recall* (Rec) and *Precision* (Prec) measures for a given property p of the cluster c can be expressed as:

$$\text{Rec}_c(p) = \frac{|c_p^*|}{|D_p^*|}, \ \text{Prec}_c(p) = \frac{|c_p^*|}{|c|} \tag{1}$$

where the notation X_p^* represents the restriction of the set X to the set members having the property p.

---

[1] Conversely to classical Recall and Precision measures that are supervised.

Then, for estimating the overall clustering quality, the averaged *Macro-Recall* (R) and *Macro-Precision* (P) measures can be expressed as:

$$R = \frac{1}{|C|}\sum_{c \in \overline{C}} \frac{1}{S_c} \sum_{p \in S_c} \text{Rec}_c(p), \ P = \frac{1}{|C|}\sum_{c \in \overline{C}} \frac{1}{S_c} \sum_{p \in S_c} \text{Prec}_c(p) \qquad (2)$$

where S_c is the set of properties which are peculiar to the cluster c that is described as:

$$S_c = \left\{ p \in d, d \in c \ \middle| \ \overline{W}_c^p = \underset{c \in C}{Max}\left(\overline{W}_c^p\right) \right\} \qquad (3)$$

where $\overline{C}$ represents the peculiar set of clusters extracted from the clusters of C, which verifies:

$$\overline{C} = \left\{ \ c \in C \ \middle| \ S_c \neq \varnothing \ \right\} \qquad (4)$$

and:

$$\overline{W}_c^p = \frac{\sum_{d \in c} W_d^p}{\sum_{c \in C}\sum_{d \in c} W_d^p} \qquad (5)$$

where W_x^p represents the weight of the property p for element x.

Macro-Recall and *Macro-Precision* measures defined by Eq. 2 can be considered as cluster-oriented measures because they provide average values of Recall and Precision for each cluster. Their main goal is thus to estimate in an overall way an optimal number of cluster for a given method and a given dataset. For evaluating more precisely the quality of a clustering result and for discriminating non homogeneous results from homogeneous one, complementary data properties oriented measures (i.e. micro-measures) should thus be used. These new averaged *Micro-Recall* and *Micro-Precision* can be expressed as:

$$R = \frac{1}{|L|}\sum_{c \in \overline{C}, p \in S_c} \text{Rec}_c(p), \ P = \frac{1}{|L|}\sum_{c \in \overline{C}, p \in S_c} \text{Prec}_c(p) \qquad (6)$$

where L represents the size of the data description space.

The role of clusters labeling is to highlight the peculiar characteristics of the clusters associated to a cluster model at a given time. Labeling can be thus used both for visualizing clustering results [11] and for optimizing or enhancing learning of a clustering method [1]. Some label relevance measures can be derivated from our former quality measures using a probabilistic approach. The *Label Recall L-R* derives directly from Eq. 5. It is expressed as:

$$L - R_c(p) = \overline{W}_c^p \qquad (7)$$

The *Label Precision P-R* can be expressed as:

$$L_c\text{-}P(p) = \frac{\sum_{d \in c} W_d^p}{\sum_{p' \in d, d \in c} W_d^p} \tag{8}$$

Consequently, the set of labels L_c that can be attributed to a cluster c can be expressed as:

$$L_c = \left\{ p \in d, d \in c \mid L_c\text{-}F(p) = \underset{c' \in C}{Max}(L_{c'}\text{-}F(p)) \right\} \tag{9}$$

where the *Label F-measure* $L_{c'}\text{-}F(p)$ can be defined as:

$$L_{c'}\text{-}F(p) = \frac{2(L_{c'}\text{-}R(p) \times L_{c'}\text{-}P(p))}{L_{c'}\text{-}R(p) + L_{c'}\text{-}P(p)} \tag{10}$$

As soon as *Label Recall* is equivalent to the conditional probability $P(c|p)$ and *Label Precision* is equivalent to the conditional probability $P(p|c)$, this former labeling strategy can be classified as an expectation maximization approach with respect to the original definition given by Dempster and al. [4]. In section 4, we will consequently propose a new original incremental exploitation of this strategy that can act as a similarity measure and thus substitute to the classical use of distance in the context of clustering.

3   First Experiments and Results

The aim of our first experiment is to compare the behavior of the neural clustering methods on two different kinds of textual datasets that are a homogeneous dataset and one heterogeneous one. The goal of this experiment is to bring more light on the effective quality and defects of these methods in a sufficiently general context.

Our homogeneous test dataset is build up from a set of 1000 patents abstracts related to the oil engineering technology and recorded during the year 1999. An index set (i.e. a vocabulary set) is generated from the full text associated to the subfield describing the domain of application of the patents by the use of a basic computer-based indexing tool. A normalization of the rough index set is performed in order to obtain the final index set by merging the synonym terms (for example oil engineering and oil fabrication, ...). Each patent abstract is finally indexed by a selection of terms issued from the final index set. The resulting dataset could be considered as a homogeneous dataset since it covers the single field of the domain of use of the patents with a limited and contextual vocabulary. A frequency threshold of 2 being finally applied on the index terms, it resulted in a data description set of 234 keywords.

Our heterogeneous test dataset is build up from a set of bibliographic records resulting from the INIST PASCAL database and covering on year of research performed in the Lorraine during the year 2005. The structure of the records makes it possible to distinguish the titles, the summaries, the indexing keywords and the authors as representatives of the contents of the information published in the corresponding article. In our experiment, the research topics associated with the keywords field are solely considered. A soon as these keywords cover themselves a large set of different topics (as far one to another as medicine from structural physics or forest cultivation, ...), the resulting experimental dataset can be considered as highly heterogeneous. Our test dataset represents a dataset of 1341 records. A frequency threshold of 3 being applied on the index terms, it resulted in a data description set of 889 keywords.

In both cases, a set of pre-processing steps is applied to the resulting index of the dataset records in order to obtain a weighted vector representation of the information it contains. The resulting index vectors associated to each record are finally weighted using the IDF-weighting scheme [16] in order to decrease the effect of more wide-spread indexes.

All the neural clustering methods that we have described, ranging from static ones, like SOM or NG, to incremental ones, like IGNG or I^2GNG, have been considered in our experimental context. We also considered the Walktrap method in order to exploit a recent reference method issued from the category of the non-neural clustering methods. The Walktrap method [14] takes its inspiration from the Random Walks paradigm. This paradigm applies to graphs whose nodes are the data to be classified and edges represent the connections between these nodes. The expected goal is to break up the graph into a certain number of communities according to similarities criteria. A community is a group of data for which the density of internal connections is stronger than the density of the external ones. The Walktrap algorithm hierarchically merges the created communities with the goal of optimizing a modularity quality criteria based on the balance between the communities internal links and their external links.

For each neural method, we do many different experiments letting vary the number of clusters in the case of the static methods and the neighborhood parameters in the case the incremental ones (see below). We have finally kept the best clustering results for each method as regards to the values of *Recall-Precision* defined at section 2. In the case of Walktrap method, one single final cluster model has been considered because the algorithm is achieving internally its own optimization process concerning the number of clusters. The situation of the IGNG method would normally have been similar because the neighborhood parameter has a theoretical optimal value σ_T. Nevertheless, by varying the value around the value of σ_T we have observed that the best clustering results are never obtained by the use of this reference value, but by the one of smaller values. We thus applied this former variation strategy to find out the optimal clustering results with the IGNG method. The same process is achieved with the I^2GNG method using a relative variation of the σ parameter instead of an absolute one.

The clustering results obtained on the homogeneous dataset and on the heterogeneous dataset are presented in table 1. The analysis of the clustering quality results on the first dataset highlights good performances for almost all the methods, except for the I^2GNG method. The best results are obtained with the methods based on a free topology, and this especially with the NG and with the IGNG method. Nevertheless, as soon as the power of synthesis of a clustering methods depends on its capacity to produce good clustering results according to a number of resulting clusters which is as small as possible, the overall quality balance tips in the favor of the IGNG which got a *Micro F-measure* which is almost as high as the one of NG, whereas producing a number of clusters which is half less. Another interesting result is also highlighted by this experiment. Thus, as soon as one can optimize its number of clusters, as in the context of this experiment, the NG learning algorithm seems to be more efficient than the GNG one (similar final number of clusters for the two methods with higher quality values for the NG method). In the case of the Walktrap method, there is a clear difference between the *Macro F-measure* and the *Micro-F-measure*. This difference illustrates the presence of unbalanced clustering results including a certain number of noisy clusters of important size. Hence, big noisy clusters cannot be detected by the *Macro F-measure* as soon as they coexist with smaller relevant ones (cf. Eq. 2). The results of I^2GNG that should be as good as those of IGNG because of their kernel similarities are only average ones. This method seems clearly to suffer of initialization problems. Thus, as soon a no initial value is given for the neighborhood influence of a newly created cluster (including only one upcoming data) each cluster can initially randomly agglomerate any kind of data, even those that are very different one to another. This might lead to the creation of heterogeneous clusters with a relatively big size that might also coexist with smaller clusters if groups of sufficiently discriminant data are present in the dataset.

Table 1. Clustering result on homogeneous and heterogenous datasets

CLUSTERING METHOD	HOMOGENEOUS DATASET			HETEROGENEOUS DATASET		
	OPTIMAL NBR OF CLUSTERS	F-MEASURE MACRO	F-MEASURE MICRO	OPTIMAL NBR OF CLUSTERS	F-MEASURE MACRO	F-MEASURE MICRO
WALTRAP	96	0.89	0.62	98	0.67	0.13
SOM	196	0.78	0.66	**389**	**0.47**	**0.40**
NG	160	0.85	0.86	160	0.59	0.33
GNG	170	0.80	0.80	--	--	--
IGNG	92	**0.90**	**0.85**	378	0.58	0.21
I^2GNG	32	0.58	0.38	294	0.52	0.16

A first analysis of the results on our second dataset shows that most of the clustering methods have huge difficulties to deal with heterogeneous data producing consequently very bad quality results, even for their optimal number of clusters, as it is illustrated by the low values of *Micro F-Measure*. The very high difference between *Micro F-measure* and *Macro F-measure* values represent an enhanced form of the phenomenon observed with homogeneous data. Hence, it illustrates the presence of garbage clusters attracting most of the data in parallel with chunks clusters representing either marginal groups or unformed clusters. This is the case for the Walktrap, I^2GNG methods, and at a lesser extent for the NG method. The IGNG method that produced the best results with homogeneous data becomes also strongly affected by this phenomenon whenever heterogeneous data have to be processed. This behavior is confirmed when one looks more precisely to the cluster content and the cluster size distribution for said methods. A very bad case occurs with the Walktrap method, whose low quality results are even being obtained at the cost of removing a large amount of documents from the final clustering model. The worst case occurs with the GNG method that does not provide any results on this dataset because of its incapacity to escape from an infinite cycle of creation-destruction of neurons (i.e. clusters). The only consistent behavior is the one of the SOM method. This is illustrated by a correct *Micro F-measure* value and by a good coherence between *Micro F-measure* and *Macro F-measure* values.

One plausible cause of the problem of insane data agglomeration occurring with almost all the tested clustering methods, whenever our heterogeneous textual dataset is used as an entry, is the nature of the similarity used by the method during the learning process. Hence, it is a known phenomenon that the usual Euclidean distance, which is the most used similarity measure for clustering, becomes weakly discriminant in highly multidimensional spaces containing sparse data: its distribution becomes biased towards the small values leading to consider almost all the data as similar one to another. Cosine distance should have better behavior in this context. Nevertheless, our complementary experiments using this distance did not enable us to obtain any significant increase in performance. Hence, on its own side, cosine distance is highly sensitive to the presence of highly polysemic terms (like age, system, human, …) embedded in small index vectors (i.e. with small number of non zero values). This context represents also one of the characteristics of your dataset. Only the grid constrained learning of the SOM method seems to be a good strategy for preventing the model of producing too bad results in such a critical context. Hence, it enforces the homogeneity of the results by splitting both data and noise on the grid. We thus propose in the next section specific alternative to be applied on the potentially best clustering algorithms, in order to cope with the observed problems.

4   Novel Adaptations of the IGNG and I^2GNG Algorithms

Random choice of the final winner neuron among multiple winners (IGNG-R): Because of the use of a non discriminating distance, at many steps of the learning process, there exist several competing neurons (i.e. clusters) which appear as potential winning neurons since these neurons have the same distance to the current input data, as it has been experimentally verified. The algorithm must thus designate a main winner thanks to its current "winner take most" learning strategy. In the original IGNG algorithm, whenever this situation occurs, the choice is made to designate as main winner the first neuron in the list of created neurons. This strategy directly leads to the apparition of a garbage cluster (i.e. the first created neuron) during learning on our heterogeneous dataset. A better strategy consists thus in applying a random selection process whenever a winner must be selected among many input data equidistant neurons. The indirect consequence of this new strategy will be also to split potential noise among many clusters.

Choice of the final winner among multiple winners using a labeling maximization approach (IGNG-M): Whenever a winner must be selected among many input data equidistant neurons, a more intelligent strategy that the random one would consist in using a label maximization approach to select the final winner. Thanks to this strategy the input data is at first attached to all the potential challengers to create "enhanced-challengers", and the average *Label F-measure* of the "enhanced-challengers" is computed on the basis of the Eq. 10. The winner is chosen as the challenger whose 'enhanced state" positively maximizes the *Label F-measure* difference with its normal state.

Direct use of a labeling maximization approach as a clustering similarity measure (IGNG-F): The latter strategy might be unable to cope with the critical influence of distance as soon as it exploits this latter as a first selection criteria. This problem will be confirmed by our experimental results (see table 3). A new strategy can thus consists in completely suppressing the use of distance in the winner selection process by considering the label maximization approach (cf. Eq. 9 and Eq. 10) as a main selection process. Another advantage of this new strategy is to provide IGNG method with efficient incremental character. Hence, no more parameters depending on the dataset need to be used in the enhanced algorithm.

Neighborhood reciprocity initialization strategy (I^2GNG-N): A potential strategy to cope with the I^2GNG method initialization problems could consist in creating initialization kernels in order to provide initial neighborhood influence parameters to the clusters. A neighborhood reciprocity based approach can be relevant for this purpose. Hence, this strategy minimizes the influence of initialization on the further evolution of clusters. Nevertheless, one of its main drawbacks is to suppress the incremental character of the algorithm.

Table 2 gives the results obtained with our new strategies. It especially proves the efficiency of our direct labeling maximization strategy (IGNG-F) that outperforms all the existing strategies by producing the most efficient results on heterogeneous data. One might also remark that a significant increase of the performance of the I^2GNG algorithm is obtained once suitable clusters neighborhood initialization strategy is employed (I^2GNG-N).

Table 2. Clustering results of enhanced methods on heterogeneous dataset

CLUSTERING METHOD	OPTIMAL NBR OF CLUSTERS	F-MEASURE MICRO
IGNG Original	378	0.21
IGNG-R (Random when equal)	382	0.43
IGNG-L (Labels max. when equal)	437	0.44
IGNG-F (Labels max. F-measure glob similarity)	**337**	**0.47**
I^2GNG Original	294	0.15
I^2GNG-N (Neighborhood reciprocity init.)	221	0.38

5 Conclusion

Neural clustering algorithms show high performance in the usual context of the analysis of homogeneous textual dataset. This is especially true for the recent adaptive versions of these algorithms, like the incremental neural gas algorithm (IGNG). Nevertheless, this paper clearly highlights the drastic decrease of performance of these algorithms, as well as the one of more classical non neural algorithms, when a heterogeneous textual dataset is fed as an input. Specific quality measures and cluster labeling techniques that are independent of the clustering method are used for performance evaluation. One of the main contributions of our paper has been to propose an incremental growing neural gas algorithm exploiting knowledge issued from clusters current labeling in an incremental way as an alternative to the original distance based algorithms. This solution enabled us to achieve a very significant increase of performance for the clustering of heterogeneous textual data. Moreover, it provides a real incremental character to the proposed algorithm. This latter capability open us clear perspectives to apply our approach in a very near future to the challenging domain of temporal mining of textual data. We also consider to apply it to other kinds of data like the ones falling in the genomics domain an as well as to adapt the label maximization similarity principle to several other clustering algorithms. The very next challenger for that optimization would naturally be the I^2GNG algorithm.

References

1. Attik, M., Al Shehabi, S., Lamirel, J.-C.: Clustering Quality Measures for Data Samples with Multiple Labels. In: Proceedings of IASTED International Conference on Databases and Applications (DBA), Innsbruck, Austria (2006)
2. Calinski, T., Harabasz, J.: A dendrite method for cluster analysis. Communications in Statistics 3, 1–27 (1974)
3. Davies, D., Bouldin, W.: A cluster separation measure. IEEE Trans. Pattern Anal. Machine Intell. 1, 224–227 (1979)
4. Dempster, A.P., Laird, N.M., Rubin, D.B.: Maximum likelihood for incomplete data via the em algorithm. Journal of the Royal Statistical Society B-39, 1–38 (1979)
5. Frizke, B.: A growing neural gas network learns topologies. In: Tesauro, G., Touretzky, D.S., leen, T.K. (eds.) Advances in neural Information processing Systems, vol. 7, pp. 625–632. MIT Press, Cambridge (1995)
6. François, C., Hoffmann, M., Lamirel, J.-C., Polanco, X.: Artificial Neural Network mapping experiments. EICSTES (IST-1999-20350) Final Report (WP 9.4), 86 p. (2003)
7. Hamza, H., Belaïd, Y., Belaîd, A., Chaudhuri, B.B.: Incremental classification of invoice documents. In: Proceedings of 19th International Conference on Pattern Recognition - ICPR (2008)
8. Kassab, R., Lamirel, J.-C.: Feature Based Cluster Validation for High Dimensional Data. In: Proceedings of IASTED International Conference on Artificial Intelligence and Applications (AIA), Innsbruck, Austria (2008)
9. Kohonen, T.: Self-Organising Maps, 3rd edn. Springer, Berlin (2001)
10. Lamirel, J.-C., Al-Shehabi, S., François, C., Hoffmann, M.: New classification quality estimators for analysis of documentary information: application to patent analysis and web mapping. Scientometrics 60(3) (2004)
11. Lamirel, J.-C., Ta, A.P., Attik, M.: Novel Labeling Strategies for Hierarchical Representation of Multidimensional Data Analysis Results. In: Proceedings of IASTED International Conference on Artificial Intelligence and Applications (AIA), Innsbruck, Austria (2008)
12. Martinetz, T., Schulten, K.: A "neural gas" network learns topologies. In: Kohonen, T., Makisara, K., Simula, O., Kangas, J. (eds.) Articial Neural Networks, pp. 397–402. Elsevier, Amsterdam (1991)
13. Merkl, D., He, S.H., Dittenbach, M., Rauber, A.: Adaptive hierarchical incremental grid growing: an architecture for high-dimensional data visualization. In: Proceedings of the 4th Workshop on Self-Organizing Maps, Advances in Self-Organizing Maps, Kitakyushu, Japan, pp. 293–298 (2003)
14. Pons, P., Latapy, M.: Computing communities in large networks using random walks. Journal of Graph Algorithms and Application (2006)
15. Prudent, Y., Ennaji, A.: An Incremental Growing Neural Gas learns Topology. In: Proceedings of ESANN 2005, 13th European Symposium on Artificial Neural Networks, Bruges, Belgium (2005)
16. Robertson, S.E., Sparck Jones, K.: Relevance Weighting of Search Terms. Journal of the American Society for Information Science 27, 129–146 (1976)

Synergies between Network-Based Representation and Probabilistic Graphical Models for Classification, Inference and Optimization Problems in Neuroscience

Roberto Santana, Concha Bielza, and Pedro Larrañaga

Departamento de Inteligencia Artificial, Universidad Politécnica de Madrid
28660 Boadilla del Monte, Madrid, Spain
roberto.santana@upm.es, pedro.larranaga@fi.upm.es, mcbielza@fi.upm.es

Abstract. Neural systems network-based representations are useful tools to analyze numerous phenomena in neuroscience. Probabilistic graphical models (PGMs) give a concise and still rich representation of complex systems from different domains, including neural systems. In this paper we analyze the characteristics of a bidirectional relationship between networks-based representations and PGMs. We show the way in which this relationship can be exploited introducing a number of methods for the solution of classification, inference and optimization problems. To illustrate the applicability of the introduced methods, a number of problems from the field of neuroscience, in which ongoing research is conducted, are used.

1 Introduction

Neural systems can often be depicted using networks where each network node represents one constitutive element of the complete represented system. In network representations of neurons, neuronal circuits and brain maps, nodes can respectively represent neuron compartments, neurons, or brain regions. Networks links between the nodes usually represent structural or functional relationships between the constitutive elements of the representation. Sometimes numerical and categorical data is added to the nodes and links, enriching the representation expressivity.

Several authors have stressed the influence that the particular connectivity patterns in neural circuits have in neurophysiological and mental activities [6,16,17]. It is especially relevant to determine how particular connectivity patterns may be related to neuronal diseases or mental disorders [3]. Research on network theory [2,9,18] has shown that network analysis can help to uncover and characterize the patterns of interactions in complex systems. Several applications of network theory have been reported in the field of neuroscience [3,6,29].

A network descriptor is a numerical value that measures a particular structural or topological characteristic of the network. Different network descriptors can offer valuable information about a single network or a family of networks.

N. García-Pedrajas et al. (Eds.): IEA/AIE 2010, Part III, LNAI 6098, pp. 149–158, 2010.

However, sometimes a concise representation of a set of networks (e.g. a set of alternative brain region structural connectivity patterns [29], a set of functional connectivity patterns derived from MEG data analysis of different individuals, etc.) is required. In these cases it is not clear to what extent the set of all single network descriptors can serve to represent common characteristics of the networks. An alternative is to construct a more general representation of the set of networks. This can be done using probabilistic modeling of the set of networks.

Probabilistic graphical models (PGMs) [20] are one of the most recurrent machine learning paradigms to specify interactions in complex systems in terms of probabilistic dependencies. They can be used to represent complex relationships between different data sets, including networks. They usually comprise two components: a graphical structure and a quantitative component. The graphical structure displays certain probabilistic conditional independence relationships between variables. The quantitative component, which is a collection of numerical parameters, usually conditional probabilities, gives an idea of the strength of the dependencies. PGMs have been used to represent different neuronal and cortical processes [21,22,24].

A PGM of a set of networks can serve to capture important regularities from the set of networks (e.g. frequent subnetworks) and patterns of interactions between the networks components. It can later be employed to make queries about different structural or topological hypotheses concerning the represented set of networks.

From another perspective, an interesting fact is that the graphical structure of commonly employed PGMs can also be seen as a network. This fact allows the application of results from network theory to this particular domain. The goal is in this case is to extract, from the analysis of the PGMs' derived network descriptors, particular structural characteristics with a possible valuable interpretation in terms of the original system represented by the PGM.

Therefore, we have that, on one hand sets of networks can be conveniently modeled using PGMs, and on the other hand network analysis of the structural component of PGMs can reveal valuable information of the modeled domain. This relationship points to a synergy between network theory and PGMs. In this paper we analyze different aspects of the relationship between these two domains and discuss a number of ways in which research in neuroscience can benefit from this synergy.

2   Networks

We will focus the analysis on undirected, directed and weighted graphs which will also be called networks.

$G = (V, E)$ will represent an *undirected graph*, where $V = \{v_1, \ldots, v_n\}$ is the set of vertices (or nodes) and $E = \{e_1, \ldots, e_m\}$ is the set of edges between the nodes. $G' = (V, E')$ will represent a *directed graph* where $E' = \{a_1, \ldots, a_m\}$ is the set of arcs (directed edges) between the nodes.

In some contexts, in which the distinction between an undirected and directed graph is not relevant, we will use the term *link* to refer to a connection between two nodes, either an edge or an arc.

A *weighted graph* is a directed or undirected graph where parameter w_{ij} represents the weight between nodes v_i and v_j, whenever e_{ij} (respectively a_{ij}) belongs to the set of edges (respectively arcs) of the network.

There are two types of network descriptors: local descriptors that provide information about a node or a link, and global descriptors that contain information about the complete network. The following are examples of network descriptors.

In an undirected graph, the *degree* of a node is the number of adjacent vertices of the node. In a directed graph, the *indegree* (*outdegree*) is the number of incoming (outgoing) arcs of the node.

A *path* is a sequence of linked nodes that never visit a single node more than once. The *path length* between two vertices is the number of vertices in the path. One node v is *reachable* from another node u if there is a path between them. The *distance* between a node v and a node u is the length of the shortest path between them if u is reachable from v, otherwise it is set to infinity.

The *characteristic path length* of a graph is the average shortest path length between every pair of reachable vertices in the graph. The *betweenness centrality* of a node is the fraction of all shortest paths in the network that traverse a given node. Similarly, *edge betweenness centrality* is the fraction of all shortest paths in the network that traverse a given edge [4]. The *clustering coefficient* of a node is defined as the fraction of the existing number of node links to the total possible number of neighbor-neighbor links [30].

A *(structural) motif* [18,29] is a connected graph or network consisting of M vertices and a set of edges with connectedness ensured forming a subgraph of a larger network. For each M there is a limited set of distinct motif classes. A *module* (also called *community*) is a densely connected subset of nodes that is only sparsely linked to the remaining network.

3 Probabilistic Modeling of Network Sets

We take a set of N directed networks $\mathcal{G} = \{G'_1, \ldots G'_N\}$ as a sample from a wider set of networks that possibly share some type of topological similarity. The number of nodes in each network G' is m. Self-loops are excluded and thus the maximal number of arcs in the network is $\frac{m(m-1)}{2}$. Our goal is to obtain a probabilistic model of networks in $\mathcal{G}$.

For probabilistic modeling, a representation of each solution is needed. We use X_i to represent a discrete random variable. A possible value of X_i is denoted x_i. Similarly, we use $\mathbf{X} = (X_1, \ldots, X_n)$ to represent an n-dimensional random variable and $\mathbf{x} = (x_1, \ldots, x_n)$ to represent one of its possible values.

Although alternative representations are possible, we will represent a network G' using a binary vector $\mathbf{x} = (x_1, \ldots, x_n)$, where $n = \frac{m(m-1)}{2}$. In this representation there is a unique mapping between each variable X_i and a unique arc of

G'. $x_i = 1$ is interpreted as the arc a_i belongs to the network. If $x_i = 0$, arc a_i is absent from the network.

The initial set $\mathcal{G}$ can be mapped to a binary data-set $\mathcal{D} = \{\mathbf{x}^{(1)}, \ldots \mathbf{x}^{(N)}\}$. From this data set it is possible to compute different statistics about the set of original networks. For instance, it is possible to determine the frequencies of all possible subnetwork configurations between a subset of nodes by computing the marginal frequencies of the variables mapping the arcs that depart from or arrive at these nodes. Similarly, we can learn a PGM from $\mathcal{D}$. This will serve as a model of the represented networks. The way in which the initial set $\mathcal{G}$ is selected will influence of the learned probabilistic model [26].

Once a PGM is constructed, it can be used to make queries related to the network class for which the data-set serves as a sample. Applications of this type to a variety of domains exist. We focus here on applications to the domain of network-based problems. Also in this domain, the PGM can be used for tasks involving *classification, inference* and *optimization*.

3.1   Classification

Using the PGM it is possible to estimate the probability that a given network G' belongs to the class of networks represented by $\mathcal{G}$. In this case, G' should be transformed into its corresponding binary representation $\mathbf{x}$, and the probability $p(\mathbf{x})$ given by the model can be taken as the class membership probability. A similar strategy can be employed to assign a given network G' to one among a set of k different classes of networks $\mathcal{G}^1 \ldots \mathcal{G}^k$.

3.2   Inference

The PGM can be used to estimate the probability of a particular subnetwork in the class of networks. In this context, partial inference is applied. It is possible, for instance, to estimate how likely is that a given arc is present in the class of networks represented by $\mathcal{G}$. Another approach allows the computation of the network that most likely belongs to the class of networks represented by $\mathcal{G}$. In this case, abductive inference is employed to compute the most probable configuration (or most probable explanation) given by the model, which is then transformed, using the variable to arc one-to-one mapping, to the corresponding network.

3.3   Optimization

Abductive inference is not the only alternative to obtain a given configuration from the PGM. Sampling methods can be also employed with that purpose. Therefore, from a PGM constructed from $\mathcal{G}$ it is possible to generate, using sampling, new solutions that are expected to be similar to those in $\mathcal{G}$. An approach that iteratively applies PGM learning and sampling steps is at the core of estimation of distribution algorithms (EDAs) [14,19], an optimization method based on the use of probabilistic models. EDAs associate a fitness function value to each possible solution. The fitness function could measure, for instance, how close are the topological characteristics of the candidate network with respect to a given target network [27].

The rationale behind the use of PGMs in EDAs is to capture similar characteristics shared by high quality solutions in order to increase the likelihood of obtaining better solutions, eventually leading to find the optimal solution. Another optimization methods based on PGMs include different applications of loopy belief propagation [31]. However, these methods usually employ a PGM to represent a single network and not a set of networks.

4   Network Analysis of PGMs

Let $P = (G', \Theta)$ be a probabilistic model, where G' and Θ are respectively the graphical and quantitative components of the model. We can assume that G' is a network (e.g. a directed graph). To obtain a weighted network G^w, a matrix of weights could be computed from Θ (e.g. a weight associated to a link can be the mutual information between the related variables in P. In the general case, we have a set of N weighted networks $\mathcal{G} = \{G_1^w, \ldots G_N^w\}$ associated to a set of PGMs $\mathcal{P} = \{P_1, \ldots P_N\}$.

Our approach considers the computation of networks descriptors for the networks in $\mathcal{G}$ and uses these descriptors to extract information about the models in $\mathcal{P}$. Local and global networks descriptors can be used for different purposes. The former can be applied to reveal characteristics of a single variable or a pair of interacting variables in the PGM. The latter can be used to reveal global characteristics of the PGM.

4.1   Classification

Local network descriptors allow the unsupervised classification of variables (respectively interaction pairs) in different groups according to their role in the system modeled by the PGM. In this case, classification operates in an undirected way: The nodes of a network (respectively, the links) are clustered according to one or more local network descriptors. The variables mapping nodes that are in the same cluster are then considered to belong to the same class. For example, given a threshold, the network links can be classified into two groups according to their betweennes centrality value: Links with low and high betweenness centrality values. We can interpret that links with a high betweenness centrality will play a more important role in PGM-based processes that involve information transmission over the links (e.g. message passing based inference algorithms like loopy belief propagation). Similarly, classification of nodes based on other local network descriptors such as the degree, the clustering coefficient or the reachability values can support additional information about the role played by variables.

Global network descriptors can be directly employed to classify different PGMs according to the topological characteristics of their graphical components. For example, structural network motifs and small cliques, both of which can be seen as a sort of network building blocks, can be used to distinguish PGMs learned from related but different classes of problems [25].

There are two general questions related to the use of network descriptors for classification. The first is the selection of an appropriate classifier. The second is the determination of the (subset of) global network descriptors that better serve to a clear discrimination between the different classes of networks. Another fundamental question is the interpretation that a given network descriptor has in terms of the relationships between the variables (respectively links) in the PGM. It is not clear that every type of network descriptor provides a meaningful interpretation. However, as one of the examples included in the next section shows, some descriptors contain useful information about the PGM.

4.2 Inference

In network theory some research has been devoted [7,8,15] to try to predict, using information about the connections already observed, which vertices are most likely to be connected. Among the network descriptors used to infer if a pair of nodes is linked are the clustering coefficient, the path length, or the vertices degree. Vertices are assumed to have a higher probability of being connected if they have many common neighbors, there are short paths between them or if the product of their degree is large [7]. Inference is not only used to predict the connectivity of missing vertices but also to detect false positive connections, i.e. links that appear in the network but which have a low probability of being connected using the network descriptors.

The application of network descriptor based inference to PGMs seems straightforward. Network descriptors such as the clustering coefficient could be applied to infer interactions between variables in PGMs which are only partially known. They could also be used to detect false interactions which are not rare in PGMs learned from data. Local network descriptors defined for weighted networks could be also applied to predict different measures of interaction strength between variables.

4.3 Optimization

In optimization based on PGMs (e.g. EDAs), the network descriptors extracted from the PGMs learned from the problem candidate solutions, can serve to identify particular characteristics of the optimization problem domain which are captured by the PGM. The network descriptors can also be used to evaluate the impact that the topological characteristics of the PGM graphical component have in the behavior of the optimization algorithm. Network descriptors have been investigated for optimization methods based on belief propagation algorithms [28] and EDAs [25].

For example, in the case of EDAs, each run may produce several PGMs learned from data while evolving. As a result, at the end of the search the user obtains a set of models which store valuable information about the optimization problem. An analysis of the network descriptors corresponding to the PGMs learned at different generations (e.g. the average vertex degree) provides information about the behavior of the algorithm (e.g. the characteristics of the data sets produced by the EDA). Similarly, we can compare the behavior of the EDA for different optimization problems using the obtained networks descriptors.

5   Applications in Neuroscience

In this section we describe a number of potential application of probabilistic modeling of networks and network analysis of PGMs in the field of neuroscience. In some cases we report ongoing work in this direction.

5.1   Applications to Classification Problems

Different measures of association between neural systems components are usually employed to learn a network from neurobiological data such as MRI or diffusion tensor imaging data [6,23]. Usually, a single network is constructed from the data collected for each individual. In many cases, the networks are a priori classified according to the experimental conditions in which the data has been collected or the characteristics of the individuals. For example, networks can correspond to two sets of healthy and pathological brains. In this case, PGMs representing each set of networks could be constructed and used for classification as described in Section 3.1. Similarly, sets of networks representing inter-neuronal relationships and derived from data corresponding to different single neurons can be used to construct PGMs of neurons and compute the probability of a given neuron configuration, as represented by the corresponding network.

5.2   Applications to Inference Problems

Network-based inference methods are particularly suitable to be applied to inter-neuronal or inter-regional network reconstruction problems. This is also supported by the fact that nodes with similar connection patterns tend to exhibit similar neuronal function.

Let us suppose an undirected (possibly loopy) PGM of a neuronal column is available. In this model, nodes represent neurons and links represent some probabilistic evidence that there is a synapse between two neurons. Due to possible errors in the neuronal column reconstruction, we know that there exist missing (false negative) and false positive links (representing missing and false synapses). In this context, different local network descriptors can be used to classify the links and identify false positives.

Not only inference can be made about links between variables. Algorithms able to determine the modular [11,12] and hierarchical structure [7] of networks have also been proposed and can be used to detect complex structural and functional organization patterns in different types of neuron networks.

5.3   Applications to Optimization Problems

In optimization problems, we have investigated the relationship between the properties of the a priori-known problem structural information and the structural information captured by the PGMs learned by EDAs. To quantify this relationship, network descriptors have been employed.

One of the problems considered has been to investigate the effect that biasing the axonal connection delay values has in the spike-timing dynamics of a class of spiking neural networks. The study of spike-timing dynamics in the brain is of interest for neuroscience since, among other reasons, it is a key issue to investigate the role that the relative timing of spikes of multiple neurons has in the temporal coding in the brain [5,10,13].

In the problem under consideration, we have started from a spiking network whose topological structure is given. Each link between two neurons has an associated numerical value which corresponds to the conductance delay between the neurons. We know that the particular distribution of the spiking network delay values may have an effect in the number of synfire chains [1] and polychronous groups [13] generated by the spiking network. Our ultimate goal is to study the influence of conduction delays in the polychronization process and in particular, to investigate whether the conduction delays can be biased to maximize the number of coexisting polychronous groups. To find networks with optimal conduction delays, an EDA that uses as PGM a tree is applied. The initial spiking network structure is kept fixed and only the delay values are modified by the EDA. Therefore the sample solutions are network delay assignments.

At the end of the EDA optimization process, the trees are processed and different average network descriptors are computed (e.g. degree of each vertex). These descriptors are compared with the network descriptors corresponding to the original spiking network topology. From this comparison we are able to determine to which extent the structural characteristics of the original problem are captured by the PGMs learned by the EDA, supporting information about the accuracy and effectiveness of the learning methods used by the optimization algorithm.

6   Conclusion and Future Work

In this paper we have presented different alternatives for the application of probabilistic modeling of network-based representations and network-based analysis of PGMs to classification, inference and optimization problems. Our proposal relies on two important properties: 1) The representational capabilities of PGMs to describe complex interactions between the components of a given system. 2) The amount of structural information that can be captured by network descriptors.

Although considerable work has been devoted to the use of PGMs to represent the behavior of neural systems and the application of network theory to study neuronal and mental processes, the combination of both approaches has not been treated in detail. The results presented in this paper about the potential application of the synergy between PGMs and network-based representations are a first, still preliminary, step. We expect more results could be obtained in this domain from the combined approach of both types of representations.

Acknowledgements

This research is part of the CajalBlueBrain project. It has been partially supported by TIN-2008-06815-C02-02, TIN2007-62626 and Consolider Ingenio 2010 - CSD2007-00018 projects (Spanish Ministry of Science and Innovation).

References

1. Abeles, M.: Local Cortical Circuits: An Electrophysiological Study. Springer, Heidelberg (1982)
2. Amaral, L.A.N., Scala, A., Barthélémy, M., Stanley, H.E.: Classes of small-world networks. Proceedings of the National Academy of Sciences (PNAS) 97(21), 11149–11152 (2000)
3. Bassett, D.S., Bullmore, E., Verchinski, B.A., Mattay, V.S., Weinberger, D.R., Meyer-Lindenberg, A.: Hierarchical organization of human cortical networks in health and schizophrenia. Journal of Neuroscience 28(37), 9239–9248 (2008)
4. Brandes, U.: A faster algorithm for betweenness centrality. Journal of Mathematical Sociology 25, 163–177 (2001)
5. Brown, E.N., Kass, R.E., Mitra, P.P.: Multiple neural spike train data analysis: State-of-the-art and future challenges. Nature Neuroscience 7, 456–461 (2004)
6. Bullmore, E., Sporns, O.: Complex brain networks: Graph theoretical analysis of structural and functional systems. Nature Reviews: Neuroscience 10, 1–13 (2009)
7. Clauset, A., Moore, C., Newman, M.E.J.: Hierarchical structure and the prediction of missing links in networks. Nature 453, 98–101 (2008)
8. Clauset, A., Moore, C., Newman, M.E.J.: Structural Inference of Hierarchies in Networks. In: Statistical Network Analysis: Models, Issues, and New Directions, pp. 1–13. Springer, Heidelberg (2008)
9. Dorogovtsev, S.N., Goltsev, A.V., Mendes, J.F.F.: Critical phenomena in complex networks. Journal of Modern Physics 80(4), 1275–1335 (2008)
10. Durstewitz, D., Gabriel, T.: Dynamical basis of irregular spiking in NMDA-driven prefrontal cortex neurons. Cerebral Cortex 17, 894–908 (2007)
11. Frey, B.J., Dueck, D.: Clustering by passing messages between data points. Science 315, 972–976 (2007)
12. Guimera, R., Amaral, L.A.N.: Functional cartography of complex metabolic networks. Nature 433, 895–900 (2005)
13. Izhikevich, E.M.: Polychronization: Computation with spikes. Neural Computation 18(2), 245–282 (2006)
14. Larrañaga, P., Lozano, J.A. (eds.): Estimation of Distribution Algorithms. A New Tool for Evolutionary Computation. Kluwer Academic Publishers, Dordrecht (2002)
15. Liben-Nowell, D., Kleinberg, J.: The link-prediction problem for social networks. Journal of American Society for Information Science and Technology 58(7), 1019–1031 (2007)
16. Lichtman, J.W., Livet, J., Sanes, J.R.: A technicolor approach to the connectome. Nature Reviews: Neuroscience 9, 417–422 (2008)

17. McIntosh, A.R.: Towards a theory of cognition. Neural Networks 13, 861–870 (2000)
18. Milo, R., Shen-Orr, S., Itzkovitz, S., Kashtan, N., Chklovskii, D., Alon, U.: Network motifs: Simple building blocks of complex networks. Science 298, 824–827 (2002)
19. Mühlenbein, H., Paaß, G.: From recombination of genes to the estimation of distributions I. Binary parameters. In: Ebeling, W., Rechenberg, I., Voigt, H.-M., Schwefel, H.-P. (eds.) PPSN 1996. LNCS, vol. 1141, pp. 178–187. Springer, Heidelberg (1996)
20. Pearl, J.: Probabilistic Reasoning in Intelligent Systems: Networks of Plausible Inference. Morgan Kaufmann, San Mateo (1988)
21. Rao, R.P.N.: Neural models of Bayesian belief propagation. In: Bayesian Brain. Probabilistic Approaches to Neural Coding, pp. 239–267. MIT Press, Cambridge (2007)
22. Rolfe, J.T.: The cortex as a graphical model. Master's thesis, Computation and Neural Systems, California Institute of Technology (2006)
23. Rykhlevskaia, E., Gratton, G., Fabiani, M.: Combining structural and functional neuroimaging data for studying brain connectivity: A review. Psychophysiology 45, 173–187 (2008)
24. Sajda, P., Baek, K., Finkel, L.: Bayesian networks for modeling cortical integration. In: Akay, M. (ed.) Handbook of Neural Engineering, pp. 585–600. Wiley Press, Chichester (2007)
25. Santana, R., Bielza, C., Lozano, J.A., Larrañaga, P.: Mining probabilistic models learned by EDAs in the optimization of multi-objective problems. In: Proceedings of the 11th Annual Genetic and Evolutionary Computation Conference GECCO 2009, pp. 445–452. ACM, New York (2009)
26. Santana, R., Larrañaga, P., Lozano, J.A.: Interactions and dependencies in estimation of distribution algorithms. In: Proceedings of the 2005 Congress on Evolutionary Computation CEC 2005, Edinburgh, UK, pp. 1418–1425. IEEE Press, Los Alamitos (2005)
27. Santana, R., Larrañaga, P., Lozano, J.A.: Evolving optimized brain networks topologies using multi-objective evolutionary computation (submmitted for publication 2010)
28. Santana, R., Mendiburu, A., Lozano, J.A.: An empirical analysis of loopy belief propagation in three topologies: Grids, small-world networks and random graphs. In: Jaeger, M., Nielsen, T.D. (eds.) Proceedings of the Fourth European Workshop on Probabilistic Graphical Models (PGM 2008), pp. 249–256 (2008)
29. Sporns, O., Kötter, R.: Motifs in brain networks. PLoS Biology 2(11), e369 (2004)
30. Watts, D.J., Strogatz, S.: Collective dynamics of small-world networks. Nature 393(6684), 440–442 (1998)
31. Yanover, C., Weiss, Y.: Approximate inference and protein-folding. In: Becker, S., Thrun, S., Obermayer, K. (eds.) Advances in Neural Information Processing Systems, vol. 15, pp. 1457–1464. MIT Press, Cambridge (2003)

Modeling Short-Time Parsing of Speech Features in Neocortical Structures

P. Gómez, J.M. Ferrández, V. Rodellar, L.M. Mazaira, and C. Muñoz

Grupo de Informática Aplicada al Procesado de Señal e Imagen
Universidad Politécnica de Madrid, Campus de Montegancedo, s/n
28660 Boadilla del Monte, Madrid
Tel.: +34913367394, Fax: +34913366601
pedro@pino.datsi.fi.upm.es

Abstract. The unveiling of neocortical short-time circuits to detect specific formant associations in Speech Processing is reviewed. The use of these specific structures to capture and parse dynamic changes taking place in the syllabic structure of speech is also presented. Results from computer simulations supporting physiological evidence are presented.

Keywords: Speech Processing, Neuromorphic Computing, Bioinspired Systems.

1 Introduction

Speech may be defined as a communication-oriented activity consisting in the production of a sequence of sounds which convey a complex information code derived from language. These sounds are radiated mainly through lips and when captured by a microphone result in recorded speech. When observed in the time domain, speech looks like as a chain of pseudo-periodic spike-like patterns, which correspond mainly to vowel bursts. If observed in the frequency domain the FFT spectrogram is composed by horizontal bands spaced by a common interval in frequency, which is the fundamental frequency f_0 or pitch. These are known as harmonics and convey information about the timbre of speech, which is ultimately related with the speaker's identity as well as with prosody. The harmonics may appear intensified by vocal tract resonances as pseudo-bands of intensity which sometimes seem more or less horizontal, and at times bend in specific patterns. These are known as formants and convey information about the coloring of speech, but besides, the three lowest formants contribute important communication or message clues. There are other intervals where speech activity distribution is mainly vertical. These patterns are known as Noise Bursts (NB) and correspond to segments where speech is produced without phonation (voice-less speech). The clues which convey the minimum amount of meaning in each part of speech are known as "information-bearing elements (IBE's)". The main IBE's with articulatory significance are the following: the presence/absence of voicing, the presence of stable formants, the dynamic behavior of unstable formants, the presence of noise bands (vertically distributed), and the duration of silences. An example of

N. García-Pedrajas et al. (Eds.): IEA/AIE 2010, Part III, LNAI 6098, pp. 159–168, 2010.
© Springer-Verlag Berlin Heidelberg 2010

what is being exposed may be found in Figure 1 below. The formant positions and trajectories of the four approximants [β, ð, ζ, γ] (front, mid-front, mid-back, back) articulated with vowel [a] are given to illustrate the stable vowel positions and the consonant loci [21].

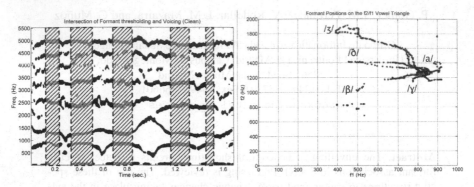

Fig. 1. Left: Sequence of formants for the group /aβa:aða:aζa:aγa/. The segments where formants are stable (shaded frames) correspond to the vowel nuclei. The complementary in-between segments correspond to the positions of the fricative voiced consonants (approximants). Right: Loci of the f2 vs f1 formant positions on the vowel triangle (the two lowest bands in the left plot): the position of the vowel [a] acts as an attractor where formant trajectories depart from and arrive to. Consonant loci of the four approximants ([β, ð, ζ, γ]) are labeled with their respective symbols.

2 The Generalized Neuromorphic Computing Unit

The determination of the specific neural structures involved in speech processing and their precise functionality is one of the most difficult problems faced in the field, as direct in vivo measuring is affected by the highly aggressive nature of the testing techniques, which motivate that most of the neurophysiologic tests have been con-ducted on animal models [22]. Other sources of knowledge are based on indirect evidence obtained studying perceptual alterations in humans after brain damage, ei-ther induced by illness or by external injuries ([17][4]). Functional magnetic reso-nance imaging (fMRI) and magneto-encephalography (MEG) have been introduced only recently as real-time introspection tools, although affected by limitations in reso-lution [7]. This overview will summarize some of the main phenomena of interest for speech processing under the perceptual point of view: tone intensity and pitch percep-tion, harmonic and formant estimation, noise-like broadband signal perception, ampli-tude and frequency modulation, vowel onset, sustain and decay detection and their relation to consonant perception, etc. For such Figure 2 will be taken into account. Speech processing in the auditory system starts when acoustic waves arrive to the cochlea through the outer and middle ear. Frequency and time separation of signal components are produced in the basilar membrane along the cochlea operating as a filter bank [2]. Low frequencies produce maximum excitation in the apical end of the membrane, while high frequencies produce maximum excitation towards the basal area. As a result, organized spike-like streams of stimuli coding frequency by place and phase locking are produced. These streams are transferred from the cochlea to the first relay stage in the Cochlear Nucleus (CN) via the Auditory Nerve (AN). The information flows to higher neural centres along auditory nerve fibres, each one being specialized in the transmission of a different characteristic frequency (CF).

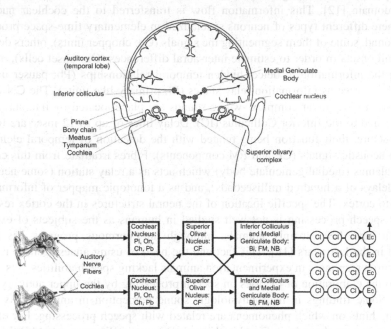

Fig. 2. Speech Perception Model. Top: Main neural pathways in the peripheral and central auditory centers adapted from [8]. Bottom: Simplified main structures. The cochlea produces time-frequency organized representations which are conveyed by the auditory nerve to the cochlear nucleus, where certain specialized neurons (Pl: Primary-like, On: Onset, Ch: Chopper, Pb: Pauser) are implied in temporal processing. Binaural information is treated in the Superior Olivar Nucleus, where selective tono-topic units (CF) may be found. Other units specialized in detecting tonal movements (FM), broadband spectral densities (NB) and binaural processing (Bi) are found in the inferior colliculus and the medial geniculate body. The auditory cortex shows columnar layered units (Cl) as well as massively extensive connection units (Ec). Their function may be related with short-time memory, being the object of Electro-Microscopy [5], [3], and High Performance Computing [6].

An interesting issue is the role played by lateral inhibition, which has to see with harmonic and formant detection in the auditory pathways. From the perceptual facts described above it seems clear that speech perception is very much based in formant perception, both static and dynamic. The transition from time-frequency detailed spatiotemporal structure of the responses of the auditory nerve to specific CF/CF and FM/FM responses found in the primary auditory cortex (AI) of the moustached bat by Suga [20] indicates that some powerful mechanism is applied to reduce spike firing rates and the number of fibres conveying information to higher auditory centres. It is believed that the mechanism for this compression coding process is based in "specific lateral inhibition networks which may exist in the anteroventral Cochlear Nucleus (CN), especially involving T-Stellate cells, which exhibit fast inhibitory surrounds and a robust representation of the input spectrum regardless of level" [19]. This belief is also supported by the strong reduction in spike firing rates found in the lower levels of the auditory pathways as compared with the firing rates in the AI areas which suggest the presence of a strong compression mechanism both in the time and in the frequency domain [12]. This information flow is transferred to the cochlear nucleus (CN) where different types of neurons specialized in elementary time-space processing are found, some of them segmenting the signals (Cp: chopper units), others detecting stimuli onsets in order to estimate inter-aural differences (On: onset cells), others delaying the information to detect hidden temporal relationships (Pb: pauser units), while others serve as information relay stages (Pl: primary-like units). The CN feeds information to the olivar complex -where sounds are place-located by interaural differences-, and to the Inferior Colliculus (IC). Delay lines of up to 12 msec are found in its structure, their function being related with the detection of temporal elements coded in acoustic signals (CF and FM components). Fibres irradiate from this centre to the thalamus (medial geniculate body) which acts as a relay station (some neurons exhibit delays of a hundred milliseconds), and as a tonotopic mapper of information arriving to cortex. The specific location of the neural structures in the cortex responsible for speech processing is not well studied in humans as the subjects of experimentation have been mainly animals, although an enormous progress has been achieved in the last years [18]. This fact and the need of using anaesthesia to record single neuron responses in experimentation animals lacking speech abilities puts some shades to the elaboration of theories on speech processing by the upper auditory system [1]. Some findings in neurophysiologic sound perception in animals may give interesting hints on which phenomena are related with speech processing. For example, certain neurons have been found in the cat's primary auditory cortex (AI) that fire when FM-like frequency transitions are present (FM elements [16]), while in macaque some neurons respond to specific noise bursts (NB components). In the moustached bat AI neurons have also been found that respond to combinations of two static tones (vowel-like structures) or even to dynamic changes in two tones (Active Voiced Dynamic structures, as were defined above [20]). The morphology and functionality of the units of interest share important features in common as the reaction to one or several inputs with an excitatory or inhibitory function which may be based in the model of Donald Hebb [13], the response expressed as a stream of firing spikes within a given time interval delayed with respect to the stimuli (causality), or the processing time-frequency representations of speech-derived neural activity. Algorithmically a definition of a Generalized Neuromorphic Computing Unit (GNCU) is that of an operator transforming an input representation space (a generalized spectrogram image as the one in Figure 5 top) mathematically described as a matrix $X(m,n) \in \mathfrak{R}^{m \times n}$ to an output representation space $\tilde{X}(m,n) \in \mathfrak{R}^{m \times n}$ where m and n correspond respectively to the indices of frequency and time accordingly with the following transformation:

$$\tilde{X}(m,n) = F\left\{ \sum_{i=-1}^{I} \sum_{j=0}^{J} w_{ij} X(m-i, n-j) \right\} \tag{1}$$

$w_{ij} \in \mathcal{R}^{IxJ}$ being a set of connection weights associated to the inputs (excitatory or inhibitory, depending on their respective value), and $F\{.\}$ being a nonlinear saturation mapping function. The structure and operation of a GNCU is represented in Figure 3.

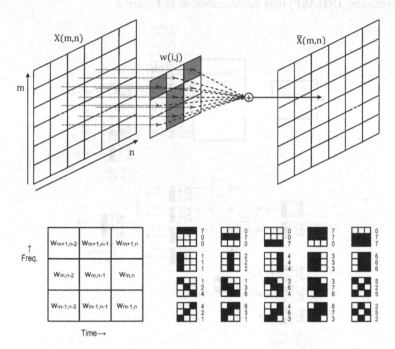

Fig. 3. Top: Structure of a Generalized Neuromorphic Computing Unit (GNCU). Bottom: image processing templates implementing some simple functions in speech spectrogram processing.

The GNCU receives a synaptic input, which may be positive or negative, the synaptic weight is expressed also as a real number. The addition of all stimuli is mapped to the output by a non-linear saturating function, and the response is produced also as a real number. The reception of inputs and the generation of outputs are supposed to be regulated by a main timing clock marking the cadence of the time instant n. The operation of a GNCU is quite similar to that of a pixel template in image processing [14]. The number of different functions which may be implemented by the GNCU's is very large, as it may be deduced examining several 3x3 templates given as examples in Figure 3 (bottom). For instance, the templates in the upper row (700, 070, 007, 770, and 077) are specifically designed to track stable formant positions, and can be considered different variants of CF units. The templates in the second row from left to right (111, 222, 444, 333, and 666) are implementing NB units. The templates 124, 136, 364 and 376 are specialized in detecting descending formants (-fM units), and similarly templates 421, 631, 463 and 673 are designed to detect ascending formants (+fM units). Under this point of view the detection of formants in audition is carried out by similar structures to the ones detecting edges in vision, and both processes can be seen as a part of powerful scene representation coding processes.

3 Neuromorphic Hierarchical Architecture for Speech Processing

A possible Neuromorphic Hierarchical Architecture to implement specific tasks in Speech Processing (NHASP) may be described as in Figure 4.

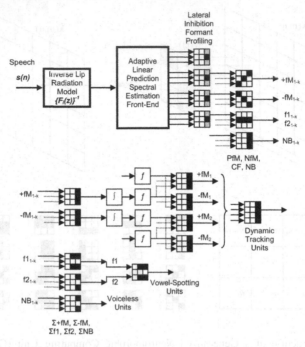

Fig. 4. Neuromorphic Hierarchical Speech Processing Architecture for a single channel

The static or dynamic nature of the consonants is fully described now in terms of formant dynamics (FM1, FM2, CF and NB). The NHSPA may be seen as different subsystems which are interconnected to process an input audio stream $s(n)$. The systemic description from top to bottom and left to right is as follows:

- LIFP: Lateral Inhibition Formant Profilers, designed to detect the presence of plausible formants by delineation and prediction.
- $+f_{M1-K}$, $-f_{M1-K}$: Positive and Negative Slope Formant Trackers detecting ascending or descending formants by masks {124-376} and {421-673}.
- $f1_{1-K}$, $f2_{1-K}$: First and Second Energy Peak Trackers, intended for formant detection mimicking CF neurons, using masks {700-077}.
- $\Sigma+fM$, $\Sigma-fM$: These are integrators or accumulators working on the inputs of previous Formant Tracker Integration Units on neighbour bands (350-650 Hz for the first formant, or 650-2300 Hz for the second formant).
- $+fM_1$, $-fM_1$, $+fM_2$, $-fM_2$: First and Second Formant Integration Units (positive and negative slopes), estimating the features FM1 and FM2.
- ΣNB: Noise Burst Integration Units ({111-666}) for wide frequency activity detection, as in voiceless consonants.

- **VSU**: Voiceless Spotting Units. These integrate the outputs of different ΣNB's acting in separate bands to pattern the activity of fricative voiceless consonants.
- **WSU**: Vowel Spotting Units. These integrate the activity of $\Sigma f1$ and $\Sigma f2$ units to detect the presence of vowels and their nature.
- **DTU**: Dynamic Tracking Units. These integrate the activity of different dynamic trackers on the first two formants to detect consonant dynamic features.

4 Results

In what follows the emphasis will be placed in showing the detection of some meaningful dynamic features of speech, leaving the interested reader to inspect other related publications ([10][9][11]). Classically to study these features, speech segments showing fast formant movements are used. In this section a typical example will be shown based on the classical sentence *–Where were you while you were away?-*. Its LPC corresponding f_2-vs-f_1 formant plot on the vowel triangle are shown in Figure 5.

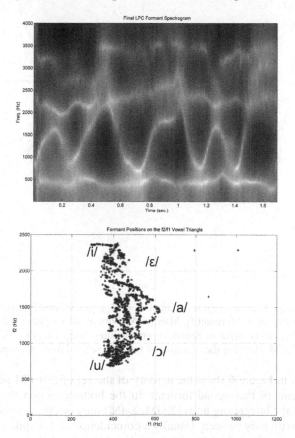

Fig. 5. Top: LPC spectrogram of the sentence *–**Where were you while you were away**?-*. Bottom: Tormant loci given by f_2-vs-f_1 showing the five reference vowels in English.

The spectrogram reveals fast up and down movements of formants (especially f_2), confined to a vowel triangle within which formant trajectories smear in time. The modelling of the two first formants by *FM+* and *FM-* units constitute a specific objective of this study. The details of the architecture used in the study are the following: $M=1024$ units are characteristic frequency outputs from LPC, with frequency resolution of 8 Hz for a sampling frequency of 8000 Hz. These are sampled each 5 msec. to define a stream of approximately 200 spikes per second. The dimensions of the +FM and -FM units are 7x7, which means that the connectivity in frequency extends from +3 to -3 neighbour neurons, whilst the delay lines in the pauser units required for temporal organization of the stimuli go from 0 to 30 msec. As the frequency distribution is linear, 38 channels are required for the detection of the first formant (350-650 Hz), and 204 for the second formant (700-2300).

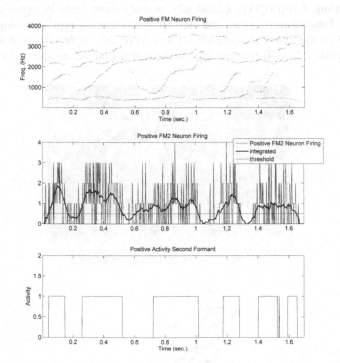

Fig. 6. FM Unit firing. Top: Activity at the input of +fM$_{700-2300}$ Second Formant Tracking Units coding the band of the second formant f_2. Middle: Activity at the output of +fM$_{700-2300}$. Integration and thresholding at the input of Second Formant Integrating Units (positive slope +fM$_2$). Bottom: Output of +fM$_2$ showing the detection of positive second formant slopes.

The templates in Figure 6 show the activity of the set of 204 FM neurons tracking the fast movements of the second formant. In the bottom section the activity at the synaptic input of the integrating units (Σ+fM, Σ-fM) may be appreciated. The granular or spike-like activity may be seen. Usually a coincidence of 2-4 spikes at a time from different neighbour units, which are integrated and thresholded over a short time period are enough to trigger the firing of integrating neurons, detecting the positive segments of the second formant.

5 Discussion and Conclusions

Through the present work it has been shown that formant-based speech processing may be carried by well-known bio-inspired mask processors (CF and FM units). The structures studied correspond roughly to the processing centres in the olivar nucleus and the inferior colliculus. The lower and mid auditory pathways have been intensively and extensively researched, and a lot of useful knowledge for neuromorphic speech processing has been produced. Nevertheless the functional role played by the cortical structure in speech processing lacks a similar description, this functionality being a great challenge even nowadays [18]. The columnar organization of the neocortex was first described by Rafael Lorente de No [15]. The main underlying question is: Why cortical columnar organization is believed to be important for speech processing by higher auditory pathways? There are some interesting answers which can only be formulated as hypotheses to be ratified by further research. On one side it is clear that short memory plays an essential role in phone time organization and parsing. Phonemic parsing demands specific resources for feature storage and time accounting in order to produce meaningful word definitions. Under this point of view a parsing analysis line would be the systemic counterpart of a micro column. The study of simple structures to emulate short-time parsing of dynamic features in the construction of representation spaces for specific speech phones is proposed as a future development.

Acknowledgments

This work is being funded by grants TEC2006-12887-C02-00 and TEC2009-14123-C04-03 from the Ministry of Education and Science, CCG06-UPM/TIC-0028 from CAM/UPM, and by project HESPERIA (http.//www.proyecto-hesperia.org) from the Programme CENIT, CDTI, Ministry of Industry, Spain.

References

[1] Ainsworth, W.A., Greenberg, S.: Auditory Processing of Speech. In: Ainsworth, S.G. (ed.) Listening to Speech: An Auditory Perspective, pp. 3–17. Lawrence Erlbaum Ass. Pub., Mahwah (2006)
[2] Allen, J.B.: Cochlear Modeling. IEEE ASSP Magazine, 3–29 (1985)
[3] Arellano, J.I., Benavides-Piccione, R., DeFelipe, J., Yuste, R.: Ultrastructure of dendritic spines: correlation between synaptic and spine morphologies. Frontiers in Neuroscience 1(1), 131–143 (2007)
[4] Corina, D.P., Gibson, E.K., Martin, R., Poliakov, A., Brinkley, J., Ojemann, G.A.: Dissociation of Action and Object Naming: Evidence from Cortical Stimulation Mapping. Human Brain Mapping 24, 1–10 (2005)
[5] Elston, G.N., Benavides-Piccione, R., DeFelipe, J.: The pyramidal cell in cognition: a comparative study in man and monkey. J. Neurosci. 21, 1–5 (2001)
[6] Friedman, R.: Reverse Engineering the Brain. Biomedical Computation Review, 10–17 (Spring 2009)

[7] Gandour, J., Tong, Y., Talavage, T., Wong, D., Dzemidzic, M., Xu, Y., et al.: Neural Basis of First and Second Language Processing of Sentence-Level Linguistic Prosody. Human Brain Mapping 28, 94–108 (2007)

[8] Goldstein, B.: Sensation and Perception. Wadsworth Publ., Belmont (1984)

[9] Gómez, P., Ferrández, J.M., Rodellar, V., Fernández, R.: Time-frequency Representations in Speech Perception. Neurocomputing, 820–830 (2009)

[10] Gómez, P., Ferrández, J.M., Rodellar, V., Álvarez, A., Mazaira, L.M.: A Bio-inspired Architecture for Cognitive Audio. In: Mira, J., Álvarez, J.R. (eds.) IWINAC 2007. LNCS, vol. 4527, pp. 132–142. Springer, Heidelberg (2007)

[11] Gómez, P., Ferrández, J.M., Rodellar, V., Álvarez, A., Mazaira, L.M., Martínez, R., et al.: Detection of Speech Dynamics by Neuromorphic Units. In: Mira, J., Ferrández, J.M., Álvarez, J.R., de la Paz, F., Toledo, F.J. (eds.) IWINAC 2009. LNCS, vol. 5601, pp. 67–78. Springer, Heidelberg (2009)

[12] Greenberg, S., Ainsworth, W.A.: Speech Processing in the Auditory System: An Overview. In: Greenberg, W.A.S. (ed.) Speech Processing in the Auditory System, pp. 1–62. Springer, New York (2004)

[13] Hebb, D.O.: The Organization of Behavior. Wiley Interscience, New York (1949 - reprinted 2002)

[14] Jähne, B.: Digital Image Processing. Springer, Berlin (2005)

[15] Lorente de No, R.: Cerebral cortex: architecture, intracortical connections, motor projections. In: Fulton, J.F. (ed.) Physiology of the Nervous System, pp. 288–330. Oxford University Press, Oxford (1949)

[16] Mendelson, J.R., Cynander, M.S.: Sensitivity of Cat Primary Auditory Cortex (AI) Neurons to the Direction and Rate of Frequency Modulation. Brain Research 327, 331–335 (1985)

[17] Ojemann, G.A.: Cortical Organization of Language. Journal of Neuroscience 11(8), 2281–2287 (1991)

[18] Rauschecker, J.P., Scott, S.K.: Maps and streams in the auditory cortex: nonhuman primates illuminate human speech processing. Nature Neuroscience 12(6), 718–724 (2009)

[19] Shamma, S.: On the role of space and time auditory processing. Trends in Cognitive Sciences 5(8), 340–348 (2001)

[20] Suga, N.: Basic Acoustic Patterns and Neural Mechanisms Shared by Humans and Animals for Auditory Perception. In: Ainsworth, E.S.G. (ed.) Listening to Speech: An Auditory Perspective, pp. 159–181. Lawrence Erlbaum Associates, Pub., Mahwah (2006)

[21] Sussman, H.M., McCaffrey, H.A., Mathews, S.A.: An Investigation of Locus Equations as a Source of Relational Invariance for Stop Place Categorization. Journal of the Acoustical Society of America 90, 1309–1325 (1991)

[22] Yin, P., Ma, L., Elhilali, M., Fritz, J., Shamma, S.: Primary Auditory Cortical Resoponses while Attending to Different Streams. In: Kollmeier, B., et al. (eds.) Hearing: From Sensory Processing to Perception, pp. 257–265. Springer, Heidelberg (2007)

Optimizing the Number of Airfoils in Turbine Design Using Genetic Algorithms

José M. Chaquet[1,*], Enrique J. Carmona[2], and Roque Corral[1]

[1] Technology and Methods Dep., Industria de TurboPropulsores S.A.
Avda. de Castilla 2, 28830, San Fernando de Henares, Madrid, Spain
Tel.: +34 91 2079147, Fax: +34 91 2079411

[2] Dpto. de Inteligencia Artificial, Escuela Técnica Superior de Ingeniería Informática,
Universidad Nacional de Eduación a Distancia, Madrid, Spain
jose.chaquet@itp.es, ecarmona@dia.uned.es, roque.corral@itp.es

Abstract. A method for optimizing the number of airfoils of a turbine design is presented. The optimization consists of reducing the total number of airfoils meanwhile a set of geometric, aerodynamic and acoustic noise restrictions are fulfilled. It is described how is possible to reduce the problem degrees of freedom to just one variable per row. Due to the characteristics of the problem, a standard Genetic Algorithm has been used. As a case study, a real aeronautical Low Pressure Turbine design of 6 stages has been optimized.

1 Introduction

A turbine of a gas turbine engine is a device that extracts work from a pressured gas stream. It is normally made up of three modules, called HPT, IPT and LPT (*High*, *Intermediate* and *Low Pressure Turbine*). The extraction of work from the fluid is done by means of several aerodynamic surfaces called *airfoils* which are placed in an annular way forming *rows*. A turbine *stage* is formed by two consecutive rows, called *stator* and *rotor*. Stator airfoils are called *vanes*, meanwhile rotor airfoils are called *blades*. The stator is attached to the casing and directs the flow towards the rotor, meanwhile the rotor transmits the power to the turbine *shaft*. The number of airfoils of a row is called *NumberOff*.

The design process of an aeronautical turbine is a very challenging task. A LPT can contribute with one third to the total weight and with up to 15% to the total cost [1]. A lot of different constraints must be taken into account when designing the LPT airfoils and usually the final decision on the optimum particular configuration requires a trade-off among different requirements.

In this work it is presented a method for optimizing the NumberOffs of a turbine. The optimization consists of reducing the total number of airfoils meanwhile a set of geometric, acoustic and aerodynamic restrictions are fulfilled. It will be demonstrated that is possible to reduce the problem *Degrees of Freedom*

---

* Corresponding author.

N. García-Pedrajas et al. (Eds.): IEA/AIE 2010, Part III, LNAI 6098, pp. 169–178, 2010.
© Springer-Verlag Berlin Heidelberg 2010

(DoF) to just the NumberOff for each row. The approach adopted to solve the optimization problem uses a Genetic Algorithm (GA).

There are several applications in the literature that make use of GAs in the design process of gas turbine components, like the control system unit [2,9], blade cooling holes [3,5,6], the combustor [4,10], rotor system [7] or the 2D and 3D design of airfoils [8,11]. Some applications use standard GA [4,8,11], while others implement specific GA, as Multi-objective GA (MOGA) which evolves a Pareto-optimal solution [2,7,9,10]. In some methods the initial strategy involves the identification of high performance (HP) regions of conceptual design spaces and the extraction of relevant information regarding the characteristics of the solutions within these regions [3,5]. HP regions are rapidly identified using the COGA approach (*Cluster-oriented* GA). Another special GA used is called GAANT, which is based upon ant colony concepts and genetic algorithms [5]. Other possible approach is a Generalized Regression GA (GRGA) which explores the relationship among the variables of the solutions belonging to any continues portion of the Pareto front using non-linear multivariable regression analysis [6].

In this paper, first a description of the problem to solve is presented (section 2). It will be shown how to reduce the problem DoF. Then the GA approach will be described (section 3) and the results obtained in the optimization of a real 6 stage aeronautical gas turbine are presented (section 4). Finally, the conclusions and future works are given (section 5).

2   Problem Description

The problem consists of the turbine total number of airfoils minimization for a given flow-path (Fig. 1a) and aerodynamic exit angles. The minimization process has to fulfil a set of aerodynamic, acoustic and geometric restrictions that may be reduced to a set of explicit analytical expressions. As a consequence, both the objective function and the restrictions are extremely fast to evaluate.

In order to parametrize the problem, a simplified geometry will be used approximating each row by a rectangle (Fig. 1b). For a turbine of M number of rows, each row is defined with only 5 parameters: NumberOff (N_i), gap (g_i), chord (c_i), mean radius (R_i) and span (S_i) where i goes from 1 to M. The mean radius is the distance of the middle point of the row to the turbine axis. It is also needed one global variable, L, which is the total axial length of the turbine. The turbine inner and outer annuli are supposed to be optimized in an outer loop and in this exercise are kept constant. Therefore the mean radius and the span of all the rows are constant. NumberOffs, gaps and chords will be modified in order to find optimum feasible configurations. Gaps for row i is the distance between the trailing edge of row i and the leading edge of next row $i + 1$, or the exit station for the last row. The initial gap, g_0, is defined as the distance between the inlet station and the leading edge of first the row (figure 1b).

The geometric constraints are defined with the following parameters for each row: maximum aspect ratio (MA_i), minimum pitch to chord ratio (mPC_i), maximum pitch to chord ratio (MPC_i), minimum gap (mG_i), minimum gap to chord

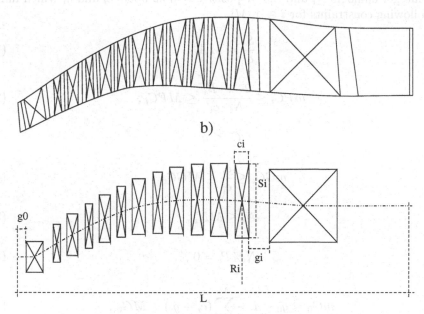

Fig. 1. Real geometry (a) and simplified one (b)

ratio (mGC_i), maximum gap to chord ratio (MGC_i), maximum NumberOff (MN_i) and the NumberOff for each package (P_i). The maximum aspect ratio should be limited by mechanic and flutter response. The pitch to chord ratio is limited in order to maintain Zweiffel coefficient bounded. Gaps are bounded in order to avoid mechanical interferences and by noise restrictions. The package parameter imposes that the NumberOff must be multiple of P_i. For the inlet gap g_0, two constraints are given for bounding its value between a minimum and a maximum value: mG_0 and MG_0.

It is well known that one way of reducing the generation of noise associated to pure tones is to force that the NumberOffs ratio for two consecutive rows lies within some specific intervals [1]. When the NumberOff ratio fulfills this conditions, the acoustic wave amplitudes decrease with the axial distance, the stage is said to be *cut-off* and the perturbations do not propagate outside the turbine. The cut-off condition depend as well on the flow variables, but in our problem these are assumed to remain constant. Noise constraints are given by four parameters: α_i, β_i, γ_i and δ_i. These parameters define two intervals $[\alpha_i, \beta_i]$ and $[\gamma_i, \delta_i]$ where the ratio of NumberOff of row i and row $i+1$ must be located. Normally $0 \le \alpha_i \le \beta_i \le 1 \le \gamma_i \le \delta_i$. When both ranges are used, the configuration is called Mixed cut-off. For *Direct* cut-off mode, $[\alpha_i, \beta_i]$ interval is chosen for even rows and $[\gamma_i, \delta_i]$ for odd rows, therefore it will be more vanes than blades. The opposite is chosen for *Reverse* cut-off mode.

Putting all together, the mathematical problem consist of finding the M positive integer numbers N_i and the M positive real numbers c_i and g_i which fulfill the following constraints for $i \in [1, M]$

$$\frac{S_i}{c_i} \leq MA_i,\tag{1}$$

$$mPC_i \leq \frac{2 \cdot \pi \cdot R_i}{N_i \cdot c_i} \leq MPC_i,\tag{2}$$

$$mG_i \leq g_i,\tag{3}$$

$$mGC_i \leq \frac{g_i}{c_i} \leq MGC_i,\tag{4}$$

$$N_i \leq MN_i,\tag{5}$$

$$N_i \% P_i = 0,\tag{6}$$

$$mG_0 \leq g_0 \equiv L - \sum_{i=1}^{M} (c_i + g_i) \leq MG_0,\tag{7}$$

$$if (i \neq M \ \& \ Mixed) \ \frac{N_i}{N_{i+1}} \in [\alpha_i, \beta_i] \cup [\gamma_i, \delta_i],\tag{8}$$

$$if \{i \neq M \ \& \ (Direct \ \& \ i\%2 = 0) \ or \ (Reverse \ \& \ i\%2 = 1)\} \ \frac{N_i}{N_{i+1}} \in [\alpha_i, \beta_i],\tag{9}$$

$$if \{i \neq M \ \& \ (Direct \ \& \ i\%2 = 1) \ or \ (Reverse \ \& \ i\%2 = 0)\} \ \frac{N_i}{N_{i+1}} \in [\gamma_i, \delta_i].\tag{10}$$

In equation (6) the symbol % means the remainder of integer division. Equation (7) computes the first gap g_0 and it imposes that g_0 must be in between mG_0 and MG_0.

Taking into account the three parameters for each row (N_i, c_i and g_i), there are $3M$ DoF. We will show that the problem may be reduced to that of finding the M DoF associated to the number of airfoils for each individual row.

Fig. 2a displays Gap-Chord space. The shaded region represents g_i and c_i feasible pairs where constraints (3) and (4) are represented. Points A and A' have the same chord, but A' has the minimum possible gap. The same happens with points B and B'. If point A is feasible regarding to all constraints except those in equation (7), point A' will be feasible as well. But point A' could be considered better than A because gives more room to other rows to increase their gaps and chords. For that reason and regardless of other considerations, gaps will be set to the minimum for a given chord:

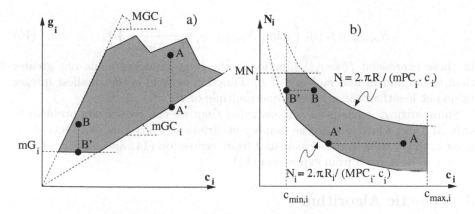

Fig. 2. Feasible domain spaces (shaded area): Gap-Chord (a) and NumberOff-Chord (b)

$$g_i \equiv g_i(c_i) = \max\left(mG_i, mGC_i \cdot c_i\right). \tag{11}$$

In Fig. 2b a typical NumberOff-Chord diagram for a specific row is plotted. The shaded region represents c_i and N_i feasible pairs without taking into account the Noise constraints. Using constraints (1), (2), (3) and (4) we obtain:

$$c_{min,i} = \max\left(\frac{S_i}{MA_i}, \frac{mG_i}{MGC_i}, \frac{2 \cdot \pi \cdot R_i}{MN_i \cdot MPC_i}\right). \tag{12}$$

Using (7), (11) and (12) expressions it is possible to compute for each row a maximum chord considering that the rest of rows have their minimum chords. It is important to notice that this limit is not absolute, but it depends on the rest the turbine rows. It is an upper limit, but will decrease if at least one row has his chord larger than his minimum chord.

$$c_{max,i} = L - \sum_{j=1, j\neq i}^{M} \left(c_{min,j} + g_j(c_{min,j})\right) - mg_0. \tag{13}$$

From Fig. 2b we can argue that if point A is feasible regarding all constraints, point A' will be feasible as well. A' is considered better because it has the minimum chord for a given NumberOff. Smaller chords give more room to other rows. The same consideration may be done for points B and B'. Then, given a NumberOff, the optimum chord can be chosen using the following expression:

$$c_i \equiv c_i(N_i) = \max\left(c_{min,i}, \frac{2 \cdot \pi \cdot R_i}{N_i \cdot MPC_i}\right). \tag{14}$$

Finally, the range of N_i to explore may be derived from expressions (2), (5) and (12):

$$N_{max,i} = floor_{P_i}\left(\min\left(MN_i, \frac{2 \cdot \pi \cdot R_i}{mPC_i \cdot c_{min,i}}\right)\right), \tag{15}$$

$$N_{min,i} = ceil_{P_i} \left(\min \left(N_{max,i}, \frac{2 \cdot \pi \cdot R_i}{MPC_i \cdot c_{min,i}} \right) \right) . \qquad (16)$$

In these expression $floor_{P_i}()$ function is the largest integer value not greater than the argument and multiple of P_i. Function $ceil_{P_i}()$ is the smallest integer value not less than the argument and multiple of P_i.

Summarizing, it has been demonstrated than we can reduce the problem to only M DoF, which will be the number of airfoils of every row, N_i. Once N_i is known, the c_i value can be calculated from expression (14) and, in turn, the g_i value can be derived from expression (11).

3   Genetic Algorithm

Once it has been demonstrated that each design configuration is determined by a set of NumberOffs, it could be possible to perform an exhaustive search computing all the possible configurations. Using expressions (15) and (16), the number of configurations to explore will be $\prod_{i=1}^{M} (N_{max,i} - N_{min,i}) / P_i$. As it will be showed in section 4, huge numbers appear in real problems.

Due to the multiple restrictions, it is difficult to define a continuous and derivable optimization function. Therefore methods based in gradient of the optimization function are not recommended. Several characteristics of the problem makes appropriate the use of a Genetic Algorithm (GA). First of all, it is easy to transform a *Constrained Optimization Problem* (COP) into a *Free Optimization Problem* (FOP). Secondly, the optimization function is not necessary to be continuous. Thirdly, the solution codification is made easily using a numeric vector.

The first step for defining a GA is to link the *real* world to the GA world. Objects forming possible solutions within the original problem context are referred to as *phenotypes*, while their encoding are called *genotypes*. In our problem, the phenotypes are vectors of natural numbers with the NumberOff for each row. Each NumberOff only can change in the range given by (15) and (16). The encoding of each genotype is a bit string for each NumberOff. The number of bit strings will be M, one for each row. Each bit string is called a *gene*. Each gene may have a different number of bits

$$B_i = ceil_1 \left[\left(\ln \frac{N_{max,i} - N_{min,i}}{P_i} \right) / \ln 2 \right] . \qquad (17)$$

The way of decoding the genotype to the phenotype consists of obtaining the integer number n_i from the bit string. A Gray coding is used instead of the usual binary coding because of its advantages, described extensively in the literature [12]. Then, the NumberOff will be $N_i = N_{min,i} + n_i \cdot P_i$. Gaps and chords are obtained using the expressions (11) and (14). Maybe it will be necessary to modify the gaps in order to fulfill restriction (7).

As it was mentioned in section 2, equation (11) does not take into account the constraint (7). A repairing process may be necessary if, in obtaining the phenotype, g_0 does not meet that constraint. If $mG_0 \leq g_0 \leq MG_0$ the fixing is not necessary. On the other hand, if $g_0 \leq mG_0$ it is not possible to repair and the individual receives a high penalty in its fitness. If $g_0 > MG_0$ a repairing process is needed. The repairing process is made in the phenotypic space and this consists of distributing the amount $\triangle g = g_0 - MG_0$ among the the rest of the gaps maintaining the constraints $g_i \leq MGC_i \cdot c_i$.

The next step in the design process of the GA is to choose the *fitness* function. The role of the fitness function is to represent the requirements to be optimized. The fitness function implemented transforms our initial COP into a FOP. With the representation of individuals adopted, all the constraints are satisfied but (7), (8), (9) and (10). Being M the number of rows, a penalty function F_R is defined as 0 for individuals placed in the feasible regions and negative values increasing exponentially in the following way

$$F_R = \begin{cases} 1 - \exp\left(\lambda \frac{mG_0 - g_0}{L}\right) + \sum_{i=1}^{M} F_i & if\ g_0 < mG_0 \\ \sum_{i=1}^{M} F_i & if\ mG_0 \leq g_0 \leq MG_0 \\ 1 - \exp\left(\lambda \frac{g_0 - MG_0}{L}\right) + \sum_{i=1}^{M} F_i & if\ MG_0 < g_0 \end{cases}, \quad (18)$$

where g_0 is computed using expression (7). The value of constant parameter λ is used for modulating the exponential decreasing in the unfeasible regions. Its value is taken experimentally and does not have a big influence in the performance of the algorithm. F_i deals with the noise restrictions depending of the cut-off mode. For instance, for Direct cut-off mode and $i\%2 = 0$ or Reverse cut-off mode and $i\%2 = 1$:

$$F_i = \begin{cases} 1 - \exp\left[\lambda\left(\alpha_i - \frac{N_i}{N_{i+1}}\right)\right] & if\ \frac{N_i}{N_{i+1}} < \alpha_i \\ 0 & if\ \alpha_i \leq \frac{N_i}{N_{i+1}} \leq \beta_i \\ 1 - \exp\left[\lambda\left(\frac{N_i}{N_{i+1}} - \beta_i\right)\right] & if\ \beta_i < \frac{N_i}{N_{i+1}} \end{cases}. \quad (19)$$

In order to perform an simple optimization among the feasible individuals, the fitness functions is defined:

$$F_N = \begin{cases} F_R & if\ F_R < 0 \\ 1/\sum_{i=1}^{N} N_i & if\ F_R \geq 0 \end{cases}. \quad (20)$$

GA uses a population of possible solutions. The parent selection mechanism implemented here is the *tournament method*, i.e. k individuals with replacement are chosen randomly from the population and the final individual chosen will be the best of these k in terms of their fitness value. Once the parents have been selected, there is a recombination probability p_r which sets if the offspring of two parents are just a copy of the parents or a real recombination is produced. Two recombination methods have been implemented: one point crossover over the genes (called *gene crossover*) and one point crossover over the bits for each gene (*bit crossover*). Another parameter that control the algorithm is the mutation probability p_m. After doing the crossover of the parents, the offspring is mutated. The mutation is done in each gene swapping a random bit. A generational model is used, so for each generation all parents are changed by their offspring. It has been implemented the feature of elitism, swapping the worst individual after the mutation operator is applied by the best individual of the previous generation.

The initialization is made by taking a random representation of possible solutions from the design space and carrying out fitness evaluations on all the individuals.

4   Case Study and Experimental Results

The GA described in the previous section has been applied to an aeronautical LPT made up of 6 stages and an *Outlet Guide Vane* (OGV), which makes a total of 13 rows (Fig. 1). The total number of airfoils of this turbine is 1486 and its axial length is 1.225 meters. The restrictions imposed has been the same used by the design team, so the study case must be considered a real one. Only the Reverse cut-off condition is considered feasible.

Using the expressions (15) and (16), it is possible to compute the possibilities of each NumberOff. The number of possible values varies greatly between each row. The minimum number is 1 possibility for the first and last row, and the maximum value is 63 for the fourth row. Multiplying all the possibilities we obtain a total number of configurations to explore of $2.8 \cdot 10^{18}$. If we use a exhaustive search and consider that each configuration was evaluated in 10^{-6} seconds, the computing time would be 73117 years. So an exhaustive search can not be used in this case.

The parameters of the GA have been chosen by trial and error. The best results are obtained for a population of $5 \cdot 10^4$ individuals, 50 generations, $k = 5$, $p_r = 0.8$, $p_m = 0.01$, gene crossover and elitism. Due to the stochastic nature of the GA, the algorithm has been run 5 times. The average total NumberOff achieved has been 1461.4, with a standard deviation of 1.96. The best total NumberOff has been 1460. The average time needed has been 2 minutes and 22 seconds using a 2.40 GHz Intel Core Duo machine with a 4 GB of RAM memory and a operative system Linux openSUSE 10.3.

Fig. 3a shows the NumberOff for each row of the original design and the new ones obtained by the best run of the GA. Several configurations with the same total NumberOff of 1460 have been found. All these solutions are indistinguishable by the algorithm. As is clear from the interpretation of equation (20), the evolving process involves two phases: an initial stage ($F_R < 0$) dedicated to satisfying the constraints, and a second stage ($F_R \geq 0$) devoted to minimizing the total number of airfoils once the constraints are satisfied. This can be seen in Fig. 3b, where the evolution of the best fitness of the population in each run is plotted against the generation number. Fig. 3c is an enlarged view of Fig. 3b and shows the border between these two stages. More specifically, 15 to 19 generations are needed for having at least one individual that meets all the restrictions. In Fig. 3d it is showed the new real geometry in meridional plane obtained by the GA.

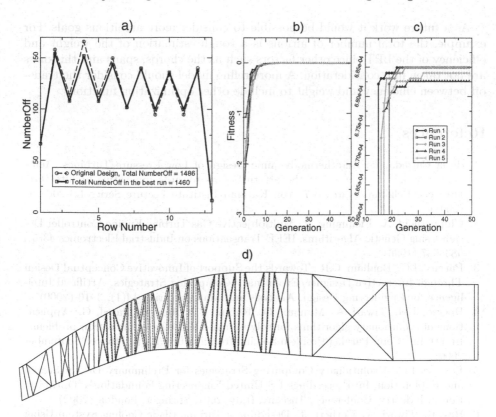

Fig. 3. Summary of experimental results: NumberOffs achieved in the best run (a), progress plots (b) and (c), where (c) shows a magnified region of (b), and optimized real geometry (continuous line) compared with the original one (dashed line) (d)

Notice that the algorithm has changed the chord and the gap of some rows in order to fulfill the constraints.

5   Conclusions and Future Work

A GA has been applied to perform the airfoil number optimization of a LPT gas turbine fulfilling a set of realistic restrictions. The turbine model used as input to the GA corresponds to the final design of a turbine made from a standard design methodology. The algorithm has reduced the total number of airfoils in 1.74%. The improvement is not bigger because the input to the GA is an already optimized final design using the same set of restrictions, so it was close to the optimum. However, from the standpoint of the real turbine design, the improvement is not negligible. With the appropriate parameters for the GA, the optimization process found the same configuration with a very low dispersion (standard deviation in the total NumberOff less than 2 blades). The time consuming of the algorithm is low, despite of dealing with a high population number.

As a future work it would be possible to consider more ambitious goals. For example, the total number of airfoils is a rough estimation of the weight and efficiency of the LPT since other factors such as the chords, spans and thickness are not taken into consideration. A more refine model should consider the trade-off between efficiency and weight to include other optimization functions.

References

1. de la Calzada, P.: Aerothermodynamic Design of Low Pressure Turbines. Aero-engine design: from state of the art turbofans towards innovative architecture, Brussels, Belgium, March 3-7. Von Karman Institute Lecture Series LS-2008-04 (2008)
2. Chipperfield, A., Flemming, P.: Multiobjective Gas Turbine Engine Controller Design Using Genetic Algorithms. IEEE Transactions on Industrial Electronics 43(5), 583–587 (1996)
3. Parmee, I.C., Bonham, C.R.: Towards the Support of Innovative Conceptual Design Through Interactive Designer/Evolutinary Computing Strategies. Artificial Intelligence for Engineering Design, Analysis and Manufacturing 14(1), 3–16 (2000)
4. Rogero, J.M., Tiwari, A., Munaux, O., Rubini, P.A., Roy, R., Jared, G.: Applications of evolutionary algorithms for solving real-life design optimisation problems. In: 6th Int. Conf. Parallel Problem Solving from Nature, Paris, France (September 2000)
5. Parmee, I.C.: Evolutionary Computing Strategies for Preliminary Design Search and Exploration. In: Proceedings US United Engineering Foundation's 'Optimisation in Industry' Conference, Tuscany, Italy, 2001. Springer, London (2002)
6. Roy, R., Tiwari, A., Corbett, J.: Designing a Turbine Blade Cooling System Using a Generalised Regression Genetic Algorithm. CIRP Annals 52(1), 415–418 (2003)
7. Angantyr, A., Aidanpaa, J.O.: A Pareto-Based Genetic Algorithm Search Approach to Handle Damped Natural Frequency Constraints in Turbo Generator Rotor System Design. J. Eng. Gas Turbines Power 126, 619 (2004), doi:10.1115/1.1760529
8. Ahuja, V., Hosangadi, A.: Design Optimization of Complex Flowfields Using Evolutionary Algorithms and Hybrid Unstructured CFD. In: 17th AIAA Computational Fluid Dynamics Conference, Toronto, Ontario, Canada, June 6-9 (2005)
9. Parrilla, M., Aranda, J., Dormido-Canto, S.: Parallel Evolutionary Computation; Application of an EA to Controller Design. In: Mira, J., Álvarez, J.R. (eds.) IWINAC 2005. LNCS, vol. 3562, pp. 153–162. Springer, Heidelberg (2005)
10. Elliott, L., Ingham, D.B., Kyne, A.G., Mera, N.S., Pourkashanian, M., Wilson, C.W.: A Novel Approach to Mechanism Reduction Optimization for an Aviation Fuel/Air Reaction Mechanism Using a Genetic Algorithm. J. Eng. Gas Turbines Power 128, 255 (2006), doi:10.1115/1.2131887
11. Varvill, R., Paniagua, G., Kato, H., Thatcher, M.: Design and Testing of the Contra-Rotating Turbine for the Scimitar precooled Mach 5 Cruise Engine. In: IAC-08-C4.5.3 (2008)
12. Eiben, A.E., Smith, J.E.: Introduction to Evolutionary Computing. Springer, Heidelberg (2007)

Branch and Bound Algorithm for a Single Vehicle Routing Problem with Toll-by-Weight Scheme

Zizhen Zhang[1], Hu Qin[1,*], Andrew Lim[1], and Songshan Guo[2]

[1] Department of Management Sciences, City University of Hong Kong,
Tat Chee Ave, Kowloon Tong, Hong Kong
{zizzhang,tigerqin,lim.andrew}@cityu.edu.hk

[2] Department of Computer Science, School of Information Science and Technology,
Sun Yat-Sen University, Guangzhou, Guangdong, PR China
issgssh@mail.sysu.edu.cn

Abstract. Most of previous studies on vehicle routing problems assume that traversal cost of each edge is simply equivalent to a constant number. Unfortunately, the models of this kind can not be applied in China because toll per kilometer of Chinese expressways varies with vehicle's weight. Motivated by rapidly increasing market of expressway transportation in China, we address a new and special vehicle routing problem that takes a single vehicle and its weight into account. To solve this problem practically, we provide a branch-and-bound algorithm with a well-designed lower bound. This algorithm can deal with any toll scheme in which toll per unit distance monotonically increases with weight. Computational results show that test instances with up to 42 vertices can be solved in reasonable computing time.

Keywords: vehicle routing problem; toll-by-weight; branch and bound.

1 Introduction

Expressway transportation has been playing an important role in promoting rapid growth of Chinese economy. By the end of 2008, China's expressway network has a total mileage of over 60,000 kilometers and its overall construction cost exceeds 240 billion US dollars. In some countries, such as Australia and United States, the majority of expressways are state-owned and toll-free. But in China, almost all of expressways are owned by for-profit corporations that raise construction funds from securities markets or banks, and recoup investments through tolls.

Tolls of Chinese expressways have been levied on basis of vehicle's type and traveling distance for a long time. This toll scheme drives transportation companies or individuals to overload their vehicles for more economic benefits and

---

* Corresponding author.

N. García-Pedrajas et al. (Eds.): IEA/AIE 2010, Part III, LNAI 6098, pp. 179–188, 2010.

accordingly leads to serious damages of expressways, dangerous driving or illegal modification of vehicles. To present a fairer method and prevent overloading, since 2003, over twenty Chinese provinces have implemented a new toll scheme, referred to as toll-by-weight, whereby expressway tolls are collected based on vehicle's weight and traveling distance. Despite the existence of various toll schemes all over the world, apart from China, few countries adopt the toll-by-weight scheme.

Most of previous studies on vehicle routing problems assume that traversal cost of each edge is simply equivalent to edge length (constant number), irrelevant to vehicle's weight [1]. Thus, one objective of these problems is to minimize the overall travel distance of single or multiple vehicles. Obviously, in China, this assumption is not reasonable because vehicle's traversal cost varies with its weight. In this paper, we investigate a new and special vehicle routing problem that takes a single vehicle and its weight into account, called the single vehicle routing problem with toll-by-weight scheme (SVRPTS). Since in more than twenty Chinese provinces all expressway transportation plans have to consider toll-by-weight schemes, the SVRPTS has innumerable applications.

2   Problem Description and Literature

The SVRPTS models the following scenario. Let $G = (V, E)$ be a complete and undirected graph, where $V = \{v_0, v_1, \ldots, v_n, v_{n+1}\}$ is the vertex set and $E = \{e_{i,j} = (v_i, v_j) : v_i, v_j \in V, i \neq j\}$ is the edge set. Vertex v_0 and v_{n+1} represent the exit from and the entrance to the depot, and $V_C = \{v_1, \ldots, v_n\}$ denotes the set of n customers. Each customer i has a demand with weight of q_i ($q_0 = q_{n+1} = 0$) to be delivered from the depot and each edge $e_{i,j}$ has a travel distance $d_{i,j}$, where distance matrix $[d_{i,j}]$ satisfies the triangularity condition. A vehicle with empty weight of Q_0 and unlimited capacity is loaded with all customer demands, $Q = \sum_{i=1}^{n} q_i$, at the depot and then successively visits each of vertices exactly once. On arriving vertex $v_i \in V_C$, the vehicle's weight is decreased by q_i to fulfill customer demand. When the vehicle passes through edge $e_{i,j}$ from v_i to v_j, its weight is denoted by $w_{i,j}$. Note that $w_{i,j} = 0$ and $w_{j,i} = 0$ if the vehicle's route does not contain edge $e_{i,j}$. Toll function $f(w)$, where w is the vehicle's weight, is applied to all graph edges for calculating transportation cost per unit distance. The traversal cost of edge $e_{i,j}$ paid by the vehicle with weight $w_{i,j}$ is calculated by $d_{i,j}f(w_{i,j})$. The objective of the problem is to find a Hamiltonian path on G, starting from v_0 and ending at vertex v_{n+1}, while minimizing the vehicle's total transportation cost.

Fig. 1 gives two typical toll functions (or schemes) in which the unit of $f(w)$ is Chinese Yuan (RMB) per kilometer and the weight unit is ton. As shown in Fig. 1(a), the tolls in Gansu province are charged directly proportional to the vehicle's weight, namely, the toll per ton per kilometer is a fixed value, 0.08 RMB. Jiangxi province uses a relatively more complex toll scheme (see Fig. 1(b)), which is expressed by the following piecewise nonlinear function:

$$f(w) = \begin{cases} 0 & \text{if } w = 0 \\ 0.4 & \text{if } 0 < w \leq 5 \\ 0.08w & \text{if } 5 < w \leq 10 \\ -0.0005w^2 + 0.07w + 0.15 & \text{if } 10 < w \leq 40 \\ 2.15 & \text{if } w > 40 \end{cases}$$

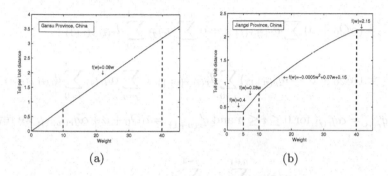

(a)   (b)

Fig. 1. (a) Linear toll function. (b) Piecewise nonlinear toll function.

Let us indicate with $r = (v_{r(0)}, v_{r(1)}, \ldots, v_{r(n)}, v_{r(n+1)})$, where $r(0) = 0$, $r(n+1) = n + 1$, a SVRPTS route on which vertex $v_{r(i)}$ $(1 \leq i \leq n)$ appears in position i. From now on, $d_{r(i),r(i+1)}$ and $w_{r(i),r(i+1)}$ represent the length and weight of edge $(v_{r(i)}, v_{r(i+1)})$, and $q_{r(i)}$ is the weight of demand at $v_{r(i)}$. The total transportation cost $z(r)$ of a given route r can be calculated by:

$$z(r) = \sum_{i=0}^{n} d_{r(i),r(i+1)} f(w_{r(i),r(i+1)}) = \sum_{i=0}^{n} d_{r(i),r(i+1)} f\left(Q_0 + \sum_{j=i+1}^{n+1} q_{r(j)}\right) \quad (1)$$

Toll function $f(w)$ can be linear, that is, $f(w) = \alpha w + \beta$, where α and β are non-negative constants. If $\alpha = 0$ and $\beta > 0$, the SVRPTS reduces to the traditional traveling salesman problem (TSP) [2], one of the most intensively studied NP-complete problems. If $\alpha > 0$ and $\beta \geq 0$, according to Proposition 1, the SVRPTS can be transformed to the minimum latency problem (MLP) [3,4,5,6,7], which is also termed the traveling repairman problem [8,9], the traveling deliveryman problem [10,11,12], and the cumulative traveling salesman problem [13]. Three types of solution approaches have been applied to the minimum latency problem, which are exact algorithms [6,8,10,11,12,13], approximation algorithms [3,4,5,7] and meta-heuristics [9].

Proposition 1. *The SVRPTS with $f(w) = \alpha w + \beta$ $(\alpha > 0, \beta \geq 0)$ is equivalent to the weighted and unweighted MLP.*

Proof. According to expression (1), for any route r, we have:

$$z(r) = \sum_{i=0}^{n} d_{r(i),r(i+1)} \left(\alpha \left(Q_0 + \sum_{j=i+1}^{n+1} q_{r(j)} \right) + \beta \right)$$

$$= (\alpha Q_0 + \beta) \sum_{i=0}^{n} d_{r(i),r(i+1)} + \alpha \sum_{i=0}^{n} d_{r(i),r(i+1)} \sum_{j=i+1}^{n+1} q_{r(j)}$$

$$= (\alpha Q_0 + \beta) \sum_{i=0}^{n} d_{r(i),r(i+1)} + \alpha \sum_{j=1}^{n+1} q_{r(j)} \sum_{i=0}^{j-1} d_{r(i),r(i+1)}$$

$$= (\alpha Q_0 + \beta + \alpha q_{r(n+1)}) \sum_{i=0}^{n} d_{r(i),r(i+1)} + \sum_{j=1}^{n} \alpha q_{r(j)} \sum_{i=0}^{j-1} d_{r(i),r(i+1)} \quad (2)$$

Letting $q'_{r(i)} = \alpha q_{r(i)}$ for $0 \leq i \leq n$ and $q'_{r(n+1)} = \alpha Q_0 + \beta + \alpha q_{r(n+1)}$, we rewrite $z(r)$ as:

$$z(r) = \sum_{j=1}^{n+1} q'_{r(j)} \sum_{i=0}^{j-1} d_{r(i),r(i+1)} \quad (3)$$

According to the definition of MLP, $z(r)$ can be viewed as the total weighted latency associated with route r, where $q'_{r(j)}$ is the weight of vertex $v_{r(j)}$. So the SVRPTS with such toll function is equivalent to the weighted MLP. As stated by [7], the weighted MLP can be further transformed to the unweighted MLP. We have therefore proved this proposition.   □

We can only find two previous articles, [14,15], that study the toll-by-weight scheme in the vehicle routing problem. Both of them apply heuristics to solve their models. As for the SVRPTS, its cases with linear toll functions have been widely investigated since they can be transformed to the TSP and the MLP. However, we can not find literature papers tackling the SVRPTS cases with nonlinear toll functions.

After in-depth analysis, we know that all Chinese provinces that have implemented toll-by-weight schemes have adopted monotonically increasing toll functions. The branch and bound algorithm proposed in this paper is the first exact approach that is able to handle the SVRPTS with any monotonically increasing toll function $f(w)$. The remainder of the paper is structured as follows. Sect. 3 introduces a lower bound of the problem, followed by the description of the branch and bound algorithm in Sect. 4. Computational results are reported in Sect. 5 and concluding remarks are discussed in Sect. 6.

3   Lower Bound

The quality of lower bound can influence the performance of the branch and bound greatly. To derive lower bound for the SVRPTS, we first present several preliminary results.

Lemma 1. *Let* $(d_0^r, \ldots, d_n^r)$, *where* $d_i^r \leq d_{i+1}^r$ *for* $0 \leq i \leq n-1$, *be increasingly sorted edge lengths of any SVRPTS route* $r = (v_{r(0)}, v_{r(1)}, \ldots, v_{r(n)}, v_{r(n+1)})$. *Given a monotonically increasing toll function* $f(w)$, *we have:*

$$z(r) = \sum_{i=0}^{n} d_{r(i),r(i+1)} f(w_{r(i),r(i+1)}) \geq \sum_{i=0}^{n} d_i^r f(w_{r(i),r(i+1)}) \qquad (4)$$

Proof. For any route r, it is obvious that $w_{r(i),r(i+1)} \geq w_{r(i+1),r(i+2)}$. And monotonically increasing toll function $f(w)$ ensures that $f(w_{r(i),r(i+1)}) \geq f(w_{r(i+1),r(i+2)})$. Thus, we have $f(w_{r(0),r(1)}) \geq f(w_{r(1),r(2)}) \geq \ldots \geq f(w_{r(n),r(n+1)})$. By the well-known *rearrangement inequality* [16], we can deduce this lemma straightforwardly. □

Lemma 2. *On a complete and undirected graph* $G = (V, E)$, *where* V *contains* n *vertices,* T *is a minimum spanning tree (MST) and* T' *is an arbitrary spanning tree. Sequence* $(d_1^T, \ldots, d_{n-1}^T)$ *and* $(d_1^{T'}, \ldots, d_{n-1}^{T'})$ *are increasingly sorted edge lengths of* T *and* T', *i.e.,* $d_i^T \leq d_{i+1}^T$ *and* $d_i^{T'} \leq d_{i+1}^{T'}$ *for* $1 \leq i \leq n-2$. *There exists* $d_i^T \leq d_i^{T'}$ *for* $1 \leq i \leq n-1$.

Proof. Letting e_i^T and $e_i^{T'}$ be the edges corresponding to d_i^T and $d_i^{T'}$, the edge sets of T and T' can be denoted by $E(T) = \{e_1^T, \ldots, e_{n-1}^T\}$ and $E(T') = \{e_1^{T'}, \ldots, e_{n-1}^{T'}\}$. According to the property of spanning tree, we know that if any $e_i^{T'} \in E(T')$ is added to T, there must exist a unique cycle $(e_i^{T'}, e_1^i, \ldots, e_{k_i}^i, e_i^{T'})$, where k_i is the number of cycle edges and $e_j^i \in E(T)$ for $1 \leq j \leq k_i$, and the length of e_j^i must be less than or equal to $d_i^{T'}$.

Construct a bipartite graph $G_B = (X, Y, E_B)$, where each vertex in X (or Y) corresponds to one edge in $E(T')$ (or $E(T)$). If e_j^T is on the cycle associated with $e_i^{T'}$, i.e., $e_j^T \in \{e_1^i, \ldots, e_{k_i}^i\}$, E_B contains an edge connecting e_j^T and $e_i^{T'}$. Take the example shown in Fig. 2 to illustrate this construction process.

Next, we will show that there exists a perfect bipartite matching on G_B. To this end, according to Hall's Theorem [17], we need to show $|N(S)| \geq |S|$ for every $S \subseteq X$, where $N(S)$ is the edge set including all elements of Y adjacent to elements of S For example, if $e_i^{T'} \in S$, $\{e_1^i, \ldots, e_{k_i}^i\} \subseteq N(S)$. Taking $V(S)$ and $V(N(S))$ to indicate the vertex sets associated with S and $N(S)$, we construct a graph $G' = (V', S)$, where $V' = V(S) \cup V(N(S))$. Obviously, this graph is a forest with $c(S)$ components, each of which may be subset of S or an isolated vertex. Since S does not contain cycles, by Corollary 3.1.8 of [18], we can deduce that $|V'| = |S| + c(S)$. In the same way, we can also construct $G'' = (V', N(S))$ and get $|V'| = |N(S)| + c(N(S))$. From the definition of $N(S)$, we can easily find that any pair of vertices connected by one edge in S must be connected by one or a couple of edges in $N(S)$ and thus $c(S) \geq c(N(S))$. Hence, we can prove $|S| \leq |N(S)|$ and each $e_i^{T'}$ can exclusively select one edge $e_j^i \in \{e_1^i, \ldots, e_{k_i}^i\}$ such that $d_i^{T'}$ is greater than or equal to the length of e_j^i.

Now we prove $d_i^T \leq d_i^{T'}$ for $1 \leq i \leq n-1$ by contradiction. Suppose $d_i^T > d_i^{T'}$. Apparently, d_i^T is at least greater than i elements in $\{d_1^{T'}, \ldots, d_{n-1}^{T'}\}$, i.e., $d_i^T >$

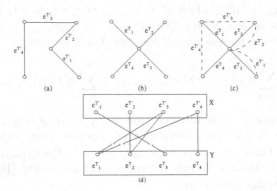

Fig. 2. (a) Spanning tree. (b) Minimum spanning tree. (c) Spanning tree (dashed lines) and minimum spanning tree. (d) Bipartite graph.

$d_i^{T'} \geq \ldots \geq d_1^{T'}$. As proved previously, each $e_i^{T'} \in E(T')$ with length $d_i^{T'}$ must exclusively have one edge $e_j^T \in E(T)$ such that $d_i^{T'} \geq d_j^T$. As a result, we can deduce that at least i elements in $\{d_1^T, \ldots, d_{n-1}^T\}$ are less than d_i^T. Nevertheless, d_i^T can only be greater than at most $i-1$ elements of $\{d_1^T, \ldots, d_{n-1}^T\}$, leading to a contradiction. Thus, d_i^T must be less than or equal to $d_i^{T'}$ for $1 \leq i \leq n-1$. □

Before continuing to the theorem, we need to define a special tree, called *minimum restricted spanning tree* (MRST).

Definition 1 (MRST). *Let $G = (V, E)$ be a complete and undirected graph, where $V = \{v_0, v_1, \ldots, v_n, v_{n+1}\}$. The MRST is constructed by first identifying the MST of $\{v_1, \ldots, v_n\}$ and then connecting vertex v_0 and v_{n+1} to their nearest neighbors on the MST.*

In MRST, the vertex v_0 and v_{n+1} are restricted to have degree of one. The reader can distinguish the MRST and MST by Fig. 3.

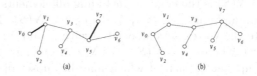

Fig. 3. (a) Minimum restricted spanning tree. (b) Minimum spanning tree.

Using the above two lemmas and the MRST, we can obtain a lower bound of the SVRPTS, which is given by the following theorem.

Theorem 1. *Let $G = (V, E)$ be a complete and undirected graph with vertex set $\{v_0, v_1, \ldots, v_n, v_{n+1}\}$. $\bar{T}$ is a MRST on G. The lengths of $\bar{T}$'s edges incident to v_0 and v_{n+1} are indicated with $d_0^{\bar{T}}$ and $d_n^{\bar{T}}$. First, sort the lengths of* *the other edges on $\bar{T}$ increasingly, thereby generating a sequence $(d_1^{\bar{T}}, \ldots, d_{n-1}^{\bar{T}})$. Then, sort the weights of customer demands in descending order and obtain a sequence $(p_1, \ldots, p_n)$, where $p_i \in \{q_1, \ldots, q_n\}$ and $p_i \geq p_{i+1}$ for $1 \leq i \leq n-1$. A polynomially computable lower bound for the SVRPTS is:*

$$LB = d_0^{\bar{T}} f(Q + Q_0) + d_n^{\bar{T}} f(Q_0) + \sum_{i=1}^{n-1} d_i^{\bar{T}} f\left(\sum_{j=i+1}^{n} p_j + Q_0 \right) \tag{5}$$

Proof. Assume r, starting from v_0 and ending at v_{n+1}, is an optimal SVRPTS route on G. After sorting all edge lengths of r, except $d_{r(0),r(1)}$ and $d_{r(n),r(n+1)}$, in ascending order, we can obtain a sequence $(d_1^r, d_2^r, \ldots, d_{n-1}^r)$. By Lemma 1, we can get:

$$z(r) = \sum_{i=0}^{n} d_{r(i),r(i+1)} f(w_{r(i),r(i+1)})$$

$$\geq d_{r(0),r(1)} f(w_{r(0),r(1)}) + \sum_{i=1}^{n-1} d_i^r f(w_{r(i),r(i+1)}) + d_{r(n),r(n+1)} f(w_{r(n),r(n+1)})$$

According to Definition 1, we know that $d_{r(0),r(1)} \geq d_0^{\bar{T}}$ and $d_{r(n),r(n+1)} \geq d_n^{\bar{T}}$. Since subroute $(v_{r(1)}, v_{r(2)}, \ldots, v_{r(n)})$ is one of spanning trees covering vertex set $\{v_1, v_2, \ldots, v_n\}$, by Lemma 2, we have $d_i^r \geq d_i^{\bar{T}}$ for $1 \leq i \leq n-1$. Subsequently, we can deduce that:

$$z(r) \geq d_0^{\bar{T}} f(w_{r(0),r(1)}) + \sum_{i=1}^{n-1} d_i^{\bar{T}} f(w_{r(i),r(i+1)}) + d_n^{\bar{T}} f(w_{r(n),r(n+1)}) \tag{6}$$

One can easily obtain that $w_{r(0),r(1)} = Q + Q_0$, $w_{r(n),r(n+1)} = Q_0$ and $w_{r(i),r(i+1)} = \sum_{j=i+1}^{n} q_j + Q_0 \geq \sum_{j=i+1}^{n} p_j + Q_0$. Since $f(w)$ is a monotonically increasing function, $f(\sum_{j=i+1}^{n} q_j + Q_0) \geq f(\sum_{j=i+1}^{n} p_j + Q_0)$. Based on the above inequalities, we can complete this proof. $\qquad\square$

4 Branch-and-Bound Algorithm

Branch-and-bound is a general technique for finding optimal solutions of various combinatorial optimization problems. In our branch-and-bound algorithm, the upper bound of the SVRPTS is firstly generated by the meta-heuristics described in [15] and then updated during the search process. Fig. 4 shows the branch-and-bound search tree. Usually, "vertex" and "node" have the same meaning and are interchangeable. But, in this paper, we specify that "vertex" represents joint point in graph G and "node" is used for search tree. The search tree is explored according to a depth-first policy while the best-first policy is applied to the unexplored nodes at the same tree level.

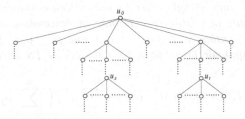

Fig. 4. Branch and bound search tree

Given a node u_s at level m of the tree, we can easily identify its path to the root. This path is essentially a partial route of the SVRPTS, denoted by $r_s = (v_{r_s(0)}, \ldots, v_{r_s(m-1)}, v_{r_s(m)})$, where $u_0 = v_{r_s(0)}$ and $u_s = v_{r_s(m)}$. The subproblem related to node u_s is also a SVRPTS with vertex set $V - \{v_{r_s(0)}, \ldots, v_{r_s(m-1)}\}$, starting from $v_{r_s(m)}$ and ending at v_{n+1}. The lower bound LB_s associated with node u_s is the sum of the transportation cost on r_s and the lower bound of its subproblem. If LB_s is greater than or equal to the current upper bound, all complete routes sharing r_s can be fathomed, that is, node u_s can be pruned, and the search procedure can backtrack to another part of the tree. Otherwise, we continue to branch and choose the children node of u_s that has the best lower bound.

In addition to lower bound pruning, one tree node can also be eliminated from consideration by dominance pruning. Let us consider two nodes u_s and u_t at a certain level of the tree as well as their paths r_s and r_t. Assuming r_s and r_t contain the same set of customers and end at the same customer, it is well-known that if the transportation cost on r_s is less than that on r_t, u_t is dominated by u_s and can be eliminated from the search tree. Therefore, before calculating the lower bound of each tree node u_s, we fix u_0, u_s and employ an $O(n^2)$ heuristics to check permutations of other customers on r_s. Therefore, before calculating the lower bound of each tree node u_s, we employ an $O(n^2)$ heuristics to check whether this node can be dominated by other nodes.

5   Computational Experiments

The algorithm described in this paper was coded in C++ and all experiments were run on a DELL laptop with 2.40 GHz Intel Duo CPU, 4Gb memory and Windows Vista. Computational times reported here were in CPU seconds on this machine.

We generated 15 test instances for the SVRPTS from TSPLIB and VRPLIB files: *ulysses16, ulysses22, gr24, fri26, bayg29, bays29, dantzig42, swiss42, E021, E022, E023, E030, E033, E036, E041*, which can be accessed at: http://www.iwr.uni-heidelberg.de/groups/comopt/software/TSPLIB95/ tsp/ and http://www.or.deis.unibo.it/research_pages/ORinstances/ VRPLIB/VRPLIB.html. Our test instances only use the vertex location information in these files and the first vertex is designated to be the depot. The distance unit and weight unit are assumed to be kilometer and ton, respectively. The weight Q_0 of empty vehicle was set to 5 and the demanding weight q_i of each vertex was randomly generated from the uniform distribution in the interval $[0.8, 1.2]$. Experiments were conducted under both toll schemes of Gansu and Jiangxi province that have been described in Sect. 2.

In Table 1, we report computational results for our branch-and-bound algorithm. The first column contains names of the TSPLIB and VRPLIB files. The other columns are divided into two blocks, corresponding to two toll schemes. Each block contains the following information: the optimal objective value (Value), the computing time (Time), the number of explored nodes in the search tree (Nodes), and the ratio of the lower bound to the optimal objective value (Ratio). From this table, we can see that instances with up to 33 vertices can be easily handled. For the instances with over 40 vertices, the computing time and the number of explored nodes increase explosively. The values in column "Time" of Gansu toll scheme is less than that of Jiangxi toll scheme. The reason of this phenomenon is highly probable that the non-linear toll function implemented by Jiangxi province makes instances harder.

Table 1. Experimental results for the branch-and-bound algorithm

Cases	Gansu Toll Scheme				Jiangxi Toll Scheme			
	Value (RMB)	Time(s)	Nodes	Ratio (%)	Value (RMB)	Time(s)	Nodes	Ratio (%)
ulysses16	57.57	0.09	14,556	61.32	54.36	0.10	23,727	62.79
ulysses22	68.20	2.87	229,467	58.82	62.01	4.03	351,701	61.00
gr24	1,517.33	1.17	37,514	76.37	1,333.97	1.48	47,932	77.08
fri26	1,150.24	0.75	18,127	80.16	978.71	0.86	16,015	82.14
bayg29	2,295.62	25.19	574,736	76.34	1,949.36	50.30	1,205,874	76.88
bays29	2,857.27	76.41	1,925,966	71.18	2,411.19	108.84	2,780,570	72.34
dantzig42	1,176.87	644.90	4,263,222	74.95	925.85	1,728.64	12,361,548	77.16
swiss42	2,227.24	649.66	4,737,059	75.54	1,749.90	2,437.59	20,244,906	77.36
E021	298.50	0.06	2,308	82.69	265.95	0.07	2,886	83.89
E022	329.46	0.14	5,496	75.76	290.40	0.14	5,869	78.06
E023	512.93	0.10	3,370	72.95	454.74	0.11	3,545	75.05
E030	525.44	4.81	134,385	64.18	439.98	5.81	170,468	67.33
E033	582.85	3.58	37,158	75.51	481.72	7.40	81,044	76.81
E036	575.21	179.77	2,176,065	82.18	465.95	308.09	4,011,228	83.07
E041	657.87	476.92	3,913,325	83.72	512.49	972.57	8,714,554	85.06

6 Conclusions

Motivated by the toll-by-weight schemes implemented by over twenty Chinese provinces, we propose a single vehicle routing problem in which transportation cost per unit distance monotonically increases with the vehicle's weight. This problem is a new variant of traditional vehicle routing problem and has been studied by few researchers. The branch-and-bound algorithm described in this paper is the first exact algorithm for the problem and is capable of solving to optimality all instances with up to 42 vertices. The study of toll-by-weight scheme in the vehicle routing problem has huge growing space because of its scarceness in the literature and also its wide application in China.

References

1. Toth, P., Vigo, D. (eds.): The vehicle routing problem. SIAM, Philadelphia (2002)
2. Gutin, G., Punnen, A. (eds.): The Traveling Salesman Problem and Its Variations. Kluwer Academic Publishers, Dordrecht (2002)
3. Blum, A., Chalasani, P., Coppersmith, D., Pulleyblank, B., Raghavan, P., Sudan, M.: The minimum latency problem. In: Proceedings of the twenty-sixth annual ACM symposium on Theory of computing (STOC 1994), Montreal, Quebec, Canada, pp. 163–171 (1994)
4. Goemans, M., Kleinberg, J.: An improved approximation ratio for the minimum latency problem. Mathematical Programming 82(1-2), 111–124 (1998)
5. Arora, S., Karakostas, G.: Approximation schemes for minimum latency problems. SIAM Journal on Computing 32(5), 1317–1337 (2003)
6. Wu, B., Huang, Z., Zhan, F.: Exact algorithms for the minimum latency problem. Information Processing Letter 92(6), 303–309 (2004)
7. Archer, A., Levin, A., Williamson, D.: A faster, better approximation algorithm for the minimum latency problem. SIAM Journal on Computing 37(5), 1472–1498 (2008)
8. García, A., Jodrá, P., Tejel, J.: A note on the traveling repairman problem. Networks 40(1), 27–31 (2002)
9. Salehipour, A., Sörensen, K., Goos, P., Bräysy, O.: An efficient grasp+vnd metaheuristic for the traveling repairman problem. Working papers, University of Antwerp, Faculty of Applied Economics (2008)
10. Minieka, E.: The delivery man problem on a tree network. Annals of Operations Research 18(1-4), 261–266 (1989)
11. Fischetti, M., Laporte, G., Martello, S.: The delivery man problem and cumulative matroids. Operations Research 41(6), 1055–1064 (1993)
12. Méndez-Díaz, I., Zabala, P., Lucena, A.: A new formulation for the traveling deliveryman problem. Discrete Applied Mathematics 156(17), 3223–3237 (2008)
13. Bianco, L., Mingozzi, A., Ricciardelli, S.: The traveling salesman problem with cumulative costs. Networks 23(2), 81–91 (1993)
14. Chen, X., Li, J., Fan, Y., Wu, Y., Ding, L.: Design and implementation of vehicle routing optimization system based on toll-by-weight. Manufacture Information Engineering of China 17, 69–72 (2007)
15. Shen, C., Qin, H., Lim, A.: A capacitated vehicle routing problem with toll-by-weight rule. In: Chien, B., Hong, T. (eds.) Opportunities and Challenges for Next-Generation Applied Intelligence. Studies in Computational Intelligence, vol. 214, pp. 311–316. Springer, Heidelberg (2009)
16. Hardy, G., Littlewood, J., Pólya, G.: Inequalities. Cambridge University Press, Cambridge (1988)
17. Hall, P.: On representatives of subsets. Journal of London Mathematical Society 10, 26–30 (1935)
18. Gross, J., Yellen, J. (eds.): Graph Theorey and Its Applications. Chapman and Hall/CRC (2005)

Near Optimal Secret Sharing for Information Leakage Maximization

Frank Yeong-Sung Lin, Kuo-Chung Chu, Pei-Yu Chen, and Guan-Wei Chen

Department of Information Management National Taiwan University
Taipei, Taiwan, R.O.C.
yslin@im.ntu.edu.tw, kcchu@ntcn.edu.tw, d96006@im.ntu.edu.tw,
r96037@im.ntu.edu.tw

Abstract. In this paper, we propose a mathematical programming model to describe an offense-defense scenario. In the offense problem, the objective of attackers is to compromise nodes in order to steal information. Therefore, the attackers try to recover secrets through compromising certain nodes and to maximize the information leakage as much as possible. During the attack actions, the attacker must allocate a limited budget to collect a large enough number of shares and decrypted keys through compromising certain nodes. Therefore, we advocate Lagrangean Relaxation algorithms and the proposed heuristics to find a near optimal solution. Through solutions from the perspective of the attacker, we then induce some efficient defense mechanisms for the network operators.

Keywords: Optimization, Lagrangean Relaxation, Resource Allocation, Network Planning, Secret Sharing, Information Security, Reliability, Survivability.

1 Introduction

The rapid growth of the Internet has made many individuals, schools and enterprises generate a great deal of demands, and how to share the information has securely become an important issue. However, rapid upgrades in technology still bring a negative side effect: computer crimes also increase rapidly [1]. Hackers engage in cyber crime by applying a variety of tools, such as injecting worms or using backdoor programs for web phishing, to steal information for fun or gaining benefits, . These cyber-crime events have already been urgent problems for a while and have caused serious damage to network security, especially regarding information leakage. In fact, sometimes the cyber crimes happen without anyone noticing until attackers announce or publicize the stolen information. Typically, an information system is a "Survivable Storage System" and should provide continuous service for each legitimate user even if the system suffers from intentional attacks or natural accidents. People access necessary data and information through digital storages frequently so that the confidentiality, reliability, availability, integrity of the data storage devices must be considered as a very important aspect of information security.

N. García-Pedrajas et al. (Eds.): IEA/AIE 2010, Part III, LNAI 6098, pp. 189–198, 2010.

In this manner, the combinative method of secret sharing [3] and replication mechanisms [4] achieves the goal of information security, and it provides users with the ability of increasing degrees of security to store critical information to ensure its persistence, continuous accessibility, indestructibility, and confidentiality [5].However, there is a tradeoff between the depth and the width of deployment to process the secret sharing scheme, such as the greater system security would result in the less availability of information when it is needed. Whoever can obtain a large enough number of shares and the corresponding decrypted key may recover the secret.

In an offense scenario, assuming the attacker is extremely skilled, he will always find the most efficient way to maximize system damage. For example, he will know which node contains what kind of shares and decrypted keys, and he will consider the nodal capability and the benefit on this node to decide whether to compromise it or not. If the attacker gets more than the threshold number of shares, he can cause serious damage to both reputation and profit. To access more information, the attacker must choose the best ratio of the attack cost to benefit gained because the budget is finite. Even though a lot of drawbacks and risks exist in networks, most enterprises still store and share data and information by means of the network system. Some problems, for example, derive from information backups, recoveries, and the sharing of information between legitimate users, while we deal with these problems then try to keep the information more secure. It is quite important to incorporate the optimal protection parameters into the defense optimization problem [6]. However, there are few researches that discuss system performance and the offense-defense scenarios in mathematical ways. Therefore, we propose a mathematical model, called the Attack Target Selecting Strategy (ATSS). The objective of this model is to recover the secret information and maximize the total damage.

The remainder of this paper is organized as follows. In next section, a mathematical formulation of the offense-defense scenario is proposed. The proposed solution approach which is based on the Lagrangean Relaxation method is presented after the problem formulation. Then we discuss the computational results and implications. Finally, the last section discusses conclusions and future works from this research.

2 Problem Formulation

Business enterprises have a lot of sensitive information and business secrets, such as customer data or core knowledge. If the information leakage occurs, the victims can lose competitive advantages and perhaps even lead to loss of reputation. Therefore, enterprises must adopt multiple mechanisms to reduce the impact of information leakage. One such mechanism is that information should be encrypted before applying a secret sharing scheme so as to further enhance confidentiality. In this case, the attacker and users must obtain enough shares and decrypted keys if they want to recover the secret to the defense capability to avoid a waste of attack cost, to compromise a node and cause information leakage,

The network we discussed is an Autonomous-System (AS) level Internet. Topology is an undirected graph, in which the nodes are connected by an undirected link, and each node represents a domain and each link represents the inter-domain connection. The attacker outside the AS must enter into the AS through compromising the entry node and compromise nodes step-by-step in the targeted network. Furthermore, the attacker constructs the attack tree or path from his initial position to the target node where all intermediate nodes on the path or tree must be compromised.

2.1 Problem Formulation of the ATSS Model

The problem of attacker behavior is formulated as a mathematical programming problem. The given parameters and decision variables are defined in Table 1 and Table 2, respectively.

Table 1. Given Parameters

Notation	Description
N_1	The index set of all actual nodes
L_1	The index set of all candidate links
W	The index set of all Origin-Destination (O-D) pairs for attack
P_w	The index set of all candidate paths for (O-D) pair w, where $w \in W$
δ_{pl}	The indicator function, which is 1 if the link or the node l is on path p, and 0 otherwise (where $l \in N_1 \cup L_1$, $p \in p_w$)
Ω_l	1 if link l is selected to implement, and 0 otherwise (where $l \in L_1$)
V	The index set of all sensitive information
m_v	The share index of the secret v, where $v \in V$
α_{imv}	1 if the node i stores shares of index m, and 0 otherwise (where $i \in N_1, m \in m_v, v \in V$)
η_{iv}	1 if the node i stores the decrypted key of the secret v, and 0 otherwise (where $i \in N_1, v \in V$)
S_v	Damage incurred by leaking at least k_v pieces of the secret v and the corresponding decrypted key, where $v \in V$
k_v	The threshold number of shares required to recover the secret v, where $v \in V$
$\bar{a}_i(b_i)$	The threshold of the attack cost leads to a successful attack, where $i \in N_1$
A	The total attack budget of attacker

Table 2. Decision Variables

Notation	Description
a_i	The attack budget allocated to compromise the node, where $i \in N_1$
Z_v	1 if both k_v shares and the key are stolen and 0 otherwise (where $v \in V$)
x_p	1 if path p is selected as the attack path; and 0 otherwise, where $p \in p_w$
y_i	1 if node i is attacked, and 0 otherwise (where $i \in N_1$)

The objective of an attacker is to maximize damage through compromising nodes and then obtaining the essential shares. In this problem, the attacker must use a finite budget to recover maximal damage in the targeted network. Hence, we model this problem as an optimization problem called the ATSS Model. The formulation is shown as follows.

Objective function:

$$\underset{Z_v,y_i,a_i,x_p}{Max} \quad (\sum_{v \in V} S_v Z_v), \qquad\qquad\qquad\qquad\qquad\qquad\qquad \text{IP 1}$$

Subject to:

$$\sum_{p \in P_w} x_p = y_i \qquad\qquad\qquad \forall i \in N_1, w = (o,i) \qquad\qquad \text{IP 1.1}$$

$$\sum_{p \in P_w} x_p \leq 1 \qquad\qquad\qquad \forall w \in W \qquad\qquad\qquad\qquad \text{IP 1.2}$$

$$x_p = 0 \ or \ 1 \qquad\qquad\qquad \forall p \in P_w, w \in W \qquad\qquad \text{IP 1.3}$$

$$y_i = 0 \ or \ 1 \qquad\qquad\qquad \forall i \in N_1 \qquad\qquad\qquad\qquad \text{IP 1.4}$$

$$\sum_{w \in W}\sum_{p \in P_w} x_p \delta_{pi} \leq (|N_1|-1)y_i \qquad \forall i \in N_1 \qquad\qquad\qquad\qquad \text{IP 1.5}$$

$$\sum_{p \in P_w} x_p \delta_{pl} \leq \Omega_l \qquad\qquad \forall l \in L_1, w \in W \qquad\qquad \text{IP 1.6}$$

$$\sum_{i \in N_1} a_i \leq A \qquad\qquad\qquad\qquad\qquad\qquad\qquad\qquad\qquad \text{IP 1.7}$$

$$0 \leq a_i \leq \hat{a}_i(b_i) \qquad\qquad\qquad \forall i \in N_1 \qquad\qquad\qquad\qquad \text{IP 1.8}$$

$$\hat{a}_i(b_i)y_i \leq a_i \qquad\qquad\qquad \forall i \in N_1 \qquad\qquad\qquad\qquad \text{IP 1.9}$$

$$k_v Z_v \leq \sum_{m \in m_v}\sum_{i \in N_1}(\alpha_{imv}y_i) \qquad \forall v \in V \qquad\qquad\qquad\qquad \text{IP 1.10}$$

$$Z_v \leq \sum_{i \in N_1} \eta_{iv} y_i \qquad\qquad\qquad \forall v \in V \qquad\qquad\qquad\qquad \text{IP 1.11}$$

$$Z_v = 0 \ or \ 1 \qquad\qquad\qquad \forall v \in V. \qquad\qquad\qquad\qquad \text{IP 1.12}$$

The attacker chooses the attack path to reach the target i, and the intermediate nodes that are all compromised are determined in Constraint (IP 1.1) to Constraint (IP 1.5). Constraint (IP 1.6) restricts the attack path p which must be constructed on the implemented link. The attacker thus allocates his budget to compromise the node. And Constraint (IP 1.7) to Constraint (IP 1.9) are constrains about the allocated budget to compromise the node of attackers. Constraint (IP 1.10) to Constraint (IP 1.12) jointly enforce that the attacker doesn't cause the information damage S_u unless he gets the decrypted key and reveals the threshold k_u of shares by compromising the nodes.

3   Solution Approach

3.1   The Lagrangean Relaxation-Based Algorithm

In this section, the Lagrangean Relaxation method [7] is applied to solve the ATSS model. First, complicating constraints are relaxed by being multiplied with the corresponding Lagrangean multipliers, the product of which is then added to the primal objective function, and then the LR problem is generated. Second, the LR problem is decomposed into four subproblems according to the decision variables. Each subproblem adopts the well-known algorithm to solve it optimally and easily. More detailed procedures about the proposed model are described in the following sections.

3.2 The Lagrangean Relaxation Problem

In the ATSS Model, we relax Constraint (IP 1.1), (IP 1.5), (IP 1.9), (IP 1.10), and (IP 1.11). The model is transformed to an optimization (LR 1). More details about (LR 1) is shown below.

Optimization problem:

$$Z_D(\mu_1,\mu_2,\mu_3,\mu_4,\mu_5) = \min_{Z_v,y_i,a_i,x_p} -\sum_{v \in V} S_v Z_v + \sum_{i \in N_1} \mu_i^1 \{ \sum_{p \in P(o,i)} x_p - y_i \}$$

$$+\sum_{i \in N_1} \mu_i^2 \{ \sum_{w \in W} \sum_{p \in P_w} x_p \delta_{pi} - (|N_1|-1)y_i \} + \sum_{i \in N_1} \mu_i^3 \{ \hat{a}_i(b_i)y_i - a_i \} \qquad \text{LR 1}$$

$$+\sum_{v \in V} \mu_v^4 \{ k_v Z_v - \sum_{m \in m_v} \sum_{i \in N_1} \alpha_{imv} y_i \} + \sum_{v \in V} \mu_v^5 \{ Z_v - \sum_{i \in N_1} \eta_{iv} y_i \},$$

Subject to (IP 1.2) to (IP 1.4), (IP 1.6) to (IP 1.8)and (IP 1.11) to (IP 1.12)

Subproblem 1 (related to decision variable x_p)

$$Z_{Sub\,1}(\mu_1,\mu_2) = \min\{\sum_{i \in N_1} \sum_{p \in P(o,i)} \mu_i^1 x_p + \sum_{i \in N_1} \sum_{w \in W} \sum_{p \in P_w} \mu_i^2 x_p \delta_{pi}\}, \qquad \text{Sub 1}$$

Subject to (IP 1.2), (IP 1.3) and (IP 1.6)

In subproblem 1, we arrange the problem (Sub 1) as Equation (1).

$$Z_{Sub\,1}(\mu_1,\mu_2) = \min \sum_{w \in W} \sum_{p \in P_w} [\sum_{j \in N_1} \mu_j^2 \delta_{pj} + \mu_i^1] x_p. \qquad (1)$$

To reduce the complexity, subproblem 1 is then decomposed in into |W| problems, which are all independent shortest path problems. We individually determine the value of x_p for each O-D pair w. In this problem, Dijkstra's minimum cost shortest path algorithm is applied the to solve it, and time complexity is $O(|N_1|^2)$.

Subproblem 2 (related to decision variable Z_u)

$$Z_{Sub\,2}(\mu_4,\mu_5) = \min\{-\sum_{v \in V} S_v Z_v + \sum_{v \in V} \mu_v^4 k_v Z_v + \sum_{v \in V} \mu_v^5 Z_v\}, \qquad \text{Sub 2}$$

Subject to (IP 1.12)

In Subproblem 2, we arrange (Sub 2) as Equation (2), and decompose it into |v| independent subproblems, where we decide the value of Z_u of the secret u.

$$Z_{Sub\,2}(\mu_4,\mu_5) = \min \sum_{v \in V}(-S_v + \mu_v^4 k_v + \mu_v^5) Z_v. \qquad (2)$$

If $(-S_v + \mu_v^4 k_v + \mu_v^5)$ is non-positive, the value of Z_u must be set to one for each sensitive information because of the minimum problem, and zero otherwise. The time complexity of (Sub 2) is $O(|v|)$.

Subproblem 3 (related to decision variable y_i)

$$Z_{Sub\,3}(\mu_1,\mu_2,\mu_3,\mu_4,\mu_5)$$

$$= \min \sum_{i \in N_1} \mu_i^1(-y_i) + \sum_{i \in N_1} -\mu_i^2(|N_1|-1)y_i) + \sum_{i \in N_1} \mu_i^3(\hat{a}_i(b_i)y_i) \qquad \text{Sub 3}$$

$$+\sum_{v \in V} \sum_{m \in m_v} \sum_{i \in N_1}(-\mu_v^4 \cdot \alpha_{imv} y_i) + \sum_{v \in V} \sum_{i \in N_1} -\mu_v^5 \eta_{iv} y_i,$$

Subject to (IP 1.1)

The same concept is presented above, and accordingly the (Sub 3) is reformed as Equation (3).

$$Z_{\text{Sub 3}}(\mu_1,\mu_2,\mu_3,\mu_4,\mu_5) = \min \sum_{i\in N_i}\{-\mu_i^1 - \mu_i^2(|N_i|-1) + \mu_i^3(\bar{a}_i(b_i)) + \sum_{v\in V}(\sum_{m\in m_v}(-\mu_v^4\alpha_{imv})-\mu_v^5\eta_{iv})\}y_i. \tag{3}$$

Then we can further decompose $Z_{\text{Sub 3}}$ in Equation (3) into $|N_I|$ independent subproblems. We must determine the value of y_i of the actual node $i \in N_I$. Since this is a minimum problem, we set one if the coefficient of y_i are non-positive, zero otherwise. The exhausting search algorithm is applied to solve this subproblem. The time complexity of (Sub 3) is $O(|N_I||v||m_u|)$.

Subproblem 4 (related to decision variable a_i)

$$Z_{\text{Sub 4}}(\mu_3) = \min \sum_{i\in N_i}-\mu_i^3 a_i,$$

Sub 4

Subject to(IP 1.7) and (IP 1.8)

Although (Sub 4) traditionally minimizes negative loss rather than maximizes positive profit, it can be viewed as a fractional knapsack problem. First, we use the parameter $-\mu_i^3$ as the weight of the artificial link, and then sort each actual node $i \in N_I$ by weight in ascending order. Second, we allocate the value of a_i to $a_i(b_i)$ from the smallest $-\mu_i^3$ to the biggest one until the sum of allocated a_i equals or exceeds A; if the last a_i is insufficient to set $a_i(b_i)$, the last a_i is set to the value of the sum of a_i subtracted from A. The time complexity of this problem is $O(|N_I|^2)$.

3.3 Getting Primal Feasible Solutions

We get the lower bound (LB) of the primal problem after solving the LR problem and further use a multiplier to adjust the original algorithm to the LR-based modified heuristic algorithm to obtain the upper bound (UB). We try to derive the tightest gap between the UB and LB with the proposed heuristic, so we iteratively use the subgradient technique to adjust the multipliers as good as possible. The basic concept of the LR-based heuristic we propose here is to extract X_p's value from the subproblem as the candidate attack path and compromise all nodes on these paths. Here, we calculate the node weight, which reflects the ratio of the attack cost to the profit gained. The smaller the node weight is, the more attractive it is to attackers. The node weight is recalculated continually according to the condition of secrets. This mechanism assists the attacker to cause information leakage more effectively.

If attack costs exceed budget, the attacker chooses the largest node weight to remove its attack cost until the attack cost is feasible. The objective of the procedure is to reserve the maximal profit on this attack tree and to abandon relatively worthless nodes. On the other hand, if the attack cost is smaller than budget, it means the attacker still has some budget to allocate. However, what differs from before is that we set the compromised nodes' weight to zero here. The resulting node weight is considered the cost to implement Prim's Algorithm, and then each node's path weight from the attacker's initial position can be known. For each unrecovered secret, we sum up the weight of the paths until the secret can be recovered, and set the smallest weight to be the targeted secret. Therefore, the attacker will attack uncompromised nodes on chosen paths to recover the targeted secret. The procedure for choosing the to-be-recovered target and constructing the attack path to unify the attack tree is repeated until the attacker has no attack power to compromise any other path.

4 Computation Experiments

4.1 Experiment Environment

To measure the effect of different damage value distributions for the attacker, we design three different patterns of damage value in this paper. The first is uniform distribution, which is the scope of the information value, from two to twelve, and there are the same secret numbers in each different level; the second is the normal distribution, which the damage value pattern is normally distributed, with a mean of 7 and a standard deviation of 1.6667; the third is the deterministic distribution, whose secret damage is the same, meaning each secret is equally important.

We also design the different number of users to measure the vulnerability. The greater the number of legitimate users that exist, the greater the reliability network operators must guarantee. Furthermore, there are three budget allocation strategies, denoted B1, B2 and B3. B1 is a uniform-based budget allocation, where for each node we allocate the same defense budget. B2 is a degree-based budget allocation, where we allocate the defense budget according to the percentage that the degree number of the node is over the total degree of the network. B3 is a share-count-based budget allocation, where we allocate the defense budget depending on how many shares and decrypted keys the node contains. The network size consists of 25, 64, 100 nodes in each scenario. The defense capability function is defined as a concave form, $2 log(6b_i+1)+\varepsilon$, where b_i is the budget allocated to node i.

4.2 Computation Experiments with the ATSS Model

To evaluate whether the performance of our proposed heuristic algorithm is effective we implement two simple algorithms for comparisons, denoted SA1 and SA2. The concept of SA1 depends on the current condition of the secret to determine which node with the smallest weight has the highest priority to be compromised. SA1 creates the Next_Attack_candidate to record the set of the neighborhood of the attack tree, and all nodes in the Next_Attack_candidate are the candidate targets. After setting the weight of the node, we apply the greedy algorithm to construct an attack tree from the attacker's initial position. The procedure is repeated until the attack budget is exhausted. The total computational complexity of the is $O(|N_I|^3)$. Briefly, the main idea of SA1 arises from the intention of the attacker to compromise nodes with the smallest weight to obtain the most beneficial effect.

The fundamental concept of SA2 is derived from the LR-based heuristic. First, the sum of paths with the smallest weight is chosen, which is set as the target to be recovered in terms of the state of all secrets. Second, for each unrecovered secret, we sum the weight of the first k_u th path, whose nodes contain shares and the decrypted key, and then sort the unrecovered secrets by the weights in ascending order. Third, we set the secret with the smallest weight of the sum of paths as the target, meaning that it obtains the most beneficial effect. Finally, the uncompromised nodes on the chosen path must be compromised if the attack budget is sufficient. The procedure is repeated until the attack budget is exhausted or all secrets are already checked, and the computational complexity of SA2 is $O(|N_I||v^2||m_u|)$.The experiment result is shown in Fig. 1 to Fig. 4. The discussions and implications of the experiment are in the next section.

4.3 Discussion of Results

From Fig. 1 to Fig. 3, the target network with the B3 strategy is the least vulnerable and the most robust in all cases. It performs more successfully than the other strategies since the defense resource is allocated according to the importance of each node. The more shares and keys that a node contains, the higher probability of it is chosen as targets by attackers. With the growth of the network, the difference between B1, B2 and B3 increase significantly for each damage value distribution. The attacker could choose more targets so that the influence of wrong defense allocation would be magnified for network vulnerability.

The trend of network vulnerability rises if the system must provide more users with QoS requirements. Take Deterministic distribution as an example. All damage value is system reliability being achieved to a certain level; the network operator must transfer some budget from defense budget. For each damage value distribution, the decision of the attacker is equally important, so the attacker chooses the targets according to the kind of shares and obtained keys. Fig. 4 illustrates the network vulnerability of our proposed algorithm is always higher than SA1 and SA2 among damage value distributions. Clearly, the proposed heuristics provide a better solution than SA1and SA2.

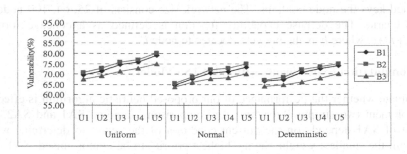

Fig. 1. The Network Vulnerability under Different Numbers of Users ($|N_I|$= 25)

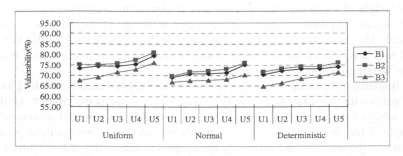

Fig. 2. The Network Vulnerability under Different Numbers of Users ($|N_I|$= 64)

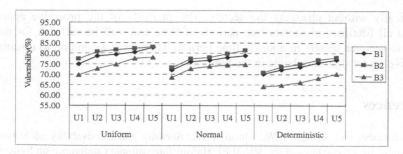

Fig. 3. The Network Vulnerability under Different Numbers of Users ($|N_l|$= 100)

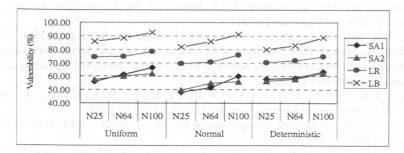

Fig. 4. Vulnerability of Different Network Sizes and Damage Distributions

5 Conclusion

In our paper, we assist defenders by constructing a robust network topology for users and minimize the vulnerability caused by information leakage. From the experiment results, the guideline of shares and decrypted keys distribution strategies increase the separation of shares in terms of the single secret and to differentiate the share patterns among nodes; the discipline of topology adjustment is to set the average degree of each node to the least and the same numbers rather than form of rendezvous points considering the concept of defense-in-depth; the best strategy is to allocate resources on relatively attractive nodes for attackers.

The main contribution of this paper is to characterize complicated attack behaviors and real-world network strategies through mathematical models. In addition, we obtain clues from Lagrangean Relaxation procedures and exploit our heuristics to find a near optimal solution. Network operators can achieve the tradeoff between the confidentiality and availability with secret sharing and replication mechanisms. The concept of defense-in-depth is considered in our paper so that the network vulnerability is reduced as a whole in terms of a holistic view. Through the experiment results, we could induce multiple defense mechanisms that were actually more efficient than a single defense mechanism. In this paper, we assume the attacker collects shares and decrypted keys to reveal secrets without time limitation. However, this would be insufficient for evaluating the survivability. To enhance security further, the proactive secret sharing scheme is advocated [8], where shares and decrypted keys are renewed periodically without changing the secrets. The property of the proactive approach divided all lifetimes of secrets into periods of time and will be difficult for the attacker to recover secrets in a single time period. Therefore, we intend to discuss the proactive secret sharing scheme in the future.

References

1. Azadmanesh, A., Krings, A.W., Oman, P.W.: Security and Survivability of Networked Systems. In: Proceedings of the 38th IEEE Hawaii International Conference on System Sciences (2005)
2. Al-Kuwaiti, M., Kyriakopoulos, N., Hussein, S.: Network Dependability, Fault-tolerance, Reliability, Security, Survivability. In: A Framework for Comparative Analysis. The George Washington University (2006)
3. Shamir, A.: How to Share a Secret. Massachusetts Institute of Technology (1979)
4. Subbiah, A., Blough, D.M.: An Approach for Fault Tolerant and Secure Data Storage in Collaborative Work Environments. School of Electrical and Computer Engineering Georgia Institute of Technology (2005)
5. Ganger, G.R., Kiliççöte, H., Strunk, J.D., Wylie, J.J., Bigrigg, M.W., Khosla, P.K.: Survivable Information Storage Systems. Garnegie Mellon University (2000)
6. Levitin, G.: Optimal Defense Strategy against Intentional Attacks. IEEE Transactions on Reliability 56(1) (2007)
7. Fisher, M.L.: An Application Oriented Guide to Lagrangean Relaxation. Interfaces 15(2), 10–21 (1985)
8. Herzberg, A., Krawczyk, H., Yung, M., Jarecki, S.: Proactive Secret Sharing or How to Cope with Perpetual Leakage. IBM T.J. Watson Research Center (1995)

Solving Non-Stationary Bandit Problems by Random Sampling from Sibling Kalman Filters

Ole-Christoffer Granmo and Stian Berg

Department of ICT, University of Agder, Grimstad, Norway

Abstract. The multi-armed bandit problem is a classical optimization problem where an agent sequentially pulls one of multiple arms attached to a gambling machine, with each pull resulting in a random reward. The reward distributions are unknown, and thus, one must balance between exploiting existing knowledge about the arms, and obtaining new information. Dynamically changing (non-stationary) bandit problems are particularly challenging because each change of the reward distributions may progressively degrade the performance of any fixed strategy.

Although computationally intractable in many cases, Bayesian methods provide a standard for optimal decision making. This paper proposes a novel solution scheme for bandit problems with non-stationary normally distributed rewards. The scheme is inherently Bayesian in nature, yet avoids computational intractability by relying simply on updating the hyper parameters of sibling Kalman Filters, and on random sampling from these posteriors. Furthermore, it is able to track the better actions, thus supporting non-stationary bandit problems.

Extensive experiments demonstrate that our scheme outperforms recently proposed bandit playing algorithms, not only in non-stationary environments, but in stationary environments also. Furthermore, our scheme is robust to inexact parameter settings. We thus believe that our methodology opens avenues for obtaining improved novel solutions.

Keywords: Bandit Problems, Kalman Filter, Bayesian Learning.

1 Introduction

The conflict between exploration and exploitation is a well-known problem in reinforcement learning, and other areas of artificial intelligence. The multi-armed bandit problem captures the essence of this conflict, and has thus occupied researchers for over fifty years [1]. In [2], a new family of *Bayesian* techniques for solving the classical two-armed Bernoulli bandit problem was introduced, akin to the *Thompson Sampling* [3] principle, and empirical results that demonstrated its advantages over established top performers were reported.

The above mentioned solution schemes were mainly designed for stationary bandit problems, leading to fixed arm selection strategies. However, in many real-life applications, such as web polling [4], the associated bandit problems are changing with time, making them non-stationary. Thus, if an algorithm with a

N. García-Pedrajas et al. (Eds.): IEA/AIE 2010, Part III, LNAI 6098, pp. 199–208, 2010.

fixed strategy is applied to bandit problem that is changing, each change may progressively degrade the performance of the algorithm [5].

In this present paper, we address the *Non-Stationary* Multi-Armed Normal Bandit (MANB) problem. In brief, we propose a Bayesian solution for non-stationary normally distributed rewards, that has sufficient flexibility to track the better actions as changes occur over time.

1.1 The Non-Stationary Multi-Armed Normal Bandit Problem

The MANB problem is a classical optimization problem that explores the trade off between exploitation and exploration in, e.g., reinforcement learning. The problem consists of an agent that sequentially pulls one of multiple arms attached to a gambling machine, with each pull resulting in a reward. The reward obtained from each *Arm i* has been affected by Gaussian noise of variance σ_{ob}^2 (observation noise), with the true unperturbed reward r_i being unknown.

This leaves the agent with the following dilemma: Should the arm that so far seems to be associated with the largest reward r_i be pulled once more, or should an inferior arm be pulled in order to learn more about *its* reward? Sticking prematurely with the arm that is presently considered to be the best one, may lead to not discovering which arm is truly optimal. On the other hand, lingering with the inferior arm unnecessarily, postpones the harvest that can be obtained from the optimal arm.

The non-stationary MANB problem renders the above problem even more intriguing because it allows the true unperturbed rewards r_i to change with time. In this paper, we address problems where each reward r_i is modified by independent Gaussian perturbations of constant variance σ_{tr}^2 (transition noise) at each time step.

In effect, a solution scheme for non-stationary MANB problems must thus both determine which action is the best one, as well as tracking any reward distribution changes that might occur.

1.2 Contributions and Paper Organization

The contributions of this paper can be summarized as follows. In Sect. 2, we briefly review a selection of the main MANB solution approaches. Then, in Sect. 3, we present our Kalman Filter based solution to MANB (KF-MANB). The KF-MANB scheme is inherently Bayesian in nature, even though it only relies on simple updating of hyper parameters and random sampling. Thus, the MANB solution scheme takes advantage of the Bayesian perspective in a computationally efficient manner. In addition, the scheme is able to track the best arms when the problem is non-stationary, relying on a set of sibling Kalman filters. In Sect. 4, we provide extensive experimental results that demonstrate that the KF-MANB scheme outperforms established top performers, both for stationary (!) and non-stationary bandit problems. Accordingly, from the above perspective, it is our belief that the KF-MANB scheme represents the current state-of-the-art and a new avenue of research. Finally, in Sect. 5 we list open KF-MANB related research problems and provide concluding remarks.

2   Related Work

From a broader point of view, one can distinguish two distinct fields that address bandit like problems, namely, the field of Learning Automata and the field of Bandit Playing Algorithms. A myriad of approaches have been proposed within these two fields, and we refer the reader to [5] and [6] for an overview and comparison of schemes. We here provide a brief review of selected top performers in order to cast light on the distinguishing properties of KF-MANB.

Learning Automata (LA) have been used to model biological systems [5] and have attracted considerable interest in the last decade because they can learn the optimal action when operating in (or interacting with) unknown stochastic environments. Furthermore, they combine rapid and accurate convergence with low computational complexity. More notable approaches include the family of linear updating schemes, with the Linear Reward-Inaction (L_{R-I}) automaton being designed for stationary environments [5]. In short, the L_{R-I} maintains an arm probability selection vector $\bar{p} = [p_1, p_2]$, with $p_2 = 1 - p_1$. The question of which arm is to be pulled is decided randomly by sampling from $\bar{p}$, which initially is uniform. Upon receiving a reward, a linear updating rule increases the probability of selecting the rewarded arm in the future, allowing the scheme to achieve ϵ-optimality [5]. A *Pursuit scheme* (P-scheme) makes this updating scheme more goal-directed by maintaining Maximum Likelihood (ML) estimates of the unperturbed rewards associated with each arm. Instead of using the rewards that are received to update $\bar{p}$ directly, they are rather used to update the ML estimates. The ML estimates, in turn, are used to decide which arm selection probability p_i is to be increased.

The ϵ-**greedy rule** is another well-known strategy for the bandit problem [7]. In short, the arm with the presently highest average reward is pulled with probability $1 - \epsilon$, while a randomly chosen arm is pulled with probability ϵ. In other words, the balancing of exploration and exploitation is controlled by the ϵ-parameter. Note that the ϵ-greedy strategy persistently explores the available arms with constant effort, which clearly is sub-optimal for the MANB problem. It is even sub-optimal for non-stationary MANB problems because the ϵ-greedy strategy maintains strongly converging ML estimates of the unperturbed rewards. As a remedy for the former (but not the latter) problem, ϵ can be slowly decreased, leading to the ϵ_n-greedy strategy described in [8]. The purpose is to gradually shift focus from exploration to exploitation.

A promising line of thought is the **interval estimation** methods, where a confidence interval for the unperturbed reward of each arm is estimated, and an "optimistic reward estimate" is identified for each arm. The arm with the most optimistic reward probability estimate is then greedily selected [6,9]. The INTEST (Interval Estimation) scheme [9] was one of the first schemes to use optimistic reward estimates to achieve exploration. Many variants of the INTEST scheme have been proposed — one for normally distributed rewards is described in [6]. In [8], several confidence interval based algorithms are analysed. These algorithms provide logarithmically increasing *Regret*, with UCB1-NORMAL targeting normally distributed rewards.

The application of a **Bayesian philosophy** for searching in such probabilistic spaces has a long and well-documented path through the mathematical literature, probably pioneered by Thompson [3] even as early as 1933, in the form of the Thompson sampling principle. According to this principle, each arm should be chosen a fraction of the time that corresponds to the probability that the action is optimal. This principle was recently rediscovered by other authors, e.g., in [1], such a Bayesian philosophy appears in the so-called *probability matching algorithms*. By using conjugate priors, these authors have resorted to a Bayesian analysis to obtain a closed form expression for the probability that each arm is optimal given the prior observed rewards/penalties. More recently, however, Wang *et al* [10] combined so-called sparse sampling with Bayesian exploration, where the entire process was specified within a finite time horizon. By achieving this, they were able to search the space based on a sparse look-ahead tree which was produced based on the Thompson Sampling principle. In [11], the author derived optimal decision thresholds for the multi-armed bandit problem, for both the infinite horizon discounted reward case and for the finite horizon undiscounted case. Based on these thresholds, he then went on to propose practical algorithms, which can perhaps be perceived to be enhancements of the *Thompson Sampling* principle. Finally, the authors of [12] take advantage of a Bayesian strategy in a related domain, i.e., in Q-learning. They show that for normally distributed rewards, in which the parameters have a prior normal-gamma distribution, the posteriors also have a normal-gamma distribution, rendering the computation efficient. They then integrate this into a framework for Bayesian Q-learning by maintaining and propagating probability distributions over the Q-values, and suggest that a non-approximate solution can be obtained by means of random sampling for the normal distribution case. In a similar vein, a scheme for Gaussian Temporal Difference learning is proposed in [13], with on-line learning of the posterior moments of a value Gaussian process. It would be interesting to investigate the applicability of these results for non-stationary MANB problems.

A more recent technique, the "Price of Knowledge and Estimated Reward" (POKER) algorithm proposed in [6], attempts to combine the following three principles: (1) Reducing uncertainty about the arm rewards should grant a bonus to stimulate exploration; (2) Information obtained from pulling arms should be used to estimate the properties of arms that have not yet been pulled; and (3) Knowledge about the number of rounds that remains (the horizon) should be used to plan the exploitation and exploration of arms. We refer the reader to [6] for the specific algorithm that incorporates these three principles.

3   Kalman Filter Based Solution to Non-Stationary Normal Bandit Problems (KF-MANB)

Bayesian reasoning is a probabilistic approach to inference which is of importance in machine learning because it allows quantitative weighting of evidence supporting alternative hypotheses, with the purpose of allowing optimal decision making. It also provides a framework for analyzing learning algorithms [14].

We here present a scheme for solving the non-stationary MANB problem that inherently builds upon the Bayesian reasoning framework, taking advantage of the tracking capability of Kalman filters [15]. We thus coin the scheme *Kalman Filter Based Solution to MANB* (KF-MANB). Essentially, KF-MANB uses the Kalman filter for two purposes. First of all, the Kalman filter is used to provide a *Bayesian estimate* of the rewards associated with each of the available bandit arms. Secondly, a novel feature of KF-MANB is that it uses the Kalman filters as the basis for a *randomized* arm selection mechanism. Being based on the Kalman filter, the normal distribution is central to KF-MANB:

$$ f(x_i; \mu_i, \sigma_i) = \alpha \, e^{-\frac{1}{2}\left(\frac{(x_i - \mu_i)^2}{\sigma_i^2}\right)} $$

with μ_i being the mean of the distribution, σ_i^2 being its variance, and α is a normalization constant. The following algorithm contains the essence of the KF-MANB approach. Note that in order to emphasize the simplicity of the KF-MANB algorithm, the Kalman filters are incorporated into the parameter updating of the algorithm itself, and do not appear as distinct entities.

Algorithm: KF-MANB
Input: Number of bandit arms q; Observation noise σ_{ob}^2; Transition noise σ_{tr}^2.
Initialization: $\mu_1[1] = \mu_2[1] = \cdots = \mu_q[1] = A$; $\sigma_1[1] = \sigma_2[1] = \cdots = \sigma_q[1] = B$; # *Typically, A can be set to* 0, *with B being sufficiently large.*
Method:
For $N = 1, 2, \ldots$ **Do**

1. For each *Arm* $j \in \{1, \ldots, q\}$, draw a value x_j randomly from the associated *normal* distribution $f(x_j; \mu_j[N], \sigma_j[N])$ with the parameters $(\mu_j[N], \sigma_j[N])$.
2. Pull the *Arm* i whose drawn value x_i is the largest one:

$$ i = \underset{j \in \{1,\ldots,q\}}{\operatorname{argmax}} \ x_j. $$

3. Receive a reward $\tilde{r}_i$ from pulling *Arm* i, and update parameters as follows:
   – *Arm* i:

$$ \mu_i[N+1] = \frac{(\sigma_i^2[N] + \sigma_{\text{tr}}^2) \cdot \tilde{r}_i + \sigma_{\text{ob}}^2 \cdot \mu_i[N]}{\sigma_i^2[N] + \sigma_{\text{tr}}^2 + \sigma_{\text{ob}}^2} $$

$$ \sigma_i^2[N+1] = \frac{(\sigma_i^2[N] + \sigma_{\text{tr}}^2)\,\sigma_{\text{ob}}^2}{\sigma_i^2[N] + \sigma_{\text{tr}}^2 + \sigma_{\text{ob}}^2} $$

   – *Arm* $j \neq i$:

$$ \mu_j[N+1] = \mu_j[N] $$
$$ \sigma_j^2[N+1] = \sigma_j^2[N] + \sigma_{\text{tr}}^2 $$

End Algorithm: KF-MANB

As seen from the above KF-MANB algorithm, N is a discrete time index and the parameters $\phi^N = \langle(\mu_1[N], \sigma_1[N]), (\mu_2[N], \sigma_2[N]), \ldots, (\mu_q[N], \sigma_q[N])\rangle$ form an infinite $2 \times q$-dimensional continuous state space, with each pair $(\mu_i[N], \sigma_i[N])$ giving the prior of the unknown reward r_i associated with *Arm i*. Within Φ the KF-MANB navigates by transforming each prior normal distribution into a posterior normal distribution, based on the reward obtained at that time step, the observation noise, and the transition noise.

Since the state space of KF-MANB is both continuous and infinite, KF-MANB is quite different from both the *Variable Structure-* and the *Fixed Structure* LA families [5], traditionally referred to as *Learning Automata*. In all brevity, the novel aspects of the KF-MANB are listed below:

1. In traditional LA, the action chosen (i.e, arm pulled) is based on the so-called action probability vector. The KF-MANB does not maintain such a vector, but chooses the arm based on the *distribution* of the components of the *Estimate* vector.
2. The second difference is that we have not chosen the arm based on the *a posteriori* distribution of the estimate. Rather, it has been chosen based on the magnitude of a *random sample* drawn from the *a posteriori* distribution, and thus it is more appropriate to state that the arm is chosen based on the *order of statistics* of instances of these variables[1].

In the interest of notational simplicity, let *Arm 1* be the Arm under investigation. Then, for any parameter configuration $\phi^N \in \Phi$ we can state, using a generic notation[2], that the probability of selecting *Arm 1* is equal to the probability $P(X_1^N > X_2^N \wedge X_1^N > X_3^N \wedge \cdots \wedge X_1^N > X_q^N | \phi^N)$ — the probability that a randomly drawn value $x_1 \in X_1^N$ is greater than all of the other randomly drawn values $x_j \in X_j^N, j \neq i$, at time step N, when the associated stochastic variables $X_1^N, X_2^N, \ldots, X_q^N$ are *normally* distributed, with parameters $(\mu_1[N], \sigma_1[N]), (\mu_2[N], \sigma_2[N]), \ldots, (\mu_q[N], \sigma_q[N])$ respectively. In the following, we will let $p_1^{\phi^N}$ denote this latter probability.

Note that the probability $p_1^{\phi^N}$ can also be interpreted as the probability that *Arm 1* is the optimal one, given the observations ϕ^N. The formal result that we will derive in the unabridged paper shows that the KF-MANB will gradually shift its arm selection focus towards the arm which most likely is the optimal one, as the observations are received.

4   Empirical Results

In this section we evaluate the KF-MANB by comparing it with the best performing algorithms from [8,6], as well as the Pursuit scheme, which can be seen

---

[1] To the best of our knowledge, the concept of having automata choose actions based on the *order of statistics* of instances of estimate distributions, has been unreported in the literature.

[2] By this we mean that P is not a fixed function. Rather, it denotes the probability function for a random variable, given as an argument to P.

as an established top performer in the LA field. Based on our comparison with these "reference" algorithms, it should be quite straightforward to also relate the KF-MANB performance results to the performance of other similar algorithms.

Although we have conducted numerous experiments using various reward distributions, we here report, for the sake of brevity, results for 10-armed stationary and non-stationary MANB problems, measured in terms of *Regret*. *Regret* is simply *the difference between the sum of rewards expected after N successive arm pulls, and what would have been obtained by only pulling the optimal arm.* For these experiment configurations, an ensemble of 1000 independent replications with different random number streams was performed to minimize the variance of the reported results. In each replication, 2000 arm pulls were conducted in order to examine both the short term and the limiting performance of the evaluated algorithms.

We first investigate the effect observation noise has on performance in stationary environments. The difficulty of stationary bandit problems is determined by the "signal-to-noise ratio" of the problem, that is, the ratio between arm *reward difference* and the *standard deviation* of the observation noise. In brief, if the arms are ranked according to their index i, we let the difference in reward between *Arm i* and *Arm i + 1* be 50.0 ($r_i - r_{i+1} = 50.0$). With the scale thus being set, we vary observation noise to achieve a wide range of signal-to-noise ratios: $\sigma_{ob} \in [\frac{1}{4} \cdot 50.0, \frac{1}{3} \cdot 50.0, \frac{1}{2} \cdot 50.0, \frac{2}{3} \cdot 50.0, \frac{4}{5} \cdot 50.0, 50.0, 1\frac{1}{4} \cdot 50.0, 1\frac{1}{2} \cdot 50.0, 2 \cdot 50.0, 3 \cdot 50.0, 4 \cdot 50.0]$. Thus, for $\sigma_{ob} = \frac{1}{4} \cdot 50.0$ the observation noise is small compared to the difference between rewards, and distinguishing which arm is best is correspondingly easier. Conversely, an observation noise of $\sigma_{ob} = 4 \cdot 50.0$ makes the true difference between arms in the ranking fall within 1/4 standard deviation of the noise. Accordingly, discriminating between the arms in this case is correspondingly more challenging.

Table 1 reports normalized *Regret* after 2000 arm pulls for each algorithm, with suitable parameter settings. As seen in the table, KF-MANB is

Table 1. Normalized regret for transition noise $\sigma_{tr} = 0$ (stationary environments)

Algorithm / σ_{ob}	12.5	16.7	25.0	33.3	50.0	75.0	100.0	150.0	200.0
BLA Kalman	*5.1*	*5.2*	*5.4*	*5.8*	*7.1*	*10.6*	*16.1*	*28.5*	*45.0*
UCB1 Normal	135.0	135.0	135.2	136.3	140.7	151.8	168.9	213.9	270.5
INTEST 0.1	608.5	595.1	537.2	515.0	450.3	367.3	298.5	229.4	188.9
INTEST 0.2	581.7	579.7	559.3	549.9	526.1	442.8	422.3	357.6	320.2
INTEST 0.05	558.6	585.6	522.0	484.3	420.1	325.4	239.7	158.1	150.0
Pursuit 0.050	45.6	41.2	45.4	47.0	50.8	52.7	71.0	85.7	114.6
Pursuit 0.010	52.3	52.2	52.3	53.0	53.3	55.5	58.6	69.0	78.1
Pursuit 0.005	101.7	101.9	102.2	102.4	103.3	105.0	106.4	112.4	122.9
POKER	5.5	5.7	5.5	7.2	10.6	19.1	29.5	42.6	58.7
ϵ_n-GREEDY $c = 0.3$	29.0	28.6	28.1	30.5	33.5	39.8	50.2	74.1	97.8
ϵ_n-GREEDY $c = 0.6$	37.9	37.7	37.9	38.3	40.4	46.1	54.1	68.0	84.4
ϵ_n-GREEDY $c = 0.9$	65.3	65.5	65.5	65.2	65.4	68.1	70.3	86.5	99.0

superior under all tested degrees of observation noise, with the POKER algorithm being a close second best. Note that POKER is given the total number of arm pulls to be used in each run. This information is used to prioritize exploitation when further exploration will not pay off due to the limited number of arm pulls remaining. The Pursuit scheme and the e_n–GREEDY-schemes provide significantly higher *Regret*. Furthermore, INTEST clearly provides the highest *Regret* among the compared algorithms. Corresponding results concerning the probability of selecting the best arm after each arm pull can be found in the unabridged paper. These results show that KF-MANB converges to selecting the best arm more accurately and more quickly than the other schemes.

The fact that KF-MANB outperforms the other schemes in stationary environments is rather surprising since most of the competing algorithms also assume normally distributed rewards (which is the sole assumption of KF-MANB in this experiment). This performance advantage can perhaps be explained by KF-MANBs capability of reasoning with the known observation noise. However, as will be seen below, the performance advantage of KF-MANB is not overly sensitive to incorrectly specified observation noise.

The advantage of KF-MANB becomes even more apparent when dealing with bandit problems that are non-stationary. In Table 2, normalized *Regret* is reported for $\sigma_{ob} = 50.0$, with varying transition noise: $\sigma_{tr} \in [0.0, \frac{1}{4} \cdot 50.0, \frac{1}{3} \cdot 50.0, \frac{1}{2} \cdot 50.0, \frac{2}{3} \cdot 50.0, \frac{4}{5} \cdot 50.0, 50.0, 1\frac{1}{4} \cdot 50.0, 1\frac{1}{2} \cdot 50.0, 2 \cdot 50.0, 3 \cdot 50.0, 4 \cdot 50.0]$. As seen in the table, KF-MANB is superior for the non-stationary MANB problems. Also, notice how the degree of transition noise affects its performance to a very small degree, demonstrating the power of the KF-MANB scheme. Conversely, the other schemes, being unable to track reward changes, are obtaining a progressively worse *Regret* as the number of arm pulls increases.

Table 2. Normalized regret for observation noise $\sigma_{ob} = 50.0$, with varying transition noise σ_{tr} (non-stationary environments)

Algorithm / σ_{tr}	0.0	12.5	16.7	25.0	33.3	50.0	75.0	100.0	150.0	200.0
BLA Kalman	7.2	43.0	44.9	45.9	47.6	48.4	49.3	49.8	49.3	49.3
UCB1 Normal	140.6	260.5	269.4	271.1	286.0	281.7	287.5	286.2	278.6	280.2
INTEST 0.1	456.4	488.1	470.2	460.6	476.3	475.3	470.6	481.9	471.5	468.6
INTEST 0.2	506.0	536.7	523.2	519.5	519.7	521.0	498.4	514.7	499.6	509.0
INTEST 0.05	429.1	446.9	431.3	439.4	441.2	463.9	447.7	454.8	449.4	460.0
Pursuit 0.050	51.8	389.0	407.5	437.9	485.9	487.7	497.7	515.4	516.0	521.3
Pursuit 0.010	53.0	365.7	400.0	407.1	451.2	456.0	448.4	452.9	456.5	440.9
Pursuit 0.005	103.1	393.3	418.8	422.0	462.1	453.5	447.5	463.0	448.7	455.4
POKER	12.0	297.2	332.8	361.4	391.2	416.1	409.7	422.9	416.8	419.7
ϵ_n-GREEDY $c = 0.3$	33.8	304.0	336.3	341.7	379.9	379.1	371.3	381.6	374.9	386.4
ϵ_n-GREEDY $c = 0.6$	39.3	304.7	320.8	335.0	368.7	374.3	374.0	378.9	364.6	370.2
ϵ_n-GREEDY $c = 0.9$	65.7	320.0	338.3	338.3	370.3	367.3	370.7	371.4	366.0	371.3

Table 3. Sensitivity to incorrectly specified observation noise with $\sigma_{tr} = 0.0$

Belief $\hat{\sigma}_{ob}$: $\left\|\,\frac{1}{4}\sigma_{ob}\,\right|\,\frac{1}{3}\sigma_{ob}\,\left|\,\frac{1}{2}\sigma_{ob}\,\right|\,\frac{2}{3}\sigma_{ob}\,\left|\,\frac{4}{5}\sigma_{ob}\,\right|\,\sigma_{ob}\,\left|\,1\frac{1}{4}\sigma_{ob}\,\right|\,1\frac{1}{2}\sigma_{ob}\,\left|\,2\sigma_{ob}\,\right|\,3\sigma_{ob}\,\left|\,4\sigma_{ob}\,\right|$

Regret: $\|\,13.2\,|\,10.3\,|\,5.7\,\,|\,\,5.9\,\,|\,\,6.4\,\,|\,7.1\,|\,\,8.3\,\,\,|\,\,10.2\,\,|\,14.9\,|\,27.1\,|\,41.3\,|$

Table 4. Sensitivity to incorrectly specified transition noise with $\sigma_{ob} = 50.0$

Belief $\hat{\sigma}_{tr}$: $\left\|\,\frac{1}{4}\sigma_{tr}\,\right|\,\frac{1}{3}\sigma_{tr}\,\left|\,\frac{1}{2}\sigma_{tr}\,\right|\,\frac{2}{3}\sigma_{tr}\,\left|\,\frac{4}{5}\sigma_{tr}\,\right|\,\sigma_{tr}\,\left|\,1\frac{1}{4}\sigma_{tr}\,\right|\,1\frac{1}{2}\sigma_{tr}\,\left|\,2\sigma_{tr}\,\right|\,3\sigma_{tr}\,\left|\,4\sigma_{tr}\,\right|$

Regret: $\|\,168.8\,|\,113.5\,|\,66.6\,|\,46.5\,|\,46.1\,|\,48.4\,|\,59.6\,|\,74.6\,\,|\,106.4\,|\,159.0\,|\,225.6\,|$

One of the advantages of KF-MANB is its ability to take advantage of knowledge about the observation noise and transition noise affecting a MANB problem. In cases where the exact observation noise and transition noise is unavailable, KF-MANB may have to operate with incorrectly specified noise. Table 3 summarizes the effect incorrect specification of observation noise has on normalized *Regret* for KF-MANB. As seen, the KF-MANB algorithm is still the top performer for the tested stationary MANB problems, provided the incorrectly specified observation noise has a standard deviation $\hat{\sigma}_{ob}$ that lies within 33% and 150% of the true standard deviation σ_{ob} (!). Also observe that the performance even improves when $\hat{\sigma}_{ob}$ is set slightly below σ_{ob}. A reasonable explanation for this phenomenon is that the KF-MANB scheme is too conservative when planning its arm pulls, probably because it does not consider the so-called *gain in information*, only the present probability of selecting the correct arm. Therefore, it is likely that a slightly too low $\hat{\sigma}_{ob}$ compensates for this by making the KF-MANB more "aggressive".

We observe similar results when transition noise is incorrectly specified, as seen in Table 4. Again, the KF-MANB is surprisingly unaffected by incorrectly specified noise. Indeed, it provides reasonable performance when operating with a standard deviation $\hat{\sigma}_{tr}$ that lies within 50% and 150% of σ_{tr}.

From the above results, we conclude that KF-MANB is the superior choice for MANB problems in general, providing significantly better performance in the majority of the experiment configurations.

5 Conclusion and Further Work

In this paper we presented a *Kalman Filter based solution scheme to Multi-Armed Normal Bandit* (KF-MANB) problems. In contrast to previous LA and *Regret* minimizing approaches, KF-MANB is inherently Bayesian in nature. Still, it relies simply on updating the hyper parameters of sibling Kalman Filters, and on random sampling from these. Thus, KF-MANB takes advantage of Bayesian estimation in a computationally efficient manner. Furthermore, extensive experiments demonstrate that our scheme outperforms recently proposed algorithms, dealing particularly well with non-stationary problems. Accordingly, in the above perspective, it is our belief that the KF-MANB represents a new promising avenue of research, with a number of interesting applications. In further work, we intend to study systems of KF-MANB from a game theory point of view, where multiple KF-MANBs interact forming the basis for multi-agent systems.

References

1. Wyatt, J.: Exploration and Inference in Learning from Reinforcement. PhD thesis, University of Edinburgh (1997)
2. Granmo, O.C.: Solving Two-Armed Bernoulli Bandit Problems Using a Bayesian Learning Automaton. To Appear in the International Journal of Intelligent Computing and Cybernetics (2010)
3. Thompson, W.R.: On the likelihood that one unknown probability exceeds another in view of the evidence of two samples. Biometrika 25, 285–294 (1933)
4. Granmo, O.C., Oommen, B.J., Myrer, S.A., Olsen, M.G.: Learning Automata-based Solutions to the Nonlinear Fractional Knapsack Problem with Applications to Optimal Resource Allocation. IEEE Transactions on Systems, Man, and Cybernetics, Part B 37(1), 166–175 (2007)
5. Narendra, K.S., Thathachar, M.A.L.: Learning Automata: An Introduction. Prentice-Hall, Englewood Cliffs (1989)
6. Vermorel, J., Mohri, M.: Multi-armed bandit algorithms and empirical evaluation. In: Gama, J., Camacho, R., Brazdil, P.B., Jorge, A.M., Torgo, L. (eds.) ECML 2005. LNCS (LNAI), vol. 3720, pp. 437–448. Springer, Heidelberg (2005)
7. Sutton, R.S., Barto, A.G.: Reinforcement Learning: An Introduction. MIT Press, Cambridge (1998)
8. Auer, P., Cesa-Bianchi, N., Fischer, P.: Finite-time Analysis of the Multiarmed Bandit Problem. Machine Learning 47, 235–256 (2002)
9. Kaelbling, L.P.: Learning in Embedded Systems. PhD thesis, Stanford University (1993)
10. Wang, T., Lizotte, D., Bowling, M., Scuurmans, D.: Bayesian sparse sampling for on-line reward optimization. In: Proceedings of the 22nd International conference on Machine learning, pp. 956–963 (2005)
11. Dimitrakakis, C.: Nearly optimal exploration-exploitation decision thresholds. In: Kollias, S.D., Stafylopatis, A., Duch, W., Oja, E. (eds.) ICANN 2006. LNCS, vol. 4131, pp. 850–859. Springer, Heidelberg (2006)
12. Dearden, R., Friedman, N., Russell, S.: Bayesian q-learning. In: AAAI/IAAI, pp. 761–768. AAAI Press, Menlo Park (1998)
13. Engel, Y., Mannor, S., Meir, R.: Reinforcement learning with gaussian processes. In: Proceedings of the 22nd International conference on Machine learning, pp. 956–963 (2005)
14. Mitchell, T.M.: Machine Learning. McGraw-Hill, New York (1997)
15. Russel, S., Norvig, P.: Artificial Intelligence - A Modern Approach, 2nd edn. Prentice-Hall, Englewood Cliffs (2003)

A Learning Automata Based Solution to Service Selection in Stochastic Environments*

Anis Yazidi[1], Ole-Christoffer Granmo[1], and B. John Oommen[2],**

[1] Dept. of ICT, University of Agder, Grimstad, Norway
[2] School of Computer Science, Carleton University, Ottawa, Canada

Abstract. With the abundance of services available in today's world, identifying those of high quality is becoming increasingly difficult. Reputation systems can offer generic recommendations by aggregating user provided opinions about service quality, however, are prone to "ballot stuffing" and "badmouthing". In general, unfair ratings may degrade the trustworthiness of reputation systems, and changes in service quality over time render previous ratings unreliable.

In this paper, we provide a novel solution to the above problems based on Learning Automata (LA), which can learn the optimal action when operating in unknown stochastic environments. Furthermore, they combine rapid and accurate convergence with low computational complexity. In additional to its computational simplicity, unlike most reported approaches, our scheme does not require prior knowledge of the degree of any of the above mentioned problems with reputation systems. Instead, it gradually learns which users provide fair ratings, and which users provide unfair ratings, even when users unintentionally make mistakes.

Comprehensive empirical results show that our LA based scheme efficiently handles any degree of unfair ratings (as long as ratings are binary). Furthermore, if the quality of services and/or the trustworthiness of users change, our scheme is able to robustly track such changes over time. Finally, the scheme is ideal for decentralized processing. Accordingly, we believe that our LA based scheme forms a promising basis for improving the performance of reputation systems in general.

Keywords: Reputation Systems, Learning Automata, Stochastic Optimization.

1 Introduction

With the abundance of services available in today's world, identifying those of high quality is becoming increasingly difficult. "Reputation Systems" (RSs)

---

* This work was partially supported by NSERC, the Natural Sciences and Engineering Research Council of Canada.
** Chancellor's Professor; Fellow : IEEE and Fellow : IAPR. The Author also holds an Adjunct Professorship with the Dept. of ICT, University of Agder, Norway.

N. García-Pedrajas et al. (Eds.): IEA/AIE 2010, Part III, LNAI 6098, pp. 209–218, 2010.

attracted a lot of attention during the last decade in the academia as well as in the industry. RSs have also emerged as an efficient approach to handle trust in online services, and can be used to collect information about the performance of services in the absence of direct experience.

In this paper we intend to study how experiences can be shared between users in a social network, where the medium of collaboration is a RS. The basic premise, of course, is that it is possible for users to expediently obtain knowledge about the nature, quality and drawbacks of specific services by considering the experiences of other users. The above premise is true if the basis of the decision is accurate, up-to-date and fair. In fact, the social network and the system itself might contain misinformed/deceptive users who provide either unfair positive ratings about a subject or service, or who unfairly submit negative ratings. Such "deceptive" agents, who may even submit their inaccurate ratings innocently, have the effect that they mislead a RS that is based on blindly aggregating users' experiences. Furthermore, when the quality of services and the nature of users change over time, the challenge is further aggravated.

Finding ways to counter the detrimental influence of unfair ratings on a RS has been a focal concern of a number of studies [1,2,3]. Dellarocas [1] used elements from collaborative filtering to determine the nearest neighbors of an agent that exhibited similar ratings on commonly-rated subjects. He then applied a cluster filtering approach to filter out the most likely unfairly positive ratings. Sen and Sajja [2] proposed an algorithm to select a service provider to process a task by querying other user agents about their ratings of the available service providers. The main idea motivating their work is to select a subset of agents, who when queried, maximizes the probability that the majority of the queried agents provide correct reputation estimates. However, comprehensive experimental tests show that their approach is prone to the variation of the ratio of deceptive agents. In contrast, in [4], Witby and Jøsang presented a Bayesian approach to filter out dishonest feedback based on an iterated filtering approach. The authors of [5] proposed a probabilistic model to assess peer trustworthiness in P2P networks. Their model, which in one sense is similar to ours, differs from the present work because the authors of [5] assume that a peer can deduce the trustworthiness of other peers by comparing its own performance with reports of other peers about itself. Though such an assumption permits a feedback-evaluating mechanism, it is based on the fact that peers provide services to one another, thus permitting every party the right to play the role of a service provider and the service consumer (a reporting agent). Our approach, which we briefly describe in the next section makes a clear distinction between these parties – the service provider and the reporting

In this paper, we provide a novel solution to the above problems based on Learning Automata, which can learn the optimal action when operating in unknown stochastic environments [6]. Furthermore, they combine rapid and accurate convergence with low computational complexity. In additional to its computational simplicity, unlike most reported approaches, our scheme does not require prior knowledge of the *degree* of any of the above mentioned problems with RSs. Rather, it adaptively, and in an on-line manner, gradually learns the identity and characteristics of the users who provide fair ratings, and of those which provide unfair ratings, even when these are a consequence of them making unintentional mistakes.

Unlike most existing reported approaches that only consider the feedback from "fair" agents as being informative, and which simultaneously discard the feedback from "unfair" agents, in our work we attempt to intelligently combine (or fuse) the feedback from fair and deceptive agents when evaluating the performance of a service. Moreover, we do not impose the constraint that we need *a priori* knowledge about the ratio of deceptive agents. Consequently, unlike most of existing work, that suffer from a decline in the performance when the ratio of deceptive agents increases, our scheme is robust to the variation of this ratio. This characteristic phenomenon of our scheme is unique.

2   Modeling the Problem

Consider a population of L services (or service providers), $\mathcal{S} = \{S_1, S_2, \ldots, S_L\}$. We also assume that the social network (or pool of users) consists of N parties (synonymously called "agents") $\mathcal{U} = \{u_1, u_2, \ldots, u_N\}$. Each service S_l has an associated quality, which, in our work is represented by an "innate" probability of the service provider performing exceptionally well whenever its service is requested by an agent. This probability is specified by the quantity θ_l, assumed to be unknown to the users/agents. For a given interaction instance between user agent u_i and service S_l, let x_{il} denote the performance value, which, for the sake of formalism, is assumed to be generated from a distribution referred to as the *Performance Distribution* of S_l. After the service has been provided, the user/agent u_i observes the performance x_{il}, where $x_{il} \in \{0, 1\}$. We assume that '0' denotes the lowest performance of the service, while '1' denotes its highest performance.

At this juncture, after the agent has experienced the quality of the service, he communicates his experience to the rest of the network. Let y_{il} be the report that he transmits to other agents after he experiences x_{il}. Obviously[1], $y_{il} \in \{0, 1\}$. To do this, we assume that agent u_i communicates his experience, x_{il}, truthfully to other agents in the population, with a probability p_i. In other words, p_i denotes the probability that agent u_i is not misreporting his experience. For ease of notation, we let $q_i = 1 - p_i$, which represents the probability that agent u_i does indeed misreport his experience. Clearly, $p_i = Prob(x_{il} = y_{il})$.

Observe that as a result of this communication model, a "deceptive" agent will probabilistically tend to report low performance experience values for high performance services and *vice versa*. Our aim is to partition the agents as being true/fair or deceptive.

Formally, the Agent-Type Partitioning Problem ($ATPP$), can be stated as follows: A social network consists of N agents, $\mathcal{U} = \{u_1, u_2, \ldots, u_N\}$, where each

---

[1] We mention, in passing, that other researchers, have used the notation y_{il} to signify the rating of the service.

agent u_i is characterized by a fixed but unknown probability p_i of him reporting his experience truthfully. The ATPP involves partitioning $\mathcal{U}$ into 2 (mutually exclusive and exhaustive) groups so as to obtain a 2-partition $\mathbb{G}_k = \{G_i \,|\, i = 1, 2\}$, such that each group, G_i, of size, N_i, exclusively contains only the agents of its own type, i.e., which either communicate truthfully or deceptively.

To simplify the problem, we assume that every p_i can assume one of two possible values from the set $\{p_d, p_f\}$, where $p_d < 0.5$ and $p_f > 0.5$. Then, agent u_i is said to be fair if $p_i = p_f$, and is said be deceptive if $p_i = p_d$.

Based on the above, the set of fair agents is $\mathcal{U}_f = \{u_i | p_i = p_f\}$, and the set of deceptive agents is $\mathcal{U}_d = \{u_i | p_i = p_d\}$.

Let y_{il} be a random variable defined as below:

$$y_{il} = \begin{cases} 1 & \text{w.p } p_i.\theta_l + (1 - p_i).(1 - \theta_l) \\ 0 & \text{w.p } p_i.(1 - \theta_l) + (1 - p_i).\theta_l. \end{cases} \tag{1}$$

Consider the scenario when two agents u_i and u_j utilize the same service S_l and report on it. Then, based on the above notation, their reports relative to the service S_l are y_{il} and y_{jl} respectively, where:

$$\begin{aligned} Prob(y_{il} = y_{jl}) &= Prob[(y_{il} = 0 \wedge y_{jl} = 0) \vee (y_{il} = 1 \wedge y_{jl} = 1)] \\ &= Prob[(y_{il} = 0 \wedge y_{jl} = 0)] + Prob[(y_{il} = 1 \wedge y_{jl} = 1)] \\ &= Prob(y_{il} = 0) \cdot Prob(y_{jl} = 0) + Prob(y_{il} = 1) \cdot Prob(y_{jl} = 1). \end{aligned}$$

Throughout this paper, we shall denote $Prob(y_{il} = y_{jl})$ to be the probability that the agents u_i and u_j will agree in their appraisal. This quantity has the following property.

Theorem 1. *Let u_i and u_j two agents. If both u_i and u_j are of the same nature (either both deceptive agents or both fair), then $Prob(y_{il} = y_{jl}) > 0.5$. Similarly, if u_i and u_j are of different nature, then $Prob(y_{il} = y_{jl}) < 0.5$.*

Proof: The proof is straightforward.   □

3   A LA-Based Solution to the *ATTP*

The input to our automaton, is the set of user agents $\mathcal{U} = \{u_1, u_2, \ldots, u_N\}$ and the reports that are communicated within the social network. With regard to the output, we intend to partition $\mathcal{U}$ into two sets, namely, the set of fair agents $\mathcal{U}_f = \{u_i | p_i = p_f\}$, and the set of deceptive agents $\mathcal{U}_d = \{u_i | p_i = p_d\}$. The intuitive principle that we use is that the agents that have the same nature (fair or deceptive) will report similar experiences about the same service, and we shall attempt to infer this phenomenon to, hopefully, migrate them to the same partition. Observe that since agents of different nature report dissimilar experiences about the same service, we hope to also infer *this*, and, hopefully, force them to converge into different partitions.

We define the Agent Migrating Partitioning Automaton (*AMPA*) as a 7-tuple as below: $(\mathcal{U}, \underline{\Phi}, \underline{\alpha}, \underline{\beta}, \mathbb{Q}, \mathbb{G}, \mathbb{L})$, where

- $\mathcal{U} = \{u_1, u_2, \ldots, u_N\}$ is the set of agents.
- $\underline{\Phi} = \{\phi_1, \phi_2, \ldots, \phi_{2M}\}$ is the set of states.
- $\underline{\alpha} = \{\alpha_1, \alpha_2\}$ is the set of actions, each representing a group into which the elements of $\mathcal{U}$ fall.
- $\underline{\beta} = \{`0`, `1`\}$ is the set of responses, where '0' represents a *Reward*, and '1' represents a *Penalty*.
- $\mathbb{Q}$ is the transition function, which specifies how the agents should move between the various states. This function is quite involved and will be explained in detail presently.
- The function $\mathbb{G}$ partitions the set of states for the groups. For each group, α_j, there is a set of states $\{\phi_{(j-1)M+1}, \ldots, \phi_{jM}\}$, where M is the depth of memory. Thus,

$$G(\phi_i) = \alpha_j \qquad (j-1)M + 1 \leq i \leq jM. \qquad (2)$$

This means that the agent in the automaton chooses α_1 if it is in any of the first M states, and that it chooses α_2 if it is in any of the states from ϕ_{M+1} to ϕ_{2M}. We assume that $\phi_{(j-1)M+1}$ is the most internal state of group α_j, and that ϕ_{jM} is the boundary state. These are called the states of "*Maximum Certainty*" and "*Minimum Certainty*", respectively.

- $\mathbb{W} = \{W_l^D(t)\}$, where, $W_l^D(t) = \{$ Last D records prior to instant t relative to service S_l $\}$.

Our aim is to infer from $\mathbb{W}$ a similarity list of agents deemed to be collectively similar. From it we can, based on the window of recent events, obtain a list of pairs of the form $< u_i, u_j >$ deemed to be similar. The question of how $\mathbb{W}$ is obtained will be discussed later.

If agent u_i is in action α_j, it signifies that it is in the sub-partition whose index is j. Moreover, if the states occupied by the nodes are given, the sub-partitions can be trivially obtained using Eq. (2).

Let $\zeta_i(t)$ be the index of the state occupied by agent u_i at the tth time instant. Based on $\{\zeta_i(t)\}$ and Eq. (2), let us suppose that the automaton decides a current partition of $\mathcal{U}$ into sub-partitions. Using this notation we shall later describe the transition map of the automaton. Since the intention of the learning process is to collect "similar" agents into the same sub-partition, the question of "inter-agent similarity" is rather crucial. In the spirit of Theorem 1, we shall reckon that two agents are similar if they are of the same nature, implying that the corresponding probability of them agreeing is greater than 0.5. Note that the latter parameter was assumed constant in [7].

We now consider the reward and penalty scenarios separately. Whenever two agents u_i and u_j test the same service, if their corresponding reports are identical (either both '0' or both '1'), and they currently belong to the same partition, the automaton is rewarded by moving u_i and u_j one state closer to the internal state. This mode of rewarding is called *RewardAgreeing* mode depicted in Figure 1. As opposed to this, if u_i and u_j are dissimilar and they currently belong to distinct partitions, the automaton is rewarded. This mode of rewarding is called the *RewardDisagreeingMode*.

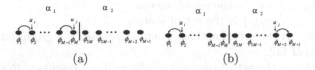

Fig. 1. (a)RewardAgreeing Mode: This is the case when both agents u_i and u_j belong to the same partition. (b) Reward Disagreeing Mode: This is the case when both agents u_i and u_j belong to different partitions.

Whenever two agents u_i and u_j test the same service, if their corresponding reports are identical (either both '0' or both '1'), and they currently belong to distinct partitions, the automaton is penalized by moving u_i and u_j one state closer to the boundary state in their respective groups. If one of the two agents is already in the boundary state, he moves to the boundary state of the alternate group. More specifically, this case is encountered when two similar agents, u_i and u_j, are allocated in distinct groups say, α_a and α_b respectively. This mode of rewarding is called the *PenalizeAgreeing* mode depicted in Figure 2.

However, if u_i and u_j are both assigned to the same subpartition, but they should rather be assigned to distinct groups, the automaton is penalized. Analogous to the above, this mode of penalizing is called the *PenalizeDisagreeing* mode, because, in this mode, agents which are actually dissimilar are assigned to the same subpartition and they are therefore penalized. This is depicted in Figure 3.

We now address the question of recording the reports associated with the various agents, which in turn, involves the set $\mathbb{W}$ defined above. In our work,

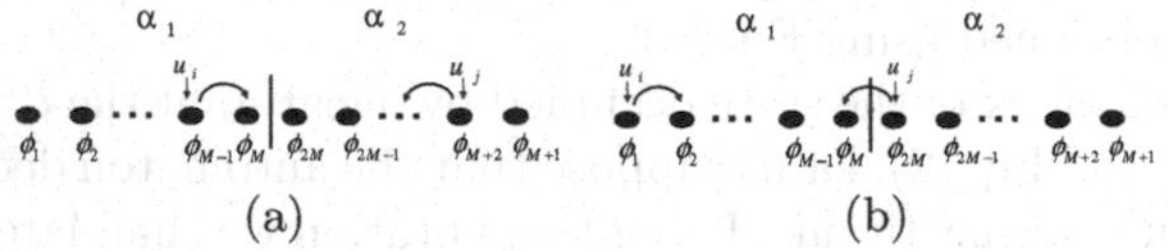

Fig. 2. PenalizeAgreeing Mode: This is the case when both agents u_i and u_j belong to different partitions. In (a), neither of them is in a boundary state. As opposed to this, in (b), the figure depicts the case when one of them, u_j, is in a boundary state.

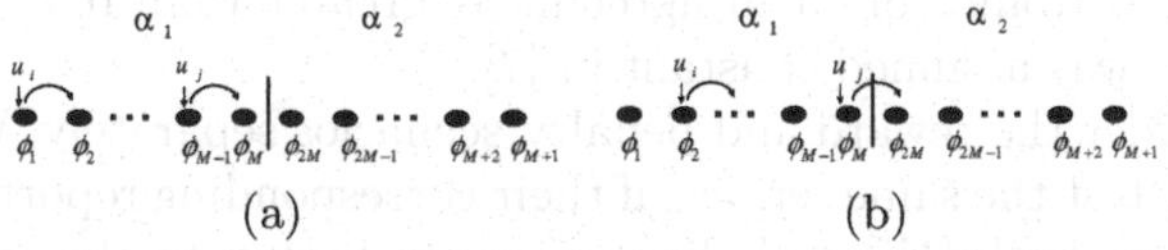

Fig. 3. PenalizingDisagreeing mode: This is the case when both agents u_i and u_j belong to the same partition, when, in actuality, they should belong to distinct partitions. In (a), neither of them is in a boundary state. As opposed to this, in (b), the figure depicts the case when one of them, u_j, is in a boundary state.

we adopt a "tuple-based" window to store the reports for a given service [8], where the window is specified in terms of the number of tuples. Observe that our approach is consistent with the work of Shapiro [9] where it was proven that in an environment in which peers can change their behavior over time, the efficiency of a reputation mechanism is maximized by giving higher weights on recent ratings and where older (stale) ratings are discounted. Clearly, this is equivalent to enforcing a sliding window model.

Despite the ability of our LA-based clustering algorithm to separate between the two groups $\mathcal{U}_f$ and $\mathcal{U}_d$, the agent can not determine which of the two groups is the fair one, $(\mathcal{U}_f)$, and which is the deceptive one, $(\mathcal{U}_d)$, unless he tries the services himself. Intuitively, if the agents knows this information, he can just take the inverse of the reports of the "liars" as being trustworthy, while he considers the rest of the reports from fair agents as also being trustworthy.

With regard to the set $\mathbb{W}$, and the decision making procedure that maximizes the likelihood of choosing high performance service, for a given service is as follows. Every agent stores the last D reports seen so far. Thus, the agent in question maintains, for every service, a sliding window over the last D reported experiences, which guarantees gathering the most recent reports. At time instant t, $W_l^D(t)$ contains the D tuples with the largest time stamps (where, if the total number d of reports seen so far is smaller than the length of the window D, the vector contains these d elements). Clearly, $W_l^D(t)$ stores the most recent D tuples[2]. Also, let $W_l^D[k]$ denote the record of index k in the vector, or the $(D - k)^{th}$ last record. Since we adopt a simple interaction model, at each time instant a random agent chooses a random service to interact with and report his experience to the rest of agents.

3.1 The Decision Making Phase

In the spirit of what we have developed so far, we assume that the services belong to two categories: High performance services and low performance services. A high performance service is a service with high value of θ, and similarly, a low performance service is a service with a low value of θ. We suppose that agent u aspires to interact with high performance services. Therefore, every time u desires to access a service, u creates a list L of the recommended services by applying a majority voting method, as explained below. Based on this list, u chooses a random service among the elements of this created list. In order to create a list of the high performance services, for every service S_l, agent u evaluates the feedback from agents that may have directly interacted with service S_l during the last D interactions. We adopt the terminology of a "witness" to denote an agent solicited for providing its feedback. In this sense, at instant t, agent u examines the service history vector $W_l^D(t)$ that contains the last reports of the witnesses regarding the performance of service S_l. For every report in the vector $W_l^D(t)$, agent u should take the reverse of the report as true if he believes that the witness

---

[2] In future, unless there is ambiguity, for ease of notation, we shall omit the time index t.

is a "liar", and consider the rest of the reports as being trustworthy. Following such a reasoning, given D trustworthy reports about a given service, we can apply a deterministic majority voting to determine if the service is of high performance or of low performance. Obviously, if the majority is '1', the service is assumed to be of a high performance, and consequently, it is added to the list L. However, a potential question is that of determining which partition is the deceptive one, and which involves the fair agents. In order to differentiate between the partitions we design a LA that learns which of the partitions is deceptive and which is fair – based on the result of the interaction between agent u with the selected service S_l. The automaton is rewarded whenever agent u selects a recommended service from the list L and the result of the interaction is a high performance (meaning '1'). Similarly, the automaton is penalized whenever agent u selects a recommended service from the list L and the result of the interaction is a low performance (meaning '0'). Again, we suppose that agent u in question is initially assigned to the boundary state. We observe the following:

- If agent u is in class α_j then u supposes that all the agents in α_j are fair, and the agents in the alternate class are deceptive.
- Whenever agent u decides to interact with a high performance service, he creates the list L of recommended services, and proceeds to choose a random service from L.
- If the result of the interaction is '1', a reward is generated, and the agent u goes one step towards the most internal state of class α_j.
- If the result of the interaction is '0', a penalty is generated and agent u goes one step towards the boundary state of class α_j.
- If agent u is already in the boundary state, he switches to the alternate class.

The automaton will converge to the action which yields the minimum penalty response in an expected sense. In our case, the automaton will converge to the class containing the fair agents, while the deceptive agents converge to the alternate class.

4   Experimental Results

To quantify the quality of the scheme, we measured the average performance of the selected services over all interactions, and this was used as the performance index. All the results reported have been obtained after averaging across 1,000 simulations, where every simulation consisted of 40,000 runs. The interactions between the agents and the services were generated at random, and at every time instant, a random agent was made to select a random service. In our current experimental setting, the number of agents was 20 and the number of services in the pool of available services was 100. The agent in question (i.e., the one which we are interested in) periodically accesses a service every 1,000 runs as per the above-mentioned decision making procedure.

4.1   Performance in Static Environments VS Dynamic Environments

We first report the results for environments which are static. In this particular setting, 10% of the services were high performance services with $\theta = 0.8$, and 90% were low performance services with $\theta = 0.1$. Further, 15 of the reporting agents were deceptive with $p_d = 0.2$, while 5 were fair agents with $p_f = 0.8$. The depth of memory used for the LA was $M = 10$, and the length of the sliding window was 100. Figure 4 demonstrates the ability of the approach to accurately infer correct decisions in the presence of the deceptive agents. Observe that the scheme achieves a near-*optimal* index that asymptotically approaches the performance of the high performance services, i.e., $\theta = 0.8$. To investigate the behaviour of the $AMPA$ with performances which changed with time, we first considered the scenario when these changes were made periodically. Indeed, we achieved this by changing all the service performances periodically every 5,000 runs. Further, the changes were made "drastic", i.e., by inverting them from their prior values as per $\theta_{l,new} = 1 - \theta_{l,old}$. From the results shown in Figure 5, the reader will observe that the scheme is able to adapt favourably to such changes. Indeed, from Figure 5, we notice that as the behavior of the services changed (i.e., at every $5,000^{th}$ step), the subsequent access by agent u resulted in choosing a low performance service.

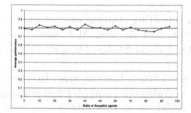

Fig. 4. The behavior of the $AMPA$, measured in terms of the average performance, in an environment when the behavior of the agents is static

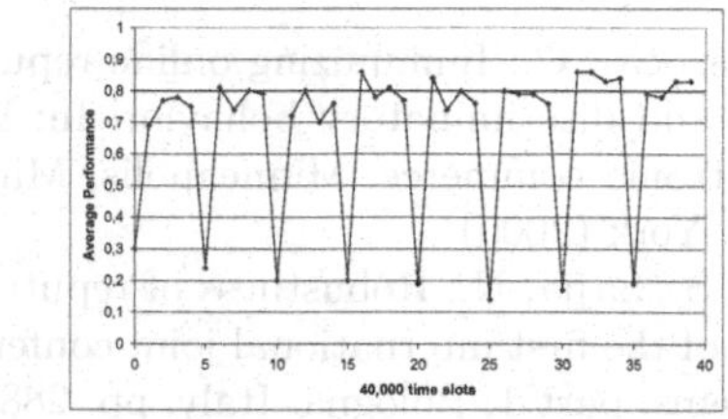

Fig. 5. The performance of the $AMPA$ with periodically changing service performances

4.2   Immunity to the Proportion of Fair Agents

We now consider the problem of investigating how "immune" our system is to the percentage of deceptive agents. Figure 6 presents the average performance of the system (over all interactions) when the ratio of deceptive agents is varied. The scheme is truly "immune" to varying the proportions of fair and deceptive agents. In fact, even if all agents are deceptive, (i.e., this is equivalent to a ratio of 100%, the average performance is stable and again achieves near optimal values that approach the index of the high performance services, $\theta = 0.8$. In our opinion, this is quite remarkable!

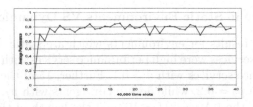

Fig. 6. The variation of the average performance under different ratios of deceptive agents

5   Conclusion

In this paper, we presented a new technique for coping with liars in reputation systems. The agents were modeled of two nature: fair and deceptive. Unlike other reported approaches, our scheme is able to counter detrimental effect of deceptive agents by intelligently combining feedback from fair and deceptive agents. The results of the simulation are conclusive and and demonstrate the potential of learning automata when applied in the area of Reputation Systems.

References

1. Dellarocas, C.: Immunizing online reputation reporting systems against unfair ratings and discriminatory behavior. In: Proceedings of the 2nd ACM conference on Electronic commerce, Minneapolis, Minnesota, United States, pp. 150–157. ACM, New York (2000)
2. Sen, S., Sajja, N.: Robustness of reputation-based trust: boolean case. In: Proceedings of the first international joint conference on Autonomous agents and multiagent systems, part 1, Bologna, Italy, pp. 288–293. ACM, New York (2002)
3. Zacharia, G., Maes, P.: Trust management through reputation mechanisms. Applied Artificial Intelligence 14(9), 881–907 (2000)
4. Whitby, A., Jsang, A., Indulska, J.: Filtering out unfair ratings in bayesian reputation systems. In: Proceedings of the 7th Int. Workshop on Trust in Agent Societies (at AAMAS 2004). ACM, New York (2004)
5. Despotovic, Z., Aberer, K.: A probabilistic approach to predict peers performance in P2P networks. In: Cooperative Information Agents VIII, pp. 62–76 (2004)
6. Narendra, K.S., Thathachar, M.A.L.: Learning Automata: An Introduction. Prentice-Hall, New Jersey (1989)
7. Oommen, B.J., Ma, D.C.Y.: Stochastic automata solutions to the object partitioning problem. The Computer Journal 35, A105–A120 (1992)
8. Mayur Datar, M., Gionis, A., Indyk, P., Motwani, R.: Maintaining stream statistics over sliding windows. SIAM J. Comput. 31(6), 1794–1813 (2002)
9. Shapiro, C.: Consumer information, product quality, and seller reputation. The Bell Journal of Economics 13(1), 20–35 (1982)

AC2001-OP: An Arc-Consistency Algorithm for Constraint Satisfaction Problems*

Marlene Arangú, Miguel A. Salido, and Federico Barber

Instituto de Automática e Informática Industrial
Universidad Politécnica de Valencia
Valencia, Spain

Abstract. Many real life problems can be modeled as constraint satisfaction problems (CSPs) and be solved using constraint programming techniques. In broad domains, consistency techniques become an important issue important since they can prune the search space and make more efficient the search of solutions. In this paper, we present AC2001-OP, an optimized version of AC2001/3.1 for arithmetic constraints, that reduces the number of propagations, the number of constraint checks and the running time meanwhile it prunes the same search space that the standard version. In inequality constraints, AC2001-OP, checks the binary constraints in both directions (full arc-consistency), but it only propagates the new constraints in one direction. Thus, it avoids checking redundant constraints that do not filter any value of variable's domains. The computational evaluation performed shows the improvement of AC2001-OP over AC2001/3.1 in both random instances as well as in domain-oriented problems of railway scheduling scenarios.

Introduction

Many combinatorial problems can be modeled as constraint satisfaction problems (CSPs) and be solved using constraint programming techniques. Constraint propagation is a common technique used to prune the search space in CSPs. Consistency-enforcing algorithms make any partial solution of a small sub-network extensible to surrounding networks. The number of possible combinations can be huge, while only very few are consistent. By eliminating redundant values in variables's domains, the size of the solution space decreases. If, as a result of reduction, any domain becomes empty, then it is known immediately that the problem has no solution [10].

Arc-consistency is considered to be the most common filtering technique. It ensures that each value in the domain of each variable is supported by a value in the domain of the variable that it constrains. The arc-consistency algorithms are used in the pre-processing step, before starting the search and are also used during the search process. Proposing efficient algorithms for enforcing arc-consistency has always been considered as a central question in the constraint reasoning community because it is frequently used in both industrial and academic solvers [2]. Most of the algorithms proposed so far put a lot of effort on identifying a support to confirm the existence of a

---

* This work has been partially supported by the research projects TIN2007-67943-C02-01 (Min. de Educacion y Ciencia, Spain-FEDER) and P19/08 (Min. de Fomento, Spain-FEDER).

N. García-Pedrajas et al. (Eds.): IEA/AIE 2010, Part III, LNAI 6098, pp. 219–228, 2010.

support [9]. Furthermore, once a domain is pruned, a propagation process is usually triggered: value propagation (fine grained) or arc-propagation (coarse grained). Thereby, there are many arc-consistency algorithms and today, the most referenced algorithms are AC3 [8] (because of its simplicity) and AC2001/3.1 [3] (because of its simplicity and optimality) [7].

After 20 years of research in fine-grained algorithms, re-emerge the interest of researchers for constraint propagation in the coarse-grain algorithms, specifically the AC3 algorithm, a greedy and fast algorithm, where its data structure is very simple (only one queue Q) but inefficient because its propagation mechanism repeats the same checking every time. To avoid these drawbacks AC2001/3.1 stores $value_j$, the smallest support for each value on each constraint. However, we have found that there are constraints whose propagations do not perform any prune, and if these propagations are avoided, the algorithm improves its performance.

We reformulate the AC2001/3.1 for inequality constraints by means of the management of the constraint propagations in only one direction instead of in both directions, as in [1]. This reformulation is named AC2001-OP. Thus, in section 1, we provide the necessary definitions and the notations to understand the rest of the paper. In section 2, we explain the AC2001/3.1 algorithm in detail. We present our AC2001-OP algorithm in section 3. In section 4, we evaluate the behavior of AC2001/3.1 and AC2001-OP empirically with random problems as well as some benchmarks on the railway scheduling problem using real-life data. Finally, we present our conclusions in section 5.

1   Definitions

By following standard notations and definitions in the literature [2,4], we have summarized both the basic definitions and the notations used in this paper:

Definition 1. Constraint Satisfaction Problem, CSP is a triple $P = \langle X, D, R \rangle$ where: X is the finite set of variables $\{X_1, X_2, ..., X_n\}$; D is a set of domains $D = \{D_1, D_2, ... , D_n\}$ such that, for each variable $X_i \in X$, there is a finite set of values that the variable can take; R is a finite set of constraints $R = \{R_1, R_2, ..., R_m\}$ which restrict the values that the variables can simultaneously take.

Definition 2. Arithmetic constraint is a constraint in the form $X_i \, op \, X_j$, where $X_i, X_j \in X$ and the operator $op \in \{<, \leq, =, \neq, \geq, >\}$. Due to the fact that any constraint $X_i\{>, \geq\}X_j$ can be written as $X_j\{<, \leq\}X_i$, without loss of generality, we can restrict the operators to $op \in \{<, \leq, =, \neq\}$.

Definition 3. Inequality constraint is a constraint in the form $X_i < X_j$.

In this paper, we restrict our attention to binary CSPs with arithmetic constraints (all arithmetic constraints involve two variables). Thus, we can represent the CSP as a directed graph, where variables are represented by nodes and binary constraints correspond to directed arcs (see Fig. 1). We denote: $R_{ij} \equiv (R_{ij}, 1)$ as the direct constraint defined over the variables X_i and X_j: $X_i\{<, \leq, =, \neq\}X_j$; $R_{ji} \equiv (R_{ij}, 2)$ as the same constraint in the inverse direction over the variables X_i and X_j (inverse constraint): $X_j\{>, \geq, =, \neq\}X_i$ and opR_{ij} as the operator of constraint R_{ij}.

Fig. 1 left shows a binary CSP with three variables X_0, X_1, and X_2; $D_0 = D_1 = D_2 = \{0, 1, 2\}$ and three direct constraints $R_{01} : X_0 < X_1, R_{02} : X_0 < X_2$ and

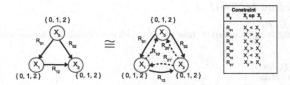

Fig. 1. Example of a Binary CSP

$R_{12} : X_1 < X_2$. It can be observed that $R_{01} \equiv (R_{01}, 1) : X_0 < X_1$ is the direct constraint while $R_{10} \equiv (R_{01}, 2) : X_1 > X_0$ is the inverse one (see Fig. 1, center). The operator of R_{01} is '$<$', so we denote $opR_{01} = '<'$. Thus, without loss of generality, we use both notations R_{ij} or $(R_{ij}, 1)$.

Definition 4. Instantiation is a pair (X_i, a), that represents an assignment of the value a to the variable X_i. We can use $(X_i = a) \equiv (X_i, a)$.

Definition 5. Arc-consistency. A **value** $a \in D_i$ is **arc-consistent** relative to X_j, iff there exists a value $b \in D_j$ such that (X_i, a) and (X_j, b) satisfy the constraint R_{ij} $((X_i = a, X_j = b) \in R_{ij})$. A **variable** X_i is **arc-consistent** relative to X_j iff all values in D_i are arc-consistent. A **CSP is arc-consistent** iff all the variables are arc-consistent, e.g., all the arcs R_{ij} and R_{ji} are arc-consistent. (Note: here we are talking about full arc-consistency).

2 AC2001/3.1

Based on the framework of AC3 [8] a new algorithm: AC2001/3.1 [3] was developed by adding a data structure which stores the last support found and re-starts the search from this value. AC2001/3.1 (see Algorithm 1) changes the *Revise* procedure and adds an initialization phase (see Algorithm 2) for *Last* vector in a dummy value. This dummy value must meet to be smaller than $minD(X_j)$. AC2001/3.1 algorithm assumes all domains are upward sorted. The way of processing of AC2001/3.1 is the basis of coarse-grain algorithms that follow: AC3.2, AC3.3 [6]; AC3rm [7], etc. The algorithm AC2001/3.1 is the only optimal coarse-grain algorithm [2]. It has $O(ed^2)$ space complexity and $O(ed)$ time complexity where e is the number of edges and d is the maximum domain size.

The *Revise* procedure (see Algorithm 3) verifies, for each value $a \in D_i$, that the value stored in $Last(R_{ij}, X_i, a)$ belongs to D_j before seeking support for a value of the variable domain. This avoids ineffective checking, since this value a, which was proved to be supported by means of the previous check, was also proved to be still supported in D_j, thus the *Revise* procedure continues with the next value of D_i. In case of $Last(R_{ij}, X_i, a)$ stores a dummy value or this value b does not belong to D_j, Revise2001 procedure proceeds to find a value $c \in D_j$ where $c > dummyvalue$, and $c > b$, and c satisfies R_{ij}. If value c is not found, the value $a \in D_i$ is pruned because a is not supported by any value of D_j and return *change*=true.

Algorithm 1. Procedure AC2001/3.1

Data: A CSP, $P = \langle X, D, R \rangle$
Result: **true** and P' (which is arc consistent) or **false** and P' (which is arc inconsistent because some domain
remains empty)

```
  begin
1 │   Initialize2001(P, Last)
2 │   for every arc R_ij ∈ R do
3 │   └   Append (Q, (R_ij)) and Append (Q, (R_ji))
4 │   while Q ≠ φ do
5 │       select and delete R_ij from queue Q
6 │       if Revise2001(R_ij) = true then
7 │           if D_i ≠ φ then
8 │           └   Append (Q, (R_ki)) with k ≠ i, k ≠ j
  │           else
9 │           └   return false /*empty domain*/
10 │   return true
  end
```

Algorithm 2. Procedure Initialize2001

Data: A CSP P' defined by two variables $X = (X_i, X_j)$, domains D_i and D_j, and constraint R_{ij}.
Result: $Last$ vector initialized in a dummy value

```
  begin
1 │   for each R_ij ∈ R do
2 │       for each a ∈ D_i do
3 │       └   Last(R_ij, X_i, a) = dummy_value
4 │       for each b ∈ D_j do
5 │       └   Last(R_ij, X_j, b) = dummy_value
  end
```

AC2001/3.1 algorithm is efficient in a support re-checks, due to: (a) it avoids constraints checks if there exist a valid value and (b) it finds a new support from the last support found. However, it is inefficient since it does not update the checked variables bidirectionally (this drawback is resolved by AC3.3 algorithm [6]). As in other arc consistency techniques, AC2001/3.1 always propagates once values are pruned, without considering whether the propagation will be effective (the re-evaluation prunes values) or ineffective (only spending time, because no prune is performed).

3   AC2001-OP

As we pointed out in section 2, we have detected ineffectiveness in AC2001/3.1 due to the fact that the constraint propagation of some inverse arithmetic constraints $(R_{ij}, 2)$ is ineffective since no values in the domain will be pruned. However, AC2001/3.1 searches for direct and inverse constraints in the set of constraints R for constraint propagation.

AC2001-OP algorithm is a reformulation of AC2001/3.1 in its propagation strategy. It uses the same Initialize2001 procedure and a similar Revise2001 procedure, but some changes are carried out to avoid the drawbacks presented in AC2001/3.1:

- we label each constraint R_{ij} between X_i and X_j as a tuple (R_{ij}, s), where $s = 1$ if it is a direct constraint $(R_{ij} \equiv (R_{ij}, 1))$ and $s = 2$ if it is an inverse constraint $(R_{ji} \equiv (R_{ij}, 2))$.

Algorithm 3. Procedure Revise2001

Data: A CSP P' defined by two variables $X = (X_i, X_j)$, domains D_i and D_j, and constraint R_{ij}.
Result: D_i, such that X_i is arc consistent relative X_j and the boolean variable $change$

```
begin
1       change ← false
2       for each a ∈ D_i do
3           if value store in Last(R_ij, X_i, a) ∉ D_j then
4               if ∄b ∈ D_j such that (X_i = a, X_j = b) ∈ R_ij then
5                   remove a from D_i
6                   change ← true
            else
7                   Last(R_ij, X_i, a) ← b

8       return change
end
```

- Q is changed by QS, where it is firstly a queue and later it is a stack. Thus, QS stored tuples (R_{ij}, s) $|s \in \{1, 2\}$.
- it presents a new propagation schema (see Algorithm 4, steps 8 to 12).

The AC2001-OP algorithm reaches arc-consistency and carries out both a smaller number of propagations in Q and a smaller number of constraint checks than AC2001/3.1. Thus, AC2001-OP has a lower running time than AC2001/3.1. The data structure QS used by AC2001-OP to store the constraints firstly acts as a queue and later acts as a stack. QS is initialized in steps 1 to 3 of Algorithm 4 by inserting the tuples $(R_{ij}, 1)$ and $(R_{ij}, 2)$ as a queue. Afterwards, QS will behave as a stack. If $s = 1$ (step 6 of AC2001-OP), then the *Revise* procedure receives the direct constraint R_{ij}. If $s = 2$ in step 6, then it receives the inverse constraint R_{ji}. AC2001-OP will add new constraints on the top of QS in three different cases:

- if the constraint operator is equal to '$<$' and $s = 1$, and also the tentative added constraint has not been included in QS yet (step 9);
- in the remaining operators $\{\leq, =, \neq\}$, the tentative added constraints will be inserted in QS if they have not been included in QS yet (step 11);
- if the operator is equal to '$<$' and $s = 2$ and the operator of the tentative added constraint is not equal to '$<$' and it has not been included in QS yet (step 12).

Added constraints will be selected again in step 5, e.g., before the rest of the constraints previously stored in the stack QS. Thus, the addition of constraints is only carried out if they have not been included in the stack yet.

Lemma: The addition of inequality constraints $(X_k < X_j)$ in the stack added by an inverse inequality constraint $(X_j > X_i)$ will be redundant and will not prune any value in the domain of variable X_k.

Proof: The study of the direct inequality constraint $(X_i < X_j)$ has pruned all values in D_i without a support in D_j. Therefore, $\forall a \in D_i$, the upper bound of D_j $(uppD_j)$ is a support of a. The study of the inverse inequality constraint $X_j > X_i$ prunes all values in D_j without a support in D_i. If a value $c \in D_j$ is pruned, the inequality constraint $(X_k < X_j)$ would be included in the stack only if it had not yet been included. Due to the fact that all direct and inverse constraints are initially inserted in the stack, this

Algorithm 4. Procedure AC2001-OP

Data: A CSP, $P = \langle X, D, R \rangle$
Result: **true** and P' (which is arc consistent) or **false** and P' (which is arc inconsistent because some domain
    remains empty)

    begin
1      $Initialize2001(P, Last)$
2   **for** *every arc* $R_{ij} \in R$ **do**
3   Append $(QS, (R_{ij}, 1))$ and Append $(QS, (R_{ij}, 2))$

4   **while** $QS \neq \phi$ **do**
5   select and delete (R_{ij}, s) from queue Q where $s = 1 \vee s = 2$
6   **if** $Revise2001(R_{ij}, s) = true$ **then**
7   **if** $D_i \neq \phi$ *and* $D_j \neq \phi$ **then**
8   **if** $((opR_{ij} =' <'$ *and* $s = 1)$ *or* $(opR_{ij} \neq' <'))$ **then**
9   Append $(QS, (R_{ki}, 1))$ with $k \neq i,\ k \neq j$

10   **else**
11   Append $(QS, (R_{ki}, 1))$ with $k \neq i,\ k \neq j,\ opR_{ki} \neq' <'$
12   Append $(QS, (R_{ki}, 2))$ with $k \neq i,\ k \neq j,\ opR_{ki} \neq' <'$
           else
13   **return** false /*empty domain*/

14   **return** true
    end

constraint was previously studied, and all the remaining values in D_k had a support in D_j. Thus, $\forall b \in D_k$, the upper bound of Dj ($uppD_j$) was a support of b. Therefore, if $c <> uppD_j$, no pruning will be carried out by the inclusion of the inequality constraint $X_k < X_j$. If $c = uppD_j$, the domain of X_j remains empty ($Dj = \emptyset$), so the problem was not previously consistent. Thus, every inequality constraint added to QS by the propagation of an inverse inequality constraint will be redundant.

4   Experimental Results

Determining which algorithms are superior to others remains difficult. Algorithms take often been compared by observing its performance on benchmark problems or on suites of random instances generated from a simple, uniform distribution. On the one hand, the advantage of using benchmark problems is that if they are an interesting problem (to someone), then information about which algorithm works well on these problems is also interesting. However, although an algorithm outperforms to any other algorithm in its application to a concrete benchmark problem, it is difficult to extrapolate this feature to general problems. On the other hand, an advantage of using random problems is that there are many of them, and researchers can design carefully controlled experiments and report averages and other statistics. However, a drawback of random problems is that they may not reflect real life situations.

In the empirical evaluation we compare the behavior of AC2001/3.1 over AC2001-OP. This evaluation was carried out with both different types of problems: benchmark problems and random problems. Here, we analyzed the number of constraint checks, the number of propagations and the running time as a measure of efficiency. All algorithms were written in C. The experiments were conducted on a PC Intel Core 2 Quad (2.83 GHz processor and 3 GB RAM).

4.1   Domain-Oriented Benchmark Problems

The railway scheduling problem is a real life problem which we have used for analyzing the behavior of arc consistency algorithms. A running map (see Figure 2) contains information regarding the topology of the railways (stations, tracks, distances between stations, traffic control features, etc.) and the schedules of the trains that use this topology (arrival and departure times of trains at each station, frequency, stops, crossing, overtaking, etc.).

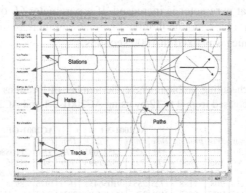

Fig. 2. Example of running map for railway scheduling problem

The scenario is a set of ordered locations $L = \{l_1, l_2, .., l_i\}$, a set of trains $T = \{t_1, t_2, ..., t_k\}$ for each direction and a journey (it is the order in which the train visits each of locations l_i) for each train . The problem is to place k trains over i locations to minimize the average transversal time satisfying: user constraints (initial departure time, frequency of departure, commercial stops, etc.), traffic constraints (exclusiveness, reception time, expedition time, precedence, etc.) and railway constraints (number of tracks between dependencies, capacity of each station closure times, etc.).

The railway scheduling problem can be solved in a centralized or distributed way [11]. Here, we present a simpler instance of the railway scheduling problem proposed in [5]. Our instances were carried out on a real railway infrastructure that joins two Spanish locations (Zaragoza and Caset) using data of the Administrator of Railway Infrastructures of Spain (ADIF). The journey between these two locations is divided in five stations and two halts. The variables are S_{ij} and $E_{(i+1)j}$: the start time and end time of train j in locations $i \rightarrow (i + 1)$, respectively. We only considered these constraints:

- Exclusiveness: A single track section must be occupied by only one train at the same time. $S_{ik} + p_{ik} < S_{hj} + 1 \vee S_{hj} + p_{hj} < S_{ik} + 1, \forall S(ik) \, and \, S(hj)$ where $i < h$.
- Precedence: Each train, that goes in one direction, employs a given time interval to cover each section. $S_{ij} + p_{ij} < S_{hj} + 1, \forall X(i, j) \rightarrow X(h, j)$.

- Journey: that specifies the ordered subset of visited locations for each train. $S_{1k} \rightarrow S_{2k} \rightarrow ...S_{ik}$.
- Duration: that specifies the duration of each train between two contiguous locations $S_{ij} + p_{ij} = E_{ij}$.

In this empirical evaluation, the constraints were generated by using the approach proposed in [12]. Each set of instances was defined by the tuple $\langle L, T \rangle$, where L was the number of locations (stations or halts) and T was the number of trains in each direction. Thus, we set one parameter and vary the other one in order to evaluate the algorithm performance when that parameter is increased. If a parameter (L or T) increases then both the number of variables and the number of constraint increase as well. The domain size (the maximum time) was fixed in 1000 seconds.

Table 1. The railway scheduling problem where the number of locations was set to 7 and the number of trains was increased from 2 to 12 by using AC2001-3.1 and AC2001-OP

				AC2001-3.1			AC2001-OP		
t_i	var	const	pruning	Time	Prop	Cc	Time	Prop	Cc
2	30	51	1896	372	225	22577693	373	158	22108862
4	58	186	3660	778	725	45217993	729	540	44236030
6	86	405	5424	1216	1501	68044248	1119	1146	66509208
8	114	708	7188	1725	2553	91056458	1621	1976	88928396
10	142	1032	8952	2191	3707	114116488	2036	2862	111384205
12	170	1356	10716	3123	4905	137178293	2861	3748	133840172

Table 1 shows the number of variables and constraints, the pruned values, the running time, the number of constraint checks and propagations in railway scheduling problem, where the number of locations was set to 7 and the number of trains was increased from 2 to 12: $< 7, t_i >$. The results of Table 1 shows that the running time, the number of propagations and the number of constraint checks were lower in AC2001-OP than in AC2001/3.1. The AC2001-OP algorithm improved the running time, propagations and constraint checks in all cases with an average of 7.48%, 23.25% and 2.34%, respectively. AC2001-OP also improved the number of constraint checks due to the strategies of modeling and propagation. These strategies allowed a pruning in early stages avoiding value checks that were subsequently pruned.

Table 2. The railway scheduling problem where the number of trains was set to 6 and the number of locations was increased from 5 to 25 by using AC2001-3.1 and AC2001-OP

				AC2001-3.1			AC2001-OP		
l_i	var	const	pruning	Time	Prop	Cc	Time	Prop	Cc
5	62	291	2796	766	822	49238934	719	642	48418203
7	86	405	5424	1216	1501	68044248	1119	1146	66509208
9	110	519	11220	1532	2382	87463824	1360	1794	84348345
11	134	633	18090	1953	3469	106931190	1719	2586	102001563
13	158	747	25596	2391	4760	126318828	2063	3522	119385798
15	182	861	34128	2891	6258	145683327	2437	4608	136401906
25	302	1431	112356	5438	16786	241617678	4250	12168	210123024

Table 2 shows the number of variables and constraints, the pruned values, the running time, the number of constraint checks and propagations in railway scheduling problem, where the number of locations was increased from 5 to 25 (Zaragoza - Calat) and the number of trains was set to 6. Again, the results of Table 2 shows that the running time, the number of propagations and the number of constraint checks were lower in AC2001-OP than in AC2001/3.1. The AC2001-OP algorithm improved the running time, propagations and constraint checks in all cases with an average of 15.57%, 26.44% and 7.04%, respectively.

4.2 Random Problems

As we pointed out, benchmark sets are used to test algorithms for specific problems, but in recent years, there has been a growing interest in the study of the relation among the parameters that define an instance of CSP in general (i.e., the number of variables, domain size and arity of constraints). Therefore, the notion of randomly generated CSPs has been introduced to describe the classes of CSPs. These classes are then studied using empirical methods.

In this case, a random CSP instance was characterized by the 3-tuple $< n, d, m >$, where n was the number of variables, d the domain size and m the number of binary constraints. We generated two classes of random problems: problems with inequality constraints and problems with arithmetic constraints.

In both types of problems, all the variables maintained the same domains. We evaluated 50 test cases for each type of problem. Thus, in all instances, we set two of the parameters and varied the other one in order to evaluate the algorithm's performance when this parameter increased.

Table 3. Time (milliseconds), propagations (Prop) and number of constraint checks (Cc) by using AC2001-3.1 and AC2001-OP with both inequality constraints $< n, 50, 800 >$ and arithmetic constraints $< n, 50, 800 >$

| | | Inequality constraints | | | | | | Arithmetic constraints | | | | | |
| | | AC2001-3.1 | | | AC2001-OP | | | | AC2001-3.1 | | | AC2001-OP | | |
n	pruning	Time	Prop	Cc	Time	Prop	Cc	pruning	Time	Prop	Cc	Time	Prop	Cc
50	1031	132.7	12443	815418	46.8	3140	809706	450	62.4	3694	907752	42.1	1762	906446
70	892	90.1	7634	921740	46.8	1963	917514	489	62.2	3597	982396	46.8	2160	981434
90	858	79.2	6264	975825	46.9	1764	972615	448	47.5	2854	1029559	46.8	1789	1029053
110	836	77.3	5319	1009727	46.5	1684	1007179	440	51.3	2591	1058073	46.5	1718	1057605
130	828	78.4	4965	1032894	46.8	1656	1030803	520	50.6	3106	1081672	46.8	2139	1076569
150	821	79.3	4476	1049576	46.8	1635	1047811	448	61.2	2392	1091545	46.8	1741	1091230

The results of Table 3 for both inequality and arithmetic constraints show that the running time, the number of propagations and the number of constraint checks were lower in AC2001-OP than in AC2001/3.1. In inequality constraints, the AC2001-OP algorithm improved the running time, propagations and constraint checks in all cases with an average of 47.75%, 71.19% and 0.34%, respectively. However, arithmetic constraints, the behavior of AC2001/3.1 and AC2001-OP was closer because both algorithms maintain the same performance for constraints with operator $op \in \{=, \neq\}$. Table 3 for inequality constraints also shows that the pruned values and the number of propagations were reduced as the number of variables increased. This is due to the fact that as the number of variables increased, the tightness of the problems decreased since the number of constraints remained constant.

5 Conclusions

Arc-consistency techniques are widely used to prune the search space of CSPs. In this paper, we present AC2001-OP, which is an optimized and reformulated version of AC2001/3.1 that improves the efficiency of previous versions by reducing the number of propagations, the number of constraint checks and the running time in CSPs with arithmetic constraints. For this type of problems, AC2001-OP prunes the same search space as AC2001/3.1, but its efficiency is given by the propagation strategy. AC2001-OP checks the binary constraints in both directions (full arc-consistency) but, in inequality constraints, it only propagates new constraints in one direction. Thus, it avoids checking redundant constraints that do not filter any value of the variable's domain. The evaluation section shows that AC2001-OP algorithm will be useful in many real problems that can be modeled with arithmetic constraints, as railway scheduling problem showed above. An important percentage of the constrains of this problem, which had to be generated in a concrete order, are inequality constraints. As a consequence of that and also due as a result of the above mentioned propagation strategy, the performance of AC2001-OP was better than AC2001/3.1's.

References

1. Arangú, M., Salido, M.A., Barber, F.: AC3-OP: An arc-consistency algorithm for arithmetic constraints. In: CCIA 2009 (2009)
2. Bessiere, C.: Constraint propagation. Technical report, CNRS (2006)
3. Bessiere, C., Régin, J.C., Yap, R., Zhang, Y.: An optimal coarse-grained arc-consistency algorithm. Artificial Intelligence 165, 165–185 (2005)
4. Dechter, R.: Constraint Processing. Morgan Kaufmann, San Francisco (2003)
5. Ingolotti, L.: Modelos y métodos para la optimización y eficiencia de la programación de horarios ferroviarios. PhD thesis, Universidad Politécnica de Valencia (2007)
6. Lecoutre, C., Boussemart, F., Hemery, F.: Exploiting multidirectionality in coarse-grained arc consistency algorithms. In: Rossi, F. (ed.) CP 2003. LNCS, vol. 2833, pp. 480–494. Springer, Heidelberg (2003)
7. Lecoutre, C., Hemery, F.: A study of residual supports in arc consistency. In: Proceedings IJCAI 2007, pp. 125–130 (2007)
8. Mackworth, A.K.: Consistency in networks of relations. Artificial Intelligence 8, 99–118 (1977)
9. Mehta, D.: Reducing checks and revisions in the coarse-grained arc consistency algorithms. CP Letters 2, 37–53 (2008)
10. Ruttkay, Z.: Constraint Satisfaction - a Survey. CWI Quarterly 11(2, 3), 123–162 (1998)
11. Salido, M., Abril, M., Barber, F., Ingolotti, L., Tormos, P., Lova, A.: Domain dependent distributed models for railway scheduling. Knowledge-Based Systems 20, 186–194 (2007)
12. Salido, M.A.: A non-binary constraint ordering heuristic for constraint satisfaction problems. Applied Mathematics and Computation 198(1), 280–295 (2008)

NFC Solution for the Development of Smart Scenarios Supporting Tourism Applications and Surfing in Urban Environments

Francisco Borrego-Jaraba, Irene Luque Ruiz*, and Miguel Ángel Gómez-Nieto

University of Córdoba. Department of Computing and Numerical Analysis
Campus de Rabanales. Albert Einstein Building. E-14071 Córdoba, Spain
{i12bojaf,iluque,mangel}@uco.es

Abstract. Ubiquitous applications have increased during the last decade thanks to the development of communication and mobile technologies. These applications cover a wide spectrum of problems, sectors, scenarios and environments that aim to build smart environments supporting many kinds of human interactions. Tourism plays a substantial role in the economies of some cities and countries. Tourism can secure employment, foreign exchange, investment and regional development, and therefore a research area where the development of ubiquitous applications is having a great interest. In this paper, we describe a pervasive solution for the innovation of the touristic sector offering the users/visitors, in a way easy, intuitive and context-awareness, support for the navigation and localization in urban smart scenarios. The solution is based in the use of Near Field Communication Technology and Smart Posters spread up along the smart environments. The model architecture is described as well as the developed software. Application to tourism in the city of Córdoba is presented.

Keywords: Ambient Intelligence, Tourism, City navigation, Near Field Communication, Pervasive system.

1 Introduction

The Ambient Intelligence (AmI) concept was developed in the ISTAG reports [1, 2] providing a vision of the Information Society future where the emphasis is on user friendliness, efficient and distributed services support, user-empowerment, and support for human interactions.

Ambient Intelligence paradigm often refers to electronic environments that are sensitive and responsive to the presence of people. The intention is to hide the technology in the background, and provide ambient means like speech and gestures to interact with these environments.

In this way, people are surrounded by intelligent intuitive interfaces that are embedded in all kinds of objects and an environment that is capable of recognizing and

---

* Corresponding author.

N. García-Pedrajas et al. (Eds.): IEA/AIE 2010, Part III, LNAI 6098, pp. 229–238, 2010.
© Springer-Verlag Berlin Heidelberg 2010

responding to the presence of different individuals in a seamless, unobtrusive and often invisible way.

In this vision of the future that forecast AmI, the model of user interaction, information visualization, access personalization and context sensitivity play a very important role that has been studied by different authors [2, 3, 4], where several models and paradigms have been proposed.

Near Field Communication (NFC) [5] is an emerging technology that provides a natural interaction way between the user and its environment that makes it the ideal candidate for the development of intelligent ambients. NFC is a standard-based, short-range wireless connectivity technology that lets different devices communicate when they are in close proximity. It is based on RFID (Radio Frequency Identification) [6]. NFC enables simple and safe two-way interactions among electronic devices, allowing users to perform contactless transactions, access digital content and connect devices with a single "touch". In other words NFC is a mobile device with RFID technology.

NFC has also the ability to write information onto the RFID-chip. This opens up for features like door authentication, transit authentication, payment or even getting downloaded trailers or information from a Smart Poster [7].

NFC offers a simple solution based in the "touching paradigm" where users touch with their NFC device to everyday life objects augmented with visual marks and RFID Tags with the aim of trigger the intelligent services offered by those objects. Nowadays, different investigations are studying the use of NFC to a wide spectrum of problems, including commerce, ticketing and payment, transport, tourism, identification and security, university [8-13], among other.

Tourism is an important social and economical activity providing huge economics resources to many cities and countries where the development of AmI and the use of NFC could enhance and improve the activity. Applications oriented to tourism activity should be oriented to improve to different kind of scenarios [14, 15]: indoors and outdoors.

Several studies and prototypes have been proposed for the development of smart environments applied to touristic sector. Combining RFID and Bluetooth technologies are used for user navigation in indoors scenarios like Museums, real traffic, transportation services, tourism guides, commerce, etc. Other proposals use GPS technology supporting the user navigation in the city or other outdoors scenarios, or augmented paper map with RFID Tags [16].

Special interests have taken applications oriented to city transport (bus and subway) also supporting transportation payment. Those systems generally propose the use of informative panels placed in transport stops allowing the user, using his/her NFC device, to obtain information about transportation schedules, waiting time for arrival, purchase tickets, and so on [17].

In this paper, we present a touristic context-aware solution for the localization and navigation in urban environments. The idea proposed in this work is that the user could design its own routes making use of a set of intelligent objects (Smart Posters) augmented by RFID Tags with information about localizations where the tourist could visit. The touristic information is shown to the user with different shapes and details, localization and navigation through different points of the scenario is provided through maps real-time downloaded. Answers to "what is this?", "where am I?", "where it is?", "what is there nearby me?" etc., are given to the user in an intuitive, quick way and without any previous manipulation of the mobile device by the user.

The proponed solution is based in the user of Smart Posters with text and visual information corresponding to the places where they are located. The Smart Posters spread up in touristic areas (see Fig. 1) are formed by a set of Tags associated to each visual element of the Smart Poster, which offers the user different touristic services and information.

Fig. 1. An example of a Smart Poster in touristic area

The information stored in the Tags (using NFC-Forum standard [18]), the user selection and the information stored in the system allows the system to offer, through maps and text information, a swift, quick and user-customized channel to navigate in the touristic environment.

The paper has been organized as follows: in section 2 the proposed model is presented, describing the interactive model and system architecture. In section 3 the intelligent scenarios using Smart Posters are described, together with the information stored in each poster and the software solution built for the NFC device and server. In section 4 an application example for the use in the touristic area of the Córdoba city is presented. Finally, we discuss the solution proposed and the possibility of application to other kind of scenarios.

2   A NFC Model for City Navigation

City Surfing is the capability of the users (visitors/tourist) to move to or between different tourist interest points in a way simple, easy, intuitive and context-awareness. In this context, tourists are immersed in smarts urban environments that provide them information and other services.

Touching paradigm is appropriate for the development of these smart scenarios. Users only need "touch" an augmented object of the scenario to obtain any information or requested service.

As Fig. 2 shows, the proposed model architecture is based on the use of three actors: a) Smart Posters disseminated in the environment containing Tags associated to different interest points, b) users, using NFC mobile phones storing appropriate software (MIDlet), and c) a back-end software in charge to dispatch the user request. Smart Posters contain different objects (visual, graphic and text information about different locations) augmented by Tags that keep information and services about themselves.

When the user "touches" with his/her NFC device any of the Tags (objects) located in the Smart Poster, a MIDlet, previously downloaded in the mobile device, is initiated establishing a communication GPRS/EDGE/UMTS with a back-end application located in the server side.

The back-end application receives the information sent by the MIDlet and moves this information to the server that answers back the MIDlet, being the MIDlet the responsible of showing the answer to the user in a proper way.

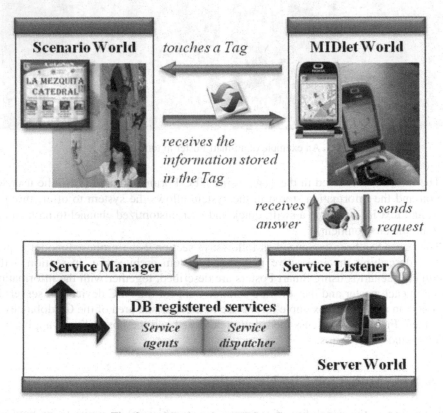

Fig. 2. Architecture for a NFC surfing system

For location and navigation applications different kind of user requests must to be answered: "where am I", "what is it", "how can I go to", "what is there around me", "how can I find", etc. So, different kind of answers must be provided by the back-end application only using the information sent by the MIDlet and captured when the user touches a Smart Poster Tag.

In order to give answer to all possible user requests the back-end application includes the functional components shown in Fig. 2. The service listener is an agent in charge of receiving any request. When the service listener receives a request, it analyzes it, checks its registry and processes it to the Service Manager, who is the responsible to execute it and answer back a response to the MIDlet stored in the NFC phone device.

The Tags, associated to the different pictograms of the Smart Posters, store text and location information corresponding with the related interest city points. This information is gathered by the MIDlet installed in the NFC phone device when the user touches the Tag.

The MIDlet is a Java application that is executed in the NFC device and that guides the interaction between the user and the scenario. When the user "touches" a Tag with its NFC device, thanks to the information stored in the Tag, the MIDlet is instantiated allowing the interaction of the system with the user. This event is carried out thanks to the "push registry" method. Through the "push registry" method, the mobile phone would activate a specific MIDlet depending of the kind of information that has been read in the Tag.

3   Augmented Environments with Smart Posters

City surfing is performed in open environments where we can disseminate Smart Posters with appropriate visual and textual information for helping in the city location and navigation.

Tags are associated with the different pictograms or icons drawn in the Smart Posters which represent different city interest points. For an easy and intuitive user interaction, clear and simple Smart Posters should be created. For instance, each Smart Poster located in a specific city location could only include attached Tags for: a) the main pictogram corresponding with the interest point where the Smart Poster is located; and b) a set of pictograms (images) related to the advice interest points located near to the actual user location.

Each Tag associated to the different Smart Posters objects should store enough information to give answer to the user requests. In our model, Tags store:

- A brief description of the interest point related with the Tag.
- Physical coordinates where the Smart Poster is placed.
- Physical coordinates of the interest point related to the Tag.
- A set of services associated with the Tag.

When the user touches a Tag, as previously mentioned, the MIDlet is initiated automatically. In case that MIDlet would not be installed in the NFC device, a message alerting about the need of the MIDlet download from the server is received. That is a service associated with any Tag in all Smart Posters. Once the MIDlet is downloaded and installed in the device, the user can configure it.

Now, the MIDlet gathers all information from the Tag and shows the user the list of associated services to the Tag as well as other default application services, as:

- The user can retrieve information about the interest points associated with the Tag. In this way, the systems shows a brief description about the interest points as well as allows to the user initiate a GPRS connection with the Web page about the interest points.

- The user can retrieve a navigation map. This map shows to the user the advice route from his/her present location to the location of the interest point selected.
- Allows the user to access the available information and services in a touristic information service, related to: a) the interest point where the Smart Poster is located, and b) any of the other interest points or locations showed in the Smart Poster.

A Java application for the developing of the city surfing scenarios has been developed. This application allows the creation of different projects (scenarios) where a non restricted number of Smart Posters can be considered. Moreover, each Smart Poster can be associated any number of Tags each one related with different Smart Posters objects.

Information about the projects (scenarios), Smart Posters and Tags is stored in a relational database in the server side. So, when the user touches a Tag, the MIDlet performs the following actions:

- Retrieves the information stored in the Tag.
- Analyzes the stored services and shows to the user a list Menu with the different options.
- Sends to the server side the service selected by the user. For instance, if the user selects a map from his/her present position to a wished interest point, the information sent to the server is two coordinates (present position and the interest points where the user whishes to go).

When the listener in the server side receives the request, it sends that request to the Service Manager. This process checks in the application database if the service is defined and if the information received is correct. If yes, the service is executed and the answer is back to the MIDlet, otherwise an error message is back.

This architecture allows us to implement different services associated with different Tags, and even services not implemented in the actual development. For instance, a Tag could have associated a service consisting in buying a ticket from a museum. In this case, the server service just would consist in a gateway to the secure portal in charge of tickets sale.

4 Application to Tourism Surfing at Cordoba City

The developed system has been tested in the tourist area of the Córdoba city. For the development of the Smart Posters Tags Mifare 1k [19], and Omnikey 5120 USB [20] have been used as read/write device. The NFC devices used have been Nokia 6131 NFC [21] mobile phones.

In this test, Smart Posters have been disseminated over a wide tourist area. Each Smart Poster is located in an interest point showing information (pictograms) about the interest point and other advices interest points nearby.

As Fig. 3 shows, different user interactions have been tested. When the user touches a Tag located in a tourist point (Fig. 3a), the MIDlet shows to the user a Menu (Fig. 3b) with the list of available services for that Tag. If the user selects, for instance, the option "Recover Map", a map with the route from his/her present location to the selected/touched interest point is shown by the MIDlet (Fig 3c). This map shows the advice route with other nearby tourist interest points. Those interest points previously visited by the user are shown with different color to the selected by the user.

The information (maps and text) received by the user in interactions with Smart Posters, can be stored for future accesses and requests. This information is stored in the mobile device, being the location chosen by the user in the "Configuration" options (Figure 3b). The user could at any time, manually or guided by the MIDlet, delete the history stored in the device.

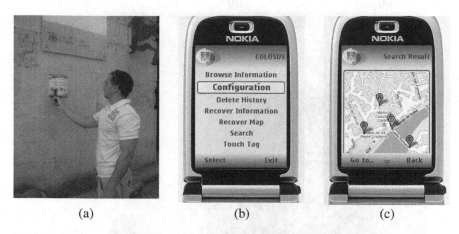

(a)   (b)   (c)

Fig. 3. Surfing across the city of Córdoba

An advantage of the system is that the tourist does not to move to an information center, connect to a Web Portal, etc., in order to know or to have the application in his/her NFC device.

So, the first time a user "touches" a Tag with his/her NFC device, the system detects that the MIDlet is not installed in the NFC device and it asks the user whether he/she wants it to be downloaded. Once the user has the MIDlet installed, he/she can configure its execution.

Other important system characteristic is its capability to give answer to different user searches. Fig. 4a shows the MIDlet Menu in charge to perform searches about interest points. In this form, the user selects:

- The category of interest point (monument, restaurant, church, garden, etc.).
- Any text to be also considered in the search criterion. This text will be matched against the information stored in the project database in the server side.
- The limit of distance in meter. This distance is taken from the last interest point accessed (Tag touched) by the user. Due to not GPS system is used by the system to know the user real location, the search area is considered the circumference of radio equal to the distance entered by the user, being the circumference center the location of the last Tag touched by the user.

Fig. 4. Snapshots corresponding with the search characteristic

Once the search criteria have been chosen, for instance search for a restaurant 200 meters around (Fig. 4b), the MIDlet sends the request to the server which answers back a map and a list with the current location and that of the interest points that fulfill the current search criteria (Fig. 4c). Now, the user can move to the new interest point (in our example, the restaurant "Bodegas Campos") to enjoy its famous cuisine, and later to touch a new Tag in the Smart Poster (Fig. 4d) located in that tourist point in order to follow with his/her tourist visit to the Córdoba city.

5 Discussion and Remarks

In this paper we have presented a pervasive and context-aware system for application to the tourism city. In this proposal the users (tourists) use mobile phones with Near Field Communication technology to interact with tourist smart environments.

Scenarios, controlled tourist city areas, are dotted of Smart Posters showing textual and graphic information (pictograms/images) of sights augmented with RFID Tags.

The system developed does not require any configuration by the user, or going to Tourist Information Points or any tourist Web portal access in order to download the system.

The system is easy and intuitive to use, just the user touches a pictograms corresponding with the wished sight to visit, the system provides textual information, and a map with the advised route or any other implemented service.

Although current NFC Mobile devices are kept to only some models from just some commercial brands is forecasted that for 2011 more than 50% of mobile phones will include NFC technology, and this kind of system could change the behavior of the tourists, offering more services than a simple paper tourist guide.

We are testing the system for application to big commercial areas, where the user has trouble with the location of the companies located there, could underpin an increase and expansion of the business in those areas.

Acknowledgments. This work was supported by the Ministry of Science and Innovation of Spain (MICINN) and FEDER (Project: TIN2009-07184).

References

1. ISTAG. Scenarios for Ambient Intelligence in 2010. European Commission Report (2001), http://www.cordis.lu/ist/istag.htm
2. ISTAG. Ambient Intelligence: from vision to reality. European Commission Report (2003)
3. Aarts, E., Marzano, S. (eds.): The New Everyday: Visions of Ambient Intelligence. 010 Publishing Rotterdam, The Netherlands (2003)
4. Ailisto, H., Pohjanheimo, L., Välkkynen, P., Strömmer, E., Tuomisto, T., Korhonen, I.: Bridging the physical and virtual worlds by local connectivity-based physical selection. Pers. Ubiquit. Comput. 10, 333–344 (2006)
5. ECMA. Near Field Communication white paper. ECMA/TC32-TG16/2004/1 (2004)
6. Finkenzeller, K.: RFID Handbook: Fundamentals and Applications in Contacless Smart Cards and Identification. Wiley, England (2003)
7. NFC Forum, http://www.nfc-forum.org/home
8. Floerkemeier, C., Langheinrich, M., Fleisch, E., Mattern, F., Sarma, S.E. (eds.): IOT 2008. LNCS, vol. 4952. Springer, Heidelberg (2008)
9. Remédios, D., Sousa, L., Barata, M., Osório, L.: NFC Technologies in Mobile Phones and Emerging Applications. In: IFIP International Federation for Information Processing, vol. 220, pp. 425–434. Springer, Heidelberg (2006)
10. Matas Miraz, G., Luque Ruiz, I., Gómez-Nieto, M.A.: Applications of Near Filed Communication Technology in University Environments. In: IASK International Conference of E-Activity and Leading technology, Seville, Spain, pp. 127–134 (2009)
11. Matas Miraz, G., Luque Ruiz, I., Gómez-Nieto, M.A.: How NFC can be used for the Compliance of European Higher Education Area Guidelines in European Universities. In: Proceedings 1st International IEEE Workshop on Near Field Communication, pp. 3–8 (2009)
12. Luque Ruiz, I., Gómez-Nieto, M.A.: University Smart Poster: Study of NFC Technology in University Ambient. In: 3rd Symposium of Ubiquitous Computing and Ambient Intelligence. Advances in Soft Computing, vol. 51, pp. 112–116 (2008)

13. Hardy, R., Rukzio, E.: Touch & Interact: Touch-based Interaction with a Tourist Application. In: Proceeding in MobileHCI 2008, Amsterdam, the Netherlands, September 2008, ACM Press, New York (2008)
14. Manes, G.: The Tetherless Tourist: Ambient Intelligence in Travel & Tourism. Information Technology & Tourism 5, 211–220 (2003)
15. Staab, S., Werthner, H.: Intelligent Systems for Tourism: Trends & Controversies. IEEE Intelligent Systems 6, 53–66 (2002)
16. Liikka, J., Lahti, J., Alahuhta, P., Rosenberg, M.: KAMO - Mobile Guide for the City Traveller. In: 4th International Conference on Intelligent Environments, Seattle, USA, July 2008, pp. 1–7 (2008)
17. Oyster mobile wallet (London underground) (2008), http://www.tflgov.uk/, Monaco City Museum. http://2009.wima-nfc.com/content/Deploying-NFC-technology-in-the-Nouveau-Musee-National-de-Monaco-/deploying_nfc_technology_in_the__nouveau_musee_national_de_monaco_UK.php
18. NFC-Forum. Record Type Definition Technical Specifications, http://www.nfc-forum.org/specs/spec_list/
19. Mifare Family by NxP, http://www.nxp.com/#/pip/pip=[pfp=53422]|pp=[t=pfp,i=5342]2|
20. Omnikey GmbH, http://www.omnikey.com/?id=3&tx_okprod_pi1[product]=67
21. Nokia 6131 NFC, http://europe.nokia.com/find-products/devices/nokia-6131-nfc

Communication Support Visual Interface for Collaborative Learning

Yuki Hayashi, Tomoko Kojiri, and Toyohide Watanabe

Department of Systems and Social Informatics,
Graduate School of Information Science, Nagoya University, Japan
{yhayashi,kojiri,watanabe}@watanabe.ss.is.nagoya-u.ac.jp

Abstract. In computer-supported collaborative learning, learners focus on particular learners/utterances in discussing exercises. However, as the communication band of information networks is restricted, learners cannot acquire much information about the situations or the behaviors of other learners in the learning environment. In this paper, we describe an interactive interface where learners are aware of the conversation flow and visually acquire information. In our interface, utterance texts are moved toward the learner view from the transition information of utterances. Focusing utterances of the learner are detected based on the target learner of utterances and stressed in the represented in the interface. Experimental results showed that participants could intuitively grasp the conversation flow by observing the moving utterances.

Keywords: Round-table interface, awareness, CSCL, focusing intention, focusing utterance.

1 Introduction

With the development of information communication technologies, learners can easily meet and study with others through networks independently of time and location. Many researches have been conducted on supporting such learning styles in the field of computer-supported collaborative learning (CSCL) [1, 2]. However, as the communication band of networks is restricted, learners cannot acquire much information about other learners' situations or behaviors. To attain communication in distributed environments, such well-known concepts as "awareness" need to be considered [3]. Since learners experience collaboration by observing interested learners and advance their exercises by listening to utterances that they think valuable, the learning environment should effectively provide awareness information so that learners can experience the learning situation and smoothly grasp the appropriate information.

To support collaboration among learners, we constructed a collaborative learning environment where learners are aware of the effective information based on their focusing intentions for other learners (focusing target) [4, 5]. In the interface, learner views are automatically changed according to focusing targets of learners and the focusing degrees of the targets. Focusing targets are estimated based on such actions as making utterances and observing the memo-sheets of other learners because they are the most fundamental learning activities. Although the learner view displayed in

N. García-Pedrajas et al. (Eds.): IEA/AIE 2010, Part III, LNAI 6098, pp. 239–248, 2010.
© Springer-Verlag Berlin Heidelberg 2010

the interface may provide a trigger for communication, conversations among learners are still not directly supported. Since learners make progress in solving exercises by exchanging utterances, they must grasp the conversation flow naturally/intuitively.

To support learner conversations, text-chat systems are commonly used in the CSCL field [6]. In general text-chat interfaces, plural messages can be sent at the same time, so successive utterances do not always refer to the same topic [7]. To support the conversation flow, Smith et al. proposed a threaded chat system in which participants select a specific thread and utterance to which to respond [8]. By observing the threaded order of utterances, participants can understand the conversation flow. However, real-time threaded chat has a temporal restriction among utterances. In addition, participants must endure the cognitive loads of watching all threads [6]. Viegas et al. proposed a chat interface where participants are represented by colored circles, and conversational topics are represented as clusters of circles in which their utterances appear [9]. Although utterances are visually organized by topics, the context between each utterance cannot be grasped from the interface. On the other hand, Muhlpfordt et al. proposed a CSCL system in which text chat and shared work areas are combined into one interface [10]. Objects in the shared work area can be indicated from the chat area by arrowed lines. The indicators simplify the direct recognition of the context between utterances and objects. However, these systems do not represent particular objects/utterances on which learners focus.

In face-to-face environments, learners perceive the conversation flow not only from utterances but also from such nonverbal information as face directions and voice volume. In addition, learners can interact with other learners in a timely fashion by listening to utterances in which they are interested. Therefore, it is desirable for learners to exhibit utterer/utterance-targets, and to distinguish focused utterances from other utterances. In this paper, we propose a conversation support interface in collaborative learning. Utterance texts move from utterer to the utterance targets in a virtual learning environment. From the moving utterance texts, learners can intuitively grasp the conversation flow. The focusing utterances, which are detected based on the target utterance, the utterer, and the utterance target information, are represented in the learner view with different colors and display times to distinguish them from other utterances.

2 Approach

2.1 Round-Table Interface

Currently, we are focusing on a learning group that is studying a common exercise. As fundamental learning activities, learners make utterances using the text-chat and write down their solutions/ideas on their own memo-sheets. Figure 1 shows the windows in our collaborative learning environment where learners exchange utterances through the chat window [5]. In the round-table window, other learners are represented visually as polygon objects attached to their video images caught by inexpensive web cameras and allocated around the round-table. Their memo-sheets are arranged on the round-table in front of their camera images. Learners write down their answers to their own memo windows and observe the content of other learner memo-sheets through the memo window of the target learner.

During learning, learners communicate among themselves by focusing on a specific learner and actively obtaining actions. In our round-table interface, learner views are changed dynamically based on the calculated focusing degrees of other learners. The focusing degrees for other learners are calculated based on each action to increase the focusing degree for the learner to whom the learner himself/herself is paying attention. The focusing target is determined as the learner who has the largest focusing degree and appeared in the center of the learner view. In Figure 1, learner C is X's current focusing target. Moreover, the size of the focusing target changes based on the focusing degree of the focusing target. Focusing targets of other learner are also reflected in the interface by facing their camera images at their focusing targets. Since the focusing target is estimated and displayed based on the general actions of learners, our learning environment can support learning activities regardless of the particular learning subject or material.

Our goal in this paper is to promote interaction among learners by reflecting the conversation flow in the round-table interface. In the following section, we discuss focusing intentions for utterances.

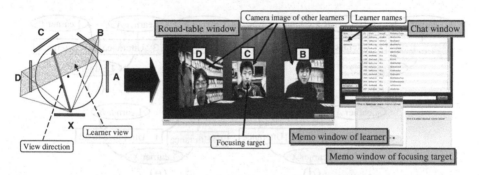

Fig. 1. Windows in our collaborative learning support system

2.2 Focusing Intention for Utterances

During the discussion, a learner focuses on particular utterances, if they are uttered to the learner or if they refer to the learner's past utterances. Such utterances may relate to answers to his questions or reactions to his ideas. Therefore, focusing utterances are detected by the context of successive utterances that are grasped by their target utterances and the target learners of the utterances (utterance targets).

Figure 2 represents the focusing utterance patterns of learner X. Learners A and B correspond to other learners. The source node of the arrow indicates the utterer, and its destination node is the utterance target. The series of utterances for determining the focusing utterances are classified into five patterns. In Figure 2, the target utterance of utterance 2 (2: Utterance) is utterance 1 (1: Utterance). Utterance 2 in all patterns is detected as the focusing utterances of X.

In face-to-face learning environments, learners can perceive the utterer and utterance target from nonverbal information. Since such awareness information cannot be represented in text-chat mediated environments, learners must visualize the conversation flow in our interface. Utterances to learner X and the utterances to all learners are related to learner X, so these utterances should be grasped by learner X. On the contrary, utterances among other learners are not focused on by the learner. For learners to recognize focusing utterances, they must distinguish among focusing utterances and display them appropriately in the virtual learning environment.

In our interface, utterance texts are moved in the learner view to visually emphasize the exchange of utterances. Figure 3 represents an example of moving utterances from utterers to utterance targets. When learners make utterances to particular learners, their texts move from utterers to the utterance targets (Figure 3(a)). On the other hand, Figure 3(b) shows the transitions of utterances to all learners from learners B and X. These utterances need to be grasped by all learners, so their texts move to the center of the round-table. If the learner is the utterance target, utterance texts come to the learner's direction and gradually become bigger. Utterance texts made by learner X move to the utterance targets and become smaller. Texts of focusing utterances are emphatically displayed in the center of the learner view.

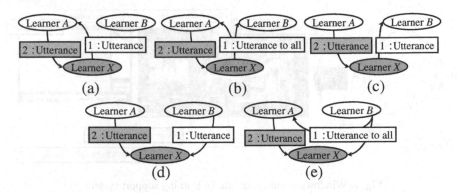

Fig. 2. Focusing utterance patterns for learner X

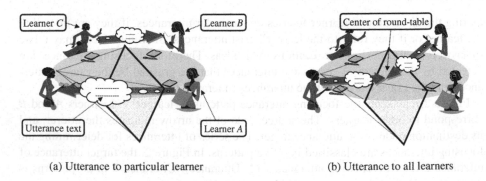

(a) Utterance to particular learner   (b) Utterance to all learners

Fig. 3. Example of moving utterances from utterers to utterance targets

3 Display Method of Utterances

To visually emphasize the exchange of utterances, utterance texts are moved to the learner view. Utterances move from utterers to their utterance targets. In our system, learners select their target learner names and target utterances when inputting their utterances in the chat window. Figure 4 shows the moving routes of utterance texts. X represents the learner, and A, B, C, and D represent other learners. In Figure 4, X's focusing target is C. The arrows under the utterance texts represent the moving directions of utterances. When an utterance to all learners occurs, its texts move from the coordinate of the utterers to the middle point between learners X and X's focusing target (Figure 4(a)). Figure 4(b) represents the utterance between X and other learners. If X makes an utterance to B, the utterance target, the utterance texts move from the coordinates of X to B. On the other hand, utterance texts move from the coordinates of C to X when an utterance is generated from C to X. Figure 4(c) shows the utterance route among other learners. Utterance texts flow from the coordinates of C to A if the utterance is uttered by C to A. In this case, utterance texts may not be observed by X when they do not traverse in X's view.

When utterance texts reach the target coordinate, these texts fade out after a certain period. Focusing utterances are represented differently from normal utterances. The color of a focusing utterance is highlighted and its font size becomes bigger. Moreover, its fading-out time is longer than that of the normal utterance.

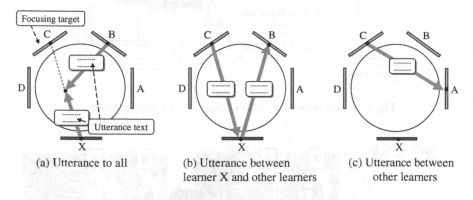

(a) Utterance to all

(b) Utterance between learner X and other learners

(c) Utterance between other learners

Fig. 4. Moving routes of utterance texts

4 System Operation

Figure 5 illustrates the system architecture of our collaborative learning system. The client-side system is constructed by an Adobe AIR application. To capture the learner real-time moving images, web cameras are needed for individual learner computers. The Apache Tomcat server on the server-side system is composed of a Red 5 server that supports the Real-Time Messaging Protocol (RTMP). A BlazeDS server enables messaging to the AIR application and the OpenID consumer server for the certification of learners. As OpenID providers, several website IDs like Google[1], Yahoo![2], and Mixi[3] can be used. In addition, web camera images of learners are distributed through the Adobe Flash Media Server. Learning records such as learner names and utterances are stored in the relational database management system (RDBMS).

Figures 6 and 7 are examples of utterance transitions and their displaying images in the round-table interface. Utterances are moved in the learner view from the utterers to the target learners of utterances. When C makes an utterance to A, the utterance texts move from the locations of C to A (Figure 6(a)). Figure 6(b1) shows the interface of X just after an utterance has been generated. X's focusing target is A, and only some of the utterance texts can be recognized. Figure 6(b2) is the interface after the utterance text has reached A. All utterance texts are seen. Figure 7 displays X's focusing utterance. Its utterance texts are represented in the learner view with a different color (red). Moreover, its font size becomes bigger to distinguish them from other utterances (Figure 7(c)).

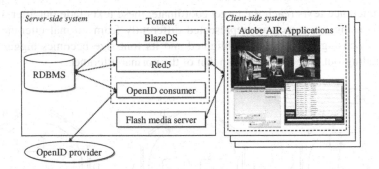

Fig. 5. System architecture of our collaborative learning system

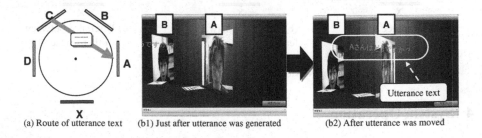

(a) Route of utterance text   (b1) Just after utterance was generated   (b2) After utterance was moved

Fig. 6. Example of moving utterance among other learners

---

[1] http://www.google.com/
[2] http://www.yahoo.com/
[3] http://mixi.jp/

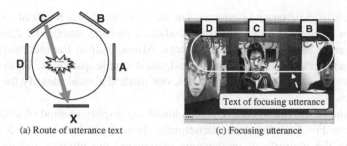

(a) Route of utterance text   (c) Focusing utterance

Fig. 7. Example of focusing utterance

5 Experiment

5.1 Experimental Setting

In this section, we evaluate the effectiveness of our display method of utterances and the appropriateness of the detected focusing utterances.

In the experiment, Groups 1 and 2 were participated, each of which is organized by four participants. They were asked to discuss current topics about Japanese society for 30 minutes. Before the experiment, participants practiced manipulating the interface. Representations of the utterance texts of both focusing and normal utterances were explained. In order for participants not to concentrate on the discussion, memo windows were not used during the experiment. After the discussion, participants were asked to select utterances on which they focused during the experiment from the chat log. The utterances selected by participants were compared with the focusing utterances detected by our system. Participants also answered questionnaires about the display method of utterances.

5.2 Experimental Result

Table 1 represents the numbers of utterance targets selected by the participants. Table 2 shows the number of correct focusing utterances in utterances detected by the system. Based on the results of Table 1, participants not only focused on utterances whose utterance targets were the learners themselves but also those whose utterance targets were all learners and other learners. This result indicates that our assumption, "focusing utterances only exist in utterances whose targets are the learner himself/herself," was insufficient. Many focusing utterances that were not detected by the system provided fresh ideas to all participants and answered questions for other learners. The mechanism of detecting focusing utterances should be modified so as to consider the contents of utterances as well.

Since our system detects focusing utterances only from utterances whose target learners are the learner himself/herself, the precision and recall rates are calculated by utterances whose target learners are the learner himself/herself. The result is shown in Table 3. Based on the result of the recall rate, our method correctly detected over the 70% of the focusing utterances. Many of the correctly detected focusing utterances were answers to their target utterances. On the other hand, the result of the precision rate was low in both groups. This result indicates that the number of detected utterances was larger than the selected utterances. Almost half of the incorrectly selected focusing utterances showed agreements and asked simple questions. To avoid detecting these utterances as focusing utterances, our method should identify the intentions of utterances.

Table 4 shows the questionnaire results about the display method of utterances and their answers. For each question, participants chose from 1 (worst) to 5 (best). For question (a), the majority of participants recognized the utterers and the utterance targets from the transitions of the utterance texts. Questions (b) and (c) asked about the readability of the moving utterance texts. Some participants gave low scores for question (b) and commented that the lengths of many utterances were so long that they could not read all texts before fading out. We need to improve the display method based on text length, e.g., to separate the utterance texts and display them in turn. On the contrary, a number of participants gave high scores to question (c). This result shows that participants could naturally observe the learning environment and communicate with other participants, even though the camera images and utterance texts were displayed. From the result of question (d), participants were able to grasp the detected focusing utterances to some extent. Participants pointed out that they focused on the chat window to read the utterance texts as they concentrated on the discussion. To cope with active discussions, we must integrate the information displayed in the chat windows into the round-table windows.

Some participants commented that they successfully recognized the reactions of other learners to utterances by monitoring the camera images with the utterance texts. Such natural reactions derived by actions are not grasped by traditional collaborative learning support systems. Therefore, our system provides learners with the feeling of sharing identical learning environments with other learners. In this experiment, we evaluated our method with only two groups through collaborative learning. To confirm our method's effectiveness, further evaluations with more groups should be conducted.

Table 1. Utterance targets of focusing utterances selected by participants

Utterance target	Group 1	Group 2
Learner himself/herself	33	21
All learners	15	12
Other learner	16	19

Table 2. Numbers of detected and correct focusing utterances

	Group 1	Group 2
Detected focusing utterance	58	63
Correct focusing utterance	27	15

Table 3. Precision and recall rates of detected focusing utterances whose target learners were the learner himself/herself

	Group 1	Group 2	Total
Recall rate	81.8%	71.4%	77.8%
Precision rate	46.6%	23.8%	34.7%

Table 4. Questionnaire results about display method of utterances

No	Questions	Average score
(a)	Could you recognize the transitions of utterances?	4.00
(b)	Could you read the utterance texts?	3.63
(c)	Did moving texts prevent smooth communication?	4.75
(d)	Could you grasp the display differences of focusing utterances?	3.25

6 Conclusion

In this paper, we proposed a collaborative learning environment in which focusing intentions for utterances can be visually reflected. Our study proposes one solution to enhance conversations among learners in CSCL systems. Utterances were moved in the learner view from the transition information of utterances. The focusing utterances of learners are detected by the target learner and the target utterance information and emphatically displayed. A questionnaire about the display method of utterances clarifies that participants intuitively grasped the flow of utterances by observing the moving utterance texts. In addition, our method detected over 70% of the correct focusing utterances. To avoid detecting incorrect focusing utterances, the intentions of utterances should be identified.

A future direction of this research is to improve the usability of our interface. Our system should support voice chat to make conversations more natural. In addition, the displayed information must be integrated; for example, transparent utterances can be displayed on the round-table window, and utterance targets can be selected by clicking camera images, and so on.

Acknowledgement

This research was supported by Grand-in-Aid for Research Fellow of the Japan Society for the Promotion of Science (No. 21-1764).

References

1. Adelsberger, H.H., Collis, B., Pawlowski, J.M.: Handbook on Information Technologies for Education and Training. Springer, Heidelberg (2002)
2. Andriessen, J.H.E.: Working with Groupware. Springer, Heidelberg (2003)

248   Y. Hayashi, T. Kojiri, and T. Watanabe

3. Gutwin, C., Stark, G., Greenberg, S.: Support for Workspace Awareness in Educational Groupware. In: Proc. of CSCL 1995, pp. 147–156 (1995)
4. Hayashi, Y., Kojiri, T., Watanabe, T.: Focusing Support Interface for Collaborative Learning. Journal of Information and Systems in Education 6(1), 17–25 (2008)
5. Hayashi, Y., Kojiri, T., Watanabe, T.: Focus Support Interface Based on Collaborative Learning Activity. In: Lovrek, I., Howlett, R.J., Jain, L.C. (eds.) KES 2008, Part I. LNCS (LNAI), vol. 5177, pp. 322–329. Springer, Heidelberg (2008)
6. Looi, C.K.: Exploring the Affordances of Online Chat for Learning. International Journal of Learning Technology 1(3), 322–338 (2005)
7. Garcia, A., Jacobs, J.B.: The Interactional Organization of Computer Mediated Communication in the College Classroom. Qualitative Sociology 21(3), 299–317 (1998)
8. Smith, M., Cadiz, J., Burkhalter, B.: Conversation Trees and Threaded Chats. In: Proc. of CSCW 2000, pp. 97–105 (2000)
9. Viegas, F.B., Donath, J.S.: Chat circles. In: Proc. of SIGCHI 1999, pp. 9–16 (1999)
10. Muhlpfordt, M., Stahl, G.: The integration of synchronous communication across dual interaction spaces. In: Proc. of CSCL 2007, pp. 522–531 (2007)

Violin Fingering Estimation Based on Violin Pedagogical Fingering Model Constrained by Bowed Sequence Estimation from Audio Input

Akira Maezawa, Katsutoshi Itoyama, Toru Takahashi, Kazunori Komatani, Tetsuya Ogata, and Hiroshi G. Okuno

Graduate School of Informatics, Kyoto University
Yoshida Honmachi, Kyoto, Japan

Abstract. This work presents an automated violin fingering estimation method that facilitates a student violinist acquire the "sound" of
his/her favorite recording artist created by the artist's unique fingering.
Our method realizes this by analyzing an audio recording played by the
artist, and recuperating the most playable fingering that recreates the
aural characteristics of the recording. Recovering the aural characteristics requires the *bowed string estimation* of an audio recording, and using
the estimated result for *optimal fingering decision*. The former requires
high accuracy and robustness against the use of different violins or brand
of strings; and the latter needs to create a natural fingering for the violinist. We solve the first problem by detecting estimation errors using
rule-based algorithms, and by adapting the estimator to the recording
based on mean normalization. We solve the second problem by incorporating, in addition to generic stringed-instrument model used in existing
studies, a fingering model that is based on pedagogical practices of violin
playing, defined on a sequence of two or three notes.
The accuracy of the bowed string estimator improved by 21 points
in a realistic situation (38% → 59%) by incorporating error correction
and mean normalization. Subjective evaluation of the optimal fingering
decision algorithm by seven violinists on 22 musical excerpts showed that
compared to the model used in existing studies, our proposed model
was preferred over existing one ($p = 0.01$), but no significant preference
towards proposed method defined on sequence of two notes versus three
notes was observed ($p = 0.05$).

1 Introduction

Fingering[1] is an important aspect of violin expression, as the choice of the bowed
string affects the sonority. For example, the highest-tuned string sounds brilliant,
and the lowest-tuned string sounds strong. Such variation in timbral quality
offers a violinist an artistic choice of playing a high-pitched note on the higher-
tuned or lower-tuned string, depending on the violinist's inclination towards

---

[1] The art of deciding one of four fingers that presses on one of four differently tuned
strings (*bowed string*) to play a note.

N. García-Pedrajas et al. (Eds.): IEA/AIE 2010, Part III, LNAI 6098, pp. 249–259, 2010.
© Springer-Verlag Berlin Heidelberg 2010

brilliant or strong tone[2]. At the same time, such choice is limited by the violinist's fingering skill because some bowed string sequences are easier to play than others. Hence, the essence of fingering decision is in deciding the sequence of right-sounding strings that is playable [1][2].

Since finding musically expressive fingering is a nontrivial task, violinist would often listen to his/her favorite recording (one whose musical style he/she finds agreeable) to imitate the sonority of the recording, as a first step towards generating a sensible fingering. Because not only the fingering but also many factors influence the generated sound, a violinist must isolate the changes in sonority due to different fingering – a difficult task for inexperienced violinists.

Therefore, we seek to develop a fingering estimation method that suggests a technically manageable fingering that recreates the bowed string sequence of a given violin recording. There are many studies in fingering decision, but these have either focused on generating a playable fingering, without considering the fingering expression unique to a particular artist as expressed through different choice of bowed strings [3][4], or have imposed unrealistic assumptions (when applied directly to the violin) on how the instrument is played [5].

Our problem is twofold: accurate estimation of bowed strings, and generation of playable fingerings. Estimation of bowed string needs robustness against use of different violins and brand of strings – an antique violin and modern violin, for example, sound very different, so do a string with silver coating and gold coating. The existing study in bowed string estimation [6] does not evaluate its performance with multiple violins or brands of strings, but our preliminary experiment suggests that it is weak against such variations. Generating a playable fingering is difficult because there are fingering issues unique to the violin, some of which cannot be dealt with by fingering decision methods without knowledge specific to a particular stringed instrument [3][4]. For example, because the violin is a relatively small unfretted instrument, rarely does a violinist play two successive notes using the same finger because such fingering is prone to intonation errors. On the other hand, this kind of motion is frequent in fretted stringed instruments such as the guitar.

This paper presents a fingering estimation method that recovers the sequence of bowed string of a given monophonic violin audio recording. Our method is robust against differences in acoustical characteristics among different violins and the brands of strings used. Our method also employs a new fingering model, the *violin pedagogical model*, that considers fingering issues that arise specifically for the violin. As shown in Fig. 1, the method is composed of two main components: estimation of bowed strings from an audio signal, and generation of the most playable fingering constrained by the estimated bowed string sequence. We perform two sets of experiments, one to evaluate the accuracy of bowed string estimation, and another to evaluate whether our proposed fingering model is more natural than the existing one.

---

[2] *Air in G*, arrangement by A. Wilhelmj of J.S.Bach's Suite No. 3, BWV1068, is an example where the arranger specifies which string the piece should be played on (i.e., the G String), in order to convey the sound characteristic of the string.

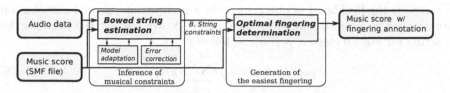

Fig. 1. Block diagram

2 Modeling and Classifying the Bowed String

We assume that existing methods are used to align the score and audio [7], and to separate out the violin part [8]. Next, we extract output energy of a filter bank from the separated signal as the feature, and model it as a F0-dependent Gaussian Mixture Model (GMM). Maximum a posteriori (MAP) estimation is then used to estimate the bowed string for each string, and voting is used to determine the bowed string for each note.

The filter bank consists of eight filters with triangular magnitude response, whose center frequencies are spaced equidistant in the log-frequency axis between 1kHz and 15kHz, and the bandwidth constant in the log-frequency axis. We extract the feature using a frame-length of 2048 samples with overlap of 441 samples, at a sampling rate of 44.1kHz. The features are based on those used in existing instrument classification systems [9,10], with the filter-bank settings tailored to discriminate violin strings.

We model the feature as a Gaussian mixture (GMM) governed by F0-dependent parameters, as they were highly dependent on the F0. We found that modeling the features by training a 5-mixture GMM for each Δc=100 cent interval was sufficient. Therefore, we first divide the frequency axis into K=50 regions spaced Δc cents apart, such that the kth ($K > k \geq 0$) region R_k is described as follows, where c_{min} is the frequency of the lowest pitch of the violin:

$$R_k = [c_{min} + (k - 0.5)\Delta c, c_{min} + (k + 0.5)\Delta c), \tag{1}$$

Every training data (x, c, i), where x is the feature, c is the pitch, and i is the string, is clustered to one of K clusters, k, such that $c \in R_k$.

For each $k \in [0, K)$, we model M GMM's, one for each string (M=4). Then, given an input data with the F0=c, we determine the likelihood by evaluating the likelihood of the GMM for each string, using dataset X_k, such that $k \in R_k$. Thus, we model the likelihood of data vector x in kth cluster for the ith string, $p(x|i, k)$, as a J-mixture (J=5) Gaussian Mixture Model (GMM):

$$p(x|i, k) = \sum_{j=1}^{J} \phi_{j,k}(i)\mathcal{N}\left(x|\mu_{j,k}(i), \Sigma_{j,k}(i)\right) \tag{2}$$

where $\sum_j \phi_{j,k}(i) = 1$, and $\phi_{j,k}(i)$, $\mu_{j,k}(i)$, $\Sigma_{j,k}(i)$ are the jth weight, mean vector and covariance matrix, respectively, for the ith string in F0 cluster k.

$\mathcal{N}(x|u, S)$ is the likelihood of observing x in a multivariate normal distribution parametrized by mean u and covariance matrix S. We also set the prior on the ith string for kth F0 cluster, $p_S(i|k)$, as follows:

$$p_S(i|k) = s(k, s_i) / \sum_{j=1}^{4} s(k, s_j) \tag{3}$$

Here, $s(k, s_i)$ is 1 if the string s_i is playable in kth F0 cluster, and 0 otherwise.

Then, for each feature x and pitch c extracted from a frame of audio, (x, c), that has been associated with cluster k, we find the maximum a posteriori (MAP) estimate of the bowed string, $\hat{s}(x, c)$ as follows:

$$\hat{s}(x, c) = \arg \max_i p(i|x, k) = \arg \max_i p_S(i|k)p(x|i, k) \tag{4}$$

For each note, we estimate the string by first evaluating the MAP estimate for each frame the note is played. Then, the string that had the greatest count of MAP estimate is chosen as the bowed string. Such voting method was chosen as it offered the greatest accuracy compared to other methods considered. Specifically, we set the estimated string for the nth note, s_n which starts at frame b_n and ends at e_n as the following, where $x^{(j)}$ and $c^{(j)}$ are the feature and the pitch, respectively, for the jth frame:

$$s_n = \arg \max_{m \in \{E, A, D, G\}} \left| \left\{ j \in [b_n, e_n] | \hat{s}(x^{(j)}, c^{(j)}) = m \right\} \right| \tag{5}$$

3 Adaptation of the Acoustic Model

Because two violins typically have significantly different acoustic characteristics, adapting the trained classifier to new violins is necessary. We adapt the model by normalizing the mean of the features for each frequency cluster.

For both the training data and the input audio, we determine the cluster-dependent mean of the entire feature set, $\text{ave}(\mathbf{X_k})$, given a data matrix $\mathbf{X}_k \in \mathbb{R}^{D \times L}$, each of the L rows containing D-dimensional feature data that has been assigned to the kth cluster. Let $\text{ave}(\mathbf{X}_{k,t})$ be the average of the training set for the kth cluster and $\text{ave}(\mathbf{X}_{k,i})$ be the average of the input. To evaluate the MAP estimate taking into consideration the differences in acoustic characteristics, we modify (6) as follows:

$$\hat{s}(x, c) = \arg \max_i p_S(i|k)p(x'|i, k)|_{x' = x - \text{ave}(\mathbf{X}_{x,i}) + \text{ave}(\mathbf{X}_{x,t})} \tag{6}$$

4 Context-Dependent Error Correction

Since the accuracy of the bowed string estimation is poor to begin with, we improve it by assuming three fundamental principles of violin playing based on empirical observations. We assume that an estimated bowed string sequence that contradicts any one of the three principles is caused by the misdetections of the bowed string estimator. We define a note that disobeys any of the following three rules as an *error*, and propose simple algorithms to fix the errors.

Let $S = \{n_1 \cdots n_N\}$ be a monophonic score of length N where n_i contains the ith pitch as a MIDI note number, and let $s = \{s_1, \cdots, s_N\}$ contain the sequence of strings identified for the score, where s_i indicates the string identified for the ith note. s_i of 1, 2, 3 and 4 respectively indicates the G-string, D, A, and E.

4.1 Rule 1: Consistency of Direction of Pitch/String Change

Given a sequence of two notes neither of which is an open-string [3], if the second note is higher than the first, it uses the same or higher-tuned string. Likewise, if the second note is lower than the first, it uses the same or lower-tuned string. Figure 2 shows an example. We detect and fix such errors as follows:

1. Repeat (2)-(4) for a fixed number of iterations.
2. Let $M = \{i \in [1, |S|] | \mathrm{sgn}(S_i - S_{i+1}) \times \mathrm{sgn}(St_i - St_{i+1}) < 0\}$.
3. If $M = \emptyset$, exit.
4. For all $j \in M$
   (a) Let $M' := |M|$.
   (b) Set $t := s_j$, and set $s_j := s_{j+1}$, and evaluate(2) to obtain new M.
   (c) If $|M| \geq M'$, set $s_{j+1} := t$, and evaluate (2) to obtain new M.
   (d) If $|M| \geq M'$, revert s_j and s_{j+1} to state before 4a.

4.2 Rule 2: Consistency of Magnitude of Pitch/String Change

Given a sequence of three notes, consecutive jumps between nonadjacent strings occur only when intervals between the first and the second, and between second and third are greater than perfect fifths (7 semitones) apart. Figure 3 shows an example. We detect and fix such errors as follows:

1. Repeat (2)-(4) for a fixed number of iterations.
2. Let $M = \{i \in [1, |S|] | |s_i - s_{i-1}| \geq 2 \wedge |s_i - s_{i+1}| \geq 2 \wedge |n_i - n_{i-1}| \geq 7 \wedge |n_i - n_{i+1}| \geq 7\}$.
3. If $M = \emptyset$, exit.
4. For all $j \in M$
   (a) If $n_j > n_{j-1}$ and...
      i. n_j is playable on string $s_j - 1$, set $s_j := s_j - 1$.
      ii. n_j is not playable on string $s_j - 1$, set $s_{j-1} := s_{j-1}+1$, and $s_{j+1} := s_{j+1}+1$.
   (b) Otherwise, if $n_j < n_{j-1}$ set $s_j := s_j + 1$.

4.3 Rule 3: Consistency of Bowed Strings on a Mordent

A mordent – a rapid change between a note and a note of close interval above or below it – is played on one string, as shown in Figure 4. We define a mordent as a sequence of three notes such that the following hold:

1. Two adjacent notes are shorter than 3/64 the duration of a quarter note.
2. The second note is no more than 2 semitones away from the first.
3. The first note and the third note share the same pitch.

We impose this constraint by using the estimated bowed string for the longest note as the estimated bowed string for all notes in a mordent.

---

[3] An *open-string* refers to a note that is played by pressing no finger against the string.

Fig. 2. Example of rule 1

Fig. 3. Example of rule 2

Fig. 4. Example of rule 3

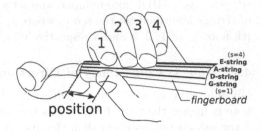

Fig. 5. Definitions of Violin Fingering

5   Violin Fingering Estimation

We treat violin fingering estimation as a combinatorial optimization problem, in which we define a cost for transition from one particular hand position to another, and find a sequence of hand motions that minimizes that cost, while being constrained to play in a given sequence of notes and bowed strings.

5.1   Formulation of the Fingering Estimation Problem

We define a *fingering* as a 4-tuple (n, s, f, p), where $n \in \mathbb{N}$ is the pitch (in MIDI note number), and $s \in \{1, 2, 3, 4\}$ the bowed string, $f \in \{0, 1, 2, 3, 4\}$ the pressed finger (0 =no finger placed), and $p \in \mathbb{N}$ the position, as shown in Fig. 5. Let $\mathcal{F}$ be a set of all possible fingerings. Also, let n(n) be a function to retrieve the pitch of $n \in \mathcal{F}$, s(n) the bowed string, f(n) the finger, and p(n) the position.

We define an *unnotated score*, $S_u \in \mathcal{N}^M$ to be a M-tuple, where M is the number of notes contained in a music score, and the i-th element, $S_u(i)$, is the i-th note of the music score. We define an *bowed string constraint*, $c_{\text{bow}} \in \{1, 2, 3, 4\}^M$, associated with note sequence S_u a M-tuple, where $M = \dim(S_u)$, and the i-th element, $c_{\text{st}}(i) \in \{1, 2, 3, 4\}$, indicates the bowed string that the i-th note of the note sequence should use. We define a *notation*, S_n be a M-tuple, where M is the number of notes contained in a note sequence, and the i-th element $S_n(i) \in \mathcal{F}$ corresponds to the i-th fingering of the note sequence.

We seek to, then, find the "best" notation F_{opt} that satisfies the given unnotated score S_u and the bowed string constraint c_{st}. Let $C_b(s_i, s_{i-1}) : \mathcal{F}^2 \to \mathbb{R}$ be a *two-note cost function*, which defines the cost of transitioning from $s_{i-1} \in \mathcal{F}$ to $s_i \in \mathcal{F}$, and $C_t(s_i, s_{i-1}, s_{i-2}) : \mathcal{F}^3 \to \mathbb{R}$ be a *three-note cost function*. We define a symbol "**0**" that satisfies the following:

$$\forall A, B \in \mathcal{F}.C_t(A, B, \mathbf{0}) = C_t(\mathbf{0}, A, B) = 0 \quad \forall A \in \mathcal{F}.C_b(\mathbf{0}, A) = C_b(A, \mathbf{0}) = 0 \quad (7)$$

Then, the *optimal fingering* is a notation F_{opt} that satisfies the following:

$$F_{opt} = \arg \min_{s_1 \cdots s_{|S_u|} \in \mathcal{F}} \sum_{i=1}^{\dim(S_u)} C_b(s_i, s_{i-1}) + C_t(s_i, s_{i-1}, s_{i-2}) \tag{8}$$

$$s.t. \forall j < 1.s_j = \mathbf{0}, \forall j > \dim(S_u).s_j = \mathbf{0}, \text{note}(s_i) = S_u(i), \text{st}(s_i) = c_{st}(i)$$

We let the two-note and three-note cost function be of form $[1; \mathbf{x}]^T \mathbf{W}[1; \mathbf{x}]$, where $\mathbf{x}$ is a feature vector that is generated from a sequence of two notes for two-note cost and three notes for three-note. We shall now define a suitable set of features for two-note and three-note models, incorporating both features from existing works and newly introduced features based on violin pedagogy.

5.2   Features

Horizontal/Vertical Model (HVM's). Existing methods model the cost of traversing from one hand position to another in terms of *horizontal/vertical cost model* [3][4], which we shall denote as *HVM-2*. It assumes that the cost of traversing from one hand position to another is the sum of (a) finger strain, (b) the movement across the fingerboard, and (c) the movement along the fingerboard.

Violin Pedagogical Models (VPM's). We introduce the *violin pedagogical model*, a fingering model inspired by violin fingering literatures [1], denoted as *VPM-2*. This model incorporates the preference towards odd positions (first and third position) and lower positions, and penalty for the half-position and a chromatic movement using one finger.

Three-note Extensions. We extend our cost model for evaluating three-note cost, which considers consecutive movements across and along the fingerboard. We extend both *HVM-2* and *VPM-2* to three-note (denoted *HVM-3* and *VPM-3*, respectively). *VPM-3* penalizes the use of 4-3-4 fingering with a position change, and rewards retaining one hand position on a sequence of three notes.

Let $\text{P}_{\min}(i, j)$, $\text{P}_{\text{nat}}(i, j)$, $\text{P}_{\max}(i, j)$ be matrices that define, respectively, the minimum playable interval between finger i and j in semitones, the most natural, and the maximum playable pitch interval. These are set as follows:

$$\text{P}_{\min} = \begin{pmatrix} 0 & 0 & 0 & 0 & 0 \\ 0 & 0 & 1 & 2.1 & 3.5 \\ 0 & 1 & 0 & 1.1 & 2.5 \\ 0 & 2.1 & 1.1 & 0 & 1.5 \\ 0 & 3.5 & 2.5 & 1.5 & 0 \end{pmatrix} ; \text{P}_{\text{nat}} = \begin{pmatrix} 0 & 0 & 0 & 0 & 0 \\ 0 & 0 & 2 & 3 & 5 \\ 0 & 2 & 0 & 1 & 2 \\ 0 & 3 & 1 & 0 & 2 \\ 0 & 5 & 2 & 2 & 0 \end{pmatrix} ; \text{P}_{\max} = \begin{pmatrix} 0 & 0 & 0 & 0 & 0 \\ 0 & 0 & 2 & 4 & 6 \\ 0 & 2 & 0 & 2 & 5 \\ 0 & 4 & 3 & 0 & 3 \\ 0 & 6 & 5 & 3 & 0 \end{pmatrix} \tag{9}$$

We furthermore define these functions for convenience:

$$\Delta_p(i, j) = \text{p}(s_i) - \text{p}(s_j) \qquad \Delta_s(i, j) = \text{s}(s_i) - \text{s}(s_j) \tag{10}$$

$$\Delta_f(i, j) = \text{f}(s_i) - \text{f}(s_j) \qquad R(i, j) = [\text{P}_{\min}(\text{f}(s_i)), \text{P}_{\max}(\text{f}(s_j))] \tag{11}$$

$$\Delta_{pr}(i, j) = |\text{n}(s_i) - \text{p}_0(\text{s}(s_i))| - |\text{n}(s_j) - \text{p}_0(\text{st}(s_j))| \tag{12}$$

where $\text{p}_0(s_i)$ is the pitch of the open-string for the bowed string $\text{s}(s_i)$.

Let $\tau_p = 3$, $\delta_{i,j}$ be Kronecker's delta, and 1_c be a function that returns 1 if condition c is true, and 0 otherwise. We define the features for model $HVM\text{-}2$, $x_{HVM\text{-}2}$, for model $VPM\text{-}2$, $x_{VPM\text{-}2}$ as follows:

$$\Delta\mathrm{pos}(i,j) = |\Delta_p(i,j)| \cdot 1_{\mathrm{f}(s_i)\neq 0 \wedge \mathrm{f}(s_j)\neq 0} \tag{13}$$

$$\mathrm{diffFinger}(i,j) = \mathrm{f}(s_i) \neq 0 \wedge \Delta_f(i,j) = 0 \wedge \Delta_p(i,j) \neq 0 \tag{14}$$

$$\mathrm{natural}(i,j) = |\Delta_{pr}(i,j)| - \mathrm{P_{nat}}(\mathrm{f}(s_i),\mathrm{f}(s_j)) = 0 \tag{15}$$

$$\mathrm{mismatch}(i,j) = \Delta_f(i,j) \cdot \Delta_{pr}(i,j) < 0 \wedge |\Delta_p| < \tau_p \tag{16}$$

$$\mathrm{stress}(i,j) = \|\Delta_{pr}(i,j)\| - \mathrm{P_{nat}}(\mathrm{f}(s_i),\mathrm{f}(s_j)) \cdot 1_{\|\Delta_{pr}(i,j)\|\in R(i,j)} \tag{17}$$

$$\mathrm{playable}(i) = \mathrm{n}(s_i) - \mathrm{p_0}(\mathrm{st}(s_i)) - \mathrm{p}(s_i) \in R(i,i) \tag{18}$$

$$x_{HVM\text{-}2,1\cdots3}(s_i,s_j) = \left(\infty \cdot 1_{\neg\mathrm{playable}(i)}, a, a^2\right)|a = \Delta\mathrm{pos}(i,j) + 1_{\mathrm{diffFinger}(i,j)} \tag{19}$$

$$x_{HVM\text{-}2,4,5}(s_i,s_j) = (\|\Delta_s(i,j)\|, \|\Delta_s(i,j)\|^2) \cdot 1_{\mathrm{f}(s_i)\cdot\mathrm{f}(s_j)\neq 0} \tag{20}$$

$$x_{HVM\text{-}2,6}(s_i,s_j) = -1_{\mathrm{natural}(i,j)} \tag{21}$$

$$x_{HVM\text{-}2,7}(s_i,s_j) = 1_{\mathrm{mismatch}(i,j)} \cdot a + 1_{\mathrm{stress}(i,j)} \cdot (1-a)|a = 1_{\mathrm{f}(i)\neq 0 \wedge \mathrm{f}(j)\neq 0} \tag{22}$$

$$\Delta_{p,\mathrm{narrow}}(i,j) = \mathrm{f}(s_i) \cdot \mathrm{f}(s_j) \neq 0 \wedge \|\Delta_p(i,j)\| < \tau_p \tag{23}$$

$$x_{VPM\text{-}2,1,2}(s_i,s_j) = (1_{\Delta_{pr}(i,j)\neq 0 \wedge \Delta_f(i,j)=0}, 1_{\|\Delta_{pr}(i,j)\|=1 \wedge \|\Delta_f(i,j)\|>1}) \cdot 1_{\Delta_{p,\mathrm{narrow}}} \tag{24}$$

$$x_{VPM\text{-}2,3}(s_i,s_j) = 1_{\mathrm{f}(s_i)\cdot\mathrm{f}(s_j)\neq 0 \wedge \Delta_p(i,j)\neq 0 \wedge \Delta_{pr}(i,j)\cdot\Delta_f(i,j)=-1} \tag{25}$$

$$x_{VPM\text{-}2,4}(s_i,s_j) = 1_{\mathrm{f}(s_i)=\mathrm{f}(s_j)=4 \wedge \|\mathrm{n}(i)-\mathrm{n}(j)\|>1} \tag{26}$$

$$x_{VPM\text{-}2,5\cdots8}(s_i,s_j) = \left(\mathrm{p}(s_i), \delta_{2,\mathrm{p}(s_i)}, \delta_{5,\mathrm{p}(s_i)}, \delta_{4,\mathrm{f}(s_i)}\right) \tag{27}$$

Features for $HVM\text{-}3$ ($x_{HVM\text{-}3}$) and $VPM\text{-}3$ ($x_{VPM\text{-}3}$) are defined as follows:

$$t_0(i,j,k) = \|\Delta_s(j,k)\| \cdot 1_{\Delta_s(i,j)\cdot\Delta_s(j,k)<0} \tag{28}$$

$$t_1(i,j,k) = \|\Delta_p(j,k)\| \cdot 1_{\mathrm{f}(s_j)\cdot\mathrm{f}(s_k)\neq 0} + 1_{\Delta_f(j,k)=0 \wedge \Delta_p(i,j)\neq 0} \tag{29}$$

$$x_{HVM\text{-}3,1\cdots4}(s_i,s_j,s_k) = \left(t_0, t_0^2, t_1/a, (t_1/a)^2\right)|a=1+1_{\mathrm{f}(s_j)=0 \wedge \|\Delta_p(i,k)\|\leq 7} \tag{30}$$

$$x_{HVM\text{-}3,5}(s_i,s_j,s_k) = 1_{\mathrm{f}(i)\cdot\mathrm{f}(k)\neq 0 \wedge \|\Delta_p(i,k)\|<\tau_p \wedge \mathrm{sgn}(\Delta_f(i,k))\cdot\mathrm{sgn}(\Delta_{pr}(i,k))<0} \tag{31}$$

$$x_{HVM\text{-}3,6}(s_i,s_j,s_k) = \|\Delta_{pr}(i,k)\| - \mathrm{P_{nat}}(\mathrm{f}(s_i),\mathrm{f}(s_k)) \cdot 1_{\|\Delta_{pr}(i,k)\|\in R(i,k)} \tag{32}$$

$$\mathrm{shift\text{-}up}(i,j,k) = \Delta_p(i,j) = 0 \wedge \Delta_p(j,k) > 0 \tag{33}$$

$$\mathrm{shift\text{-}down}(i,j,k) = \Delta_p(i,j) < 0 \wedge \Delta_p(j,k) = 0 \tag{34}$$

$$x_{VPM\text{-}3,1}(s_i,s_j,s_k) = 1_{(\mathrm{f}(s_i),\mathrm{f}(s_j),\mathrm{f}(s_k))=(4,3,4)\wedge(\mathrm{shift\text{-}up}\vee\mathrm{shift\text{-}down})} \tag{35}$$

$$x_{VPM\text{-}3,2}(s_i,s_j,s_k) = 1_{\mathrm{f}(s_i)\cdot\mathrm{f}(s_k)\neq 0 \wedge \|\Delta_p(i,k)\|<\tau_p \wedge \Delta_{pr}(i,k)\neq 0 \wedge \Delta_f(i,k)=0} \tag{36}$$

6   Experiments

We perform two sets of experiments. The first experiment assesses the performance of adaptation and error correction algorithms on bowed string estimation, and the second the playability of our new fingering model.

6.1   Experiment 1: Bowed String Estimation

We prepared two fingerings for three pieces of classical music (414 notes total). For each fingering, we recorded it using the same violin and strings used to record the training data (denoted as setup SS), another on the same violin but with different brand of strings (setup SD), and another played on different violin with different brand of strings (setup DD). We evaluated the accuracy of the bowed string estimatior with and without the adaptation, each time evaluating the accuracy with and without error correction. The result is shown in Figure 6.

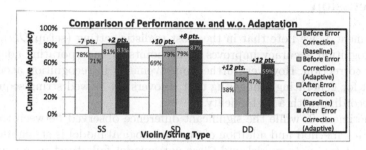

Fig. 6. Recognition accuracies with and w/o adaptation and error correction

6.2   Experiment 2: Playability of Fingering Estimator

First, 10 excerpts from three classical repertoires were prepared (approx. 200 notes). For each repertoire, we generated a fingering using four set-ups, (1)HVM-2, (2)HVM-2+VPM-2, (3) HVM-$2/3$, and (4) HVM-$2/3$+VPM-$2/3$. We assume that bowed string estimation is perfectly accurate, by not incorporating constraints based on the estimated bowed string. The feature weight matrix W was manually tuned, by first adjusting the parameters for (1) until it generated satisfactory fingerings for the repertoires considered. Then, parameters pertaining to (2) were adjusted, followed by (3) and (4). Excerpts that generated different fingerings for each of the setups were then extracted (10 excerpts, consisting of approx. 200 notes).

Next, seven violinists of various skills (amateur and professional, 10+ years of experience) evaluated the generated fingerings. First, each violinist was presented with fingerings generated using VPM-2 and VPM-2+HVM-2, and was asked to choose the better of the two, if any. Table 1 shows the result of the survey. Sign test shows that HVM-2 and VPM-2+HVM-2 are not equally favored ($p = 0.01$), which suggests that our proposed model (HVM-2+VPM-2) is favored over the baseline (HVM-2 only). Next, the evaluators were asked to evaluate 11 excerpts (approx. 200 notes) in addition to the 10 excerpts used previously, using HVM-2+VPM-2 and HVM-$2/3$+VPM-$2/3$. Fingerings that contained no difference were discarded. The results are shown in Table 2. Sign test fails to reject the null hypothesis that three-note and two-note are equally favored ($p = 0.05$).

Table 1. Count of the preference of violin
pedagogical model vs. baseline. 66 of 70
questions were answered.

Setup	Total Count
HVM-2	5
HVM-2+VPM-2	54
No preference	7

Table 2. Count of the preference of two-note vs. three-note. 117 out of 147 questions were answered.

Setup	Total Count
HVM-2+VPM-2	43
HVM-2/3+VPM-2/3	49
No preference	25

7   Discussion

In Experiment 1, we note that in the most realistic setting (setup DD), bowed string recognition accuracy improves by 21 points by incorporating adaptation and error correction. However, further improvements in recognition accuracy is important for generating a fingering that recovers the bowed string sequence of a given recording with a high fidelity.

In Experiment 2, while the significant difference observed between the baseline fingering method and addition of our pedagogical model is straightforward, the fact that two-note model and three-note model fails to show a significant difference is counter-intuitive. We believe this occurs because two-note model tends to generate fingerings that quickly alternate between natural and unnatural hand postures, while the three-note model tends to stay in one moderately natural hand posture. Hence, the result is sensitive to the user's preference towards natural hand position and transition between two hand positions.

8   Conclusion

This work presented a method for analyzing a monophonic violin audio recording to estimate a playable fingering that recreates its bowed string sequence. For bowed string estimation, robustness against use of different violins and brand of strings were improved by up to 21 points by combining model adaptation and rule-based error correction algorithm. To recommend a natural, playable fingering, we introduced the violin pedagogical model, whose features are inspired by practices of violin playing. We also introduced three-notes models, which uses a sequence of three tones as a basis for determining the finger transition costs. We found that the proposed pedagogical model was capable of generating more playable fingering, while no significant differences were observed between existing two-note-based features and three-note features.

For future work, we seek to improve the bowed string classifier and support estimation of fingerings involving double-stops from a polyphonic mixture of sound. Moreover, we would like to evaluate our method as a pedagogical tool for aiding beginning to intermediate-level violinists acquire the aural characteristics of their favorite violinists.

Acknowledgement. We would like to acknowledge violinists P. Klinger, P. Sunwoo, and J. Choi for their valuable inputs, and the volunteers who have evaluated the fingering decision algorithm and also offered valuable inputs. This work was funded by Grand-in-Aid of JST-CREST.

References

1. Yampolsky, I.M.: Principles of Violin Fingering. Oxford University Press, Oxford (1967)
2. Stowell, R.: The Cambridge Companion to the Violin. Cambridge University Press, Cambridge (1992)
3. Radicioni, D.P., et al.: A Segmentation-Based Prototype to Compute String Instruments Fingering. In: Parncutt, R., Kessler, A., Zimmer, F. (eds.) CIM 2004, Graz, Austria (2004)
4. Sayegh, S.: Fingering for string instruments with the optimum path paradigm. Computer Music Journal 13(3), 76–84 (1989)
5. Traube, C., Smith, J.O.: Extracting the fingering and the plucking points on a guitar string from a recording. In: IEEE Workshop on the Applications of Signal Processing to Audio and Acoustics, pp. 7–10 (2001)
6. Krishnaswamy, A., Smith, J.O.: Inferring control inputs to an acoustic violin from audio spectra. In: ICME '03, vol. 1, pp. 733–736 (2003)
7. Hu, N., et al.: Polyphonic audio matching and alignment for music retrieval. In: WASPAA 2003, October 2003, pp. 185–188 (2003)
8. Itoyama, K., et al.: Integration and adaptation of harmonic and inharmonic models for separating polyphonic musical signals. In: ICASSP '07, April 2007, vol. 1, pp. I-57–I-60 (2007)
9. Herrera-Boyer, P.: Automatic classification of musical instrument sounds. J. of New Music Research 32(1) (19), 3–21 (2003)
10. Kitahara, T., et al.: Pitch-dependent identification of musical instrument sounds. App. Intelligence 23(3), 267–275 (2003)

Intelligent Processing of K-Nearest Neighbors Queries Using Mobile Data Collectors in a Location Aware 3D Wireless Sensor Network

Prem Prakash Jayaraman[1], Arkady Zaslavsky[1,2], and Jerker Delsing[2]

[1] Caulfield School of Information Technology, Monash University,
900 Dandenong Road, Melbourne, Australia
[2] Lulea University of Technology, Lulea, Sweden
Prem.Jayaraman@infotech.monash.edu.au,
{Arkady.Zaslavsky,Jerker.Delsing}@ltu.se

Abstract. The increased acceptance of sensor networks into everyday pervasive environments has lead to the creation of abundant distributed resource constrained data sources. In this paper, we propose an intelligent mobile data collector-based K-Nearest Neighbor query processing algorithm namely 3D-KNN. The K-Nearest Neighbor query is an important class of query processing approach in sensor networks. The proposed algorithm is employed over a sensor network that is situated within a 3 dimensional space. We propose a novel boundary estimation algorithm which computes an energy efficient sensor boundary that encloses at least k nearest nodes. We then propose a 3D plane rotation algorithm that maps selected sensor nodes on different planes onto a reference plane and a novel k nearest neighbor selection algorithm based on node distance and signal-to-noise ratio parameters. We have implemented the 3D-KNN algorithm in GlomoSim and validate the proposed algorithm's cost efficiency by extensive performance evaluation over well defined system criteria.

Keywords: KNN Query, Sensor Networks.

1 Introduction

Sensor networks have gained vast interest in recent years [1] with wide range of applications focusing on data collection, processing and disseminating. The characteristics of sensor networks and their varied application domains project them as a distributed site of information. The sensor nodes are tiny low powered devices with communication capabilities. Hence the cost of collecting data from the sensor networks is very high [3]. A centralized approach is to relay the data from all the sensors to the sink while applications access the sink to obtain any data from specific sensor site. The sink is responsible for processing incoming data. This approach has proved to be inefficient and expensive [3]. To overcome the shortfall of the centralized approach, in-network data processing techniques have been proposed [2, 8]. These techniques use sensor's storage and processing capabilities to sense and store data within the network. This data is forwarded to the sink only when a request is received. Many

N. García-Pedrajas et al. (Eds.): IEA/AIE 2010, Part III, LNAI 6098, pp. 260–270, 2010.

research projects focus on extracting the stored sensor data efficiently [8, 3]. K-Nearest Neighbor queries are one such class of queries that has been employed to retrieve spatially distributed data [16, 17]. A sensor network is a typical example of such spatially distributed data.

KNN queries have been traditionally used in databases that require maintenance of complex index structures to identify nearest neighbors [8]. This approach is inefficient and expensive for sensor networks as sensors are energy constrained devices with limited communication and processing capabilities. This renders them incapable to maintain complex index structures to process KNN queries as opposed to databases approach. KNN queries within sensor networks have been studied in the literature [2, 4, 5, 18, 19]. The proposed approaches use sink based KNN query processing. This approach faces the short fall of the sink based [3] approach discussed earlier. Thus we propose the use of mobile data collector that employs mobile processing of KNN queries. The mobile data collectors [7] are intelligent devices that posses better communication and processing capabilities (e.g. mobile phone, robot) than the sensor nodes. These data collectors are part of the sensor network infrastructure having the capability to dynamically process KNN queries by moving closer to the point of interest (KNN point of interest) thus savings energy consumed to route the KNN query from the sink to point of interest. Our proposed KNN algorithm takes into consideration energy efficiency, dynamic network topology and query performance. More specifically our proposed algorithm makes the following contributions: (1) Reduces overall communication by selecting only a sample (k) of sensors hence reducing energy consumption of the entire network; (2) Employs a mobile data collector to propagate and execute KNN queries hence increasing query performance and reducing query propagation energy; (3) Adapts to changing network infrastructure by employing a non infrastructure-based approach i.e. an approach that does not require prior network information.

Motivated by the above requirements, we propose our 3 dimensional K-Nearest Neighbor Algorithm (3D-KNN). Our proposed KNN algorithms is employed over 3D sensor network (e.g. buildings) going by recent investigations that sensors are spatially irregular [6]. None of the current approach investigates a 3D sensor network. The proposed 3D-KNN algorithm employs a boundary estimation technique [4, 5] to estimate a sensor boundary that encompasses the sample (k) sensors. Once the boundary is estimated, an initial query is propagated to obtain pre-sensor information i.e. sensor location, signal-to-noise ratio. This information is then used by the 3D-KNN algorithm to merge sensors on different 3D planes to a reference plane. Once the mapping is completed, the k nearest nodes is selected. The boundary estimation, pre-sensor data collection and k nearest node selection are computed by the mobile data collector which is assumed to be near the point of interest.

The rest of the paper is organized as follows. In section 2, we present related work and identify the major contributions of our paper. Section 3 presents a motivating scenario behind employing KNN queries using mobile data collectors. Section 4 presents the proposed 3D-KNN algorithms. Section 5 presents extensive evaluation and results validating the proposed algorithms over different evaluation parameters. Section 6 concludes the paper with remarks on future extensions.

2 Related Work

The literature on in-network KNN processing in sensor networks can be classified into infrastructure-based and infrastructure-less approaches [5]. The work presented in [8, 18, 19] are infrastructure-based approaches where the network needs to constantly update network data structures (node index). These approaches assume a sensor network with fixed network dynamics, hence with changing network infrastructure, the overheads to maintain the network index is expensive. Also none of the proposed approaches investigate the advantages of using a mobile data collector-based KNN query processing approach.

Winter et.al [4] propose an infrastructure-based and a partial infrastructure-based 2D KNN algorithm. The infrastructure-based algorithm is based on the GeoRouting Tree (GRT) approach which requires spatial indexes to run the KNN search. This raises the problem of requiring large amount of storage capabilities to maintain index structures in dense sensor networks. To improve the performance of the GRT based KNN algorithm, Winter et.al [4] propose a partial infrastructure-based KNN algorithm namely KBT. KBT uses TreeHeight based approach to estimate the KNN boundary. The TreeHeight is a maximum hop distance that the query can propagate from the query point that encloses the set of k nearest neighbors. It uses restricted flooding and timers to achieve energy efficient query processing. But the proposed approach does not adapt well for changing network dynamics as it uses a fixed KNN boundary (Tree Height). The use of hop count as a metric to determine the KNN boundary results in higher energy consumption as two nodes with large distance might still be one hop neighbors. Both KBT and GRT based KNN approaches assumes a 2D sensor network. The proposed 3D-KNN approach uses a 3D sensor network and computes the KNN boundary based on node density. This makes the KNN boundary estimation dynamic, adapting for changing network topologies.

Wu et.al [5] propose an infrastructure-less itinerary based KNN (DKINN) where nodes are not required to maintain network data structures. The DKINN propagates the KNN query from the sink to a node closer to the point of interest (query point). While the query routes to the nearest node, it collects network information like node location and node density. Once the query arrives with initial information to the closest node, the closest node estimates the KNN boundary around the query point. The results of DKINN are better than GRT. But DKINN requires certain pre-requisites before it can be employed. The DKINN approach is based on a trajectory based data forwarding within sensor networks [14]. The trajectory provides the path the query needs to take to reach the node nearest to the query point. The trajectory computing algorithm involves electing Q-node and D-nodes. Q-node is similar to cluster heads that are responsible for forwarding the query to the next Q-node collecting information from surrounding nodes (D-nodes). To compute the initial trajectory path, the sensor needs to be equipped with specialized hardware (parallel array antennas) [14]. This may not be always feasible in every sensor network. Hence DKINN applies to a specific class of sensors.

Both GRT [4] and DKINN [5] use the sink to propagate the KNN query to a node closest to the query point. Once the query is processed, the result is propagated back to the sink. Our proposed approach avoids the use of sink to propagate the query. Instead we propose the use of mobile data collectors [7] to issue the query where the query point is centered about the mobile data collector. To our best knowledge, none of the work in the literature investigates the use of mobile data collectors to process KNN queries within a 3D sensor network. Our proposed idea is the initial step to explore an infrastructure-less 3D KNN using intelligent mobile data collectors. The key contributions of this paper is a cost-efficient intelligent[1] 3D-KNN algorithm that

- Employs an intelligent data collector to propagate KNN query within the sensor network centered around it
- Estimates the KNN boundary using the network density
- Collects initial sensor information (location, SNR) from nodes within the estimated network boundary (routing phase)
- Maps sensor nodes on 3D planes to a reference plane and compute the k nearest neighbors based on heuristic information collected during the routing phase.

3 Preliminaries

3.1 Motivating Scenario Using Mobile Data Collectors

Our proposed approach to employ mobile data collectors for KNN query processing is motivated from our previous work [7]. The intelligent mobile data collector is a part of the sensor network infrastructure having better communication, processing and battery recharging capabilities. Our motivating scenario to employ KNN query in a 3D sensor network using mobile data collector is depicted in Figure 1. The building environment is our motivating scenario where sensors are located at different levels of the building i.e. spatially distributed. The mobile data collector could be a robot that moves within the building infrastructure employing KNN queries from various points of interest. The use of 3D sensor infrastructure helps in discarding sensor nodes which are on different level and are of no interest to the user even if they fall within the KNN boundary.

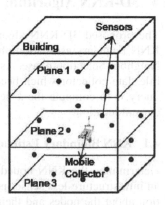

Fig. 1. A Motivating Scenario: Building Environment with Mobile Data Collector

3.2 Assumptions and Definitions

An illustration of the 3D sensor network model with a mobile data collector on which the 3D-KNN algorithm is proposed was presented in Figure 1. Our assumptions are, the sensor network is in a 3D plane and sensors are location aware. A mobile data

---

[1] We use the term intelligent as the mobile data collector has intelligence to compute KNN queries on the fly from a location closet to the point of interest. The cost is a cumulative function representing KNN query energy efficiency and performance. In our view, the terms intelligence and cost are used interchangeably to represent efficient KNN query processing.

collector [7] is within the network infrastructure and has the capability to issue KNN query from any point within the network centered about it. Once the initial KNN data is propagated back to the mobile data collector, it uses the collected network data to determine the k nearest nodes.

Hence the proposed approach investigates an inner to outer boundary selection based KNN algorithm rather than the traditional sink to query point based i.e. outer to inner boundary based approach.

Definition 1 (Nearest Neighbor): Given a set N of n sensors, location of mobile collector L, find a set N' of n' nodes such that n' $\in$ N', n $\in$ N where N' $\subseteq$ N and dist dist ($\forall$n', L) <= KNN_BOUNDARY.

Definition 2 (K-Nearest Neighbor): Given the set N' of n' sensors, find a set K of k sensor nodes such that k $\in$ K, n' $\in$ N' and dist ($\forall$k, L) < dist ($\forall$n', L).

The nearest neighbor defines the set of N' sensor nodes that fall within the estimated KNN_BOUNDAY determined using the network density. From the set of N' nodes, we determine the k (sample size) nearest neighbors.

4   3D-KNN Algorithm

The proposed 3D-KNN algorithm is executed in three phases namely, namely: (1) KNN boundary estimation phases; (2) Pre-routing phase; (3) 3D Plane Rotation and Neighbor Selection phase. As mentioned earlier, the KNN query is issued by the mobile data collector which becomes the point of interest. Hence the aim of the KNN query is to compute the *k* nearest nodes with respect to the mobile data collector's current location.

4.1   KNN Boundary Estimation Phase

Determining the KNN boundary is a major challenge in an infrastructure-less sensor network as no prior information about the nodes and their layouts are available. The KNN boundary is a sphere with radius R encompassing at least k sensors. With the assumption that nodes are spread over a 3D area (building) whose spatial characteristics are available, we use (1) to determine the density of nodes within the area. With known node density D from (1) and no of nodes (sample size) k, we compute area (A) of the space that covers at least k sensor nodes. Having computed the area, we use (2) to determine the radius R of the sphere that encloses the k nearest neighbors.

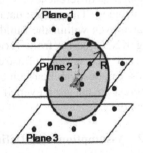

Fig. 2. Estimated KNN boundary (Shaded Area)

$$Node\ Density\ D(per\ m^3) = \frac{No\ of\ nodes\ N}{Area\ of\ Terrain} \quad (1) \qquad Radius\ (R) = \sqrt[3]{\frac{Covered\ Area\ (A)*3}{4*\pi}} \quad (2)$$

Figure 2 illustrates the KNN boundary estimation using known node density and sample search size k. The highlighted sphere is the estimated KNN boundary that comprises at least k sensor nodes. This approach requires no knowledge of sensor locations to determine the area of the KNN boundary and is computed at the mobile data collector without any interaction with the surrounding sensor nodes.

4.2 Pre-routing Phase

Once the KNN search boundary is computed, an initial data collection phase is used to collected the following information

- Node Location
- Signal-to-Noise Ratio (a cumulative function for each hop from mobile data collector to destination sensor node)

Algorithm 1: Boundary Estimation and Pre-Routing Phase

Require: Node neighbor list nec_i, A_T terrain area, N total number of nodes in the terrain, L mobile data collector location

BEGIN 3DKNN

  Compute $D = N/A_T$
  Get k (sample size)
  Compute A such that $A = k/D$
  $R = A/2$
  Compute $maxKNNDIST = DIST(L \pm R)$
  Send initial broadcast message
  For each node I receiving the broadcast
    Compute $distance = DIST(I, L)$
    If $distance < maxKNNDIST$
    Set $timer = maxKNNDIST / distance$
      Add nodeID to ROUTE
      Forward broadcast message to nec_i
    Else
      Mark KNN search boundary
      Add nodeID to ROUTE with BOUNDARY marker
      return location, snr
    End if
  End For
  On Timer Expiry for each node I
      Aggregate results of location and snr
      Send it to mobile data collector at location L
      through the path ROUTE
  End
END

Fig. 3. 3DKNN Algorithm to Estimate KNN Search Boundary and Execute Pre-Routing Phase

Given our assumption that no infrastructure information is required, the pre-routing phase is used to collect initial information required to determine the k nearest neighbors. The pre-routing is initiated by the mobile data collector broadcasting simple message beacon requesting the above information. Each broadcast message is marked with an expiry time (determined by the mobile data collector while initiating broadcast) and a maximum search distance (computed during the KNN boundary estimation). The maximum search distance is the maximum distance between the mobile data collector and a sensor node at the boundary of the KNN boundary. E.g. the kth hop node i at location loc_i on receiving the message determines the distance from the mobile collector. If the distance is less that maximum search distance, it sets a timer computed as a function of its distance and the maximum search distance and forwards the packet to rest of its neighbors. If the computed distance is greater than the search boundary, the nodes routes its location and SNR values back to the mobile data collector using the same path through which it received the message. The timer function is used to improve energy consumption by achieving data aggregation at each node closer to the mobile data collector. Since the data collector is mobile and moves closer to the next point of interest, different groups of nodes are chosen to be data aggregators hence tackling the problem of depleting the energy of relay nodes. The boundary estimation and pre-routing phase algorithms are presented in Figure .

4.3 3D Plane Rotation and k Nearest Sensor Selection

The pre-routing phase allows collection of node information from a selected set of nodes within the KNN boundary. The SNR along with the node location is used to map the sensor nodes on various planes of the 3D terrain to a reference plane. The reference plane is the plane on which the mobile data collector moves. Assuming the mobile data collector moves across the XY plane with a constant Z value (E.g. $Z = 1$ if mobile data collector is in level 1), the sensor nodes enclosed within the sphere that lie on various 3D planes are mapped to the XYZ plane of the data collector namely the reference plane. The distance between the data collector and the sensor node is given by (3).

$$Boundary\ Distance\ B_D = \sqrt{(X_2 - X_1)^2 + (Y_2 - Y_1)^2 + (Z_2 - Z_1)^2} \quad (3)$$

The plane rotation and neighbor selection algorithm computes distances of nodes on different planes with respect to the reference plane. TO achieve our plane rotation and node selection, we use two metrics namely distance (D) and SNR. The SNR is a good indicator to estimate link quality which is related to energy consumption. Hence identifying the most energy efficient nodes over various 3D planes is achieved by the 3D Plane rotation and neighbor selection algorithm. To achieve exact selection and mapping of nodes, we propose $KNN\text{-}METRIC$ given by

$$KNN - METRIC = c * \frac{\alpha * SNR}{\beta * Boundary\ Distance\ (B_D)} \quad (4)$$

c is a constant and α, β are weights assigned to each metric by the application user. To compute a value for the constant c, we assume an ideal case where the $KNN\text{-}METRIC = 1$, $\alpha = 0.4$, $\beta = 0.6$ and ideal case values for B_D and SNR being 100 and 60 respectively

$$c = 1 * \frac{0.6 * 100}{0.4 * 60} = 2.5 \quad (5)$$

By obtaining both distance and SNR during pre-routing phase, the plane rotation and neighbor selection achieves mapping selected sensor nodes on the reference plane. None of the previous approaches consider a 3D network nor incorporate a function of distance and SNR to compute nearest neighbors while processing KNN queries. Our argument is that the $KNN\text{-}METRIC$ given by (4) employed by our proposed 3D-KNN algorithm provides higher efficient energy which is validated by extensive evaluation presented in section 5.

5 Simulation and Evaluation

To validate the proposed 3D-KNN approach, we simulate our algorithm using GlomoSim [11, 12]. GlomoSim is a parallel discrete system simulator based on Parsec [13]. GlomoSim has the capability to simulate mobile wireless nodes using a random walk model. For the simulation we use the parameters presented in table 1. Our

Table 1. Simulation Parameters

Parameter	Value
Number of Nodes (N)	20 to 200
Terrain Size (A_T)	1000 x 1000 and 2000 x 2000
Radio T_x Power	15 dBm
k	Number of Nearest nodes
c	2.5

terrain is a building where nodes are spread across a 3D terrain. Neighbor discovery is done at runtime by the sensors. This is a not a requirement to process the KNN query as this can also be determined during the pre-routing phase. This approach facilitates the 3D-KNN algorithm to adapt to changing network infrastructure. The sensor nodes are assumed to be static with the mobile data collector moving on plane with changing X, Y and constant Z.

5.1 Boundary Estimation Algorithm Evaluation

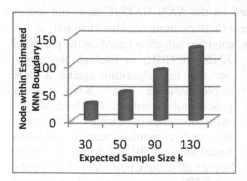

Fig. 4. Nodes Found within the KNN Boundary for request K using 3D-KNN algorithm

The KNN query is disseminated into the sensor network by the mobile data collector. The boundary area is computed by the mobile data collector based on the sample size k. It is important to evaluate the boundary estimation algorithm as the boundary area computed needs to cover at least k sensor nodes. The result of evaluation is presented in Figure 4. As seen in the graph, for given sample size k, the estimated boundary covers at least k sensor nodes. Also the search boundary is not too big enclosing the entire network. This result is also an indication of the efficiency of the boundary estimation algorithm's capability to cover the least area that comprises at least k required sensor nodes.

5.2 Query Latency and Energy Consumption

The query latency is the time taken to process a KNN query for varying sizes of k and energy consumption is the overall energy consumed by the entire sensor network to process the KNN query for varying k. To validate and prove the energy efficiency and query performance of the proposed 3D-KNN algorithm, we compare the results of this evaluation with KBT (Fixed Tree Height) [4]. The simulation results are presented in Figure and Figure .

The results in figure 5 and 6 validate the performance improvement of the proposed 3D-KNN algorithm over KBT. A trend line projected on the results indicate the exponential increase in energy consumption and query latency using KBT against a linear increase in energy consumption and query latency using 3D-KNN for varying values of k. The energy efficiency of the proposed 3D-KNN algorithm is primarily due to 1) Proposed boundary estimation based on network density that covers at least k sensor

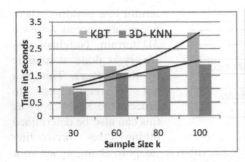
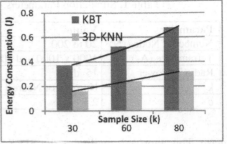

Fig. 5. 3D-KNN vs. KBT: Query Latency Comparison

Fig. 6. 3D-KNN vs. KBT: Energy Consumption Comparison

nodes hence reducing the amount of message broadcast in the network; 2) Plane rotation and k nearest neighbor selection based on the *KNN-METRIC* choosing sensor nodes that are both closer and energy efficient (better communication channel).

To further evaluate the plane rotation and neighbor selection based on the proposed KNN-METRIC, we evaluate the neighbor selection algorithm against a basic implementation of KNN query processing algorithm. The basic implementation does not employ SNR heuristics and computes nearest neighbors based only on distance hence not taking energy efficiency into account, while the 3D-KNN computes nearest neighbors taking both distance and SNR which from previous evaluations prove to be a good indicator to predict energy consumption while computing KNN queries. The result of this evaluation is presented in Figure . The highlighted

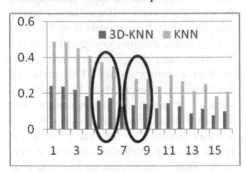

Fig. 7. 3D-KNN using proposed heuristics (SNR, Distance) vs base KNN Implementation

part of the graph illustrated by red circles indicates the metric values computed using the two approaches. Investigating the results, node 9 which is at a longer distance than 8 (deduced from basic KNN metric) would be much energy efficient nearest neighbor as its SNR and distance metric is higher than node 8. The similar outcome is observed for nodes 5 and 6. This evaluation proves and validates the energy efficient k nearest neighbor selection employed by the proposed the 3D-KNN algorithm.

6 Conclusion

This paper has proposed an approach to compute cost-efficient K-Nearest Neighbor queries in a 3D sensor network using intelligent mobile data collectors. Our proposal envisages the use of mobile data collectors to disseminate and process KNN queries. The proposed 3D-KNN algorithm employs KNN boundary estimation based on node density of the network, thus restricting the number of sensor covered by the KNN boundary to at least k sensor nodes. To compute the KNN boundary, our algorithm does not require prior knowledge of network infrastructure. The 3D-KNN algorithm employs a plane rotation algorithm that maps sensor nodes on 3D planes to a reference plane identified by the mobile data collector. Finally, we propose a neighbor selection algorithm that employs *KNN-NETRIC*, a function of SNR and distance to select the k nearest neighbors.

The proposed algorithms have been implemented in GlomoSim, a discrete parallel event simulator and extensive evaluations have been performed to validate and prove the cost efficiency of the proposed 3D-KNN algorithm. We have compared the results of the simulations with KBT (a partial infrastructure-based KNN algorithm) from both communication (energy) and performance (query latency) point of view. The 3D-KNN algorithm performs better than KBT under given simulation parameters proving to be higher energy efficient and performance oriented primarily attributed to the proposed cost-efficient boundary estimation, plane rotation and novel neighbor selection algorithms. The results are promising and we look to extend our work into non-broadcast based sensor nodes namely Bluetooth [15] based sensor nodes.

References

1. Shen, C.-C., Srisathapornphat, C., Jaikaeo, C.: Sensor information networking architecture and applications. IEEE Personal Communications, 52–59 (2001)
2. Yao, X.T., Lim, E.-P.: In-Network Processing of Nearest Neighbor Queries for Wireless Sensor Networks. In: Li Lee, M., Tan, K.-L., Wuwongse, V. (eds.) DASFAA 2006. LNCS, vol. 3882, pp. 35–49. Springer, Heidelberg (2006)
3. Bonnet, P., Gehrke, J., Seshadri, P.: Towards sensor database systems. In: Proceedings of IEEE, MDM 2001, Hong Kong, China, pp. 3–14 (2001)
4. Winter, J., Xu, Y., Lee, W.: Energy Efficient Processing of K Nearest Neighbor Queries in Location-aware Sensor Networks. In: Proceedings of the Second Annual international Conference on Mobile and Ubiquitous Systems: Networking and Services, Washington, DC, July 17-21, pp. 281–292 (2005)
5. Wu, S.-H., Chuang, K.-T., Chen, C.-M., Chen, M.-S.: DIKNN: An Itinerary-based KNN Query Processing Algorithm for Mobile Sensor Networks. In: IEEE 23rd International Conference on Data Engineering, ICDE 2007, April 15-20, pp. 456–465 (2007)
6. Ganesan, D., Ratnasamy, S., Wang, H., Estrin, D.: Copingwith irregular spatio-temporal sampling in sensor networks. ACM SIGCOMM Computer Communication Review 34(1) (2004)
7. Jayaraman, P.P., Zaslavsky, A., Delsing, J.: Cost Efficient Data Collection of Sensory Originated Data using Context-Aware Mobile Devices. In: MDM 2008, Ninth International Conference on Mobile Data Management Workshops, pp. 190–200 (2008)
8. Liu, B., Lee, W., Lee, D.: Distributed caching of multidimensional data in mobile environments. In: Proc. of MDM (2005)
9. Lee, W., Zheng, B.: Dsi: A fully distributed spatial index for location-based wireless broadcast services. In: Proc. of ICDCS (2005)
10. Patil, S., Das, S., Nasipuri, A.: Serial data fusion using space-filling curves in wireless sensor networks. In: Proc. of SECON (2004)
11. GloMoSim: Global Mobile Information Systems Simulation Library,
   http://pcl.cs.ucla.edu/projects/glomosim/

12. Gerla, M., Bajaj, L., Takai, M., Ahuja, R., Bagrodia, R.: GloMoSim: A Scalable Network Simulation Environment. Technical Report 990027, University of California, 13 (1999)
13. UCLA Parallel Computing Laboratory, PARSEC,
    http://pcl.cs.ucla.edu/projects/parsec/ (August 25, 2009)
14. Niculescu, D., Nath, B.: Trajectory based forwarding and its applications. In: Proc. of MOBICOM 2003 (2003)
15. Johansson, J., Volker, M., Eliasson, J., Ostmark, A., Lindgren, P., Delsing, J.: Mulle: A minimal sensor networking device - implementation and manufacturing challenges. In: IMAPS Nordic 2004, pp. 265–271 (2004)
16. Mouratidis, K., Hadjieleftheriou, M., Papadias, D.: Conceptual partitioning: an efficient method for continous nearest neighbor monitoring. In: Proceedings SIGMOD 2005, Baltimore (June 2005)
17. Mouratidis, K., Papadias, D., Bakiras, S., Tao, Y.: A threshold based algorithm for continuous monitoring of k nearest neighbors. IEEE Trans. Knowl. Data Eng (TKDE) 17(11), 1451–1464 (2005)
18. Yao, Y., Tang, X., Lim, E.: Localized monitoring of kNN queries in wireless sensor networks. The VLDB Journal 18(1), 99–117 (2009)
19. Soheili, A., Kalogeraki, V., Gunopulos, D.: Spatial queries in sensor networks. In: Proceedings of the 13th Annual ACM international Workshop on Geographic information Systems, GIS 2005, Bremen, Germany, November 4-5, pp. 61–70. ACM, New York (2005)

An Intelligent Interface with Composite Dominant Directed Graph Based Petri Nets Controller for Rotatable Solar Panel in Integrated PHEV System

Jian-Long Kuo[1], Kun Shian Su[2], Jing-Hsiung Yang[2], and Wen-Pao Chen[2]

[1] Institute of Mechanical A.E. and System Information and Control, National Kaohsiung First University of Sci. and Tech., Nan-Tze, Kaoh-Siung 811, Taiwan
[2] Department of Electrical Engineering, National Kaohsiung University of Applied Sciences, Sanmin, Kaoh-Siung 807, Taiwan
JLKUO@CCMS.NKFUST.EDU.TW

Abstract. This paper proposes an intelligent dominant directed graph (DDG) based Petri nets (PN) controller to increase the efficiency of the plug-in hybrid electric vehicle (PHEV) by using rotatable solar panel. Conventionally, the PHEV with solar panel has a critical problem of putting on the roof of a PHEV. Since the limited space on the roof of the vehicle is not large enough. Rotatable structure is considered to track the sunlight by intelligent dominant directed graph based Petri nets controller. The mechanical maximum power point tracking (MPPT) function can be achieved. A stepping motor is used to control the rotating angle of the rotating solar panel. With the composite mechanical MPPT with DDG+PN control algorithms, the maximum power in a limited roof space of the vehicle is possible. The solar panel has not to be very large. This increases the efficiency of the PHEV. It is convinced that the proposed DDG+PN MPPT algorithms are applicable to the PHEV system.

Keywords: Dominant directed graph(DDG), Petri nets (PN), Maximum power point tracking (MPPT), Plug-in hybrid electric vehicle (PHEV).

1 Introduction

1.1 Plug-In Hybrid Electric Vehicle

The electric vehicle (EV) becomes more and more important in our real life due to the energy saving and carbon reduction issue. Among, various many EVs, The plug-in hybrid electric vehicle (PHEV) is a hybrid vehicle with an integrated mechatronic system and also with batteries that can be recharged by connecting a plug to an electric power source. The PHEV has the characteristics of both hybrid electric vehicles and battery electric vehicles.

There are an electric motor and internal combustion engine (ICE) in the hybrid EV system. There is a plug for the EV to connect to the electric grid. The cost for electricity to power plug-in hybrid EV for all-electric operation has been estimated at less than one quarter of the cost of gasoline [1]-[9]. As compared to conventional

N. García-Pedrajas et al. (Eds.): IEA/AIE 2010, Part III, LNAI 6098, pp. 271–280, 2010.

vehicles, PHEV can reduce the problem of air pollution, dependency on petroleum, and greenhouse gas emissions that contribute to global warming [2][3][4].

There is great potential for the PHEV. It is more efficient than conventional hybrids. [5]. By controlling the PHEV's ICE, the engine can keep its maximum efficiency all the time. A PHEV is likely to convert to motive energy on average at about 30% efficiency. The engine of a PHEV would be likely to operate far more often near its peak efficiency. The batteries can serve the modest power needs at times when the ICE would be forced to run well below its peak efficiency. The actual efficient achieved depends on losses from electricity generation, inversion, battery charging/discharging, the motor controller and motor itself, the way a vehicle is used, and the opportunity to recharge by connecting to the electric grid.

1.2 Directed Graph

Basically, the dominant directed graph (DDG) is a graph theory. It is used to determine the winner in a tournament. The winner represents the maximum solar power value in this problem. The teams in a tournament represent a series of sampling signals to calculate the dynamic time-varying solar power value. Eight sampling signals are sampled from the A/D converter. Eight teams represent the eight sampling signals.

Therefore, the maximum solar power value can be determined. The directed graph has the benefit of graphical representation which can provide better understanding for the designer. The eight signals in the eight directions are sampled sequentially. Therefore, the sampling is time-dependent and keeps changing all the time.

1.3 Petri Nets

For the discrete distributed systems, Petri nets method is a good method to describe the dynamics [10]-[16]. Petri nets method is used to implement an intelligent logic controller in a rotatable solar panel system. The Petri nets approach is a very popular technique for digital control system in recent years. Since the tremendous programmable logic design for the system integration, the Petri nets approach provides a systematic matrix approach to handle the synchronization problem for logic control. When considering a large system, the conventional logic design is usually quite complicated. The programming of an intelligent logic controller is designed by using C language.

2 Structure of Proposed PHEV System

This paper proposes an intelligent composite DDG Petri nets controller to control the solar cell panel putting on the roof of the vehicle. The DDG is the first step algorithm, and the Petri nets is the second algorithm. Both of them are intelligent control algorithms. With the intelligent composite controller, the mechanically maximum power point tracking can be achieved.

For a series of continuous solar power values sensing from the voltage and current sensors, the strength of the solar power is sensed into A/D of MCU, the solar power value is calculated. There are totally eight sensors in the eight directions. In other words, there are eight teams in a tournament. Many rounds of the tournaments are going continuously due to continuous sampling data from A/D of MCU.

The major new design concept is the rotatable solar panel above the vehicle as shon in fig 1(a). The rotatable solar panel is put on the roof of the vehicle. Since the vehicle is possible to move in any directions, the rotating structure is considered here to track the sunlight by mechanical approach. By defining eight directions on the roof of the vehicle, the Petri nets based control is used to track the eight directions when the vehicle is going. The eight directions are coded in a special number sequence as denoted in Fig. 1(b). With the special number sequence, the output matrix in the Petri nets method can be equal to an identity matrix. This makes the Petri nets formulation easier.

By defining the appropriate system matrices, the controller can be implemented by using intelligent DDG+PN algorithms in embedded C language as shown in Fig. 2(a).

3 Directed Graph Formulation

3.1 Directed Graphs

A directed graph or digraph is a pair defined as $G = (V, A)$ with the following definition [17]-[20]:

A set V is defined whose elements are called vertices or nodes. A set A is defined including ordered pairs of vertices, called arcs, directed edges, or arrows. There is difference as compared to an ordinary or undirected graph. The directed graph is defined in terms of edges, which are unordered pairs of vertices.

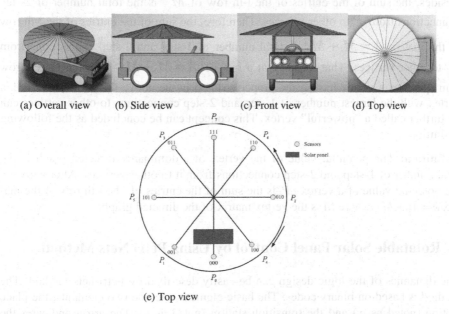

(a) Overall view   (b) Side view   (c) Front view   (d) Top view

(e) Top view

Fig. 1. (a)-(d) Three-dimensional view of the intelligent PHEV system. (e) Definition of eight directions for rotatable solar panel in top view.

3.2 Dominant-Directed Graphs

There is a definite dominance relation between any two members of the group. For given any two individuals A and B, either A dominates B or B dominates A, but not both. The directed graph can describe the same fact in the same way. The relation $P_i \to P_j$ means P_i dominances P_j, this means that for all different pairs, either $P_i \to P_j$ or $P_j \to P_i$, but not both. In general, the following fact is defined.

Definition: A dominant-directed graph is a directed graph such that for any different pair of vertices P_i and P_j, either $P_i \to P_j$ or $P_j \to P_i$, but not both. The directed graph can be applied onto a league with n sports team. They play each other exactly one time, as in one round of a round-robin tournament in which no ties are allowed. The relation $P_i \to P_j$ means that team P_i beat team P_j in their single match. The definition of a dominant-directed group is satisfied. Therefore, dominant directed graphs are sometime called tournaments.

Theorem: In any dominance-directed graph, there is at least one vertex from which there is a 1-step or 2-step connection to any other vertex. A vertex with the largest total number of 1-step and 2-step connections to other vertices has the above property stated in the theorem. There is a simple way to find such vertices using the vertex matrix M and its square matrix M^2. The sum of the entries in the i-th row of M is the total number of 1-step connections from P_i to other vertices.

Besides, the sum of the entries of the i-th row of M^2 is the total number of 2-step connections from P_i to other vertices. Therefore, the sum of the entries of the i-th row of the matrix $A = M + M^2$ is total number of 1-step and 2-step connections from P_i to other vertices. That means that a row of $A = M + M^2$ with the largest row sum specifies a vertex having the property stated in the above theorem. Therefore, a vertex with the largest number of 1-step and 2-step connections to other vertices can be further called a "powerful" vertex. This concept can be concluded as the following definition.

Definition: The potential value of the vertex of a dominance-directed graph is the total number of 1-step and 2-step connections from it to other vertices. Alter natively, the potential value of a vertex $..P_i$ is the sum of the entries of .the i-th row of the matrix $A = M + M^2$, where M is the vertex matrix of the directed graph.

4 Rotatable Solar Panel Control by Using Petri Nets Method

The dynamics of the logic design can be easily described by Petri nets method. The method is based on binary codes. The basic elements include two elements: the place station (noted as p_i) and the transition station (noted as t_i). The arrow indicates the input and output operation for the transition station. The place station can be a specific process or a state. The active place station moves to the next active place station after the firing operation. The original active station becomes inactive. The transition station handles the control logic transition. The Petri nets method has the capability of simulating the dynamic logic operation.

C is a complete Petri nets graph defined in the following:

$$C = (S, T, W) \tag{1}$$

The notation S means the place station in the Petri nets method. The station T means the transition station in the in the Petri nets method. The transition station T and the relation between station S and station T have to be found in the logic system. The input and output relation matrices are defined as W and W^+. The W matrix represents the input relation for the station S into the station T. The W^+ matrix represents the output relation for the S station out to the T station. The switching status of the directions of the vehicle in the eight directions $P_0 \sim P_7$ are defined as the elements of the place station vector.

$$S = \{p_0, p_1, ..., p_7\}, \tag{2}$$
$$p_0 = P_0, p_1 = P_1, ..., p_7 = P_7,$$

The transition station vector is expressed as follows for the time sequence $t_0 \sim t_7$.

$$T = \{t_0, t_1, ..., t_7\} \tag{3}$$
$$W : (S \times T) \to C, \ W^+ : (T \times S) \to C, \tag{4}$$

There are two key matrices required to be defined. The first matrix W is an input relation matrix that maps from station S to station T. The second matrix W^+ is an output relation matrix that maps from station T to station S. The marked points represent tokens. That means the station is under operation. The marked matrix is represented as:

$$M_i = (m(p_1), m(p_2)...m(p_j)...m(p_n))^T \tag{5}$$

M_i is the station status after the j-th firing process. If the p_j is under operation, then $m(p_j) = 1$. The initial state is defined as

$$M_o = (1 \ 0 \ 0 \ 0 \ 0 \ 0 \ 0 \ 0)^T \tag{6}$$

If the input status is changed, the transition station begins to perform the firing operation. The firing vector is defined as:

$u_i = (u(t_1), u(t_2)...u(t_j)...u(t_m))^T$, for i=1,2,3,....

If the t_j is fired, then the $u(t_j) = 1$. The S and T can be expressed as follows:

$$S = \{p_0, p_1, ... p_n\}, \text{ for } n=7, \tag{7}$$
$$T = \{t_0, t_1, ... t_m\}, \text{ for } m=7, \tag{8}$$

The M_0 for the initial state is expressed as

$$M_o = (1 \ 0 \ 0 \ 0 \ 0 \ 0 \ 0 \ 0)^T \tag{9}$$

and $W : (S \times T) \to C$ and $W^+ : (T \times S) \to C$ can be expressed as

$$
W^-_{S\times T} = \begin{array}{c} \\ P_0 \\ P_1 \\ P_2 \\ P_3 \\ P_4 \\ P_5 \\ P_6 \\ P_7 \end{array}
\begin{bmatrix}
t_0 & t_1 & t_2 & t_3 & t_4 & t_5 & t_6 & t_7 \\
0 & 1 & 0 & 0 & 1 & 0 & 0 & 0 \\
1 & 0 & 0 & 0 & 0 & 1 & 0 & 0 \\
0 & 0 & 0 & 0 & 1 & 0 & 1 & 0 \\
0 & 0 & 0 & 0 & 0 & 1 & 0 & 1 \\
1 & 0 & 1 & 0 & 0 & 0 & 0 & 0 \\
0 & 1 & 0 & 1 & 0 & 0 & 0 & 0 \\
0 & 0 & 1 & 0 & 0 & 0 & 0 & 1 \\
0 & 0 & 0 & 1 & 0 & 0 & 1 & 0
\end{bmatrix}
\quad
W^+_{S\times T} = \begin{array}{c} \\ P_0 \\ P_1 \\ P_2 \\ P_3 \\ P_4 \\ P_5 \\ P_6 \\ P_7 \end{array}
\begin{bmatrix}
t_0 & t_1 & t_2 & t_3 & t_4 & t_5 & t_6 & t_7 \\
1 & 0 & 0 & 0 & 0 & 0 & 0 & 0 \\
0 & 1 & 0 & 0 & 0 & 0 & 0 & 0 \\
0 & 0 & 1 & 0 & 0 & 0 & 0 & 0 \\
0 & 0 & 0 & 1 & 0 & 0 & 0 & 0 \\
0 & 0 & 0 & 0 & 1 & 0 & 0 & 0 \\
0 & 0 & 0 & 0 & 0 & 1 & 0 & 0 \\
0 & 0 & 0 & 0 & 0 & 0 & 1 & 0 \\
0 & 0 & 0 & 0 & 0 & 0 & 0 & 1
\end{bmatrix} \quad (10)
$$

There are two nonzero elements for each row or each column in the matrix W^-. The W^+ is an identity matrix under the proposed number sequence definition for controlling the rotatable solar panel.

5 Verification

5.1 Dynamic Behavior of Dominant Directed Graph

To verify the effect of the dominant directed graph, an example of sampling data is illustrated in Fig 2(b). The rotating behavior is not very simple since the vehicle is possibly going in any directions. The solar panel cell is also rotating relative to the vehicle. Therefore, the exact relative directions for the solar panel cell should have to consider two factors. 1) The direction of the solar panel cell relative to the vehicle. 2) The direction of the vehicle relative to the ground. Therefore, the voltage values of the sensors on the rotatable board keep changing all the time. Sometimes, it depends on the vehicle speed or the rotating speed of the rotatable board. Therefore, a more intelligent tracking method should be developed. In this paper, an intelligent composite DDG Petri nets based controller is developed to overcome this problem. Two methods are mixed together to handle the complex logic design problem in a systematic and intelligent way. The DDG is in charge of the responsibility of the determining the maximum solar power value. The intelligent Petri nets controller is in charge of the switching to the rotating desired direction. Results show that the tracking performance can be proved to be effective.

The eight sensed signals are similar to eight teams in a tournament playing games each other. The final results are indicated in the dominance directed graph. The vertex matrix of the graph is expressed as:

$$
M = \begin{array}{c} \\ P_0 \\ P_1 \\ P_2 \\ P_3 \\ P_4 \\ P_5 \\ P_6 \\ P_7 \end{array}
\begin{bmatrix}
P_0 & P_1 & P_2 & P_3 & P_4 & P_5 & P_6 & P_7 \\
0 & 1 & 0 & 0 & 1 & 0 & 0 & 0 \\
0 & 0 & 0 & 0 & 0 & 1 & 0 & 1 \\
0 & 1 & 0 & 0 & 0 & 0 & 1 & 0 \\
1 & 0 & 1 & 0 & 0 & 0 & 0 & 0 \\
0 & 0 & 1 & 0 & 0 & 0 & 0 & 0 \\
0 & 0 & 0 & 1 & 1 & 0 & 1 & 0 \\
1 & 0 & 0 & 0 & 0 & 0 & 0 & 1 \\
0 & 0 & 0 & 1 & 1 & 0 & 0 & 0
\end{bmatrix}
\quad A = M + M^2 = \begin{array}{c} \\ P_0 \\ P_1 \\ P_2 \\ P_3 \\ P_4 \\ P_5 \\ P_6 \\ P_7 \end{array}
\begin{bmatrix}
P_0 & P_1 & P_2 & P_3 & P_4 & P_5 & P_6 & P_7 \\
0 & 1 & 1 & 0 & 1 & 1 & 0 & 1 \\
0 & 0 & 0 & 2 & 2 & 1 & 1 & 1 \\
1 & 1 & 0 & 0 & 0 & 1 & 1 & 2 \\
1 & 2 & 1 & 0 & 1 & 0 & 1 & 0 \\
0 & 1 & 1 & 0 & 0 & 0 & 1 & 0 \\
2 & 0 & 2 & 1 & 1 & 0 & 1 & 1 \\
1 & 1 & 0 & 1 & 2 & 0 & 0 & 1 \\
1 & 0 & 2 & 1 & 1 & 0 & 0 & 0
\end{bmatrix} \quad (11)
$$

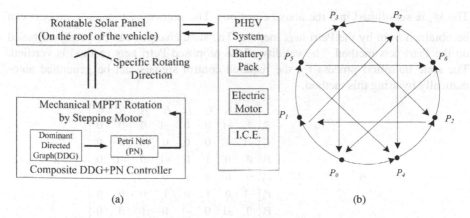

(a)   (b)

Fig. 2. (a) Control scheme in PHEV system. (b) Definition of the directed graph with eight vertices for the intelligent rotatable solar panel controller scheme.

Then, the rows sums of A are: First rows sum = 5, second rows sum = 7, third rows sum = 6, fourth rows sum = 6, fifth rows sum = 3, sixth rows sum = 8, seventh rows sum = 6, eighth rows sum = 5. Since the sixth row has the largest row sum, the vertex P_5 must have a 1-step or 2-step connection to any other vertex. This can be easily verified from the directed graph.

The eight sensed signals can be ranked in the above case according to their potential values. From the calculations of the row sums in the above case, the potential value can be calculated. Therefore, the ranking of the sensed signals according to their potential values are: P_5 (first), P_1 (second), P_2 P_3 P_6 (third), P_0 and P_7 (fourth), P_4 (last).

5.2 Dynamic Behavior of Proposed Petri Nets

There is a corresponding marked matrix for every Petri nets graph to describe the station status in the Petri nets graph. As shown in Fig. 3, the dynamic operation for the M_i and u_i can be revealed.

The sequential firing vector is u_i. The state changes from M_0 to $M_1, M_2 \cdots M_7$, then goes back to $M_7 = M_0$. A periodic process can be observed. A complete Petri nets method is expressed as follows:

$$M_k = M_{k-1} + W^+ u_k - W^- u_k \tag{12}$$

$$= M_{k-1} + (W^+ - W^-) u_k$$

The $W^T = W^+ - W^-$ is an incidence matrix. The equation can be rewritten as

$$M_7 = M_0 + W^T \sum_{k=0}^{7} u_k \tag{13}$$

The M_0 is substituted into the above equations. The sequential transition process can be obtained from by the Petri nets method. The state changes can be predicted based on the Petri nets method. The validity of the proposed Petri nets method is verified. The state transition process for the required control signals can be generated automatically by using this method.

$$
W^T = W^+ - W^- = \begin{array}{c} \\ P_0 \\ P_1 \\ P_2 \\ P_3 \\ P_4 \\ P_5 \\ P_6 \\ P_7 \end{array}
\begin{array}{cccccccc}
t_0 & t_1 & t_2 & t_3 & t_4 & t_5 & t_6 & t_7 \\
\begin{bmatrix}
1 & -1 & 0 & 0 & -1 & 0 & 0 & 0 \\
-1 & 1 & 0 & 0 & 0 & -1 & 0 & 0 \\
0 & 0 & 1 & 0 & -1 & 0 & -1 & 0 \\
0 & 0 & 0 & 1 & 0 & -1 & 0 & -1 \\
-1 & 0 & 1 & 0 & 1 & 0 & 0 & 0 \\
0 & -1 & 0 & -1 & 0 & 1 & 0 & 0 \\
0 & 0 & 1 & 0 & 0 & 0 & 1 & -1 \\
0 & 0 & 0 & -1 & 0 & 0 & -1 & 1
\end{bmatrix}
\end{array}
\tag{14}
$$

$$
M_1 = (0\ \ 1\ \ 0\ \ 0\ \ 0\ \ 0\ \ 0\ \ 0)^T
\tag{15}
$$

$$
M_2 = (0\ \ 0\ \ 1\ \ 0\ \ 0\ \ 0\ \ 0\ \ 0)^T
$$

$$
\cdots\ M_7 = (0\ \ 0\ \ 0\ \ 0\ \ 0\ \ 0\ \ 0\ \ 1)^T
$$

5.3 Case Study under Light Load Condition

The light load condition is tested first. The load condition can be regulated by varying the duty of the boost converter. In order to calculate the electric power, the voltage and the current of the solar panel are required for the microcontroller. The maximum power occurs when the output voltage is 16V in Table 1.

The influence of the intelligent DDG+PN controller is verified in Table 2. The dynamic power tracking is measured when t=2.5 sec. It keeps tracking to the maximum power value all the time. Experimental results show that the DDG+PN control algorithm can perform very well.

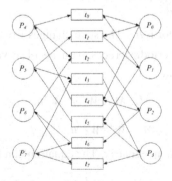

Fig. 3. The interrelation of intelligent Petri nets controller scheme

Table 1. Electric power measurement for testing case

Voltage(V)	Current (A)	Power (W)
11	0.51	5.61
12	0.49	5.88
13	0.47	6.11
14	0.46	6.44
15	0.44	6.6
16	0.41	6.56
17	0.38	6.46
18	0.26	4.68
19	0	0
11	0.51	5.61

Table 2. Power tracking sampling at t=2.5 s for testing case

No.	Voltage(V)	Current(A)	Power (W)	Percentage
1	16.8	0.38	6.384	0.9684
2	15.6	0.41	6.396	0.9702
3	17.4	0.35	6.09	0.9238
4	17.8	0.35	6.23	0.9450
5	15.4	0.42	6.468	0.9811
6	16.8	0.38	6.384	0.9684
7	16.6	0.39	6.474	0.9821
8	15.4	0.42	6.468	0.9811
9	15.4	0.42	6.468	0.9811

6 Conclusion

This paper has successfully proposed the mechanical DDG+PN MPPT methods with two control algorithms. In the composite algorithms, the first algorithm, DDG algorithm, is used to determine the maximum solar power value. Then, the second algorithm, PN algorithm is used to rotate the ratatable solar panel on the roof of the vehicle. "If…, then…" logic description is not necessary in this algorithm. The associated logic control is easier.

The smaller ratable panel on the roof of the vehicle is designed to lighten the weight of the vehicle. Also, the proposed algorithm can increase the power tracking capability in a mechanical way. By the two composite DDG+PN algorithms, it is not required to put a large panel on the top of the vehicle. The two composite algorithms are used to increase the overall electrical energy of the PHEV. They can increase the overall electrical energy by using intelligent composite DDG+PN controller. The developed intelligent DDG+ PN MPPT controller has been successfully implemented to harvest maximum solar power in PHEV system.

References

1. Frank, A.: What are Plug-In Hybrids? Team Fate. University of California, Davis (retrieved August 7, 2007)
2. Archer, D.: Fate of fossil fuel CO_2 in geologic time. Journal of Geophysical Research 110, C9: C09S05.1– C09S05.6 (2008), doi:10.1029/ 2004JC 002625
3. Boschert, S.: Plug-in Hybrids: The Cars that Will Recharge America. New Society Publishers, Gabriola Island
4. Friedman, T.: Hot, Flat, and Crowded: Why We Need a Green Revolution–and How It Can Renew America. Farrar, Straus & Giroux, New York (2008)
5. Gonder, J., Markel, T.: Energy Management Strategies for Plug-In Hybrid Electric Vehicles, technical report NREL/CP-540-40970 presented at SAE World Congress, Detroit, Michigan (2007)
6. Chau, K.T., Chan, C.C., Liu, C.: Overview of Permanent-Magnet Brushless Drives for Electric and Hybrid Electric Vehicles. IEEE Transactions on Industrial Electronics 55(6), 2246–2257 (2008)
7. Lukic, S.M., Cao, J., Bansal, R.C., Rodriguez, F., Emadi, A.: Energy Storage Systems for Automotive Applications. IEEE Transactions on Industrial Electronics 55(6), 2258–2267 (2008)
8. Emadi, A., Lee, Y.J., Rajashekara, K.: Power Electronics and Motor Drives in Electric, Hybrid Electric, and Plug-In Hybrid Electric Vehicles. IEEE Transactions on Industrial Electronics 55(6), 2237–2245 (2008)
9. Haddoun, A., El Hachemi Benbouzid, M., Diallo, D., Abdessemed, R., Ghouili, J., Srairi, K.: Modeling, Analysis, and Neural Network Control of an EV Electrical Differential. IEEE Transactions on Industrial Electronics 55(6), 2286–2294 (2008)
10. Peterson, J.L.: Petri nets. ACM Computing Surveys 9(3), 223–252 (1977)
11. Peterson, J.L.: Petri net theory and the modeling of systems. Prentice-Hall, Englewood Cliffs (1981)
12. Lee, J.S.: A Petri Net Design of Command Filters for Semiautonomous Mobile Sensor Networks. IEEE Transactions on Industrial Electronics 55(4), 1835–1841 (2008)
13. Lee, J.S., Zhou, M.C., Hsu, P.L.: An application of Petri nets to supervisory control for human-computer interactive systems. IEEE Transactions on Industrial Electronics 52(5), 1220–1226 (2005)
14. Zurawski, R.: Petri net models, functional abstractions, and reduction techniques: applications to the design of automated manufacturing systems. IEEE Transactions on Industrial Electronics 52(2), 595–609 (2005)
15. Wai, R.J., Chu, C.C.: Motion Control of Linear Induction Motor via Petri Fuzzy Neural Network. IEEE Transactions on Industrial Electronics 54(1), 281–295 (2007)
16. Wai, R.J., Chu, C.C.: Robust Petri Fuzzy-Neural-Network Control for Linear Induction Motor Drive. IEEE Transactions on Industrial Electronics 54(1), 177–189 (2007)
17. Bang, J., Gutin, G.: Digraphs: Theory, Algorithms and Applications. Springer, Heidelberg (2000)
18. Bondy, J.A., Murthy, U.S.R.: Graph Theory with Applications. North-Holland, Amsterdam (1976)
19. Diestel, R.: Graph Theory, 3rd edn. Springer, Heidelberg (2005)
20. Harary, F., Norman, R.Z., Cartwright, D.: Structural Models: An Introduction to the Theory of Directed Graphs. Wiley, New York (1965)

An Autonomous Fault Tolerant System for CAN Communications

Armando Astarloa, Jesús Lázaro, Unai Bidarte,
Aitzol Zuloaga, and José Luis Martín

Department of Electronics and Telecommunications, Faculty of Engineering,
University of the Basque Country
Alameda de Urquijo s/n, 48013 Bilbao - Spain
armando.astarloa@bi.ehu.es

Abstract. In this paper, an Autonomous Fault Tolerant System that
implements a communication gateway between a CAN bus and asynchronous communication interface is presented. This gateway has been
implemented using a Triple Modular Redundancy architecture at IP core
level. The system can respond to an error detected by a voter in a Triple
Modular Redundancy architecture reconfiguring the module that fails
using pre-defined bitstreams. The whole system has been implemented
in a Virtex-4 FPGA and the reconfiguration system is based on a hard
PowerPC microprocessor.

1 Introduction

An *Autonomous Computing System* (ACS) is a system that runs with a large
degree of independence [1]. An *Autonomous Fault Tolerant System* (AFTS) has
this large degree of autonomy and it is able to configure its own resources in
presence of an error in order to maintain its functionality. The SRAM-based
FPGAs with partial reconfigurable capabilities make it possible.

Furthermore, the latest platform FPGAs have enabled the integration of whole
digital systems in a single device: hardware cores, microprocessors, on-chip buses,
etc. G. Martin in the chapter "The History of the SoC Revolution" [2] emphasized how the core-based design with commercial reconfigurable FPGA platforms
was a strong reality in the System-on-Chip (SoC) [3] design, and it would continue in the future. Now, in 2009, the SoCs are widely extended, specially the
SoCs implemented in reconfigurable logic: the System-on-Programmable-Chips
(SoPCs).

The use of the partial reconfiguration in SRAM FPGA platform based designs, replacing a part of the configuration memory while the remaining digital
system implemented in the chip continues running, will lead to more flexible
systems. Futhermore, all the reconfiguration infrastructure (reconfiguration controller, bitstreams memory, etc.) may be embedded in the same chip, emerging
the self-reconfigurable SoPCs (Configurable System-on-Programmable-Chips -
CSoPCs-). During the last decade, there has been many academic approaches in
this field [4], and thanks to the integration of reconfiguration interfaces inside the

N. García-Pedrajas et al. (Eds.): IEA/AIE 2010, Part III, LNAI 6098, pp. 281–290, 2010.

FPGAs, like the ICAP in Xilinx FPGAs, the research on self-reconfiguring platforms was boosted [5]. Recently, new approaches are emerging with very useful contributions, like new design tools and mechanisms to interconnect properly the static and dynamic sections in the FPGA [6], or self-reconfiguration control systems to be applied to Mixed Cores (IP cores with embedded tiny 8 bit processors) [7].

This advancement in production technology does not come without penalties. Unfortunately SRAM technology is specially sensitive to radiation-induced Single Event Upsets (SEUs) and also, there are permanent errors in the chip's silicon fabric due to aging problems. These permanent errors are more frequent each day due to the advancement in fabrications processes that produce smaller transistors with narrower dielectrics and that use lower voltage levels [8]. According to some reliability reports a 90nm FPGA can have a FIT(One FIT is equal to one failure per 10^9 hours of system operation) of 3 [9], although some other reports state that an FPGA begins to be faulty much earlier in continuous operation mode [10,11,12]. Thus, FPGA chips experimented scaling technology reduction and switching activity increase make these devices more vulnerable to aging effects (i.e. Electromigration and Time-Dependent Dielectric Breakdown), which may cause permanent Single Hardware Errors in the chip's substratum [8].

Thus, on one hand, the SRAM-based FPGA is the most suitable technology to implement AFTSes that offer higher levels of reliability but on the other hand, its susceptibility to SEUs must be taken into account.

In order to solve failures generated by SEUs, a technique called *scrubbing* has been developed [13]. This technique reconfigures the matrix in order to replace the changed configuration bits with the correct ones. There are different strategies regarding to *scrubbing*. It can be applied continuously [14] or only when it is needed [15]. *Scrubbing* technique combined with conventional Triple Module Redundancy (TMR) techniques to mitigate SEU effects has been proposed in [16]. There are other combination of techniques, like *Partial TMR* [17] or dynamic reconfiguration for DSP diagnosis [18]. Recently, in [19] we have proposed a combination of the TMR and Dynamic Reconfiguration to mitigate SEU effects and permanent hardware errors. This approach is oriented to core based design, applying redundancy at core level, and takes advantage from the new facilities for partial reconfiguration of the Virtex-4 family FPGAs.

ACSes in general, and AFTSes in particular are complex systems and the proposed shift to autonomy is ambitious. In [1], a roadmap for ACSes is proposed. Although there are defined 8 theoretical levels of autonomy and intelligence, nowadays it has been reported only an experimental proof-of-concept level 2 ACS [20]. At level 2, the system can accept netlists and autonomously generate a partial bitstream. However, due to the limited available place and route tools for embedded systems the evolution in this roadmap is limited. Other systems, like [21] were designed to demonstrate specific techniques, like simultaneous scrubbing with partial reconfiguration.

The main contributions of the work presented in this paper are: the definition of a surveillance operation for AFTSes and the implementation of an AFTS for widely used communication standards. We present an AFTS that implements a communication gateway between CAN bus and asynchronous communication link (UART). Attending to roadmap set in [1], this AFTS is defined as a Level 1 ACS. Thus, is able to reconfigure using pre-defined bitstreams. But also, attending to this roadmap it could be identified as a limited Level 4 ACS, due it can respond to condition changes within the system or within the environment (an error detected by the voter).

The remainder of this article is organized into four sections. Section 2 presents the system architecture of the CAN GATEWAY AFTS. Section 3 details the surveillance operation for the reconfiguration controller. In Section 4, the implementation results of the AFTS implemented in a Virtex-4 FPGA are summarized. The paper ends at Section 5 with the conclusions and future work in this field.

2   System Architecture

The system architecture of the CAN GATEWAY AFTS is depicted in Figure 1. All the system is implemented using a single FPGA. The modules that compose the system are the following:

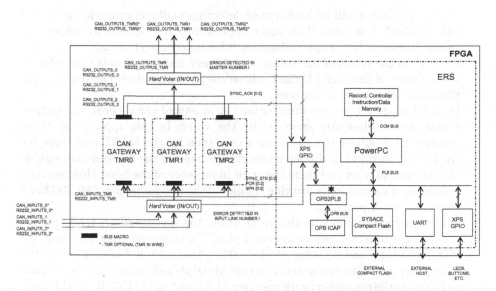

Fig. 1. Block Diagram of the CAN GATEWAY AFTS

– CAN GATEWAY: This is the critical core. In general, this is defined as Dynamic Reconfigurable IP (DR-IP) core [22]. As it can be identified in Figure 1, inside the FPGA three implementations of the CAN GATEWAY run in parallel with the same functionality (but not necessary with the same layout) in different locations to provide triple redundancy (CAN GATEWAY TMR0, CAN GATEWAY TMR1 and CAN GATEWAY TMR2). The internal architecture of the CAN

GATEWAY is depicted in Figure 2. Each core embeds a modified Picoblaze soft CPU (MTM microprocessor [7]), a UART and a Wishbone CAN communication controller [23]. MTM and the UART are linked to the Wishbone CAN controller through a Wishbone on-chip bus (internal to the CAN GATEWAY core). The processor controls the communication between the UART and the CAN controller in order to provide gateway functionality.

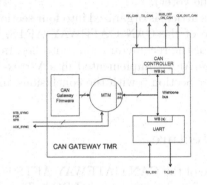

Fig. 2. Internal architecture of a CAN GATEWAY core

- Voter: This voter will be in charge of detecting malfunctioning in any of the CAN GATEWAY TMR cores. This voter applies majority scheme to output the result. It allows three triple redundant 9 bit independent signals. It outputs, apart from the result of the voting, two binary codified signals that informs the number of the CAN GATEWAY whose output value does not match with the values of the remaining ones.
  In order to detect an abnormal situation in any of three cores, the output signals are continuously analyzed by the voter. In this application, there are four 1 bit output signals for each core (one for the UART and three for the CAN controller). If discrepancies are detected in the transmission signals the system can react and avoid the error in presence of the fault. However, the communication continues working thanks to the two remaining CAN GATEWAY cores that work properly.
  Additionally, depending on the application, the system allows triple redundancy in the communications lines and pins. The input signals can be analyzed (CAN_INPUTS and RS232_INPUTS -_0*, _1* and _2*- in Figure 1) using the same voter, and also, the system can provide triple redundancy at the outputs to facilitate the connection with another AFTS system (CAN_OUTPUTS and RS232_OUTPUTS -_0*, _1* and _2*-).
- Embedded Reconfiguration System (ERS): It enables both *scrubbing* and partial bitstream downloading operations. This section has been built using Xilinx Platform Studio and it based on the hard PowerPC microprocessor embedded on Virtex-4 FX FPGAs. The software and data are embedded on the dedicated RAM of the FPGA (BlockRAMs). This memory is connected directly to the PowerPC through a dedicated On-Chip-Memory (OCM) bus and protected using ECC. All this reconfiguration system is implemented in

the static section of the design and it is completed with the Compact Flash controller (SysAce) for storage of the bitstreams, with the internal reconfiguration port (OPB ICAP), with an UART for debug functionalities and with two General Purpose Input/Output (GPIO) cores. One of this GPIO cores (on the right at Figure 1) connects all the miscellaneous logic to the system (bottoms, leds, etc.). The second GPIO manages the communication signals between the dynamic CAN GATEWAY modules, the voter and the reconfiguration system. All this peripherals, except the OPB ICAP are connected to the PowerPC using the 64 bit Peripheral-Local-Bus (PLB).

3   Autonomous Fault Tolerant Surveillance Operation

Figure 3 summarizes the Fault surveillance operation carried out by the ERS and the Voter. The proposed sequence is application independent and it has been enunciated using the following parameters:

j It is a number between 0 and 2 that identifies the DR-IP core that will be addressed in the following operation.

i This parameter is equivalent of j for predictive *scrubbing* operation.

z_j It represents the implementation number (partial bitstream) z for the DR-IP core number j.

z_{max} It is the maximum number of different implementations (partial bitstreams) for a given DR-IP core. For this design, all the three DR-IP cores have the same maximum number of implementations (z_{max}).

After the system initialization, the system will run in **Normal operation**. It is defined as the operation of the system in absence of faults generated by an error. In this situation, the three DR-IP cores run in parallel (in this application three CAN GATEWAY cores). In the absence of fault, all three cores output the same values, so there are no discrepancies detected by the voter. Thus, the ERS should not perform any reactive action.

However, for some aero-spatial applications, a predictive *scrubbing* operation can be programmed in order to mitigate SEU effects that could not generate directly an error in the output. This operation has been represented in the left branch from the **Normal Operation**. If predictive *scrubbing* operation is enabled, when a dedicated timer for this task overflows, one of the DR-IP cores is refreshed with the partial bitstream that implements the layout (that is placed in error free resources (z_i)). The number of the DR-IP core that is refreshed each time is determined by i. This counter takes the values 0,1 and 2 cyclically.

If the voter detects discrepancies, the system will enter **Faulty Operation** mode. The fault can be localized at two scenarios:

– In the first scenario the fault is located at the input signals of the DR-IP cores. If the AFTS uses physical triple redundancy at the communications lines and pins, the voter can detect discrepancy at the values of the redundant input lines. In this situation, the reconfiguration controller can detect it, and

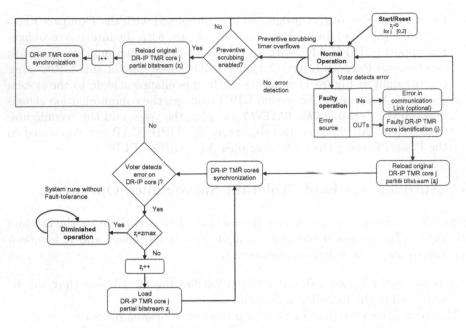

Fig. 3. Autonomous Fault Tolerant surveillance operation

inform about this failure to higher level software layers (or to an external host). But, thanks to the TMR voting scheme, the system can run properly. This feature is optional, and it makes sense depending on the application and depending on the safety strategy used in the communication lines.

- The second faulty scenario is set when a discrepancy is detected at the output of one DR-IP core output signal. In this case, the voter will inform to the reconfiguration controller about the module that fails. This core is identified by the core number (j) and the ERS will perform a *scrubbing* operation to the j DR-IP core that fails. In this attempt, it will load the partial bitstream with the same layout as the one that was running properly before the fault (partial bitstream defined by the value set in the z_j counter). If the error was generated by a SEU, the AFTS could continue working properly after the *scrubbing* operation and the synchronization stage.

However, if the fault is not solved by *scrubbing*, the source of this malfunctioning is as a permanent error. Thus, the ERS will repeat the partial bitstream loading operation, but instead of using the original partial bitstream, it will load for the same DR-IP core a different bitstream with a different layout. The value that identifies the partial bitstream that will be loaded is defined by z_j, that is incremented each time that the reconfiguration system attempts another try. With this operation, the system will try to avoid logic or routing resources that could be permanently damaged. These versions are generated using VHDL attributes that fix resources to specific and relative locations.

The different versions of the partial bitstreams are stored into the Compact Flash. Thus, the fixing capability of the system is limited (Level 1: Capability to load pre-implemented bitstreams). If none of the options fixes the error, the system will continue running but without its Fault-Tolerance capability. However, the AFTS could warn about this situation to higher level software layers or to a remote host. This situation is called **Diminished Operation**.

4   Implementation Results

The hardware design was done using the following CAD tools: ISE 9.2, Partial Flow 9.2 PR12, Xilinx Embedded Development Kit (EDK) 9.2 and Planahead 10.1. The software design was done using EDK for the ERS and PblazeIDE for the microcontroller embedded in the CAN GATEWAY core. The target board used for the prototype is a Xilinx ML405, that populates a Virtex-4 FX20 FPGA.

Table 1 summarizes the implementation results for the system. The static section, where the ERS and the voter is placed has been simplified as maximum in order to obtain a compact implementation (it uses less than 11% of the general purpose resources of the FPGA) and to increment its robustness against SEU effects. The utilization of the hard PowerPC microcontroller and the protection of its data and software by ECC enhance the robustness of this section.

Also, in Table 1 the implementation results of one CAN GATEWAY core is presented. It is an heterogeneous core that uses general purpose resources and one BlockRAM to store the firmware of the embedded tiny microprocessor. The partial reconfigurable regions selected for each CAN GATEWAY core have more available resources than the strictly needed for the implementation in order to have different Place & Route alternatives.

Figures 4(a) and 4(b) depict the layout of the FPGA with and without the three CAN GATEWAY cores respectively. As it can be observed, each partial reconfigurable region assigned to each CAN GATEWAY core can be different because there is a subset of partial bitstreams for each region.

As it has been described in previous sections, each CAN GATEWAY core runs autonomously performing a gateway operation. In order to allow dynamic loading of a new CAN GATEWAY core, the system must ensure time and signal consistency

Table 1. CAN Gateway AFTS implementation on a Virtex-4 FX20 FPGA

Resources type	Static Section	CAN GATEWAY core
4 input LUTs	1.173 (6%)	804 (4%)
Slice Flip-Flops	1.194 (6%)	359 (2%)
Virtex-4 Slices	991 (11%)	496 (5%)
18K BlockRAM	41 (60%)	1 (1%)
DSP48	2 (6%)	0 (0%)
PowerPC	1 (100%)	0 (0%)
ICAP ports	1 (50%)	0 (0%)
Maximum running speed	108 MHz	104 MHz

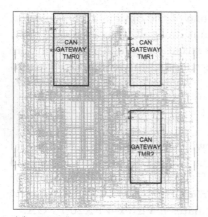 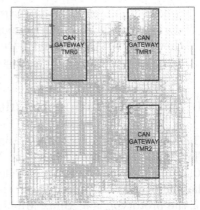

(a) FPGA layout without CAN
GATEWAY TMR cores loaded.

(b) FPGA layout with CAN
GATEWAY TMR cores loaded.

Fig. 4. AFTS layouts

and synchronization. In the current stage of the design, these issues have been solved as follow:

- Signal consistency: The communication signals between the dynamic and static sections are connected using Bus Macros that provide signal consistency. In this system, they have been identified as critical and their security should be improved using specific TMR Bus Macros.
- Timing consistency: In the proposed AFTS, all the system uses the same timing reference, driven by clock dedicated nets. So, after the insertion of a new core, it will share the same clock as the other ones.
- Core synchronization: This issue must be carefully analyzed for each application. It must be taken into account that after a partial reconfiguration, all the values stored in the Flip-Flops and LUTs used as distributed memory are initialized in the partial reconfigurable region. So the system must provide means to communicate to the new core the values that are using the remaining two cores and to set a common synchronization point. In this application, the synchronization is applied only to the tiny microprocessor embedded in each CAN GATEWAY core. Thus, the values stored into the CAN controller and UART FIFO are lost after a partial reconfiguration. This microprocessor is a modified Picoblaze CPU in order to support synchronization. It includes the control signals strobe, ack, Program Counter Reset (PCR) and Stack Pointer Reset (SPR) that allow different synchronization approaches [7].

5 Conclusions

A detailed AFTS that protects a complex core from temporal and permanent errors has been presented. It is able to auto-reconfigure using pre-defined bitstreams and it can respond to condition changes within the system or within the environment and respond to them.

An Autonomous Fault Tolerant surveillance operation for the reconfiguration controller has been detailed and proposed. This operation is general and can be applied to any Level 1 AFTS.

The implementation results validate the proposed design and offer valuable information about the maturity level of the development tools and technology for the implementation of AFTS.

In order to shift to higher levels of autonomy, Place & Route software tools for embedded systems should be provided by the reconfigurable device vendors. However, taking into account that AFTS systems are in an early stage, also at Level 1 there is a lot of research work. Future work in this field includes: Research on strategies to optimize the generation of behavioral equivalent partial bitstreams with different layouts; more sophisticated synchronization schemes and reliability enhancement of the static area and Bus Macros.

Acknowledgment

This work has been partially supported by the research program DIPE-BEAZ 2009 (DIPE09/02).

References

1. Adraka, R., Steiner, N., Athanas, P.: Autonomous Computing Systems: A Proposed Roadmap. In: Proceedings of the 2007 International Conference on Engineering of Reconfigurable Systems and Algorithms, ERSA 2007 (2007)
2. Martin, G., Chang, H. (eds.): Winning the SoC Revolution: Experiences in Real Design. Kluwer Academic Publishers, Massachusetts (2003)
3. Bergamaschi, R.A., Bhattacharya, S., Wagner, R., Fellenz, C., Muhlada, M.: Automating the Design of SOCs Using Cores. IEEE Design & Test of Computers 18(5), 32–45 (2001)
4. Astarloa, A.: Dynamic Partial Reconfiguration of Multi-processor Modular Systems in SoPC devices. PhD thesis, University of the Basque Country (July 2005)
5. Blodget, B., James-Roxby, P., Keller, E., McMillan, S., Sundararajan, P.: A Self-reconfiguring Platform. In: Y. K. Cheung, P., Constantinides, G.A. (eds.) FPL 2003. LNCS, vol. 2778, pp. 565–574. Springer, Heidelberg (2003)
6. Silva, M.L., Canas Ferreira, J.: Support for partial run-time reconfiguration of platform FPGAs. Journal of Systems Architecture (52), 619–639 (2006)
7. Astarloa, A., Zuloaga, A., Bidarte, U., Martín, J.L., Jiménez, J., Lázaro, J.: Tornado: A self-reconfiguration control system for core-based multiprocessor CSoPCs. Journal of Systems Architecture 53(9), 629–643 (2007)
8. Constantinescu, C.: Trends and challenges in VLSI circuit reliability. IEEE Micro 23(4), 14–19 (2003)
9. Xilinx Inc. Device reliability report, fourth quarter 2008. UG116 (2009)
10. Quinn, H., Graham, P., Krone, J., Caffrey, M., Rezgui, S.: Radiation-induced multi-bit upsets in SRAM based FPGAs. IEEE Transactions on Nuclear Science 52(6), 2455–2461 (2005)
11. Suresh, S., Prasanth, M., Yuan, X., Vijaykrishnan, N., Karthik, S.: FLAW: FPGA lifetime awareness. In: IEEE Design Automation Conference, pp. 630–635 (2006)

12. Adell, P., Allen, G.: Assessing and mitigating radiation effects in Xilinx FPGAs. JPL Publication (2008)
13. Carmichael, C., Caffrey, M., Salazar, A.: Correcting Single-Event Upsets Through Virtex Partial Configuration. Xilinx Application Notes (June 2000), http://www.xilinx.com
14. Charmichael, C.: Correcting single-event-upsets throught Virtex partial reconfiguration. XAPP216, Xilinx Inc. (2000)
15. Chapman, K., Jones, L.: SEU strategies for Virtex-5 devices. XAPP864, Xilinx Inc. (2009)
16. Bolchini, C., Miele, A., Santambrogio, M.D.: TMR and Partial Dynamic Reconfiguration to mitigate SEU faults in FPGAs. In: 22nd IEEE International Symposium on Defect and Fault Tolerance in VLSI Systems, pp. 87–95 (2007)
17. Pratt, B., Caffrey, M., Graham, P., Morgan, K., Wirthlin, M.J.: Improving FPGA Design Robustness with Partial TMR. In: IEEE International Reliability Physics Symposium (IRPS 2006), April 2006, pp. 226–232 (2006)
18. Girardey, R., Hübner, M., Becker, J.: Dynamic Reconfigurable Mixed-signal Architecture for Safety Critical Applications. In: 19th International Conference on Field Programmable Logic and Applications (FPL 2009), September 2009, pp. 503–506 (2009)
19. Iturbe, X., Azkarate, M., Martinez, I., Perez, J., Astarloa, A.: A Novel SEU, MBU and SHE Handling Strategy for XILINX VIRTEX-4 FPGAs. In: 19th International Conference on Field Programmable Logic and Applications (FPL 2009), September 2009, pp. 569–573 (2009)
20. Adraka, R., Steiner, N., Athanas, P.: Autonomous Computing Systems: A Proof-of-Concept. In: Proceedings of the 2007 International Conference on Engineering of Reconfigurable Systems and Algorithms, ERSA 2007 (2007)
21. Heiner, J., Sellers, B., Wirthlin, M., Kalb, J.: FPGA Partial Reconfiguration via configuration Scrubbing. In: 19th International Conference on Field Programmable Logic and Applications (FPL 2009), September 2009, pp. 99–104 (2009)
22. Astarloa, A., Lázaro, J., Bidarte, U., Zuloaga, A., Jiménez, J.: PCIREX: A Fast Prototyping Platform for TMR Dynamically Reconfigurable Systems. In: Proceedings of the International Conference on Reconfigurable Computing and FPGAs, ReConFig 2009, December 2009, pp. 54–58 (2009)
23. Shehryar, S., Mohor, I.: OpenCores CAN Protocol Controller (2009), http://www.opencores.org/project,can

A DICOM Viewer with Capability for Flexible Retrieval of Medical Images from Fuzzy Databases

Juan Miguel Medina, Sergio Jaime-Castillo, and Esther Jiménez

Department of Computer Science and Artificial Intelligence. University of Granada
C/ Periodista Daniel Saucedo Aranda s/n, 18071 Granada, Spain
medina@decsai.ugr.es, sjaime@decsai.ugr.es,
estherj@correo.ugr.es
http://idbis.ugr.es

Abstract. This paper presents a medical image viewer implemented in Java, whose innovative features are: capability for visual edition and storing of spine's deviation measures of patients suffering from scoliosis, and flexible retrieval of stored images based on these measurements, which are the standard descriptor for this pathology. The viewer is a useful tool for physicians in diagnosis and treatment of scoliosis.

Keywords: DICOM viewer, medical CBIR, Fuzzy Databases.

1 Introduction

Images are a fundamental tool in health care for diagnosis, clinical studies, research and learning. Currently, there are multiple techniques to capture images from patients to help diagnostic tasks such as X-Ray images, Computer Tomography (CT), Magnetic Resonance Imaging (MRI), Positron Emission Tomography (PET), Ultrasonography, etc. Diagnostic task generates a large amount of images which must be archived for future evaluations. Fortunately, most of these techniques produce digital images, which are more efficiently archived and handled, by means of computer systems, than physical ones. In medical imaging, these computer systems are called Picture Archiving and Communication Systems (PACS). PACS consist of a network of computers devoted to the storage, retrieval, distribution and presentation of images. The most common format for image storage is DICOM (Digital Imaging and Communications in Medicine). The main parts of PACS are: PACS servers that store and send the images and, PACS workstations, that can use local peripherals for scanning image films into the system, printing image films from the system and interactively displaying digital images. PACS workstations offer means of manipulating the images (cropping, rotating, zooming, windowing, and others) and the software used for this purpose is called DICOM viewer. PACS systems solve the problem of storing digital images but do not provide mechanisms to retrieve them based on the pathology's information items they contain. Instead, the single available mechanism is querying the server by patient's name or patient's file number.

Content-Based image retrieval (CBIR) [1] is the application of computer vision techniques to the problem of digital image search in large databases. In [2] we proposed a CBIR system that allows automatically extracting measures of the spine curvature starting from X-Rays of patients with scoliosis. These measures are represented

N. García-Pedrajas et al. (Eds.): IEA/AIE 2010, Part III, LNAI 6098, pp. 291–300, 2010.

and stored into the Fuzzy Object-Relational Database System (FORDBMS) proposed in [3,4], which provides a flexible way of querying X-rays based on the spine curve measures stored on it [5].

This paper describes a prototype of DICOM viewer, an important element of the proposed CBIR system. This viewer provides physicians with a tool to visually edit and measure curves and to perform queries to retrieve DICOM images of patients based on the parameters of the spine deformity. The client DICOM viewer has been developed starting from Tudor DICOM viewer [6]. Because of this, our viewer also includes all features provided by the Tudor DICOM viewer (see Section 3.1).

The rest of the paper is organized as follows. Section 2 describes the most important modules of the CBIR system to which the viewer belongs. Section 3 describes the viewer, and illustrates the use and functioning of the novel features that it provides. Finally, the main conclusions and future works are summarized in section 4.

2   Architecture of the CBIR System

The proposed DICOM viewer belongs to a CBIR system that permits the user to perform flexible queries that search for images of patients who present a similar curve pattern or Cobb angle measure [7] to a given one (Section 3.3 will provide a description of this

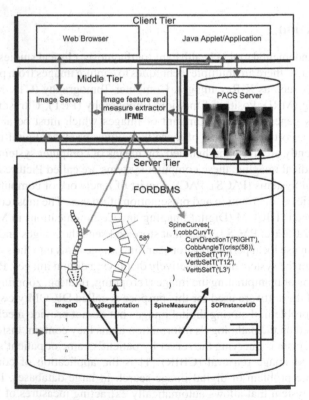

Fig. 1. Schema of the CBIR System

measurement). To achieve this functionality, the system integrates a module that can perform automatic spine measurements starting from X-rays. These measures together with their X-Rays references are stored into the FORDBMS, for later flexible retrieval.

Fig. 1 shows the general schema of this CBIR system. It is organized in a three tier architecture, although some of them could operate into the same computer. Each tier includes several modules, whose roles are described below:

- **FORDBMS**: It is into the server tier. The FORDBMS, proposed in [3,4], is a general purpose database server extended with fuzzy data handling capabilities built on Oracle® DBMS. It stores references to DICOM X-rays images, the vectorial description of the spine extracted by the IFME module and the spine measures processed by this module. The FORDBMS can solve flexible queries on this kind of content using an extension of the SQL dialect of the Oracle® DBMS. It is important to mention that the FORDBMS does not store any DICOM image, but their DICOM IDs, that permit retrieving them from a standard PACS Server that can run on any server on the network.

- The **IFME** (Image Feature and Measure Extractor) module is in the middle tier and implements the algorithms needed to automatically extract the Cobb measures from X-rays. Also, this module generates the DML statements to store these measures into the FORDBMS and to perform queries based on them. Finally, a vectorized representation of the extracted spine and vertebra shapes is generated by this module and stored into FORDBMS for display purposes.

- The **Image Server** is an application server that processes the requests of the clients to the FORDBMS. It invokes IFME module when the client requests the extraction of the spine measures for an X-ray image to perform a query based on an image prototype or to insert it into the FORDBMS together with the DICOM ID. The image server can generate dynamic html pages and can serve JAVA applets for browser based clients.

- The **client application** is a modified PACS workstation capable to visualize and handle DICOM images. It can be implemented into the middle tier; in this case, the image server provides the application to the browser, or it can be a JAVA applet/application running on the client tier. The client application adds specific functionality to the basic features of a PACS workstation. We describe this specific functionality below:

  • The user can retrieve from FORDBMS patient studies based on Cobb angle measures of the spine in a flexible way. The client application generates a flexible SQL query based on the conditions set by the user, searching into the spine description extracted from images.

  • The user can provide an image and request the client application to retrieve those with similar spine curvature. To do this, the application invokes the IFME module to extract spine parameters from the sample image. With this information, the client builds and sends the query to the FORDBMS.

  • For the retrieved images, the application can show the Cobb angle measures and the matching degree with the query. The user can visually edit this measures and store them with the image references into the FORDBMS.

  • The application provides options to set parameters into FORDBMS for flexible querying and to process DICOM studies from/to file system or from/to another

PACS. The application can extract and store the spine parameters by invoking IFME module; this processing can be done on the fly or in batch mode.

This paper shows a JAVA implementation of this client, whose description and use will be detailed in next Section.

3   Description and Use of the DICOM Viewer

In this Section we will describe some aspects of the implementation of the DICOM viewer and the use of its specific features.

3.1   Basic Features of the Viewer

As we said in Section 1, our viewer has been implemented starting from Tudor DICOM viewer [6]. This viewer, developed by SANTEC, a department of the public research centre Henri Tudor, is written in Java and it is distributed under the LGPL license. Tudor DICOM viewer uses Tudor DICOM tools, a Java library based on dcm4che version 2 [8], the Java Advanced Imaging API (JAI) [9] and ImageJ [10]. Our modification of this viewer also uses these tools and the functionality of Tudor DICOM viewer is mantained.

The paper [11] describes the most important features and capabilities of the Tudor DICOM viewer, some of which are: fetching images from several PACS Servers, sending images to any configured PACS Server, support of multiple image compression types (VR, RLE, JPEG Lossless, etc.), an integrated DICOM Store to receive images from network and support for several DICOM services (Storage-SCP, Storage-SCU, Query/Retrieve-SCU); for the viewing of images it provides windowing, zooming, shifting, measuring via mouse, several split-screen or multi-monitor configurations, managing of images series, etc. As we have mentioned, to these capabilities we have added support to retrieve from PACS, in a flexible way, DICOM images of patients suffering scoliosis using their spine's curves description. Also, we have added capability for measuring Cobb angles and storing these measures into the system. These added capabilities and their use are illustrated in next subsections.

3.2   Configuring the DICOM Viewer for Flexible Querying

The DICOM viewer interacts with another systems: PACS servers, that store the X-Ray images, and FORDBMS, that stores the fuzzy representation for the Cobb angle measures and provides flexible querying based on them. To connect to these systems the viewer provides the forms shown in Fig. 2 a) and b). By using the first form, we set the parameters of the PACS servers that can be accessed by the viewer for retrieving and sending DICOM files. Also, in this form we can test the accessibility of the configured servers. The second form allows setting the parameters to access the FORDBMS: we can save several configurations and we can load a particular one. Finally, we need to establish the configured connection by clicking the "CONNECT" button. If everything is correct, we get the message "Database Connected"; if not, an error message is shown and we cannot access the capabilities for edition of Cobb angles or querying based on angle parameters.

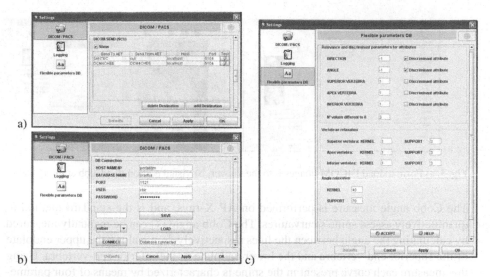

Fig. 2. Forms for configuration of: a) PACS Servers, b) Database Server and, c) parameters to set the flexible behavior of the database for queries

On the form with label c) in Fig. 2, we can set the parameters that specify the flexible default behavior for querying, according to the functionality described in the paper [5]. In this form, we can set the weight (relevance) of each attribute describing Cobb angles when computing flexible equality operations. All attributes have the same relevance, 1, for this parameter in the example shown in Fig. 2 c), except the two first, that have negative values (these attributes also appear marked in the discriminant column). This means that these attributes are discriminant, i.e., when computing flexible equality operations, a FEQ (Fuzzy equality) value equal to 0 for any of these attributes determines a FEQ value of 0 for the whole Cobb angle comparison. The sixth row in Fig. 2 c), shows the value 3 for the parameter "number of values different to 0", which means that, if the number of comparisons of pairs of attributes that get a value greater than 0 is less than 3, then the whole Cobb angle comparison returns a value equal to 0. By means of the "Vertebrae relaxation" parameters, we can set the flexible behavior of FEQ by default when comparing two vertebrae. In Fig. 2 c), the first column has set the value 1 for all vertebra kernels, which means that FEQ returns 1 when the compared vertebrae are equal or adjacent; the value 3 in the support column sets that FEQ returns 0 when the compared pair of vertebrae is separated by four or more vertebrae; if the compared vertebrae are separated by three vertebrae then FEQ returns 0.33 and, when separation is two, FEQ returns 0.66. Finally, in the "Angle relaxation" parameters we can set the values that determine the behavior of the FEQ comparison for angles. The values set in Fig. 2 c), relax the angle value for FEQ comparisons, in a 40% for the kernel and in a 70% for the support.

3.3   Measuring Cobb Angles

Our DICOM viewer provides the capability to perform Cobb angle measurements on the retrieved images using the mouse and, to store these measures into the FORDBMS.

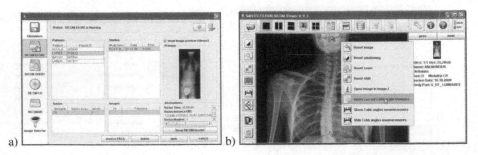

Fig. 3. a) Form to load DICOM images into the viewer, b) visual edition of a Cobb angle measure

The Cobb angle measure is performed on AP X-rays, and is the standard method to quantitatively assess spine's curvatures. The Cobb angle [7] can be manually measured by calculating the angle between the lines respectively drawn along the upper endplate of the superior end-vertebra and the lower endplate of the inferior end-vertebra. Using this measure each curve present in the spine is characterized by means of four parameters: the side of the convexity of the curve (right or left), the superior end-vertebra, the inferior end-vertebra and the angle's value. Also, it is important to identify the apical vertebra associated with the adjacent disc interspaces that have the greatest segmental angulation of all interspaces in the curve.

To perform Cobb angle measures with this tool, we first need to retrieve the image into the main panel. There are several ways to get images: Fig. 3 a) shows the use of the file chooser to retrieve a given image from the local DICOM Store. Once we have selected the desired image, we can send it to any configured PACS Server, we can delete it or we can open it into the thumbnails panel located in the right side of the main window of the viewer. In this example, we have selected the last option. Then, by clicking its thumbnail in the mentioned panel, we will retrieve it into the main panel of the viewer. By right-clicking on this panel a contextual menu appears, see Fig. 3 b). The last two menu items provide options to show/hide Cobb angle measures previously performed on this image.

To visually perform a Cobb angle measure, we need to click the angle icon located into left tools panel. Then, by clicking the ends of each segment that delimits the angle into the image, the program automatically computes the angle's value. To store this measure into the FORDBMS we need to show the contextual menu and select the "Insert current Cobb angle measure" option. The viewer will show the form displayed in Fig. 4 a). The value and direction of the angle are automatically taken from the previous edition and the user only needs to set the value for the vertebrae that delimits the curve and the apical vertebra. Also, the user can attach comments related to the curve. Finally, to store this Cobb curve measure, we need to click the associated button. To perform the measures for all curves present into the image, we need to repeat the described procedure. To finalize and to store the whole measurement of the spine, we have to click on the down arrow icon located into the upper tools panel. The viewer will show the form shown in Fig. 4 b) to save the measurement and its vectorial description. In this form the user has to set the author of the measurement and he/she can add comments.

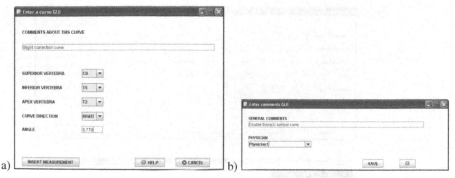

Fig. 4. a) Form to set the vertebrae of the Cobb angle and to add comment to this measure, b) Form to set the author of the measurement and, add comments to this measure

3.4 Performing Flexible Queries

The DICOM viewer allows performing two kinds of flexible queries looking for similar images:

1. Searching images that include a certain curve. To perform this kind of query, we need to click on the database icon, located into the upper tools bar (Fig. 3 b)). Then, the viewer provides the form shown in Fig. 5 a) wherein the user can set the values for the curve that the X-Rays images he/she is looking for must include. Note that the curve parameters are affected by imprecise values. These values are computed using the default flexible parameters, that are set by means of the form shown in Fig 2 c). For each query, the form showed in Fig. 5 a), allows adjusting these flexible parameters to the user needs.

   Once we have set the query parameters, we can perform the query looking for images measured manually (by specialists), automatically (by the system), or both. Then, the viewer will show in the right side of the main window the images thumbnails that match the query (see Fig. 6). In the caption of each thumbnail appears the degree to which the image satisfies the query condition, and the specialist that has performed the measure of this image. The user can click on the desired thumbnail to display it into the main panel of the viewer.

2. Searching images whose curve pattern is similar to the one present into a sample image. To perform this kind of query we need to click on the pencil icon, located into the upper tools bar (Fig. 3 b)). Fig. 5 b) shows the form that appears with the X-Ray image and the spine curves drawn on the left. Also, the form shows into each tab the values for the Cobb angles. The user can edit these values and their flexible parameters, computed from default values set into the configuration form (Fig. 2 c)). There is the option of unmark each curve: if so, the system will perform the query looking for images that include the set of marked curves; otherwise, the query will be based on flexible equality of the pattern of curves. Next, for query execution, the user has three options like in the previous case: manual, automatic, or both measurements. Then, the viewer will show, in the right side of the main window, the images thumbnails that match the query (see Fig. 6). The process for working with each retrieved image is like the one describe in the previous item.

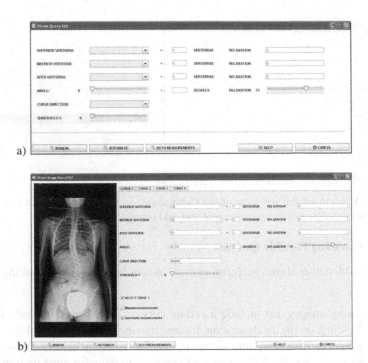

Fig. 5. Alternatives to perform flexible image retrieval: a) form to set curve parameters that sought images must include, b) form that shows the curve parameters of the sample image, used for retrieving similar images

Computation of the flexible query. The viewer uses the fuzzy description of the curves present into the spine to perform the two kinds of queries mentioned above. These queries are translated into Fuzzy SQL queries using the dialect implemented into our FORDBMS. The detailed description of this process is outside the scope of this paper, for further details the reader should refer to [5]. Nevertheless, with the help of Fig. 6, we are going to explain how the FORDBMS computes the similarity degree between the spine curves of the two images compared. The set of curves measured from the spine is represented into the FORDBMS by means of a fuzzy datatype called Conjunctive Fuzzy Collection. Therefore, the FORDBMS must evaluate the fuzzy equality for the two instances of this datatype that represent the spine curves measured on each image. To do this, the FORDBMS evaluates the fuzzy inclusion of the curves collection of the left image into the curves collection of the right image, and then evaluates the fuzzy inclusion of the curves collection of the right image into the curves collection of the left image, and returns the min value as FEQ degree. In this example: $FInclusion(LeftImage, RightImage) = FInclusion(RightImage, LeftImage)$ $= 0.736$ and, therefore, $FEQ(LeftImage, RightImage) = 0.736$. To evaluate, for example, $FInclusion(LeftImage, RightImage)$, the FORDBMS computes the fuzzy equality for the curve 1s on LeftImage with respect to each curve in RightImage, (1c, 2c, 3c) , and takes the maximum; then, it evaluates the same for the curve 2s and for the curve 3s; finally, it takes the minimum of these three values as the FInclusion

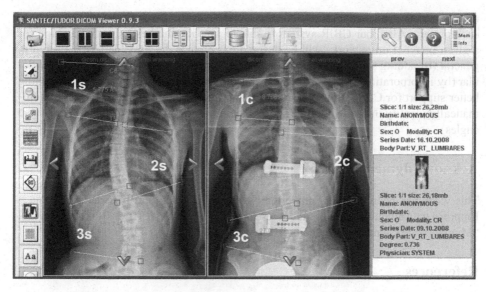

Fig. 6. Image retrieved (right) with respect to the sample image (left)

degree. In the example shown in Fig. 6, the computations are: $FInclusion(LeftImage,$ $RightImage) = min(max(FEQ(1s, 1c), FEQ(1s, 2c), FEQ(1s, 3c)), max(FEQ($ $2s, 1c),$ $FEQ(2s, 2c),$ $FEQ(2s, 3c)),$ $max(FEQ(3s, 1c),$ $FEQ(3s, 2c), FEQ(3s,$ $3c))) = min(max(0.866, 0, 0), max(0, 0.736, 0), max(0, 0, 0.934)) = 0.736.$ To compute the fuzzy equality of two curves, the FORDBMS evaluates the fuzzy equality between the values of each attribute and, then, computes a weighted average from the five degrees obtained. For example, in the images shown in Fig. 6, the computations to evaluate FEQ(1s,1c) are: $FEQ(1s, 1c) = (FEQ('RIGHT','RIGHT') * |-1| +$ $FEQ(5.775, 8.706) * |-1| + FEQ(C6, T2) * |1| + FEQ(T2, T3) * |1| + FEQ(T5, T6) *$ $|1|)/(1 + 1 + 1 + 1 + 1) = (1 + 0.99 + 0.34 + 1 + 1)/5 = 0,866.$ In each previous attribute comparison we have used the flexible parameters set by default that Fig. 2 c) shows.

4   Concluding Remarks and Future Work

The DICOM viewer described in this paper is integrated into an innovative Flexible CBIR System and provides the user with the capacity to perform Cobb angles measurements visually and to store them. In addition, by using this tool the user can perform flexible queries to retrieve X-Ray images with similar spine curvature to a given one. These capabilities are useful to help physicians in diagnosis and treatment of scoliosis.

Physicians classify spine deformities using patterns proposed by several authors, it is not difficult to represent on our CBIR system each spine pattern by means of a linguistic description. For example, the "thoracic curve" pattern, proposed in [12], can be described by the following approximate parameters: the convexity of the curve is on the right side, the superior end-vertebra is between T4 and T6, the apex vertebra is between T8 and T9 and, the inferior end-vertebra is between T11 and L2. It is possible the use of this linguistic description to perform queries searching images that match such pattern. Also, our CBIR system is able to provide the best pattern matching for a given image. Future works will be devoted to enhance the Flexible CBIR system in general (by adding semantic capabilities), and to improve the DICOM viewer in particular (by incorporating these semantic capabilities into the searching module, providing better support for Cobb angle measurement and adding segmentation features to automatically identify the end vertebrae of Cobb angles and the segments that delimit these angles).

Acknowledgment

This work has been partially supported by the "Consejería de Innovación Ciencia y Empresa de Andalucía" (Spain) under research project P06-TIC-01570 and the Spanish "Ministerio de Ciencia e Innovación" (MICINN) under grants TIN2009-08296.

References

1. Lew, M.S., Sebe, N., Lifl, C.D., Jain, R.: Content-based multimedia information retrieval: State of the art and challenges. ACM Transactions on Multimedia Computing, Communications, and Applications 2(1), 1–19 (2006)
2. Jaime-Castillo, S., Medina, J.M., Sánchez, D.: A system to perform cbir on x-ray images using soft computing techniques. In: Proc. FUZZ-IEEE 2009, Korea, August 20-24, pp. 1314–1319 (2009)
3. Cubero, J., Marín, N., Medina, J., Pons, O., Vila, M.: Fuzzy object management in an object-relational framework. In: Proc. 10th Int. Conf. on Information Processing and Management of Uncertainty in Knowledge-Based Systems, IPMU 2004, pp. 1767–1774 (2004)
4. Barranco, C.D., Campaña, J.R., Medina, J.M.: Towards a fuzzy object-relational database model. In: Galindo, J. (ed.) Handbook of Research on Fuzzy Information Processing in Databases, pp. 435–461. IGI Global (2008)
5. Medina, J.M., Jaime-Castillo, S., Barranco, C.D., Campaña, J.R.: Flexible retrieval of x-ray images based on shape descriptors using a fuzzy object-relational database. In: Proc. IFSA-EUSFLAT 2009, Lisbon, Portugal, July 20-24, pp. 903–908 (2009)
6. SANTEC: Tudor dicom tools, SANTEC. Public Research Centre Henri Tudor (2009), http://santec.tudor.lu/project/optimage/dicom/start
7. Cobb, J.: Outline for the study of scoliosis. Am Acad Orthop Surg Inst Course Lect 5, 261–275 (1948)
8. DCM4CHE.org: Dcm4che-v2. open source clinical image and object management, http://www.dcm4che.org/
9. SUN: Java advanced imaging api, http://java.sun.com/javase/technologies/desktop/media/jai
10. IMAGEJ: Imagej. image processing and analysis in java, http://rsbweb.nih.gov/ij
11. Hermen, J., Moll, C., Jahnen, A.: Solving annoying dicom problems using imagej and the tudor dicom tools. In: Med-e-Tel 1-3.04.2009. Luxembourg, vol. 2, Global Telemedicine and eHealth Updates: Knowledge Resolurces (2009)
12. Ponseti, I., Friedman, B.: Prognosis in idiopathic scoliosis. J. Bone Joint Surgery 32, 381–395 (1950)

License Plate Detection Based on Genetic Neural Networks, Morphology, and Active Contours

Joaquín Olivares, José M. Palomares, José M. Soto, and Juan Carlos Gámez

Department of Computer Architecture, Electronics, and Electronic Technology,
University of Córdoba, Córdoba, Spain
{olivares,jmpalomares,jmsoto,jcgamez}@uco.es

Abstract. This paper describes a new method for License Plate Detection based on Genetic Neural Networks, Morphology, and Active Contours. Given an image is divided into several virtual regions sized 10×10 pixels, applying several performance algorithms within each virtual region, algorithms such as edge detection, histograms, and binary thresholding, etc. These results are used as inputs for a Genetic Neural Network, which provides the initial selection for the probable situation of the license plate. Further refinement is applied using active contours to fit the output tightly to the license plate. With a small and well–chosen subset of images, the system is able to deal with a large variety of images with real–world characteristics obtaining great precision in the detection. The effectiveness for the proposed method is very high (97%). This method will be the first stage of a surveillance system which takes into account not only the actual license plate but also the model of the car to determine if a car should be taken as a threat.

1 Introduction

Pattern Recognition is an Artificial Intelligence technique which allows to find and classify objects or structures contained inside bigger structures. Nowadays, there are several techniques based on Pattern Recognition, for License Plate Recognition (LPR) on digital images. These techniques are used in many systems [1], for example, in car parking access control, to measure average vehicle speed over long distances, to detect border crossings, to detect a stolen car with a list that can be updated in real time, for electronic toll collection on pay-per-use roads or for its use by the police to detect vehicle infringements.

Nowadays, most LPR systems [2] are split in two different parts: the Capture Unit which takes the image of the vehicle, and the Process Unit (PU) which carries out the recognition of the license plate. In the same way, the PU is split in two different sub–problems: License Plate Detection (LPD) and Digit/Character Recognition. In the LPD step, correct results are very difficult to obtain, due to the great variety of characteristics that can be present in each image: poor resolution, blurry images, objects obscuring (part of) the plate and different contrast due to reflection, rays of light, or shadows, among others.

N. García-Pedrajas et al. (Eds.): IEA/AIE 2010, Part III, LNAI 6098, pp. 301–310, 2010.
© Springer-Verlag Berlin Heidelberg 2010

In this work, a new method for LPD is proposed. This method is an hybridization of Genetic Neural Network (GNN), Morphology, and Active Contours. The article is divided in six different sections. In section 2, some methods developed by other authors are revised. The proposed method is described in section 3, showing the three main modules. The following two sections (Sec. 4 and 5) present the parameters of the model and some experimental results, respectively. Finally, in section 6, main conclusions of the article are discussed and some future research is proposed.

2   Background

Duan et al. [3] proposed an efficient boundary–based method for license plate detection combining the Hough transform and Active Contour algorithms. According to authors, this method optimizes speed and accuracy. Furthermore, the method has a preprocessing module based on three algorithms, graying, normalizing, and histogram equalization to improve the rate of LPD and a module responsible for license plate verification. The detection module was evaluated and obtained an error rate of 1.8%.

Kahraman et al. [4] presented an algorithm for LPD using the Gabor transform. In this algorithm, the images are convolved with 12 different Gabor filters. In the convolved images, the license plates show a high value of intensity and can be segmented with a thresholding algorithm, some morphological operators, and a simple utilization of an eight–connected blob. The authors evaluated the performance of this algorithm and achieved a correct detection in 98% of cases.

Cano et al. [5] proposed a method for automatic location of the license plate based on a supervised classifier. An equalization, a Sobel filtering, and a simple thresholding are previously applied to the images. Next, a feature extraction technique is applied. It consists in the processing of a small window centered on each pixel, applying PCA (Principal Component Analysis), which detects whether the pixel is an inner pixel of a license plate region or not. Finally, for license plate location, a classifier based on the $k–nearest\ neighbours$ rule is used.

Clemens et al. [6] presented a module for LPD divided in three parts: a detector that combines the AdaBoost–algorithm with Haar–like features (this detector provides multiple detections for a single license plate), the post–processing stage which merges all those detections and the tracker stage for constraining the search of the detector to certain areas of the image.

A two–stage method based on Adaboost classifier followed by a SIFT descriptor and a SVM filter has been recently described by Ho et al. [7]. They discovered that Adaboost is able to detect almost all license plates, up to 95% of correct detections, although Adaboost provides a large number of false positives (precision, 35%). Their two–stage method still obtains high values of correct detection (92%) whilst improving the precision of the detection (91%).

Anagnostopoulos et al. [8] made a categorization of the methods for LPD into different classes. The first type of method is based on binary image processing and includes all those algorithms that are based on many different techniques like edge statistics, morphology, or connected component analysis. The second type is based on gray–level processing and includes all those algorithms for LPD that are based on other techniques like region segmentation, image transformations, or statistical measurements. The third type is based on color processing which works with the expected plate appearance. This type contains algorithms regarding color model transformation, fuzzy sets theory, or histogram processing. The last type is based on classifiers and contains algorithms based on computational intelligence such as artificial neural networks, genetic programming, or genetic algorithms.

Feng and Shuoben [9] recently proposed a LPR method based on local shape and color. The method they proposed have some key points similar to the one proposed in this work, such as vertical and horizontal edge extraction and further thresholding of pixels based on their illuminance and color. The method also manages properly slanted and oblique plates, providing a 96.3% acuracy. In the abstract, they state that the method has little influence on light and blur, however, no further explanations are included in their work.

The GNN, used in the first step of the proposed method, is based on that presented by Montana and David [10]. These authors created a Genetic Algorithm for Neural Network weight optimization. This algorithm has five principal components: chromosome encoding, evaluation function, initialization procedure, operators, and parameter settings.

Odeh et al. [11] developed a method to classify different lesions in medical images. Several techniques were used to extract visually relevant characteristics, which were used as inputs for a Genetic Algorithm for pattern classification. Some parts of their method are based in morphology and edge extraction, which are also used in the proposed method in this work.

3   Proposed Method

In this section, a system for LPD based on GNN, Morphology, and Active Contours is described. This system is divided into three main modules: Preprocessing, Processing, and Postprocessing.

3.1   Preprocessing

In this stage, the images are processed using several different algorithms to obtain modified images or computed data, which will be used as the inputs to the GNN of the following phase. These algorithms are binary thresholding, horizontal and vertical Sobel edge filtering, Prewitt edge filtering, and white, gray, and black pixel histograms.

3.2   Processing

In this module, the preprocessed images are divided into 10×10 virtual regions (each region with the same size). The optimum size and amount of the virtual regions were determined applying a large number of experiments, obtaining the best results for that size and number of regions.

For each region, the following information is extracted using the images from the preprocessing stage: number of edge pixels obtained by the Sobel operator, amount of edge pixels obtained by the Prewitt edge filtering (applied with a lower threshold that the one used with Sobel), number of edge pixels provided by a horizontal Sobel edge detector, amount of white pixels obtained from a binarized image, and the amount of white, gray, and black pixels of the original (non binarized) image. Prior to use the GNN to detect license plates, it has to be trained. In the following paragraph, the training of the GNN will be described.

Training. The extracted information is introduced in a previously created GNN for training. In each iteration of training, the algorithm obtains the information of one virtual region. The GNN processes the information and gives an output for each virtual region to indicate whether a part of the license is contained in this region or not.

The training phase is made with a set of 6–10 images and their respective virtual regions. These images have to be selected meticulously, in order to train the GNN with highly representative images of different license plates and situations. It means that in the training set of images there should be included at least one image with a sloping license plate, another one with a dark plate, another image with a very bright plate, etc. besides including some images of "standard" license plates. Using this simple hint, the system is able to obtain a quite robust GNN. Furthermore, the training phase can be accomplished fast (ranging from 21 to 35 seconds for the whole training stage in an AMD Turion 64 x2 Dual Core 1.9Ghz running Linux Ubuntu 7.04).

Execution. Once that GNN is trained properly, it is able to process a large set of different images. This module also makes use of the previously defined virtual regions of each image. The information extracted of each virtual region is introduced in the previously trained GNN. It determines whether each region contains all or a part of the searched license plate. In that case, the output of the network for that region is activated. Otherwise, the output for that region is deactivated. Finally, all activated regions are joined and combined together to obtain the final region, inside of which the whole plate is located.

3.3   Postprocessing

The final region is usually bigger than the license plate, therefore, it is necessary to apply further processing of the image in order to obtain a more accurate detection of the plate.

The first step in the postprocessing stage is to obtain a binarization of the final processing–stage region. Several morphology operators are applied sequentially on the binarized image: an horizontal opening and closing and two consecutive vertical closings and openings. These operations are designed to remove all unnecessary information from the final region, like loose pixels. The result from this step is a rectangle, which is very similar and quite close to the searched plate.

After that, an active contour (or *snake*) is initialized using the contour of the rectangle as seed. With this final step, the *snake* adapts itself to the border of the license plate, with very little or no error. In Fig. 1, the output of the GNN is represented in a gray rectangle, and the output of the *snake* is represented with a set of black (or white, if the image is too dark to be able to detect black) points.

Sometimes the *snake* cannot be generated due to odd characteristics in the image: license plates too dark or too bright. For this case, the images are processed again to enhance their features. First of all, the histogram of each image is analyzed. If the image is very dark, the system makes a shift of the histogram to make the image lighter. On the opposite, if the image is very bright, the system makes a displacement of the histogram to darken the image. After that, the image is introduced again in the GNN to obtain a new output.

The whole system has an average response time of 3.87 seconds (in the same platform as the training phase) for images without second processing and 7.98 seconds for those images that need histogram displacement, because a whole new processing is needed.

4   Parameters of the Model

There are some parameters that have an influence on the obtained results:

- Activation threshold: it determines whether the output of the network is activated or deactivated. If this parameter is very close to 0, some virtual region (that should not be activated) will be activated. However, if it is very close to 1, some virtual region (that should be activated) will not be activated.
- Number of nodes per layer: nodes of each hidden layer of the network. This parameter has an influence in the accuracy of the results given by the GNN.
- Mutation probability: mutation probability of the genetic algorithm. This parameter has a direct influence with the training process.
- Training images: number of images used in the training phase of the neural network. This parameter also has an influence on the accuracy of the results given by the GNN.

The best values of the activation threshold and the number of nodes per layer have been determined with a genetic algorithm. The optimum value of the amount of training images and the mutation probability have been determined by codifying many configurations and proving each configuration of the GNN to compare which one obtains the best results. These values have the same influence in both training and execution phases.

The experiments have been carried out using a large set of images taken in many different situations: night shots with flash, light underexposition/ overexposition, inclined licensed plates, different positions of the license plates, different sizes of the license plates, different models of the license plates, etc.

5   Experimental Results

In Tab. 1, the results of the experiments are shown. For each experiment, this table shows the number of images used in the training phase of the GNN, the number of nodes in the two hidden layers, the mutation probability, and the percentage of plates properly detected (with images not used in the training phase). In some cases, the genetic algorithm is not able to find an optimized neural network for the training set of images, because the training images have so different features that they produce unstable changes in the weights of the GNN. In the best case, the system provided 97% of effectiveness (the license plate was correctly detected in 194 out of 200 images). In Tab. 2, the experiment which obtained best results is described. The set of images is divided into six different types of images, according to the features they show. As can be observed, all of the types of images are above 92% of effectiveness in the detection. Moreover, several types of images achieved 100% of detection. The system was unable

Table 1. Experimental Results

Training images	Nodes-Layer	Mutation Prob.	% Plates detected
1	20/10	0.1	75%
3	20/10	0.1	82%
10	20/10	0.1	75%
6	20/10	0.1	97%
6	10/5	0.1	92%
6	50/25	0.1	92%
6	100/50	0.1	91%
6	500/100	0.1	92%
6	30/30	0.1	92%
6	20/10	0.1	75%
6	20/10	0.01	94%
6	20/10	0.05	95%
6	20/10	0.15	92%
6	20/10	0.25	86%
6	20/10	0.35	85%

Table 2. Results of the 4th experiment

Type of images	Total Images	Plates Detected	% Plates Detected
Standard Images, no special features	94	92	97.9%
Images with sloping plate	21	21	100%
Images with square plate	3	3	100%
Images with dark plate	26	25	96.2%
Images with light plate	31	30	96.8%
Night images	25	23	92%
Total Images	200	194	97%

Fig. 1. Examples of License Plate Detection

to provide accurate results for some night images shot with flash. This wrong behavior is due to the great amount of light reflected by the plate, which makes the digits undetectable. However, the method shows great accuracy in the rest of images.

In Fig. 1, some examples of detected plates are depicted. The first case shows an example of the detection of a standard plate. The central image shows how the *snake* has been designed to be able to expand outside the GNN output (the gray rectangle in Fig. 1), because in some cases, the region given by the GNN does not contain the whole plate. The second case presents an example of a plate with a special shape, different from the rest of the plates. In that image, the license plate is composed of two rows of digits and the *snake* adapts itself around them without any problem. The third type is an example of a light overexposed image. In this type of images, the license plates show greater difference between the license plate background and the digits than in other types of images. This behavior also occurs in night shots with flash, depicted in the following row. In both types of images, the *snake* cannot be generated initially sometimes, due to the great quantity of brightness or darkness in the image. When this happens, the method analyzes the histogram to enhance the image features. The fourth case presents an example of an image taken during night with flash. In this type of images, most of the picture, except for the plate, is very dark and an histogram shifting is applied to make the image brighter. The fifth case shows a sloping plate, for which the *snake* adapts itself accurately. Finally, in some cases, the system is unable to find the proper plate as in the one shown in the sixth row. In it, a large name appears in a similar position than an standard plate and the font of the large name is quite similar to the font used in the license plate, thus, the GNN selects the large name as a plate. Therefore, in order to detect this kind of plates, further processing (i.e. digit recognition) has to be applied to reject plates that do not fit approved license plate models. This situation is not a common case, it has been specifically selected to stress the detection method to the limit. Nevertheless, if the GNN is trained with this type of images, it would be able to detect properly the plate, rejecting the large name.

6   Conclusions

In this article, a new system for LPD has been proposed. This method shows large effectiveness on plate detection, as in the best case, 97% of license plates were properly detected. Furthermore, in most of the cases, the result of the detection presented great precision, with little or even no error, and was very close to the actual license plate. Effectiveness depends on the parameters of the model, whilst precision depends basically on the pictures themselves. It is very important to note that this system provides accurate results even in bad situations, such as, (bright) overexposed images, (dark) underexposed images, and night shots with flash. The method also behaves properly with different positions and models of the license plate (sloping, not centered, square plates, rectangular plates, etc.). Other authors provide better results in terms of percentage of correct detections, however, the set of images they used is unknown and, thus, it cannot be compared with the proposed method. Most of those methods are not tested against night images, oblique plates, etc. and thus, high detection values are obtained. However, this method has been proved with a real–world dataset with a large variety of cars, license plates and situations.

It is worth noting that with a very small subset of well–chosen images, the system is able to handle properly many different images with different characteristics. This has been proved using just 6 images in the training phase and obtaining a correct detection of the license plate in 194 out of 200 images. The images used in the training phase were not used in the execution phase, and thus, this method shows a quite robust behavior. This system requires little configuration in the training phase, except for fine–tuning of the parameters.

6.1   Future Research

This method is the first stage of a larger intelligent surveillance system for police and other security forces. With this method, every car could be detected and the license plate would be compared with the model of the car for which the license plate was emitted. Thus, any car with a "repeated" license plate (often used by terrorists for bomb–cars) which do not match the real model of the car, would be marked as a suspicious one.

Besides, due to the use of quite simple computation (summation, multiplication, comparisons, look–up tables, and fixed–point mathematical operations), this system is suitable for embedded development. Because of the high precision of the LPD module, this system can be used as the first step of a new module for digit recognition [12].

References

1. License Plate Recognition, http://www.licenseplaterecognition.com/
2. Automatic Number Plate Recognition, http://www.anpr-tutorial.com/
3. Duan, T.D., Hong Du, T.L., Phuoc, T.V., Hoang, N.V.: Building an automatic vehicle license plate recognition system. In: Proceedings of International Conference on Computer Science RIVF, pp. 59–63 (2005)
4. Kahraman, F., Kurt, B., Gökmen, M.: License plate character segmentation based on the Gabor transform and vector quantization. In: Yazıcı, A., Şener, C. (eds.) ISCIS 2003. LNCS, vol. 2869, pp. 381–388. Springer, Heidelberg (2003)
5. Cano, J., Perez-Cortes, J.C.: Vehicle license plate segmentation in natural images. In: Perales, F.J., Campilho, A.C., Pérez, N., Sanfeliu, A. (eds.) IbPRIA 2003. LNCS, vol. 2652, pp. 142–149. Springer, Heidelberg (2003)
6. Arth, C., Limberger, F., Bischof, H.: Real-Time License Plate Recognition on an Embedded DSP-Platform. In: Procs. of the IEEE Conf. on Computer Vision and Pattern Recognition (CVPR '07), pp. 1–8 (2007)
7. Ho, W.T., Lim, H.W., Tay, Y.H.: Two–stage License Plate Detection using Gentle Adaboost and SIFT–SVM. In: 2009 First Asian Conf. on Intelligent Information and Database Systems, pp. 109–114 (2009), doi:10.1109/ACIIDS.2009.25

8. Anagnostopoulos, C.-N.E., Anagnostopoulos, I.E., Psoroulas, I.D., Loumos, V., Kayafas, E.: License Plate Recognition From Still Images and Video Sequences: A Survey. IEEE Transactions on Intelligent Transportation Systems 9(3), 377–391 (2008)
9. Feng, J., Shuoben, B.: License Plate Location Based on Characteristic of Local Shape and Color. In: WRI World Congress on Computer Science and Information Engineering, CSIE, vol. 5, pp. 279–282 (2009)
10. Montana, D.J., Davis, L.D.: Training feedforward Networks using Genetic Algorithms. In: Procs. of the Intl. Joint Conf. on Artificial Intelligence. Morgan Kauffman, San Francisco (1989)
11. Odeh, S.M., Ros, E., Rojas, I., Palomares, J.M.: Skin Lesion Diagnosis Using Fluorescence Images. In: Campilho, A., Kamel, M.S. (eds.) ICIAR 2006. LNCS, vol. 4142, pp. 648–659. Springer, Heidelberg (2006)
12. Fan, X., Fan, G., Liang, D.: Joint Segmentation and Recognition of License Plate Characters, Image Processing. In: Procs. of ICIP 2007, vol. 4, pp. 353–356 (2007)

System for Supporting Web-based Public Debate Using Transcripts of Face-to-Face Meeting

Shun Shiramatsu[1], Jun Takasaki[1], Tatiana Zidrasco[1], Tadachika Ozono[1], Toramatsu Shintani[1], and Hiroshi G. Okuno[2]

[1] Graduate School of Engineering, Nagoya Institute of Technology,
Gokisho-cho, Showa-ku, Nagoya, Japan
[2] Graduate School of Informatics, Kyoto University,
Yoshida-honmachi, Sakyo-ku, Kyoto, Japan
siramatu@nitech.ac.jp

Abstract. We propose a public debate support system through iterative alternation of face-to-face meetings and Web-based debates. Web-based facilitation of public debates is suitable for complementary question and answering when the debate in face-to-face meetings is insufficient due to time restriction. Since transcripts of public meetings tend to be lengthy and specialized, sharing public concerns among citizens and stakeholders requires much time and effort. To solve this problem, we propose two approaches. First, supporting the sharing of public concerns with structuration of public debate based on rhetorical structure theory (RST). It enables a user to manually specify his/her intention of a question, e.g., the question requires more evidence. An intention tag is effective for facilitating public debate. Second, supporting reading with visualization of topic transition, using our developed SalienceGraph. Moreover SalienceGraph retrieves passages related to a transient topic from past meeting records or documents. These approaches support citizens and stakeholders in finding, tracking, and sharing public concerns.

1 Introduction

We are developing a framework for supporting public debate to facilitate public involvement. Public involvement in building consensus for community development requires much effort and time for sharing public concerns among citizens and stakeholders. This is because understanding long transcripts of face-to-face public debates requires much time and effort for non-expert citizens. Moreover, Web-based asynchronous debate is suitable for complementary question and answering when the debate in face-to-face meetings is insufficient due to time restriction. Hence, our framework consists of iterative alternation of face-to-face meetings and Web-based debates.

Over the past few decades, there has been a growing debate about the role of the public in determining policy regarding health and environmental risk management [1]. To build consensus through public involvement, aggregating and sharing opinions aired in public debates is important [2,3]. In this process,

N. García-Pedrajas et al. (Eds.): IEA/AIE 2010, Part III, LNAI 6098, pp. 311–320, 2010.

public concerns can be managed according to the spiral process for knowledge creation[4] by using meeting records as shown in Figure 1.

For example, transcripts of the Yodo River Basin Committee, which include long public meetings, are published as lengthy PDF files on the Web [5]. Meetings in the committee have been held over 200 times and each meeting transcript has hundreds of sentences and several dozens pages. Although there are manual summaries, they are no effective way of finding an argument because the summaries cannot include all arguments of a debate.

Moreover, to reduce the amount of time and effort needed to understand the arguments, support for grasping the background of the arguments is needed. Since background information is often omitted by meeting participants, readers of meeting records often need to check relevant information. To complement ommited information, citizens need asynchronous question and answering and searching relevant information when they read the meeting transcripts. This study focuses on the rhetorical structure of a meeting to facilitate asynchronous question and answering.

This study deals with the following issues for supporting public debate.

(1) Facilitate asynchronous debate to complement insufficiency of face-to-face debate and to share public concerns included in meeting transcripts
(2) Provide an overview of transition of a long meeting to reduce the time and effort needed to track and find arguments
(3) Reduce the amount of time and effort needed to understand background or relevant information of arguments

To address issue (1), we have developed a Web-based interface for commenting an meeting transcripts based on rhetorical structure theory (RST). To address issue (2), we have developed a visualizer for transitions of a topic in a meeting based on a metric for focus of attention on each term in the meeting. Since joint attention among meeting participants and readers dynamically changes sentence by sentence, the metric is designed to deal with dynamic transition. To address issue (3), we have developed a method for retrieving information related to a transient topic based on the above-mentioned metric.

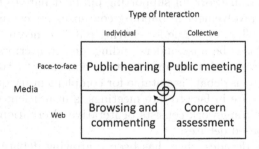

Fig. 1. Iterative alternation of face-to-face meetings and Web-based debates for sharing public concerns

2   Literature Reviews

Malone et al. developed on-line debate system called Climate Collaboratorium [6] to harness the collective intelligence of citizens. Their aim is similar to ours, that is, complement debate to share public concerns (issue (1)). Although their main approach is to use user-created plans for debate, they do not focus on the rhetorical structure of a debate.

To enable users to track and find arguments from a long meeting (issue (2)), visualizing an overview of transition is more effective than conventional methods for visualizing arguments. There are several argument visualization tools [7], such as ArguMed [8], Araucaria [9], Semantic Editor [10], etc. Typically, these tools produce "box and arrow" diagrams in which premises and conclusions are formulated as statements [11]. We have developed a method for visualizing the transitions of a topic because solving issue (2) requires an overview of transition of a long meeting.

Several debate browsers for a multimodal record of a meeting have been developed [12,13]. Furthermore, several environments for online argumentation based on "box and arrow" diagrams have also been developed [14,15]. Although we need to deal with multimodal meeting records and constructing argumentation environment is necessary, we focus on the transcription of a meeting record.

To help the user understand the background of arguments (issue (3)), our method for visualizing topic transition can be naturally expanded to a new method for finer-grain retrieval of information related to transient topics. This retrieval method does not require text segmentation. Several topic mixture methods for finer-grain information retrieval have been proposed [16,17,18]. These conventional methods require text segmentation to deal with dynamic transition. Although these methods can be used to provide topic-related information for issue (3), we use a new method naturally expanded from our visualization method for issue (2).

Furthermore, solving issues (2) and (3) also supports a corpus-based analysis of public debate [19] because solving them can reduce the time and effort needed for researchers to read a long public debate.

3   Web-based Interaction for Sharing Public Concerns

To complement insufficiency in face-to-face meetings, we are developing a prototype called SalienceGraph, shown in Figure 2. Citizens can write comments about meeting transcripts into the right-side of the figure via the Web. Transcripts of face-to-face meetings are stored as Global Document Annotation (GDA) files to represent linguistic structure [20]. Comments written via Web are stored as Resource Description Framework (RDF) files to represent rhetorical structure.

The rhetorical relation tags between the comments and statements in the transcripts are manually assigned by users. Although the tag set is designed based on rhetorical structure theory (RST) [21], we introduce a set of novel tags representing intentions of questions, that is, *require-evidence, require-example,*

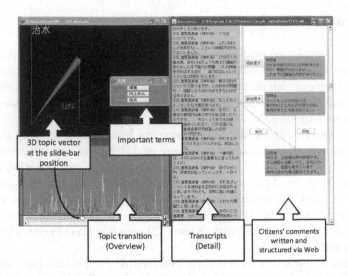

Fig. 2. SalienceGraph: Public debate browser for commenting via Web

and *require-background*. Since rhetorical structure indicates whether the answer matches the intention of the question, we presume that the novel relations are effective for facilitateing appropriate on-line debate. For example, when a negative conflict occurs in an on-line debate, we presume that users tend to provide an inappropriate answer, which does not satisfy the intention of the question. Hence, the design of the commenting interface assumes that users are motivated to specify a rhetorical relation tag to recieve their desired kind of answers.

4   Salience-based Visualization of Topic Transition

To reduce the time and effort needed to track and find arguments, we developed a visualizer for visualizing dynamic topic transition in a long meeting. Since the topic and joint attention dynamically change sentence by sentence, a metric for focus of attention on each term at each sentence needs to be designed (Figure 3). On the basis of this metric, a visualizer for topic transition in a meeting can be developed (Figure 4).

4.1   Design of Salience Metric

The horizontal axis of Figure 3 and the vertical axis of Figure 4 represent the *salience* of discourse entities [22]. We simply call it the "salience of terms". In our past research [23,24], a metric for salience is designed as the *reference probability* under the assumption that a salient entity tends to be referred to in the subsequent utterance unit, and we use it here as well. Let w be a word, U_i be the current utterance unit, U_{i+1} be the subsequent one, and $\mathrm{pre}(U_i) = [U_1, \cdots, U_i]$ be the preceding discourse. Let $w' \xrightarrow{\mathrm{coref}} w$ in U_{i+1} denote that a word in U_{i+1} has a coreference relation with w. The discourse salience of w at U_i is defined as the reference probability:

$$(\text{Salience of } w \text{ at } U_i) = p(\exists w' \xrightarrow{\text{coref}} w \text{ in } U_{i+1}|\text{pre}(U_i))$$
$$= \Pr(w|\text{pre}(U_i)), \tag{1}$$

where $\Pr(w|\text{pre}(U_i))$ is a simplified notation for the reference probability. This probabilistic definition quantifies salience.

The consistency of the definition of salience with the centering theory, which is a theory of the continuity of the attentional state and pronominalization [22], is empirically verified using large English and Japanese corpora [23]. The reference probability $\Pr(w|\text{pre}(U_i))$ is statistically calculated from a corpus by logistic regression:

$$\Pr(w|\text{pre}(U_i)) = \frac{1}{1+\exp\left(-(\beta_0+\sum_k \beta_k \cdot \text{feat}_k(\langle w, U_i\rangle))\right)}, \tag{2}$$

where $\text{feat}_k(\langle w, U_i\rangle)$ denotes feature values for the calculation, which is defined by using grammatical functions, part-of-speech, frequency, and recency [25]. The feature values are weighted by the recency effect [26] because the recent appearance of a target term should be emphasized over the old one [25]. The regression

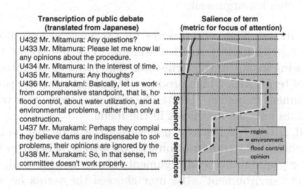

Fig. 3. Salience of term changes sentence by sentence

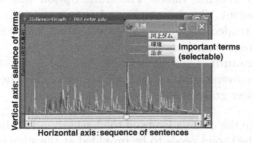

Fig. 4. Visualizing topic transition in long meeting to support overviewing, tracking, and finding arguments

weight for each feat_k is denoted by β_k in Equation (2). It is obtained from a corpus with the maximum-likelihood method.

Using this definition of salience enables us to deal with the transition on a sentence-by-sentence basis and to visualize the transition of topics (Figure 4). As shown in Figure 2, we developed a prototype of a debate browser, SalienceGraph, based on visualization scheme for topic transition, which is implemented using Java. It requires preprocessing for the transcription of a public debate as follows:

1. Analyze dependency structure using CaboCha, a Japanese dependency parser [27].
2. Annotate the result using CaboCha with GDA.
3. Calculate salience value $\Pr(w|\text{pre}(U_i))$ for each term w and sentence U_i. The calculation target $\langle w, U_i \rangle$ is only such that w appears in $\text{pre}(U_i)$, the preceding context of U_i.
4. Annotate salience value $\Pr(w|\text{pre}(U_i))$ with GDA for each term w and each sentence U_i.

4.2 Design of Graphical User Interface (GUI)

The GUI of SalienceGraph is designed based on Shneiderman's *Visual Information-Seeking Mantra* [28]. It supports an overview of transition of topics and finding an intended argument.

- **Overview first:** The user recieves an overview of transition in a long meeting using the topic transition window. The important terms can be chosen by using menus in the terms box. The menus have fifteen candidates of important terms with a high product of the total reference probability and inverse document frequency (IDF). The user can input other terms than the candidate ones into the text fields in the menu.
- **Zoom and filter:** When the user drags the slide bar under the topic transition window, the transcription window scrolls by being interlocked with the slide bar position. To read arguments about specific topics, e.g., "flood control" and "environment", the user chooses the terms he/she wishes to find from the menus and drag the slide bar to the position in which the terms have high salience values. The transcription window then scrolls to the argument about "flood control" and "environment", and the user can read her/his intended argument. Moreover, the transition window can be zoomed onto the intended argument.
- **Details on demand:** Thus, the user can find the detail of her/his intended argument. The movement of the 3D topic vector around the slide bar position also helps the user grasp the local transition of topics.

Furthermore, to help the user understand the background of the argument, information related to the topics needs to be provided at the slide bar position in the "Details on demand" phase. The next section describes a method for retrieving related information based on the salience of terms.

4.3   Retrieval of Topic-Related Information

We developed a method for retrieving information related to the transient topics at the slide bar position in SalienceGraph [24]. Finer-grain information related to the transient topics can be retrieved based on the salience metric. A salience vector $[p(w_1|\text{pre}(U_i)), \cdots, p(w_n|\text{pre}(U_i))]$, i.e., a vector comprising the salience of terms, represents topics at the moment of the sentence U_i. Because $\text{pre}(U_i)$ is calculated using the preceding context $\text{pre}(U_i)$, the vector can be used as a query vector representing the transient topic affected by the preceding context Since the salience vectors are calculated for each sentence, the nearest neighbor search based on salience vector enables finer-grain information retrieval.

Note that large calculation is necessary for the nearest neighbor search because the vocabulary size n is in the tens of thousands. Therefore, we use a probabilistic Latent Semantic Analysis (pLSA) [29] to compress the dimensions of a salience vector and approximate nearest neighbor (ANN) [30] to search the nearest neighbors. The procedure is as follows.

1. For each meeting transcript and retrieval-targeted document, e.g., other meeting transcripts and newspaper articles, annotate dependency structure and salience values with GDA.
2. Extract n terms whose product of the total reference probability and IDF are higher ranked from the records of meeting.
3. Compress the dimensions of n-dimensional salience vectors for each sentence in meetings and targeted documents by pLSA.
4. Retrieve candidate sentences with nearest neighbor vectors to provide topic-related information by ANN on the basis of the compressed salience vectors.
5. Show the 5 best candidates using a tab window chosen by the user. In a tab, a candidate sentence and several preceding sentences are shown. The user can use them to choose the information they need from the candidates.

5   Experimental Results

5.1   Evaluation of Salience Metric

To evaluate our salience metric, the reference probability, we prepared two corpora in Japanese, which are annotated with GDA tags.

CSJ: Four interview dialogues from the Corpus of Spontaneous Japanese (CSJ) [31], which contain
  - 1,780 utterance units (IPUs; inter-pause units),
  - 6.92 morphemes per utterance unit, and
  - 1,180 anaphora relations annotated manually.

Mainichi: 3,000 newspaper articles in Japanese from the Mainichi Shinbun for 1994 (GSK2004-A [32]), which contain
  - 63,221 utterance units (predicate clauses), 37,340 sentences,
  - 10.79 morphemes per utterance unit, and
  - 86,541 anaphora relations annotated manually.

We designed a metric $evalSal(m)$ to evaluate a target method m for calculating salience.

$$\text{evalSal}(m) = \text{cor}\Big(\big[\text{sal}_m(w|\text{pre}(U_i))\big]_{\langle w, U_i \rangle}, \big[\text{isRef}(w, U_{i+1})\big]_{\langle w, U_i \rangle} \Big), \qquad (3)$$

where $\text{isRef}(w, U_{i+1})$ is the dummy variable defined above (i.e., 1 if $\exists w \xrightarrow{\text{ref}} e$ in U_{i+1}, otherwise 0), and $\text{cor}(x, y)$ denotes Pearson's correlation coefficient between x and y.

We compared the evaluation scale, $evalSal(m)$, of our method for calculating the reference probability to that of the baseline method for the term frequency (TF) measured in an optimal rectangular window. The evaluation measures with the naive TF were 0.105 for *CSJ* and 0.301 for *Mainichi*. The evaluation measures with our proposed method (0.365 for *CSJ* and 0.368 for *Mainichi*) were greater. This means that our method can be used to more effectively predict whether the target entity is referred to in the subsequent U_{i+1} than with the naive TF. The increase in effectiveness with our method was more significant for *CSJ* than for *Mainichi*. This indicates that handling spoken language needs more integration of the features than handling written language.

6   Concluding Remarks

We proposed SalienceGraph, a prototype system for supporting public debate with iterative alternation of face-to-face meetings and Web-based debates towards facilitating public involvement. To complement insufficiency of face-to-face debate, SalienceGraph includes a Web-based interface for commenting about meeting transcripts based on rhetorical structure theory. To support grasping of an overview of whole transition to track and to find intended arguments, we designed a salience metric and developed a novel method for visualizing topic transition. Our prototype system, SalienceGraph, was designed based on *Visual Information-Seeking Mantra*. The design visually helps the users to grasp an overview of topic transition and to find arguments from a lengthy debate.

Moreover, to support understanding of background of the arguments, we developed a method for salience-based retrieval of information related to transient topic specified by a user. The method for finer-grain retrieval does not need text segmentation because the salience vectors are annotated for each sentence. It is a natural expansion of the method for visualizing topic transition, which deals with topic transition and effects from the preceding context. Furthermore, we conducted experiments for retrieving topic-related information and instantiated the relevant information provided with our method. Our proposed framework reduces the amount of time and effort needed to aggregate and share arguments for public involvement.

As future work, we are planning to evaluate the efficiency of the Web-based commenting interface for sharing public concerns among citizens and stakeholders.

Acknowledgment

The authors are grateful to Kiyoshi Kobayashi and Hayeong Jeong, who told us about the meeting records of the Yodo River Basin Committee, and Kôiti Hasida, who designed GDA tag set. This work was supported by Grant-in-Aid for Scientific Research (No. 19100003, No. 09152946).

References

1. Rowe, G., Frewer, L.: Public participation methods: A framework for evaluation. Science Technology Human Values 25(1), 3–29 (2000)
2. Renn, O., Webler, T., Rakel, H., Dienel, P., Johnson, B.: Public participation in decision making: A three-step procedure. Policy Sciences 26(3), 189–214 (1993)
3. Rowe, G., Frewer, L.: A typology of public engagement mechanisms. Science Technology Human Values 30(2), 251–290 (2005)
4. Nonaka, I., Toyama, R., Konno, N.: SECI, Ba and Leadership: a Unified Model of Dynamic Knowledge Creation. Long Range Planning 33(1), 5–34 (2000)
5. Yodo River Basin Committee: List of meeting minutes (2007) (in Japanese), http://www.yodoriver.org/doc_list/gijiroku.html
6. Malone, T., Laubacher, R., Introne, J., Klein, M., Abelson, H., Sterman, J., Olson, G.: The climate collaboratorium: Project overview. CCI Working Paper No. 2009-003 (2009), http://cci.mit.edu/publications/CCIwp2009-03.pdf
7. Kirschner, P., Shum, S., Carr, C.: Visualizing Argumentation: Software Tools for Collaborative and Educational Sense-Making. Springer, Heidelberg (2003)
8. Verheij, B.: Artificial argument assistants for defeasible argumentation. Artificial Intelligence 150(1-2), 291–324 (2003)
9. Reed, C., Rowe, G.: Araucaria: Software for argument analysis, diagramming and representation. International Journal of AI Tools 13(4), 961–980 (2004)
10. Hasida, K.: Semantic Authoring and Semantic Computing. In: Sakurai, A., Hasida, K., Nitta, K. (eds.) JSAI 2003. LNCS (LNAI), vol. 3609, pp. 137–149. Springer, Heidelberg (2007)
11. van den Braak, S.W., van Oostendorp, H., Prakken, H., Vreeswijk, G.A.W.: A critical review of argument visualization tools: Do users become better reasoners? In: Workshop Notes of the ECAI 2006 Workshop on CMNA, pp. 67–75 (2006)
12. Bouamrane, M.M., Luz, S.: Navigating multimodal meeting recordings with the meeting miner. In: Larsen, H.L., Pasi, G., Ortiz-Arroyo, D., Andreasen, T., Christiansen, H. (eds.) FQAS 2006. LNCS (LNAI), vol. 4027, pp. 356–367. Springer, Heidelberg (2006)
13. Bouamrane, M.M., Luz, S.: Meeting browsing: State-of-the-art review. Multimedia Systems 12(4-5), 439–457 (2007)
14. Oinas-Kukkonen, H.: Debate browser — an argumentation tool for metaedit+ environment. In: Proceedings of the Seventh European Workshop on Next Generation of CASE Tools (NGCT '96), pp. 77–86 (1996)
15. Kamimaeda, N., Izumi, N., Hasida, K.: Evaluation of Participants' Contributions in Knowledge Creation Based on Semantic Authoring. The Learning Organization 14(3), 263–280 (1999)
16. Blei, D.M., Moreno, P.J.: Topic segmentation with an aspect hidden Markov model. In: Proceedings of SIGIR, pp. 343–348 (2001)

17. Canny, J.F., Rattenbury, T.L.: A dynamic topic model for document segmentation. Technical report, EECS Department, University of California, Berkeley (2006)
18. Caracciolo, C., Hage, W.V., Rijke, M.D.: Towards topic driven access to full text documents. In: Proceedings of European Digital Library Conferences, pp. 495–500 (2004)
19. Jeong, H., Shiramatsu, S., Kobayashi, K., Hatori, T.: Discourse analysis of public debates using corpus linguistic methodologies. Journal of Computers 3(8), 58–68 (2008)
20. Hasida, K.: Global Document Annotation (GDA) (2004),
    http://i-content.org/GDA/
21. Mann, W., Thompson, S.: Rhetorical Structure Theory: Towards A Functional Theory of Text Organisation. Text 8(3), 243–281 (1988)
22. Grosz, B., Joshi, A., Weinstein, S.: Centering: A Framework for Modeling the Local Coherence of Discourse. Computational Linguistics 21(2), 203–226 (1995)
23. Shiramatsu, S., Komatani, K., Hasida, K., Ogata, T., Okuno, H.G.: A Game-Theoretic Model of Referential Coherence and Its Empirical Verification Using Large Japanese and English Corpora. ACM Transactions on Speech and Language Processing (ACM-TSLP), Article 6, 5(3) (2008)
24. Shiramatsu, S., Kubota, Y., Komatani, K., Ogata, T., Takahashi, T., Okuno, H.: Visualization-based Approaches to Support Context Sharing towards Public Involment Support System. In: Opportunities and Challenges for Next-Generation Applied Intelligence. Studies in Computational Intelligence, vol. 214, pp. 111–117. Springer, Heidelberg (2009)
25. Shiramatsu, S., Komatani, K., Ogata, T., Okuno, H.G.: SalienceGraph: Visualizing Salience Dynamics of Written Discourse by Using Reference Probability and PLSA. In: Ho, T.-B., Zhou, Z.-H. (eds.) PRICAI 2008. LNCS (LNAI), vol. 5351, pp. 890–902. Springer, Heidelberg (2008)
26. Murdock, B.B.: The Serial Position Effect in Free Recall. Journal of Experimental Psychology 64, 482–488 (1962)
27. Kudo, T., Matsumoto, Y.: Japanese dependency analysis using cascaded chunking. In: Proc. of CoNLL 2002, COLING 2002 Post-Conference Workshops, pp. 1–7 (2002)
28. Shneiderman, B.: Designing the User Interface: Strategies for Effective Human-Computer Interaction. Pearson Addison Wesley, London (1998)
29. Hofmann, T.: Probabilistic latent semantic analysis. In: Proc. of UAI 1999, pp. 289–296 (1999)
30. Arya, S., Mount, D.M.: Approximate Nearest Neighbor Queries in Fixed Dimensions. In: Proceedings of the Fourth Annual ACM/SIGACT-SIAM Symposium on Discrete Algorithms, pp. 271–280 (1993)
31. Maekawa, K.: Corpus of Spontaneous Japanese: Its Design and Evaluation. In: Proceedings of the ISCA & SSPR 2003, pp. 7–12 (2003)
32. GSK (Gengo Shigen Kyokai): Linguistic resourse catalogue (in Japanese),
    http://www.gsk.or.jp/catalog.html

Psychophysical Evaluation for a Qualitative Semantic Image Categorisation and Retrieval Approach

Zia Ul-Qayyum*, A.G. Cohn, and Alexander Klippel

ziaqayyum@uaar.edu.pk, a.g.cohn@leeds.ac.uk, klippel@psu.edu

Abstract. This paper details the behavioral evaluation of a qualitative image categorisation and retrieval approach using semantic features of images. Content based image retrieval and classification systems are highly active research areas and a cognitively plausible image description can improve effectiveness of such systems. While most approaches focus on low level image feature in order to classify images, humans, while certainly relying on some aspects of low level features, also apply high-level classifications. These high-level classification are often qualitative in nature and we have implemented a qualitative image categorisation and retrieval framework to account for human cognitive principles. While the dataset, i.e. the image database that was used for classification and retrieval purposes contained images that where annotated and therefore provided some ground truth for assessing the validity of the algorithm, we decided to add an additional behavioral evaluation step: Participants performed similarity ratings on a carefully chosen subset of picture implemented as a grouping task. Instead of using a predefined number of categories, participants could make their own choice on a) how many groups they thought were appropriate and b) which icons/images belong into these groups. The results show that the overall underlying conceptual structure created by the participants corresponds well to the classification provided through the algorithm.

Keywords: Qualitative spatial representation, qualitative similarity, image categorisation and retrieval, psychophysical evaluation.

1 Introduction

Content based image classification and retrieval systems have gained more importance and have been an active research area in recent years with an increasing requirement of robust and flexible techniques to handle dynamic and complex visual content in large volumes of digital data at a higher semantic level. Most of the research in this area is primarily based on the use of low level image features like colour, texture, shape etc [1,2,3]. Although low level image processing algorithms and methodologies are quite mature, such systems are hard to be used effectively by a novice due to the semantic gap between user perception

---

* Corresponding author.

N. García-Pedrajas et al. (Eds.): IEA/AIE 2010, Part III, LNAI 6098, pp. 321–330, 2010.

and understanding, and system requirements. Furthermore, humans tend to describe scenes using natural language semantic keywords/concepts like sky, water etc and specify retrievals "an image with water next to fields and having sky at the top ..." or ".... has a small lake with high peaks of mountains behind and fields on left....". This suggests that the use of underlying semantic knowledge in a qualitative representation language may provide a way to model the human context and a natural way to bridge this semantic gap for better image understanding, categorization and retrieval capabilities. In an earlier work, we had, therefore proposed a qualitative knowledge driven framework for image categorisation and retrieval using local semantic content of images [4,5].

There are number of methods discussed in the literature to assess the similarity of objects, events and spatial relations [6,7,8]. Keeping in the characteristics of the proposed categorisation and retrieval framework [4,5], a psychophysical evaluation is an obvious choice and is therefore used as an alternative evaluation approach in order to perform:

Categorization Evaluation: The participants were provided with an appropriately chosen set of images and asked to group images into as many number of images as they deemed fit, and to assign a label/keyword to each group.
This provides an evaluation of whether the number of classes from data set matches those selected by the study participants. Moreover, it provides a validation of the *'ground truth'* as participants will place images in a group based on their notion of 'similarity'; so comparing the images in a group created by a participant vs the pre-assigned class labels provides a cognitive evaluation of the *'ground truth'*. Moreover, it can reveal level of confusion between certain existing classes of images in ground truth.

Retrieval Evaluation: The above task provides an evaluation of the image retrieval approach as well, because if the participants *'mostly'* place the images of the same pre-assigned class in one group - it implies that humans also choose certain images to belong to particular group if they are 'visually similar (in qualitative terms)'. Furthermore, the participants are requested to give a natural language description of sampled images in each group they create to get an idea about their notion of 'relative similarity' in images of each group. This provides an assessment of the QSD-based approach for categorization and *'qualitative similarity measure'*-based retrieval tasks.

A metric based evaluation of qualitative approaches is always regarded a difficult task because of the nature of qualitative representations. In order to evaluate the overall performance of our qualitative knowledge driven approach to image categorization and retrieval [4,5], manually assigned categories for the image data were used. However, to evaluate the efficiency and effectiveness of the qualitative representations based categorisation and retrieval framework , a psychophysical evaluation approach is proposed. Qualitative representations of image content is a cognitively more plausible way to describe images; psychophysical evaluation of such approaches, therefore is an obvious choice and is used as an alternative approach.

Before discussing these psychophysical evaluation experiments, the baseline approach used in our previous work on *qualitative semantic image description* based categorisation and retrieval is briefly described to make this paper self-contained.

1.1 Baseline Approach for Qualitative Categorisation and Retrieval

There has been substantial work done in areas like computer vision, pattern recognition etc on detecting, recognising and categorizing objects of interest in images and other application domains. Most of the techniques in image description and categorisation has been based on describing the image using low level features such as colour and texture [9,10,11,1,2,12], whereas semantic scene description is arguably a natural way to describe image features and it may bridge the gap between a human's description and that of a computer. Although, there has been more recent work on the use of semantic content in such systems [13,14,15,4,16,17] and using spatial context and spatial relations in image analysis/automatic annotation [18,19,20], the need to bridge the semantic gap between low level synthetic features and high level semantic meanings has been regarded as an open problem [21].

In an earlier work, we had proposed a qualitative knowledge-driven semantic modelling approach for image categorisation and retrieval [4,5]. It was demonstrated that how category descriptions for a set of images can be learned using qualitative spatial representations over a set of local semantic concepts (LSC) such as sky, grass and categorizing the images into one of six global categories (e.g. Coasts, Landscapes with Mountains etc). Four kinds of qualitative spatial representations, namely *'RSizeRep'* based on relative size of each of concept occurences in each image, *'AllenRep'* based on Allen relations [22] and are measured on the vertical axis between the intervals representing the maximum vertical extent of each concept occurrence, *'ChordRep'* based on Morchen and Ultsch's work [23] in which each row in grid like image is a *chord* which is labelled by concatenating the corresponding patch labels in that row and the *'TouchRep'* to model whether one patch type is spatially in contact with another in the image, were used in these experiments.

Qualitative semantic image descriptions were obtained by applying the above QSRs and their variants to learn class descriptions and categorise images into one of a fixed number of semantic classes (such as sky_clouds, coasts, landscapes_with_mountains (lwm), fields, forests and waterscapes) [4]. It demonstrated that supervised learning of a pure qualitative and spatially expressive representation of semantic image concepts can rival a non-qualitative one for image categorization [24]. In order to evaluate the performance of this approach to image categorization, manually assigned categories for the images were used.

Image categorisation is one of the critical steps for retrieving images. We used the same semantic descriptions as in the categorization work summarized above to evaluate the validity of our hypothesis that the qualitative representations which were able to effectively support categorization may also provide an effective and natural way to support content-oriented querying approach [5]. Further details of this approach can be viewed in our previously published work [4,5].

A collection of seven hundred natural scenes images was used in this work. The labelled data set was provided by Julia Vogel who has developed a quantitative semantic modelling framework for image categorisation and retrieval [16].

2   Psychophysical Experimental Setup

As already argued previously, a qualitative representation of image content is cognitively plausible way to describe images and perform categorization and retrieval based on such descriptions. Moreover, it was argued that the *qualitative similarity measure* used to accomplish image retrieval tasks is a natural way to arrange the images in order of their respective *typicality* with respect to a query image. Psychophysical evaluation of such approaches, therefore, is an obvious choice and is used as an alternative approach to evaluate our qualitative knowledge driven approach for categorisation and retrieval of images. The details of these experiments and corresponding results are presented in the following sections.

2.1   Experiments

This sections details the behavioural validation of the algorithm discussed in the above section. The goal is to provide validation, or the ground truth for the algorithm that has been advised on the basis of a qualitative spatial representation.

Participants: Twenty students including two females were used to conduct these experiments. They were selected from different subject areas like chemistry, medevial studies, mathematics, geography, computing etc with average age of about thirty two years (age of participants ranges between 24 to 52 years). The reason to choose participants with such diverse academic backgrounds was to achieve a varied understanding and perception of the participants with regard to the type of experiment and the nature of the data.

Materials: We used 72 icons to depict landscapes. The 72 icons were chosen from a data set that contains 700 pictures of natural landscapes. The following procedure was applied to make this selection and to obtain a representative example. A representative example should be first of all be related to the six groups: landscape with mountains, forest, field, coast, waterscape, and sky_ clouds; corresponding to the hypothesis that the algorithm classifying images into these six categories is operating on cognitively adequate principles. Hence, we adopted the following strategy: Consider the average penalty weights for all images in a class in the corpus based on all four base qualitative representations used in actual categorization and retrieval experiments. It is worth reporting here again that the sequence of penalty weights for each image in each of the six classes is generated by taking each image of the corpus as a query image iteratively in a leave-one-out fashion and k such sequences per class are generated, where k is the total number of images in each class. The penalty weights for each image are then averaged to get a single sequence of weights for each class.

This approach rules out bias due to choice of query image in these experiments. The respective average penalty weights sequences for each of the pre-assigned category of images are then sorted in ascending order to arrange images in decreasing order of qualitative similarity. For each image category, twelve images are selected by taking six, four and three images from top, middle and bottom of the sorted sequence of k images for each category which means that the selected images have varied typicality level with respect to a class. The sampled data set thus contained seventy two images from all six categories in the corpus.

Procedure: The icons were integrated into the grouping tool. Figure 1 shows a screenshot of a mimicked ongoing experiment. The grouping tool divides the screen into two parts. On the left side, participants find the stimulus material, consisting of all icons 72 depicting different landscapes, which are placed in a different random order for each participant. The number of icons required scrolling to access all items. (Scrolling is a common procedure in interacting with computer interfaces; no problems were expected nor found during the experiments.) The right side of the screen is empty at the start; participants move icons to this side in order to group them during the experiment. The interface was kept simple so that participants could perform only the following three actions: Create a new group, Delete an existing group, Finish. The experiment took place in the participants' workplace and were tested individually. After arriving and obtaining some basic information, we explained to them the general procedure of the experiments and demonstrated the functionality of the grouping tool in form of a mock-up grouping task using different animal. Participants were advised that there is no right or wrong number of groups. In contrast to other grouping tasks

Fig. 1. The grouping tool (snapshot from an ongoing experiment). On the left side, icons representing landscapes are presented in random order. On the right side, a participant has started to group icons according to her categories of landscapes.

[24] there was no predefined set of groups that participant had to create. The algorithm, though, assigns six different labels for groups. We therefore tested two aspects of validity at the same time: on the one hand, whether the categorization of landscapes into 6 distinct groups is something that is reflected in the behavioral data created by the participants, and, on the other hand, whether the category boundaries are comparable to the judgment of human cognitive agent.

After the grouping task, participants were presented with the groups that they had created and were asked to provide two verbal labels for each group, i.e., a linguistic description for the kind of landscape a particular group represents. They were first asked to provide a global or general label and additionally for a slightly more elaborate description of the content within each group. Again, the participants were free in their choice of labels (compared to other experiments in this a predefined set of labels had to be assigned). The participants had a varied linguistic background and we refrain here from an in depth discussion and just use example of the labels participants provided.

2.2   Results

The groupings of each participant result in a 72 x 72 similarity matrix, the number of the icons used in this experiment on each axis. This matrix allows us to code all possible similarities between two icons simultaneously for all icons in the data set; it is a symmetric similarity matrix with 5184 cells. Similarity is coded in a binary way; any pair of icons is coded as '0' if its two items are not placed in the same group and '1' if its two items are placed in the same group. The overall similarity of two items is obtained by summing over all the similarity matrices of individual participants. For example, if two icons (called A and B) were placed into the same group by all 20 participants, we add 20 individual '1's to obtain an overall score of 20 in the respective cells for matrix position AB and BA.

This data was subjected to several agglomerative hierarchical cluster analysis. Cluster analysis identifies "natural" groupings within data that minimize within-group and maximize between-group variation. Agglomerative cluster analysis initially treats each case as a separate cluster, recursively combining the most similar clusters until all clusters are combined. After Aldenderfer and Blashfield [25], the cluster analysis used can be summarized according to the following five criteria:

1. Software: CLUSTAN software were used to perform the cluster analysis.
2. Similarity measure: Squared Euclidean distance was used as the analysis similarity measure.
3. Cluster method: Four common cluster methods were used and compared: complete linkage (minimizes the maximum distance between clusters), average linkage (minimizes the average distance between clusters), and Ward's methods (minimizes the distance to the center mean).
4. Number of clusters: In many studies, deciding on the appropriate number of clusters is a critical step in the analysis. Our results confirm a clear 6 cluster solution (see below).
5. Validation: The results were initially validated through the comparison of the results of several cluster methods (item 3 above) suggested by Kos and

Psenicka [26]. Further validation was performed by repeating the analysis with two randomly selected sub-groups (a procedure suggested by Clatworthy et al. [27]).

Figure 2 shows a cluster analysis using Ward's method. The dendrogram shows a clear 6 cluster solution. The labels on the left side of the dendrogram provide the picture (running) number and the ground truth that was calculated through the algorithm, i.e. the category in which they would have been placed based on the algorithm. This classification shows the successful categorization of pictures by the algorithm compared to the results of this user study, i.e. the dendrogram on the left side. From the 72 pictures all picture in the category sky-clouds were categorized correctly, all pictures in the category forest, all pictures in the category field, all but two pictures in the category landscape-with-mountain (lwm), all but two pictures in the category waterscape, and all but one picture in the category coast. Hence, we have a total of 5 out of 72 pictures placed in other than expected groups.

Validation. As indicated above, the validation was performed by comparing different clustering methods as suggested by Kos and Psenicka [26]. Figure 3 compared the results of Ward's, average linkage, and complete linkage. This comparison shows nearly identical cluster structure. The cluster structure at the cut-off

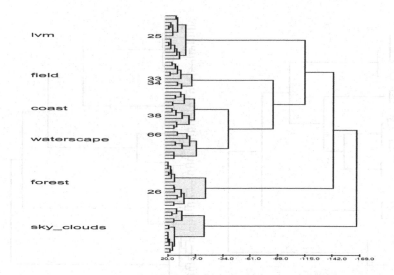

Fig. 2. The figure shows a dendrogram as the result of a cluster analysis using Wards method. Indicated is a six cluster solution. On the left side the predicted categories based on the algorithm are indicated: landscape with mountain (lwm), field, coast, waterscape, forest, and sky-clouds. The derived clustering structure indicates strong agreement between the human participant test and the results of the algorithm, i.e. only 6 pictures are not grouped according to the expected grouping provided by the algorithm. The numbers of the misclassified pictures are written next to the dendrogram.

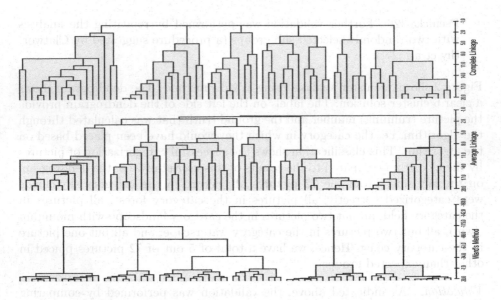

Fig. 3. Depicted are the results from three different cluster methods: Wards, average linkage, and complete linkage. While average and complete linkage to not exhibit the same clear 6 cluster solution, the assignment of pictures into 6 clusters is nearly identical across all three methods.

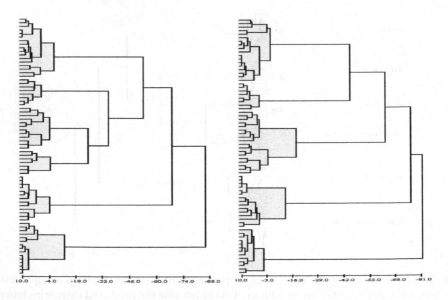

Fig. 4. Participants were randomly assigned to two groups. Both groups were subjected to Wards method. Depicted are dendograms for both groups (i.e. 10 participants each).

point for the six-cluster solution (shaded areas) is shown (the number of misplaced pictures is: 6 for Ward's method, 7 for average linkage, and 8 for complete linkage).

A further validation technique was applied (which also can be seen as a means to test whether the number of participants was sufficient), i.e. the participants were split into two groups using numbers from the website random.org. We performed Ward's method on both groups and the results show that both sub-groups exhibited nearly identical cluster structures. In both groups some icons were 'incorrectly' (compared to the algorithm) placed into groups (7 and 10) (see Figure 4).

3   Conclusion

The results of the above experiments provide an evaluation of our approach of categorization and retrieval in natural scene images using qualitative semantic image descriptions - QSID. It was argued that an expressive image description is key to success in categorization and retrieval approaches and that humans tend to describe different categories using qualitative terms and relations. Qualitative representations provide a natural way to model human cognition and therefore, QSID's based on an image's local semantic content provide a more plausible way to represent/describe the images. (The verbal descriptions of each group in these experiments has not been formally analysed, but participants used qualitative keywords like *more, above, below, meet etc* and local semantic features like *sky, grass, water etc* in their descriptions which is similar to QSIDs used to model the image content in our categorization and retrieval approach.) The proposed framework also helps to reduce the semantic gap between humans and most of content based image retrieval systems. Moreover, the results of these experiments tend to validate the *ground truth* of the preassigned category label in terms of number of classes and indicate , at the same time, the confusion in pre-assigned image labelling.

References

1. Rui, Y., Huang, T.S., Chang, S.F.: Image Retrieval: Past, Present and Future. Journal of Visual Communication and Image Representation 10, 1–23 (1999)
2. Veltkamp, R.C., Tanase, M.: Content-Based Image Retrieval Systems: A Survey. Tech. Rep. UU-CS-2000-34, Univ. Utrecht, Utrecht, The Netherlands (2000)
3. Deb, S., Zhang, Y.: An Overview of Content-based Image Retrieval Techniques. In: Proceedings of 18th Int. Conf. on Advanced Information Networking and Application (AINA 2004), vol. 1, pp. 59–64 (2004)
4. Qayyum, Z.U., Cohn, A.G.: Qualitative Approaches to Semantic Scene Modelling and Retrieval. In: Proceedings of 26th SGAI Int. Conference on Innovative Techniques and Applications of Artificial Intelligence, Research and Development in Itelligent Systems, XXIII, pp. 346–359. Springer, Heidelberg (2006)
5. Qayyum, Z.U., Cohn, A.G.: Image Retrieval through Qualitative Representation over Semantic Features. In: Proceedings of 18th British Machine Vision Conference (BMVC '07), pp. 610–619 (2007)
6. Rogowitz, B.E., Frese, T., Smith, J.R., Bouaman, C.A., Kalin, E.: Perceptual Image Similarity Experiments. In: Rogowitz, B.E., Thrasyvoulos, N.P. (eds.) Proceedings of SPIE: Human Vision and Electronic Images III, pp. 576–590 (1998)

7. Tversky, A.: Features of Similarity. Psychological Review 84, 327–352 (1977)
8. Knauff, M., Rauh, R., Renz, J.: "A Cognitive Assessment of Topological Spatial Relations: Results from an Empirical Investigation". In: Hirtle, S.C., Frank, A.U. (eds.) COSIT 1997. LNCS, vol. 1329, pp. 193–206. Springer, Heidelberg (1997)
9. Szummer, M., Picard, R.: Indoor Outdoor Image Classification. In: Proceedings of IEEE Int. Workshop on Content-based Access of Image and Video Databases (CAIVD), India, pp. 42–51 (1998)
10. Vailaya, A., Jain, A., Zhang, H.: On Image Classification: City vs Landscape. Pattern Recognition 31(12), 1921–1935 (1998)
11. Vailaya, A., Figueiredo, M., Jain, A., Zhang, H.J.: Image Classification for Content-based Indexing. IEEE Transactions on Image Processing 10(1), 117–130 (2001)
12. Enser, P., Sandom, C.: Towards a Comprehensive Survey of the Semantic Gap in Visual Image Retrieval. In: Bakker, E.M., Lew, M., Huang, T.S., Sebe, N., Zhou, X.S. (eds.) CIVR 2003. LNCS, vol. 2728, pp. 279–287. Springer, Heidelberg (2003)
13. Serrano, N., Savakis, A., Luo, J.: Improved Scene Classification using Efficient Low Level Features and Semantic Cues. Pattern Recognition 37(9), 1773–1784 (2004)
14. Pal, N.R., Pal, S.K.: A Review of Image Segmentation Techniques. Pattern Recognition 26, 1277–1294 (1993)
15. Picard, R., Minka, T.: Vision Texture for Annotation. ACM Journal of Multimedia Systems 3(1), 3–14 (1995)
16. Vogel, J., Schiele, B.: Semantic Modelling of Natural Scenes for Content-Based Image Retrieval. International Journal of Computer Vision 72(2), 133–157 (2006)
17. Wang, W., Song, Y., Zhang, A.: Semantics-Based Image Retrieval by Region Saliency. In: Lew, M., Sebe, N., Eakins, J.P. (eds.) CIVR 2002. LNCS, vol. 2383, pp. 29–37. Springer, Heidelberg (2002)
18. Papadopoulos, G.T., Mezaris, V., Dasiopoulou, S., Kompatsiaris, I.: Semantic Image Analysis using a Learning Approach and Spatial Context. In: Avrithis, Y., Kompatsiaris, Y., Staab, S., O'Connor, N.E. (eds.) SAMT 2006. LNCS, vol. 4306, pp. 199–211. Springer, Heidelberg (2006)
19. Millet, C., Bloch, I., Hede, P., Moellic, P.A.: Using Relative Spatial Relationships to Improve Individual Region Recognition. In: European Workshop on the Integration of Knowledge, Semantics and Digital Media Technologies, EWIMT '05, pp. 119–126 (2005)
20. Hollink, L., Nguyen, G., Schreiber, G., Wielemaker, J., Wielinga, B., Worring, M.: Adding Spatial Semnatics to Image Annotatins. In: Proceedings of 4th Int. Workshop on Knowledge Markup and Semantic Annotation at ISWC '04 (2004)
21. Aghbari, Z., Makinouchi, A.: Semantic Approach to Image Database Classification and Retrieval. NII J. (Natl. Inst. Inform.) 7, 1–8 (2003)
22. Allen, J.F.: Maintaining Knowledge About Temporal Intervals. Commun. ACM 26(11), 832–843 (1983)
23. Mörchen, F., Ultsch, A.: Mining Hierarchical Temporal Patterns in Multivariate Time Series. In: Biundo, S., Frühwirth, T., Palm, G. (eds.) KI 2004. LNCS (LNAI), vol. 3238, pp. 127–140. Springer, Heidelberg (2004)
24. Vogel, J., Schiele, B.: A Semantic Typicality Measure for Natural Scene Categorization. In: Rasmussen, C.E., Bülthoff, H.H., Schölkopf, B., Giese, M.A. (eds.) DAGM 2004. LNCS, vol. 3175, pp. 195–203. Springer, Heidelberg (2004)
25. Aldenderfer, M.S., Blashfield, R.K.: Cluster Analysis. Sage, Newbury Park (1984)
26. Kos, A.J., Psenicka, C.: Measuring cluster similarity across methods. Psychological Reports 86, 856–862 (2000)
27. Clatworthy, J., Buick, D., Hankins, M., Weinman, J., Horne, R.: The Use and Reporting of Cluster Analysis in Health Psychology: A Review. British Journal of Health Psychology 10, 329–358 (2005)

Features Extraction and Classification of Cartridge Images for Ballistics Identification

Jinsong Leng, Zhihu Huang*, and Dongguang Li

School of Computer and Security Science,
Edith Cowan University, WA, Australia
j.leng@ecu.edu.au,
zh_huang@yeah.net,
d.li@ecu.edu.au

Abstract. Ballistics identification is a quite challenging task from both theoretical and practical point of view. The premise underlying firearms and toolmark identification is that each firearm owns its unique toolmarks, resulting in some unique characteristic markings left on the fired projectile and cartridge case. Although various techniques have been applied to firearm identification, the major problems are still unsolved and further improvement and development are required. In other words, the ability of extracting useful features and the intelligently identification is still a major concern. This paper addresses the difficulties with respect to feature extraction and intelligent ballistics recognition. In this paper, various image processing techniques are employed for image digitizing and preprocessing the ballistics images. A novel feature set known as Circle Moment Invariants has been proposed for extracting features in cartridge images. We utilize two feature sets to characterize the ballistics images. A neural network based intelligent system is designed for classifying the extracted features of ballistics images. The experimental results indicate that the proposed approaches and feature criteria are capable of classifying the cartridge images very efficiently and effectively.

Keywords: Ballistics Identification, Digital Image Processing, Texture Feature, Circle Moment Invariant, Neural Network.

1 Introduction

The markings on the ballistics cartridges and projectiles are the most important characteristics of ballistics specimens for forensic identification. Those characteristic markings are often referred as a 'fingerprint' for ballistics recognition. The premise underlying firearms and toolmark identification is that each firearm has its unique toolmarks [11], resulting in the unique characteristic markings on the fired ballistics specimen. Consequently, each firearm can produce some unique characteristic markings on the fired projectiles and cartridge cases.

---

* Zhihu Huang is also with Distance Education Center, Chongqing Radio & TV University, ChongQing, China.

N. García-Pedrajas et al. (Eds.): IEA/AIE 2010, Part III, LNAI 6098, pp. 331–340, 2010.

Developing intelligent computerized systems for ballistics identification has motivated various organizations and researchers for decades [11,13,14]. Since 1990s, several ballistics identification systems have been developed and implemented for commercial and testing purposes. One of the international ballistics imaging systems known as IBIS (Integrated Ballistics Identification System) has been widely used by FBI in USA. Another commercial system called "Bulletproof" was developed by a Canadian company called Walsh Automation, which can acquire and store images of projectiles and cartridge cases by searching the image database for particular striations on projectiles. In 1995, the firearm identification system called Fireball (Firearm Identification System) [12] was developed by Edith Cowan University. Fireball has been used by Australia Police for identifying, storing, and retrieving the images of projectiles and cartridge cases. Due to the inherent nature of firearm identification, the fundamental difficulty remains to be unsolved from both theoretical and practical point of view [11]. In general, the major limitation of existing systems is the lack of good feature extraction techniques and the related intelligent methods, and thus the precision of comparisons relies heavily on the expertise and experience of the examiners. Until now, the existing ballistics systems can only rank a short list based on the correlations among ballistics images, which lack high level intelligent techniques. In this respect, the ability of extracting useful features and the intelligently identification is still a major problem, and thus further improvement and development of those systems are highly demanded for ballistics identification.

The popular way of intelligent firearm identification is to generate 2D or 3D images by digitizing the profiles of class characteristics and individual characteristics of ballistics specimens [13,14,1]. Precise 2D and 3D profilometry of features on ballistics cartridge cases and projectiles can be made by rotating cylindrical forensic ballistics specimens through Line-Scan imaging technique. Then the ballistics metrics can be applied to identification of the firearm [13,1]. For analyzing the ballistics images, a variety of techniques have been proposed in different disciplines. In [3], some statistical techniques were employed to compare the similarity of ballistics images, including subtraction of two cartridge case images, correlation-parameter, invariant image descriptors, and invariant moment calculation. However, the use of what type of correlation technique is dependent on the kind of markings. In [9], the spectral features of ballistic projectiles are analyzed using the fast Fourier transform (FFT), but without further analysis on features and the related classification. For identifying cartridge cases, there are only few approaches available. Kou et al. [8] described a neural network based model for the identification of the chambering marks on cartridge cases, but that paper did not provide any experimental analysis . Kong et al. [7] proposed a Self-Organizing Feature Map (SOFM) neural network only for the rim-firing pin marks. Apparently, all of those approaches are limited to some specific circumstances and also lack some systematic analysis on intelligent firearm identification.

This paper aims to address those difficulties by presenting a novel approach for intelligent ballistics recognition. In doing so, we utilize various techniques to address the problems of intelligent identification of cartridge cases. The 2D ballistics images are obtained using single wavelength ring light. The removal of noise and enhancement of the 2D images are conducted using smoothing spatial filter and power-law (gamma) transformation. We employ the Sobel technique for edge detection and Otsu [10] method for binarizing the 2D ballistics images. The features of 2D cartridge images are specified using the statistical method and the circle moment invariant technique. Finally, the neural network based intelligent system is trained and used to classify the different cartridge cases. We present a new criterion called circle moment invariant for the circle-centralized images; The experimental results indicate that the neural network based intelligent system can converge very quickly and precisely classify the cartridge cases, indicating that the proposed feature sets are very efficient and effective on intelligent ballistics recognition.

The rest of paper is organized as follows: Section 2 introduces the cartridge image preprocessing of 2D and cartridge images are also detailed. Statistical texture features and circle moment invariants are discussed in Section 3. Section 4 describes the neural network based classification system. The experimental results are explained and discussed in Section 5. Section 6 concludes the paper.

2   Preprocessing Cartridge Images

The marking on cartridge cases consists of important characteristics, which can be broadly specified as follows [16]:

- Firing pin marks on the back of the cartridge case.
- Ejector marks on the back and side of the cartridge case.
- Breach face marks on the cartridge case.
- Magazine feed marks on the side of the cartridge case.
- Power patterns on fabric have attributes of particular size, particle distribution, and chemical composition.

The purpose of image processing is to extract the interesting features from the cartridge images. The original images are required to be transfered into binary images for conducting the further analysis of the features. The quality of binary image depends on the use of the refining and the contrast enhancing techniques. The image preprocessing utilizes different methods to binarize the images, including the contrast enhancement, the Sobel edge detection and optimum global threshold known as Otsu [10].

The steps of image preprocessing are detailed as follows:

1. Reduce noise to the original image using the smoothing spatial filter;
2. Convert the original image into gray image;
3. Enhance the contrast using power-law (gamma) transformation;
4. Detect edges of the gray image using Sobel edge detection technique;
5. Binarize the refined image using Otsu method;
6. Remove the small areas on the binary image.

Based on the steps described, the cartridge images are converted into the binary images, as shown in Fig. 1.

Fig. 1. Binary Cartridge Images

3   Statistical Texture Features and Circle Moment Invariants

Statistical texture methods consider the texture as a random phenomenon with identifiable local statistics. One statistical method [4] uses six characteristics to describe texture features, i.e., mean, standard deviation (StdDev), R (normalized), third moment, uniformity, and entropy. Suppose that z be a random intensity variable, and $p(z_i)$ be the corresponding probability, where $i = 0, 1, 2, \cdots, L-1$ (L is the number of distinct intensity levels).

The first measure is the mean m, which represents the average intensity.

$$m = \sum_{i=0}^{L-1} z_i p(z_i) \tag{1}$$

The second measure is the standard deviation σ^2, indicating the intensity contrast.

$$\sigma^2 = \sum_{i=0}^{L-1} (z_i - m)^2 p(z_i) \tag{2}$$

The third measure is the normalized R, normalizing the large values of σ^2.

$$R = 1 - \frac{1}{1 + \sigma^2} \tag{3}$$

The fourth measure is the third moment μ^3, measuring the skewness of the histogram.

$$\mu^3 = \sum_{i=0}^{L-1}(z_i - m)^3 p(z_i) \tag{4}$$

The fifth measure is the "uniformity" U, representing the uniformity of the histogram.

$$U = \sum_{i=0}^{L-1} p(z_i)^2 \tag{5}$$

The sixth measure is the average entropy E, measuring the variability and uncertainty.

$$E = -\sum_{i=0}^{L-1} p(z_i) log_2 p(z_i) \tag{6}$$

The six measures form a set of statistical texture features of the ballistic projectile image. Every firearm should have a distinct set of texture features.

3.1   Circle Moment Invariants

Moment invariants are very effective features because they are independent of position, size and orientation but also independent of parallel projection. Moment invariants are firstly introduced by Hu [5]. Hu derived six absolute orthogonal invariants and one skew orthogonal invariant based upon algebraic invariants. The moment invariants have been proved to be the adequate measures for tracing image patterns regarding the images translation, scaling and rotation.

As Hu's seven moment invariants are independent of image translation, scaling and rotation, the cartridge images however do not follow the assumptions of Hu's derivation. The position of the firing pin mark is randomly distributed at the cartridge when the firearm strikes the detonator in the cartridge, as indicated in Fig. 2.

It is clear that the marks such as firing pin impression, the ejector marks, and the initials of the manufacturer stamped on its head are systematically distributed by the cartridge's geometrical circular center. Clearly, Hu's central moment invariants are not suitable to describe the features of the cartridge images. So we present the new criteria called the circle moment invariants based on the circular center.

Theorem 1. *The circle moment invariants are constant for circle-based geometrical distributed images. The circle moment invariants μ_{pq} can be defined as:*

$$\mu_{pq} = \sum_{x=0}^{M-1}\sum_{y=0}^{N-1} |(x - x_0)^p| \, |(y - y_0)^q| \, f(x, y)$$

where $p = 0, 1, 2, \cdots$ and $q = 0, 1, 2, \cdots$, x_0 and y_0 represent the center of the circle of the image.

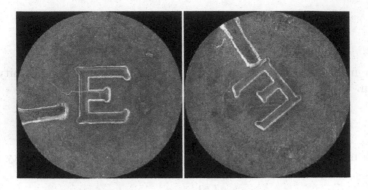

Fig. 2. Circle Systematic Cartridge Images

Proof. Let ρ and θ be the polar variables and r is the radius of the image, the circle moment invariants can be proved as follow:

$$\mu_{pq} = \sum_{x=0}^{M-1} \sum_{y=0}^{N-1} |(x - x_0)^p| \, |(y - y_0)^q| \, f(x, y)$$

$$\approx \int_0^{M-1} \int_0^{N-1} |(x - x_0)^p| \, |(y - y_0)^q| \, f(x, y) \, dx \, dy$$

$$= \int_0^{2\pi} \int_0^r |(\rho \cos\theta - x_0)^p| \, |(\rho \sin\theta - y_0)^q| \, f(\rho \cos\theta, \rho \sin\theta) \, d\rho \, d\theta$$

$$= \int_0^{2\pi} d\theta \int_0^r |(\rho \cos\theta - x_0)^p| \, |(\rho \sin\theta - y_0)^q| \, f(\rho \cos\theta, \rho \sin\theta) \, d\rho$$

So, the circle moment invariants are constant for circle-based geometrical distributed images.

Now, we further develop eight circle moment invariants for describing the features of cartridge images, details as follows:

$$\mu_{00} = \sum_{x=0}^{M-1} \sum_{y=0}^{N-1} f(x, y) \tag{7}$$

$$\mu_{11} = \sum_{x=0}^{M-1} \sum_{y=0}^{N-1} |(x - x_0)| \, |(y - y_0)| \, f(x, y) \tag{8}$$

$$\mu_{20} = \sum_{x=0}^{M-1} \sum_{y=0}^{N-1} (x - x_0)^2 f(x, y) \tag{9}$$

$$\mu_{02} = \sum_{x=0}^{M-1} \sum_{y=0}^{N-1} (y - y_0)^2 f(x, y) \qquad (10)$$

$$\mu_{21} = \sum_{x=0}^{M-1} \sum_{y=0}^{N-1} (x - x_0)^2 |(y - y_0)| f(x, y) \qquad (11)$$

$$\mu_{12} = \sum_{x=0}^{M-1} \sum_{y=0}^{N-1} |(x - x_0)| (y - y_0)^2 f(x, y) \qquad (12)$$

$$\mu_{03} = \sum_{x=0}^{M-1} \sum_{y=0}^{N-1} |(y - y_0)^3| f(x, y) \qquad (13)$$

$$\mu_{30} = \sum_{x=0}^{M-1} \sum_{y=0}^{N-1} |(x - x_0)^3| f(x, y) \qquad (14)$$

4   Neural Network Based Classification System

The three-layer back-propagation neural network (BP NN) includes input layer, hidden layer and output layer, as shown in Fig. 3.

The algorithm of BP NN was a major breakthrough in neural network research. However, the basic algorithm has two main drawbacks, i.e., the convergence is too slow and it is usually unable to reach global minimum for absorption of local minimum. To resolve these issues, two algorithms are considered in this

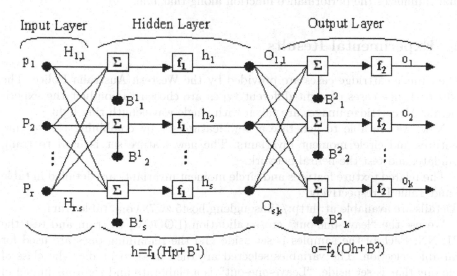

Fig. 3. Three-Layer Back Propagation Neural Network

paper. One [6,15] uses the heuristic technique, including the changes of the learning rate and the number of hidden neurons, the introduction of momentum etc. Another algorithm uses the standard numerical optimization techniques such as the conjugate gradient algorithm [2].

In basic BP NN algorithm, the learning rate is held constant throughout training. However, the performance of the algorithm is very sensitive to the proper setting of the learning rate. If the learning rate is too high, the algorithm can oscillate and become unstable. If the learning rate is too small, the algorithm takes too long to converge. It is very difficult to determine the optimal value before training. In fact, the convergence can be speed up if we increase the learning rate on flat error surfaces and then decrease the learning rate when the slope increases.

Like a low-pass filter, momentum is able to reduce the amount of oscillation or smooth out the oscillations in the trajectory. Momentum not only maintains the stability of the algorithm but also accelerate convergence because the trajectory is moving in a consistent direction. The basic back propagation algorithm adjusts the weights in the steepest descent direction (negative of the gradient). Although the function decreases most rapidly along the negative of the gradient, it may not produce the fastest convergence. Therefore, the steepest descent is often slow in convergence. Benefit from the search along conjugate direction, conjugate gradient algorithm is able to produce generally faster convergence than steepest descent one.

Conjugate gradient algorithms have been proposed to overcome those drawbacks. In most of the training algorithms discussed up to this point, a learning rate is used to determine the length of the weight update (step size). In most of the conjugate gradient algorithms, the step size is adjusted at each iteration. A search is made along the conjugate gradient direction to determine the step size that minimizes the performance function along that line.

5   Experimental Results

The sample cartridge cases are provided by the Western Australia Police. The fifty cartridge cases of eight different types are chosen to conduct the experiments. All cartridge images are taken with single wavelength ring light.

Now, we are able to generate a new feature set by combining the texture features and circle moment invariants. The new feature set is used to train, validate, and test the neural network.

The related texture features and circle moment invariants are detailed in table I and Table II respectively.
(Details are available at: http://jinsongleng.host5.zw78.com/tables.rar).

We use the "leave-one-out" cross-validation (LOOCV) to train and test the BP NN. Each of the samples is set aside and the remaining ones are used for variable selection. The variables selected are then used to predict the class of the one that is set aside. "Leave-one-out" is a elaborate and rigorous model of cross-validation that involves leaving out all possible subsets of cases.

The BP NN is trained and validated with three types of algorithms, i.e., basic BP NN, BP NN with momentum and adaptive learning rate, and BP NN with conjugate gradient algorithm.

The BP NN with conjugate gradient algorithm is used to train and validate the samples. The convergence diagram is shown in Fig. 4.

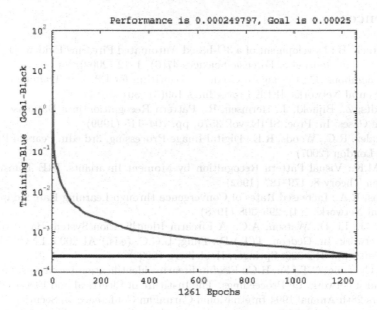

Fig. 4. Convergence Diagram of BP NN with Conjugate Gradient Algorithm

We perform LOOCV to train, validate, and test the feature set. There is one sample (A3) that is misidentified out of 50 cartridge samples, indicating that the accuracy of positive identification is 98%. Clearly, the model of BP NN with conjugate gradient algorithm can classify the cartridge images with very high accuracy.

6 Conclusion and Future Work

This paper presents a novel intelligent system for cartridge identification. The cartridge images are taken using the single wavelength ring light. The images are transformed into binary images using different techniques, including contrast enhancement, Sobel edge detection method, image binarization using Otsu, and so on. Our ultimate goal is to develop an intelligent firearm identification system that can identify both ballistics projectile and cartridge cases. The quality of ballistics cartridge images heavily depends on the types of illumination. Even though several illuminators have been used in this research, it is worthwhile to further investigate the influence of the conditions of illumination. The 3D imaging techniques can produce more accurate surface profiling of characteristic markings on cartridge cases and projectiles. Clearly, 3D diagrams can provide more unique characteristics that relate to a specific firearm. The further development for comparing 3D diagrams is highly demanded for precisely recognizing the unique features of individual firearm.

References

1. Bachrach, B.: Development of a 3D-based Automated Firearms Evidence Comparison System. Journal of Forensic Sciences 47(6), 1–12 (2002)
2. Charalambous, C.: Conjugate Gradient Algorithm for Efficient Training of Artificial Neural Networks. IEEE Proceedings 139(3), 301–310 (1992)
3. Geradts, Z., Bijhold, J., Hermsen, R.: Pattern Recognition in a Database of Cartridge Cases. In: Proc. SPIE, vol. 3576, pp. 104–115 (1999)
4. Gonzalez, R.C., Woods, R.E.: Digital Image Processing, 3rd edn. Pearson Prentice Hall, London (2007)
5. Hu, M.K.: Visual Pattern Recognition by Moment Invariants. IRE Trans. Information Theory 8, 179–187 (1962)
6. Jacobs, R.A.: Increased Rates of Convergence through Learning Rate Adaptation. Neural Networks 1(4), 295–308 (1988)
7. Kong, J., Li, D., Watson, A.C.: A Firearm Identification System Based on Neural Network. In: Gedeon, T(T.) D., Fung, L.C.C. (eds.) AI 2003. LNCS (LNAI), vol. 2903, pp. 315–326. Springer, Heidelberg (2003)
8. Kou, C., Tung, C.T., Fu, H.C.: Fisofm: firearms identification based on sofm model of neural network. In: Proceedings. The Institute of Electrical and Electronics Engineers 28th Annual 1994 International Carnahan Conference on Security Technology, pp. 120–125 (1994)
9. Li, D.: Ballistics Projectile Images Analysis for Firearm Identification. The IEEE Transactions on Image Processing 15(10), 2857–2865 (2006)
10. Otsu, N.: A Threshold Selection Method from Gray-Level Histograms. IEEE Transactions on Systems, Man and Cybernetics 9(1), 62–66 (1979)
11. Schwartz, A.: A Systemic Challenge to the Reliability and Admissibility of Firearms and Toolmark Identification. The Columbia Science and Technology Law Review VI, 1–42 (2005)
12. Smith, C.L.: Fireball: A Forensic Ballistics Imaging System. In: Proc. of IEEE 31st Annu. Int. Carnahan Security Technology, pp. 64–70 (1997)
13. Smith, C.L.: Linescan Imaging of Ballistics Projectile Markings for Identification. In: Proc. of IEEE 36th Annual 2002 International Carnahan Conference on Security Technology, pp. 216–222 (2002)
14. Smith, C.L., Li, D.: Intelligent imaging of forensic ballistics specimens for id. In: Proc. of the 2008 Congress on Image and Signal Processing, vol. 3, pp. 37–41 (2008)
15. Vogl, T.P., Mangis, J.K., Zigler, A.K., Ziink, W.T., Alkon, D.L.: Accelerating the Convergence of the Backpropagation Method. Biological Cybernetics 59, 256–264 (1988)
16. Zographos, A., Robinson, M., Evans, J.P.O., Smith, C.L.: Ballistics Identification using Line-Scan Imaging Techniques. In: IEEE Int. Carnahan Conf. Security Technology Canberra, Australia, pp. 82–87 (1997)

A-IFSs Entropy Based Image Multi-thresholding

Pedro Couto[1], Humberto Bustince[2], Miguel Pagola[2], Aranzazu Jurio[2], and Pedro Melo-Pinto[1]

[1] CITAB - UTAD University
Quinta dos Prados, 5001-801 Vila Real, Portugal
pcouto@utad.pt
[2] UPNA - Dept. de Automática y Computación,
Campus de Arrosadía, s/n, 31006 Pamplona, Spain

Abstract. In this work, a computationally efficient segmentation framework is proposed. The proposed methodology is able to auto determine the optimal number of required thresholds in order to achieve a good and accurate segmentation. Atanassov's intuitionistic fuzzy sets and intuitionistic fuzzy entropy in particular, play an important role in the determination of both the threshold value and the number of required thresholds. Experimental results and their evaluation according to uniformity measures are presented.

1 Introduction

Image segmentation, due to its importance in many image applications and due to the difficulty in finding and algorithm that performs well for all kinds of images, is still an important research field.

Recently, fuzzy sets theory and Atanassov's intuitionistic fuzzy sets have been sucessfully applied to image segmentation and, within the framework of fuzzy theory [3,6,9,10,12,13,15] the most popular thresholding algorithms are those that use the concept of fuzzy entropy [3,9,8].

In previous works [5,7] we have presented some new approaches to image thresholding based on A-IFSs [1,2,4]. In these works, Atanassov's intuitionistic fuzzy index values are used for representing the uncertainty on determining whether a pixel of the image belongs to the background or the object of the image.

In the present work, we present an extension of the general image thresholding framework presented in [5,7] intended for multi-level image segmentation that is also able to determine the number of computed thresholds. The determination of the number of computed thresholds is based on the intuitionistic fuzzy entropy values of the regions pixels in the image.

2 Proposed Methodology

The proposed methodology uses a divide and conquer strategy that successively divides the image into n sub-images by means of a threshold that is computed

N. García-Pedrajas et al. (Eds.): IEA/AIE 2010, Part III, LNAI 6098, pp. 341–349, 2010.

using the general framework for image thresholding presented in [5,7] that, considering an image Q with L gray levels, is made up of the following steps:

- Construct L fuzzy sets associated with the image Q for representing the background of the image.
- Construct L fuzzy sets associated with the image Q for representing the object of the image.
- Represent the unknowledge/ignorance of the expert in the construction of the fuzzy sets by means of Atanassov's intuitionistic fuzzy index.
- Construct the L Atanassov intuitionistic fuzzy sets associated with the background of the image.
- Calculate the entropy ε_T of each one of the L A-IFSs.
- Take as best threshold the gray value associated with the A-IFS of lowest entropy ε_T.

This algorithm will be referred as the thresholding algorithm. At this point it is important to stress that this algorithm uses intuitionistic entropy in the same sense as fuzzy entropy is used in fuzzy algorithms and, most of all, the choice of the threshold value is based on the image gray levels entropy values.

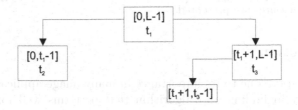

Fig. 1. Algorithm's computational process progress

In Fig. 1 the computational process of the proposed methodology is shown. In this example, the thresholding algorithm is applied to an image with gray levels $\in \{0, 1, \cdots, L-1\}$ resulting in the determination of the threshold value t_i that corresponds to the image gray-level of lowest entropy. Using the value of t_i the image is divided in two sub-images: the sub-image that contains all the pixels with gray levels less or equal to t_i and, the sub-image that contains all the pixels with gray levels greater than t_i. At this stage, one of the sub-images is selected for further processing (application of the thresholding algorithm). The selected sub-image is the one that has the greatest amplitude between gray-levels entropy values (sub-image with the greatest difference between the gray-level of maximum entropy and the one of minimum entropy). Each sub-image can only be sub-divided once.

These sub-divisions will be made $n-1$ times and, in order endow the algorithm with the capability of auto-stopping the process, a stopping criteria based on the sub-images gray levels entropy values was established. To better illustrate this stopping criteria, in Fig. 2 a flow chart of the algorithm is shown and, a detailed description of the flow chat blocks is given in section 2.1.

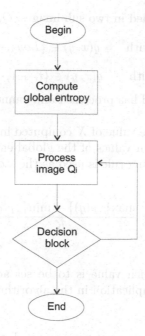

Fig. 2. Algorithm's flowchart

2.1 Algorithm Description

Being (x, y) the coordinates of each pixel on the image Q, and being $q(x, y)$ the gray level of the pixel (x, y) so that $0 \le q(x, y) \le L-1$ for each $(x, y) \in Q$ where L is the image grayscale, the implementation of the flow chart blocks of Fig. 2 goes as follows:

Compute global entropy Block: Calculate the global entropy $\varepsilon_T(q)$ of all $q(x, y) \in \{0, 1, \cdots, L-1\}$ of the original image Q.

Process image Q_i Block: In this block, the threshold value t_i for the image Q_i with gray-levels $q(x, y) \in \{Low_i, \cdots, High_i\}$ is computed. Note that, in the first iteration, the image Q_i will be the original image with gray-levels $q(x, y) \in \{Low_i, \cdots, High_i\}$ where $Low_i = 0$ and $High_i = L-1$. This computed threshold is the gray-level of lowest local entropy (see [5,7]), meaning that, this entropy values are calculated taking into account only the pixels of the sub-image Q_i, that is, the pixels with gray-levels $q(x, y) \in \{Low_i, \cdots, High_i\}$.

At this stage, using the maximum value of the global entropy $\varepsilon_T(q)$ for image Q_i, that is, for all $q(x, y) \in \{Low_i, \cdots, High_i\}$ and the global entropy $\varepsilon_T(t_i)$ of the computed threshold, the following value is computed and stored for later use in the decision block:

$$X = |\varepsilon_T(t_i) - \max\{\varepsilon_T(q)\}|$$

Then, the image Q_i is divided in two sub-images, Q_{i+1} and Q_{i+2}:

$$Q_{i+1} \quad \text{with} \quad q(x,y) \in \{Low_i, \cdots, t_i - 1\}$$

$$Q_{i+2} \quad \text{with} \quad q(x,y) \in \{t_i + 1, \cdots, High_i\}$$

Finally, image Q_i is marked has processed and cannot be processed again.

Decision Block: Using the value of X computed in the previous block and the maximum and the minimum values of the global entropy $\varepsilon_T(q)$ of all $q(x,y) \in \{0, 1, \cdots, L-1\}$ the following rule is used as the stopping criteria:

IF

$$X \geq \frac{\max\{\varepsilon_T(q)\} - \min\{\varepsilon_T(q)\}}{K},$$

$$\forall q(x,y) \in \{0, 1, \cdots, L-1\}.$$

where K is a constant which value is to be set according to the purpose of the algorithm. It's value implication in the algorithm performance will be later discussed.

THEN

calculate, for all the sub-images not yet processed, the following value:

$$Y_{Q_i} = \max\{\varepsilon_T(q)\} - \min\{\varepsilon_T(q)\},$$

$$\forall q(x,y) \in \{Low_i, \cdots, High_i\}.$$

and, select the sub-image of lowest Y_{Q_i} to be processed next.

ELSE

stop the algorithm.

Overview: The algorithm stops when the difference between the entropy of the computed threshold value t_i and the maximum entropy of the sub-image that generated it, is inferior to the difference between the maximum and minimum entropies of the entire image divided by K. When this occurs, since this sub-image was chosen because the difference between its gray-level of maximum entropy and the one of minimum entropy was greater then all the other sub-images, under our interpretation, there's no need of further sub-divisions and, no other sub-image is processed.

3   Results and Evaluation

In order to test the performance of the proposed approach, a hundred randomly selected images from image databases http://www.cs.cmu.edu/~cil/vision.html and http://www.eecs.berkeley.edu/Research/Projects/CS/vision/grouping/segbench/ were used as test images. In Fig. 3 we show a small representation of the set of tested images, namely, a nine images set, witch we will use

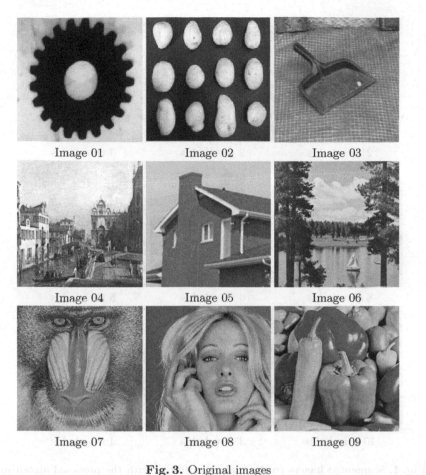

Image 01   Image 02   Image 03

Image 04   Image 05   Image 06

Image 07   Image 08   Image 09

Fig. 3. Original images

to illustrate the results of the presented algorithm. In the presented results the value of the constant K was set to 2 after experimental tests. However, the value of this constant can be changed in order to fine tune the algorithm according to the application where the algorithm is to be applied, since this value is directly related with the number of computed thresholds.

To evaluate the performance of the proposed algorithm the generalized uniformity measure (UM) [14,11,16] of Eq. 1 was used:

$$UM = 1 - \frac{1}{N \times M} \times U \tag{1}$$

Where,

$$U = \sum_{j=0}^{T} \sum_{(x,y)\in R_j} \frac{|A_j|}{|A|} \cdot \frac{(q(x,y) - \nabla_j)^2}{(q_{max} - q_{min})^2}$$

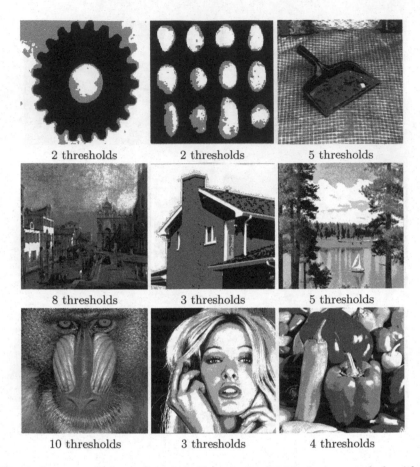

2 thresholds	2 thresholds	5 thresholds
8 thresholds	3 thresholds	5 thresholds
10 thresholds	3 thresholds	4 thresholds

Fig. 4. Segmented images (n thresholds), obtained with the proposed algorithm

In Eq. 1, T is the number of thresholds, R_j is the jth segmented region, $|A_j|$ is the pixel area of the jth segmented region, $|A|$ is image pixel area, $q(x, y)$ is the gray level of the pixel (x, y), ∇_j is the mean of gray levels of the pixel in the segmented region j, $N \times M$ is the image total number of pixels and, q_{max} and q_{min} are, respectively, the maximum and minimum gray levels of the image pixels.

The performance measurement value $UM \in [0, 1]$ assumes the value 1 when the segmentation is optimal and this value decreases as the segmentation quality decreases.

The numerical values of the performance measure value UM for the segmented images shown in Fig. 4, the number of computed thresholds and their gray values are presented in Table 1.

The segmented images at Fig. 4 and the uniformity measure values in Table 1 show that the proposed algorithm performs well in multi-level thresholding making it a suitable algorithm for segmentation applications. Results show that the

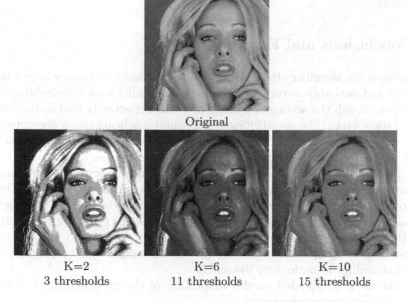

Original

K=2   K=6   K=10
3 thresholds   11 thresholds   15 thresholds

Fig. 5. Segmented images (n thresholds), obtained with different K values

Table 1. Numerical values

Image n°	of thresholds	threshold gray levels	UM values
01	2	71;203	0.998970
02	2	158;218	0.994199
03	5	87;124;148;164;181	0.999661
04	8	67;96;168;228;239;245;248;251	0.999404
05	3	97;163;204	0.999096
06	5	45;61;113;182;202	0.999334
07	10	51;69;94;129;160;177;187;194;199;203	0.999720
08	3	94;130;164	0.998936
09	4	67;127;166;185	0.998990

algorithm computed more thresholds, i.e. divided the images in more regions, for the more complex images (images 4 and 7) and less thresholds for simpler images (images 1 and 2) which denote less complexity/multiplicity regarding their gray levels.

For segmenting the images in Fig. 4, the value of K was set to 2 but, other values could have been chosen. The setting of this value is of uttermost importance since it is closely related to the number of computed thresholds. To better illustrate this relation, in Fig. 5 the results of segmenting the same image with different K values are shown. Looking at Fig. 5 it is clear that for higher values of K the algorithm produces a higher number of thresholds.

Moreover, the algorithm is computationally efficient, having sub-second execution times.

4   Conclusions and Future Work

A segmentation algorithm that works well for all kind of images is yet to be proposed and probably never will. In this work a multi-level thresholding algorithm that, trough the setting of a constant K, can effectively lead us to optimal segmentation within the specificities of particular applications, is presented.

The proposed methodology successively apply the thresholding algorithm presented in [5,7] an undetermined number of times to an image, subdividing the image into several disjoined regions. Regarding time efficiency and uniformity measures, the algorithm shows a good performance. Moreover, the algorithm is able to auto-determine the number of required thresholds in order to achieve a good segmentation depending on the application where the algorithm is to be applied.

Experimental results show that all the tested images can be properly segmented according to uniformity measures.

Further work is intended on the adaptation of the proposed methodologies towards color image segmentation.

References

1. Atanassov, K.: Intuitionistic fuzzy sets. VII ITKR's Session, Deposed in Central Sci. Techn. Library of Bulg. Acd. of Sci., Sofia, pp. 1684–1697 (1983)
2. Atanassov, K.: Intuitionistic fuzzy sets. Fuzzy Sets and Systems 20, 87–96 (1986)
3. Bezdek, J., Keller, J., Krisnapuram, R., Pal, N.: Fuzzy Models and algorithms for pattern recognition and image processing. The Handbooks of Fuzzy Sets Series. Kluwer Academic Publishers, Dordrecht (1999)
4. Burillo, P., Bustince, H.: Construction theorems for intuitionistic fuzzy sets. Fuzzy Sets and Systems 84, 271–281 (1996)
5. Bustince, H., Pagola, M., Melo-Pinto, P., Barrenechea, E., Couto, P.: Image threshold computation by modelizing knowledge/unknowledge by means of A-IFSs. In: Fuzzy Sets and Their Extensions: Representation, Aggregation and Models, Studies in Fuzziness and Soft Computing, pp. 627–644. Springer, Heidelberg (2007)
6. Chi, Z., Yan, H., Pham, T.: Optimal image thresholding. In: Fuzzy algorithms: with application to image processing and pattern recognition, pp. 45–84 (1998)
7. Couto, P.: Image segmentation using Atanassov intuitionistic fuzzy sets. PhD thesis, Trás-os-Montes e Alto Douro University, Vila Real, Portugal (2006)
8. Forero, M.: Fuzzy thresholding and histogram analysis. In: Fuzzy Filters for Image Processing, pp. 129–152. Springer, Heidelberg (2003)
9. Huang, L., Wang, M.: Image thresholding by minimizing the measure of fuzziness. Pattern Recognition 28(1), 41–51 (1995)
10. Jan, J., Sun, C., Mizutani, E.: Fuzzy sets. Neuro-fuzzy and Soft Computing, 13–46 (1997)

11. Levine, M., Nazif, A.: Dynamic measurement of computer generated image segmentations. IEEE Transactions on Pattern Analysis and Machine Intelligence 7, 155–164 (1985)
12. Lin, C., Lee, G.: Fuzzy measures. In: Neural fuzzy systems: A neuro-fuzzy synergism to intelligent systems, pp. 63–88. Prentice Hall, Upper Saddle River (1996)
13. Pal, N., Pal, S.: A review on image segmentation techniques. Pattern Recognition 26, 1277–1294 (1993)
14. Sezgin, M., Sankur, B.: Survey over image thresholding techniques and quantitative performance evaluation. Journal of Electronic Imaging 13(1), 146–165 (2004)
15. Zenzo, S., Cinque, L., Levialdi, S.: Image thresholding using fuzzy entropies. IEEE Transactions on Systems, Man and Cybernetics 28(1), 15–23 (1998)
16. Zhang, Y.: A survey on evaluation methods for image segmentation. Pattern Recognition 29(8), 1335–1346 (1996)

Method for Polygonal Approximation through Dominant Points Deletion

A. Carmona-Poyato, R. Medina-Carnicer, N.L. Fernandez-Garcia,
F.J. Madrid-Cuevas, and R. Muñoz-Salinas

Departament of Computing and Numerical Analisis, Cordoba University, Spain
malcapoa@uco.es

Abstract. A method for polygonal approximation of digital planar curves is proposed. This method is relied on the supression of dominant points. Initially, the method uses the set of all breakpoints as dominant points. The method eliminates dominant points until a final condition is satisfied. The residuary dominant points are the polygonal approximation. This aproximation is compared with other classical algorithms. The experimental results show that this method works well for digital planar curves with features of several sizes.

Keywords: Computer vision, digital planar curves, polygonal approximation, dominant points.

1 Introduction

Dominant points detection is an important research area in contour methods of shape analysis [1]. Joining the dominant points a polygonal approximation is obtained. The advantages of using dominant points in computer vision are clear: in an aerial image, dominant points indicate man-made objects; in a time sequence, dominant points can be used to compute the displacement between each pair of consecutive images [7].

Polygonal approximation is used in important recognition planar object applications:

- Goyal et al. [4] for recognition of numerals of car number plates and aircrafts.
- Grumbach et al. [5] for representation of geographic information.
- Semyonov [20] for electrooculographic biosignal processing.
- Shape understanding [1].
- Image analysis by providing a set of feature points [14].
- Image matching algorithms [8,21,25].

In this paper a method, relied on dominant points deletion, to obtain an efficient polygonal approximation is proposed. To obtain the initial set of dominant points, all the collinear points are deleted. For deletion of redundant dominant points a variable distance as threshold value is used. An iterative process is used, varying the threshold value, until a final condition is satisfied.

N. García-Pedrajas et al. (Eds.): IEA/AIE 2010, Part III, LNAI 6098, pp. 350–358, 2010.

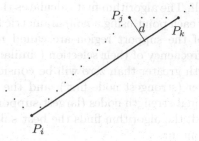

Fig. 1. Support region of point P_i and unit vectors to compute bending value r_i

In sections 2 and 3 the compared methods and proposed methods are described. The experimental results are shown in section 4 and, finally, the main conclusions are summarized in section 5.

2   Dominant Point Detection

Dominants points are usually identified as the points with local extreme curvature. In the continous case, the curvature of a point is defined as the rate of change between the tangent angle and the arc length:

$$\kappa = \frac{d\theta}{ds} \qquad (1)$$

In discrete space, many algorithms have been proposed to estimate the curvature using the neighboring points. Those neighboring points are designated as region of support of a point.

Teh and Chin [22] used the ratio of distance between P_i and the chord P_{i-k}, P_{i+k} ($d_{i,k}$), and the length of the chord ($l_{i,k}$), to determine the support region. This ratio can be considered a measure equivalent to curvature.

Ray and Ray [15] proposed a k−cosine ([17]) based method to estimate the support region.

Cornic[3] proposed an adaptive algorithm that does not rely on curvature to detect dominant points. The main idea is to measure the significance of each point for describing the contour and to evaluate this significance not by the point itself but by the other points of the curve.

Latecki et al. [9] proposed a method based in the supression of vertex with minimal relevance measure, using a discrete curve evolution (DCE). Relevance measure was based on difference in the lenght of neighboring vertices and their turn angle.

Wu [23] proposed a simple measurement to detect corners. He used an adaptive bending value to determine the region of support of each point in the contour. The estimated curvature can be obtained by smoothing bending value.

Marji and Siy [10] proposed a new algorithm that detects a set of dominant points of a contour, which constitute the vertices of a polygonal approximation of the contour itself. The algorithm first calculates the independent left and right support region for each point using a nonparametric least-squares error criterion. The end points of the support region are called *nodes* and their strength is measured by the frecuency of their selection (similar to Cornic's method). Only nodes with strength greater than zero will be considered. The nodes are sorted in descending order (strongest node first), and the length of support region is used to sort the equal-strength nodes (largest support region first). Once the set of nodes are sorted, the algorithm finds the best subset of these nodes that can cover the entire contour.

Carmona et al. [2] proposed a new algorithm to search for dominant points using some significant measure other than curvature. First the support region for each point was calculated. Left and right support regions for each point were independents. An adaptive bending value, r_i, to calculate the estimated curvature in a point P_i was used. If the value of r_i is 0 or close to 0, the i-th point is on a straight line and cannot be considered a corner. If the value of r_i is 1 or close to 1, the i-th point can be considered a corner. The corner points are the candidates of dominant points. P_i is considered a dominant point if r_i is a local maximum and the highest value in its support region. Therefore, a dominant point can only exist in a support region of a point.

Masood [11,12] proposed a new method relied in dominant point deletion. An initial set of dominant point was used. All the break points were selected as initial set, because they produce a zero deviation from original contour, wich was the basic requeriment of his algorithm. He obtained these break points using Freeman's chain code. Deletion of any dominant point would increase the sum of squared error ISE (distance of all curve points from polygonal approximation). Perpendicular squared distance of any point $P_k(x_k, y_k)$ from the straight line conecting the point $P_i(x_i, y_i)$ and $P_j(x_j, y_j)$ is calculated as:

$$\frac{((x_k - x_i)(y_j - y_i) - (y_k - y_i)(x_j - x_i))^2}{(x_i - x_j)^2 + (y_i - y_j)^2} \tag{2}$$

He used an algorithm, where the dominant point, that increased a minimum value of ISE, was deleted.

Masood [13] improved his method, using a local optimization algorithm to reduce the error (ISE), after each deletion.

2.1   Efficiency of Dominant Points Detectors

The quality of polygonal approximation can be measured by the amount of original dominant points reduction and the closeness to original boundary. These measures are the two most important used for assesing the results of polygonal approximation algorithms. For this reason many authors [19,23,24,10] used these measures to evaluate the efficiency of dominant points detectors, and to compare them. These measures are:

- Compresion Ratio (CR).

$$CR = \frac{n}{n_d} \tag{3}$$

where n is the number of points in the contour, and n_d is the number of points of the polygonal approximation. A small number of dominant points implies a large compression ratio.

- Sum of square error (ISE). This is defined as

$$ISE = \sum_{i=1}^{n} e_i^2 \qquad (4)$$

where e_i is the distance from P_i to the approximated line segment.

- Sarkar [19] combined these two measures as a ratio, producing a normalized figure of merit (FOM). This is defined as

$$FOM = \frac{CR}{ISE} \qquad (5)$$

- Maximum error $(MaxErr)$. ISE can hide large error at particular point due to closeness of the polygonal approximation to other parts of the curve. This is not desirable which may result in hiding important features of given boundary. Therefore maximum error is also an important error measurement.

Rosin [18] shows that the two terms in FOM are not balanced causing the measure to be biased towards approximations with lower ISE (which can be easily attained by increasing the number of detected dominant points) and hence is not the best measure for comparing contours with different numbers of dominant points.

To avoid this problem, Marji and Syi [10] used a modified version of this measure. The new measure is defined as

$$WE_2^x = \frac{E_2}{CR^x} \qquad (6)$$

where x is used to control the contribution of the denominator to the overall result in order to reduce the imbalance between the two terms. They used $x = 1$, 2 and 3.

3   Proposed Method

Our method first estimates the original set of dominant points, by deletion of the collinear points. Using an iterative algorithm, the redundant dominant points are deleted according to the following steps:

1. An initial distance d_t is set as threshold value.
2. An initial point P_{ini} is estimated to begin the iterations. Horng [6] pointed out the significance of the initial point to achieve the minimum error fitting. The initial point must be within the final set of dominant points. To estimate the initial point, the dominant point which sum of distances to next and previous break point is maximum is selected.

3. The redundant dominant points, with a distance (d) lower than threshold value (d_t), are deleted. This elimination proccess can be summarized as follows:
   - Select initial point as P_i, and the second and third dominant point as P_j and P_k.
   - repeat
     - perpendicular distance d of P_j from the straight line conecting the point P_i and P_k is calculated using equation 2 (Figure 1):
     - if $d <= d_t$ then
     - P_{i+1} is eliminated
     - $j \leftarrow k$ and $k \leftarrow NextDominantPoint$
     - else
     - $i \leftarrow j$, $j \leftarrow k$ and $k \leftarrow NextDominantPoint$
     - end-if
     - until $P_j = P_{ini}$
   - end-repeat
4. increase the threshold value d_t
5. repeat steps 3 to 4 until a final condition is satisfied.

4   Experimental Results

Four contours commonly used curves in many previous and recent studies [12,13,11,2,10,23,24] have been used to obtain experimental results: chromosome,

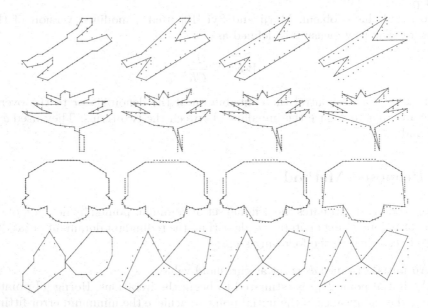

Fig. 2. Dominant points of the chromosome, leaf, semicircle and infinity contours: (a) threshold 0.5, (b) threshold 1.0, (c) threshold 1.5, (d) threshold 2.0

Table 1. Evolution of ratio decrease of length by dominant point in studied contours

Contour	thres.	n	ratio	Contour	thres.	n	ratio	Contour	thres.	n	ratio	Contour	thres.	n	ratio
Chromosome	0.45	23	0.08	Leaf	0.45	41	0.05	Semicircles	0.45	34	0.07	Infinity	0.45	18	0.08
(n=60)	0.52	22	0.01	(n=120)	0.49	40	0.01	(n=102)	0.49	30	0.02	(n=45)	0.52	15	0.03
	0.56	18	0.03		0.56	38	0.01		0.64	26	0.04		0.59	14	0.01
	0.60	16	0.02		0.57	37	0.01		0.66	24	0.01		0.64	13	0.02
	0.64	15	0.01		0.59	36	0.01		0.73	21	0.02		0.69	12	0.01
	0.69	14	0.01		0.64	28	0.05		1.00	18	0.06		0.73	11	0.03
	0.79	13	0.02		0.66	26	0.01		1.41	17	0.03		0.77	10	0.04
	0.90	12	0.02		0.73	23	0.03		1.56	11	0.25		0.98	9	0.03
	0.96	11	0.02		0.75	22	0.01							1.62	8	0.08
	1.48	9	0.11		0.79	21	0.01							1.79	7	0.16
					0.99	19	0.05									
					1.18	18	0.02									
					1.54	17	0.02									
					1.76	16	0.03									
					3.01	14	0.76									

Fig. 3. Dominant points before and after termination condition. The accepted polygonals approximation are shown on the left side.

infinity, leaf and semicircles curves. An initial value 0.5 for distance threshold with a 0.5 increment is used. The resultant contours are shown in figure 2.

Elimination of dominant points can be continued in this way till required level of approximation is obtained. Termination condition can depend upon the requeriments of end user. We propose a termination condition based on the length of the boundary. The length evolution shows the deformation of the boundary when dominant points are eliminated. In the first step, a great number of noisy dominant points are supressed, and the length of the boundary is significatively reduced. The ratio, decrease of length by dominant point, is high. In the next iterations, when threshold is increased, this ratio is reduced and the obtained boundary is very similar to the original boundary. When this ratio is higher than the ratio of the initial iteration, the obtained initial boundary is not properly adjusted to the original boundary, and the termination condition is satisfied.

Table 1 shows the results when different thresholds are considered and termination condition is satisfied.

The resultant contours before and after the termination condition is satisfied are shown in figure 3.

On the right side of the figure 3, we show the non-accepted polygonal approximation, because important dominant points have been eliminated. In shape of chromosome, an important dominant point was deleted in the top of the contour.

Table 2. Comparison with other methods

Contour	Method	n	CR	MaxErr	ISE	FOM
Chromosome	Ray-Ray[15]	18	3.33	0.71	5.57	0.60
	Ray-Ray[16]			0.65	4.81	0.69
	Latecki and Lakamper[9]			1.99	27.06	0.12
	Masood[12]			0.52	2.88	1.16
	Masood[13]			0.51	2.83	1.18
	Proposed			0.51	3.01	1.11
	Latecki and Lakamper[9]	16	3.75	1.98	32.02	0.12
	Wu[24]			0.69	4.70	0.61
	Masood[12]			0.52	3.84	0.98
	Masood[13]			0.63	3.49	1.07
	Proposed			0.51	3.97	0.95
	Teh and Chin[22]	15	4.00	0.74	7.20	0.56
	Latecki and Lakamper[9]			1.98	38.58	0.10
	Masood[12]			0.63	4.14	0.97
	Masood[13]			0.76	3.88	1.03
	Proposed			0.63	4.27	0.94
	Marji and Siy[10]	12	5.00	0.90	8.03	0.62
	Zhu and Chirlian[26]			0.89	8.92	0.56
	Latecki and Lakamper[9]			2.16	45.61	0.11
	Masood[12]			0.88	7.76	0.65
	Masood[13]			0.79	5.82	0.86
	Proposed			0.89	7.92	0.63
Leaf	Latecki and Lakamper[9]	28	4.20	2.83	54.05	0.08
	Masood[12]			0.66	6.91	0.62
	Masood[13]			0.92	6.19	0.69
	Proposed			0.74	6.83	0.63
	Wu[24]	23	5.22	1.00	20.34	0.26
	Latecki and Lakamper[9]			2.83	60.40	0.09
	Carmona et al.[2]			*	15.63	0.33
	Masood[12]			0.74	10.61	0.49
	Masood[13]			0.92	9.46	0.55
	Proposed			0.74	10.68	0.49
	Marji and Siy[10]	22	5.45	0.78	13.21	0.41
	Latecki and Lakamper[9]			2.83	60.55	0.09
	Masood[12]			0.74	11.16	0.49
	Masood[13]			0.95	10.66	0.51
	Proposed			0.74	11.16	0.49
Semicircles	Cornic[3]	30	3.40	*	9.19	0.37
	Latecki and Lakamper[9]			1.00	4.54	0.75
	Masood[12]			0.49	2.91	1.17
	Masood[13]			0.49	2.64	1.29
	Proposed			0.49	2.91	1.17
	Wu[24]	26	3.92	0.88	9.04	0.43
	Marji and Siy[10]			0.74	9.01	0.44
	Zhu and Chirlian[26]			0.63	4.91	0.80
	Latecki and Lakamper[9]			1.21	13.04	0.30
	Masood[12]			0.63	4.91	0.80
	Masood[13]			0.49	4.05	0.97
	Proposed			0.63	4.91	0.80
Infinity	Teh-Chin[22]	13	3.46	*	5.93	0.58
	Wu[24]			1.11	5.78	0.60
	Proposed			0.63	2.65	1.30
	Cornic[3]	10	4.50	*	4.30	1.05
	Carmona et al.[2]			*	5.56	0.81
	Proposed			0.90	5.29	0.90

(*)Value not provided

In shape of leaf, a important peak was deleted. In shape of semicircles, the little down semicircles have lost its shape. In shape of infinity an important dominant point was deleted in the bottom of the contour.

Due to the proposed method can obtain polygonal approximation with different number of dominant points, the approximation was performed such that the number of dominant points is equal to the dominant points of compared algorithm. Comparative results, with other methods, for the popular boundaries of chromosome, leaf, infinity and semicircles are listed in table 2.

For the shape of chromosome, results of proposed algorithm are listed (in table 2), with 18, 16, 15 and 12 dominant points to compare with other algorithms. From this table, maximum error ($MaxErr$) of proposed method is less than or equal to all algorithms except for Masood [12,13] with 12 dominant points. The best results are obtained by the Masood algorithm [13], followed by our proposed method, which is better than the rest of algorithms, in ISE and FOM.

For the shape of leaf, results of proposed algorithm are listed (in table 2), with 28, 23 and 22 dominant points. From this table, maximum error ($MaxErr$) of proposed method is less than or equal to all algorithms except for Masood [13] with 28 dominant points. Masood algorithm [12] was similar, the other Masood algorithm [13] was the best, and the proposed method is better than the rest of algorithms, in ISE and FOM.

For the shape of semicircles, results of proposed algorithm are listed (in table 2), with 30 and 26 dominant points to compare with other algorithms. From this table, maximum error ($MaxErr$) of proposed method is less than or equal to all algorithms except for Masood [13] with 26 dominant points. Masood algorithm [12] was similar, the other Masood algorithm [13] was the best, and the proposed method is better than the rest of algorithms, in ISE and FOM.

Finally, for the shape of infinity, the results of proposed algorithm are listed (in table 2), with 13 and 10 dominant points. Maximum error ($MaxErr$) of proposed method is less than all algorithms. The proposed method is better than the rest of algorithms, in ISE and FOM.

The proposed algorithm produces very good results, similar to the best algorithms, when the number of dominant points is higher than 20 or lower than 12.

5   Conclusions

An efficient and simple approach to polygonal approximation is presented in this paper. Initially, our method calculates all the dominant points. The redundant dominant points are deleted when they are quasi-collinear points with previous and next dominant points. For this propose a threshold distance is used. This threshold is increased until a termination condition is satisfied. The algorithm produces efficient polygonal approximations with different number of dominant points. This algorithm have been compared with some recent and commonly referred algorithms. The results are similar to Masood algorithm [12,11] and better than other compared algorithms. The results only are worse than optimizated Masood algorithm [13], but this algorithm has more computational complexity than proposed algorithm because it uses an optimization algorithm.

References

1. Attneave, F.: Some informational aspects of visual perception. Phychol. Rev. 61, 189–193 (1954)
2. Carmona-Poyato, A., Fernandez-Garcia, N.L., Medina-Carnicer, R., Madrid-Cuevas, F.J.: Dominant point detection: A new proposal. Image and Vision Computing 23, 1226–1236 (2005)
3. Cornic, P.: Another look at dominant point detection of digital curves. Pattern Recognition Letters 18, 13–25 (1997)
4. Goyal, S., Kumar, M.P., Jawahar, C.V., Narayanam, P.J.: Polygon approximation of closed curves across multipleviews. In: Indian Conference on Vision, Graphics and Image Processing (2002)

5. Grumbach, S., Rigaux, P., Segoufin, L.: The DEDALE system for complex spatial queries. In: Proceedings of ACM SIGMOD Symposium on the Management of Data, pp. 213–224 (1998)
6. Horng, J.H., Li, J.T.: An automatic and efficient dynamic programming algorithm for polygonal approximation of digital curves. Pattern Recognition Letters 23, 171–182 (2002)
7. Hsin-Teng, S., Wu-Chih, H.: A rotationally invariant two-phase scheme for corner detection. Pattern Recognition 29, 819–828 (1996)
8. Hu, X., Ahuja, N.: Matching point features with ordered geometric, rigidity, and disparity constraints. IEEE Transactions on Pattern Analysis and Machine Intelligence 16, 1041–1049 (1994)
9. Latecki, L.J., Lakamper, R.: Convexity Rule for Shape Decomposition Based on Discrete Contour Evolution. Computer Vision and Image Understanding 73, 441–454 (1999)
10. Marji, M., Siy, P.: Polygonal representation of digital planar curves through dominant point detection – a nonparametric algorithm. Pattern Recognition 37, 2113–2130 (2004)
11. Masood, A., Haq, S.A.: A novel approach to polygonal approximation of digital curves. Journal of Visual Comunication and Image Representation 18, 264–274 (2007)
12. Masood, A.: Dominant point deletion by reverse polygonization of digital curves. Image and Vision Computing 26, 702–715 (2008)
13. Masood, A.: Optimized polygonal approximation by dominant point deletion. Pattern Recognition 41, 227–239 (2008)
14. Neumann, R., Teisseron, G.: Extraction of dominant points by estimation of the contour fluctuations. Pattern Recognition 35, 1447–1462 (2002)
15. Ray, B.K., Ray, K.S.: Detection of significant points and polygonal aproximation of digitized curves. Pattern Recognition Letters 22, 443–452 (1992)
16. Ray, B.K., Ray, K.S.: An algorithm for detecting dominant points and polygonal approximation of digitized curves. Pattern Recognition Letters 13, 849–856 (1992)
17. Rosenfeld, A., Johnston, E.: Angle detection on digital curves. IEEE Transactions on Computers C-22, 875–878 (1973)
18. Rosin, P.L.: Techniques for assesing polygonal approximation of curves. IEEE Transactions on Pattern Analysis and Machine Intelligence 19(6), 659–666 (1997)
19. Sarkar, D.: A simple algorithm for detection of significant vertices for polygonal approximation of chain-coded curves. Pattern Recognition Letters 14, 959–964 (1993)
20. Semyonov, P.A.: Optimized unjoined linear approximation and itsapplication for Eog-biosignal processing. In: 12th IEEE International Conference on Engineering in Medicine and Biology Society, pp. 779–780 (1990)
21. Sethi, I.K., Jain, R.: Finding trajectories of feature points in a monocular image sequence. IEEE Transactions on Pattern Analysis and Machine Intelligence 9, 56–73 (1987)
22. Teh, C.H., Chin, R.T.: On the detection of dominant points on digital curves. IEEE Transactions of Pattern Analysis and Machine Intelligence 11, 859–872 (1989)
23. Wu, W.Y.: Dominant point detection using adaptive bending value. Image and Vision Computing 21, 517–525 (2003)
24. Wu, W.Y.: An adaptive method for detecting dominant points. Pattern Recognition 36, 2231–2237 (2003)
25. Yuen, P.C.: Dominant points matching algorithm. Electronic Letters 29, 2023–2024 (1993)
26. Zhu, P., Chirlian, P.M.: On critical point detection of digital shapes. IEEE Transactions of Pattern Analysis and Machine Intelligence 17(8), 737–748 (1995)

An Integrated Formulation of Zernike Representation in Character Images

Norsharina Abu Bakar, Siti Mariyam Shamsuddin, and Aida Ali

Soft Computing Research Group,
K-Economy Research Alliance
Universiti Teknologi Malaysia, Skudai, Johor
norsharina85@gmail.com, mariyam@utm.my, aida@utm.my

Abstract. Many studies have been done on improving Geometric Moment Invariants proposed by Hu since 1962 for pattern recognition. However, many researchers have found that there are some drawbacks with this geometric moment. Hence, this paper presents an integrated formulation of United Moment and Aspect Moment into Zernike Moment Invariant to seek the invarianceness of the solutions. The proposed method will be validated mathematically and experimentally. The validity invarianceness of the proposed method is measured by conducting the intra-class and inter-class analysis. The results of the proposed method are promising and feasible in identifying the similarity and differences of the images accordingly.

Keywords: Pattern Recognition, Zernike Moment Invariant, Zernike United Aspect Moment Invariant, Intra-class, Inter-class.

1 Introduction

Pattern Recognition can be defined as a study of how machines can observe the environment, can learn to distinguish patterns of interest from their background, and can make sound and reasonable decisions about the categories of patterns [10]. There are few phases involve in typical pattern recognition process. These include preprocessing, feature extraction and classifications. Feature extraction is the most critical step in any pattern recognition domains. There are two types of extracting the features in pattern recognition; either structural approach or global approach. Among the common methods widely used for extracting global shape is Moment Invariant (MI), which was proposed by Hu in 1962 [1]. MI is useful tool for mining the granularity of the global shape such as insect images, character images and others.

However, there are some issues with the usage of geometric scaling [2][6][7][8] of Hu's invariants. Due these shortcomings, this paper proposes mathematical integration of Aspect Moment Invariant and United Moment Invariant into Zernike Moment Invariant. This proposed method is capable of producing promising results for images with unequal scaling that have undergone various orientations and rotations. The remainder of this paper is organized as follows: Section II describes the drawbacks of Geometric Moment Invariants in pattern recognition; Section III provides mathematical integration of Zernike Moments with United Moment Invariant and Aspect

N. García-Pedrajas et al. (Eds.): IEA/AIE 2010, Part III, LNAI 6098, pp. 359–368, 2010.
© Springer-Verlag Berlin Heidelberg 2010

Moment Invariant. Section IV presents the experimental result by using inter-class and intra-class analysis, and finally, Section VI concludes the study.

2   Zernike Moment Invariants in Pattern Recognition

Some other moment functions are widely used in pattern recognition, and these include Legendre moments, Affine moments, Complex moments, Zernike Moments and others. Many comparisons have been done on moment functions by previous researchers in pattern recognition [8][9][11][12]. However, Zernike moments are among the common method widely used for images that undergo various rotations.

Zernike moments are based on the orthogonal functions; polynomial Zernike [5]. This moment has been proven better in terms of offering the ability features and low sensitivity to the noisy phase despite its complex computations. Polynomial Zernike is a set of orthogonal unit sphere and widely used in the analysis of the system optically. Orthogonal set of functions with a simple round function with a more weighted is known as polynomial Zernike, and it is denoted by $Vnl\ (x, y)$. Polynomial Zernike in polar coordinates is given as [9],

$$V_{nl}(x, y) = V_{nl}(r, \phi) = R_{nl}(r)e^{il\phi},$$

with $i = \sqrt{-1}$, and

n : positive integer or empty; i.e. n = 0, 1, 2 ... ∞,

l : integer positive to curb in n - l, including l ≤ n,

R : distance to the vertices of a starting point to pixel (x, y), ie

      where, $r = \sqrt{x^2 + y^2}$,

$\emptyset$: angle between vectors r and the x-axis in the direction of the lap hours, and

$Rnl\ (r)$: radius real value for polynomial can be explained as:

$$R_{nl}(r) = \sum_{s=0}^{(n-l)/2} (-1)^s \cdot \frac{(n-s)!}{s!\left(\frac{n+l}{2} - s\right)!\left(\frac{n-l}{2} - s\right)!} r^{n-2s} .$$

(1.0)

Real radius value for polynomial is written as:

$$R_{nl} = \sum_{\substack{k=1 \\ n-k=even}}^{n} B_{nlk} r^k ,$$

(1.1)

Where,

$$B_{nlk} = (-1)^s \frac{(n-s)!}{s!\left(\frac{n+l}{2} - s\right)!\left(\frac{n-l}{2} - s\right)!}$$

(1.2)

Zernike moments are shown in the form of a concentrated moment as follows [5]:

$$\phi_1(ZM_1) = \frac{3}{\pi}[2(\eta_{20} + \eta_{02} - 1)]$$

$$\phi_2(ZM_2) = \frac{9}{\pi^2}[(\eta_{20} - \eta_{02})^2 + 4\eta_{11}^2]$$

$$\phi_3(ZM_3) = \frac{16}{\pi^2}[(\eta_{03} - 3\eta_{21})^2 + (\eta_{30} - 3\eta_{12}^{\ 2})]$$

$$\phi_4(ZM_4) = \frac{144}{\pi^2}[(\eta_{03} - 3\eta_{21})^2 + (\eta_{30} + \eta_{12})^2]$$

$$\phi_5(ZM_5) = \frac{13824}{\pi^4}\{(\eta_{03} - \eta 3\eta_{21})(\eta_{03} + \eta_{21})[(\eta_{03} + \eta_{21})^2 - 3(\eta_{30} + \eta_{12})^2] - (\eta_{30} - 3\eta_{12})(\eta_{30} + \eta_{12})[(\eta_{30} + \eta_{12})^2 - 3(\eta_{03} + \eta_{21})^2]\}$$

$$\phi_6(ZM_6) = \frac{864}{\pi^3}\{(\eta_{02} - \eta_{20})[(\eta_{30} + \eta_{12})^2 - (\eta_{03} + \eta_{21})^2] + 4\eta_{11}(\eta_{03} + \eta_{21})(\eta_{30} + \eta_{12})\}$$

(1.3)

where η_{pq} is defined as scaling factor from geometrical moments [5],

$$\eta_{pq} = \frac{\mu_{pq}}{(\mu_{00})^{\frac{p+q+2}{2}}}.$$

The detail explanations of the proposed integration are given in the next section.

3   The Proposed Method

United Moment Invariant (UMI) was derived from Geometric Moment Invariant (GMI) (Hu, 1969) and Improve Moment Invariant (IMI) (Chen, 1993). GMI is useful for region representation in discrete condition but high in computational times for boundary representation (Chen, 1993). Therefore, Chen (1993) proposed IMI that is usable for boundary representation which could increase the computation speed [4]. However, Yinan (2003) proposed a new technique that was effective for both region and boundary in discrete and continuous condition [3].

ZMI was outperforming in terms of noise resilience, information redundancy and reconstruction capability. However, ZMI used scaling factor as proposed by Hu (1962) which was proved to be variant for images of unequal scaling. Therefore, the alternative scaling factor of Aspect Moment Invariant (AMI) by Feng and Keane (1994) is used in this study. The rationale of this combinations is due to the invarianceness of Aspect Invariants in dealing images of unequal scaling in X and Y direction [7].

This paper aims to propose integrated solutions of Zernike Moment Invariant, Aspect Moment Invariant and United Moment Invariant that can give better results with various factors such as boundary, region, scaling and rotation accordingly.

In this study, η_{pq} is defined as equal scaling, η'_{pq} represents discrete condition, η''_{pq} is defined as boundary and η'''_{pq} represent unequal scaling. These equations are significant in the integration process for obtaining the invarianceness of the proposed method. This is illustrated in the next paragraph where the invarianceness of $\theta'''_1 = \theta''_1 = \theta'_1 = \theta_1$ is preserved. The process of the integration is shown below.

$$\eta_{pq} = \frac{\mu_{pq}}{(\mu_{00})^{\frac{p+q+2}{2}}},$$

(1.4)

$$\eta'_{pq} = \rho^{p+q}\eta_{pq} = \frac{\rho^{p+q}}{(\mu_{00})^{\frac{p+q+2}{2}}}\mu_{pq},$$

(1.5)

$$\eta''_{pq} = \frac{\mu_{pq}}{(\mu_{00})^{p+q+1}}.$$

(1.6)

$$\eta'''_{pq} = \frac{\mu_{00}^{\frac{p+q}{2}+1}}{\mu_{20}^{\frac{p+q}{2}+1}\mu_{02}^{\frac{p+q}{2}+1}}\mu_{pq}.$$

(1.7)

From the above equation, we find that, each term has μ_{pq}. According to [3], we can contemporary avoid the influence of μ_{00} to obtain the invarianceness. Hence, the eight formulas for United Moment Invariants (UMI) is given as,

$$\theta_1 = \sqrt{\phi_2}/\phi_1 \qquad \theta_2 = \phi_6/\phi_1\phi_4$$
$$\theta_3 = \sqrt{\phi_5}/\phi_4 \qquad \theta_4 = \phi_5/\phi_3\phi_4$$
$$\theta_5 = \phi_1\phi_6/\phi_2\phi_3 \qquad \theta_6 = (\phi_1 + \sqrt{\phi_2})\phi_3/\phi_6,$$
$$\theta_7 = \phi_1\phi_5/\phi_3\phi_6 \qquad \theta_8 = (\phi_3 + \phi_4)/\sqrt{\phi_5}$$

In the proposed integration, the ϕ values are substituted by Zernike's moments as shown in Equation (1.3).

For example,

$$\phi_1 = \frac{3}{\pi} \times [2(\eta_{20} + \eta_{02}) - \eta_{00}]$$
$$= \frac{3}{\pi} \times \left[2\frac{1}{(\mu_{00})^2} \times (\mu_{20} + \mu_{02})\right) - 1\right],$$

$$\phi_2 = \left(\frac{3}{\pi}\right)^2 \times \left[(\eta_{20} - \eta_{02})^2 + 4\eta_{11}^2\right]$$
$$= \frac{9}{\pi^2} \times \left[\frac{1}{(\mu_{00})^4} \times (\mu_{20} - \mu_{02})^2 + 4\mu_{11}^2\right],$$

$$\theta_1 = \frac{\sqrt{\phi_2}}{\phi_1}$$
$$= \frac{\sqrt{\left(\frac{3}{\pi}\right)^2 \times \left[(\eta_{20} - \eta_{02})^2 + 4\eta_{11}^2\right]}}{\frac{3}{\pi} \times [2(\eta_{20} + \eta_{20}) - \eta_{00}]}$$

$$\theta'_1 = \frac{\sqrt{\left(\frac{3}{\pi}\right)^2 \times \left[(\eta'_{20} - \eta'_{02})^2 + 4\eta'_{11}^2\right]}}{\frac{3}{\pi} \times [2(\eta'_{20} + \eta'_{20}) - \eta_{00}]}$$
$$= \frac{\sqrt{\frac{9}{\pi^2} \times \left[\frac{\rho^4}{(\mu_{00})^4} \times \frac{(\mu_{20} - \mu_{02})^2}{(\mu_{00})^2} + 4\mu_{11}^2\right]}}{\frac{3}{\pi} \times \left[2\left(\frac{\rho^2}{(\mu_{00})^2} \times \frac{(\mu_{20} + \mu_{02})}{(\mu_{00})^2}\right) - 1\right]}$$

$$= \frac{\sqrt{\frac{9}{\pi^2} \times \left[\frac{1}{(\mu_{00})^4} \times (\mu_{20} - \mu_{02})^2 + 4\mu_{11}^2\right]}}{\frac{3}{\pi} \times \left[2\left(\frac{1}{(\mu_{00})^2} \times (\mu_{20} + \mu_{02})\right) - 1\right]}$$

$$= \frac{\sqrt{\frac{9}{\pi^2} \times \left[\frac{(\mu_{20} - \mu_{02})^2}{(\mu_{00})^2} + 4\mu_{11}^2\right]}}{\frac{3}{\pi} \times \left[2\left(\frac{(\mu_{20} + \mu_{02})}{(\mu_{00})} \times\right) - 1\right]},$$

$$= \frac{\sqrt{\frac{9}{\pi^2} \times \left[\frac{(\mu_{20} - \mu_{02})^2}{(\mu_{00})^2} + 4\mu_{11}^2\right]}}{\frac{3}{\pi} \times \left[2\left(\frac{(\mu_{20} + \mu_{02})}{(\mu_{00})} \times\right) - 1\right]}$$

$$\theta''_1 = \frac{\sqrt{\left(\frac{3}{\pi}\right)^2 \times \left[(\eta''_{20} - \eta''_{02})^2 + 4\eta''_{11}^2\right]}}{\frac{3}{\pi} \times [2(\eta''_{20} + \eta''_{20}) - \eta_{00}]}$$

$$\theta'''_1 = \frac{\sqrt{\left(\frac{3}{\pi}\right)^2 \times \left[(\eta'''_{20} - \eta'''_{02})^2 + 4\eta'''_{11}^2\right]}}{\frac{3}{\pi} \times [2(\eta'''_{20} + \eta'''_{20}) - \eta_{00}]}$$

$$= \frac{\sqrt{\frac{9}{\pi^2} \times \left[\frac{1}{(\mu_{00})^6} \times (\mu_{20} - \mu_{02})^2 + 4\mu_{11}^2\right]}}{\frac{3}{\pi} \times \left[2\left(\frac{1}{(\mu_{00})^3} \times (\mu_{20} + \mu_{02})\right) - 1\right]},$$

$$= \frac{\sqrt{\frac{9}{\pi^2} \times \left[[(\frac{\mu_{00}^2}{\mu_{20}^{3/2}\mu_{02}^{1/2}})(\mu_{20})] - [(\frac{\mu_{00}^2}{\mu_{20}^{1/2}\mu_{02}^{3/2}})(\mu_{02})]\right]^2 + 4[(\frac{\mu_{00}^2}{\mu_{20}^1\mu_{02}^1})(\mu_{11})]^2}}{\frac{3}{\pi} \times \left[2[(\frac{\mu_{00}^2}{\mu_{20}^{3/2}\mu_{02}^{1/2}})(\mu_{20})](\mu_{20})] + [(\frac{\mu_{00}^2}{\mu_{20}^{1/2}\mu_{02}^{3/2}})(\mu_{02})]\right] - (\frac{\mu_{00}^1}{\mu_{20}^{1/2}\mu_{02}^{1/2}})(\mu_{00})}$$

$$= \frac{\sqrt{\frac{9}{\pi^2} \times \left[\frac{(\mu_{20} - \mu_{02})^2}{(\mu_{00})^2} + 4\mu_{11}^2\right]}}{\frac{3}{\pi} \times \left[2\left(\frac{(\mu_{20} + \mu_{02})}{(\mu_{00})} \times\right) - 1\right]}$$

$$= \frac{\sqrt{\frac{9}{\pi^2} \times \left[\frac{(\mu_{20} - \mu_{02})^2}{(\mu_{00})^2} + 4\mu_{11}^2\right]}}{\frac{3}{\pi} \times \left[2\left(\frac{(\mu_{20} + \mu_{02})}{(\mu_{00})} \times\right) - 1\right]}$$

From the above derivations, we found that $\theta'''_1 = \theta''_1 = \theta'_1 = \theta_1$. Hence, this has proven that θ_1 can be applied for both region and boundary in discrete and continues condition for variation of orientation with unequal scaling data.

4 Experimental Design

Fig 1 shows the example standard database for character images that used in this study. All the characters are scanned with 300 dpi (dot per inch) and 150 dpi resolutions.

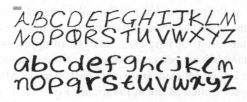

Fig. 1. Sample of Characters

Table 1 shows the criteria's of the character images that will used in this study. This images must cover all characteristics among these methods (Zernike Moment Invariant, Aspect Moment Invariant and United Moment Inavariant) to get the effectiveness result for this study.

Table 1. Characteristics of the images

Images	Charaterictics
	Criteria of United Moment Invariant -Usable in region images -Usable in boundary images
	Criteria of Aspect Moment Invariant -Covered the unequal scaling data $x1 \neq x2, y1 \neq y2$
	Criteria of Zernike Moment Invariant -Covered the rotation images

5 Result and Analysis

The invariancess of the proposed integrated formulations is presented in terms of intra-class and the inter-class concept.In this study, invarianceness is defined as the best result for the intra-class and inter-class analysis. These analysis cover the shape and rotation of unequal scaling images. The measurements are based on Mean Absolute Error (MAE) as given below:

$$MAE = \frac{1}{n}\sum_{i=1}^{n}\left|(x_i - r_i)\right|,$$

where n is number of image, x_i is the current image and r_i is the reference image. In our study, the first image is the reference image.

5.1 Intra-class Analysis

Intra-class is defined as the process that gives similar images with smaller MAE values. Table 2 shows the result for intra-class analysis of lowercase character images and Table 3 depicts the result for intra-class analysis of uppercase character images. In this study, four methods have been conducted for comparisons (AMI: Aspect Moment Invariant, UMI: United Moment Invariant, ZMI: Zernike Moment Invariant and ZAUMI: Zernike Aspect United Moment Invariant). From these tables, it shows that the bold words give smaller MAE values.

Table 2. Intra-Class Analysis (lowercase character images)

	AMI	UMI	ZMI	ZAUMI
a	1.683299	2.820876	4.899467	**0.475941**
b	4.06097	2.675798	38.36238	**1.229013**
c	**1.418656**	0.531447	7.241842	3.523945
d	1.921816	0.933289	9.500966	**0.767127**
e	1.21639	0.653731	1.437383	**0.385327**
f	3.22597	**1.711614**	9.485567	7.033327
g	2.360283	0.863246	5.449352	**0.650749**
h	1.098175	**0.680351**	27.21004	0.790359
j	3.493187	**0.996929**	59.52517	1.596386
i	2.676193	**1.713414**	83.31634	2.398335
k	1.085357	1.774266	8.666278	**0.678246**
l	**1.712419**	2.19402	90.99872	1.872845
m	1.378298	1.406635	4.494424	**1.244012**
n	1.357423	1.297179	15.86073	**1.144767**
o	2.286847	1.575373	2.449911	**0.322856**
p	2.922072	**1.049065**	24.24812	5.024553
q	1.689905	1.184756	3.506299	**0.863837**
r	3.712511	**1.105685**	10.21371	13.12731
s	0.846587	1.642202	6.458625	**0.688386**
t	3.507612	**0.929813**	14.90048	1.61419
u	1.511638	1.248238	6.941306	**0.557261**
v	1.542767	**0.667775**	8.034618	0.76355
w	1.543769	0.967629	9.635414	**0.745195**
x	2.674534	1.535252	3.569825	**0.616772**
y	2.64184	1.150224	11.13917	**0.776925**
Z	2.032676	1.690529	3.920627	**0.486137**

Table 3. Intra-Class Analysis (uppercase character images)

	AMI	UMI	ZMI	ZAUMI
A	2.025344	3.27944	45.16599	**0.788243**
B	3.200387	1.448709	24.95112	**1.084759**
C	1.602722	1.206423	21.97463	**0.604008**
D	1.289315	**0.704838**	16.97781	1.575602
E	1.467166	**0.374994**	35.24637	13.15725
F	**1.287974**	1.368695	8.755773	3.14615
G	1.103529	1.587565	19.89788	**0.596796**
H	1.01371	2.834178	12.76827	**0.353403**
I	2.25128	**1.491554**	30.27587	2.378569
J	0.852756	**0.255395**	2.167779	0.800696
K	1.852554	**0.590778**	6.980908	0.666748
L	1.27848	1.240672	33.57352	**0.839633**
M	1.476325	0.966486	21.99051	**0.751326**
N	2.591287	2.74794	20.15975	**0.60069**
O	2.374956	1.483993	23.86374	**0.711018**
P	1.757894	1.914063	13.9396	**2.784411**
Q	1.7627	2.160555	2.533339	**1.04476**
R	1.685409	**0.88277**	2.431493	0.897634
S	3.384336	1.803952	6.757688	**1.492251**
T	1.781631	1.548865	18.98232	**0.768609**
U	1.048332	**0.783356**	4.185653	0.937166

Table 3. (*Continued*)

	AMI	UMI	ZMI	ZAUMI
V	1.479768	**1.045367**	27.70079	1.36651
W	2.437513	1.098726	3.911504	**0.839645**
X	2.189803	1.805238	8.943161	**0.52088**
Y	1.352667	**0.855837**	32.42845	1.121096
Z	1.650519	0.869527	10.85404	**0.672644**

5.2 Inter-class Analysis

Inter-class is defined as the process of obtaining higher value of MAE with different images. Four comparisons have been conducted for lowercase character images ("w and m", "n and u", "i and l", "d and p") and three comparisons for uppercase character images ("U and V", "W and M", "Z and N"). From Table 4, it shows that Zernike Moment Invariant (ZMI) gives higher values for all characters. Therefore, Zernike Moment Invariant (ZMI) is good for inter-class analysis of character images.

Table 4. Inter-Class Analysis for Characters

Character Images	AMI	UMI	ZMI	ZAUMI
w and m	3.138557	1.474733	**4.129714**	0.771642
n and u	0.545484	0.65454	**24.88633**	1.196048
i and l	2.937681	0.659015	**56.44773**	0.714089
d and p	0.473237	0.04813	**20.30946**	5.105696
U and V	2.676369	2.842667	**10.1573**	0.857431
W and M	2.621361	0.980653	**39.3378**	1.505079
Z and N	1.789902	3.805524	**15.50854**	0.916444

Table 5. Summary of the Results

Technique	Invarianceness	Result	Images
The proposed Integrated Formulation (Zernike United Aspect Moment Invariant)	Intra-class	Better	Uppercase:(A,B,C,G,H,L,M,N,O,P,Q,S,T,W,X,,Z) Lowercase: (a, b, d, e, g, k, m ,n, o, q, s, u, w, x, y, z)
	Inter-class	Bad	All Characters images
Zernike Moment Invariant	Intra-class	Bad	All Characters images
	Inter-class	Better	All Characters images
United Moment Invariant	Intra-class	Better	Uppercase:(D,E,I,J,K,R,U,V,Y) Lowercase:(f, h, j, i , p, r ,t ,v)
	Inter-class	Bad	All Characters images
Aspect Moment Invariant	Intra-class	Better	Uppercase:(F) Lowercase:(c, l)
	Inter-class	Bad	All Characters images

6 Conclusion

In this study, we propose integrated formulations for better invariancenesss. From the experiments, we found that Zernike United Moment Invariants and United Moment Invariants are better in terms of intra-class for characters that are based on various shapes and orientations with unequal scaling. However, Zernike Moment Invariant is good for the inter-class analysis for these characters accordingly. Table 5 summarizes the findings of this study.

For better clarification, we give the definitions of the intra-class analysis as illustrated in fig 2. It defines that:

Better : the techniques have smaller MAE values.
Bad   : the techniques have larger MAE values.

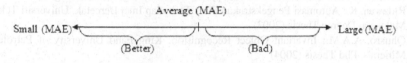

Fig. 2. Intra-class Analysis

Fig 3 provides the definition of inter-class analysis used in this study. It defines that:

Better : the techniques have larger MAE values.
Bad   : the techniques have smaller MAE values.

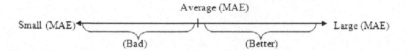

Fig. 3. Inter-class Analysis

Acknowledgments. This work is supported by Ministry of Higher Education (MOHE) under Fundamental Research Grant Scheme (Vote No.78499). Authors would like to thank Research Management Centre (RMC) Universiti Teknologi Malaysia, for the research activities, and *Soft Computing Research Group* (SCRG) for the support in making this study a success.

References

1. Hu, M.-K.: Visual pattern recognition by moment invariants. IRE Transactions on Information Theory 8(2), 179–187 (1962)
2. Muda, A.K., Shamsuddin, S.M., et al.: Invariancenes of higher order united scaled invariants. Advances in Computer Science and Engineering 1(2), 105–118 (2007)

3. Sun, Y., Liu, W., et al.: United moment invariants for shape discrimination. In: Proceedings of 2003 IEEE International Conference on Robotics, Intelligent Systems and Signal Processing (2003)
4. Chen, C.-C.: Improved Moment Invariant for Shape Discrimination. Pattern Recognition 26, 683–686 (1993)
5. Teague, M.R.: Image analysis via the general theory of moments. J. Opt. Soc. Am. 70(8), 920 (1980)
6. Shamsuddin, S.M., Sulaiman, M.N., Darus, M.: Invarianceness of Higher Order Centralised Scaled-invariants Undergo Basic Transformations. International Journal of Computer Mathematics 79, 39–48 (2002)
7. Pang, F., Keane, M.: A new set of moment invariant for Handwritten Numeral Recognition. In: IEEE Intern. Conf. on Image Processsing, pp. 154–158 (1994)
8. Pamungkas, R.P., Shamsuddin, S.M.: Weighted Aspect Moment Invariant in Pattern Recognition. In: Gervasi, O., Taniar, D., Murgante, B., Laganà, A., Mun, Y., Gavrilova, M.L. (eds.) ICCSA 2009. LNCS, vol. 5593, pp. 806–818. Springer, Heidelberg (2009)
9. Ridzwan, K.: Automasi Pengekstrakan Fitur Terhadap Imej Bercetak, Universiti Teknologi Malaysia: Degree Thesis (2003)
10. Qhusro, A.A.M.: Invariant Object Recognition, King Fahd University of Petroleum & Minerals: Phd Thesis (2004)
11. Muda, A.K., Shamsudin, S.M., Darus, M.: Invariants Discretization for Indviduality Representation in Handwriiten Authorship. In: Srihari, S.N., Franke, K. (eds.) IWCF 2008. LNCS, vol. 5158, pp. 218–228. Springer, Heidelberg (2008)
12. Bakar, N.A., Shamsuddin, S.M.: United Zernike Invariants for Character Images. In: Badioze Zaman, H., et al. (eds.) IVIC 2009. LNCS, vol. 5857, pp. 498–509. Springer, Heidelberg (2009)

Aggregation of Color Information in Stereo Matching Problem: A Comparison Study

Mikel Galar*, Miguel Pagola, Edurne Barrenechea, Carlos López-Molina, and Humberto Bustince

Universidad Pública de Navarra,
Campus Arrosadía s/n, 31006, Pamplona, Spain
mikel.galar@unavarra.es

Abstract. In this paper we present a comparison study between different aggregation functions used in stereo matching problem. We add color information from images to the stereo matching algorithm by aggregating the similarities of the RGB channels which are calculated independently. We compare the accuracy of different stereo matching algorithms when using different aggregation functions. We show experimentally that the best function to use depends on the stereo matching algorithm considered.

Keywords: Stereo matching, color, aggregation functions.

1 Introduction

The stereo matching problem consists in obtaining three-dimensional information from two bidimensional images of the same scene taken from different views, trying to imitate the human vision.

To obtain the depth from the two images, we first have to estimate the correspondence between the pixels in each image. This step consist in identifying the same physical point in both projections to determine the difference between the position of this point in each image. This difference is called *disparity*. The disparity together with the parameters of the camera allows us to obtain the depth of the point.

The main problem of the stereo matching is the difficulty to find the correspondence correctly. The images are taken from different cameras with different viewing angles that sometimes produce occlusions, perspective distortion, different lighting intensities, reflections, shadows, repetitive patterns, sensory noise, etc. All these facts convert a simple correspondence task in a very difficult one.

Usually, an ideal configuration of the cameras is supposed, this means that they are only horizontally displaced and the focus lines are parallel. An ideal configuration and epipolar geometry allow to restrict the search of one point in the first image to the epipolar line in the second image.

An exhaustive overview on stereo matching can be found in [1]. Stereo matching algorithms can be classified into local and global methods. The local approaches

---

* Corresponding author.

N. García-Pedrajas et al. (Eds.): IEA/AIE 2010, Part III, LNAI 6098, pp. 369–378, 2010.

compare the intensity levels of a finite window to determine the disparity for each pixel. These methods use different metrics or similarities to compare intensity levels such as SAD [2] or SSD [3]. Global approaches apply some global assumptions about smoothness and try to determine all the disparities together by using different optimization techniques such as, graph cuts [4,6,7], belief propagation [5], etc. (these methods usually start from a local disparity estimation).

In [8,9] the utilization of color information from images improves the stereo matching results achieved from gray scale images. The extra information provided by color removes some ambiguities avoiding false correspondence matches.

When we are dealing with color digital images, each pixel has three intensity values. The color is represented by different channels in the image, each one of them has a meaning depending on the color representation used. The most familiar representation is the *RGB* (Red, Green, Blue), but there are other known color representation that can be used like, HSV (Hue, Saturation, Value), CMYK (Cyan, Magenta, Yellow, Key) etc. There exist several techniques to calculate the disparity map using the color information, but there is no agreement about which is the best color space to work with. In this work *RGB* representation is used.

Local search matching algorithms assign to every pixel of the right image a correspondence with another pixel of the left image. If we use the local search algorithm with color images it will find for a pixel in the right image three correspondences (one per channel) in the left image, and usually they will not match. A simple and efficient solution is to aggregate the similarity information of the three channels and then choose the correspondence pixel which has the highest similarity value. In this work we study the performance of different aggregation operators, such as, the arithmetic mean, the median, the minimum, etc. To do so, we use several test images from [1] which have been taken using the ideal configuration of the cameras.

This work is organized as follows: In Section 2 we remain the classical stereo matching algorithm using three different metrics. In Section 3 we present the aggregation operators that we are going to use in Section 4 where the experiments and the comparison are carried out. Section 5 presents the conclusions and future research.

2   Stereo Matching for Color Images

Next we recall the typical steps of the classical stereo matching algorithm. In the case of gray scale images, for every pixel of the right image, the algorithm computes the similarity of the window surrounding the pixel with several windows in the left image (considering only the pixels in the epipolar line of the left image). The pixel which surrounding window has the highest similarity is chosen as the corresponding one. If color images are considered, minor changes have to be applied. We can summarize the algorithm for color images as follows (in Figure 1 we depict an overall view of the method):

```
Algorithm Stereo Matching
   const
      Window size := n x m
   begin
      For each pixel  right image
         For each pixel in the epipolar line left image
            For each color channel
               Calculate the similarity between the window centered
               at the pixel of the right image and the window
               centered at the pixel of the left image
            end For
         Aggregate similarities
      end For
      Set correspondence:= arg max{value of aggregation of similarities}
      Disparity:= difference between the x-position of two pixels
   end For
   Create a disparity map from all the disparities obtained
end.
```

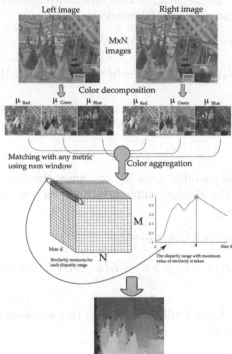

Fig. 1. Stereo matching algorithm scheme using color information from RGB channels. Where $\mu_{Red}, \mu_{Green}, \mu_{Blue}$ are the intensities of each in the channels red, green and blue respectively.

There are many different versions of the classical stereo matching algorithm. However, all of them use the scheme we have presented. The metric or the similarity measure used is usually the biggest difference between algorithms. It is also very important the aggregation function used to aggregate the color similarities. In the following subsection we present three usual similarity measures for stereo matching problem. Section 3 presents the aggregation functions that we consider for the empirical study.

2.1   Similarity between Windows

There exist several methods to compute the similarity between the windows of the right and left image. The obtained disparity maps directly depends on these measures, and also the performance of these measures usually depends on the features of the images. Our objective is to find an aggregation for color similarities that works well whichever method (similarity measure) is used. Next we show three well known similarity measures commonly used stereo matching algorithms.

SSD. The sum of square differences [3] computes the matching score as the sum of the square differences between all pixels intensities from left window respect to right window. Then, the disparity is computed with the one with the lowest value, which indicates the most similar window.

$$SSD(I_r(x,y), I_l(x+k,y)) =$$
$$\sum_{m,n \in W} (I_r(x+m, y+n) - I_l(x+m+k, y+n))^2 \qquad (1)$$

being x, y the position of the pixel, k the displacement of the left window respect to the right window, W the window (size $n \times m$) considered and I_r, I_l right and left images respectively.

SAD. The sum of absolute differences [2], computes the disparity in the same way as SAD, but using the absolute differences between pixel intensities instead of the square differences:

$$SSD(I_r(x,y), I_l(x+k,y)) =$$
$$\sum_{m,n \in W} |I_r(x+m, y+n) - I_l(x+m+k, y+n)| \qquad (2)$$

Fuzzy similarity. The fuzzy similarity between two windows is computed with the following expression [8]:

$$SM_{FS}(I_r(x,y), I_l(x+k,y)) =$$
$$\frac{1}{m \times n} \sum_{m,n \in W} \left(1 - \frac{|I_r(x+m,y+n) - I_l(x+m+k,y+n)|}{\alpha} \right) \qquad (3)$$

the parameter $\alpha = 16$ is used generally [8]. Disparity is computed with the pixel which similarity measure attains its maximum value.

3   Aggregation Functions

In our experiments we use RGB representation as in [8,9]. Similarly to [8] we treat each color channel separately until we aggregate their similarity values. By adding color information to stereo matching algorithm we can avoid some false correspondence produced by color ambiguities.

In [8] they propose to use the minimum as aggregation function for this task but some inconsistencies can be produced. For example, a pixel with low similarity values in all channels will have a larger matching score than another pixel with a great value of similarity in two channels and the other value near (but under) the similarities of the first pixel. Hence, the minimum would cause some undesirable matches (mismatches). Therefore, it is necessary a study of several aggregation functions to find which one is the most suitable to aggregate the color similarities in the stereo matching problem. Next we present different aggregation functions that we will analyze in the experimental study presented in Section 4.

Note: We denote a vector of n elements with $\mathbf{x} = \{x_1, x_2, \ldots, x_n\}$.

- **Minimum**
$$M(\mathbf{x}) = min(x_1, x_2, \ldots, x_n) \tag{4}$$

- **Product**
$$M(\mathbf{x}) = \prod_{i=1}^{n} x_i \tag{5}$$

- **Arithmetic Mean**
$$M(\mathbf{x}) = \frac{1}{n} \sum_{i=1}^{n} x_i \tag{6}$$

- **Weighted Mean**
$$M(\mathbf{x}) = \frac{1}{n} \sum_{i=1}^{n} x_i \cdot w_i \tag{7}$$

where $\mathbf{w} = \{w_1, w_2, \ldots, w_n\}$ is the weight vector that satisfies $\sum_{i=1}^{n} w_i = 1$. In our comparison we consider different weight vectors to compute the final similarity:

$$\mu(x) = w_R \cdot \mu_R(x) + w_G \cdot \mu_G(x) + w_B \cdot \mu_B(x) \tag{8}$$

For example if $w_R = 0.1$, $w_G = 0.8$ and $w_B = 0.1$, we obtain

$$\mu(x) = 0.1 \cdot \mu_R(x) + 0.8 \cdot \mu_G(x) + 0.1 \cdot \mu_B(x) \tag{9}$$

If $w_R = 0,299$, $w_G = 0,5870$ and $w_B = 0,1140$, we obtain

$$\mu(x) = 0,299 \cdot \mu_R(x) + 0,5870 \cdot \mu_G(x) + 0,1140 \cdot \mu_B(x) \tag{10}$$

The weights values of equation (10) belong to the computation of the luminance of a RGB image [10]. The expression of luminance is used to transform RGB color images into gray scale. The purpose of luminance is to represent the brightness of colors just as human perceive them. For example, humans consider the color green brighter than the color blue.

- **Harmonic Mean**

$$M(\mathbf{x}) = n \left(\sum_{i=1}^{n} \frac{1}{x_i} \right) \tag{11}$$

- **Median**

$$M(\mathbf{x}) = \begin{cases} \frac{1}{2}(x_{(k)} + x_{(k+1)}), & \text{if } n = 2k \text{ is even} \\ x_{(k)}, & \text{if } n = 2k \text{ is odd,} \end{cases} \tag{12}$$

where $x_{(k)}$ is the k-th largest (or smallest) component of $\mathbf{x}$.

- **Geometric Mean**

$$M(\mathbf{x}) = \left(\prod_{i=1}^{n} x_i \right)^{(1/n)} \tag{13}$$

- **Mode**
The mode is the most frequent value in $\mathbf{x}$.

4   Experimental Results

In our experimental study, we compare the behavior of the different aggregation functions in color aggregation. We have two main objectives:

- To check if using color information by aggregating the similarities improves the results of using gray scale images.
- To study which is the best aggregation function in order to aggregate color similarities.

To evaluate the performance we use the Middlebury test bed proposed by Scharstein and Szeliski [1] (http://cat.middlebury.edu/stereo). In this test, the disparity maps obtained from our algorithm are compared with the ideal disparity maps.

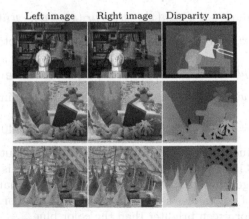

Left image   Right image   Disparity map

Fig. 2. Test images from Middlebury test bed

The test images are shown in Figure 2 with their corresponding ideal disparity maps. We refer to each image pair by the name given in [1]: "Tsukuba", "Teddy" and "Cones". We have to recall that the stereo matching algorithms do not use any type of preprocessing or postprocessing steps (such as, optimization techniques, occlusion detection or image filtering).

In Table 1 we present the quantitative results for the stereo matching algorithm using the fuzzy similarity measure (expression 3) and different aggregation functions to join color channels similarities. The first column of Table 1 is the aggregation function used. Then, three columns for each image pair are presented. These columns represent the percentage of absolute disparity error greater than one for three different regions in the image:

- **no-oc.**: only non-occluded pixels are considered.
- **all**: whole image is considered.
- **disc.**: pixels near discontinuities are considered.

The last column is an overall performance of the algorithm calculated with the mean of all other columns. In the first row, the results obtained by the stereo algorithm applied to gray scale images are depicted. Such a way we can notice the improvement of the performance using color images. Following rows show the algorithms listed in descending order of total error.

In Table 2 we present the total error obtained for each metric considered. The last column presents the mean error for each aggregation. Bold numbers indicate the best aggregation.

Table 1. Quantitative evaluation results for different aggregation functions to add color similarities using fuzzy similarity measure. * Where Weighted Mean 262 means that $w_R = 0.2$, $w_G = 0.6$ and $w_B = 0.2$.

Aggregation function	Tsukuba			Teddy			Cones			$\%E_t$
	%no-oc	%tot	%disc	%no-oc	%tot	%disc	%no-oc	%tot	%disc	
Gray scale	7,84	9,71	18,66	20,07	28,18	30,85	15,57	24,61	26,35	20,21
Aritmetic Mean	7,44	9,27	18,21	18,35	26,67	31,56	12,47	21,96	23,07	18,78
Product	7,46	9,31	18,11	18,59	26,87	31,72	12,49	21,96	22,83	18,81
Geometric Mean	7,46	9,31	18,11	18,59	26,87	31,72	12,49	21,96	22,83	18,81
Harmonic Mean	7,45	9,33	18,10	18,87	27,11	31,91	12,56	22,02	22,72	18,90
Weighted Mean Luminance	7,37	9,23	17,85	18,01	26,37	30,63	14,04	23,32	24,43	19,03
Weighted Mean 262*	7,45	9,26	18,10	18,37	26,68	30,79	13,46	22,83	24,36	19,03
Weighted Mean 622*	7,48	9,34	17,99	19,07	27,34	32,33	13,61	22,93	23,55	19,29
Weighted Mean 181*	7,63	9,43	18,39	19,41	27,60	31,04	14,87	24,10	25,83	19,81
Weighted Mean 226*	8,26	9,97	19,38	21,38	29,36	33,76	12,29	21,90	23,94	20,02
Weighted Mean 811*	7,82	9,71	18,00	20,71	28,81	33,69	15,11	24,25	24,98	20,34
Median	8,12	9,91	19,11	21,93	29,88	33,92	15,56	24,76	25,73	20,99
Min	8,18	10,10	18,32	26,02	33,49	36,18	16,02	25,07	25,03	22,04
Mode	8,40	10,32	18,52	26,73	34,12	36,56	16,40	25,42	25,31	22,42
Weighted Mean 118*	9,29	10,95	21,15	25,82	33,35	37,03	14,40	23,84	26,72	22,51

Table 2. Total error obtained for each color aggregation and similarity measure. *
Where Weighted Mean 262 means that $w_R = 0.2$, $w_G = 0.6$ and $w_B = 0.2$.

Aggregation function	SAD metric	SSD metric	Fuzzy Sim.	Mean error
Gray scale	23, 20	24, 87	20, 21	22, 76
Aritmetic Mean	22, 32	24, 32	**18,78**	21, 81
Geometric Mean	**22,06**	**23,83**	18, 81	**21,57**
Harmonic Mean	22, 13	24, 24	18, 90	21, 76
Median	24, 00	25, 57	20, 99	23, 52
Min	24, 83	26, 70	22, 04	24, 52
Mode	25, 11	26, 74	22, 42	24, 76
Product	**22,06**	**23,83**	18, 81	**21,57**
Weighted Mean 118*	24, 93	26, 64	22, 51	24, 05
Weighted Mean 181*	23, 14	24, 72	19, 81	23, 20
Weighted Mean 226*	23, 07	25, 32	20, 02	22, 80
Weighted Mean 262*	22, 47	24, 32	19, 03	21, 94
Weighted Mean 622*	22, 43	24, 30	19, 29	22, 01
Weighted Mean 811*	23, 10	24, 69	20, 34	22, 71
Weighted Mean Luminance	22, 41	24, 24	19, 03	22, 23

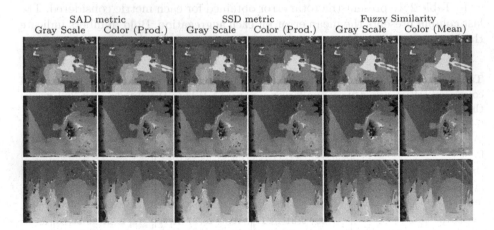

SAD metric　　　　　　SSD metric　　　　　　Fuzzy Similarity
Gray Scale　Color (Prod.)　Gray Scale　Color (Prod.)　Gray Scale　Color (Mean)

Fig. 3. Best disparity maps for each method compared with the disparity map extracted from gray scale images

Figure 3 shows the comparison of the best disparity maps obtained with color aggregation and the ones obtained from gray scale images.

We conclude from this experiment, that the aggregation function to use strongly depends on the stereo matching algorithm considered. None of the aggregation functions have outperformed all the others in all three methods. However, it is clear that the selection of the aggregation function is a key factor. It can improve the results obtained from gray scale images. Taking into account these tests, we recommend using the luminance, the product and the geometric mean, which are the aggregations with better overall performance in our test sets.

Also the total error obtained using the weighted arithmetic mean based on the luminance formula is always better than using gray scale images. To obtain the gray scale images we have used the RGB luminance formula. We observe that is advisable to use the three color channels to compute the matching and then aggregate that information instead of aggregating the information first and then applying the algorithm for a unique color channel.

5   Conclusions and Future Research

We carried out a comparison study of the perfomance of different aggregation functions in the stereo matching algorithm to aggregate the similarities from different color channels. We conclude that is better to make the color aggregation after the similarities are computed in order to avoid ambiguities (produced by color) than to aggregate the color to obtain gray scale images and then compute the similarities.

The experiment shows that the optimum aggregation function depends on the metric used. However, there are aggregation functions such as the weighted arithmetic mean based on the luminance, the geometric mean or the product which performs properly for all three metrics.

For future work, we will perform similar comparisons analyzing the perfomance using different color spaces. We will also consider more test images to confirm our experimental results.

Acknowledgments. This paper has been partially supported by the National Science Foundation of Spain, Reference TIN2007-65981.

References

1. Scharstein, D., Szeliski, R.: A taxonomy and evaluation of dense two-frame stereo correspondence algorithms. International Journal of Computer Vision 47(1-3), 7–42 (2002)
2. Zabih, R., Woodfill, J.: Non-parametric local transforms for computing visual correspondence. In: Third European Conference on Computer Vision, Sweden (1994)
3. Trucco, E., Roberto, V., Tinonin, S., Corbatto, M.: SSD disparity estimation for dynamic stereo. In: Proceedings of the British Machine Vision Conference (1996)
4. Bleyer, M., Gelautz, M.: Graph-based surface reconstruction from stereo pairs using image segmentation. In: SPIE, vol. 5665, pp. 288–299 (2005)
5. Felzenszwalb, P.F., Huttenlocher, D.P.: Efficient belief propagation for early vision. In: CVPR, vol. I, pp. 261–268 (2004)
6. Hong, L., Chen, G.: Segment–based stereo matching using graph cuts. In: CVPR, vol. I, pp. 74–81 (2004)

7. Kolmogorov, V., Zabih, R.: Computing visual correspondence with occlusions via graph cuts. In: ICCV, vol. II, pp. 508–515 (2001)
8. Tolt, G., Kalaykov, I.: Measures based on fuzzy similarity for stereo matching of colour images. Soft Computing 10, 1117–1126 (2006)
9. Klaus, A., Sormann, M., Karner, K.: Segment-Based Stereo Matching Using Belief Propagation and a Self-Adapting Dissimilarity Measure. In: ICPR, vol. 3, pp. 15–18 (2006)
10. Deza, E., Deza, M.M.: Image and Audio Distances, Dictionary of Distances, pp. 262–278. Elsevier, Amsterdam (2006)

Fast HDR Image Generation Technique Based on Exposure Blending

Andrey Vavilin, Kaushik Deb, and Kang-Hyun Jo

Dept. Electrical Engineering and Information Systems, University of Ulsan,
Mugeo-dong, Nam-ku, Ulsan 689-740, Korea
{andy,debkaushik99,jhk2009}@islab.ulsan.ac.kr

Abstract. In the proposed work a method for generating HDR images based on exposure blending is described. Using three differently exposed images a single image with recovered details in shadows and highlights is generated. Input images are analyzed to locate over and underexposed regions based on pixels intensity. Local contrast of input images is also considered in order to generate the output image with correct color transactions between differently exposed areas. Then images are merged using blending function. The proposed method requires a single pass thru the image to generate the result, which allows to process one image for less than 100 milliseconds. The proposed method requires no information about camera or shutting conditions, such as shutter speed or aperture size.

Keywords: HDR images, exposure blending, bilateral filtering, box blur.

1 Introduction

The high dynamic range (HDR) imaging techniques are designed to produce images that faithfully depict the full visual dynamics of real world scenes. Most of the algorithms are based on reconstructing the real luminance of the scene using several input images taken with different exposure. All the algorithms could be classified into two main categories: spatially uniform (non-local) and spatially varying (local).

A spatially varying approach is based on the fact that humans are capable of viewing high contrast scenes thanks to the local control sensitivity in the retina. This suggests that a position-dependent scale factor might reduce a scene contrasts acceptably for displaying them on a low dynamic range device. This approach converts the original scene of real-world intensities to the displayed image intensities, using a position-dependent multiplying term. The examples of spatial varying approach were described in [1,3,4,6].

A non-local approaches do not imitate local adaptation. Instead, almost all image synthesis, recording, and display processes use an implicit normalizing step to map the original scene intensities to the target display intensities without disturbing any scene contrasts that fall within the range of the display device. This normalization consists of a single constant multiplier. Image normalization has two important properties: it preserves all reproducible scene contrasts and it discards the intensities of the original scene or image. A contrast, the ratio of any two intensities, is not changed if

N. García-Pedrajas et al. (Eds.): IEA/AIE 2010, Part III, LNAI 6098, pp. 379–388, 2010.

the same multiplier scales both intensities. Normalizing implicitly assumes that scaling does not change the appearance, as if all the perceptually important information was carried by the contrasts alone, but scaling display intensities can strongly affect a viewer's estimates of scene contrasts and intensities. Although this scaling is not harmful for many well-lit images or scenes, discarding the original intensities can make two scenes with different illumination levels appear identical. Normalization also fails to capture dramatic appearance changes at the extremes of lighting, such as gradual loss of color vision, changes in acuity, and changes in contrast sensitivity. The examples of global-based approach could be found in [2,5,7].

Another technique is a block-based approach presented in [8,9,10,11]. It is based on decomposing of input images into a set of rectangular blocks of the same size. Then the best exposure is selected for each block. Resulting image is a mosaic combined with selected exposures. This technique was improved by using clusters of arbitrary shape instead of rectangular blocks in [13].

The proposed algorithm is based on similar approach. Each pixel of output image is computed as a weighted sum of corresponding pixels of input images. Weights are selected according to intensity of pixel itself and its neighborhood. However, the proposed method blends exposures for each pixel separately. It allows to reduce the number of operations and computational time.

In the current work the goal was to introduce an algorithm with the ability to generate an image with recovered details in shadowed and highlighted parts of a scene in less than 100ms. Such algorithm could be used as a prefiltering operation in different applications in which result must be robust under various lighting conditions. One of possible application was described in [14].

2   Algorithm Description

In the proposed paper we describe a method to generate an image with improved dynamic range properties based on simple exposure blending technique. For most applications it is enough to use 3 input images with exposure difference in 2EV. Let's denote an image with normal exposure as I^0. Underexposed (darker) and overexposed (brighter) images are denoted as I^{-2} and I^{+2} respectively. Normally exposed image is an image taken in fully automatic mode. It will be used as a reference to evaluate the quality of result. Overexposed and underexposed images are taken with the same aperture as the normally exposed one but with exposure compensation in $\pm 2EV$ and -2EV respectively. The exposure compensation changes the shutter speed while all other parameters are fixed.

The proposed method generates an output image by blending the input images. Normally exposed image is selected as a reference one. Overexposed pixels of this image are combined with same pixels in underexposed image. And underexposed pixels of normally exposed image are combined with an overexposed one. In other words, we combine dark pixels of normally exposed image with pixels in over exposed image which are brighter. Similar bright pixels in a reference image are combined with the darker image. This idea could be illustrated by Fig.1.

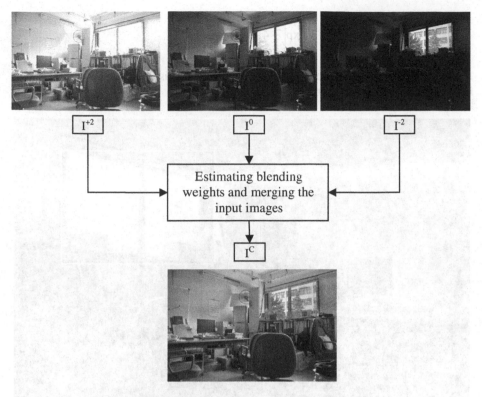

Fig. 1. Exposure blending scheme for 3 input images

Over and underexposed pixels indicate regions with possible losses of information due to shadows or highlights. The confidence of the pixel value is decreasing, while its intensity is approaching to 0 or to 255 (see Fig.2 for the details). Thus, intensities in the middle of the feasible range are considered to be more confident comparing with the intensities at the ends. In the proposed framework we consider pixels with intensity close to 0 to be underexposed, and pixels with intensity close to 255 to be overexposed. Pixels with intensity close to 127 are considered to be normally exposed and used as a reference. This idea is used to select the coefficients for the blending function. Using normally exposed image as a reference we combine its pixels with the pixels of over and underexposed images. The proportions of a blending depends on how close the intensity of the reference pixels are with regard to the over and the underexposed ones. Mathematically this could be formalized as (1).

$$I_{i,j}^{C} = \begin{cases} b(I_{i,j}^{0}) \cdot I_{i,j}^{0} + (1 - b(I_{i,j}^{0})) \cdot I_{i,j}^{+2}, & if \ \ I_{i,j}^{0} < 127.5 \\ b(I_{i,j}^{0}) \cdot I_{i,j}^{0} + (1 - b(I_{i,j}^{0})) \cdot I_{i,j}^{-2}, & if \ \ I_{i,j}^{0} > 127.5 \end{cases} \tag{1}$$

where I^{C} is the combined image, I^{-2}, I^{+2} and I^{0} are underexposed, overexposed and normally exposed images respectively and b is blending coefficient, computed by a Gaussian-like function (2) centered at 127.5. The peak of the function is selected to be in the middle of feasible intensity range.

$$b(x) = \exp\left(-4\frac{(x-127.5)^2}{127.5^2}\right) \qquad (2)$$

As an alternative, linear function could be used. Comparison between different blending functions is given in Section 3.

Fig. 2. Losses of information in overexposed (yellow rectangle) and underexposed (red rectangle) regions

The computational time, required to obtain a HDR image using the described idea, is very small: just one pass required to obtain the result image. However, the output could contain color artifacts and local contrast of such image will be very low. This problem is illustrated by Fig.3 (a).

This could be solved by using average value of window, centered on the pixel, to compute the weight instead of single pixel. Thus, equation (1) could be transformed into:

$$I_{i,j}^C = \begin{cases} b\left(I_{i,j}^{avg}\right)\cdot I_{i,j}^0 + \left(1-b\left(I_{i,j}^{avg}\right)\right)\cdot I_{i,j}^{+2}, & if \ I_{i,j}^0 < 127.5 \\ b\left(I_{i,j}^{avg}\right)\cdot I_{i,j}^0 + \left(1-b\left(I_{i,j}^{avg}\right)\right)\cdot I_{i,j}^{-2}, & if \ I_{i,j}^0 > 127.5 \end{cases} \qquad (3)$$

where $I_{i,j}^{avg}$ is an average intensity for a window with radius *size* centered at *i,j*.

$$I_{i,j}^{avg} = \frac{1}{N}\sum_{m=i-size}^{i+size}\sum_{n=j-size}^{j+size}I_{m,n}^0 \qquad (4)$$

Using average value allows preserving local contrast. However, it produces halos in the areas where intensities are rapidly changed. Increasing windows size results in smoother color transactions and increasing size of halos. Example of average-based blending is shown in Fig.3 (b). Detailed comparison is given in Section 3.

Problem of halos could be solved by using idea of bilateral filtering: average value is changed to a weighted average. Weight coefficient depends from distance from the pixel to the center of the window and from the difference in intensities with the central pixel. To compute it we transform (4) into:

$$I_{i,j}^{avg} = \frac{1}{n} \sum_{m=i-size}^{i+size} \sum_{n=j-size}^{j+size} I_{i,j}^0 \cdot w_I\left(\left|I_{i,j}^0 - I_{m,n}^0\right|\right) \cdot w_D\left(\sqrt{(i-m)^2 + (j-n)^2}\right) \tag{5}$$

where n is normalizing coefficient defined as

$$n = \sum_{m=i-size}^{i+size} \sum_{n=j-size}^{j+size} w_I\left(\left|I_{i,j}^0 - I_{m,n}^0\right|\right) \cdot w_D\left(\sqrt{(i-m)^2 + (j-n)^2}\right) \tag{6}$$

and $w_I(x)$ and $w_D(x)$ are intensity weighting function and spatial weighting function respectively. Result for weighted-based approach is shown in Fig.3 (c).

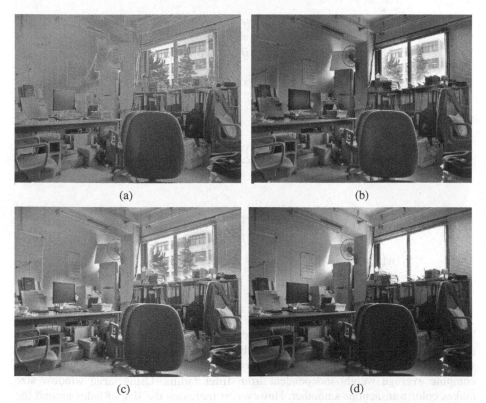

(a)   (b)

(c)   (d)

Fig. 3. Output images produced by direct mapping – (a), average-based approach – (b), weighted average approach – (c) and a single reference image taken with a camera in automatic mode – (d). Window size 41x41 pixels was used for average and weighted-average approaches.

3 Experimental Results

All the experiments were done on Pentium-IV with 1 GB RAM. The algorithm was implemented using C++ under Borland Developer Studio environment. The test images were taken under different lighting conditions by different cameras. Exposure difference between images of the same scene varied from 0.3EV to 4EV. To evaluate the quality of result, images with resolution from 800x600 up to 3000x2000 were used. Computational time was measured for the images with the resolution 800x600 pixels.

In first group of tests we tried to select the blending function which will produce the most accurate results. Besides blending function defined by equation (2), the following functions were used:

$$b(x) = \begin{cases} \dfrac{1}{127.5}x & ,if\ x < 127.5 \\ -\dfrac{1}{127.5}x + 2 & ,otherwise \end{cases} \tag{7}$$

$$b(x) = \begin{cases} \dfrac{1}{75}x & ,if\ x < 75 \\ 1 & ,if\ x \in [75,181] \\ -\dfrac{1}{75}x + 3.4 & ,x > 181 \end{cases} \tag{8}$$

$$b(x) = \begin{cases} 1 & ,if\ x \in [75,181] \\ 2\exp\left(-4\dfrac{(x-127.5)^2}{127.5^2}\right) & ,otherwise \end{cases} \tag{9}$$

$$w(x) = \begin{cases} \exp\left(-15\dfrac{(x-75)^2}{75^2}\right) & ,if\ x < 75 \\ 1 & ,if\ x \in [75,181] \\ \exp\left(-15\dfrac{(x-181)^2}{75^2}\right) & ,x > 181 \end{cases} \tag{10}$$

The weights were computed using average of intensity for some pixel environment (see description of average-based approach in Section 2 for more details). Window size was varied from 5x5 to 41x41. However, technique described in [15] allows to compute average weight independent from filter radius. Using large window size makes color transactions smoother. However, it increases the size of halos around the areas with rapidly changed exposure.

Our experiments indicated that blending function defined by equation (2) produces best result for the average-based filter with window size 41x41 pixels. Comparison for blending with (2) using averaging windows of different size is shown in the Fig.4.

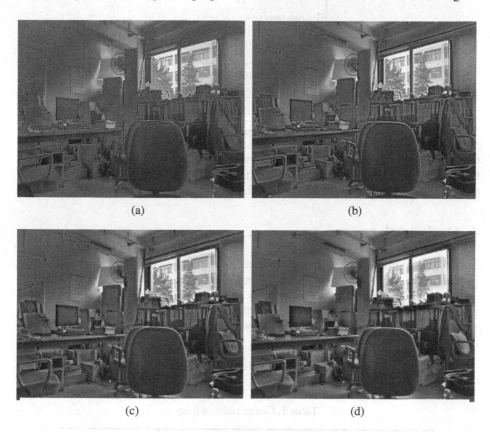

(a)   (b)

(c)   (d)

Fig. 4. Comparing results for the different window size (a) – 5x5, (b) – 11x11, (c) – 21x21, (d) – 41x41

To reduce the halos weighted-average technique described by (5) and (6) was applied. We compared 3 functions for computing intensity weight $w_I(x)$ (equations (11)~(13)) and 2 functions for computing the spatial weight $w_D(x)$ (equations (14)~(15)).

$$w_I(x) = \begin{cases} 1 - \dfrac{1}{127}x & , if\ x < 127 \\ 0 & , otherwise \end{cases} \tag{11}$$

$$w_I(x) = 1 - \frac{1}{256}x \tag{12}$$

$$w_I(x) = \begin{cases} \exp\left(-4\dfrac{x^2}{127.5^2}\right), if\ x < 127 \\ 0\ , otherwise \end{cases} \qquad (13)$$

$$w_D(x) = 1 - \frac{x}{window\_size} \qquad (14)$$

$$w_D(x) = \exp\left(-4\frac{x^2}{2 \cdot window\_size^2}\right) \qquad (15)$$

Our experiments showed that images generated with (11) as intensity weighting functions and (14) as a spatial weighting function produce less halos comparing to other mapping while preserving the local contrast.

4 Optimizations

To make our program work faster we used lookup tables for $b(x)$, $w_I(x)$ and $w_D(x)$. Instead of recalculating weight values for each pixel during the exposure blending we added an initialization step in which arrays with all feasible values for weighted were generated. For example, the intensity weighting function $w_I(x)$ is a discreet function which takes the values from 0 to 255 as an argument could be changed to one-dimensional array TI defined as

$$TI[x] = w_I(x),\ x = 0,1,2,...,255 \qquad (16)$$

Table 1. Computational time

Method	Average time (ms)
Pixel based blending	22
Average	37
Weighted average (intensity)	51
Weighted average (intensity and spatial)	79

5 Conclusions

According to our experiments, using weighted average with intensity weighting function defined by (11) and spatial weighting function defined by (14) and blending function (2) produces better images with higher local contrast and smallest halos. However it increase computational time and makes the process dependent from the filter radius. For the applications, which are not sensitive to halos but crucial to computational time, we recommend to use average-based approach without weighting or with intensity weighting only.

The proposed method allows generating images with improved dynamic range properties in a real-time. Computational time for a 800x600 pixels image is less then 80 ms.

Algorithm takes 3 differently exposed images as an input. Our experiments show the exposure difference between the images in 2EV to be the most effective in detail recovering.

In further works we would like to improve the efficiency of algorithm by using more than 3 images.

Acknowledgements

This work was supported (in a part) by a Ministry of Knowledge Economy of Korea under Human Resources Development Program for Convergence Robot Specialists.

References

1. Chiu, K., Herf, M., Shirley, P., Swamy, S., Wang, C., Zimmerman, K.: Spatially Nonunifrom Scaling Functions for High Contrast Images. In: Proceedings of Graphics Interface 1993, pp. 245–254 (1993)
2. Ferwerda, J., Pattanaik, S.N., Shirley, P., Greenberg, D.P.: A Model of Visual Adaptation for Realistic Image Synthesis. In: Proceedings of SIGGRAPH 1996, pp. 249–258 (1996)
3. Qiu, G., Guan, J., Duan, J., Chen, M.: Tone Mapping for HDR Image using Optimization – A New Closed Form Solution. In: Proceedings of the 18th International Conference on Pattern Recognition (2006)
4. Pattanaik, S.N., Ferwerda, J., Fairchild, M.D., Greenberg, D.P.: A Multiscale Model of Adaptation and Spatial Vision for Realistic Image Display. In: Proceedings of SIGGRAPH 1998, pp. 287–298. ACM, New York (1998)
5. Pattanaik, S.N., Tumblin, J.E., Yee, H., Greenberg, D.P.: Time-Dependent Visual Adaptation for Realistic Real-Time Image Display. In: Proceedings of SIGGRAPH 2000, pp. 47–54 (2000)
6. Rahman, Z., Jobson, D.J., Woodell, G.A.: Multi-scale retinex for colour image enhancement. In: Proceedings of International Conference on Image Processing, Lausanne, Switzerland, September 16-19, vol. 3, pp. 1003–1006 (1996)
7. Tumblin, J., Hodgings, J.K., Guenter, B.: Two Methods for Display of High Contrast Images. ACM Transactions on Graphics 18(1), 56–94 (1999)
8. Vavilin, A., Jo, K.-H.: Recursive HDR Image Generation from Differently Exposed Images. In: Proceedings of Graphicon 2008, Moscow, Russia, June 23-27, pp. 156–160 (2008)
9. Vavilin, A., Jo, K.-H.: Recursive HDR Image Generation from Differently Exposed Images. In: Proceedings of ICCAS 2008, Seoul, Korea, October 14-17 (2008)
10. Rovid, A., Varkonyi-Koczy, A.R., Hashimoto, T., Balogh, S., Shimodaira, Y.: Gradient Based Synthesized Multiple Exposure Time HDR Image. In: IMTC 2007, Warsaw, Poland, May 1-3 (2007)
11. Wang, T.-H., Ke, W.-M., Zwao, D.-C., Chen, F.-C., Chiu, C.-T.: Block-based Gradient Domain High Dynamic Range Compression Design for Real-time Applications. In: ICIP 2007 Proceedings, September 16 - October 19, vol. 3, pp. 561–564 (2007)

12. Mertens, T., Kautz, J., Reeth, F.: Exposure Fusion. In: Proceeding of 15th Pacific Conference on Computer Graphics and Applications, PG 2007, October 29 - November 2, pp. 382–390 (2007)
13. Vavilin, A., Jo, K.-H.: HDR Image Generation based on Intensity Clustering and Local Feature Analysis. In: ICIC 2009, Ulsan, Korea, September 16-19 (2009)
14. Vavilin, A., Jo, K.-H.: Graph-based Approach for Robust Road Guidance Sign Recognition from Differently Exposed Images. Journal of Universal Computer Science 15(4), 786–804 (2009)
15. Lukin, A.: Tips&Tricks: Fast Image Filtering Algorithms. In: Proceedings of Graphicon 2007, Moscow, Russia, June 23-27 (2007)

Parallelizing and Optimizing LIP-Canny Using NVIDIA CUDA

Rafael Palomar, José M. Palomares, José M. Castillo, Joaquín Olivares, and Juan Gómez-Luna

Department of Computer Architecture, Electronics and Electronic Technology
Computer Architecture Area
University of Córdoba

Abstract. The Canny algorithm is a well known edge detector that is widely used in the previous processing stages in several algorithms related to computer vision. An alternative, the LIP-Canny algorithm, is based on a robust mathematical model closer to the human vision system, obtaining better results in terms of edge detection. In this work we describe LIP-Canny algorithm under the perspective from its parallelization and optimization by using the NVIDIA CUDA framework. Furthermore, we present comparative results between an implementation of this algorithm using NVIDIA CUDA and the analogue using a C/C++ approach.

1   Introduction

Feature extraction is one of the earlier stages that many computer vision related algorithms perform. Among the features commonly extracted, edges are especially important due to their relevance in subsequent stages. There are many methods available to perform this feature extraction, but the image filtering for obtaining the gradient map is one of the most frequently used.

The *Canny* algorithm [1] is an effective edge detector that is widely used. The application of this algorithm in a certain kind of images (i.e. images presenting gaussian noise) shows better results than other algorithms such as the Sobel edge detector [2,3].

The *Logarithmic Image Processing* (LIP) is a robust mathematical model that presents certain desirable properties among which we can find the adjustment into a determined range of results of the operations, as well as obeying of some laws applicable to the human vision system. In the work of Palomares *et al.* [4] a Canny algorithm based on LIP (LIP-Canny) is proposed. This new approach improves the traditional Canny algorithm in terms of edge detection, but it is a slower algorithm.

The most remarkable disadvantage of the Canny algorithm is that it requires more processing power than others like Sobel. This can be a problem in the processing of a large set of images or large images, a fact that motivates the development of new implementations that lead to new improvements of performance.

N. García-Pedrajas et al. (Eds.): IEA/AIE 2010, Part III, LNAI 6098, pp. 389–398, 2010.

Regarding the problem of performance improvement, researchers are paying special attention to to GPGPU (General Purpose Graphic Processing Units) processing, that allows the execution of conventional algorithms in specialized graphic processing hardware. This technology has evolved rapidly and since NVIDIA developed CUDA, the interest around this technology has grown in many research fields. Examples of this fact could be the works of Riegel et al.[5] in fluid mechanics and Kavanagh et al.[6] in astrophysics.

This work pretends to cover the LIP-Canny algorithm under the perspective of its parallelization and optimization to archieve improvements of performance. It is based on Palomares et al.[4] and Luo and Duraiswami[7], and can be integrated as part of more complex algorithms that use an edge detection stages like Gómez-Luna et al.[8].

2   The LIP Model

In the late 80's and early 90's Jourlin and Pinoli[9,10] exhibit a new paradigm for the processing of images using the projection of light (as in the case of microscope images). The aim was to solve common problems like the overflow that could be produced when two images are added. This new approach was named LIP (*Logarithmic Image Processing*).

Jourlin and Pinoli describe new mathematical operators to perform the addition and amplification of microscope images. These operators not only perform the operations that they were designed for, but they also preserve the physical nature of the images to be processed.

2.1   Definitions, Naming Conventions and Ranges

Before starting to detail the underliying mathematical model of LIP, it is convenient to describe the ranges and the meaning of some variables.

M is referred to as the upper limit of the possible values of a pixel could have, which depends on the image depth. For instance, an 8-bit image (grayscale) would use an M value (unreachable) of 256 and a minimum value of 0 (Note that absolute darkness and absolute brightness do not occur in the real world). Gray-level images are denoted as capitalized letter such as I, J, etc. Gray-level functions are denoted as lowercase letters such as f where $f \in (0, M)$, while the *gray tone* of a gray-level function is denoted as the corresponding letter with a hat and in the case of f it is defined as $\hat{f} = M - f$. Finally, the LIP transformed gray tone function will be denoted as the corresponding lowercase letter with a tilde such as $\tilde{f}$.

2.2   A Brief Outline of LIP

There are two possible ways to apply the LIP model to any digital image processing technique. In this section, we include a brief introduction to each of these methods.

Operating images in LIP space with traditional operators. The first method comes from the tranformation of the "original" image (image expressed in natural space) to an special space called LIP. This is carried out by an *isomorphic transform* defined by

$$\tilde{f} = \varphi(\hat{f}) = -M \cdot \log\left(1 - \frac{\hat{f}}{M}\right) \tag{1}$$

Once the corresponding processing technique is applied, the image has to be transformed though an *inverse transformation* defined by

$$\hat{f} = \varphi^{-1}(\tilde{f}) = M \cdot \left(1 - \exp\left(-\frac{\tilde{f}}{M}\right)\right) \tag{2}$$

Operating images in linear space with modified operators. The second method operates directly on the images expressed in natural space. For this purpose, we define:

- A new image with an inversion of the scale ($\hat{I} = M - I$).
- A special sum operator $\triangle$ defined as $\hat{f} \triangle \hat{g} = \hat{f} + \hat{g} - \frac{\hat{f} \cdot \hat{g}}{M}$
- A special scalar product operator $\triangle$ defined as $\alpha \triangle \hat{f} = M - M \cdot \left(1 - \frac{\hat{f}}{M}\right)^{\alpha}$
- Further operators have been proposed, for example the LIP-Difference $\triangle$ or the LIP-Summation $\overset{\Sigma}{\triangle}$.

3   A Briefly on Parallel Processing with CUDA

A common trend in the videogames industry and more concisely into the graphics industry, is to develop architectures based on processors capable to process a great amount of data parallely. These "graphics" processors were originally designed to rapidly transform complete 3D scenes into 2D graphics. Obviously, in an architecture especially designed for such a purpose, the tasks performed are specialized, but recent tests have demonstrated that these architectures have obtained processing speeds of more than one order of magnitude compared with CPUs. Nowadays new technologies such as NVIDIA CUDA provides the developers with tools for programming algorithms for their execution in graphic architectures, thus obtaining higher performance rates than the analogous algorithms executed on CPUs.

3.1   Architecture

The architecture is based on special processors called *streaming multiprocessors* (SMs) capable of keeping a huge number of threads running parallely, which allows developers to easily implement data-parallel kernels. Each SM contains a set of *streaming processors* (SPs), 32-bit units especially designed to perform profitable multiply-add operations of single-precision floating-point numbers. In addition the SMs have two special function units (SFUs) that execute more complex operations such as square root, sine, cosine, etc.

Because of SMs' high demand of data the system memory is divided physically in different spaces. The GPU has a *global memory* shared by all the processing units (SPs) whereas each SM has a small on-chip *shared memory* used by all the SPs of the SM. For read-only data that is accessed simultaneously by many threads there is a *constant memory* per SM[1] and a *texture memory* shared by clusters of SMs.

3.2   Execution Model

The CUDA execution model fits around two execution modes. Certain pieces of code of a CUDA program would be executed sequentially by the CPU while another code would do it as kernels executed parallely by de GPU.

The kernels are organized in a two-level hierarchy, threads in the lower level that maps directly with the SPs and block of threads in the higher level that map directly with the SMs. In order to feed the execution threads the data space will be divided in a SIMD-like style.

The maximum efficiency of the kernels can be reached when the occupancy of the SMs is as high as possible, the memory hierarchy is properly used and the correct access patterns for the different memory spaces is preserved. For further details about the architecture, execution model, access patterns and optimizations see [11] and [12].

4   Implementing LIP-Canny with CUDA

The Canny algorithm and its variants that use LIP present certain features that enables its parallelization on GPUs. A common strategy to implement image processing algorithms using CUDA is to separate the implementation in kernels that individually, load the data in *shared memory*, perform some operations on the data and finally store the results back into the *global memory*.

In this section we present both the changes needed for applying LIP to the Canny algorithm as well as some additional changes applicable to the Canny algorithm, with regard to Luo[7].

4.1   LIP-Canny Using a Traditional Operators' Approach

As mentioned previously, using traditional operators to implement LIP-Canny requires a direct transformation to LIP space, processing of the image and a inverse transformation to linear space. The first intuitive approximation is to implement two separate kernels, one for the direct transformation operating

---

[1] Altough this memory exist per SM, the content is common to and replicated for all SMs.

Table 1. Kernels for LIP-Canny using a traditional operators' approach

Kernel	Development
Loading Data and Performing the LIP Transformation	Custom
Gaussian Row Convolution	Based on [13]
Gaussian Column Convolution	Based on [13]
Derivative Gaussian Row Convolution	Based on [13]
Derivative Gaussian Column Convolution	Based on [13]
Gradient Mag. and Dir. Computation + Inverse LIP Transformation	Custom
Non-Max. Suppression	Based on [7]
Hysteresis	Based on [7]
Unloading Data	Based on [7]

before the filtering stages and another for the inverse transformation operating before the gradient computation stage. In order to avoid undesirable memory transferences between *global* and *shared* memories, each kernel must perform all the operations possible when the data is in *shared memory*, therefore some kernels have to be merged. Table 1 shows the kernels used in our implementation and their development nature.

Loading Data and Performing LIP Transformation Kernel. Usually the images are given in a 1-byte per pixel (gray-scale) format. As mentioned previously, the processing units are especially designed to perform 32-bit floating-point operations, hence these image data must be represented in a more convenient format. Luo[7] presents a conversion technique based on logical AND and shift operations while mantaining the correct memory access patterns, in addition we have included the LIP transformation operations based on the Equation 1. Fig. 1 shows a case in which a thread reads 4 bytes from an image formatted as 1-byte per pixel, performs the transformations needed while the data are on registers and finally stores the data back in their corresponding positions to forming a 4-bytes per pixel image.

Filtering Operations. The filtering operations widely differ from the Luo[7] proposal. While the authors have used fixed length filters we propose a pseudo-parameterization which allows the processing to benefit from a variable filter length. This pseudo-parameterization establishes a wide filter length and fills it with the corresponding centered gaussian or derivative gaussian function, which avoids some of the calculations needed for pure variable length filters. Fig. 2 shows examples of this pseudo-parameterization. Regarding the convolution operation, Podlozhnyuk [13] offers an efficient approach that has been used in this work.

Gradient Magnitude and Direction Computation and Inverse LIP Transformation. This kernel arises from including of the inverse LIP transformation operations in the gradient and direction computation processes. The philosophy of the kernel is the same as that of the rest of the kernels, that is, loading from *global* to *shared* memory, processing and storing data back into

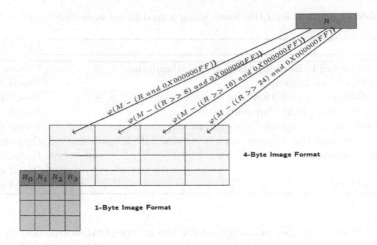

Fig. 1. Data conversion performed by a thread

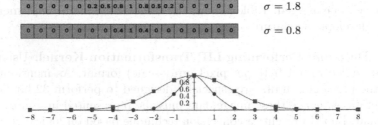

Fig. 2. Pseudo-parameterized kernel generation

the *global* memory. Luo[7] uses the classical magnitude of the gradient equation and a discretization for the direction, but we have included the inverse LIP transformation for each vector component, according with the Equation 2.

4.2 LIP-Canny Using a Modified Operators' Approach

Using modified operators requires a new convolution composed from the LIP operators previously introduced. However Palomares et al.[14] demonstrate that it is possible to obtain a new operation $conv2D_\Delta$ from traditional separable filter convolution operations and by using "transformed" images. This new operation is equivalent and more efficient than the pure LIP operators' approach. Furthermore the authors establish a new operation $grad_\Delta$ that requires the definition of $conv2D_\Delta$ in terms of its LIP transformed

$$\varphi(conv2D_\Delta(\hat{I}, F)) = M \cdot \left(K \cdot \log M - conv1D \left(conv1D \left(lnI, \mathbf{a}^T \right), \mathbf{b} \right) \right) \quad (3)$$

where $K = \sum_{j=0}^{m-1} \mathbf{a}(m-j) \cdot \sum_{i=0}^{n-1} \mathbf{b}(n-i)$. We can keep the derivative filtering operations invariant to the *Traditional Operators* approach, but it is necessary

Table 2. Kernels for LIP-Canny using a modified operators' approach

Kernel	Development
Loading Data + Obtaining the Logarithm Image	Custom
Gaussian Row Convolution	Based on [13]
Gaussian Column Convolution	Custom
Derivative Gaussian Row Convolution	Based on [13]
Derivative Gaussian Column Convolution	Based on [13]
Gradient Mag. and Dir. Computation + Inverse LIP Transformation	Custom
Non-Max. Suppression	Based on [7]
Hysteresis	Based on [7]
Unloading Data	Based on [7]

to obtain a new "transformed" image resulting from the application of the logarithm to the original image as well as that of performing gaussian filtering as seen Equation 3. As in the *Traditional Operators* approach, we take advantage of this in order to add some processing in the load data kernel and the gaussian filtering (y) kernel. Below, we further develop these changes.

Loading Data and Getting the Logarithm Image. As we explained in the analogous kernel for the traditional operators' approach, the data must be converted into a more convenient format. The difference introduced in this kernel is the application of the logarithm operation to all the pixels of the original image, which we have included in the loading data kernel.

Gaussian Column Convolution. Concerning the $conv2D_\Delta$, we have used the Podlozhnyuk[13] convolution for the row filtering while some modifications are introduced for the column filtering. These modifications consist of the addition of the extra operations needed to perform $\varphi(conv2D_\Delta)$ as seen in the Equation 3.

Gradient Magnitude and Direction Computation and Inverse Transformation. Here we apply the same principles that lead the gradient magnitude and direction computation previously explained in the *Traditional Operators* approach. This time, the magnitude computation is performed using the $grad_\Delta$ operator defined as:

$$grad_\Delta(\hat{\mathbf{g}}) = M \cdot \left(1 - \exp\left(-\frac{\sqrt{\varphi(\hat{g}_x)^2 + \varphi(\hat{g}_y)^2}}{M}\right)\right) \qquad (4)$$

5 Results

In order to evaluate the performance of the different proposals, the two approaches previously described have been implemented using the NVIDIA CUDA framework for their execution on GPU just as we are using C/C++ for their execution on CPU. The hardware platform used for the CPU execution is *Intel P8400 (2.26GHz), 4GB RAM DDR2* while the hardware used for the GPU execution is *NVIDIA 9200GS, 512GB global memory*.

A maximum length filter of 15 for the pseudo-parameterized filtering process has been used with $\sigma = 1$. As Luo[7] states, the implementation of hysteresis using NVIDIA CUDA has to be iterated sometimes. We did not experimented a significant improvement over 4 iterations for our test images, hence we fixed this number of iterations.

The experimentation process consisted of 100 executions per implementation. The results obtained are expressed in terms of average time in milliseconds, *speedup* and time consumption percentage.

Comparing NVIDIA CUDA and C/C++ implementations. Fig. 3 and 4 exhibit the average execution times for all the implementations. The NVIDIA CUDA implementations behave better in terms of execution time compared to the C/C++ approaches. Generally, the *speedup* grows as the image size becomes larger.

The *Modified Operators* approach give more efficient implementations. Fig. 5 shows the *speedup* obtained upon comparing this approach with the *Traditional Operators* approach, revealing that the NVIDIA CUDA implementation makes a better exploitation of the *Modified Operators* approach than C/C++.

The behaviour of the *speedup* curve is different for the NVIDIA CUDA implementation than for the C/C++ implementation. The former decreases as the image size increases while the latter slightly increases with the image size.

Execution time distribution using NVIDIA CUDA. As mentioned previously, the NVIDIA CUDA executions are distributed around kernels. Figs. 6

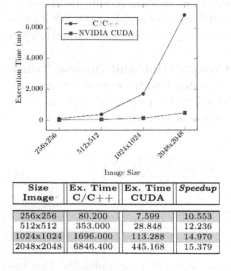
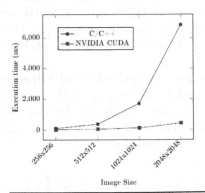

Size Image	Ex. Time C/C++	Ex. Time CUDA	Speedup
256x256	80.200	7.599	10.553
512x512	353.000	28.848	12.236
1024x1024	1696.000	113.288	14.970
2048x2048	6846.400	445.168	15.379

Size Image	Ex. Time C/C++	Ex. Time CUDA	Speedup
256x256	79.000	6.786	11.640
512x512	346.200	26.448	13.089
1024x1024	1660.600	104.533	15.885
2048x2048	6704.100	418.563	16.016

Fig. 3. Results for the *Traditional Operators* approach

Fig. 4. Results for the *Modified Operators* approach

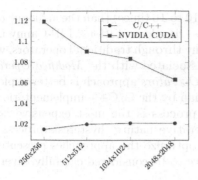

Image Size	C/C++	CUDA
256x256	1.015	1.119
512x512	1.020	1.090
1024x1024	1.021	1.083
2048x2048	1.021	1.063

Fig. 5. *Speedup* for the *Modified Operators* approach compared to the *Traditional Operators* approach

and 7 show the distribution for LIP-Canny using both approaches for a 512×512 input image. The distribution of the kernels may vary slightly for different image sizes, but the order of time consumption remains invariant except for the memory transfers. The results exhibit similar distributions for the different LIP-Canny implementations using NVIDIA CUDA. Hysteresis takes a special importance due to its high time consumption.

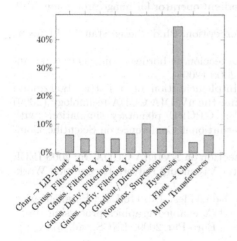

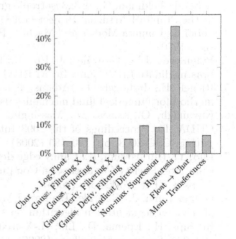

Fig. 6. Distribution for the *Traditional Operators* approach

Fig. 7. Distribution for the *Modified Operators* approach

6 Conclusions

In this work, we have presented two different approaches to implement LIP-Canny using NVIDIA CUDA, one through traditional operators applied to modified images and another through modified operators applied to traditional images.

Comparative results between C/C++ implementations and NVIDIA CUDA implementations are presented. These results show that NVIDIA CUDA implementations are faster (aproximately 10 to 16 times) than the analogue using C/C++. Furthermore, as occurs in C/C++ implementations, LIP-Canny using modified operators is faster than LIP-Canny through traditional operators, when based on NVIDIA CUDA. The *speedup* associated with the *Modified Operators* approach compared with the *Traditional Operators* approach is better exploited by the NVIDIA CUDA implementation than by the C/C++ implementation.

The results show that the hysteresis process is the most expensive kernel in terms of execution time due to its iterative nature (hysteresis process was repeated 4 times). For further efforts to optimize the approaches presented in this work, the hysteresis process could have to be considered carefully, given the relevance of the process in terms of execution time.

The impact of the distribution when choosing another number of iterations will be significant, making the existing difference between the hysteresis kernel an the other kernels grow upon increasing the number of iterations, obtaining thus the opposite effect when decreasing this number which is highly dependent on the image to be processed.

References

1. Canny, J.: A computational approach to edge detection. IEEE Transactions on Pattern Analysis and Machine Intelligence 8(6), 679–698 (1986)
2. Sobel, I., Feldman, G.: A 3x3 isotropic gradient operator for image processing. Talk at the Stanford Artificial Project (1968)
3. Sobel, I.: Camera Models and Machine Perception. Ph.d. thesis, Standford University (1970)
4. Palomares, J.M., González, J., Ros, E.: Detección de bordes en imágenes con sombras mediante LIP–Canny. In: AERFAI 2005 (2005)
5. Riegel, E., Indinger, T., Adams, N.: Implementation of a Lattice-Boltzmann method for numerical fluid mechanics using the nVIDIA CUDA technology (2009)
6. Kavanagh, G., Lewis, M., Massingill, B.: GPGPU planetary simulations with CUDA. In: Proceedings of the 2008 International Conference on Scientific Computing, CSC 2008, pp. 180–185 (2008)
7. Luo, Y., Duraiswami, R.: Canny edge detection on NVIDIA CUDA. In: 2008 IEEE Computer Society Conference on Computer Vision and Pattern Recognition Workshops, CVPR Workshops (2008)
8. Gómez-Luna, J., González-Linares, J.M., Benavides, J.I., Guil, N.: Parallelization of a video segmentation algorithm on CUDA–enabled graphics processing units. In: Sips, H., Epema, D., Lin, H.-X. (eds.) Euro-Par 2009. LNCS, vol. 5704, pp. 924–935. Springer, Heidelberg (2009)
9. Jourlin, P.: A model for logarithmic image processing. Journal of Microscopy 149, 21–35 (1988)
10. Pinoli, J.: The logarithmic image processing model: Connections with human brightness perception and contrast estimators. Journal of Mathematical Image Processing 7, 341–358 (1997)
11. NVIDIA: NVIDIA CUDA Programming Guide (2009)
12. NVIDIA: NVIDIA CUDA C Programming Best Practices Guide. CUDA Toolkit 2.3. (2009)
13. Podlozhnyuk, V.: Image Convolution with CUDA
14. Palomares, J.M., González, J., Ros, E., Prieto, A.: General logarithmic image processing convolution. IEEE Transactions on Image Processing 15(11), 3602–3608 (2006)

Some Averaging Functions in Image Reduction

D. Paternain[1], H. Bustince[1], J. Fernandez[1], G. Beliakov[2], and R. Mesiar[3,4]

[1] Department of Automatic and Computation,
Public University of Navarra, Pamplona, Spain
{daniel.paternain,bustince,fcojavier.fernandez}@unavarra.es
[2] School of Information Technology, Deakin University, Australia
gleb@deakin.edu.au
[3] Department of Mathematics and Descriptive Geometry, Slovak University of
Technology, SK-813 68 Bratislava, Slovakia
[4] Institute of Information Theory and Automation, Czech Academy of Sciences,
CZ-182 08 Prague, Czech Republic
mesiar@math.sk

Abstract. In this work we propose a definition of weak local reduction operators and an algorithm that uses such operators to reduce images. We show how to construct local reduction operators by means of different aggregation functions. We also present several experimental results obtained using these aggregation functions-based reduction operators.

Keywords: Image reduction, local reduction operators, aggregation functions.

1 Introduction

Image reduction consists in diminishing the resolution of the image while keeping as much information as possible. Image reduction can be used to accelerate computations on an image ([12,8]), or just to reduce its storage cost ([9]).

We know that in the literature, there exist many different image reduction methods. Some of them consider the image to be reduced globally ([9]). Some others divide the image in pieces and act on each of these pieces locally ([7]). In this work we focus on the latter.

The problem we consider is the following: given an image, create a new, smaller image such that the intensity of each of the pixels of the smaller image reflects the interrelation between the elements of a particular region of the original image, in such a way that the new pixel preserves as much information as possible from the considered region in the original image. This problem has led us to axiomatically define the concept of local reduction operator.

In this work, as a particular case, we obtain weak local reduction operators by means of aggregation functions, since these functions have been extensively considered in the literature ([1,4,6]).

We also present an image reduction algorithm. We study experimentally point of view the effect of using some of the most common averaging functions in this algorithm.

N. García-Pedrajas et al. (Eds.): IEA/AIE 2010, Part III, LNAI 6098, pp. 399–408, 2010.

There is no an exact way of determining which is the best reduction method. It depends on a particular application we are considering. In this work, to decide whether a reduction is better than another, we reconstruct the original image from the reduction using the bilinear interpolation of MATLAB. We choose this reconstruction method since we also do the implementation of our methods with MATLAB.

2   Preliminaries

We start by recalling some concepts that will be used along this work.

Definition 1. *An aggregation function of dimension n (n-ary aggregation function) is a non-decreasing mapping $M : [0,1]^n \to [0,1]$ such that $M(0,\ldots,0) = 0$ and $M(1,\ldots,1) = 1$.*

Definition 2. *Let $M : [0,1]^n \to [0,1]$ be a n-ary aggregation function.*

(i) M is said to be idempotent if $M(x,\ldots,x) = x$ for any $x \in [0,1]$.
(ii) M is said to be homogeneous if $M(\lambda x_1,\ldots,\lambda x_n) = \lambda M(x_1,\ldots,x_n)$ for any $\lambda \in [0,1]$ and for any $(x_1,\ldots,x_n) \in [0,1]^n$.
(iii) M is said to be shift-invariant if $M(x_1 + r,\ldots,x_n + r) = M(x_1,\ldots,x_n) + r$ for all $r > 0$ such that $0 \le x_i + r \le 1$ for any $i = 1,\ldots,n$.

A complete characterization for shift-invariantness and homogeneity of aggregation functions can be seen in [10,11].

We know that a triangular norm (t-norm for short) $T : [0,1]^2 \to [0,1]$ is an associative, commutative, non-decreasing function such that $T(1,x) = x$ for all $x \in [0,1]$. A basic t-norm is the minimum ($T_M(x,y) = \wedge(x,y)$). Analogously, a triangular conorm (t-conorm for short) $S : [0,1]^2 \to [0,1]$ is an associative, commutative, non-decreasing function such that $S(0,x) = x$ for all $x \in [0,1]$. A basic t-conorm is the maximum ($S_M(x,y) = \vee(x,y)$).

3   Local Reduction Operators

In this work, we consider an image of $n \times m$ pixels as a set of $n \times m$ elements arranged in rows and columns. Hence we consider an image as a $n \times m$ matrix. Each element of the matrix has a value in $[0,1]$ that will be calculated by normalizing the intensity of the corresponding pixel in the image. We use the following notation.

- $\mathcal{M}_{n \times m}$ is the set of all matrices of dimension $n \times m$ over $[0,1]$.
- Each element of a matrix $A \in \mathcal{M}_{n \times m}$ is denoted by a_{ij} with $i \in \{1,\ldots,n\}$, $j \in \{1,\ldots,m\}$.
- Let $A, B \in \mathcal{M}_{n \times m}$. We say that $A \le B$ if for all $i \in \{0,\ldots,n\}, j \in \{0,\ldots,m\}$ the inequality $a_{ij} \le b_{ij}$ holds.

– Let $A \in \mathcal{M}_{n \times m}$ and $c \in [0,1]$. $A = c$ denotes that $a_{ij} = c$ for all $i \in \{1, \ldots, n\}, j \in \{1, \ldots, m\}$. In this case, we will say that A is constant matrix or a flat image.

Definition 3. *A weak local reduction operator* WO_{RL} *is a mapping* $WO_{RL} :$ $\mathcal{M}_{n \times m} \to [0,1]$ *that satisfies*

(WORL1) For all $A, B \in \mathcal{M}_{n \times m}$, *if* $A \leq B$, *then* $WO_{RL}(A) \leq WO_{RL}(B)$.
(WORL2) If $A = c$ *then* $WO_{RL}(A) = c$.

Remark: We call our operators weak local reduction operators since we demand the minimum number of properties that, in our opinion, a local reduction operator must fulfill.

Definition 4. *We say that a weak reduction operator* WO_{RL} *is:*

(WORL3) homogeneous if $WO_{RL}(\lambda A) = \lambda \cdot WO_{RL}(A)$ *for all* $A \in \mathcal{M}_{n \times m}$ *and* $\lambda \in [0,1]$
(WORL4) stable under translation (shift-invariant) if $WO_{RL}(A + r) = WO_{RL}$ $(A) + r$ *for all* $A \in \mathcal{M}_{n \times m}$ *and* $r \in [0,1]$ *such that* $0 \leq a_{ij} + r \leq 1$ *whenever* $i \in \{1, \ldots, n\}, j \in \{1, \ldots, m\}$.

4   Image Reduction Algorithm

In this section we present a possible algorithm for image reduction.

Given an image $A \in \mathcal{M}_{n \times m}$ and a reduction block size $n' \times m'$ (with $n' \leq n$ and $m' \leq m$), we propose the following algorithm:

(1) Choose a local reduction operator.
(2) Divide the image A into disjoint blocks of dimension $n' \times m'$.
If n is not a multiple of n' or m is not a multiple of m' we suppress the smallest number of rows and/or columns in A that ensures that these conditions hold.
(3) Apply the local reduction operator to each block.

Example 1. In Figure 1 we show a scheme of this algorithm. On a 9×9 image we take reduction blocks of size given by $n' = m' = 3$. The reduced image will hence have 3×3 dimension.

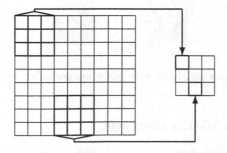

Fig. 1. Example of reduction of a matrix

5   Construction of Weak Local Reduction Operators from Averaging Functions

Proposition 1. *Let M be an idempotent aggregation function. The operator defined by*

$$WO_{RL}(A) = M(a_{11}, a_{12}, \ldots, a_{1m}, \ldots, a_{n1}, \ldots, a_{nm})$$

for all $A \in \mathcal{M}_{n \times m}$ is a weak local reduction operator.

Example 2. a) Take $M = T_M$. In Figure 2 we apply the weak local reduction operator obtained from T_M to the image (a) and we obtain image (a1). In image (b) we add some salt and pepper type noise. Applying the same weak local reduction operator as before we obtain image (b1)

b) Take $M = S_M$. In the same figure, we apply the weak local reduction operator obtained from S_M to image (a) and we obtain image (a2). The same process is done for image (b), getting image (b2).

Observe that these two operators minimum and maximum are not good local reduction operators. If we take the minimum over a block with noise we always obtain the value 0. Analogously, if we consider the maximum and apply it to a block with noise, we always recover the value 1. In this way we lose all information about the elements in the block that have not been altered by noise. This fact leads us to study other aggregation functions.

(a)   (b)

(a1)   (b1)

(a2)   (b2)

Fig. 2. Reduction of Lena and Lena with noise images using minimum and maximum and block size of 2×2

Proposition 2. *The following items hold:*

(1) $WO_{RL}(A) = T_M(a_{11}, a_{12}, \ldots, a_{1m}, \ldots, a_{n1}, \ldots, a_{nm})$ is a weak local reduction operator that verifies (WORL3) and (WORL4).

(2) $WO_{RL}(A) = S_M(a_{11}, a_{12}, \ldots, a_{1m}, \ldots, a_{n1}, \ldots, a_{nm})$ is a weak local reduction operator that verifies (WORL3) and (WORL4).

Proof: It follows from the fact that both weak local reductions operators constructed from minimum and maximum satisfies (WORL3) and (WORL4).

5.1   Weighted Quasi Arithmetic Means

Definition 5. Let $g : [0, 1] \rightarrow [-\infty, \infty]$ be a continuous and strictly monotone function and $w = (w_1, \ldots, w_n)$ a weighting vector such that $\sum_{i=1}^{n} w_i = 1$. A weighted quasi-arithmetic mean is a mapping $M_g : [0, 1]^n \rightarrow [0, 1]$ defined as

$$M_g(x_1, \ldots, x_n) = g^{-1}\left(\sum_{i=1}^{n} w_i g(x_i)\right)$$

Proposition 3. Let $M_g : [0, 1]^{n \cdot m} \rightarrow [0, 1]$ be a weighted quasi-arithmetic mean. The operator defined as

$$WO_{RL}(A) = g^{-1}\left(\sum_{i=1}^{n}\sum_{j=1}^{m} w_{ij} g(a_{ij})\right)$$

for all $A \in \mathcal{M}_{n \times m}$ is a weak local reduction operator.

Notice that from Definition 5 we can generate well-known aggregation functions as, for instance, the weighted arithmetic mean $(g(x) = x)$ and the weighted geometric mean $(g(x) = \log(x))$.

Proposition 4. A weak local reduction operator built from a weighted quasi-arithmetic with $w_{ij} = \frac{1}{n \cdot m}$ satisfies (WORL3) if and only if

$$WO_{RL}(A) = \left(\prod_{i=1}^{n}\prod_{j=1}^{m} a_{ij}\right)^{\frac{1}{n \cdot m}} \qquad or$$

$$WO_{RL}(A) = \left(\sum_{i=1}^{n}\sum_{j=1}^{m} \frac{a_{ij}^{\alpha}}{n \cdot m}\right)^{\frac{1}{\alpha}} \qquad with \ \alpha \neq 0$$

for all $A \in \mathcal{M}_{n \times m}$.

Proof: See page 118 of [6]   □

In Figure 3 we illustrate property (WORL3). Image (a) is Cameraman image with random noise (white pixels). Image (b) has been obtained multiplying the intensity of each of the pixels of (a) by $\lambda = 0.5$. That is, $(b) = 0.5 \cdot (a)$. Under these conditions, we consider the following weak local reduction operators.

- the geometric mean in the second row.
- the following quasi arithmetic mean

$$M_g(x_1,\ldots,x_n) = \begin{cases} \dfrac{\sqrt[n]{\prod_{i=1}^{n} x_i}}{\sqrt[n]{\prod_{i=1}^{n} x_i} + \sqrt[n]{\prod_{i=1}^{n}(1-x_i)}} & \text{if } \{0,1\} \nsubseteq \{x_1,\ldots,x_n\} \\ 0 & \text{otherwise} \end{cases}$$

in the third row

We see that $(b1) = 0.5 \cdot (a1)$, so they keep the same proportion than images (a) and (b). However, it is visually clear that $(b2) \neq 0.5 \cdot (a2)$. This is due to the fact that the second aggregation function that we have used does not satisfy $(WORL3)$.

(a)   (b)

(a1)   (b1)

(a2)   (b2)

Fig. 3. Test of property $(WORL3)$ of weak local reduction operators. Reduction block size 2×2.

Proposition 5. *A weak local reduction operator built from a weighted quasi-arithmetic mean with $w_{ij} = \frac{1}{n \cdot m}$ satisfies $(WORL4)$ if and only if*

$$WO_{RL}(A) = \frac{1}{n \cdot m} \sum_{i=1}^{n} \sum_{j=1}^{m} a_{ij} \quad or$$

$$WO_{RL}(A) = \frac{1}{\alpha} \log \left(\sum_{i=1}^{n} \sum_{j=1}^{m} \frac{e^{\alpha a_{ij}}}{n \cdot m} \right) \quad with \ \alpha \neq 0$$

for all $A \in \mathcal{M}_{n \times m}$

Proof: See page 118 in [6]   □

In Figure 4 we illustrate property $(WORL4)$. The normalized intensity of the pixels in image (a) vary from 0 to 0.5. Image (b) corresponds to add $r = 0.5$ to each of the intensities of the pixels in image (a). That is, $(b) = (a) + 0.5$. We apply the following weak local reduction operators:

- the arithmetic mean in the second row
- the geometric mean in the third row.

Observe that $(b1) = (a1)+0.5$. However, it is visually clear that $(b2) \neq (a2)+0.5$. This is due to the fact that the arithmetic mean satisfies $(WORL4)$ whereas the geometric mean does not.

(a)   (b)

(a1)   (b1)

(a2)   (b2)

Fig. 4. Test of property $(WORL4)$ of weak local reduction operators. Reduction block size 2×2.

5.2   Median

Proposition 6. *The operator defined as*

$$WO_{RL}(A) = Med(a_{11}, \dots, a_{1m}, \dots, a_{n1}, \dots, a_{nm})$$

for all $A \in \mathcal{M}_{n \times m}$, where Med denotes the median, is a weak local reduction operator verifying $(WORL3)$ and $(WORL4)$.

Proof: It is straight forward   □

In Figure 5 we show the original House image (image (a)). We take as weak local reduction operator the one defined from the median and obtain image (a1). We add salt and pepper noise to image (a) to get image (b). We apply the same weak local reduction operator and obtain (b1). Observe that for this kind of reduction operators, noise does not have as much influence as for others. The reason for this is that salt and pepper noise adds black and white pixels randomly. As the median gives back the value "in the middle", it is not affected by black and white pixels.

Remark: Observe that we can build weak local reduction operators based in Choquet integral. In particular, if we impose symmetry, we get OWA operators, of which the mean is a prominent case.

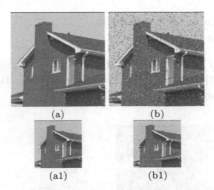

(a)   (b)

(a1)   (b1)

Fig. 5. Reduction of image House using the median operator with block sizes of 2×2

6   Experimental Results

As we have said in the Introduction, there is no exact way of determining which is the best reduction method. It depends on the particular application we are considering ([7,8,9]). In this section we analyze different reductions by reconstructing them to their original size using the two-dimensional bilinear interpolation from MATLAB.

There exist many methods to calculate the similarity between the original image and the reconstructed one. In fact, we know that there is a relation between the different types of errors (absolute mean error, quadratic mean error, etc.) and the aggregation function to be considered in each case ([4]). We will study in the future the relationship between the error measure and the aggregation function in image comparison. On the other hand, we can consider an image as a fuzzy set ([3]). For this reason, we are going to use fuzzy image comparison indexes. In [2] an in depth study of such indexes is carried out. In our work we are going to consider the Similarity measure based on contrast de-enhancement. This index has been used, for instance, in [5] and it satisfies the six properties demanded in [2] to similarity indexes. With the notations we are using, given $A, B \in \mathcal{M}_{n \times m}$, this index is given by:

$$S(A, B) = \frac{1}{n \cdot m} \sum_{i=1}^{n} \sum_{j=1}^{m} 1 - |a_{ij} - b_{ij}|.$$

In the experiments we are going to reduce images in Figure 6 using as weak local reduction operators those based on: minimum, geometric mean, arithmetic mean, median and maximum. In Table 1 we show the results of the comparison by means of the S index between the original images in Figure 6 and the reconstructed ones.

Notice that, in general, the results are very good. In particular, for all the images we obtain the best result with the median. We also obtain similar results with the geometric and the arithmetic means. On the contrary, we get the worst results with the minimum and the maximum. This is due to the fact that with

Table 1. Comparison between reconstructed images and images in Figure 6

	Minimum	Geom. Mean	Arith. Mean	Median	Maximum
Image (a)	0.9586	0.9748	0.9750	0.9759	0.9582
Image (b)	0.9832	0.9854	0.9848	0.9866	0.9803
Image (c)	0.9429	0.9650	0.9651	0.9673	0.9393
Image (d)	0.9509	0.9708	0.9706	0.9719	0.9482

(a)   (b)   (c)   (d)

Fig. 6. Original images of size 256×256

(a)   (b)   (c)   (d)

Fig. 7. Images with salt and pepper noise of size 256×256

Table 2. Comparison between reconstructed images and images in Figure 7

	Minimum	Geom. Mean	Arith. Mean	Median	Maximum
Image (a)	0.8517	0.8696	0.9621	0.9757	0.8729
Image (b)	0.9116	0.9129	0.9639	0.9865	0.8509
Image (c)	0.8586	0.8819	0.8536	0.9671	0.8457
Image (d)	0.6824	0.8851	0.9607	0.9717	0.8569

these two operators we only take into account a single value for each block, which needs not to be representative of the rest of values in that block.

In Table 2 we show the comparison of the images in Figure 7 and the reconstructed ones. Images in Figure 7 have been obtained by addition of salt and pepper noise to images in Figure 6. In these conditions, the best result is also obtained using the median as weak local reduction operator. This is due to the fact that the value provided by the median is not affected by salt and pepper noise. Moreover, we observe that the operators given by the minimum, the geometric mean and the maximum are very sensitive to this noise. For the first two ones, a single pixel of 0 intensity determines that the value for the corresponding block is also 0. For the maximum, if there is a pixel with intensity equal to 1, then the result is also equal to 1.

So, from the analysis of Tables 1 and 2 and with the considered reconstruction method, we can say that the best weak local reduction operator is that based on the median. Moreover, we must remark that whenever we study noisy images, the best comparison measures are those given in [2] since one of the axioms demanded by the authors is precisely that of reaction in the presence of noise.

7   Conclusions

In this work we have axiomatically defined local reduction operators. We have studied how to construct these operators by means of averaging functions. We have analyzed which properties are satisfied by some of these aggregation-based reduction operators.

From our operators, we have proposed an image reduction algorithm. To settle which is the best local reduction operator, we have proposed an application based on reconstructing the original images from the reduced ones. To compare images we have used a fuzzy similarity index. We have seen that, in all of the cases, the best weak local reduction operator is provided by the median. Moreover, this operator is not affected by salt and pepper noise.

Acknowledgments. This work has been partially supported by grants TIN2007-65981, VEGA 1/0080/10 and APVV-0012-07.

References

1. Beliakov, G., Pradera, A., Calvo, T.: Aggregation Functions: A Guide for Practitioners. Studies in Fuzziness and Soft Computing, vol. 221 (2007)
2. Bustince, H., Pagola, M., Barrenechea, E.: Construction of fuzzy indices from DI-subsethood measures: Application to the global comparison of images. Information Sciences 177, 906–929 (2007)
3. Bustince, H., Barrenechea, E., Pagola, M., Fernandez, J.: Interval-valued fuzzy sets constructed from matrices: Application to edge detection. Fuzzy Sets and Systems 160, 1819–1840 (2009)
4. Calvo, T., Beliakov, G.: Aggregation functions based on penalties. Fuzzy sets and Systems (in press), doi:10.1016/j.fss.2009.05.012
5. Chaira, T., Ray, A.K.: Fuzzy measures for color image retrieval. Fuzzy Sets and Systems 150, 545–560 (2005)
6. Fodor, J., Roubens, M.: Fuzzy Preference Modelling and Multicriteria Decision Support. Kluwer Academic Publishers, Dordrecht (1994)
7. Loia, V., Sessa, S.: Fuzzy relation equations for coding/decoding processes of images and videos. Information Sciences 171, 145–172 (2005)
8. Di Martino, F., Loia, V., Sessa, S.: A segmentation method for image compressed by fuzzy transform. Fuzzy Sets and Systems 161, 56–74 (2010)
9. Perfilieva, I.: Fuzzy transform and their applications to image compression. In: Bloch, I., Petrosino, A., Tettamanzi, A.G.B. (eds.) WILF 2005. LNCS (LNAI), vol. 3849, pp. 19–31. Springer, Heidelberg (2006)
10. Rückschlossová, T.: Aggregation operators and invariantness. PhD thesis, Slovak University of Technology, Bratislava, Slovakia (June 2003)
11. Rückschlossová, T., Rückschloss, R.: Homogeneous aggregation operators. Kybernetika (Prague) 42(3), 279–286 (2006)
12. Xiang, S., Nie, F., Zhang, C.: Learning a Mahalanobis distance metric for data clustering and classification. Pattern Recognition 41, 3600–3612 (2008)

A Method for Weighting Multi-valued Features in Content-Based Filtering

Manuel J. Barranco and Luis Martínez

University of Jaén, Campus Las Lagunillas, 23071, Jaén, Spain
barranco@ujaen.es, martin@ujaen.es
http://sinbad2.ujaen.es

Abstract. Content-based recommender systems (CBRS) and collaborative filtering are the type of recommender systems most spread in the e-commerce arena. A CBRS works with two sets of information: (i) a set of features that describe the items to be recommended and (ii) a user's profile built from past choices that the user made over a subset of items. Based on these sets and on weighting items features the CBRS is able to recommend those items that better fits the user profile. Commonly, a CBRS deals with simple item features such as key words extracted from the item description applying a simple feature weighting model, based on the TF-IDF. However, this method does not obtain good results when features are assessed in multiple values and or domains. In this contribution we propose a higher level feature weighting method based on entropy and coefficients of correlation and contingency in order to improve the content-based filtering in settings with multi-valued features.

1 Introduction

Recommendation systems are excellent tools to customize information in settings where the vast amount of information overloads users. Particularly, content-based recommender systems, CBRS [1,4,12,13], are one of the traditional types of such systems, which uses the available information about the choices that the user made in the past. This information is used to build a user profile that exposes the user's preferences or necessities. Besides, it is necessary a database of descriptive information about the items, each item is described by a set of features.

Typically, a CBRS works with textual analysis so that the features are words or terms that describe the items. In this way, given a set of features or terms, the vector describing an item is filled by ones and zeros that indicates whether or not a term appears in the text description of that item. Nevertheless, in a more general case, the features can be assessed by multi-valued variables or different domains: numeric, linguistic or nominal, boolean, etc.

Similar to other recommendation systems, the content-based ones present advantages and disadvantages. So they often are combined with other models such as collaborative or knowledge-based in order to improve its performance.

N. García-Pedrajas et al. (Eds.): IEA/AIE 2010, Part III, LNAI 6098, pp. 409–418, 2010.

The basic functions of a CBRS consists of (i) updating the profile of each user (ii) filtering the available products with the user's profile and (iii) recommending the products that better fits the profile. The filtering process should consider that not all features are equally important. Obviously, when a user selects an item, he/she is watching some features that are important and ignoring others that are worthless to him/her. This consideration represents an implicit feature weighting which is subjective and different for each user.

The aim of this paper is to introduce a new method to obtain these weights, in recommendation settings where the features can be assessed with multi-valued variables or in multiple domains, by using the implicit ratings obtained from the users in the past. Thus, assigning weights to the features, according to the weighting that the user has implicitly provided, the profile will be more useful in the recommendation process. Our proposal computes two measures for weighting each feature. First we take into account the entropy or amount of information for each feature, the more entropy the more weighting should have. And second we consider the correlation (for quantitative features) and contingency (for qualitative features), between items chose by the user in the past and the values of some features of the set of items. The greater the relationships, the higher the weight for the feature.

This paper is structured as follows. Section 2 reviews necessary concepts for our proposal. Sections 3 describes in further detail our proposal for weighting multi-valued features which is illustrated by an example in Section 4. Finally, Section 5 points out some conclusions.

2   Preliminaries

In this section we review briefly content-based recommender systems and methods commonly used for weighting features in this setting.

2.1   Content-Based Recommender Systems

First we will review briefly content-based recommendation systems [1,11,13]. Those systems use a database with a set of items $A = \{a_i, i = 1...n\}$ described by a set of features $C = \{c_j, j = 1...m\}$ defined each one in a domain D_j, so that each item a_i is described by a vector $V_i = \{v_{ij} \in D_j, j = 1..m\}$ (see Table 1).

Table 1. Data for a CBRS

	c_1	...	c_j	...	c_m
a_1	v_{11}	...	v_{1j}	...	v_{1m}
...	...	...	...	...	...
a_n	v_{n1}	...	v_{nj}	...	v_{nm}

For each user, u, there exists a set $A_u = \{a_i^u \in A, i = 1, \ldots, n_u\}$, where a_i^u are the items experienced by the user, u. The assessments of their features are described by, v_{ij}^u, and a user's preference assessments, $r_i^u \in D_u$ (implicit or explicit) being D_u the expression domain (see Table 2).

Table 2. User data for a CBRS

	c_1	...	c_m	R_u
a_1^u	v_{11}^u	...	v_{1m}^u	r_1^u
...	...	...	...	...
$a_{n_u}^u$	$v_{n_u1}^u$	...	$v_{n_um}^u$	$r_{n_u}^u$
P_u	p_1^u	...	p_m^u	
W_u	w_1^u	...	w_m^u	

By using the user's information, the CBRS computes a user profile P_u that represents the user preferences and a weighting vector W_u that includes the weights of each feature according to their relevance in the user's needs:

- $P_u = \{p_j^u \in D_j, j = 1..m\}$ are the user's values for item features. They can be obtained in different ways [1,11,13].
- $W_u = \{w_j^u, j = 1..m, 0 \leq w_j^u \leq 1\}$ are the weights that show the relevance of each feature, according to user's needs.

Once we know the available data for a CBRS, we will describe its working:

1. Acquisition of the items' features and users' profiles. The system updates the user profiles based on implicit information obtained in the past.
2. Filtering process. For each item and feature the system calculates the similarity with the user profile. The values obtained are then aggregated to obtain the similarity with each item.
3. Recommendations. The system selects the most similar items to user's necessities.

2.2 Feature Weighting in CBRS

We have aforementioned that the user profile, P_u, is used to filter the most suitable items together a weighting vector, W_u. In the literature is common a feature weighting method based on item descriptive words [13,15] based on the Term Frequency - Inverse Document Frequency (TF-IDF) [2] that has been used as a weighting scheme in Information Retrieval [7], Decision-Making problems [5], etc.

The use of TF-IDF feature weighting in CBRS [15], consists of user's profiles with zeros and ones that indicate the existence or absence of key words in the item description. The weights are computed for each user, u and each feature, c_j by using two factors: (i) A quantification of the intra-user similarity, FF (feature frequency), which indicates the characteristic frequency of c_j for user u and (ii) a quantification of the inter-user dissimilarity, IUF (inverse user frequency) which provides a higher value to the distinctive characteristics, i.e., the least repeated in the set of users.

$$W(u, c_j) = FF(u, c_j) * IUF(c_j) \tag{1}$$

Commonly, the factor $FF(u, c_j)$, is computed by using the number of times that feature c_j appears in the items that user u has rated positively. The second factor, according to the TF-IDF scheme [2], is computed as $IUF(c_j) = Log \frac{|U|}{UF(c_j)}$ being $UF(c_j)$ the number of users that have rated positively any item that has the feature c_j, and $|U|$ the total number of users registered in the system. Such weights are used in the filtering process to match the user's profile and the items descriptions.

This feature weighting method is useful in CBRS dealing with binary features based on text descriptions, i.e., a feature is a word that can appear (value 1) or not appear (value 0) in an item's description. However, for those systems dealing with multi-valued features, the previous approach is not appropriate because a richer modelling with more than 2 values is necessary. The problem of weighting multi-valued features has been addressed in other areas like information retrieval and machine learning [9,10]. Nevertheless, this problem has been performed poorly in recommender systems settings. Our aim is to provide a proposal to address satisfactorily this issue in CBRS.

3   Feature Weighting Based on Entropy and Dependency Measures

Our aim is to propose a new feature weighting method for CBRS that can cope with multi-valued features. This proposal uses the data structure showed in Tables 1 and 2. We consider the item descriptions $V_{i.}^u = \{v_{ij}^u, j = 1 \ldots m\}$ and the features descriptions $V_{.j}^u = \{v_{ij}^u, i = 1 \ldots n_u\}$.

Our proposal consists of a feature weighting method that computes a weight for each feature according to (i) the amount of information provided by itself (multi-valued features can provide different amount of information), and (ii) the correlation between the items experienced by the user and the features of items. The feature weighting method follows the phases described below (see Figure 1):

1. Calculation of inter-user similarity. It is computed to know which features are more relevant to the user. For each feature c_j, we propose the use of the entropy H_j to compute the amount of information that it can offer.
2. Calculation of intra-user similarity. It is calculated the correlation between user's past items and the features values on the set of items. This calculation will depend on the nature of the features (qualitative, quantitative). For a feature c_j and a user u, it is calculated a coefficient of dependency, DC_{uj}, between the ratings obtained from the user, $R_u = \{r_i^u, i = 1, \ldots n_u\}$, and the valuations of the feature in the items rated, $V_{.j}^u = \{v_{ij}^u, i = 1 \ldots n_u\}$:
   – Correlation coefficient: for quantitative features.
   – Contingency coefficient: for qualitative features.

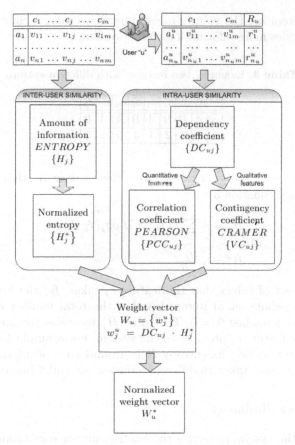

Fig. 1. Feature weighting based on entropy and dependency measures

3. Calculation of weights. Finally, it is obtained the feature weight as a result of the product of entropy and degree of dependency.

In the coming sections we show in further detail each phase.

3.1 Inter-user Similarity

To compute how informative is each feature we propose the use of the entropy.

Definition 1[6,14]. Entropy of information is the average amount of information, measured in bits, which contains a random variable. Given a random variable x, its entropy is given as:

$$H(x) = -\sum_i p(x_i) \, Log_2 \left(p(x_i) \right) \tag{2}$$

Features with a greater entropy are most interesting and should have a greater weight. For example, given two features, c_1 and c_2 (see Table 3), if a user rates positively the item a_1, the value $c_2 = 1$ must have more weight than $c_1 = A$ because it provides more information to the system.

Table 3. Example: two features with different entropy

	a_1	a_2	a_3	a_4	a_5	a_6	a_7	a_8
c_1	A	B	B	A	B	A	A	B
c_2	1	3	2	4	4	5	6	5

For each feature c_j the system computes the entropy H_j that is normalized in $H_j^* \in [0,1]$ (see equation 3):

$$H_j = -\sum_{k_j} (f_{k_j}/n) Log_2(f_{k_j}/n)$$

$$H_j^* = \frac{H_j}{\sum_i H_i}$$

(3)

being $\{k_j\}$ the set of values that the feature c_j takes, f_{k_j} the frequency of the value k_j in the whole set of items A and n the total number of items. This calculation consideres Log $0 = 0$. The value H_j^* indicates the amount of information that the feature c_j provides to the system. For example, for an attribute that only take two values, its entropy H is around 1 bit of information. While, another attribute that takes 16 different values is around 4 bits of information.

3.2 Intra-user Similarity

In this phase, the system measures the contingency or correlation between the ratings in the user's profile and the values of a feature c_j on the set of items. If there is a dependency between these variables, it suggests that the feature is important for the user. Depending on the nature of the feature we propose different measurements. For quantitative features is used a correlation coefficient. For qualitative features is used a coefficient of contingency. We propose to use two well known coefficients of dependency for measuring the intra-user similarity: Pearson's correlation coefficient for correlation, and Cramer's V coefficient for contingency [3].

Pearson's correlation coefficient should be used when data are approximately distributed according to a normal distribution. We assume this premise. In other cases we may use other coefficients, like Spearman's one [3], instead of Pearson's coefficient.

Definition 2 [3]: Pearson's correlation coefficient measures the linear relationship between two variables. Unlike the covariance, the Pearson correlation is independent of the scale of measurement of variables:

$$r = \frac{\sigma_{XY}}{\sigma_X \sigma_Y}$$

(4)

$$s.t. \begin{cases} \sigma_{XY} = \frac{1}{n}\sum_{i=1}^{n} x_i y_i + \bar{x}\bar{y} \\ \sigma_X = \sqrt{\sum_{i=1}^{n}\frac{x_i^2}{n} - \bar{x}^2} \\ \sigma_Y = \sqrt{\sum_{i=1}^{n}\frac{y_i^2}{n} - \bar{y}^2} \end{cases}$$

Definition 3 [3]: Cramer's V coefficient . It is a contingency ratio that measures the dependence between two random variables, X and Y, where at least one of them is qualitative.

$$V = \sqrt{\frac{\chi^2}{n \cdot min\,(I-1, J-1)}} \tag{5}$$

$$s.t. \begin{cases} \chi^2 = \sum_{i=1}^{I}\sum_{j=1}^{J}\frac{(p_{ij}-q_{ij})^2}{q_{ij}} \\ n \text{ is the total number of occurrences} \\ I \text{ is the number of distinct values of the variable } X \\ J \text{ is the number of distinct values of the variable } Y \\ p_{ij} \text{ is the frequency of the pair } (i,j) \\ q_{ij} = \frac{p_{X=i}\cdot p_{Y=j}}{n} \text{ is the theoretical frequency of the pair } (i,j) \\ p_{X=i} \text{ is the frecuency of } X = i \\ p_{Y=j} \text{ is the frecuency of } Y = j \end{cases}$$

The dependence coefficient, DC, between the ratings made by the user u and the values of items for the feature, c_j, is given by the following expression

$$DC_{uj} = \begin{cases} |PCC_{uj}| & \text{if } c_j \text{ is quantitative} \\ VC_{uj} & \text{if } c_j \text{ is qualitative} \end{cases}$$

being PCC_{uj} the Pearson's correlation coefficient corresponding to the variables R_u and $V_{.j}^u$.

$$PCC_{uj} = \frac{\sum_i r_i^u v_{ij}^u - \frac{\sum_i r_i^u \sum_i v_{ij}^u}{n_u}}{\sqrt{\left(\sum_i (r_i^u)^2 - \frac{(\sum_i r_i^u)^2}{n_u}\right)}\sqrt{\left(\sum_i (v_{ij}^u)^2 - \frac{(\sum_i v_{ij}^u)^2}{n_u}\right)}} \tag{6}$$

and VC_{uj} is the Cramer's V, contingency coefficient corresponding to the same variables for qualitative features.

$$VC_{uj} = \sqrt{\frac{\sum_{k_u}\sum_{k_j}\frac{\left(f_{k_u,k_j} - \frac{f_{k_u}f_{k_j}}{n_u}\right)^2}{\frac{f_{k_u}f_{k_j}}{n_u}}}{n_u \; min\,(|D_u|, |D_j|)}} \tag{7}$$

where k_u and k_j are indexes for the set of different values in R_u and $V_{.j}^u$ respectively, f_{k_u}, f_{k_j} are the frequencies of values indexed by k_u and k_j respectively and f_{k_u,k_j} is the frequency of simultaneous occurrences of the two values indexed by k_u and k_j.

The Pearson coefficient is bounded on the interval [-1,1] providing information on the degree of dependence and also the type of dependence, direct or inverse. For our purposes it is not important the type of dependence. So, we take the absolute value, thus the result is in the interval [0,1]. In this way, and because of the Cramer V is also bounded in [0,1], DC coefficient will be bounded in that interval, being the value 1 the maximum dependence degree.

3.3   Calculation of Features' Weights

Once the factors H_j^* and DC_{uj} have been obtained, the system will compute the weight of a feature c_j as the product of both factors:

$$w_j^u = DC_{uj} \cdot H_j^* \tag{8}$$

Since a vector of weights $\{w_i\}$ must satisfy the property $\sum w_i = 1$, the final vector of weights W_u^* is given by:

$$W_u^* = \left\{ w_j^{*u} \mid j = 1, \ldots, m, \ w_j^{*u} = \frac{w_j^u}{\sum_i w_i^u} \right\} \tag{9}$$

4   Example

Let us consider an example with a set of items $A = \{a_1, \ldots, a_{20}\}$ where each item is described by a set of features or characteristics $C = \{c_1, \ldots, c_5\}$ being $c_1, \ldots, c_4$ quantitative features assessed in the domains $\{1, \ldots, 4\}$, $\{1, \ldots, 6\}$, $\{1, \ldots, 20\}$ and $\{1, \ldots, 30\}$ respectively, and c_5 a qualitative feature assessed in the domain $\{A, B, C, D\}$. In Table 4 it is shown the description of each item according to such a set of features.

Table 4. Item-Feature matrix

	a_1	a_2	a_3	a_4	a_5	a_6	a_7	a_8	a_9	a_{10}	a_{11}	a_{12}	a_{13}	a_{14}	a_{15}	a_{16}	a_{17}	a_{18}	a_{19}	a_{20}
c_1	1	3	2	2	4	2	1	1	4	2	2	1	1	3	4	1	2	4	1	2
c_2	2	6	2	3	4	4	2	6	5	4	3	6	2	4	5	2	2	4	2	4
c_3	2	5	12	14	8	16	4	4	15	14	18	17	10	13	17	1	1	19	9	11
c_4	5	20	10	11	25	13	5	2	28	12	9	4	6	18	27	3	10	29	1	14
c_5	A	C	B	B	D	B	A	A	D	B	B	A	A	C	D	A	B	D	A	B

On the other hand, we have a set of user's ratings in the domain $\{1, \ldots, 5\}$ that are shown in Table 5. These are the items that the user has rated in the past. In our case we assume 10 items have been already rated.

Our goal is to obtain a vector of weights for the five features given, to be used during the search of the items that best fit the user profile. So, we will apply entropy based weighting method.

Table 5. User's ratings

a_1	a_2	a_3	a_4	a_5	a_6	a_7	a_8	a_9	a_{10}
1	5	2	3	4	3	1	1	5	2

Calculation of entropies. We obtain: $H = \{H_j\} = \{1.86, 2.13, 3.92, 4.12, 1.86\}$. Its normalization provides a vector of relative entropies:

$$H^* = \{H_j^*\} = \{0.13, 0.15, 0.28, 0.30, 0.13\}$$

Calculation of dependence degrees. For the features $c_1, \ldots, c_4$ we calculate the correlation coefficient by using equation (6) obtaining the values:

$PCC_{u1} = 0.91$, $PCC_{u2} = 0.52$, $PCC_{u3} = 0.40$, $PCC_{u4} = 0.93$

For the qualitative feature c_5, the contingency coefficient obtains, $VC_{u5} = 0.73$. Therefore, the vector of dependence degrees will be:

$$DC_u = \{DC_{uj}\} = \{0.91, 0.52, 0.40, 0.93, 0.73\}$$

Calculation of features' weights. Finally, applying the formula (8) we obtain the vector of weights

$$W_u = \{w_j^u\} = \{0.12, 0.08, 0.11, 0.28, 0.10\}$$

We then normalize it according to (9) and obtain the final vector of weights for the features considered. That will be used by the CBRS in order to compute the recommendations.

$$W_u^* = \{w_j^{*u}\} = \{0.18, 0.12, 0.16, 0.40, 0.14\}$$

5 Conclusions and Future Works

The use of feature weighting methods in content based recommender systems has been a usual solution for their filtering processes. Additionally, the most common weighting method has been the TF-IDF, but it presents some drawbacks when the information manages by the recommender system is multi-valued or assessed in different domains.

In this contribution we have proposed a new method for calculating weights of features for content-based recommendation systems, where the features can be both quantitative and qualitative. The new method is based on two factors: intra-user similarity and inter-user dissimilarity that in our proposal the former is computed either by the Pearson correlation for quantitative features or by the Cramer's V for qualitative ones. And the latter is computed by the entropy that measures the amount of information of each feature.

Acknowledgements

This work is partially supported by the Research Project TIN2009-08286, P08-TIC-3548 and FEDER funds.

References

1. Adomavicius, G., Tuzhilin, A.: Toward the Next Generation of Recommender Systems: A Survey of the State-of-the-Art and Possible Extensions. IEEE Trans. on Knowledge and Data Engineering 17(6), 734–749 (2005)
2. Aizawa, A.: An information-theoretic perspective of TF-IDF measures. Information Processing and Managemente 39, 45–65 (2003)
3. Bishop, Y.M.M., Fienberg, S.E., Holland, P.W.: Discrete Multivariate Analysis: Theory and Practice. The MIT Press, England (1995)
4. Bogers, T., Bosch, A.: Comparing an evaluating information retrieval algorithms for news recommendation. In: Proc. of the 2007 ACM Conference on Recommender Systems, Minneapolis, USA, pp. 141–144 (2007)
5. Chung Wu, H., Pong Luk, R.W.: Interpreting tf-idf term weights as making relevance decisions. ACM Trans. on Information Systems 26(3), Article No. 13, 1–37 (2008)
6. Cover, T.M., Thomas, J.A.: Elements of Information Theory. John Wiley & Sons, Inc., Chichester (1991)
7. Fang, H., Tao, T., Zhai, C.: A formal study of information retrieval heuristics. In: Proc. of the 27th annual int. ACM SIGIR conf. on Research and depvelopment in information retrieval, pp. 49–56 (2004)
8. Hayes, C., Massa, P., Avesani, P., Cunningham, P.: An On-line Evaluation Framework for Recommender Systems. Technical Report TCD-CS-2002-19, Department of Computer Science, Trinity College Dublin (2002)
9. Hong, T.P., Chen, J.B.: Finding relevant attributes and membership functions. Fuzzy Sets and Systems 103, 389–404 (1999)
10. John, G.H., Kohavi, R., Pfleger, K.: Irrelevant features and the subset selection problem. In: Machine Learning: Proc. of the 11th int. conf., pp. 121–129. Morgan Kaufmann Publishers, San Francisco (1994)
11. Martínez, L., Pérez, L.G., Barranco, M.J.: A Multi-granular Linguistic Content-Based Recommendation Model. International Journal of Intelligent Systems 22(5), 419–434 (2007)
12. Mooney, R.J., Roy, L.: Content-based book recommending using learning for text categorization. In: Proc. of the 15th ACM conf. on Digital libraries, Texas, USA, pp. 195–204 (2000)
13. Pazzani, M.J., Billsus, D.: Content-Based Recommendation Systems. In: Brusilovsky, P., Kobsa, A., Nejdl, W. (eds.) Adaptive Web 2007. LNCS, vol. 4321, pp. 325–341. Springer, Heidelberg (2007)
14. Shannon, C.E.: A mathematical theory of communication. The Bell System Technical Journal 27, 379–423, 623–656 (1948)
15. Symeonidis, P., Nanopoulos, A., Manolopoulos, Y.: Feature-weighted user model form recommender systems. In: Conati, C., McCoy, K., Paliouras, G. (eds.) UM 2007. LNCS (LNAI), vol. 4511, pp. 97–106. Springer, Heidelberg (2007)

Virtual Doctor System (VDS):
Medical Decision Reasoning Based on Physical and Mental Ontologies[*]

Hamido Fujita, Jun Hakura, and Masaki Kurematsu

Iwate Prefectuarl University, Intelligent Software Systems Laboratory
152-52 Sugo, Takizawa, Iwate-gun, Iwate, 020-0173, Japan
HFujita-799@acm.org, {hakura,kure}@iwate-pu.ac.jp

Abstract. Human computer Interaction based on emotional modelling and physical views, collectively; has been investigated and reported in this paper. Two types of ontology have been presented to formalize a patient state: mental ontology reflecting the patient mental behavior due to certain disorder and physical ontology reflecting the observed physical collected exhibited consequences of such disorder. These two types of ontology have been mapped and aligned using OWL-S and SWRL for reasoning purposes. We have constructed an integrated computerized model which reflects a human diagnostician as computer model and through it, an integrated interaction between that model and the real human user (patient) is utilized for 1st stage diagnosis purposes. The diagnostician knowledge has been utilized through UMLS for testing, and the integrated mapping of the two views been represented through OWL-S framework. The reasoning instantiation is done using SWRL and RACER integrated on Protégé 4.

Keywords: Semantic Web, OWL, Medical diagnosis, knowledge based reasoning, cognitive model, human interaction.

1 Introduction

There have been extensive move towards changing the way health care is delivered, financed and regulated [13] Medical innovations have become an important lever inquest of improving efficiency. The main purpose is to improve the efficiency so that more patients could receive treatment more quickly without reducing the quality of care [8]. How to cope with a rise in the need for the elderly care services is a formidable issue facing all the industrialized countries.

The proportion of the population 65 and over has doubled from 10% in 1985 to 20% in 2005, and is projected to be 30% in 2023 [9].

---

[*] This research is supported by the Ministry of Internal Affairs and Communications of Japan under the Strategic Information and Communications R&D Promotion Programme (SCOPE).

N. García-Pedrajas et al. (Eds.): IEA/AIE 2010, Part III, LNAI 6098, pp. 419–428, 2010.

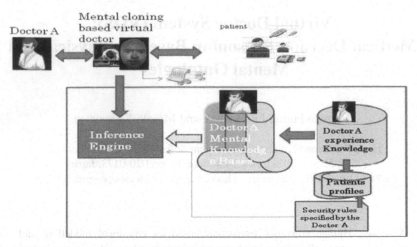

Fig. 1. Simple outline of the VDS

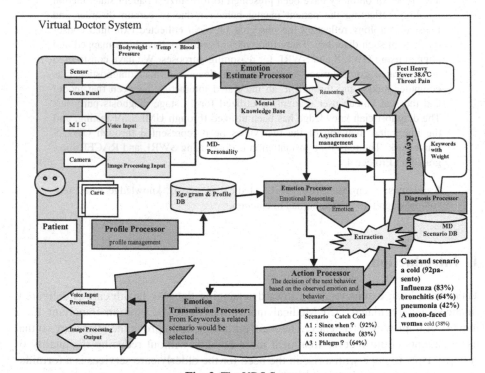

Fig. 2. The VDS System

The system proposed in this paper participates in helping physicians to manage the diagnosis procedure using the same knowledge that that physicians have by copying (mimic) his/her style, mentality, diagnosis routines and medicine recipes. It is not replacing the physicians but it would participate to utilize his/her knowledge for preliminary diagnosis and health care services to patient for efficiency purpose.

Fig. 3. VD avatar   **Fig. 4.** VDS experiment style

This paper contributes to present part of our experimental work on building a virtual system based or what we called as Virtual doctor System (VDS) Fig.2, to act as a physical or medicinal doctor for diagnosis purposes.

1.1 VDS Outline

The system we called here as VDS (Virtual Medical System) (Fig.2) is to work together with the corresponding medical doctor that the system is mimicking. So the system (VDS) and the MD are working together in comprehensive coherency; the former is complementary to the latter but not vice versa. The former is to diagnose outpatient 1st and classify these diagnosis into classes according to a defined ontology explained in next section. *Simple* cases classes that the VDS would take conclusion

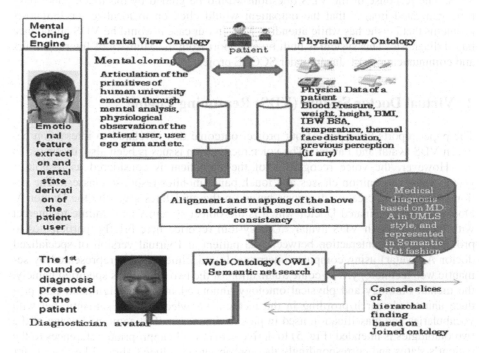

Fig. 5. System architecture of the inference engine

and set the diagnosis procedure and accordingly take action (e.g., issue drugs to the patient) are examined.

The cloning of medical doctor behavior is based on analysis of human medical doctor (HMD). The analysis is projected using his/her observed styles as a person and also as expert in medical diagnosis related practices. The system would create a virtual face (i.e., screen mask) of an actual doctor to interact with a patient. Physical doctor face is masked copied and attached on manikin (as shown in Fig 4). Inside it there is a projector that reflects the 3 dimensional generated images on the mask screen that reflects the actual facial real-time created images and voices of the medical doctor namely, Doctor A (Fig. 4). The style mimics the actual doctor emotional expression as well his/her diagnosis scenario. Also, the MD would speak [6] in natural accent with emotions based on the outpatient mental mode, estimated by the patient profile class (age, gender, ego data), and his/her situation automatically measured by data resembled to classes in the physical ontology (blood pressure, body weight, body temperature, and thermal analyzer). The devices read outpatient physical data are all attached to chair with nearby touch panel. These devices (equipments) are assembled to a patient desk chair that the patient would sit on, and automatically these measurements are collected and transferred through serial connection to the virtual doctor system. These physical data are all measured and sent online to the VDS together with the mental status data (situation) of the user (outpatient), with estimated ego state retrieved from the databases. The touch panel monitor would be used to create an active interaction to enter data (response to diagnosis initiated by the VDS) by the outpatient according to the interoperability generated scenario by the VDS. The response of the VDS questions would be guided by the touch panel real-time generated images that the outpatient would click on to localize the diagnosis problems that he/she has while attending MD, in our case it would be VDS attendance based diagnosis. This system is built by a support from the Ministry of Interior affairs and communications of Japan under SCOPE project.

2 Virtual Doctor System (VDS) Reasoning Engine

The paper reports here, part of our project outcome that is related to interaction between VDS avatar and Patient. The voice recognition issues is been also, discussed in [6]. However, the voice recognition of the outpatient is considered as responses yes/no voice recognition classes and touch panel monitor response classes. The action scenario is to create a diagnosis based on the guidelines given by the Doctor A. Doctor A is a nominated Doctor which is the object system would mimic to interact with patient through VDS avatar. Our system reported here briefly, participates to provide cognitive interaction between real patient and virtual version of specialized doctor A (avatar) using computer interpretable guidelines (CIGs) represented by semantic web technology. The contextualization of the two ontologies specified namely, the mental ontology and physical ontology annotated mapping alignment, that produce annotated search profiling in the medical knowledge base semantic net with vocabularies and classification used in patient diagnosis. The combined usage of the two ontologies is intended (Fig. 5) to derive semantically appropriate references to the patient's status and correspondingly the appropriate concluded aligned key words for relative diagnosis search. The diagnosis retrieval from the knowledge base would be related to the specialization of the patient case through the combined ontology. This in turn would lead to derive the validated correspondence related to patient condition.

The patient ID file would have information related to the, personal information, like name, gender, age, employment type, tallness, address, marital status, special information and other type of personal related medical information. This represents the *patient module* that would have related information to the *mental state* of that patient, his/her *physiological* state definition shown in Fig. 5 as ego gram and profile database [2]. This would establish a template that also stored as part of the patient module structure. Such Templates is related to the mental cloning aspects: The user ego gram, his/her universal templates, and six basic templates of Ekman emotion and the neutral state (no emotion recognized state) [3]. As part of the language issues we have defined other modes that are needed during the diagnosis procedure. These states estimated appearance can be specified as pain(x), x would be a percentage values that to be extracted from the combination of other observed cognitive state. We have six primitives' cognitive states. {*Happy, sad, disgust, fear, surprise, anger*}. Each state can be attributed with a value representing rates among: *high, low medium*. These cognitive states are primitive's states, due to their characteristic nature to express human emotion, universally. Albeit, the degree of exposing these states are different among people due to several factors. The digestion of these primitive values and localization is verified using the touch panel monitor and/or responding to questions from the VDS as yes/no voice by outpatient. These cognitive states values can be predicated and estimated (i.e., computed) based on specialization and symmetrical projection through people characteristic, observed through other disciplinary, like Type_Age, Type_Gender, Type_Ego-gram and so [5]. In this paper, we call these as *stereo data* as typed Meta data related to complex representation for emotional states. For example: Type-Fear:(Type_Age:20th,Type_Gender:male,Meta_Type_perosnality). This is a stereo type (i.e., class definition) on Class:fear be characterized. For sickness related issues, the pain (user) can be a stereo type of a combination of *{disgust (medium), (sad (low)), neutral}*. The combinations of the emotional related states can be extracted in real-time from the frame video collected from user images labeled on the spoken sentences that he/she articulates to present his/her condition, synthesized by the touch panel through emotion transmission processor (Fig.5).

Also, articulation representation through the outpatient's voice to extract user physical status or/and mental status in spoken language is considered. This time the spoken language is Japanese. The spoken language is arbitrary set of sound's words (sound of spoken words). The sound is a stereotype collecting the emotional feature of the patient (i.e., user) measured by pitch and power [6]. For example the strep throat with nasal secretions or sore throat due to viral infection would have a certain pattern of pitch and power sounds characterize the throat soaring and depth of infection.

The facial and related situational information collected by the system would reflect the status of the patient observed appearance. Here, is the stereotype of the emotion of the user. So the patient status is a combination of the pair:

```
{StereoType_Voice(pitch, power), Stereotype_ (Face(happy,
sad,..), situation (gender(Boolean), temperature(integer),
blood pressure(integer,integer), BMI(integer))}.
```

The Face(…) class definition would participate to reason for example to the type of headache The pain type is; Pain (burning, steady, sharp) can be collected from the articulation of the six primitives of face emotion. However, particular expressions to painful stimulation occurred with regularity and that the durations of these expressions changed differentially with age [16].

These two different ontology stereotypes information represent the mental cloning of the user for reasoning purpose. The wording (key word extraction by the mapping alignment between the two view schemata related to the two ontologies), are to be concluded by the system. These wording would construct the situation related abstraction useful to be articulated to construct the schema needed to establish the conceptual view of the user diagnostic situation. Words collected from patient through different means as shown in Fig.2, and conceptualized. For example Headache; as a concept is conceptualized into mental view (facial, sound, touch panel..), and physical view (temperature, blood pressure, BMI, touch panel). Each view would have a set of condition and assertion to be fulfilled collectively as assertions. The observed behavior represented by these merged two views based, are temporal order related situational reasoning.. It is sequent cascade incremental reasoning, based on regenerative schema at the functional correspondence mapping. It is cyclic iterative reasoning based on the same schema's structure for diagnosis. The 1st structure pattern would be used to collect the best response, and accordingly the related diagnosis pattern is fetched and customized with diagnostician template to readout, to the patient with emotion mimicking the MD namely A. The response from the patient would lead to another incremental schema that is semantically consistent with the previous schema with similar partial set semantically consistent fragmented diagnosis outcome, with extra key word, extracted from the patient response derived from patient performance due to the readout, role-act diagnosis initiated by the schema of the alignment of the two ontologies. The incremental schema generation from the mapping alignment constructed through the patient and computed by system due to the VDS generated scenarios derived from the semantic net, and shown in Fig. 5, is cascading and incremented schema type generation, in nature. This would provide structured interoperability through such integration.

Medical diagnosis process is built by merging a set of fragments instances of the mental views instances with the corresponding physical views instances.

The VDS doctor would express these synchronized stereo types using avatar which is 3D generated graphics and synchronized voice sounds as shown in Fig. 2 and Fig.3. The 1st response would be presented through the avatar using the representation of the stereotypes (emotion and voice) mentioned above. Then the collected information for the patient user is also represented in the next cycle of diagnosis hierarchy, for another round of reasoning in the search engine. The domain knowledge is specified by automatic retrieval in establishing a link between the ontology and the patient database, as shown in Fig.2.

We formalized OWL based reasoning of the system using these two types of ontology, to establish the semantic relation between procedures and entities among the mapped ontologies based on the previously explained stereotype views. We align the properties of physical diagnosis specified by the medical doctor with those related to cognitive reasoning based on the patient mental cloning articulation [2]. Features expressed by stereotype Meta data definition are used to make such alignment. The mapping is an abstraction that encapsulate the features (properties) related to certain abstraction in an ontology and reflect or map that feature into other ontology such that to qualify the related features through such mappings. This would enhance and smooth the interoperability on service through different schema reflected on different type ontologies. This mapping is incremental process as the patient produce new schema and also the VDS consume this schema to produce another request by which the patient user would correspond to produce another schemata to be correspondingly, consumed again by the diagnostician (the system).

3 Implementation Aspects

Ontologies used in semantic web consist of hierarchical description of concepts and their properties in a domain (nest of concepts organized due to the nature of the situation instantiated from the integrated ontologies). Fig. 2 shows the components of system implementation. This section explains the implementation that is: formalizing the medical knowledge, mental knowledge of the MD, diagnosis knowledge of MD and user profile knowledge according to the mental ontology classes and physical ontology classes, as OWLS's XML documents. Individual axioms, facts based on OWL'XML syntax are represented. Axioms in the clinical knowledge documents containing facts about patient that to be matched due to rules. Facts are matched against XML rules to provide reasoning support so to provide interoperability (automatic reasoning) using semantic net. This can be provided using Protégé 4[20][21] to build the ontology on the OWL using OWL2 plugins. All knowledge bases on Fig. 2 marked and linked (i.e., annotated) to the semantic type marked due to physical ontology and mental ontology for reasoning (instantiation) using SWRL (semantic Web rule language). The RDF based instantiation is ABOX and the annotation objects are instances of the semantic types (e.g., HEADACHE <-> Catch_Cold; Catch_Cold is Semantic Type, and HEADACHE is RDF based keyword).

The benefit on using the ontologies as separate resources would provide great flexibility to the system in contrast to systems that implement the ontologies as part of the application. The ontologies are OWL RDF files in our context. The access to high level of ontologies using API based on OWL-API [24] and Protégé API. Ontology would define the service of medical diagnosis as service API. This service API uses and reason inside the service API. The reasoned would response to question asserted in the ontology.

In term of OWL-S [19], Web service is defined in the context of medical application as the system that provides diagnosis to patient user as a service based on process ontology defined by merging the two ontologies, namely the physical and mental ones explained in Fig. 5. The Semantic Web should enable users to locate, select, employ, compose, and monitor Web-based services automatically.

Diagnosis of medical doctors as provider of a diagnosis service to patient is presented in OWL-S markup services. Ontology-enhanced search engine is used to locate the appropriate service automatically. So OWL-S enables declarative repository of services properties to be used for automatic service discovery. Program invokes web service by another program or agent. Execution of web service is a sort of a collection of remote procedure calls. An OWL-S markup Web service provides a declarative computer-interpretable API. Software agent is to interpret this markup to understand what input is necessary to invoke the service and what information will be returned. The service profile through the usage of OWL subclasses would create a representation of medical services. The definition of the services as stated by the OWL-S[19] would be specified as below:

(1) The medical entity provides the service. In our case it is a typical hospital for outpatient, namely "Matsuzono_Clinic".
(2) The function the service computes: Diagnosis of Outpatient based of Doctor_namcd_A. The input is patient medical records, defined by the patient ontology. The output generated defined by the MD ontology. The preconditions are specified as valid patient condition: Valid_Insurance_policy, Valid_Age,Valid_with_specific_medical_records. These are the preconditions that need to be checked by the system to have the validity needed to provide the service to the patient user.
(3) The profile of service describing its feature, and its category to reflect the quality of the service, is named as grounding.

The ontology vocabulary in terms of OWL is defined by RDF. The ontology is hierarchical definition and representation of knowledge domain with relevant entities and relations. This is the language that would interpret the MD diagnosis profile and patient data through the merged ontology vocabulary, namely mental vocabulary and physical vocabulary. Our two typed ontologies are described in OWL-S. The description logic used in OWL is to classify resources (e.g. patient profile ego gram, pain_type and etc.) that defined in RDF documents. OWL has two main categories: Classes and properties. The SWRL API provides a deductive logic based mechanism to create and manipulate OWL knowledge base. API used by the SWRL editor in Protege4. Rules is been defined and applied to OWL database and composed of antecedent (body) (called as A-Box in RACER), and consequent (head) (called as T-Box). A Fever:-Headache→Immediate; Painful_URGENT_if_Temp_is_39 then go to …
Loading these rules using SWRL editor in Protégé4 and execute them as well.

OWL API rules are to be executed by FACT++ which is Description Logic(DL) reasoner on Protégé 4, also may use external reasoner through OWL API with other type of available reasoner through DIG (Description login Implementation Group)[25]. A DIG compliant reasoner is a DL reasoner that provides a standard access interface enables the reasoner to be accessed over HTTP, using the DIG language.

The interaction in our system is based on inquiry search scenarios through the ontology representation of both the physical and mental ontologies. Based on patient condition and 1st impression reasoning, the system would establish a set of antecedent variants' as search inquiry words in used by the diagnosis processor in Fig. 3 to knowledge discovery in the ontology related to emotion and in the ontology related to diagnosis, and select the best scenario or cascade of scenarios suitable as consequent in the directed graph based RDF network.

The scenarios handled by the scenario processor are decomposed as network of tasks representing the control flow of diagnosis scenarios and related ontology, namely the physical and mental ontologies.

The OWL-S has been used in such representation to provide web services with reasoning support that deals with facts and rules annotated from RDF based medical documents. The three elements composing the service according to the OWL-S are: service profile, process model (how to use the service), and service grounding (how to access or invoke the service).

MD doctor diagnosis routines, as well as the MD personality (mental view) are added to the action scenario related to diagnosis (Fi.g.2). All these knowledge based are to be represented as a concept in DL in structural formal way using the stereotype based views mentioned above. The reasoning would be reflected through what we called as diagnosis map: reflects the clustering of different knowledge map articulated through the mapping of the two previously mentioned views (mental and physical) shown in Fig.5.

4 Conclusion

The MD is a real person that based on interviews, we extract her/his personality that is to be used into the system and act on his/her behalf on mental basis using her/his routine diagnosis procedure (knowledge and scenarios). Using this with other related information we created a system that interacts with the patient user based on Transaction analysis protocol. The system would be examined in Beta space at a hospital where that MD is working. We have represented the patient mental view and physical view using OWL style ontology. We have aligned and mapped these two views to discover the best integrated correspondence that resulted in a set of key words that would be used in searching the best action scenario relative to patient case. All diagnosis knowledge of MD is stored in the knowledge base as semantic net using Protégé 4+OWL2. For testing purposes we are collecting cases studies through MD committee board established as part of this project consisting of 6 MDs. The system is under construction and to be installed in a hospital in Morioka city Iwate, Japan by 2010.

Aknowledgment. We would like to give our gratitude to the Medical Doctors Committee board of VDS of SCOPE project as the medical application board advisory of this research.

References

[1] ten Teije, A. (ed.): 2008 Computer-Based Medical Guidelines and Protocols: A Primer and Current Trends. Studies in Health Technology and Informatics. IOS Press, Amsterdam (2008)

[2] Fujita, H., Hakura, J., Kurematsu, M.: Intelligent human interface based on mental cloning-based software. International Journal on Knowledge-Based Systems 22(3), 216–234 (2009)

[3] Fujita, H., Hakura, J., Kurematsu, M., Chida, S., Arakawa, Y.: Empirical based Techniques for Human Cognitive Interaction Analysis: Universal Template Design. In: The 7th New Trends in Software Methodologies, tools and Techniques (Proceedings of SoMeT 2008), pp. 257–277. IOS Press, Amsterdam (2008)

[4] Hakura, J., Kurematsu, M., Fujita, H.: 2008 An Exploration toward Emotion Estimation from Facial Expressions for Systems with Quasi-Personality. International Journal of Circuits, Systems and Signal Processing 1(2), 137–144 (2008)

[5] Hakura, J., Kurematsu, M., Fujita, H.: 2009 Facial Expression Invariants for Estimating Mental States of Person. In: New Trends in Software Methodologies, tools and Techniques (SoMeT 2009). Frontiers in Artificial Intelligence and application series, vol. 199. IOS Press, Amsterdam (2009)

[6] Kurematsu, M., Ohashi, M., Kinoshita, O., Hakura, J., Fujita, H.: An Approach to implement Listeners Estimate Emotion in Speech. In: New Trends in Software Methodologies, tools and Techniques (SoMeT 2009). Frontiers in Artificial Intelligence and application series, vol. 199. IOS Press, Amsterdam (2009)

[7] Leflar, R.B., Iwata, F.: Medical Error as Reportable Event, as Tort, as Crime: A Transpacific Comparison. Widener Law Review 189(25) (2005)

[8] Mikkola: Hospital Pricing reform in the public health care system- an empirical case study from Finland. International journal of Health Care Finance and Economics 3(4), 267–286 (2003)

[9] NIPSSR, 2006; National Institute of Population and Social Security Research, Population Statistics of Japan, NIPSSR, Tokyo (2006)

[10] Horowitz: Introduction to Psychodynamics. In: Horowitz, M.J. (ed.) A New Synthesis. Basic Books, Inc., New York (1988)

[11] Kalfoglou, Y., Scholermmer: Ontology Mapping: the state of the art. The knowledge Engineering review (2003)

[12] Tanaka, M., Noguchi, M.: Concept Retrieval of Medical Text using UMLS. Japan Journal of Medical Informatics 20, 934–935 (2000)

[13] Smith: Reforming Markets in Health Care-An Economic Perspective. Open University Press, Buckingham (2000)

[14] Trautmann, R.L., Erskine, R.G.: Ego state analysis: A comparative view. Transactional Analysis Journal 11, 178–185 (1981)

[15] Weizenbaum, J.: ELIZA - A Computer Program for the Study of Natural Language Communication Between Man and Machine. Communications of the Association for Computing Machinery 9, 36–45 (1966)

[16] Izard, C.E., Hembree, E.A., Huebner, R.R.: Infants' emotion expressions to acute pain: Developmental change and stability of individual differences. Developmental Psychology 23(1), 105–113 (1987)

[17] Rodríguez, M.A., Egenhofer, M.J.: Determining semantic similarity among entity classes from different ontologies. IEEE Transactions on Knowledge and Data Engineering 15(2), 442–456 (2003)

[18] Arguello, M., Des, J.: Clinical practice guidelines: a case study of combining OWL-S, OWL, and SWRL. Knowledge-Based Systems 21, 247–255 (2008)

[19] OWL-S, http://www.w3.org/Submission/OWL-S/

[20] Protégé, http://protege.stanford.edu/

A Model for Generating Related Weighted Boolean Queries

Jesus Serrano-Guerrero, Jose A. Olivas, Enrique Herrera-Viedma,
Francisco P. Romero, and Jose Ruiz-Morilla

Department of Information Technologies and Systems
University of Castilla-La Mancha, 13071, Ciudad Real, Spain
and
Department of Computer Science and Artificial Intelligence
University of Granada, 18071 Granada, Spain
{jesus.serrano,joseangel.olivas,franciscop.romero}@uclm.es,
viedma@decsai.ugr.es,
joaquin.ruiz@panel.es
http://smile.esi.uclm.es

Abstract. In this paper a model for polyrepresenting weighted boolean queries based on reformulation is presented. This model tries to generate a set of boolean queries for completing the meaning of the original query instead of modifying the query adding, changing or removing terms as techniques such as query expansion propose. This model is specially designed for those systems which do not support very large queries such as the Web search engines.

The input of the model are boolean queries which have been weighted by the user in order to express some semantics that the set of polyrepresented queries have to satisfy. The user is able to fix a threshold for limiting the minimum resemblance of the polyrepresented queries and the original one. From the original query, using a reformulation strategy which guarantees that length of the new queries is not enlarged excessively, the proposed model generates a set of candidate queries/concepts for representing the original one. That set is reduced by a bottom-up process based on the semantics established by the user in order to choose the best queries for representing the original one.

Keywords: Query polyrepresentation, Weighted boolean queries, Fuzzy logic.

1 Introduction

The attention of this work is focused on the problem of improving the process of query formulation in order to deal with some of the obstacles found during the development of the metasearch engine called BUDI [14].

BUDI works with typical web search engines such as Google or Yahoo and therefore it is assumed that the web user queries can be very short and unstructured to express a complete idea and consequently are quite ambiguous.

N. García-Pedrajas et al. (Eds.): IEA/AIE 2010, Part III, LNAI 6098, pp. 429–438, 2010.
© Springer-Verlag Berlin Heidelberg 2010

But the web search engines present other handicaps, one of them is the number of terms of a query. Some search engines restrict the number of terms, for example, the Google's API[1] does not allow more than 10 terms, the first ten terms, the rest are ignored. Another handicap is the necessary time for submitting a query and retrieving the result using this kind of APIs. This task is time-consuming and for this reason, strategies like query expansion are very difficult to be implemented.

Hence in order to improve the performance of the system solving partially the previously-mentioned constraints, we present an approach which intends to simulate several users expressing the same request by using different concepts that are able to retrieve relevant information to be merged generating the final list of results. Every concept will have a similar length and all of them can be submitted on a search engine concurrently.

Therefore a model for generating a set of new boolean queries related to an original query is presented. This model is based on a query language which allows the user to express his boolean queries assigning weights to the different terms or concepts of the queries. From this user query a reformulation strategy can generate new queries and the semantics associated with these weights guide the process to decide if the query is related enough w.r.t. the original query.

The output of this model is a set of related queries which could represent the same information of an expanded query with thousands of added terms but in this case the length of the queries is similar to the length of the original one.

The rest of the paper is organized as follows. Section 2 presents the state of the art of the topic treated in the paper. Section 3 describes the main aspects of the fuzzy polyrepresentation query system that has been proposed. Section 4 comments an example of the application of the proposed model and finally some conclusions and future works are pointed out.

2   Related Work

Concept-based retrieval arises because it is getting more difficult to satisfy users with only keyword-based retrieval. Its objective is to treat query terms as concepts, rather than as strings of letters [5]. These works are focused on retrieving relevant documents even if they do not contain the words used in the original query, that is, both, documents and queries, are represented by their fundamental concepts and not only based on lexical representations.

Hence it is necessary an appropriate representation of queries and documents. The representation of the information from different points of view can be an interesting approach; distinct query formulations could improve the retrieval performance better than any individual query formulation [13], [7].

Belkin [1] suggests that it is a good idea to take advantage of as many interpretations as possible. Each different representation means a different interpretation of the user's underlying information problem. Kekalainen [11] tested the effects of different query structures and query expansion on retrieval performance using

---

[1] Application Programming Interface.

the InQuery system. Another work about polyrepresentations could be [15], but in this case the main focus is the representation of documents.

In order to represent the information from different points of view techniques such as query expansion/reformulation can be very interesting. Jansen [8] defines query reformulation as the process of altering a given query to improve search or retrieval performance.

Efthimiadis has developed a lot of experiments about interactive query expansion [4], Javerlin [10] presents a tool named ExpansionTool to support automatic constructing and expanding concept-based queries whereas Xu [16] uses the local analysis and the global analysis of documents for query expansion.

Query expansion can have sense with short queries specially which are a well-known phenomenon on the Web [9]. Bruza [3] categorized query reformulation into 11 types and found that users frequently repeated the query they had already submitted. They also found that other main categories of reformulation were, in order of frequency, term substitutions, additions, and deletions. Rieh [12] described Web query reformulation based on three main facets: concepts, formats and resources and identified eight types of patterns: (i)specified reformulation, (ii)generalized reformulation, (iii) parallel reformulation, (iv) building-block reformulation, (v) dynamic reformulation, (vi) multi-tasking reformulation, (vii) recurrent reformulation and (viii) format reformulation.

3   Model for Polyrepresenting Weighted Boolean Queries

The aim of this model is to generate a set of queries/concepts whose meaning is very similar to the original query and which can help to maximize the search process. Each new query can be submitted as an individual request and the final results retrieved by the queries could be merged in order to build a final list of results.

A polyrepresentation set consists of four elements (T, Q, F, SDQ) where T is a set of index terms (single words or phrases) and Q is a set of weighted boolean queries which consists of three main elements (q_o, Q_r, S_r). q_o is the original user query and Q_r is the set of reformulated queries generated from the original one following a reformulation strategy S_r. F is a numeric function which measures the relationship degrees between the original query terms and the reformulated query terms whereas SDQ is a numeric function that measures the similarity between the original query q_o and each reformulated query $q \in Q_r$.

A polyrepresentation query system consists of three main subsystems, the query subsystem, the reformulation subsystem and the filtering subsystem. These components are the core of the next subsections.

3.1   Definition of the Query Subsystem

We define the queries by means of an extended boolean model as the proposed by Bordogna [2] where two distinct levels for the concept of weight were defined: *query term weight* and *query weight*, with associated semantics.

Each query can be defined following a fuzzy query language which allows the user to incorporate semantics to the queries. The semantic associated with the weights are restrictions on the set of reformulated queries that will be the final result of the Fuzzy Polyrepresentation Query System.

Usually in Information Retrieval many authors propose the use of semantics on the documents that the Information Retrieval Systems have to satisfy during the search process [2], [6].

The proposed language allows the interpretation of the queries as concepts and not only as a list of terms. A query can express several concepts in distinct levels, for example, each individual term can be considered as a concept but a set of terms connected by logical operators can be considered a concept as well. Moreover some of them are more important than the others according to the user opinion. This fact can be modeled by the user thanks to the incorporation of semantic to the subclauses, then it is possible to distinguish and rank which the most meaningful concepts are.

Query representation

User queries are weighted boolean queries. Every query is expressed as a combination of the weighted index terms connected by the logical operators AND ($\land$), OR ($\lor$) and NOT ($\neg$). The weights are numeric values which can be associated with individual terms, subclauses and the whole query. This language allows the user to treat the queries as a set of concepts rather than a set of individual terms that can be weighted. To complete the formulation of the query subsystem it is necessary to study the semantic of the weights and the rules for formulating queries. Both are analyzed in the following subsections.

The semantics of the weights

Usually in Information Retrieval, the weights of the queries are associated with restrictions on the documents that have to be retrieved, however, in this case the associated weights express restrictions on the reformulated queries.

In this approach the semantics of each query weight are *threshold semantics*, however, the meaning is different than in [6]. The semantic does not define a minimum requirement that the matching between documents and queries has to fulfill but means the minimum value of the relationship degree between the weighted term or concept and its corresponding reformulated term or concept.

Therefore when a new query is reformulated, this one has to preserve a minimum resemblance w.r.t. the original one. If the resemblance is not acceptable between both then the reformulated query should be rejected to not belong to the set of polyrepresented queries.

Let C be the set of possible concepts that compose a query q_j, i.e., individual terms T, subclauses and whole query, the query representation q_j is defined as a fuzzy set of C and characterized by a membership function:

$$\mu_{q_j} : C \to [0,1], i.e., q_j = \sum_{i=1}^{m} \mu_{q_j}(c_i)/c_i.$$

$q_j \in Q$ is a set of m concepts where μ_{q_j} is a numerical weight that represents a degree of significance of $c_i \in q_j$. Depending on the kind of query the weights can have different interpretations. Thus in the original query q_o the degree of significance of c_i indicates the importance of the concept in the query according to the user opinion.

From the original query q_o a set of reformulated queries Q_r with similar length can be generated, in this case the significance of each term c_i indicates the relationship degree w.r.t. the concept of the original query in the position i.

Example. Assume a user query q_o that is composed by 5 terms $T = \{t_1 = c_1, t_2 = c_2, t_3 = c_3, t_4 = c_4, t_5 = c_5\}$, two subclauses $\{c_6, c_7\}$ and the whole query c_8; and a set of 2 queries $Q_r = \{q_1, q_2\}$ reformulated from the original query. The original query has been weighted by the user:

$$q_o = 0.5/c_1 + 0.7/c_2 + 0.3/c_3 + 0.2/c_4 + 0.9/c_5 + 0.5/c_6 + 0.55/c_7 + 0.6/c_8$$

The reformulated queries Q_r can be generated using an ontology, thesaurus or any other source which provides a set of related terms $\{t_{i'} = c_{i'}, t_{i''} = c_{i''}, \ldots\}$ for each term t_i of the original query. All the terms of the reformulated queries have been associated with a weight assigned by a numeric function F which measures the relationship degree between each original term and the reformulated one. The concepts which are weighted in the reformulated query are the individual terms/concepts by means of a knowledge source and the subclauses and the whole query are weighted ($\{x_{i'}, x_{i''}, \ldots, x_{j'}, x_{j''}, \ldots, x_{k'}, x_{k''}, \ldots\}$) depending on the weights of the terms/concepts and the aggregation functions used for representing the boolean operators, this calculus is commented in subsection 3.2.

$$q_1 = 1.0/c_{1'} + 1.0/c_{2'} + 0.5/c_{3'} + 0.3/c_{4'} + 0.7/c_{5'} + x_{i'}/c_{6'} + x_{j'}/c_{7'} + x_{k'}/c_{8'}$$
$$q_2 = 0.4/c_{1''} + 0.7/c_{2''} + 1.0/c_{3''} + 0.4/c_{4''} + 0.8/c_{5''} + x_{i''}/c_{6''} + x_{j''}/c_{7''} + x_{k''}/c_{8''}$$

Analyzing the original query (q_o) the terms c_2 and c_5 are the most important terms of the query according to the user opinion, on the contrary the terms c_3 and c_4 are the least meaningful of the query, maybe they are adjectives or prepositions.

Analyzing the relation between the original query (q_o) and the reformulated queries (q_1, q_2), on the one hand the relationship degree between the terms c_1 and $c_{1'}$ is 1 because maybe both terms are the same word or express the same idea, for instance, a synonym. On the other hand the relationship degree between the terms c_4 and $c_{4''}$ is very low, this fact can indicate that both terms can be found in the same context but do not express very similar or related terms.

Rules for formulating queries

We denote by R the set of all legitimate queries, i.e., boolean expressions on pairs (t, w) defined by the following syntactic rules:

1. $\forall \langle t, w \rangle \in T x [0, 1] \rightarrow \langle t, w \rangle \in R$.
2. $\forall q_1, q_2, \ldots, q_n \in R$ and $w \in [0, 1] \rightarrow \langle q_1 \wedge q_2 \wedge \ldots \wedge q_n, w \rangle \in R$.
3. $\forall q_1, q_2, \ldots, q_n \in R$ and $w \in [0, 1] \rightarrow \langle q_1 \vee q_2 \vee \ldots \vee q_n, w \rangle \in R$.
4. $\forall q_1 \in R \rightarrow \neg q_1 \in R$.

5. All legitimate boolean queries $q \in R$ are only those obtained by applying rules $1 - 4$ inclusive.

Remark. The weights of the rules 2 and 3 are not relevant for the reformulated queries, only for the original query.

3.2 Definition of the Reformulation Subsystem

The aim of this subsystem is to generate a set of queries which can be related to a certain extent w.r.t. the original query. These new queries present concepts similar to the original one that allow the representation of the same idea but using a different set of terms. In order to generate those queries it is necessary to choose a strategy for reformulating queries and a knowledge source for providing terms related to the terms of the original query. The knowledge source, apart from providing terms/concepts, must have mechanisms to measure the relationship degree between concepts in order to model the weights of the reformulated query.

An example of strategy could be the replacement of each term/concept with all related terms from the knowledge source. Thus given the query $q_o = c_1 \vee c_2 \vee c_3$ and a set of terms/concepts with associated weights $\{\langle c_{1'}, w_{1'} \rangle, \langle c_{1''}, w_{1''} \rangle\}$ related to the original term/concept c_1, the new reformulated queries are:

$$q_1 = \langle c_{1'}, w_{1'} \rangle \vee \langle c_2, 1.0 \rangle \vee \langle c_3, 1.0 \rangle$$
$$q_2 = \langle c_{1''}, w_{1''} \rangle \vee \langle c_2, 1.0 \rangle \vee \langle c_3, 1.0 \rangle$$

3.3 Definition of the Filtering Subsystem

The aim of the filtering subsystem is to evaluate the reformulated queries w.r.t. the original query in terms of capability of representing the original query according to the semantics assigned to the different concepts of the original query (terms and subclauses). As a result this subsystem has to return a set of queries Q_f that represents a set of alternatives to the original query.

Evaluation of the weighted boolean queries

Definition. Similarity Degree between Queries (*SDQ*). The similarity degree between two queries (q_1, q_2) assesses the capability of replacing the query q_1 using the query q_2 without losing the meaning of the first one.

$$SDQ : Q \times Q \rightarrow [0, 1]$$

The value 0 indicates that both queries are totally different, are expressing different ideas, not necessarily contrary; whereas the value 1 indicates that both queries are expressing exactly the same idea, that is, both share the same meaning instead of using different terms.

The queries are evaluated following a bottom-up process where the atomic components $\langle t, w \rangle$ are evaluated first, each boolean subclause that composes the query second and so on, until the whole query is evaluated.

The function SDQ describes the evaluation of the relationship degree between a term of the original query and a term of the reformulated query.

$$SDQ : \langle t, w \rangle \times \langle t, w \rangle \rightarrow [0, 1]$$

Let S be a set of related terms provided by a knowledge resource, for a given pair $\langle t, w \rangle$, the function SDQ can be seen as a membership function:

$$M(\langle t, w \rangle) = \{ \langle s_i, SDQ(s_i, \langle t, w \rangle) \rangle \, | s_i \in S \}$$

SDQ is based on the evaluation of the atomic components of the query q_i. The function SDQ has to be extended (SDQ^*) in order to evaluate the subclauses of the query and the whole query. This new definition is recursive following these rules:

$$SDQ^*(\neg q_1, \neg q_2) = SDQ^*(q_1, q_2)$$
$$SDQ^*(q_1 \wedge q_2) = min(SDQ^*(q_1), SDQ^*(q_2))$$
$$SDQ^*(q_1 \vee q_2) = max(SDQ^*(q_1), SDQ^*(q_2))$$

The first rule states that the negation is not important because the objective of the evaluation process is to compare the resemblance between two terms, and that comparison is independent of the negation.

Assuming the aforementioned characteristics, the filtering subsystem evaluates a query following the subsequent steps:

1. Evaluation of terms/atoms through the function SDQ.
2. Evaluation of subexpressions by the function SDQ^*.
3. Evaluation of the whole query by the function SDQ^*.

1. Evaluation of terms/atoms. The filtering process starts with the evaluation of the lowest level, the individual terms/concepts. In this stage it is necessary to differentiate the semantics of the weights of the terms/concepts of the original query and the reformulated query. The weights of the original query represents the minimum relationship degree that the corresponding weights of the reformulated query have to fulfill, that is, these weights represent thresholds that the weights of the reformulated have to surpass. Whereas the semantic of the weights of the reformulated queries means the relationship degree between the original query terms and the reformulated terms which has to be provided by the used knowledge source.

If one of the thresholds is greater than its corresponding relationship degree in the reformulated query $((t_1, w_1) \geq (t_{1'}, w_{1'}))$, then the query is rejected as possible member of the set Q_f, otherwise, the evaluation process continues.

2. Evaluation of subclauses. Once the terms/concepts of the lowest level have been evaluated successfully, it is necessary to evaluate more complex concepts grouped by logical operators. Each subclause of the original query has an associated weight that indicates the minimum degree of resemblance between the original subclause and the reformulated one.

On the contrary, in the reformulated query the subclauses have not associated weights, for that reason, it is necessary to calculate the relationship degree w.r.t.

the original subclause. This calculus is computed through the weights from the knowledge sources. Thus the boolean operator AND and OR are computed as aggregation functions and the value computed from the relationship degrees of each subclause represents the relationship degree of that subclause.

That new relationship degree has to be compared with the threshold assigned by the user in the original query for that subclause, if the relationship degree is greater than the threshold then the process has to continue with the rest of subclauses of the reformulated query, otherwise, the query must be rejected as possible member of the set Q_f. If all queries have been evaluated successfully, the evaluation of the whole query is the last step of the evaluation process.

3. Evaluation of the whole query. Once all subclauses have been evaluated, this is the final step which determines if the reformulated query is member of Q_f or not. The whole query has to be evaluated from the relationship degrees of the subclauses by the aggregation function used for executing the main operator of the query, the root of the tree that represents the query.

Finally if the relationship degree of the query is greater than the threshold fixed by the user to accept a reformulated query then the query is considered as an alternative to the original one and included into the set Q_f.

The evaluation process is repeated with all the queries $q_j \in Q_r$ and the final result of the evaluation of the polyrepresentation query system is a fuzzy subset Q_f of the set Q_r which contains the queries that represent the meaning of the original one in a accurate way.

4   Example of Application of the Proposed Model

Given the original query

$$q_o = ((t_1, 0.5) \langle \vee, 0.6 \rangle (t_2, 0.8)) \langle \wedge, 0.5 \rangle ((t_3, 0.7) \langle \vee, 0.5 \rangle (t_4, 0.3))$$

and a reformulated query q_r from the previous query

$$q_r = ((t_{1'}, 0.8) \langle \vee, 0.6 \rangle (t_{2'}, 1.0)) \langle \wedge, 0.5 \rangle ((t_{3'}, 0.9) \langle \vee, 0.5 \rangle (t_{4'}, 0.6))$$

the process to assess if the reformulated query q_r can belong or not to the set Q_f is described in the following subsections.

4.1   Evaluation of the Atomic Atoms

The evaluation of each atomic atom is processed taking into account the relationship degree established during the reformulation process and the threshold assigned by the user. If at least one of the atomic atoms of the query q_r does not exceed the thresholds of the atomic atoms of the query q_o then the whole query q_r will be rejected as possible member of the set of more similar queries Q_f.

Therefore each term from the original query t_i has to be compared with its corresponding reformulated term $t_{i'}$. As can be seen all the atomic $t_{i'}$ atoms exceed the threshold selected by the user for each atomic atom t_i.

$$(t_1, 0.5) < (t_{1'}, 0.8); (t_2, 0.8) < (t_{2'}, 1.0); (t_3, 0.7) < (t_{3'}, 0.9); (t_4, 0.3) < (t_{4'}, 0.6)$$

Thus the evaluation process can continue with the analysis of the following level of the query: the subclauses.

4.2   Evaluation of Subclauses

The original query q_o presents two subclauses with their associated threshold semantic:

$$q_{o1} = (t_1, 0.5) \langle \vee, 0.6 \rangle (t_2, 0.8)$$
$$q_{o2} = (t_3, 0.7) \langle \vee, 0.5 \rangle (t_4, 0.3)$$

In this case the *threshold semantic* associated with the atomic atoms is not considered but the semantic associated with the subclauses, that is, the weight close to the boolean operators. These weights represent the threshold that the relationship degree of each reformulated concept q_{r1}, q_{r2} has to exceed in order to continue the evaluation process.

The reformulated query q_r presents two subclauses:

$$q_{r1} = (t_{1'}, 0.5) \langle \vee, 0.6 \rangle (t_{2'}, 0.8)$$
$$q_{r2} = (t_{3'}, 0.7) \langle \vee, 0.5 \rangle (t_{4'}, 0.3)$$

In the previous evaluation level, each atom is considered as a concept, in this case, the whole subclause is considered as a more complex concept and the relationship degree of both concepts q_{o1}, q_{o2} w.r.t. the original concept is calculated from the atomic concepts. The operation for assessing the relationship degree of each concept is the aggregation of relationship degrees w_i of the reformulated terms t_i w.r.t. the original one.

In this case the aggregation is computed by the classic MAX operator:

$$OR((t_i, w_i), \dots, (t_m, w_m)) = MAX_{i=1,\dots,m}(t_i, w_i)$$
$$OR(q_{r1}) = MAX((t_{1'}, 0.5), (t_{2'}, 0.8)) = 0.8$$
$$OR(q_{r2}) = MAX((t_{3'}, 0.7), (t_{4'}, 0.3)) = 0.7$$

4.3   Evaluation of the Whole Query

Once the subclauses have been evaluated the whole query $q_{r1} \langle \wedge, 0.6 \rangle q_{r2}$ can be evaluated through the partial results of the subclauses. In this case the aggregation is computed by the classic MIN operator:

$$MIN(q_{r1}, q_{r2}) = MIN(0.7, 0.8) = 0.7$$

The evaluation of the whole query exceeds the threshold that was fixed by the user $MIN(q_{r1}, q_{r2}) = 0.7 > 0.6$, therefore the query q_r is considered as part of the solution Q_f.

5   Conclusions and Future Works

A new model for generating new boolean queries related to the original one has been presented. This model is specially designed to compare queries in a conceptual way and can only work with queries which preserve the same conceptual structure of the original query. For that reason the reformulation process is proposed as mechanism to generate new candidate queries. The model is specially useful in those systems where the length of the queries is limited to a short number of terms such the Web search engines. As future work the addition of new semantics is proposed in order to model the characteristics of the original query with more detail.

Acknowledgments. Partially supported by TIN2007-67494 F-META project, MEC-FEDER, Spain and PEIC09-0196-3018 SCAIWEB-2 excellence project, JCCM, Spain.

References

1. Belkin, N.J., Kantor, P., Fox, E.A., Shaw, J.A.: Combining the evidence of multiple query representations for information retrieval. Information Processing and Management 31, 431–448 (1995)
2. Bordogna, G., Carrara, P., Pasi, G.: Query term weights as constraints in fuzzy information retrieval. Information Processing and Management 27, 15–26 (1991)
3. Bruza, P., Dennis, S.: Query Reformulation on the Internet: Empirical Data and the Hyperindex Search Engine. In: Proceedings of RIAO '97 - Computer Assisted Information Searching on the Internet, pp. 500–509 (1997)
4. Efthimiadis, E.N.: A user-centred evaluation of ranking algorithms for interactive query expansion. In: SIGIR '93: Proceedings of the 16th annual international ACM SIGIR conference, New York, NY, USA, pp. 146–159 (1993)
5. Grootjen, F.A., Van Der Weide, T.P.: Conceptual query expansion. Data and Knowledge Engineering 56, 174–193 (2006)
6. Herrera-Viedma, E.: Modeling the retrieval process for an information retrieval system using an ordinal fuzzy linguistic approach. Journal of the American Society for Information Science and Technology 52, 460–475 (2001)
7. Ingwersen, P., Jarvelin, K.: The Turn: Integration of Information Seeking and Retrieval in Context. Springer, Secaucus (2005)
8. Jansen, B.J., Booth, D.L., Spink, A.: Patterns of query reformulation during Web searching. Journal of the American Society for Information Science and Technology 60, 1358–1371 (2009)
9. Jansen, B.J., Spink, A.: An analysis of web searching by European AlltheWeb.com users. Information Processing and Management 41, 361–381 (2005)
10. Jarvelin, K., Kekalainen, J., Niemi, T.: ExpansionTool: Concept-Based Query Expansion and Construction. Information Retrieval 4, 231–255 (2001)
11. Kekalainen, J., Jarvelin, K.: The Co-Effects of Query Structure and Expansion on Retrieval Performance in Probabilistic Text Retrieval. Information Retrieval 1, 329–344 (2000)
12. Rieh, S.Y., Xie, H.: Analysis of multiple query reformulations on the web: The interactive information retrieval context. Information Processing and Management 42, 751–768 (2006)
13. Saracevic, T., Kantor, P.: A study of information seeking and retrieving. III. Searchers, searches and overlap. Journal of the American Society for Information Science 3, 197–216 (1988)
14. Serrano-Guerrero, J., Romero, F.P., Olivas, J.A., De La Mata, J., Soto, A.: BUDI: Architecture for Fuzzy Search in Documental Repositories. Mathware and Soft Computing 16, 71–85 (2009)
15. Skov, M., Larsen, B., Ingwersen, P.: Inter and intra-document contexts applied in polyrepresentation for best match IR. Information Processing and Management 44, 1673–1683 (2008)
16. Xu, J., Croft, B.W.: Improving the effectiveness of information retrieval with local context analysis. ACM Transactions on Information Systems 18, 79–112 (2000)

Web Usage Mining for Improving Students Performance in Learning Management Systems

Amelia Zafra and Sebastián Ventura

Department of Computer Science and Numerical Analysis,
University of Cordoba, Spain
{azafra,sventura}@uco.es

Abstract. An innovative technique based on multi-objective grammar guided genetic programming (MOG3P-MI) is proposed to detect the most relevant activities that a student needs to pass a course based on features extracted from logged data in an education web-based system. A more flexible representation of the available information based on multiple instance learning is used to prevent the appearance of a great number of missing values. Experimental results with the most relevant proposals in multiple instance learning in recent years demonstrate that MOG3P-MI successfully improves accuracy by finding a balance between specificity and sensitivity values. Moreover, simple and clear classification rules which are markedly useful to identify the number, type and time of activities that a student should do within the web system to pass a course are provided by our proposal.

Keywords: Web Usage Mining, Educational Data Mining, Multiple Instance Learning, Multi-objective Evolutionary Algorithm, Grammar Guided Genetic Programming.

1 Introduction

As an increasingly powerful, interactive, and dynamic medium for delivering information, the World Wide Web in combination with information technology has found many applications. One popular application has been for educational use, as in Web-based, distance or distributed learning. The use of the Web as an educational tool has provided learners and educators with a wider range of new and interesting learning experiences and teaching environments, that were not possible in traditional education. These platforms contain a considerable amount of e-learning materials and provide some degree of logging to monitor the progress of learning keeping track of learners' activities including content viewed, time spent at a particular subject and activities done. This monitoring trawl provides appropriate data for many different contexts in universities, like providing assistance for a student at the appropriate level, aiding the student's learning process, allocating relevant resources, identifying exceptional students for scholarships and weak students who are likely to fail.

A normal situation in the web-based learning systems is that instructors provide different resources and learners are encouraged to participate in the variety

N. García-Pedrajas et al. (Eds.): IEA/AIE 2010, Part III, LNAI 6098, pp. 439–449, 2010.

of activities. However, it becomes difficult for the instructors to track and identify all the activities performed by the learners and subsequently, it is hard to evaluate the structure of the course content and its effectiveness in the learning process. It would be very helpful to have an automatic tool for detecting those activities which improve the learning process and appraise the web-based course structure effectiveness. With this purpose, our research proposes a new method based on multiple instance learning (MIL) representation to classify students into two groups: the *low performance* students, who have a high probability of failing a course and the *high-performance* students, who have a high probability of passing a course. Our technique generates rules IF-THEN that allow the establishment of relationships between the student's work in web systems and passing a certain course. In this manner, instructors and students could be guided and recommended about what activities or resources would support and improve their learning.

The paper is structured as follows: section 2 reviews the works of data mining applied over academic scenarios; section 3 describes the problem that we aspire to solve showing its multiple instance representation and the available information to carry out this study; section 4 presents and explains the proposed model for solving the problem; section 5 shows experimental results and the rules obtained; finally, in section 6, the conclusion and further works are described.

2   Web Usage Mining in Academic Computing

Web usage mining [1] refers to non-trivial extraction of potentially useful patterns and trends from large web access logs. In the specific context of web-based learning environments, the increasing proliferation of web-based educational systems and the huge amount of information that has been made available has generated a considerable scientific activity in this field. Delavaire et al. [2], given the large amounts of data collected in academic institutions, propose a model with different types of education-related questions and the data-mining techniques appropriate for them. An example of a specific case study of clustering students who have similar characteristics (such as *self starters* and *high interaction*) is given in [3]. Anjewierden et al. [4] investigate the application of data mining methods to provide learners with real-time adaptive feedback on the nature and patterns of their on-line communication while learning collaboratively. Lazcorreta et al. [5] propose a new method for automatic personalized recommendation based on the behavior of a single user in accordance with all other users in web-based information systems. Chanchary et al. [6] analyze students' logs of a learning management system with data mining and statistical tools to find relationships between students' access behavior and overall performances. Finally, studies about the prediction of students' marks or their academic success have also been developed in this area [7,8,9,10]. Further information can be found in the survey carried out by Romero and Ventura [11].

3   Determination of Factors Influencing the Students' Academic Achievements

In this section, we will first present the definition of the problem that we want to solve. Then, we will describe the representation of the problem using MIL and finally, the specific data considered in this study will be set out in detail.

3.1   Definition of the Problem

A student could do different activities in a course to acquire and strengthen the concepts acquired in class. Later, at the end of the course, there is a final exam. A student with a mark over a fixed threshold passes a module, while a student with a mark lower than that threshold fails that module. With this premise, the problem consists of studying the work carried out by students to find interesting relationships that can suggest activities and resources for students and educators that can favour and improve both their learning and effective learning process.

To carry out this study the students will be classified into two groups: *high performance* students who have a high probability of succeeding and *low performance* students, with a high probability of failing (or dropping out). We will have information on every student which describes her/his work done on the web-based learning system. The idea is to determine the activities that are needed so that a student passes or fails the module taking into consideration the time dedicated and the number and type of activities done by the student during the course. Concretely, the types of activities considered in this study are quizzes considering the number of quizzes consulted, passed and failed, assignments considering the number of practices/tasks submitted or consulted and forums considering the number of messages sent and read.

3.2   A Multi-instance Perspective

In this problem, the different resources available to the student are not compulsory but rather are presented as a support to strengthen concepts before the final exam. Thus, each student can execute a different number of activities: a hard-working student may do all the activities available and on the other hand, there can be students who have not done any activities at all. Moreover, there are some courses which contain only a few activities and others which contain an enormous variety and number of them.

The characteristics of this problem make the information of each pattern different depending on the student and course. Traditional supervised learning would use the same structure with the same number of attributes for all patterns independently of the real information about each student and course and therefore, most patterns would have empty values. On the other hand, MIL [12] allows a representation that adapts itself perfectly to the concrete information available for each student and course, eliminating the missing values that appear in traditional representation. The key factor in MIL representation lies in the concepts

Table 1. Attributes for MIL representation of the student

INFORMATION ABOUT BAGS

Attribute	*Description*
User-Id	Student Identifier.
Course	Course identifier.
FinalMark	Final mark obtained by the student in this course.

INFORMATION ABOUT INSTANCES

Attribute	*Description*
Type Activity	Type of activity which represents the instance. Eight type of activities are considered: FORUMS: read, written or consulted, QUIZZES: passed or failed and ASSIGNMENTS: submitted or consulted.
TimeActivity	Time spent to complete the tasks of this type of activity.
NumberActivity	Number of activities of this type completed by the student.

of pattern and instances. In this learning a pattern (called bag) could contain different numbers of instances. Thus, the correspondence is one-to-several and not one-to-one as in traditional supervised learning. In this problem, each pattern or bag represents a student registered in a course. Each student is regarded as a bag which represents the work carried out. Each bag is composed of one or several instances and each instance represents the different types of work that the student has done. Therefore, each pattern will have as many instances as different types of activities that have been done by the student. Information about the attributes of bags and instances could be consulted in Table 1.

3.3 Case Study

This study employs the students' usage data from the web-based learning environment at Cordoba University considering Moodle platform [13]. The available information on the web usage log files for students was collected during an academic year from September to June, just before the Final Examinations. Seven different courses are considered with 419 students. The details about the different courses are given in Table 2, only considering about each student his/her identifier, activity with respect to forums, assignments and quizzes and final mark obtained in this course although more information is stored by the system.

4 The Proposed Model for Using Web Usage Mining in Education Data

In this section, we propose a new model based on multi-objective grammar guided genetic programming to predict the students' academic performance

Table 2. General Information about Data Sets

Course Identifier	ICT-29	ICT-46	ICT-88	ICT-94	ICT-110	ICT-111	ICT-218
Number of Students	118	9	72	66	62	13	79
Number of Assignments	11	0	12	2	7	19	4
Number of Forums	2	3	2	3	9	4	5
Number of Quizzes	0	6	0	31	12	0	30

based on features extracted from logged data in a web-based education system. The motivation to include this algorithm called MOG3P-MI is on one hand, the use of multi-objective proposal that allows us to find a set of optimal solutions considering different contradictory measurements. We search to find a solution with the best balance between sensitivity and specificity values to achieve the most accuracy models. The objective is to determine the most relevant resources to improve the learning process from the classification model obtained by this proposal. Thus, it is very important for the model to be precise and correctly classify both students who pass and those who fail the course, because otherwise the conclusions would not be significant. On the other hand, this algorithm allows to work in MIL scenario using a more flexible representation that eliminates the missing values of other representations which hinder algorithms from achieving the highest accuracy in the classification. Finally, another advantage of this proposal is that grammar-guided genetic programming (G3P) [14] is considered a robust tool for classification in noisy and complex domains and allows us to obtain representative information about the knowledge discovered to identify the most relevant activities for supporting and improving students' learning.

The design of the system will be examined in more detail in continuation with respect to the following aspects: individual representation, genetic operators, fitness function and evolutionary process.

4.1 Individual Representation

Individuals in our system represent classifiers which classify students into two classes (students who have a high probability of passing a course and students who have a low probability of doing so). The classifier is composed of IF-THEN rules whose antecedent determines the time, number and type of activities that the students have to do, if they want to have a high probability of passing the course. Those students who do not satisfy these requirements will have a low probability of passing the course. The rule generated has the following structure:

If (*condition*(student)) **then**
    the student will have a high probability of passing the course.
End-If

$\langle$S$\rangle$ $\rightarrow$ $\langle$condition$\rangle$
$\langle$condition$\rangle$ $\rightarrow$ $\langle$cmp$\rangle$ | **OR** $\langle$cmp$\rangle$ $\langle$condition$\rangle$ | **AND** $\langle$cmp$\rangle$ $\langle$condition$\rangle$
$\langle$cmp$\rangle$ $\rightarrow$ $\langle$op-num$\rangle$ $\langle$variable$\rangle$$\langle$value$\rangle$ | $\langle$op-int$\rangle$ $\langle$variable$\rangle$$\langle$value$\rangle$$\langle$value$\rangle$
$\langle$op-num$\rangle$ $\rightarrow$ **GE** | **LT**
$\langle$op-int$\rangle$ $\rightarrow$ **IN** | **OUT**
$\langle$variable$\rangle$ $\rightarrow$ **TypeOfActivity** | **NumberOfActivity** | **TimeOfActivity**
$\langle$value$\rangle$ $\rightarrow$ *Any valid value*

Fig. 1. Grammar used for representing individuals' genotypes in G3P-MI

The *condition* clause is represented by means of the grammar shown in Figure 1. Thus, the *condition* consists of several comparisons of attribute-value attached by conjunction and/or disjunction that inform about the number, type and time that should be dedicated by a student to be successful in a course.

4.2 Genetic Operators and Fitness Function

MOG3P-MI uses a crossover and mutator operator to generate new individuals in a given generation of the evolutionary algorithm based on selective crossover and mutation as proposed by Whigham [14].

The fitness function combines two commonly used indicators, namely sensitivity (*Se*) and specificity (*Sp*) to measure the classifier's effectiveness. Sensitivity is the proportion of cases correctly identified as meeting a certain condition and specificity is the proportion of cases correctly identified as not meeting a certain condition.

$$sensitivity = \frac{t_p}{t_p + f_n}, \quad specificity = \frac{t_n}{t_n + f_p}$$

where, t_p is the number of positive bags correctly identified, f_p is the number of positive bags not correctly identified, t_n is the number of negative bags correctly identified and f_n is the number of negative bags not correctly identified.

The goal of MOG3P-MI is to maximize both Sensitivity and Specificity at the same time. These two measurements evaluate different and conflicting characteristics in the classification process where a value of 1 in both measurements represents perfect classification.

4.3 Evolutionary Algorithm

The main steps of this algorithm are based on the well-known Non-Dominated Sorting Genetic Algorithm (NSGA2) [15] philosophy, but it is designed to use a grammar guided genetic programming and multi-instance learning to add more flexibility and clarity to the representation of the individuals. The general outline of our algorithm is shown in Algorithm 1.

Algorithm 1. MOG3P-MI Algorithm

1: Set P_0 = an initial population of rules, $A_0 = \phi$ (empty external set) and t = 0.
2: P_0 is sorted based on the concept of non-domination fronts.
3: Assign fitness to P_0, the fitness is equal to its non-domination level.
4: **repeat**
5:     $R_t = P_t \cup Q_t$. Combine parent and children population.
6:     All non-dominated fronts of R_t are constructed.
7:     **repeat**
8:       **if** $|P_{t+1}| < N$ **then**
9:         Calculate crowding distance of in Front i, F_i.
10:         $P_{t+1} = P_{t+1} \cup F_i$
11:       **end if**
12:     **until** $|P_{t+1}| < N$
13:     Sort in descending order using the crowding distance value.
14:     $P_{t+1} = P_{t+1} [0 : N]$. Choose the N first elements of P_{t+1}.
15:     Use selection, crossover and mutation to create a new population, Q_{t+1}.
16:     Set t = t + 1
17: **until** acceptable classification rule is found or the specified maximum number of generations is reached.

5   Experimentation and Results

The commented case study is used to evaluate our proposal and to compare it with other similar models. Our primary objective is to determine whether the results of our model are accurate enough compared to the rest of the proposals. Then we determine the most relevant activities to help the professor and students to improve the learning process by analyzing the information provided by our system about the number, type and time that student has to devote to have a high probability of passing a course.

5.1   Results and Discussion

The most relevant proposals based on MIL presented to date are considered to solve this problem and compared to our proposal designed in JCLEC framework [16]. The paradigms compared include methods based on diverse density, on Logistic Regression, on support vector machines, on distance, on rules, on decision trees, on naive Bayes and on evolutionary algorithms [17]. More information about the algorithms considered could be consulted at the WEKA workbench [18] where these techniques are designed.

All experiments are carried out using 10-fold stratified cross validation and the average values of accuracy, sensitivity and specificity [19] are reported. Moreover, evolutionary algorithms performed five different runs with different seeds and the average values of sensitivity, specificity and accuracy are reported. Table 3 shows the average results of accuracy, sensitivity and specificity values for each method considered in the study.

Table 3. Experimental results to compare MOG3P-MI with other methods based on MIL

Paradigm based on	Algorithm	Accuracy	Sensitivity	Specificity
	PART	0.7357	0.8387	0.5920
	AdaBoostM1&PART	0.7262	0.8187	0.5992
Rules	Bagging&PART	0.7167	0.7733	0.6361
	AdaBoostM1&PART	0.7071	0.7735	0.6136
	PART	0.7024	0.7857	0.5842
Naive Bayes	NaiveBayes	0.6786	0.8515	0.4371
SVM	SMO	0.6810	0.8644	0.4270
Distances	MIOptimalBall	0.7071	0.7218	0.6877
	CitationKNN	0.7000	0.7977	0.5631
Decision Tree	DecisionStump	0.6762	0.7820	0.5277
	RepTree	0.6595	0.7127	0.5866
Logistic Regression	MILR	0.6952	0.8183	0.5218
	MIDD	0.6976	0.8552	0.4783
Diverse Density	MIEMDD	0.6762	0.8549	0.4250
	MDD	0.6571	0.7864	0.4757
Evolutionary Algorithms	G3P-MI	0.7429	0.7020	0,7750
	MOG3P-MI	**0.7952**	**0.7209**	**0.8500**

As can be seen, MOG3P-MI obtains the most accurate models. This classification problem has an added difficulty since it deals with a variety of courses with different numbers and types of exercises which makes it more costly to establish general relationships among them. Nonetheless, MOG3P-MI in this sense is the one that obtains the best trade-off between the two measurements, obtaining the highest values for specificity without a relevant fall in sensitivity values. If we observe the results of the different paradigms, it can be seen how they optimize the sensibility measurement in general at the cost of a decrease in the specificity values (excepting G3P-MI that also achieves a balance between the different measurements, although the results are worse). This leads them to an incorrect prediction of which students will not pass the course.

Moreover, MOG3P-MI obtains interpretable rules to find pertinent relationships that could determine if certain activities influence the student's ability to pass, if spending a certain amount of time on the platform is found to be an important contributing factor or if there is any other interesting link between the work of the student and the final results obtained. These relationships will be studied in the next section.

5.2   Determining Activities That Improve the Learning Process

One of the advantages of our system is that it generates a classifier consisting of IF-THEN rules which provide knowledge about the requirements that a student must satisfy to have a high probability of passing a course. These rules are simple, intuitive, easy to understand and provide representative information about the type, number and time necessary for a student to pass the course.

By the following examples, we are going to study the information provided by the model and analyze the activities that are the most efficient for acquiring knowledge.

IF [((*TimeOfActivity* < 1508) ∧ (*NumberOfActivity* = 7)) ∨
(((*TypeOfActivity* = QUIZ_P) ∧ (*NumberOfActivity* ≥ 6)) ∨
(*TimeOfActivity* ∈ [3007, 9448])]
THEN *The student has a high probability to pass the course.*
ELSE *The student has a low probability to pass the course.*

According to this rule, students who have a high probability of passing a course have to satisfy one of the following requirements: *a)* do at least six quizzes correctly, *b)* perform seven activities of some kind devoting at least 1508 minutes in the web-based system consulting resources or making activities or *c)* spend between 3007 and 9448 minutes to perform different activities in the web-based system or consult the resources available.

IF [((*NumberOfActivity* ∈ [3, 12]) ∧ (*TypeOfActivity* = QUIZ_P) ∧
(*TimeOfActivity* ∈ [516, 1727])) ∨ (*TimeOfActivity* ∈ [2998, 7143]) ∨
((*TypeOfActivity* = QUIZ_P) ∧ (*NumberOfActivity* ≥ 7))]
THEN *The student has a high probability to pass the course.*
ELSE *The student has a low probability to pass the course.*

Another of the rules obtained indicates that to pass a course it is necessary to satisfy some of the following constraints: *a)* perform at least three quizzes correctly justifying a time on the web-based system between 516 and 1727 minutes, *b)* take at least seven quizzes, or *c)* have spent at least between 2998 and 7143 minutes on the web system carrying out different activities or consulting the resources.

IF [((*NumberOfActivity* ≥ 8) ∧ (*TypeOfActivity* = QUIZ_P)) ∨
(*TimeOfActivity* ∈ [3009, 6503])]
THEN *The student has a high probability to pass the course.*
ELSE *The student has a low probability to pass the course.*

Finally, the last rule that we analyzed indicates that to pass a course it is necessary: *a)* perform at least eight quizzes correctly or *b* devote between 3009 and 6503 minutes to consult resources and make activities on the system.

We see that in general all the rules establish similar requirements. In conclusion, the development of quizzes is one of the most crucial activities in all rules to predict whether a student will pass a course, the number of them is a value approximating seven correct quizzes. Therefore, the relevance of performing quizzes correctly becomes obvious to consolidate the students' knowledge. In the case of quizzes that are not carried out because the course has no available quizzes or because students have carried out quizzes but not correctly, or because directly the student has not wanted to do them, it is necessary to justify at between least 3000 and 7000 minutes on the web-based system consulting different resources or doing different activities (with this amount of time would be indifferent the particular type or number of activities that student should do). Finally, if the time spent on the system is lower, it is necessary to specify a minimum number of activities carried out. This number is nearly to seven different activities during the time devoted to the system, although the type of activities do not matter (therefore they could be both assignments and quizzes and forums).

6 Conclusion

In this paper a new method to determine the most relevant activities to get a high probability of passing a course based on the students' work carried out on a web-based learning system is proposed. The proposal consists of multi-objective grammar guided genetic programming algorithm, MOG3P-MI, in a MIL scenario. The most representative algorithms in MIL are compared with our proposal and experimental results show that MOG3P-MI achieves the most accurate models finding a solution with a balance between sensitivity and specificity values. Moreover, representative information is provided that allows us to see which activities presented to students are really relevant for improving the learning process and allow students to consolidate the concepts studied in the classroom to then pass the course.

The results obtained are very interesting, but the work only considers if a student passes a course or not. It is would be interesting to expand the problem to predict students' grades (classified in different classes) in an e-learning system. Another interesting issue consists of determining how soon before the final exam a student's marks can be predicted. If we could predict a student's performance in advance, a feedback process could help to improve the learning process during the course.

Acknowledgments

The authors gratefully acknowledge the financial support provided by the Spanish department of Research under TIN2008-06681-C06-03 and P08-TIC-3720 Projects.

References

1. Srivastava, J., Cooley, R., Deshpande, M., Tan, P.N.: Web usage mining: discovery and applications of usage patterns from web data. SIGKDD Explor. Newsl. 1(2), 12–23 (2000)
2. Delavari, N., Beikzadeh, M., Shirazi, M.: A new model for using data mining in higher educational system. In: ITHET'04: Proceedings of 5th International Conference on Information Technology Based Higher Education and Training, Istanbul, Turkey (2004)

3. Luan, J., Zhao, C.M., Hayek, J.: Exploring a new frontier in higher education research: A case study analysis of using data mining techniques to create nsse institutional typology. California Association for Institutional Research, California, USA (2004)
4. Anjewierden, A., Kollöffel, B., Hulshof, C.: Towards educational data mining: Using data mining methods for automated chat analysis to understand and support inquiry learning processes. In: ADML'07: International Workshop on Applying Data Mining in e-Learning, pp. 27–36 (2007)
5. Lazcorreta, E., Botella, F., Fernández-Caballero, A.: Towards personalized recommendation by two-step modified apriori data mining algorithm. Expert Systems with Applications 35(3), 1422–1429 (2008)
6. Chanchary, F., Haque, I., Khalid, S.: Web usage mining to evaluate the transfer of learning in a web-based learning environment. In: WKDD'08: International Workshop on Knowledge Discovery and Data Mining, pp. 249–253 (2008)
7. Fausett, L., Elwasif, W.: Predicting performance from test scores using backpropagation and counterpropagation. In: WCCI 1994: IEEE World Congress on Computational Intelligence, Washington, USA, pp. 3398–3402 (1994)
8. Minaei-Bidgoli, B., Punch, W.: Using genetic algorithms for data mining optimization in an educational web-based system. Genetic and Evolutionary Computation 2, 2252–2263 (2003)
9. Kotsiantis, S., Pintelas, P.: Predicting students marks in hellenic open university. In: ICALT'05: The 5th International Conference on Advanced Learning Technologies, Kaohsiung, Taiwan, pp. 664–668 (2005)
10. Superby, J., Vandamme, J., Meskens, N.: Determination of factors influencing the achievement of the first-year university students using data mining methods. In: EDM 2006: Workshop on Educational Data Mining, Hong Kong, China, pp. 37–44 (2006)
11. Romero, C., Ventura, S.: Educational data mining: A survey from 1995 to 2005. Expert System Application 33(1), 135–146 (2007)
12. Dietterich, T.G., Lathrop, R.H., Lozano-Perez, T.: Solving the multiple instance problem with axis-parallel rectangles. Artifical Intelligence 89(1-2), 31–71 (1997)
13. Rice, W.H.: Moodle e-learning course development. Pack Publishing (2006)
14. Whigham, P.A.: Grammatically-based genetic programming. In: Proceedings of the Workshop on Genetic Programming: From Theory to Real-World Applications, Tahoe City, California, USA, September 1995, pp. 33–41 (1995)
15. Deb, K., Agrawal, S., Pratap, A., Meyarivan, T.: A fast elitist non-dominated sorting genetic algorithm for multi-objective optimisation: NSGA-II. In: Deb, K., Rudolph, G., Lutton, E., Merelo, J.J., Schoenauer, M., Schwefel, H.-P., Yao, X. (eds.) PPSN 2000. LNCS, vol. 1917, pp. 849–858. Springer, Heidelberg (2000)
16. Ventura, S., Romero, C., Zafra, A., Delgado, J.A., Hervás, C.: JCLEC: A java framework for evolutionary computation soft computing. Soft Computing 12(4), 381–392 (2007)
17. Zafra, A., Ventura, S.: G3P-MI: A genetic programming algorithm for multiple instance learning. Information Science (submitted 2009)
18. Witten, I., Frank, E.: Data Mining: Practical machine learning tools and techniques, P2nd edn. Morgan Kaufmann, San Francisco (2005)
19. Kantardzic, M.: Data Mining. Concepts, Models, Methods and Algorithms. John Wiley and Sons, Chichester (2003)

Strategies for Incorporating Knowledge Defects and Path Length in Trust Aggregation

Nele Verbiest[1], Chris Cornelis[1], Patricia Victor[1], and Enrique Herrera-Viedma[2]

[1] Dept. of Appl. Math. and Comp. Sci., Ghent University, Gent, Belgium
{Nele.Verbiest,Chris.Cornelis,Patricia.Victor}@UGent.be
[2] Dept. of Comp. Sci. and AI, University of Granada, Granada, Spain
viedma@decsai.ugr.es

Abstract. The ability for a user to accurately estimate the amount of trust to be placed in a peer user is gaining more and more attention in social network applications. Trust aggregation provides this ability by identifying paths that connect users in the network, and by merging trust opinions expressed by users along these paths. However, as individual trust opinions are not always based on perfect knowledge, and since the quality of a trust estimation propagated along a given path may diminish as its length increases, mechanisms are needed to handle these imperfections. In this paper, we propose a set of trust aggregation operators that take into account knowledge defects and path length. We investigate their properties, and discuss how they may be implemented in practice, taking into account characteristics of the network such as the availability of a central authority, or the need to preserve users' privacy by not publically disclosing their trust information.

1 Introduction

A trust network consists of agents (users) that can express their opinion about other agents through trust scores. Trust networks are emerging as an important tool to improve web applications such as recommender systems [1,2,3,4], e-mail filtering [5], financial transactions [6] and many more.

Generally, not all agents are connected in a trust network. In order to predict an agent's trust score in one of its peers, we can search for a path linking them and propagate trust scores along this path to obtain an estimated trust score. If more than one path is available, we need to aggregate these trust scores to obtain a final estimated trust score. In the aggregation process, not all trust scores may be equally useful, due to the way in which they were obtained. In this paper, we consider two characteristics that affect a trust score's relative importance:

- *Knowledge defects.* Sometimes, an agent has insufficient information to establish a clear trust opinion in a peer, while at other times his opinion is based on conflicting information sources. Both cases are examples of defective knowledge, and can be modelled by drawing trust scores from a bilattice as proposed in [4]. In this way, trust scores not only reflect the intensity of the trust relation, but also the amount of information on which it is based.

N. García-Pedrajas et al. (Eds.): IEA/AIE 2010, Part III, LNAI 6098, pp. 450–459, 2010.

- *Path length.* As the number of propagation steps needed to obtain a trust score increases, so does the chance of errors occurring and accumulating in the process. This is also endorsed by the experiments in [2], which show that shorter paths lead to more accurate trust estimations and recommendations.

The remainder of this paper is structured as follows: in Section 2, we recall necessary preliminaries on (ordered) weighted average aggregation operators, the bilattice-based trust model and trust score propagation, while in Section 3, we propose new classes of aggregation operators taking into account knowledge defects and path length. In Section 4, we discuss their application in a trust network; we distinguish between "big brother" approaches in which a central authority performs all propagation and aggregation steps, and distributed ones in which agents process trust information autonomously and do not need to disclose the provenance of this information to their peers. The latter approaches become especially relevant in the light of preserving users' privacy in web-based applications. In Section 5, we conclude and discuss future work.

2   Preliminaries

2.1   Aggregation Operators

In this section, we review a number of frequently used strategies for aggregating a vector $\langle a_1, \ldots, a_n \rangle$ of scalar arguments.

The simple Weighted Average (WA) operator associates weights to the values that have to be aggregated. Let $W = \langle w_1, \ldots, w_n \rangle$ be a weight vector such that $\forall i \in \{1, \ldots, n\}$ $w_i \in [0,1]$ and $\sum_{i=1}^{n} w_i = 1$. Then the WA-operator associated with W is defined as:

$$WA_W(a_1, \ldots, a_n) = \frac{\sum_{i=1}^{n} w_i a_i}{\sum_{i=1}^{n} w_i} \tag{1}$$

The Ordered Weighted Average (OWA, [7]) operator associates weights to the ordered positions of the values that have to be aggregated. Let $W = \langle w_1, \ldots, w_n \rangle$ be defined as above. Then the OWA-operator associated with W is defined as:

$$OWA_W(a_1, \ldots, a_n) = \sum_{i=1}^{n} w_i b_i \tag{2}$$

where b_i is the i-th largest element in $\{a_1, \ldots, a_n\}$.

The Induced Ordered Weighted Average (IOWA, [8]) operator associates weights to the ordered positions of the values of an order inducing variable. Let $W = \langle w_1, \ldots, w_n \rangle$ be defined as above, and $\langle v_1, \ldots, v_n \rangle$ a vector of values drawn from a linearly ordered space $(V, \leq_V)$. Then the IOWA-operator associated with W is defined as:

$$IOWA_W(\langle a_1, v_1 \rangle, \ldots, \langle a_n, v_n \rangle) = \sum_{i=1}^{n} w_i b_i \tag{3}$$

where $b_i = a_j$ iff v_j is the i-th largest element in $\{v_1, \ldots, v_n\}$.

2.2 Bilattice-Based Trust Network Model

According to the proposal in [4], we model a trust network as a triplet (A, E, R) where (A, E) is a directed graph with the agents as nodes, and directed trust links as edges. The mapping $R : E \to [0, 1]^2$ associates a trust score $R(e) = (t, d)$ with every edge e between agents x and y, such that t represents the degree of trust of x in y, and d the degree of distrust. The set of trust scores can be endowed with the following bilattice structure:

$$BL^{\square} = ([0, 1]^2, \leq_t, \leq_k, \neg) \tag{4}$$

where $\leq_t$ is a trust ordering, $\leq_k$ is a knowledge ordering and $\neg$ a negation operator, defined as follows:

$$(t_1, d_1) \leq_t (t_2, d_2) \text{ iff } t_1 \leq t_2 \text{ and } d_1 \geq d_2$$
$$(t_1, d_1) \leq_k (t_2, d_2) \text{ iff } t_1 \leq t_2 \text{ and } d_1 \leq d_2$$
$$\neg(t_1, d_1) = (d_1, t_1)$$

$\leq_t$ orders trust scores ranging from full distrust $(0, 1)$ to full trust $(1, 0)$. $\leq_k$ orders trust scores ranging from ignorance/no knowledge $(0, 0)$ to fully conflicting knowledge $(1, 1)$. Trust scores (t, d) with $t + d < 1$ are called *incomplete*, while those with $t + d > 1$ are called *inconsistent*. In both cases, there is a *knowledge defect*, which can be quantified by the following $[0, 1]$-valued measure:

$$kd(t, d) = |1 - t - d| \tag{5}$$

Trust scores with $kd(t, d) = 0$, i.e., $t + d = 1$, are said to have *perfect knowledge*. When explicit trust and distrust values in $[0, 1]$ are given for every trust relation in the network, these can be used for t and d. Otherwise, t and d should be derived from the given numerical or linguistic values that represent trust statements in the given trust network.

2.3 Trust Score Propagation

In trust networks, propagation operators are used to handle the problem of estimating a trust score in an unknown agent by inquiring through third party agents. For our purposes, a trust score propagation operator $Prop$ is a $([0, 1]^2)^2 \to [0, 1]^2$ mapping; given the trust score of agent x in agent y, and the trust score of y in z, it predicts the trust score of x in z. Trust score propagation operators have been studied extensively in [4]; here we mention just one example of such an operator, defined by, for $(t_1, d_1), (t_2, d_2)$ in $[0, 1]^2$,

$$Prop((t_1, d_1), (t_2, d_2)) = (\min(t_1, t_2), \min(t_1, d_2)) \tag{6}$$

This operator reflects the basic strategy of taking over information only from trusted sources: it copies the opinion of y in z, but only to the extent that x trusts y.

Although *Prop* defined by (6) is associative, this is not required in general. For propagation over paths with more than 2 edges, it is therefore necessary to fix the evaluation order. Here, as in [9], we assume that a right-to-left evaluation order is used for propagation, illustrated below for a three-edge path:

$$Prop((t_1, d_1), (t_2, d_2), (t_3, d_3)) = Prop((t_1, d_1), Prop((t_2, d_2), (t_3, d_3))) \quad (7)$$

With this order, each agent along the path combines its trust score in its successor with the propagated trust score it receives from this successor. In this way, an agent needs to have access only to the trust scores it has issued, and propagation does not require the intervention of a central authority.

3   Trust Score Aggregation

In general, a trust score aggregation operator is a mapping $\Omega : ([0, 1]^2)^n \rightarrow [0, 1]^2$ ($n \geq 1$), where the arguments are trust scores as defined in Section 2.2. Note that the operators from Section 2.1 require scalar values as arguments. As such, they are not directly applicable to aggregate a set of trust scores. Therefore, in accordance with the proposal from [9], we propose trust score aggregation operators that consist of two separate operators, one applied to the trust component and one to the distrust component. Before presenting their definition, we list a number of desirable properties that a trust score aggregation operator should ideally satisfy, based on the recommendations in [9].

3.1   Properties

A trust score aggregation operator Ω may satisfy the following properties:

1. *Idempotence* (**RQ1**). For (t, d) in $[0, 1]^2$,

$$\Omega((t, d), \dots, (t, d)) = (t, d) \quad (8)$$

2. *Knowledge-invariant trust monotonicity*[1] (**RQ2**). For $(t_i, d_i), (t_i', d_i')$ in $[0, 1]^2$, if $(t_i, d_i) \leq_t (t_i', d_i')$ and $t_i + d_i = t_i' + d_i'$ ($i = 1, \dots, n$), then

$$\Omega((t_1, d_1), \dots, (t_n, d_n)) \leq_t \Omega((t_1', d_1'), \dots, (t_n', d_n')) \quad (9)$$

3. *Commutativity* (**RQ3**). If π is a permutation of $\{1, \dots, n\}$, then for (t_i, d_i) in $[0, 1]^2$ ($i = 1, \dots, n$),

$$\Omega((t_1, d_1), \dots, (t_n, d_n)) = \Omega((t_{\pi_1}, d_{\pi_1}), \dots, (t_{\pi_n}, d_{\pi_n})) \quad (10)$$

4. *Neutral element* $(0, 0)$ (**RQ4**). For (t_i, d_i) in $[0, 1]^2$ ($i = 1, \dots, n - 1$),

$$\Omega((t_1, d_1), \dots, (t_{n-1}, d_{n-1}), (0, 0)) = \Omega((t_1, d_1), \dots, (t_{n-1}, d_{n-1})) \quad (11)$$

5. *Opposite arguments* (**RQ5**).

$$\Omega(\underbrace{(1, 0), \dots, (1, 0)}_{n \text{ times}}, \underbrace{(0, 1), \dots, (0, 1)}_{n \text{ times}}) = (1, 1) \quad (12)$$

---

[1] The original property (**RQ2**) from [9] required monotonicity of Ω w.r.t. both $\leq_t$ and $\leq_k$, but is restricted here to monotonicity of $\leq_t$ in case the amount of knowledge in the trust scores remains invariant; monotonicity of $\leq_k$ then becomes trivial.

3.2   Aggregation Operators

Below, we discuss various strategies for trust aggregation based on WA, OWA and IOWA operators. We first describe the generic procedure for their application:

1. Given are n trust scores $\langle (t_1, d_1), \ldots, (t_n, d_n) \rangle$. Determine m, the number of arguments (t_i, d_i) $(i = 1, \ldots, n)$ such that $kd(t_i, d_i) < 1$. If $kd(t_i, d_i) = 1$, the trust score does not take part in the remainder of the aggregation process.
2. If $m = 0$, the aggregation process terminates at this step, and the final result is set to $(1, 1)$ if at least one of the arguments equals $(1, 1)$, and to $(0, 0)$ otherwise.
3. Renumber the remaining m trust scores to $\langle (t_1, d_1), \ldots, (t_m, d_m) \rangle$.
4. With the same conditions as in Section 2.1, determine weight vectors $W = \langle w_1, \ldots, w_m \rangle$ and $W' = \langle w'_1, \ldots, w'_m \rangle$ and, in the case of an IOWA operator, vectors $\langle v_1, \ldots, v_m \rangle$ and $\langle v'_1, \ldots, v'_m \rangle$ of values for an order inducing variable.
5. The final aggregated trust score equals, for WA, OWA and IOWA, respectively:

$$WA_{W,W'}((t_1, d_1), \ldots, (t_m, d_m)) = (WA_W(t_1, \ldots, t_m), WA_{W'}(d_1, \ldots, d_m))$$

$$OWA_{W,W'}((t_1, d_1), \ldots, (t_m, d_m)) = (OWA_W(t_1, \ldots, t_m), OWA_{W'}(d_1, \ldots, d_m))$$

$$
\begin{aligned}
IOWA_{W,W'}(\quad &(\langle t_1, v_1 \rangle, \langle d_1, v'_1 \rangle), \\
&\ldots, \\
&(\langle t_m, v_m \rangle, \langle d_m, v'_m \rangle))
\end{aligned}
=
\begin{aligned}
&(IOWA_W(\langle t_1, v_1 \rangle, \ldots, \langle t_m, v_m \rangle), \\
&IOWA_{W'}(\langle d_1, v'_1 \rangle, \ldots, \langle d_m, v'_m \rangle))
\end{aligned}
$$

The principle of eliminating all $(0, 0)$ and $(1, 1)$ scores beforehand corresponds to the intuition that these trust scores do not contribute any usable information, because they represent total ignorance and complete inconsistency, respectively, and should thus not participate to the aggregation process.

Weighted Average Trust Score Aggregation. As stated in the introduction, trust scores that exhibit a high knowledge defect (too little, or too much knowledge), are considered less useful in deriving a final trust estimation. In order to penalize this knowledge defect, we can construct weight vectors $W = W'$, such that, for $i = 1, \ldots, m$,

$$w_i = \frac{1 - kd(t_i, d_i)}{\sum_{j=1}^{m} 1 - kd(t_j, d_j)} \tag{13}$$

It is also possible to construct weights based on the path length associated with a trust score. In this scenario, we additionally need the vector $\langle p_1, \ldots, p_m \rangle$, such that p_i is the number of propagations (path length) needed to obtain the trust score (t_i, d_i). The longer a trust score's path length, the smaller its associated weight should be. This can be obtained by putting $W = W'$, such that $\forall i, j = 1, \ldots, m$, $p_i w_i = p_j w_j$. That is, for $i = 1, \ldots, m$,

$$w_i = \frac{\frac{1}{p_i}}{\sum_{j=1}^{m} \frac{1}{p_j}} \tag{14}$$

Both weighting strategies can easily be combined to take into account both knowledge defect and path length, i.e., for $i = 1, \ldots, m$,

$$w_i = \frac{\frac{1-kd(t_i,d_i)}{p_i}}{\sum_{j=1}^{m} \frac{1-kd(t_j,d_j)}{p_j}} \tag{15}$$

It may be verified that the resulting $WA_{W,W'}$ have properties (**RQ1**) (on condition that all path lengths are equal), (**RQ2**) (on condition that path lengths remain invariant), as well as (**RQ3**) and (**RQ4**). Only (**RQ5**) does not hold; for instance, using (13), under the premises of this property, the outcome will be $\left(\frac{1}{2}, \frac{1}{2}\right)$ rather than $(1, 1)$. In general, it is difficult to impose this property using a WA operator.

Ordered Weighted Average Trust Score Aggregation. Ordering the trust (resp., distrust) values decreasingly prior to computing their weighted average offers additional flexibility to the aggregation process. As an example, the following weighting strategy generalizes the proposal made in [9]; for $i = 1, \ldots, m$,

$$w_i = \frac{\max(0, \lceil \frac{m}{m_t} \rceil - i + 1)}{\frac{\lceil \frac{m}{m_t} \rceil(\lceil \frac{m}{m_t} \rceil + 1)}{2}}, w_i' = \frac{\max(0, \lceil \frac{m}{m_d} \rceil - i + 1)}{\frac{\lceil \frac{m}{m_d} \rceil(\lceil \frac{m}{m_d} \rceil + 1)}{2}} \tag{16}$$

with $m_t, m_d \in \{2, \ldots, m\}$. For instance, if $m_t = 2$, it means that half of the trust degrees receive a strictly positive weight. Because of the way the weights are constructed, the weight for the highest trust degree will be strictly greater than the second one, etc. Different values for m_t and m_d may be chosen; for instance, if $m_t < m_d$, the distrust degree of the aggregated trust score will depend on fewer arguments than the trust degree. Using these weights, $OWA_{W,W'}$ satisfies all properties from Section 3.1, including (**RQ5**).

It is also possible to combine the WA weighting strategies (13)–(15) with OWA weights. In this case it is important to realize that the WA weights are associated to a fixed argument, and the OWA weights to an ordered position. In particular, let w_i^{OWA} and $w_i'^{OWA}$ be weights defined as in (16) and $w_{\pi_i}^{WA}$ and $w_{\pi_i}'^{WA}$ weights defined as in (13)–(15), where π (resp. π') permutes the weights in a way that $t_{\pi_1} \geq t_{\pi_2} \geq \ldots \geq t_{\pi_n}$ (resp. $d_{\pi_1'} \geq d_{\pi_2'} \geq \ldots \geq d_{\pi_n'}$). Then combined weights can be calculated as:

$$w_i = \frac{w_i^{OWA} w_{\pi_i}^{WA}}{\sum_{j=1}^{n} w_j^{OWA} w_{\pi_j}^{WA}}, w_i' = \frac{w_i'^{OWA} w_{\pi_i'}^{WA}}{\sum_{j=1}^{n} w_j'^{OWA} w_{\pi_j'}^{WA}} \tag{17}$$

Using these combined weights, however, $OWA_{W,W'}$ no longer satisfies (**RQ2**).

Induced Ordered Weighted Average Trust Score Aggregation. Since the order inducing variable appearing in the IOWA approach does not need to be scalar, further flexibility can be introduced in the trust aggregation process. In particular, we may consider combinations of trust/distrust degrees, path length and/or knowledge defect as potential order inducing variables, provided a suitable linear order can be imposed on them.

As a first example, we define the value of the order inducing variables as

$$v_i = (kd(t_i, d_i), t_i), \ v_i' = (kd(t_i, d_i), d_i), \tag{18}$$

$i = 1, \ldots, m$, and order these values decreasingly according to the linear order $\leq_{kd}$ on $[0, 1]^2$ defined by, for $(k_1, r_1), (k_2, r_2)$ in $[0, 1]^2$,

$$(k_1, r_1) \leq_{kd} (k_2, r_2) \Leftrightarrow (k_1 > k_2) \vee (k_1 = k_2 \wedge r_1 \leq r_2) \tag{19}$$

In other words, trust scores with lower knowledge defects are ordered first, and in case of equal knowledge defect, the higher trust (resp., distrust) value prevails.

Another option is to define $v_i = (p_i, t_i)$ and $v_i' = (p_i, d_i)$, $i = 1, \ldots, m$, and order these values decreasingly according to the linear order $\leq_p$ on $\mathbb{N} \times [0, 1]$ defined by, for $(p_1, r_1), (p_2, r_2)$ in $\mathbb{N} \times [0, 1]$,

$$(p_1, r_1) \leq_p (p_2, r_2) \Leftrightarrow (p_1 > p_2) \vee (p_1 = p_2 \wedge r_1 \leq r_2) \tag{20}$$

In this case, trust scores associated to the shortest path are ordered first, and the trust/distrust degrees are used to determine the order in case of equal path length.

Weight vectors W, W' can be constructed in the same way as for the OWA operators, with the same properties fulfilled. For instance, using (16), trust scores with the highest associated value for the order inducing variable get the highest weights. It is also possible to consider combined approaches that take into account both knowledge defect and path length, but as we have seen before, the combination of (16) with (13)–(15) results in the loss of (**RQ2**).

Instead, we may incorporate path length and knowledge defect simultaneously using alternative order inducing variables $v_i = (p_i kd(t_i, d_i), t_i)$ and $v_i' = (p_i kd(t_i, d_i), d_i)$, and ordering their values decreasingly according to the linear order $\leq_{p,kd}$ on $\mathbb{R}^+ \times [0, 1]$ defined as follows for $(s_1, r_1), (s_2, r_2)$ in $\mathbb{R}^+ \times [0, 1]$:

$$(s_1, r_1) \leq_{p,kd} (s_2, r_2) \Leftrightarrow (s_1 > s_2) \vee (s_1 = s_2 \wedge r_1 \leq r_2) \tag{21}$$

Using these order inducing variables, and weights W, W' defined by (16), we can verify that $IOWA_{W,W'}$ fulfils all requirements in Section 3.1.

4   Application to Trust Networks

In this section, we discuss how the proposed aggregation operators can be used within a trust network (A, E, R) as defined in Section 2.2 to estimate trust scores. Assume a and x are two agents in A such that there is at least one path from a to x, but no directed edge from a to x. Examples of this situation are given in Figure 1. We now consider two strategies to predict the trust score of a in x.

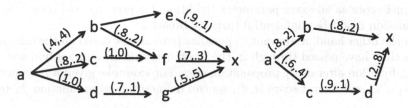

Fig. 1. Examples of trust networks

4.1 Aggregation with a Central Authority ("Big Brother")

In the first approach, all acyclic paths between a and x are considered. For every path, a propagated trust score is calculated, and at the end, all of these propagated trust scores are aggregated. This approach is called a *Big Brother* approach, since a central authority that maintains all trust information (network topology and trust scores) is needed. Any of the aggregation operators introduced in Section 3 can be used to compute the final estimated trust score.

Example 1. In the left hand side network in Figure 1, there are four a-x paths, all of them of length 3 ($abex$, $abfx$, $acfx$ and $adgx$). If we use Eq. (6) to propagate, then the trust scores corresponding to these paths are $(0.4, 0.1)$, $(0.4, 0.3)$, $(0.7, 0.3)$ and $(0.5, 0.5)$, with knowledge defects 0.5, 0.3, 0 and 0, respectively. Constructing the weight vectors $W_1 = W_1'$ by Eq. (13), we get

$$WA_{W_1,W_1'}((0.4, 0.1), (0.4, 0.3), (0.7, 0.3), (0.5, 0.5)) = (0.525, 0.331) \qquad (22)$$

If we construct weights W_2 and W_2' as in (16) with $m_t = 2, m_d = 4$ we get

$$OWA_{W_2,W_2'}((0.4, 0.1), (0.4, 0.3), (0.7, 0.3), (0.5, 0.5)) = (0.633, 0.5) \qquad (23)$$

The same result is obtained if we combine these weights with those in (13) using (17) , and also if we use W_2 and W_2' in the IOWA strategy where the order inducing variables v_i and v_i' are defined as in (18).

4.2 Aggregation without a Central Authority

If a central authority is lacking, a distributed strategy may be pursued in which agent a asks all agents it is connected to for their opinion of x. Whenever a successor s is directly connected to x, it returns the corresponding trust score to a. Otherwise, it returns a recursively calculated trust score that represents its opinion about x. Agent a then applies propagation to its own trust score in s, and the trust score supplied by s. Finally, a aggregates the trust scores established for its various successors. This is an example of a privacy-preserving approach, since the agents do not have to reveal their trust opinions to a central authority. In this case, aggregation operators incorporating path length may not be suitable, since they require the path length to be transferred along with the trust score as an extra parameter (additional overhead), and moreover this information might be confidential (privacy breach).

On the other hand, if we want to penalize trust scores based on the amount of nodes they have passed through in the trust network, we can apply a so-called ageing function after every propagation step. For example, given a parameter α $(0 < \alpha < 1)$ and a trust score (t, d), we can define the ageing function f_α by

$$f_\alpha(t, d) = \begin{cases} (\alpha t, \alpha d) & \text{if } t + d \leq 1; \\ (1 - \alpha(1 - t), 1 - \alpha(1 - d)) & \text{else.} \end{cases} \tag{24}$$

It is clear that the ageing function increases the knowledge defect; if we subsequently aggregate the results using an aggregation operator that incorporates knowledge defect, trust scores that have come a longer way through the network will have a smaller associated weight.

Example 2. In the right hand side network of Figure 1, a asks c and b for an opinion of x; b responds by returning its trust score in x, to which a applies propagation and ageing (assume $\alpha = 0.9$), i.e., $f_{0.9}(Prop(0.8, 0.2), (0.8.0.2)) = (0.72, 0.18)$. Agent c applies the same operation to the score it gets from d, i.e., it returns $(0.18, 0.72)$ to a; by another propagation and ageing step, a transforms this score to $(0.162, 0.54)$. If we construct weights $W = W'$ as in (13), we obtain

$$WA_{W,W'}((0.72, 0.18), (0.162, 0.54)) = (0.475, 0.338). \tag{25}$$

5   Conclusion and Future Work

In this paper, we have presented and investigated a range of strategies that can be used to aggregate trust scores, and which take into account aspects of the trust network such as the relative knowledge defect of trust scores, and the length of the path that is needed to obtain them. We have also investigated their properties and illustrated their application within a trust network.

In a next step, we plan to validate the introduced aggregation operators experimentally. In particular, we will set up a series of leave-one-out experiments in which a particular edge in the trust network is hidden, and the goal is to predict the corresponding trust score using the remaining connections. On the other hand, we also want to establish the usefulness of the proposed aggregation operators in recommender systems; in this case, the use of a given operator is measured by means of the accuracy it achieves in predicting a user's ratings for given items.

As another part of our future work, we plan to further refine the aggregation strategy to take into account other aspects of the trust network. One possible extension includes the incorporation of an authority function, which reflects that in obtaining a trust score, some agents are always more important than others (e.g., because they have built up a strong reputation).

Acknowledgments

Chris Cornelis would like to thank the Research Foundation—Flanders for funding his research. Patricia Victor would like to thank the Institute for the Promotion of Innovation through Science and Technology in Flanders (IWT-Vlaanderen) for funding her research. Enrique Herrera-Viedma would like to thank the financing of andalucian excellence project TIC05299, Feder Funds in FUZZYLING project (TIN2007-61079) and PETRI project (PET 2007-0460).

References

1. Bedi, P., Kaur, H., Marwaha, S.: Trust based recommender system for the semantic web. In: Proc. of IJCAI 2007, pp. 2677–2682 (2007)
2. Golbeck, J.: Computing and applying trust in web-based social networks. PhD thesis (2005)
3. Massa, P., Avesani, A.: Trust-aware recommender systems. In: Proc. of the ACM Recommender Systems Conference, pp. 17–24 (2007)
4. Victor, P., Cornelis, C., De Cock, M., Pinheiro da Silva, P.: Gradual trust and distrust in recommender systems. Fuzzy Sets and Systems 160(10), 1367–1382 (2009)
5. Golbeck, J., Hendler, J.: Reputation network analysis for email filtering. In: Proceedings of the First Conference on Email and Anti-Spam (2004)
6. Josang, A.: Trust-based decision making for electronic transactions. In: Proceedings of the Fourth Nordic Workshop on Secure IT Systems (1999)
7. Yager, R.R.: On ordered weighted averaging aggregation operators in multicriteria decision making. IEEE Transactions on Systems, Man, and Cybernetics 18, 183–190 (1988)
8. Yager, R.R., Filev, D.: Induced ordered weighted averaging operators. IEEE Transactions on Systems, Man, and Cybernetics 29(2), 141–150 (1999)
9. Victor, P., Cornelis, C., De Cock, M., Herrera-Viedma, E.: Aggregation of gradual trust and distrust. In: Proceedings of EUROFUSE 2009 (Preference Modelling and Decision Analysis), pp. 259–264 (2009)

Enhancing Context Sensitivity
of Geo Web Resources Discovery
by Means of Fuzzy Cognitive Maps

Carmen De Maio[1], Giuseppe Fenza[1], Matteo Gaeta[2],
Vincenzo Loia[1], and Francesco Orciuoli[2]

[1] Department of Mathematics and Informatics &
CORISA (Consorzio Ricerca Sistemi ad Agenti),
University of Salerno, 84084 Fisciano (SA), Italy
{cdemaio,gfenza,loia}@unisa.it
[2] Department of Information Engineering and Applied Mathematics &
CRMPA (Centro di Ricerca in Matematica Pura ed Applicata),
University of Salerno, 84084 Fisciano (SA), Italy
{gaeta,orciuoli}@diima.unisa.it

Abstract. In situations where emergencies have to be handled, it's vital
to provide a vision, shared by all involved actors, on everything happens
near the geographic area interested by the emergency and on the availability of resources like hospitals, ambulances, fire fighters, volunteers
and so on. This work introduces an approach for the smart discovery of
geo-located resources (i.e. people, services, etc.) with respect to specific
emergency requirements. The proposed approach is strongly based on
the semantic modeling of geo-spatial data, geo-localized services, people's skills and geo-positions and on a novel method exploiting Fuzzy
Cognitive Maps (FCMs) in order to suitably elicit resource plans according to the occurred event. Semantic modeling of resources highlights
value added in term of support to human resources managers. In the
next future the discovery performance will be tested in real conditions.

Keywords: Emergency Management, Fuzzy Cognitive Maps, Geo Semantic Web Services, Geosocial Networking, Semantic Web.

1 Introduction

Emergency management is investigating the possibility of taking balanced decisions on interventions as early as possible. There are many requirements to
support decision making and to accomplish emergency operation: time, space,
resources and means availability and so on. Emergency response plans play an
important role in the response to emergency process, but how to evaluate emergency plan is currently no systematic approach. The wide range of involved
resources requires coordinated and collaborative approaches to the information
and knowledge sharing. On the light of desrcribed needs, this paper focus on
two aspects of emergency process response: the semantic modeling of geo-located

N. García-Pedrajas et al. (Eds.): IEA/AIE 2010, Part III, LNAI 6098, pp. 460–469, 2010.

resources; the emergency response plans evaluation according to resources availability, geo-locations and skills.

On the one hand, awareness about availability people, services, organisms and their localization are useful information in order to support resources management, planning, scheduling and coordination. Furthermore, standard approaches to the information exchanging among involved actors are need. Recently, W3C has activated the Emergency Information Interoperability Framework Incubator Group (EIIF XG)[1] whose main missions are to review and analyze the current state-of-the-art in vocabularies used in emergency management functions. EIIF XG have introduced some XML based technical protocols in order to standardize the comunication and knowledge sharing about emergency situation. Nevertheless, these standards lack of semantic models in order to automate handling of information and support decision makers. Again, geographical dimension of information must to be covered in order to optimize resources allocation and moving on the emergency area. In order to fill the gap, Semantic Web stresses the binomial "meaning and content", adding semantics to web resources to support information sharing and interoperability. In fact, our previous studies [1] has focused at the reconciliation and collaborative processing of semantics and content of Web information. Nowadays, the introduction of semantics in the description of Web resources reflects new achievements in Web Services and social networks technologies. Semantic web services allow to automate services selection, composition, monitoring and recovery from failure [2]. Semantic social networks approaches integrate with geo-located information in order to geographically localize people. In fact, there exist some thematic social networks organized around actual geo-positions of participants, namely Geo-social Network Services [3].

On the other hand, the emergency response plans define linkage between emergency requirements and what kinds of resources are need to manage the situation. So, mashing semantic models of emergency situation and skills with updated information about resources availability enable systematic and sensitivity detection of right set of resources. Thus, by means of emergency response plans coding a software agent can perform resources discovery in order to matchmake the specific emergency and to accomplish the operation.

This work proposes an architecture (see Section 2) attaining a synergy among semantic technologies and soft computing techniques. In particular, the approach deals with fuzzy discovery in order to find eligible available resources (i.e. people and services) which appropriately meet the emergency requirements. It stresses the situation, when no exact match occurs [4]. Specifically, it presents a novel approach by means of exploitation of FCMs in order to support decision making [5] and suitably elicit the resource plan according to the occurred event. At the end of paper, an sample scenario allows the description of the query answering workflow (see Section 3). The conclusions and future works (see Section 4) are mainly related to the application of the FCMs in the emergency domain.

---

[1] http://www.w3.org/2005/Incubator/eiif/

2   Architectural Overview

Semantic Web schemas and vocabularies, based on the stack composed by RDF, RDFS and OWL, are used in order to model and represent information in machine-understandable, interoperable and standards-accessible ways. Specifically, there exist three key elements: domain ontologies (i.e. geographic information, human skills, emergency environment, etc), upper ontologies (OWL-S [2], Friend of a Friend - FOAF[3] and ResumeRDF[4]) and emergency plans described by means of mathematical models of FCMs. The most crucial role is played by FCMs in order to enable a discovery of resource (peoples and services) according to the occured event. The following sections describe in details these components.

2.1   Domain Ontologies and Taxonomies: Emergency

Generally, a domain ontology models a specific domain, or part of the world. It represents the particular meanings of terms as they apply to that domain. Specifically, this work deals with domain ontologies (based on OWL) and taxonomies (based on SKOS[5]) useful to semantically model the concepts and the relative relationships applied on emergency domain.

In order to guarantee standards compatibility, the development of the domain ontologies and taxonomies relies on the existing emergency standard, as well as TSO[6](Tactical Situation Object) and CAP[7](Common Alerting Protocol) defined in the EIIF XG initiative. According to TSO and CAP, we define emergency environment taxonomies in terms of: occurring events, involved actors (i.e. animals, childs, female, etc.), involved structures (i.e. hospital, dwelling place, etc.), degree of emergency and so on. Analogously we define a taxonomy model that representing peoples skills coherently to the emergency scenario. The taxonomy modeling operations are performed using SKOS schema.

2.2   Upper Ontologies: Semantic Models of Services and People

In this section we will provide upper semantic models enabling representation of services and people by means of instantiation of Upper Ontologies: FOAF, ResumeRDF to semantically represent people profiles, OWL-S to semantically model available services. Details about these models are given follow.

Modeling of people's information. To discover located people, in this work we present an Augmented Geo-social Network Model where individuals (volunteers, professionals, etc.) provide their profile data to some authorized organizations that can exploit it to face emergencies. Profile data mainly consist of

---

[2] http://www.daml.org/services/owl-s/
[3] http://www.foaf-project.org/
[4] http://lsdis.cs.uga.edu/ aleman/efw2007/bojars__efw2007.html
[5] Simple Knowledge Organization System - http://www.w3.org/TR/skos-reference/
[6] http://www.tacticalsituationobject.org/
[7] http://www.w3.org/2005/Incubator/eiif/XGR-EIIF-20090806/

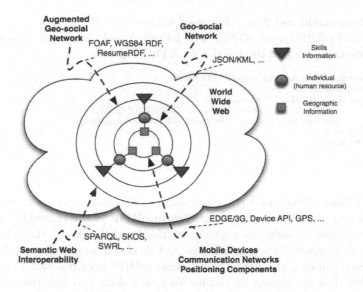

Fig. 1. Conceptual model of Augmented Geo-social Networks

competencies and geographic position. Fig. 1 shows the conceptual model of Augmented g Networks. It represents the ontology based modeling of people constructed on the top of the model of Geo-social Networks defined in [3], by considering the skills dimension and by exposing information using Semantic Web schemas to support semantic interoperability, inference and RDF Query languages (e.g. SPARQL).

In order to satisfy interoperability issues and to exploit existing modeling efforts and tools we introduce the harmonized use [6] of FOAF and ResumeRDF in order to model human resource in the proposed architecture. The **FOAF** project has become a widely accepted standard vocabulary for representing social networks, and many large social networking websites use it to produce Semantic Web profiles for their users. The way it is used satisfies the goal of using an ontology to represent considerable amounts of distributed data in a standard form. However, for FOAF to truly serve as an example of the Semantic Webs full potential, reasoning over the data must lead to the discovery of connections between what are represented as distinct data sets. FOAF provides a way to organize basic information about a person [7] (e.g. Person, firstName, surname, nick, title, mbox, etc.), other personal data (e.g. interest, knows, etc.), online accounts (e.g. icqChatID, msnChatID, jabberID, etc.), groups information (e.g. Organization, Group, Project, etc.) and documents information (e.g. Personal-ProfileDocument, Image, etc.).

In order to describe the typical latitute and longitude of an individual of type *foaf:Person* it is possible to use the RDF version of the World Geodetic System from 1984 (WGS84)[8]. WGS84 is a standard way of representing points on the

---

[8] http://www.w3.org/2003/01/geo/#vocabulary

surface of the earth, and it is widely used because it is the encoding used by the Global Positioning System (GPS). The following code fragment shows how to geo-localize an individual modelled with a FOAF profile.

```
<foaf:Person rdf:ID="FrancescoOrciuoliFOAFPerson">
    <geo:location>
        <geo:Point rdf:ID="Position_01">
            <geo:lat rdf:datatype="#string">-76.850706</geo:lat>
            <geo:long rdf:datatype="#string">39.184543</geo:long>
        </geo:Point>
    </geo:location>
    ...
</foaf:Person>
```

Nevertheless, FOAF does not cover aspects like skills. So we need the use, in sinergy with the FOAF schema, of **ResumeRDF** [8]. ResumeRDF is an ontology developed in order to express, on the Semantic Web, the information contained in a resume, such as business and academic experience, skills, publications, certifications, etc. For instance, ResumeRDF provides *cv:CV*, *cv:Person* and *cv:Skill* that are classes we can use to model skills and link them to FOAF profiles. The link between a FOAF Profile and a ResumeRDF instance could be set by using the *owl:sameAs* properties supported to perform inference using common OWL reasoners. So, if A *owl:sameAs* B then in any triple (RDF) where we see A, we can infer the same triple with A replaced by B. The following code fragment shows how to link FOAF profiles with skills information.

```
<foaf:Person rdf:ID="FrancescoOrciuoliFOAFPerson">
    <owl:sameAs rdf:resource="#FrancescoOrciuoliResumePerson"/>
</foaf:Person>
<owl:Thing rdf:ID="FirstAidSkill">
    <rdf:type rdf:resource="cv_rdfs#Skill"/>
    <skos:related rdf:resource="#FirstAid"/>
</owl:Thing>
<owl:Thing rdf:about="FrancescoOrciuoliPerson">
    <rdf:type rdf:resource="cv_rdfs#Person"/>
</owl:Thing>
<owl:Thing rdf:about="#FrancescoOrciuoliCV">
    <rdf:type rdf:resource="cv_rdfs#CV"/>
    <cv_rdfs:hasSkill rdf:resource="#FirstAidSkill"/>
    <cv_rdfs:aboutPerson rdf:resource="#FrancescoOrciuoliPerson"/>
</owl:Thing>
<skos:Concept rdf:about="FirstAid">
    <skos:definition>First Aid</skos:definition>
</skos:Concept>
```

Modeling of services. Deploying the semantics embedded in Web Services is a mandatory step in the automation of discovery, invocation and composition activities. The semantic annotation is the "add-on" to cope with the actual interoperability limitations and to assure a valid support to the interpretation of services capabilities. Nevertheless many issues have to be reached to support semantics in the Web Services and to guarantee accurate functionality descriptions. There are several studies and projects aiming at adding semantics to Web Service infrastructures. OWL-S [9] provides a qualified OWL-based support for semantic Web Services advertising and process capabilities; analogously Web Service Modeling Framework (WSMF)[10] exploit ontologies in order to solve the interoperability problems among heterogeneous web services; METEOR-S [11] has moved to the same direction, adding an interface to UDDI [12] for concept-based querying. This work exploits the OWL-S for describing the Web Services capabilities. OWL-S is an OWL-based upper ontology used to apply semantic descriptions to Web Services. OWL-S supports the dynamic discovery, invocation, composition and mediation of web services. OWL-S allows the providers to deploy a complete description of the web services capabilities, through the following three modules: Service Profile, the Service Model and Service Grounding. In particular, Service Profile represents the high level description of the specifications of a Semantic Web Services. It declares the functional description of an advertised Web Service, through its own IOPR (Input-Output-Precondition-Result) specifications. Indeed, a set of conditions holds in order to guarantee the proper execution of a service (Precondition), a set of post-conditions is defined too, after the service execution (Result), and finally the Input and Output describes I/O functional descriptions. The OWL-S Profile provides a mechanism for adding other parameters (e.g. quality guarantees, geographic availability, category and so on). The following code lines shows an example OWL-S profile that defines characterization of service in terms of the geo-localization and classification:

```
<profile:Profile rdf:ID="Profile_RedCross_Rescue">
    < profile:serviceParameter>
        <geoParam:GeoParameter>
            < profile:sParameter>
                <geo:Point rdf:ID="Position_01">
                    < geo:lat rdf:datatype="#string">-70.850706 </geo:lat>
                    < geo:long rdf:datatype="#string">45.184543 </geo:long>
                < /geo:Point>
            < /profile:sParameter>
        < /geoParam:GeonamesReference>
    < /profile:serviceParameter>

    < profile:hasInput rdf:resource="#input"/>
    < profile:hasOutput rdf:resource="#output"/>
    < profile:hasPrecondition rdf:resource="#output"/>
    < profile:hasResult rdf:resource="#output"/>
    < profile:serviceCategory rdf:resource="#PeopleRescue"/>
< /profile:Profile>

< process:AtomicProcess rdf:about="#Process_RedCross_Rescue">
    < process:hasInput>
        < process:Input rdf:ID="input">
            < process:parameterType rdf:resource="&tso;#HUM_CAPAB_MED_ClassType"/>
        < /process:Input>
    < /process:hasInput>
    < process:hasOutput>
        < process:UnConditionalOutput rdf:ID="output">
            < process:parameterType rdf:resource="&tso;#TSOAcknowledgement"/>
        < /process:UnConditionalOutput>
    < /process:hasOutput>
< /process:AtomicProcess>
```

2.3 Emergency Resource Plans Based on Fuzzy Cognitive Maps

As shown in [13],[5] FCMs have been successfully exploited in several application domains. Usually, emergency management activities foresee that resource plans are designed and applied in order to answer to the occurring events. In particular, given a specific emergency event there exists a suitable assignment of resources (i.e. organisms, actors, skills, vehicle, etc.) according to the intervention with respect to emergency type, geographic information, current availability of resources and so on. So, this section presents FCMs as a convenient mathematical model able to support the design of emergency resource plans. The FCMs support the evaluation of fuzzy discovery of available resources and emergency's requirements. Then, the evaluation of FCMs allows to retrieve the right set of resources among the available ones according to the event.

From theoretical point of view, a FCM is a fuzzy signed oriented graph with feedback that models systems by means of a collection of concepts and causal relations among concepts. In details, variable concepts are represented by nodes in a directed graph and the graphs edges represent the casual influences between the concepts. The value of a node reflects the degree to which the concept is active in the system at a particular time. This value is a function of the sum of all incoming edges and the value of the originating concept at the immediately preceding state. It is important to mention that all the values in the graph are fuzzy, i.e, concepts take values in the range between $[0, 1]$ and the arcs weights are in the interval $[-1, 1]$.

This work defines three layered FCMs as follows:

- First level:*Emergency Events* - In this layer there are concepts that represent emergency events (i.e. fire, earthquake, smash up, inundation, etc.) in terms of ontologycal entities. These concepts are activated when a specific event occurs.
- Second level: *Types of Resource* - This layer is represented by concepts in the domain ontologies that characterize people's skills (i.e. medical, firefighter, volunteer, policeman, etc.), services(i.e. People Rescue, Animal Rescue, etc.), vehicle (i.e. ambulance, fire engine, airplane etc.) and so on.
- Third level:*Available Resources* - The layer is represented by FOAF profiles' instances and OWL-S services available in the architecture. According to the upper ontology, as described above (see section 3.2) the resources are characterized by references to the domain ontologies and taxonomies.

Among concepts in the three layered FCMs, there are two kinds of relationships:

- *"Causal"*, is the relationship between first and second level. Specifically, relationships have to be defined according to the effective emergency plans adopted in the specific geographic area. The weights of the edges represent involvement degree of that kind of resource to specific event's requirements. The relationships are based on expertise.
- *"Reference"*, is the relationship between second and third level. References from specific service or profile to domain ontologies allow to automatically elicit the edges in the FCMs.

So, according to the occurred event some concepts of the first level are activated and by means of FCMs, the system retrieves a ranked list of resources in the third level. A workflow example is given in the following section.

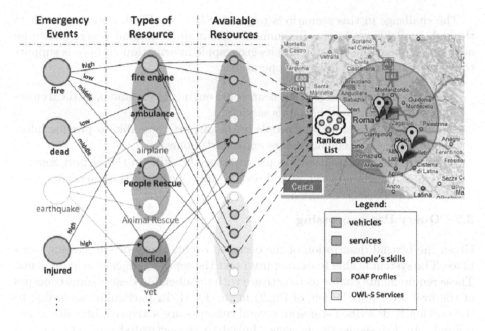

Fig. 2. An example of three layered Fuzzy Cognitive Map evaluation according to the emergency scenario

3   Query Answering Activity

When an emergency occurs in a given geographic area, it needs to find nearest and most suitable available resources (i.e medical, fireman, etc.). This section describes the query answering workflow by showing an example of emergency scenario. Fig.2 skecthes a part of emergency plan modeled by means of three layered FCMs (see Section 2.3). In particular, the figure emphasizes (red filled circle) concepts that are activated depending on a specific event. Concepts on the left of the figure represent ontologycal characterization of events. Concepts in the middle represent types of resource needs to manage the event. Finally, on the right there are concepts that represent available resources in the database. In the next section we discuss a presumed scenario of an airplane accident and the building of an emergency plan in order to assign the right resources.

3.1   Scenario Description: Airplane Accident

Let us consider the following emergency scenario:

"Today at Rome Airport, the concurrence of events leads to an airplane crashing into Terminal A. This accident causes a large number of casualties resulting in death and injuries of different degrees. A fire flares up in the Terminal. The situation at the site of the accident and nearly is becoming very chaotic."

The challenge in this scenario is to provide fast, qualified, and effective help through available resources. In summary, the main command centre has to be acquainted about the collision and its geographic information and needs support to perform at least the following operations:

- checking the availability of the nearest fire engine, ambulances, medical emergency, volunteers and hospitals services;
- checking the availability of people in the airport zone able to provide information by using cellular phones and smartphones;
- checking the availability of people with specific skills in the airport zone;
- activating available services and people and coordinate their actions;

3.2   Query Pre-processing

Given the textual description of the occurred event, query pre-processing takes place. The system is able to extract from text the set of emergency requirements. These requirements enable us to activate with membership degree some concepts of the first level (on the left of Fig.2) in the FCM. In particular, according to the previously described scenario, several concepts are activated, like: fire, dead, injured, etc. Consequently, concepts linked to the activated ones are selected with specific membership value as described follow.

3.3   Answer Evaluation, Ranking and Filtering

According to the FCM in Fig.2, after the query pre-processing phase, the activation of *Emergency Events* concepts take place. Consequently, *Types of Resources* concepts are activated with specific membership degree. So, the system selects several types of resource in order to face up to the emergency scenario occurred. In particular, as shown in Fig. 2 some concepts in the second level (in the middle of the picture), like: fire engine, ambulance, People Rescue, medical, and so on are fired. The activation depends on causal relationships between first and second level concepts.

Then, the *Available Resources* concepts in the third level (i.e FOAF Profiles and OWL-S Services) are activated. The selected list of resources have been ranked according to the FCM evaluation. Next, the third layer concepts are filtered respect to the geographic nearly to the emergency event location. The filtered list contains the scheduled resources to the emergency intervention.

4   Conclusions and Future Works

This work introduces a synergic approach of semantic technologies and soft computing techniques in order to improve emergency management performances. In particular, the architecture deals with information sharing and discovery by means of strongly usage of semantic web technologies (i.e. Domain Ontologies,

Taxonomies, Upper Ontologies, etc.). A novel approach to the discovery exploiting three layered FCMs in order to suitably model and elicit the resources available according to the emergency requirements is defined. In particular, the work exploits location-based filtering activity respect to the emergency geo-location.

In the next future, the research will deal with two main aspects. The first one is related to adaptive evolution of FCMs, by exploiting users' feedbacks, to improve resources retrieval. The second one, is related to automatic acquisition of emergency requirements from unstructured and multimedia content (e.g. SMS, images, audio clips, etc.) alternative to the textual description considered in the query pre-processing phase (see Section 3.2).

References

1. Loia, V., Pedrycz, W., Senatore, S.: Semantic web content analysis: a study in proximity-based collaborative clustering. IEEE Transaction on Fuzzy Systems 15(6), 1294–1312 (2007)
2. Martin, L.D., Paolucci, M., McIlraith, S.A., Burstein, M.H., McDermott, D.V., McGuinness, D.L., Parsia, B., Payne, T.R., Sabou, M., Solanki, M., Srinivasan, N., Sycara, K.P.: Bringing semantics to web services: the OWL-S approach. In: Cardoso, J., Sheth, A.P. (eds.) SWSWPC 2004. LNCS, vol. 3387, pp. 26–42. Springer, Heidelberg (2005)
3. Huang, Q., Liu, Y.: On geo-social network services. In: 2009 17th International Conference on Geoinformatics, August 12-14, pp. 1–6 (2009)
4. Fenza, G., Loia, V., Senatore, S.: A Hybrid approach to Semantic Web Services Matchmaking. Accepted on Intl. Journal of Approximate Reasoning (2007)
5. Stylio, C.D., Georqopoulos, V.C., Malandraki, G.A., Chouliara, S.: Fuzzy cognitive map architectures for medical decision support systems. Applied Soft Computing Journal 8(3), 1243–1251 (2008)
6. Aleman-Meza, B., Bojars, U., Boley, H., Breslin, J.G., Mochol, M., Nixon, L.J., Polleres, A., Zhdanova, A.V.: Combining RDF Vocabularies for Expert Finding. In: Franconi, E., Kifer, M., May, W. (eds.) ESWC 2007. LNCS, vol. 4519, pp. 235–250. Springer, Heidelberg (2007)
7. Golbeck, J., Rothstein, M.: Linking social networks on the web with FOAF: a semantic web case study. In: Cohn, A. (ed.) Proceedings of the 23rd National Conference on Artificial intelligence, Chicago, Illinois, July 13-17, 2008. Aaai Conference on Artificial Intelligence, vol. 2, pp. 1138–1143. AAAI Press, Menlo Park (2009)
8. Bojars, U.: Extending FOAF with Resume Information. In: 1st Workshop on FOAF, Social Networks and the Semantic Web (2004)
9. OWL Services Coalition. OWL-S: Semantic Markup for Web Services (2004); http://www.daml.org/services/owl-s/
10. Lausen, H., Roman, D., Keller, U.: Web Service Modeling Ontology WSMO - Standard, http://www.w3.org/Submission/WSMO/
11. Sheth, A., Patil, A., Oundhakar, S., Verma, K., Sivashanmugam, K., Miller, J.: METEOR-S WSDI: A Scalable Infrastructure of Registries for Semantic Publication and Discovery of Web Services
12. UDDI. Universal Description, Discovery, and Integration, http://uddi.org/
13. Acampora, G., Loia, V.: A dynamical cognitive multi-agent system for enhancing ambient intelligence scenarios. In: IEEE International Conference on Fuzzy Systems, FUZZ-IEEE 2009, August 20-24, pp. 770–777 (2009)

Finding an Evolutionarily Stable Strategy in Agent Reputation and Trust (ART) 2007 Competition

Javier Carbo and José Manuel Molina

Group of Applied Artificial Intelligence, Computer Science Department, University
Carlos III of Madrid
{javier.carbo,josemanuel.molina}@uc3m.es

Abstract. Our proposal is to apply a Game Theoretic approach to the
games played in Agent Reputation and Trust Final Competitions. Using
such testbed, three international competitions were successfully carried
out jointly with the last AAMAS international Conferences. The corresponding way to define the winner of such competitions was to run a
game with all the participants (16). Our point is that such game does
not represent a complete way to determine the best trust/reputation
strategy, since it is not proved that such strategy is evolutionarily stable.
Specifically we prove that when the strategy of the winner of the two first
international competitions (2006 and 2007) becomes dominant, it is defeated by other participant trust strategies. Then we found out (through
a repeated game definition) the right equilibrium of trust strategies that
is evolutionarily stable. This kind of repeated game has to be taken into
account in the evaluation of trust strategies, and this conclusion would
improve the way trust strategies have to be compared.

1 Introduction

The way agents achieve cooperation solving complex tasks is a design key factor
in MultiAgent Systems. However, since Agent Systems intend to be open, agents
have to establish some kind of social control that could be defined as designed
or emergent [1]. The former implemented through Electronic Institutions, such
as Certification Authorities, when trust/ is concluded from the observation of
universal and objective norms, but in many real-world interactions trust is emergent, depends on local and subjective evaluations shared between partners (reputation). In recent years, trust/reputation research community has grown a lot,
many trust/reputation models have been proposed [5]. Since it was very difficult
to compare their respective performances as many ad-hoc implementations and
metrics have been applied, a testbed platform for agent trust/reputation models
was developed: the Agent Reputation and Trust (ART) Testbed [2][1]. Using such
testbed, three international competitions were successfully carried out jointly
with the last AAMAS international Conferences. During these years the ART

---

[1] $http://megatron.iiia.csic.es/art-testbed$

N. García-Pedrajas et al. (Eds.): IEA/AIE 2010, Part III, LNAI 6098, pp. 470–477, 2010.

testbed has been used by dozens of researchers, and the ART-testbed members have discussed, patched and updated the platform using the feedback from the Competitions (see discussion notes on ART web page) and from the agent trust community (through the discussion Board of ART). These criticism produced some changes in protocols [6], and outlined new directions of work [4]. This criticism is essentially focused on the scalability of ART games since with more agents the right use of reputation would make more sense playing an increasing role to win the game. Additionally a differentiation between the way trust is acquired/modeled/updated (trust model) and the way trust is used/applied in decisions (trust strategy) would be desirable.

This paper suggests a new way ART can be used in competitions to evaluate agents. In section 2 we explain our domain: the ART testbed. Afterwards, in section 3, We show how a game-theoretic approach can be applied in this domain. In [6] and [4] did not even mention the possibility of applying a game-theoretic approach, they just remark the needing of thinking on new different ways to evaluate trust/reputation models. Our contribution is to define a way to determine the ability of a trust strategy to win when it is dominant in the society of agents. With such intention, we propose in section 4 a new different kind of repeated games with ART testbed. In order to achieve this goal the corresponding games have been run with the participant agents of ART competitions in section 5.

2   ART Testbed

The ART testbed compared different trust strategies using reputation models in the art appraisal domain. In this domain, agents are players/competitors that appraise paintings and implement trust strategies. Figure 1 shows an outline of ART domain.

In each timestep, the simulator engine presents each appraiser agent with paintings (generated by the simulation engine) to be appraised, paying a fixed fee f for each appraisal request. Very close valuations of paintings to the real value would lead to more future clients, and therefore to more earnings to win the competition. The corresponding steps of a turn in ART games is shown in figure 2.

Each painting belongs to an era among a set of artistic eras while agents have different levels of expertise (ability to appraise) in each era. An agent can appraise its own paintings and may request opinions (at a fixed cost) from other appraisers to get its valuation of the painting close to the real value (specially useful in the eras where the agent has low expertise). An agent can act also as provider of appraisals in response to opinion (about paintings) requests from other agents Additionally, an agent can similarly request reputation information about other appraisers (at a fixed and much lower cost than opinions). The winner of an ART game is the agent who earned more money along the number of iterations that were run in the game. Such earnings come from different sources: paintings appraised to the own clients (Client Fee), paintings appraised to other appraiser agents (Opinion Cost) and reputations shared with other appraiser

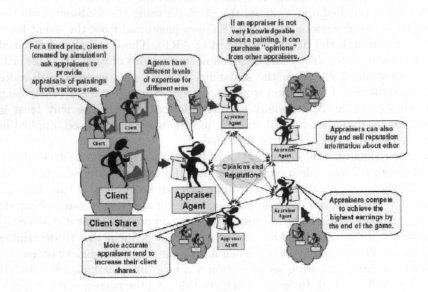

Fig. 1. ART domain outline. Source [2]

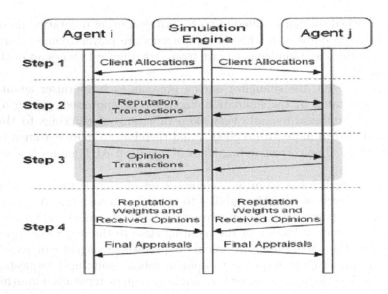

Fig. 2. Steps of a gameturn in ART domain. Source: [3]

agents (Reputation Cost), where Client Fees are the main source of income since: Client Fee >> Opinion Cost >> Reputation Cost.

3   Evolutionarily Stable Trust Strategies in ART

3.1   Trust and ESS

In game theory and behavioural ecology, an evolutionarily stable strategy (ESS) is a strategy which, if adopted by a population of players, cannot be invaded by any alternative strategy. An ESS is a Nash equilibrium which is "evolutionarily" stable meaning that once it is fixed in a population, natural selection alone is sufficient to prevent alternative (mutant) strategies from successfully invading. The ESS was developed in order to define a class of solutions to game theoretic problems, equivalent to the Nash equilibrium, but which could be applied to the evolution of social behaviour in animals. Our proposal is to apply this Game Theoretic approach to the games played in Agent Reputation and Trust Final Competitions. Although in ART games there is no reproduction neither evolution, this approach make sense since the goal of trust strategies is to establish some kind of social control over malicious/distrustful agents through the exchange of local and subjective evaluations between partners (the so called reputation in ART terms). So the idea of applying trust strategies in agent societies is to filter out the agents who do not behave properly in such society. Therefore, we could state that the loser of the direct confrontation between/among trust strategies would be expelled out of such society of agents. We can even think in terms of evolution if we assume that agents may change of trust strategy. Following that line, it seems to be reasonable that agents with a failing trust strategy would get rid of it and they would adopt a successful trust strategy in the future. Through this analogy we can define a repeated game in ART domain that would allow us to evaluate the ability of participant agents in past competitions to be an evolutionarily stable trust strategy. Furthermore, we can define as an evolutionarily stable trust strategy is a strategy which, if becomes dominant (adopted by a majority of agents) can not be defeated by any alternative strategy.

3.2   Repeated Game Definition to Find a ESS in ART

Using ART testbed, three international competitions were successfully carried out jointly with the last AAMAS international Conferences. The corresponding way to define the winner of 2007 competitions was to run the same game with all the participants (16) several times (until 10 times) plus some dummy agents (9) with enough timesteps per game (defined as 60 minuted length to complete each game)[2]. Our point is that such game does not represent a complete way to determine the best trust strategy, since it is not proved that such trust strategy is evolutionarily stable. Therefore we propose a simulation of the evolution of

---

[2] $http://megatron.iiia.csic.es/art-testbed/competition2007.html$

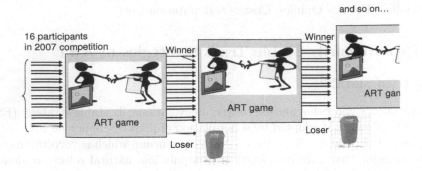

Fig. 3. Evolution Simulation in ART games

a society of ART participant agents through a set of consecutive games, where evolution is implemented assuming that agents with a failing trust strategy would get rid of it and they would adopt a successful trust strategy in the next ART game. Where we consider a failing trust strategy the one who lost (earning less money than the others) the last ART game, and we consider the successful trust strategy to the one who won the last ART game (earning more money than the others). By this way replacing in consecutive games the participant who lost the game by the one who won it. We will then find out if there is a trust strategy among the participant agents in ART competitions that is evolutionarily stable. An outline of the ART game defined to simulate a evolutive society of agents applying trust strategies is shown in figure 3.

3.3   Finding a ESS among 2007 ART Competitors

Once the type of game to be run has been defined, we have applied it to the participant agents of 2007 ART competition (the code of last competition (2008) participants is not public and we want our experiments to be repeatable). First we show in table 1 the participants and the resulting earnings of such competition[3]:

As we consider these participants (without dummy agents) as the first game in our evolutive simulation, then, if the relative positions are similar we have 2 iam2 agents, no xerxes agent and the other 14 agents as participants of the second game. We proceed in same way including an extra winner agent and excluding the loser agent in consecutive games. Next we show in table 2 the agents that win and lose each consecutive game with the corresponding earnings. The earnings showed in table 2 are computed in same way as the competition, as a normalized bank balance (bank balance divided by number of timesteps in the game), and game length and game repetition defined in the same way (60m maximum, 10 times) so all the experiments shown here can be easily repeated. As it was expected, since there are no dummies to easily cheat, the earnings of

---

[3] $http : //megatron.iiia.csic.es/art - testbed/competition\_results2007.html$

Table 1. 2007 ART Competition Results

Rank	Agent name	Affiliation	Earnings
1	iam2	Univ. Southampton	539377
2	jam	Univ. Tulsa	353700
3	blizzard	Bogazici Univ.	335933
4	zecariocales	Pontificia Univ. Rio	319564
5	spartan	Univ. Girona	311777
6	artgente	Univ. Trento	298897
7	uno	Univ. Girona	293324
8	reneil	Nanyang Tech. Univ.	269905
9	marmota	Univ. Girona	264356
10	novel	Univ. Murcia	229501
11	alatriste	Univ. Carlos III Madrid	225276
12	rex	Univ. Warwick	211467
13	IMM	Univ. Carlos III Madrid	200440
14	lesmes	Univ. Carlos III Madrid	183655
15	agentevicente	Univ. Carlos III Madrid	181932
16	xerxes	U.S. Airforce Research Lab.	148610

Table 2. Evolution Simulation Results

Game Number	Winner	Earnings	Loser	Earnings
1	iam2	17377	xerxes	-8610
2	iam2	14321	lesmes	-13700
3	iam2	10360	reneil	-14757
4	iam2	10447	blizzard	-7093
5	agentevicente	8975	Rex	-5495
6	iam2	8512	alatriste	-999
7	artgente	8994	agentevicente	2011
8	artgente	10611	agentevicente	1322
9	artgente	8932	novel	424
10	iam2	9017	IMM	1392
11	artgente	7715	marmota	1445
12	artgente	8722	spartan	2083
13	artgente	8966	zecariocales	1324
14	artgente 8372	7285	iam2	2599
15	artgente	7475	iam2	2298
16	artgente	8384	UNO	2719
17	artgente	7639	iam2	2878
18	iam2	6279	JAM	3486
19	iam2	14674	artgente	2811
20	artgente	8035	iam2	3395

Table 3. Comparison of Rankings of agents

Competition Rank	Evolution Rank	Agent name	Excluded in game number
6	1	artgente	-
1	2	iam2	-
2	3	JAM	18
7	4	UNO	16
4	5	zecariocales	13
5	6	spartan	12
9	7	marmota	11
13	8	IMM	10
10	9	novel	9
15	10	agentevicente	8
11	11	alatriste	6
12	12	rex	5
3	13	Blizzard	4
8	14	reneil	3
14	15	lesmes	2
16	16	xerxes	1

agents are much lower than those of the competition and the differences between winners and losers becomes closer in the last games.

Specifically with this experiment we have proved that although the strategy of the winner of the 2007 international competitions spreads in the society of agents (until 6 agents implementing iam2 trust strategy out of 16 participant agents), it never becomes dominant (there is no majority of iam2 agents). In fact it is defeated by other trust strategy artgente, which becomes dominant (11 artgente agents out of 16). Therefore iam2 is not an evolutionarily stable trust strategy, so its superiority as winner of 2007 competition is, at least, relative. We also found out that the right equilibrium of trust strategies that form an evolutionarily stable society is composed by 10-11 Artgente agents and 6-5 iam2 agents. Finally, from the order in which agents are excluded from the society, we can propose an alternative ranking of trust strategies in table 3 which :is very different from the competition ranking.

4   Conclusions

Due to the relative success of the trust and reputation research, and specifically of ART testbed, a good design foundation of fair comparisons among trust strategies will spread the inclusion of reputation and trust communications into more general service-oriented systems that would be truly distributed. According to that intention, we have defined what an evolutionarily stable strategy would be in trust domain, and how it can be proved in ART competitions through a repeated game with a simulation of evolution. We have applied such game definition to the participant agents of 2007 competition and we found out that the winner of such competition was not implementing an evolutionarily stable strategy. As a conclusion we stated that this kind of repeated game has to be taken into account in the evaluation of trust strategies, and this conclusion would improve the way trust strategies have to be compared, not just thinking about the testbed, also about the games definition.

Acknowledgments

This work was supported in part by Projects CICYT TIN2008-06742-C02-02/ TSI, CICYT TEC2008-06732-C02-02/TEC, SINPROB, CAM MADRINET S-0505/TIC/0255 and DPS2008-07029-C02-02.

References

1. Conte, R., Paolucci, M.: Reputation in Artificial Societies. Kluwer Academic Publishers, Dordrecht (2002)
2. Fullam, K., Klos, T., Muller, G., Sabater, J., Schlosser, A., Topol, Z., Barber, K.S., Rosenschein, J., Vercouter, L., Voss, M.: A specification of the agent reputation and trust (art) testbed: Experimentation and competition for trust in agent societies. In: The Fourth International Joint Conference on Autonomous Agents and Multiagent Systems (AAMAS 2005), pp. 512–518 (2005)
3. Fullam, K., Klos, T., Muller, G., Sabater, J., Topol, Z., Barber, K.S., Rosenschein, J., Vercouter, L.: The agent reputation and trust (art) testbed architecture. In: Workshop on Trust in Agent Societies at The Fourth International Joint Conference on Autonomous Agents and Multiagent Systems (AAMAS 2005), pp. 50–62 (2005)
4. Gomez, M., Sabater-Mir, J., Carbo, J., Muller, G.: Improving the art testbed, thoughts and reflections. In: Procs. of 12th CAEPIA Conference, pp. 1–15 (2007)
5. Ramchurn, S.D., Huynh, D., Jennings, N.R.: Trust in multi-agent systems. Knowl. Eng. Rev. 19(1), 1–25 (2004)
6. Sabater, J., Gomez, M., Muller, G., Carbo, J.: Changes for the 2008 competition (2008), http://megatron.iiia.csic.es/art-testbed/changes_2008.htm

A Proposal for News Recommendation Based on Clustering Techniques

Sergio Cleger-Tamayo[1], Juan M. Fernández-Luna[2], Juan F. Huete[2],
Ramiro Pérez-Vázquez[3], and Julio C. Rodríguez Cano[1]

[1] Department of Informatics. University of Holguín, Cuba
{sergio,jcrodriguez}@facinf.uho.edu.cu
[2] Departamento de Ciencias de la Computación e Inteligencia Artificial - CITIC
E.T.S.I Informática y de Telecomunicación – CITIC. Universidad de Granada,
18701, Granada, Spain
{jmfluna,jhg}@decsai.ugr.es
[3] Departament of Computer Science. University Central de las Villas, Cuba
rperez@uclv.edu.cu

Abstract. The application of clustering techniques in recommendation systems is discussed in the present article, specifically in a journalistic context, where multiple users have access to categorized news. The aim of this paper is to present an approach to recommend news to the readers of an electronic journal according to their profile, i.e. the record of news accessed. The Aspect Model, as well as the K-Means clustering algorithm are applied to this problem and compared empirically.

Keywords: Collaborative Filtering, Cognitive Filtering, RS, Collaborative Recommendation Systems, Clustering Techniques, K-Means, Aspect Model.

1 Introduction

The last 25 years have been marked by two opposite situations: on one hand, the inadequate and insufficient sources of information; later, on the other hand, the age of communications: the available information wearied the daily lives of hundreds of thousands of internet users.

The growth of the Internet, and in parallel, the great amount of generated materials (science, leisure, electronic commerce, etc.) have been the reason why in the last decade of the twentieth century, systems were designed with the aim of suggesting relevant items to the users, giving them a step ahead in the context of information retrieval. It was at this moment when Recommendation Systems (RS) surfaced, being able of recommending or suggesting specific items (books, songs, documents, hotels, restaurants, web sites) according to the preference of the users [1]. RS are framed into the domain of Artificial Intelligence, although it is an interdisciplinary area. Researchers are making efforts to design more accurate techniques to compute the relevance of those elements that the user is least acquainted with.

The tendency in the last few years with respect to the research in the area of news filtering in daily newspapers and other means of information have increased notably,

N. García-Pedrajas et al. (Eds.): IEA/AIE 2010, Part III, LNAI 6098, pp. 478–487, 2010.

becoming a very active research line within the Web, where new personalization techniques are designed and applied [2], [3], [4].

Broadly speaking, the reasons why people visit web sites are very diverse, which implies that their interests generally differ. Therefore, RS have to be endowed with mechanisms to identify the users, in a first stage, and later, to show news to them that they may be unacquainted with and which may be of interest to them.

In this paper a proposal framed in the field of news recommendation is presented. The basic input of the RS is the profiles of the users, i.e. the list of news read, plus the new news items that are included in the journal web site daily. All news is classified in specific categories, and can be recommended to the users according to their interests, inferred from their previous visits. More specifically, all the news accessed by the journal site user is recorded, together with their category. This information is used to generate groups of users with similar navigation profiles. The final objective is to classify the users to offer them news items that are adequate to their interests.

One of the objectives of this article focuses on describing Recommendation Systems, its objectives and characteristics, as well as techniques and models utilized in its implementation, making emphasis on the utilization of clustering techniques, which is presented in section 2. Section 3 is dedicated to illustrate the problem at hand. The experimentation and the obtained results are presented in section 4. This article concludes with section 5, where the elements that will be used as guidance for future works are presented.

2 Recommender Systems

These systems are applicable to several domains and can be separated into two types: based on the content (cognitive filtering) and collaborative filtering (social filtering). The first type provides recommendations based upon a description of the item and a profile of the user's interests. The systems generate recommendations from the features associated with products and the ratings that a user has given them [5].

Focusing on the second class, collaborative filtering RS, as it is the type in which this model is presented, their key elements are the mechanisms of prediction (filtering) based on the interests of a user, plus the preferences of several similar users (collaborators) [6]. The aim is to predict the usefulness of new items for an active user supported by that previously mentioned information.

These can be split into two principal categories, depending on the calculation algorithm: based on memory (or heuristic) and based on item/model. The first operates on the entire user database to make predictions; the algorithms based on modeling, on the contrary, use the user database to estimate or to learn a model, which is then used to give the predictions. The algorithms based on memory usually learn quickly but are slow to make predictions, while the other type makes predictions quickly but learns slowly.

The memory-based algorithms predict a user rating for a particular item by using a similarity-weighted sum of the other user ratings. The method used to calculate weighs a distinguishing characteristic of the algorithms in this category. These are the most popular prediction techniques in the applications of collaborative recommendation, also known as the nearest K neighbors method or collaborative filter based on users [7].

The model-based algorithms firstly develop a model of the users' ratings, which is assumed as a statistical prediction problem, and calculate the expected value for each item among the previous "rating". The model can be constructed offline during several hours or days according to the data source, proving to be very small, fast, and essentially as exact as the memory-based methods. They can even be faster than these except that they need an intensive learning process [8, 19].

When starting to work with data in these types of systems, its great dispersion can be noticed, given by the difference and diversity with regard to the number of valuations or accesses realized by users. Another interesting situation is the continuous increment of the number of users and their accesses, which tends to reduce the efficiency of a lot of the applicable techniques. These situations present themselves as the principal RS limitations [8], [9].

The application of clustering techniques improves the already mentioned problems, since the total data is divided into small groups, which under determined characteristics show some similarities. Obtaining those small subgroups allows on them the application of recommendation techniques. The efficiency of the clustering techniques is proved in multiple works [7], [10], [11], through which it presents an adequate alternative in high dimensionality problems. Therefore, predictions will be done in terms of the objects that compose the cluster belonging to the active object, and not with all the objects, alleviating the application of the recommender technique, and consequently increasing the performance [11].

Sarwar et al. present in [11] an algorithm utilizing neighboring formations by means of clustering techniques, which can be compared to classical techniques of neighborhood formations in RS, demonstrating in their experiments a good predictive quality of their proposal. In [12] a recursive density-based clustering algorithm on web documents based only on the log data is presented, this algorithm does not require the pre-determination on the number of clusters and is characterized by being linearly complex. Another algorithm is proposed in [13], where a clustering algorithm is utilized, being recursive it begins by dividing the space of the objects in rectangles of smaller size and in this way cells are obtained in which the cluster representatives are located.

In this article it is proposed the application of the ASPECT MODEL and K-Means clustering algorithms to the problem of identifying groups of users and performing news recommendations. Using these models we can group the IPs into a set of classes in function of the behavior that they follow when accessing the news. In this way, knowing the class to which each user belongs, would make easier the prediction of the user's behavior. As a consequence we can use the information from the group to determine, for example, whether a particular news item would be of interest to the user or, inversely what users (IPs) would be interested in a particular news item.

The K-Means algorithm is a clustering technique largely used and capable of rapidly finding a solution [14]. It starts with a random initial partition and keeps reassigning the patterns to clusters based on the similarity between the pattern and the cluster centers until a convergence criterion is met (e.g., there is no reassignment of any pattern from one cluster to another). In [15], Vicente, Erick et al. proposed a technique that makes good use of the fast convergence of the K-Means algorithm avoiding the inconvenience of reaching optimal sites. In the proposal they attain comparable results with regard to efficiency with respect to other heuristic goals.

The objective of the K-Means clustering is to partition the IPs into a set of K clusters that ideally represent the user's behaviour when visiting the news site. Each IP belongs to only one cluster, the nearest or the most similar cluster. Given an initial set of k means $\mathbf{m}_1^{(1)},\dots,\mathbf{m}_k^{(1)}$, which are specified randomly, the algorithm proceeds by alternating between two steps:

Assignment step: Assign each IP´s accesses to the cluster with the closest mean.

Update step: Calculate the new means to be the centroid in the cluster.

The algorithm ends when the assignments no longer change. Once the clusters have been learned, we can borrow information about the behaviour of the IPs in the cluster to predict the interests of the users in a given category.

While many techniques assume the membership of an object to only one cluster, others allow the object to belong to more than one cluster. In [16], Hofmann proposes a statistical technique applicable in information filtering and retrieval applications, natural language processing, and related areas. In the mentioned article the technique is applicable in the Information Retrieval context. The starting point of this technique is a statistical model which has been called ASPECT MODEL. This is a latent variable model for concurrent data which associates a hidden variable z that belongs to Z = $\{z_1\dots z_k\}$ with each observation. In the context where the model is applied, there are documents $D = \{d_1,\dots,d_m\}$ and words that conform them $W = \{w_1,\dots,w_n\}$. While other clustering models set each document in only one of the formed groups, this model assumes that each document can have multiple aspects and therefore it should have a certain grade of belonging to one specific K group that they may decide to form, at the same time the n words that are present in the documents will have a determined degree of membership towards the formed groups. This model and other variants are detailed by their own author in [17], where it is shown that good performance is gained with respect to other traditional variants.

Popescul et al. extends [18] the model proposed by Hofmann in [16]. They show a hybrid proposal of a recommendation system, incorporating in their proposal the referent data to the users, the items and their contents. Shein et al. in [19] shows the development of a hybrid model for the recommendation of items, tackling with it one of the problems of these systems, the cold start, this is the well-known problem of handling new items or new users. In a RS, the new items cannot be recommended to any user until they have been rated by some one. They make use of the ASPECT MODEL in the context of persons-actors-movies, obtaining better results than others with approximations on the same problems.

ASPECT MODEL for collaborative prediction considers a latent variable (Z) relating the IPs and category variables. The purpose is to automatically look for the potential reasons that determine which causes are likely to be relevant for a specific IP address or category and in each individual case assign a probability to this fact. Thus, from the IPs x Categories matrix (Table 1), it will be obtained three conditional probability distributions P(IP|Z), P(Z) and P(C|Z). P(IP|Z) would encode for each IP the likelihood that it belongs to a class. For example, if we assumed three classes z_1, z_2 and z_3 we would have for ip_1 P(IP= ip_1 | Z= z_1), P(IP= ip_1 | Z= z_2) and P(IP= ip_1 | Z= z_3), these likelihoods also would be encoded for ip_2, for ip_3, etc, within the matrix P(IP|Z). P(Z) is the prior likelihood that we have for the three classes P(Z= z_1), P(Z= z_2) and P(Z= Z_3). Finally, P(C|Z) would encode the likelihood about each

category given the class. Having for the Sport category, for example, P(C= "Sport" |
Z= z_1), P(C= "Sport"| Z= z_2) and P(P= "Sport"| Z= z_3).

Once the model is learned, it can be used to perform inferences. For instance, we
can compute the likelihood that each IP reads news from the categories (C) that are
arranged according to data:

$$P(IP,C) = \sum_z P(z)P(IP \mid z)P(C \mid z) \qquad (1)$$

Once at this step it is possible to determine the categories that can be more relevant
for an IP: it is calculated for all the categories P(C=Cat_n|ip_1) and from all of these
the i best are selected. Also it is possible to determine given a category, the users that
would be interested in that news. This would be equivalent to compute for all the IPs,
Pr(IP=ip_m | C = "Sports").

3 Problem Description: Recommending News

In the news web sites, avid persons frequently visit for new information. In a general
manner all the users hope to find news that satisfies them when concluding a visit, but
many times the structuring of the web application, the abstracts that may emerge from
articles or simply the fact that the user did not notice the news, may be the reason for
which the state of desired satisfaction was not attained.

Various mechanisms with the aim of increasing the user's satisfaction may be applied. Perhaps, the most direct approach consists of registering the users so we can
know their interests, i.e. the user profile, either explicitly (questionnaire) or implicitly
(analyzing their browsing patterns). Then, in each visit and after a user's identification, we can advice him/her about those news items that might be relevant to his/her
profile. This is the approach in [4] where users indicate their opinions in the form of
ratings on different articles in an online newspaper. With this information, a hybrid
approach for recommending is used. Nevertheless, the main problem of this approach
is that it is complex to get people to register in these types of systems, because a high
percent reveals some personal data that goes against privacy or it is an unnecessary
waste of time, proving to be more practical visiting anonymously.

In order to attenuate this situation we will study a different approach. Our hypothesis is that by considering the IP address, a number assigned to every device connected
to the public Internet, is enough to recognize not the user itself, but instead the kind of
user which is connected to the news server. Obviously, this identification should be
possible when the IP is permanent and therefore we shall restrict our research to a set
of static IPs which has had some connections to the newspaper site.

The idea is that it can be found different sets of IPs presenting a very similar visiting behavior in their navigation sessions, independently of the real users who are
connected. For example, we might expect to distinguish between those IPs that occasionally visit the Web site (motivated by a cultural event or some event that in that
moment captured their attention) from those IPs having frequent connections, and
among them we expect to distinguish between those IPs used by a single user from
those IPs used by many users, as for example it might be an IP in a university campus.

The objective of this paper is to study whether the above hypothesis can be used to make news recommendations according to the user's interests (the user connected in a particular IP). In order to do our research we propose the use of a model-based collaborative filtering approach. The main reason for using this approach is the large number of users (IPs) that can be connected to the site and the difficulty of searching the neighborhood for each user when he/she is logged on to the system, as memory-based approaches do. Note that the time devoted to search the neighborhood tends to be greater than that which a user would wait to receive a recommendation.

3.1 The Input Data: The "Ahora" Data Set

Generally, the input in a collaborative framework is a user-item matrix (usually very sparse) where we have for some pairs of user-items the value representing his/her interest for that item. On one hand, the items in our system are the news, particularly the category that they belong to, $C = \{Cat\_1,...,Cat\_n\}$. The categorization has been done by the editorial board of the online Daily News Website "Ahora" in Holguin, Cuba. We have a total of 49 different categories. On the other hand, the users in our data sets are represented by the IPs from where the users accessed. We will assume the $IP\ address = \{ip_1,...,ip_m\}$. The matrix values represent the number of news from a determined category that has been accessed from an IP $address$. Each session reflects an access realized in a time interval by a user from an IP address. For example:

Sesion_0: ip_1 + { (News_A,Cat_10), (News_B,Cat_10), (News_C,Cat_12), (News_D,Cat_18) .... }

Sesion_1: ip_2 + { (News_B,Cat_10), (New_H,Cat_40), (News_E,Cat_36).... }

Sesion_2: ip_1 + { (News_A,Cat_10),(New_H,Cat_40),(News_M,Cat_18) .... }

....

where it is indicated that a user has accessed news_A from the IP_1 that belongs to the category 10, news_B which belongs to the category 10, etc. With this data the IP-Categories matrix is then formed, as shown in Table 1.

Table 1. Accesses IPs x Categories matrix

...	Cat_10	Cat_12	Cat_18	Cat_36	Cat_40	...	Cat_n
ip_1	12	4	19				
ip_2	1			12	7		
...							
ip_m	20	6	36				19

The "Ahora" data set contains information of a year's time period, which includes a total of 2,262,163 petitions carried out from a total source of 3,153 pages. Petitions were accomplished from 137,314 different IP addresses for a total of 540,503 user sessions. The obtained data were analyzed removing petitions from internal IPs or other accesses that were not categorized. The final data set contains 102,631 different IP addresses and 2,036,449 observed total accesses. Figure 1 is a histogram showing the mean number of accesses for each category.

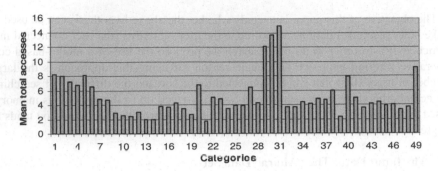

Fig. 1. Mean total access per categories

4 Evaluation

In order to evaluate the application of the above techniques to the problem of news recommendation and to determine the usefulness for the problem at hand, we have selected a data set from the electronic edition of the Daily News "Ahora" from Holguín, Cuba. We are going to discuss about the experimental setting (experimentation aims, evaluation data sets and used performance measures):

- Experimentation aim: In order to test the performance of the models we propose to measure their capability of finding those IPs that might be interested in a given category. Particularly, given a category, our objective is to rank the IPs in decreasing order of their interest in the category. We consider this problem relevant because it is quite common in many e-commerce applications.
- Test and Training sets: The "Ahora" data set is divided into test and training sets. In order to form these data sets, for each IP we select randomly an observed category. This category is located in the test data set (we are using a leave-one-out approach) while the rest of the categories are located in the training set. By means of this partition we might assume that the IPs have not revealed their interest in those categories in the test set. The described process is accomplished until obtaining a total of 10 test partitions and its respective training partitions. Similar protocol was used by Hofmann [20].
- Evaluation measures: In order to evaluate the performance of the model we will use two different measures: The first one, the Spearman's rank correlation coefficient, with the idea of comparing the obtained rankings and the second one, the Kullback-Leibler divergence, to obtain the similarity degree among the obtained likelihoods. Each ranking (likelihood) obtained for the proposed models will be compared with the *real ranking (likelihood)* that is obtained by considering those IPs that rated the target category in the test set, ordered using the number of accesses (normalized number of accesses) to the site. Particularly, a test ranking is obtained (RK_T) for each category in the test set. Thus, RK_T = IP_1, IP_2, ..., IP_r, being the IPs that have observed this category ordered by the frequency of the number of accesses, this is $f(IP1) <= f(IP2) <= ... <= f(IPk)$. The likelihood of all the IPs, Pr_Test(IP), is also calculated as the ratio.

$$Pr\_Test(IP\_i) = \frac{f(IP\_i)}{\sum_j f(IP\_j)} \tag{2}$$

In this paper we will consider three different models, the ones that will permit us validating against the test data: In the first one, that will be called Baseline (BL), we do not use any collaborative (group) information when predicting. Particularly, we will assume that the interest of an IP in a given category is proportional to the mean number of accesses from this IP to the site. The idea is that those IPs accessing more frequently have more interest in reading an unobserved category. The other two models are the ones discussed in this paper, i.e. K-Means and ASPECT MODEL, using the information of the group (class) in order to perform their prediction:

- ASPECT MODEL (AM): For each category C, the ranking (RK_AM) is obtained by ordering the IPs using Pr_AM (Ip_i | C) (see equation 1).
- K-Means (KM): Given an IP, equation 3 shows how to compute the expected number of accesses to an unobserved category C, N_Acc (IP). This value is computed in a similar way to the rating prediction done in [7], where n is the number of IPs in the cluster, $\omega_{IP,u}$ represents the similarity between IPs and $\overline{n\_acc(IP)}$ represents the mean number of accesses for the IP. Once the expected number of accesses is known, we can compute the likelihoods using equation 4.

$$N\_Acc(IP) = \overline{n\_acc(IP)} + \frac{\sum_{u=1}^{n} \left(n\_acc_{u,C} - \overline{n\_acc(u)} \right) * \omega_{IP,u}}{n} \tag{3}$$

$$Pr\_KM(IP) = \frac{N\_Acc(IP)}{\sum_{IP\_j \in C} N\_Acc(IP\_j)} \tag{4}$$

Table 2 shows the performance of each algorithm in the "Ahora" data set, for Spearman's rho and the Kullback-Leibler divergence. In Spearman's rho the positive correlation signifies that the ranks of both the variables are increasing. On the other hand, the negative correlation signifies that as the rank of one variable is increased, the rank of the other variable is decreased. The Kullback-Leibler divergence always obtains a positive value, being void if analyzed distributions are equal; values closer to zero are considered better. The evaluation measures are complementary. The Spearman's rho considers the absolute position of the elements, while the Kullback-Leibler divergence considers the values of the elements in the ranking.

We have run the experiment using 2, 3, 5 and 10 clusters. In the Baseline model, results are equal independent of the number of clusters. The values obtained in each experiment have been averaged, showing the mean value over the ten test data sets. As shown in Table 2, for K-Means, the Kullback-Leibler divergence is less than that of the ASPECT MODEL. A detailed analysis of all the obtained values permits observing the behaviour by categories. In the case of K-Means it is very inconsistent, it behaves very well in the categories that are not frequently accessed but not so well for those that are. In the ASPECT MODEL a good correspondence exists amongst the evaluation measures for all the categories, which is not so in the case of K-Means.

From these results we can conclude that the use of collaborative information helps to predict the IP´s interest. Nevertheless, the number of clusters does not seem to be very important. In general, the ASPECT MODEL is the best performing algorithm, particularly for those common categories.

Table 2. Performance of algorithm in the **Ahora** data set. Z denotes the number of classes.

Algorithm	Spearman 's rho	Kullback-Leibler divergence
Baseline	-0.11103271	2.2269938
K-Means	*-0,096400011*	*1,286405112*
Z = 2	-0,09640187	1,30158247
Z = 3	-0,096401622	1,301584936
Z = 5	-0,09639678	1,27112606
Z = 10	-0,09639977	1,27132698
ASPECT MODEL	*0,161667426*	*1,448927652*
Z = 2	0.160349855	1.462472934
Z = 3	0.162353762	1.441541524
Z = 5	0.163573011	1.458416052
Z = 10	0.160393074	1.433280097

5 Conclusions and Future Works

This paper presents an experimental study of the employment of clustering techniques, K-Means and Aspect Model in the journalistic context. These techniques were employed in the "Ahora" data set for 2, 3, 5, and 10 classes. The idea was assumed to predict the interest of a user for a category that he had not already seen, granted that he belonged to a user group. Results indicate that in general with Aspect Model better results are obtained, and the most visited categories are the ones that permit predicting in an even better way, in addition it is highly scalable, and extremely flexible.

In future works, more experiments will be conducted with other collections and algorithms, with the objective of improving the performance, for example, considering news terms instead of news categories.

Acknowledgments. This work has been jointly supported by the Spanish Ministerio de Ciencia e Innovación, under project TIN2008-06566-C04-1. The authors would like to acknowledge and thank AUIP.

References

1. Linden, G., Smith, B., York, J.: Amazon.Com Recommendations Item-to-Item Collaborative Filtering. IEEE 7(1), 76–80 (2003)
2. Lee, H.J., Park, S.J.: MONERS: A news recommender for the mobile web. Expert Systems with Applications 32(1), 143–150 (2007)

3. Bordogna, G., Pagani, M., Pasi, G., Antoniolli, L., Invernizzi, F.: An Incremental Hierarchical Fuzzy Clustering Algorithm Supporting News Filtering. In: Proceedings of the Information Processing and Management of Uncertainty in Knowledge-based Systems IPMU 2006, Paris Les Cordeliers, France, vol. I, pp. 1040–1045 (2006)
4. Claypool, M., Gokhale, A., Miranda, T., Murnikof, P., Netes, D., Sartin, M.: Combining content-based and collaborative filters in an online newspaper. In: Proc. ACM SIGIR workshop on Recommender Systems - Implementations and evaluation (1999)
5. Pazzani, M.J., Billsus, D.: Content - Based Recommendation Systems. In: Brusilovsky, P., Kobsa, A., Nejdl, W. (eds.) Adaptive Web 2007. LNCS, vol. 4321, pp. 325–341. Springer, Heidelberg (2007)
6. Schafer, J., Frankowski, D., Herlocker, J., Sen, S.: Collaborative Filtering Recommender Systems. In: Brusilovsky, P., Kobsa, A., Nejdl, W. (eds.) Adaptive Web 2007. LNCS, vol. 4321, pp. 291–324. Springer, Heidelberg (2007)
7. Konstan, J., Miller, B., Maltz, D., Herlocker, J., Gordon, L., Riedl, J.: GroupLens: Applying Collaborative Filtering to Usenet News. Communications of the ACM 40(3), 77–87 (1997)
8. Adomavicius, G., Tuzhilin, A.: Toward the Next Generation of Recommender Systems: A Survey of the State-of-the-Art and Possible Extensions. IEEE Transactions on Knowledge and Data Engineering 17(6), 734–749 (2005)
9. Xu, R., Wunsch II, D.: Survey of Clustering Algorithms. IEEE Transactions on Neural Networks 16(3) (2005)
10. Ungar, L.H., Foster, D.P.: Clustering Methods for Collaborative Filtering. In: Workshop on Recommender Systems in 15th National Conf. on Artificial Intelligence (1998)
11. Sarwar, B.M., Karypis, G., Konstan, J., Riedl, J.: Recommender Systems for Large-scale E.Commerce: Scalable Neighborhood Formation Using Clustering. In: Computer Science in Fifth International Conference on Computer and Information Technology (2002)
12. Su, Z., Yang, Q., Zhang, H., Xu, X., Hu, Y.: Correlation-based Document Clustering using Web Logs. In: Proceedings of the 34th International Conference on System Sciences (2001)
13. Goldberg, K., Roeder, T., Gupta, D., Perkins, C.: Eigentaste: A Constant Time Collaborative Filtering Algorithm. Information Retrieval 4(2), 133–151 (2001)
14. McQueen, J.B.: Some methods for classification and analysis of multivariate observations. In: Proceeding of the Fifth Berkeley Symposium on Mathematical Statistics and Probability, pp. 281–297 (1967)
15. Vicente, E., Rivera, L., Mauricio, D.: Grasp en la resolución del problema de clustering (2005) (in Spanish)
16. Hofmann, T.: Probabilistic Latent Semantic Analysis. In: Uncertainty in Artificial Intelligence, Stockholm, pp. 289–296 (1999)
17. Hofmann, T.: Latent Semantic Models for Collaborative Filtering. ACM Transactions on Information Systems 22(1), 89–115 (2004)
18. Popescul, A., Ungar, L.H., Pennock, D.M., Lawrence, S.: Probabilistic Model for Unified Collaborative and Content Based Recommendation in Sparse-Data Environments. In: Proc. of the 7th Conference on Uncertainty in Artificial Intelligence, pp. 437–444 (2001)
19. Schein, A.I., Popescul, A., Pennock, D.M., Unger, L.H.: Methods and Metrics for Cold-Star Recommendations. In: Proceedings of the 25th annual international ACM SIGIR conference on Research and development in information retrieval, Tampere, Finland (2002)
20. Hofmann, T.: Learning What People (Don't) Want. In: Flach, P.A., De Raedt, L. (eds.) ECML 2001. LNCS (LNAI), vol. 2167, pp. 214–225. Springer, Heidelberg (2001)

Analysis and Evaluation of Techniques for the Extraction of Classes in the Ontology Learning Process

Rafael Pedraza-Jimenez, Mari Vallez, Lluís Codina, and Cristòfol Rovira

Department of Communication, Pompeu Fabra University
Campus de la Comunicació, Roc Boronat 138
08018 Barcelona, Spain
{rafael.pedraza,mari.vallez,lluis.codina,
cristofol.rovira}@upf.edu

Abstract. This paper analyzes and evaluates, in the context of Ontology learning, some techniques to identify and extract candidate terms to classes of a taxonomy. Besides, this work points out some inconsistencies that may be occurring in the preprocessing of text corpus, and proposes techniques to obtain good terms candidate to classes of a taxonomy.

Keywords: Semantic Web, Ontology engineering, Ontology learning, Text mining, Language processing.

1 Introduction

In 2001 Berners-Lee and his colleagues made known to the public at large the Semantic Web [1], a short, medium and long term project of the most important agency for the Web standardization: the World Wide Web Consortium (W3C). This proposal implied deep changes that would affect, and, in fact are already affecting, the fields of creation, edition and publication of web pages and sites.

The main goal of this project is to make understandable for machines the Web content [2]. However, three requirements would be necessary to make it possible: a) Web contents must be described: to this end different languages have been created, such as RDF [3], which allows the description of any resource on the Web with metadata. b) The different knowledge domains must be structured and formalized using ontologies [4]. c) Tools to interpret, compare, and merge data on a semantic base are needed: these tools work over ontologies, and they can be built using different languages. The most important of them is OWL [5].

Nevertheless, the formalization of Semantic Web [6], on the one hand describing their resources and on the other hand making ontologies, entails a high cost in time and money. As a result, in 2010 the Semantic Web is not yet a reality [7] and, although many of its technologies are already among us [8], the W3C has recently announced that the entire project can not be achieved in less than 10 years.

To solve the first of these problems several research groups, namely, the one that the authors of this paper belong to, DigiDoc (http://www.upf.edu/digidoc), are working in the development of editors and automatic extractors of metadata (such as

N. García-Pedrajas et al. (Eds.): IEA/AIE 2010, Part III, LNAI 6098, pp. 488–497, 2010.
© Springer-Verlag Berlin Heidelberg 2010

DigiDocMeta: http://www.metaeditor.net). Regarding the second issue, in 2001 a new discipline developed, the Ontology Engineering [9], devoted to the study and the design of applications that help to develop, maintain and use these tools semi-automatically.

In this new discipline, the process called "Ontology learning" [10] is very important, which focuses on the generation of tools to import, extract, prune, refine and evaluate the taxonomy of an ontology semi-automatically.

This work is carried out in the Ontology learning field, and focuses on the analysis and evaluation of techniques commonly used to propose terms [11] that constitute the classes of the taxonomy resulting from this process.

This paper is structured as follows: the next section explains the ontology learning process; the following section sets out the main objectives of this research; the third section describes the methodology and tools used in experimentation. Then a discussion concerning the main results of this research is presented. Finally, some conclusions are stated.

2 Ontology Learning

The Ontology learning [12] is a process carried out initially by a human expert, and consists basically of three stages. First, the expert gathers a corpus of documents from the specific domain for which we want to develop the ontology. Then he applies language processing techniques [13] to extract the candidate terms to "classes" or "categories" of the taxonomy. And finally, using classification algorithms he generates a tree or graph that represents the relationships between the most significant terms of the domain [14], and that constitute the taxonomy of the ontology (see Figure 1).

Unfortunately, the implementation of this process usually concludes with taxonomies composed by inappropriate "classes" or "categories", in many cases by their high

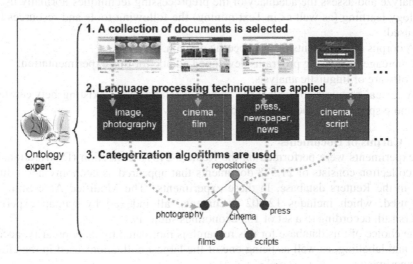

Fig. 1. Outline of the taxonomy extraction process

degree of specificity, which usually also involves the generation of an excessive number of them.

3 Objectives

As already mentioned, Ontology learning is a process, and as such, its quality is determined by the quality of the worst of its stages. Thus, its success depends, among other things, on: a) having a corpus of documents from the domain to which we want to develop the ontology; b) preprocessing properly the documents to extract the most suitable terms to be used as classes or categories of the resulting taxonomy.

This paper emphasizes the latter aspect with two aims: first, to point out some inconsistencies that may be occurring in the preprocessing of text collections; second, demand a greater attention to this stage in the text mining field, and particularly in the Ontology learning process.

With these objectives, this research analyzes and evaluates some of the preprocessing techniques most commonly used for the extraction of the classes of a taxonomy. These techniques come mainly from the Information Retrieval field, eg. the statistical measure tf-idf, *Term Frequency - Inverse Document Frequency,* whose use is widespread in Textual Data Mining.

Finally, some new preprocessing techniques are presented, which could help to envision and propose new approaches to obtaining better terms candidate to classes or categories of the taxonomies.

4 Methodology

4.1 Tools

To analyze and assess the adequacy of the preprocessing techniques normally used in Ontology learning (as well as in Text mining) the following tools and resources have been used:

a. A corpus of documents from a specific domain.
b. Language processing programs developed ad hoc for this experimentation.
c. Software of linguistic analysis.
d. A lexical resource to control the semantic relationships existing between terms (more specifically, the relationship of hyperonymy).

4.1.1 Corpus of Documents

The experiments were performed on the Reuters-21578 collection (Distribution 1.0). This collection consists of 21,578 documents that appeared as economy news during 1987 in the Reuters database. In these experiments "The Modified Apte Split" has been used, which includes 12,902 documents, all indexed by human experts of Reuters Ltd. according to a set of 135 economics subjects.

The choice of this database for this research is motivated by its popularity, accessibility and labelling, as well as being one of the largest collections used in the clustering experiments.

4.1.2 Language Processing Programs

Tools made ad hoc to facilitate the statistical processing of documents (experiment 1). Their objectives are: a) Removing text labels (or stripping). b) Standardization of texts (control of lower and uppercase letters, stop words, punctuation marks, acronyms, dates and numeric quantities). c) The application of a stemming algorithm (specifically Morphy [15], the algorithm used by WordNet).

4.1.3 Software of Linguistic Analysis

A tool that enables the linguistic processing of documents has been also used (experiments 2, 3, 4, and 5). This tool is Freeling (version 3.0), a software developed by the "Center de Tecnologies i Aplicacions of Llenguatge i la Parla" (TALP) (http://www.talp.cat/) from the Polytechnic University of Catalunya (UPC).

Some of its main functionalities are: tokenization, morphological analysis, treatment of suffixes, identification of n-grams (Multiword); recognition of dates, numbers and currencies; annotations based on WordNet sense, etc.

4.1.4 Lexical Resource

The lexical resource used is **WordNet** (WordNet 3.0, http://wordnet.princeton.edu/) [16]. It is a data base of lexical references. It groups words (nouns, verbs, adjectives and adverbs) into sets of synonyms called 'synsets', each representing a lexical concept. The senses are synsets associated with the different entries (words) of WordNet. Also, different semantic relations (meronymy, hyperonymy, hyponymy, etc.) relate the sets of synonyms.

4.2 Experiments

In this section five experiments have been defined, each one corresponding to a different preprocessing technique, and all of them defined to contrast, compare and evaluate the terms obtained as candidates for classes with them.

The characteristics of these five experiments can be seen in table 1, which specifies:

a. **Terminology Extraction Method:** i.e., the type of preprocessing that has been applied to documents to extract the most important terms.
b. **Vocabulary:** it is the number of terms extracted to represent the content of the collection.
c. **Term Weighting:** it is the statistical measure to determine the importance of terms [17] that describe the contents of each document in the collection. The assignment of weights is made using one of the following techniques:
   i. **Term frecuency**: this technique assigns to each term a value equal to its frequency of repetition within the document.
   ii. **Tf-idf**: it is the measure most commonly used in the Information retrieval and Text mining fields. This measure assigns to terms the value obtained after dividing the frequency of a term in the document between the frequency of the same term throughout the entire collection.
   iii. **Tf-Mod1**: This measure has been proposed by the authors. Here, each term obtains the value from the sum of its frequency in the document and the frequency of the same term throughout the collection.

iv.   **Tf-Mod2**: this measure has been also proposed by the authors, and supposes a slight variation from the previous one. In this case, the weight of each term is obtained by dividing the value obtained in Tf-Mod1 between the quantity of terms contained in the document.

d. **Relevance of terms in the collection**: it is the method used to propose the most representative terms of the collection as a whole. Basically, this measure helps to generate, for each experiment, a ranking that sorts the terms of the vocabulary according to their importance (or significance) for the collection. To do that, two measures have been used:

i.   **Mutual information (MI)**: is a measure widely used in the Information Theory and the Probability Theory fields, which estimates, from the weights of the terms, which are the most significant terms to represent the contents of the collection [18].

ii.   **Overall frequency of the terms (OF)**: we have applied this measure in the experiments that use the term weighting techniques proposed by the authors. Here the terms are arranged in a ranking based on their overall frequency in the collection.

Table 1. Characteristics of the preprocessing techniques

	Exp. 1	*Exp. 2*	*Exp. 3*	*Exp. 4*	*Exp. 5*
Terms Extraction Method	Statistical processing of documents: stripping, control of lower and uppercase letters, stop words, punctuation marks, acronyms, dates and numeric quantities, application of stemming algorithms	Software of linguistic analysis "Freeling"	Software of linguistic analysis "Freeling"	Software of linguistic analysis "Freeling"	Software of linguistic analysis "Freeling"
Vocabulary	10.877	3.787	3.787	3.787	3.787
Term Weighting	Term frecuency	Term frecuency	Tf-idf	Tf-Mod1	Tf-Mod2
Relevance of terms	MI	MI	MI	OF	OF

5 Results

Once the terms candidate to classes have been extracted, it is necessary to begin the analysis of results based on the following criteria:

1. Similarity among terms proposed by each experiment.
2. Coverage of keywords assigned by human expert indexers.
3. Semantics of the terms proposed.

5.1 Similarity of the Terms Proposed by the Experiments

The first analysis involves the comparison of the terms proposed by each experiment, to determine their degree of similarity. To this end, the extracted terms are sorted according to their degree of relevance and are grouped into sets, so as to obtain the 10, 50, 100, 200, 300, 400 and 500 most significant terms of each experiment.

Then, these sets are compared with each other, obtaining the percentages of similarity between the different experiments (Table 2).

When analysing the data of this table we must bear in mind that when we increase the number of terms compared, the similarities also increase, especially among the experiments 2, 3, 4 and 5, since all work on the same set of terms, but each of them sort these terms differently. Therefore, if all terms are compared, the level of coincidence of these four experiments would necessarily be 100%.

Note also that the data from those experiments that share a high similarity with the analyzed experiment have been marked in bold, and in italics those data (specially Exp. 3) which are characterized by low similarity.

Table 2. Similarity of the terms proposed by the experiments

		T10	T50	T100	T200	T300	T400	T500
Exp. 1 vs.	Exp. 2	30%	32%	34%	34,50%	42%	43%	42%
	Exp. 3	*0*	*6%*	*10%*	*15,50%*	*19,30%*	*26,25%*	*28,20%*
	Exp. 4	40%	44%	47%	51,50%	50,30%	50%	48,40%
	Exp. 5	30%	48%	47%	49%	49,60%	49,50%	47,80%
Exp. 2 vs.	Exp. 3	30%	**60%**	**61%**	65,50%	66,60%	75,50%	77%
	Exp. 4	40%	42%	48%	58,50%	65,30%	67,50%	70,20%
	Exp. 5	20%	40%	46%	57,50%	62,60%	67,25%	69,60%
Exp 3 vs.	*Exp. 4*	*0*	*8%*	*15%*	*27%*	*33,60%*	*42,75%*	*48%*
	Exp. 5	*0*	*8%*	*15%*	*26,50%*	*32,60%*	*44,25%*	*48%*
Exp. 4 vs.	**Exp. 5**	**60%**	**72%**	**84%**	**87,50%**	**87%**	**87,75%**	**89,80%**

In table 2 we can see that the Exp. 1 has a low percentage of matching up with the Exp. 3, but presents a relatively high percentage of similarity with the rest of experiments.

Exp. 2 also has a high degree of coincidence with other experiments, being quite significant its similarity with Exp. 3, especially from fifties terms (T50).

Exp. 3 shows a high coincidence with Exp. 2 (at T50 they already share the 60% of their terms) and low matching with other experiments.

Exp. 4 has a high percentage of similarity with experiments 1, 2 and 5, and particularly with the latter, with which shares 60% of its terms from tenth terms (T10). However, it is also significant its low rate of coincidence with Exp. 3.

Exp. 5 has the same behaviour than Exp. 4, with a remarkable percentage of similarity with Exp. 4.

The analysis of these results reveals that there are experiments with a high similarity, such as the Exp. 2 and Exp. 3, which from now on will be called "Group 1", and Exp. 4 and Exp. 5, and that from here on in will be called "Group 2".

5.2 Coverage of Keywords Assigned by Human Experts

The corpus of documents used in these analyses was described by human experts from Reuters Ltd., using 135 keywords from the economic field. In this work is interesting to evaluate the degree of coverage that these five experiments make of these keywords. The fewer words an experiment needs to cover keywords used by human experts, the better its coverage. The table 3 shows the percentages of coverage of these experiments.

Table 3. Coverage of the keywords assigned by human experts

		Group 1		Group 2	
Coverage	Exp. 1	Exp. 2	Exp. 3	Exp. 4	Exp. 5
10	0	0	0	0	0
50	0,74%	3,70%	3,70%	0,74%	1,48%
100	1,48%	8,14%	8,14%	2,22%	2,96%
200	8,88%	22,96%	25,92%	12,59%	14,07%
300	14,07%	26,66%	31,85%	16,29%	17,77%
400	16,29%	31,11%	34,81%	19,25%	22,96%
500	17,77%	34,07%	37,03%	24,44%	27,40%
600	18,51%	36,29%	37,03%	26,66%	28,88%
700	20%	37,03%	37,77%	30,37%	32,59%
800	21,48%	39,25%	38,51%	32,59%	34,07%
900	24,44%	41,48%	42,96%	32,59%	34,07%
1000	26,66%	42,22%	44,44%	34,07%	35,55%
2000	38,51%	52,59%	52,59%	51,11%	51,11%
3787	50,37%	55,55%	55,55%	55,55%	55,55%

Table 3 shows that none of these experiments extract all keywords proposed by human indexers, being the maximum coverage of them of 55%. This percentage is obtained only by experiments that extracted their terms using the software of linguistic analysis (Exp. 2, 3, 4, and 5). Furthermore, experiments in Group 1 achieved greater coverage of these keywords, being the Exp. 3 the one that provides the best coverage with a lower number of terms.

5.3 Semantics of the Terms Proposed

Finally, it is analyzed the semantic value of the terms proposed by each experiment. Table 4 shows the top ten terms each experiment proposed as more representative of the collection:

Table 4. The ten most relevant terms proposed by experiments

Terms	Group 1			Group 2	
	Exp. 1	Exp. 2	Exp. 3	Exp. 4	Exp. 5
1	say	nil	cattle	pct	pct
2	dollar	pct	cooperative	year	year
3	pct	rate	nil	share	share
4	year	bank	buffer	company	company
5	bank	bond	cocoa	loss	rate
6	ct	stock	beef	bank	profit
7	billion	cattle	soybean	price	loss
8	share	trade	cotton	market	sale
9	company	buffer	acre	rate	country
10	US	dollar	farm	stock	month

A human expert analysis of these data conclude that Group 1, and especially Exp. 3, is characterized by its high level of specificity. This is because Exp. 3 extracts its terminology using the technique tf.idf, which is designed to identify those terms that best discriminate a document from others. This technique, combined with the calculation of mutual information, makes its terms to be very specific.

In contrast, Group 2 recommends sets of terms that are apparently more general, and, a priori, closer to classes of a taxonomy. However, these observations are made by human experts (authors, in this case), and could be subjective. It would be interesting to be able to evaluate automatically the degree of specificity of these sets of terms.

WordNet has been used with this aim, and we have searched the number of hypernyms that this linguistic resource associates to the first 20 terms proposed by Exp. 3 and Exp. 5. As a result, 92 hypernyms has been obtained for Exp. 3, and 71 hypernyms for Exp. 5. This finding confirms that the terms proposed by Exp. 5 are more general and, in consequence, probably closer to classes or categories, that was the original goal of this experiment.

6 Conclusions

From the results observed in the analyses performed we conclude that:

a. The experiments that used an application of linguistic analysis, and specifically through the selection of nouns that appear in the texts, obtained a greater coverage of keywords proposed by human experts. Also, they extracted a lower number of terms and, in consequence, entailed a lower computational cost. Besides, terms proposed for these experiments showed semantics closer to that required by the classes of a taxonomy.

b. As a consequence of what is mentioned in the previous section, we remove from this analysis the Exp. 1. The rest of experiments can be divided into two groups according to their similarity. In the case of Group 1, this similarity may be due to the use of techniques from the Information retrieval field, which let us to extract a terminology characterized by its level of specificity. In contrast, in Group 2 the similarity is motivated by the importance given to the cumulative frequency of the terms in the collection, which the authors propose to identify terms closer to classes or categories.

c. In each one of these two groups there is an experiment that stands out for its high coverage of the keywords proposed by human indexers. In the case of Group 1 the Exp. 3 has the greatest coverage, whereas in the case of Group 2 the experiment with more coverage is Exp. 5. Furthermore, since the level of coincidence between the terms of these experiments is very low, it could be interesting to join them in a new approach, that would increase the percentage of keywords covered with a smaller number of terms.

d. Finally, the results obtained in this work show that if we want to identify terms closer to classes or categories, it is better to use preprocessing techniques such as those proposed in Exp. 4 and Exp. 5, better than approaches from the Information Retrieval field.

Acknowledgments

The development of this research is partially supported by projects CSO 2008-02627 and CSO2009-13713-C05-04 of the Spanish Ministry of Science and Innovation.

References

1. Berners-Lee, T., Hendler, J., Lassila, O.: The Semantic Web. Scientific American 284(5), 34–43 (2001)
2. Codina, L., Marcos, M.C., Pedraza-Jimenez, R. (coords.): Web semántica y sistemas de información documental. Trea (2009)
3. RDF Working Group. Resource Description Framework (RDF) (2004), http://www.w3.org/rdf
4. Pedraza-Jimenez, R., Codina, L., Rovira, C.: Web semántica y ontologías en el procesamiento de la información documental. El Profesional de la Información 16(6), 569–578 (2007)
5. OWL Working Group. OWL Web Ontology Language (2004), http://www.w3.org/2004/owl
6. Codina, L., Rovira, C.: La Web semántica. In: Tramullas, J., (eds). Tendencias en documentación digital, ch. 1. Trea (2006)
7. Pedraza-Jimenez, R., Codina, L., Rovira, C.: Semantic web adoption: online tools for web evaluation and metadata extraction. In: The 8th International FLINS Conference on Computational Intelligence in Decision and Control, Madrid (2008)
8. Feigenbaum, L., Herman, I., Hongsermeier, T., Neumann, E., Stephens, S.: The Semantic Web in Action. Scientific American 297(6), 90–97 (2007)
9. Maedche, A., Staab, S.: Ontology learning for the Semantic Web. IEEE Intelligent Systems 16(2), 72–79 (2001)
10. Maedche, A., Staab, S.: Ontology learning. In: Staab, S., Studer, R. (eds.) Handbook on Ontologies, pp. 173–189. Springer, Heidelberg (2003)
11. Buitelaar, P., Cimiando, P., Magnini, B.: Ontology Learning from Text: Methods, Evaluation and Applications. Frontiers in Artificial Intelligence and Applications Series, vol. 123. IOS Press, Amsterdam (2005)

12. Gómez-Pérez, A., Manzano-Macho, D.: An overview of methods and tools for ontology learning from texts. The Knowledge Engineering Review 9(3), 187–212 (2005)
13. Vallez, M., Pedraza-Jimenez, R.: Natural Language Processing in Textual Information Retrieval and Related Topics. "Hipertext.net", 5 (2007), http://www.hipertext.net/english/pag1025.htm
14. Hotho, A., Staab, S., Stumme, G.: Explaining text clustering results using semantic structures. In: Lavrač, N., Gamberger, D., Todorovski, L., Blockeel, H. (eds.) PKDD 2003. LNCS (LNAI), vol. 2838, pp. 217–228. Springer, Heidelberg (2003)
15. Beckwith, R., Miller, G.A., Tengi, R.: Design and Implementation of the WordNet Lexical Database and Searching Software. Description of WordNet. Technical report (1993)
16. Miller, G.: WordNet: A lexical database for english. Communications of the ACM 38(11) (1995)
17. Chisholm, E., Kolda, T.: New term weighting formulas for the vector space method in information retrieval. Technical report, Oak Ridge National Laboratory (1999)
18. Church, K.W., Hanks, P.: Word association norms, mutual information, and lexicography. Computational Linguistics 16(1), 22–29 (1990)

Air Traffic Control: A Local Approach to the Trajectory Segmentation Issue

José Luis Guerrero, Jesús García, and José Manuel Molina

Group of Applied Artificial Intelligence (GIAA), Computer Science Department
Carlos III University of Madrid, Colmenarejo - Spain
{joseluis.guerrero,jesus.garcia,josemanuel.molina}@uc3m.es

Abstract. This paper presents a new approach for trajectory segmentation in the area of Air Traffic Control, as a basic tool for offline validation with recorded opportunity traffic data. Our approach uses local information to classify each measurement individually, constructing the final segments over these classified samples as the final solution of the process. This local classification is based on a domain transformation using motion models to identify the deviations at a local scale, as an alternative to other global approaches based on combinatorial analysis over the trajectory segmentation domain.

Keywords: Air Traffic Control, segmentation, movement model, model fitting.

1 Introduction

Air Traffic Control (ATC) is a critical area related with safety, requiring strict validation in real conditions [3]. The basic considered data are sensor plots having the following components: stereographic projections of their x and y components, covariance matrix and detection time. The coordinates may be affected by errors, containing biases and noise. These sensor plots are then divided into segments sharing the same mode of flight or MOF (this division is known as the segmentation process, not to be mistaken for the one in contexts like [8]). The difficulty of that process is to differentiate accurately the different segments, especially at their edges (where it is difficult to determine whether position variation is caused by the measuring errors or by a different MOF). To improve that accuracy, as we are handling recorded data, we may use both past and future measures for our estimations.

Even though we have presented it for the ATC domain, this problem is presented in a wide range of domains such as tracking and segmentation of an object's trajectory in video data [2] (relating it to dimensionality issue), or the pattern recognition domain [9], (presenting segmentation as an optimization problem which trades off model fitting error versus the cost of introducing new segments, and introducing a solution based on dynamic programming).

In our current domain, some of the ideas we will be proposing in our segmentation algorithm are already found in available works, but in different contexts and applications. Machine learning techniques are applied in [5], but with very different attributes for our trajectory's measurements (in the reference they are based on IMM filtering [10]). Also the idea of needing several basic MM's (or movement models, a

N. García-Pedrajas et al. (Eds.): IEA/AIE 2010, Part III, LNAI 6098, pp. 498–507, 2010.
© Springer-Verlag Berlin Heidelberg 2010

simplification of the MOF's) is commonly covered ([5], [12], [6]), but their use differs to the one included in our proposal (for example, as individual models on an IMM filter or in the reconstruction process). It is interesting, as well, to consider that this segmentation problem is usually presented as a first step in the larger issue of trajectory reconstruction [12], [6].

In this study we will discuss an approach to the segmentation of trajectories where the three possible MM's are uniform, turn and accelerated movements [7]. With the presented input attributes, we will look for an algorithm that will sequentially use a different model to classify the measures belonging to each individual MM. This paper will be centered in the uniform MM.

In most cases available in the current literature on this topic, this segmentation problem and its solution are exposed as a global optimization issue [9]. Even so, all through this paper a local approach will be used. This implies that each of the trajectory's measurements will be individually classified according to the local information around it, and segments built with the classified isolated measurements will be the last step of our solution.

The formalization for our problem will be explained in the second section of this paper. The third section will present our general approach to the solution, while the fourth will analyze some initial issues of that proposal. The fifth section will present the validation experiments for the solution presented, along with some general results using that solution. Finally we will present the conclusions obtained from the solution's design and the overall results.

2 Problem Definition

2.1 General Problem Definition

As we presented in the introduction section, each analyzed trajectory (T^i) is composed by a collection of sensor reports (or measurements), which are defined by the following vector:

$$\vec{x}_j^i = \left(x_j^i, y_j^i, t_j^i, R_j^i \right), j \in \{1, \dots, N^i\} \tag{1}$$

where the j sub-index indicates the measurement number, the i super-index indicates the trajectory number, x_j^i, y_j^i are the stereographic projections, t_j^i is the detection time, R_j^i is the covariance matrix and N^i is the last measurement of the analyzed trajectory. From this problem definition our objective is to divide our trajectory into a series of segments (B_k^i), according to our estimated MOF. This is performed as an off-line process (meaning that we may use past and future information from our trajectory). The segmentation problem is formalized in (2)

$$T^i = \cup B_k^i \qquad B_k^i = \{x_j^i\} \qquad j \in [k_{min}, k_{max}] \tag{2}$$

where k is the segment number and k_{min}, k_{max} the given measurement boundaries for that segment. In the general definition of this problem these segments are obtained by the comparison with a test model of some windows of measurements coming from our trajectory, in order to obtain a fitness value, deciding finally the segmentation operation as a function of that fitness value [5], [9].

On the one hand, the segments obtained can be seen as the problem's basic division unit (using a global approach [9]), being division the basic operation of the algorithm, or we may consider classifying each of the measurements from the trajectory alone (along with their local information) and obtaining the segments as a synthesized final solution, built upon the classification of the measurements (basically, by joining those adjacent measurements sharing the same MM into a common segment, being this the approach chosen in this paper).

2.2 Local Approach Problem Definition

We have presented our problem as an offline processing, meaning that we may use information both from our past and our future. Introducing this fact into our local representation, we will restrict that information to a certain local segment around the measurement which we would like to classify. These intervals are centered on that measurement, but the boundaries for them can be expressed either in time (4) or in number of measurements (3).

$$S_j^i = \{\vec{x}_k^i\}, k\epsilon\{j - p, ..., j + p\} \quad p\epsilon[j - 1, N - j] \tag{3}$$

$$S_j^i = \{\vec{x}_k^i\}, \quad t_k^i\epsilon\{t_j^i - m, t_j^i + m\} \quad m\epsilon[t_j^i - t_0^i, t_N^i - t_j^i] \tag{4}$$

Once we have chosen a window around our current measurement, we will have to apply a function to that segment in order to obtain its classification. This general classification function $F(\vec{x}_j^i)$, using measurement boundaries, may be represented with the following formulation:

$$F(\vec{x}_j^i) = F(\vec{x}_j^i|T^i) \Rightarrow F(\vec{x}_j^i|S_j^i) = F_p(\vec{x}_{j-p}^i, ..., \vec{x}_j^i, ..., \vec{x}_{j+p}^i) \tag{5}$$

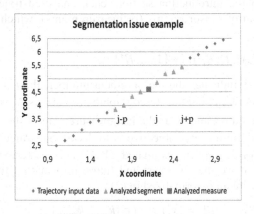

Fig. 1. Problem example

From this formulation of the problem we can already see some of the choices available: how to choose the segments (according to (3) or (4)), which classification function to apply in (5) and how to do the final segment synthesis.

3 Solution Proposal

As presented in the introduction section, we will consider three basic MM's and classify our measurements individually according to them [7]. If a measurement is classified as unknown, it will be included in the input data for the next model's analysis. This general algorithm introduces a design criterion based on the concepts of true positives rate (TPR, determining how many measurements belonging to our model are correctly classified) and false positives rate (FPR, determining how many unknown measurements we incorrectly classify), respectively equivalent to the type I and type II errors explained in [1]. The design criterion will be to keep a FPR as low as possible, understanding that those measurements, already assigned to a wrong model, will not be analyzed by the following ones. The proposed order for this analysis is the same in which we have introduced our MM's, and the choice is based on how accurately we can represent each of them.

In the local approach problem definition section, the segmentation problem was divided into two different sub-problems: the definition of the $F_p(\vec{x_j^i})$ function (to perform measurement classification) and a final segment synthesis over that classification.

We will divide our classification function $F(\vec{x_j^i})$ in a domain transformation $Dt(\vec{x_j^i})$ (domain specific, which may be seen as a data preprocessing [4]) and a final classification $Cl(Dt(\vec{x_j^i}))$ (based on general classification techniques). The domain transformation, $Dt(\vec{x_j^i})$ will convert our input data into a transformed domain (based on model fitting value) where a classification threshold will be chosen to determine whether our measurement belongs to the analyzed model or not. The output of that first phase will be several possible pre-classifications (according to parameters such as segment resolution, which will be explained in the first phase section) for each measurement of the trajectory $(\vec{x_j^i})$. For this first phase we will need to perform an analysis over the different parameters involved and a design of their value for the final algorithm proposition. This paper will be centered on these parameters' analysis.

The introduced final classification, $Cl(Dt(\vec{x_j^i}))$, will use the output data from the first phase to obtain a final classification for each measurement. After that classification has been performed, the isolated measurements will be joined into different segments, according to that classification (segment synthesis).

The formalization of these phases and the subsequent changes performed to the data is presented in the following vectors, representing the output data for our three processes:

Input data: $T^i = \{\vec{x_j^i}\}$, $j \epsilon \{1..N^i\}$ $\vec{x_j^i} = (x_j^i, y_j^i, t_j^i, R_j^i)$.

Domain transformation: $Dt(\vec{x_j^i}) \Rightarrow F(\vec{x_j^i}|T^i) \Rightarrow F(\vec{x_j^i}|S_j^i) = \{Pc_k^j\}$, $k \epsilon \{1..M\}$

Pc_k^j = pre-classification k for measurement j.

Classification process: $Cl(Dt(\vec{x_j^i}))) = Cl(\{Pc_k^j\}) = C_j$

C_j = automatic classification result for measurement j.

Final output: $T^i = \cup B_k^i$ $B_k^i = \{x_j^i\} j \epsilon [k_{min}, k_{max}]$

B_k^i = Final segments obtained by the union process.

4 First Phase: Domain Transformation

The first phase of our algorithm covers the process where we must synthesize an attribute from our input data to represent each of the trajectory's measurements in a transformed domain and choose the appropriate thresholds in that domain to effectively differentiate those which belong to our model from those which do not do so. This process has the following representative parameters: transformation function, segment management, extension and resolution, and threshold choosing technique.

The transformation function decision is the most crucial one involving this first phase of our algorithm. In [7] the discussion of whether introducing noise information in the domain transformation function allows us to improve our results was presented. The results proved that, as expected, that noise information improves the overall results. The transformed value presented was a normalized BLUE residue (6).

$$res = \frac{1}{(kmax-kmin+1)} \sum_{k=kmin}^{k=kmax} (x(k) - x_{int}(k) \ y(k) - y_{int}(k)) \ R_k^{-1} \begin{pmatrix} x(k)-x_{int}(k) \\ y(k)-y_{int}(k) \end{pmatrix} \quad (6)$$

where $x(k)$, $y(k)$ are the sensor measurements values, R_k is the covariance matrix (associated to the sensor) and $x_{int}(k)$, $y_{int}(k)$ are interpolated values using BLUE equations.

The rest of the parameters were briefly covered in [7] as well, even though we will review them here. The segment management determines whether we analyze the measurements alone or classify their surrounding segment according to the center measurement value. The segment extension is defines how we choose the units and boundaries for our segments (basically number of measurements or time interval constraints). Segment resolution refers to the choice of the length of those segments, and how it affects our results. The threshold choosing technique involves how we determine if a measurement belongs to our model or not. This parameter, not covered in previous works, will be covered in the next section.

4.1 Threshold Choosing Technique

The threshold choice involves determining the boundary above which transformed measurements will be considered as unknown. According to our design criterion, we would like to obtain a TPR as high as possible keeping our FPR ideally at a zero value. Graphically over figure 2, that implies getting the red line as low as possible, leaving only the central section over it (where the maneuver takes place, making its residue value high enough to get over our threshold).

The presented residue value in (6) follows a Chi-squared probability distribution function (pdf) normalized by its degrees of freedom, n. "n" is given by twice the number of 2D measurements contained in the interval minus the dimension of P (P=4 in uniform segment). For a valid segment residual, "res" behaves with distribution $\frac{1}{(kmax-kmin+1)} \chi^2_{2(kmax-kmin+1)-P}$, which has the following mean and variance:

$$\mu = 2 - \frac{P}{(kmax-kmin+1)} \qquad \sigma^2 = \frac{4}{(kmax-kmin+1)} - \frac{2P}{(kmax-kmin+1)^2} \quad (7)$$

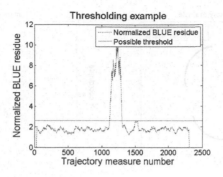

Fig. 2. Threshold choosing example

The residue distribution allows us to establish our criterion based on the TPR value, but not the FPR (we have a distribution over the uniform measurements, not the unknown ones), which is the one constrained by the design criterion. We may use the Chevychev's inequality [11] to determine a threshold which should leave the 99% of the measurements belonging to our model above it (TPR>=0.99), with $\mu + 3\sigma$ value. From the values exposed in (7) we get the following threshold value:

$$\text{thres} = 2 - \frac{4}{N} + 3\sqrt{\frac{4}{N} - \frac{8}{N^2}} \quad N = (kmax - kmin + 1) \tag{8}$$

This threshold depends on the resolution of the segment (N), which also influences the residue value in (6). It is interesting to notice that the highest threshold value is reached with the lowest resolution. This is a logical result, since to be able to keep our TPR (having fixed it with the inequality at 99%) with short segments, we need to have a high threshold, in order to counteract the noise effects (while longer segments are more resistant to that noise and thus the threshold value may be lower).

We would like to determine how precisely our χ^2 distribution represents our normalized residue in non-uniform trajectories with estimated covariance matrix. In the following figures we compare the optimal result of the threshold choice (dotted lines), manually chosen, to the results obtained with equation (8). Figure 3 shows the used trajectories for this comparison, whereas figure 4 shows the actual comparison for the proposed trajectories between the optimal TPR and the one obtained with (8) for increasing threshold values.

In the two trajectories in figure 4 we may appreciate two distortion effects introduced by our approximation. The turn trajectory shows an underestimation of our TPR due to the inexactitude in the covariance matrix R_k. This inexactitude assumes a higher noise than the one which is present in the trajectory, and thus will make us choose a higher threshold than necessary in order to obtain the desired TPR margin.

In the racetrack trajectory we perceive the same underestimation at the lower values of the threshold, but then our approximation crosses the optimal results and reaches a value over it. This is caused by the second distortion effect, the maneuver's edge measurements. The measurements close to a maneuver beginning or end tend to have a higher residue value than the theoretical one for a uniform trajectory (due to their proximity to the non-uniform segments), making us increase the threshold value

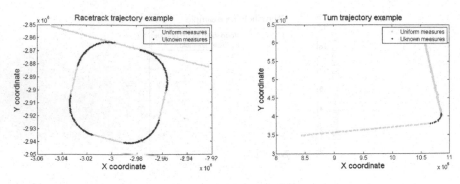

Fig. 3. Considered trajectories

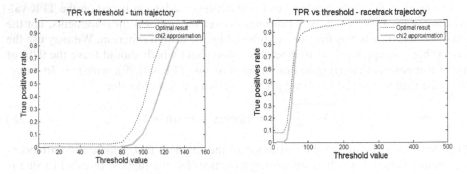

Fig. 4. χ^2 approximation comparison

to classify them correctly (which causes the optimal result to show a lower TPR in the figure). These two effects show that we may need a heuristic tuning in our χ^2 distribution in order to adapt it to these distortion effects.

5   Experimental Algorithm Design and Validation

The first step for the validation of the proposal is the generation of a set of test trajectories as representative as possible. We will include specific trajectories for each particular MM and also racetrack ones, which represent typical situations during landing procedures. To carry out the validation process we will add an additional component C_j^i to our measurement's data, which contains the real classification value of the measurement (one of our analyzed MM's), to obtain the results of the TPR and FPR indicators. This validation must be based on two different processes: the experiments performed in order to determine the design of the algorithm and those used to validate that design's results, covered in the next two sections.

5.1 Algorithm Design Parameters

This section will present the validation experiments needed to determine the design of the algorithm in the first phase section. Each of these alternatives must be compared and a decision over its value taken. One of the main difficulties arising in that process is that most of those parameters are related, so that global elections need to be made.

According to previous sections, we will use a BLUE reside, with the number of measurements as our segment extension and a χ^2 approximation based threshold choice. Resolution values allow us to obtain different effects according to their values, so a multi-resolution approach is chosen. Figure 5 shows the results for a sample turn trajectory of this pre-classifications, appreciating that high resolutions allow us to have better results (91 measurements) up to a certain limit, above which our maneuvers' boundaries start to increase, obtaining worse TPR results (121 measurements)

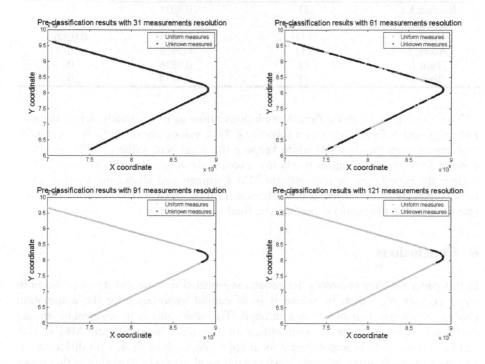

Fig. 5. Pre-classification results with different resolutions

5.2 Initial Validation Overview

Validation over our first phase pre-classification is a rather difficult process, as the complete solution algorithm must be validated as a whole. Even so, each of the different steps needs individual performance assessment in order to be able to design it correctly, so "ad hoc" validation methods are required. This is particularly true for this first phase, where the algorithm is required to find the input data for a second phase in order to be able, after that second phase, to classify each measurement correctly.

To make this achievement possible, we will choose a representative set of trajectories (two examples of each of the non-uniform possibilities presented) and obtain their TPR and FPR results over a set of different resolution values: 11, 31, 51, 71, 91 and 111. Due to space requirements we will only show the best result for each trajectory and its associated resolution. The idea behind this validation is to test the representativeness of our results for different resolutions, being able to measure whether, by joining these results, we will be able to obtain an accurate final classification. Table 1 shows these results.

Table 1. Classification results over simulated data

Trajectory	Resolution chosen	Results	
		TPR	FPR
Racetrack 1	31	0,9031	0
Racetrack 1	51	0,7591	0
Accel. 1	111	0,9935	0,0206
Accel. 2	111	0,9928	0
Turn 1	11	0,9876	0
Turn 2	91	0,9874	0

These results show that different resolutions allow us to accurately define the uniform segments of our trajectories (obtaining TPR values above 90 % in 5 out of 6 trajectories from the data set) while keeping the ideal zero value of FPR in almost every case (even in the trajectory where it exceeds the zero value, it is very low). This defines the boundaries for non-uniform MM segments and allows the application to those segments of the different possible non-uniform models (less accurate than the one presented in this work) to perform the final reconstruction

6 Conclusions

In this paper we have presented the general segmentation issue and its formulation in our particular ATC domain, where it is of capital importance for the automation process which the domain is going through. The basic idea is to segmentate an aircraft's trajectory, by means of a simplification into three basic different MM's. This can be performed from a global or a local approach, each of them with different advantages and difficulties. We have performed a local approach, covering in this paper its main issues: the domain transformation (along with the parameters determining how to choose the local information to classify each measurement), the classification techniques required and the final classification refinement needed (some of these only introduced, due to space restrictions). We have shown as well validation experiments over some critical parameters and a final overview over the quality of the general classification results, where we have obtained encouraging TPR and FPR values. Future work includes the complete description of the algorithm, introducing non-uniform models, along with its application to real data, in order to test its complete performance in real environments.

Acknowledgements

This work was supported in part by Projects CICYT TIN2008-06742-C02-02/TSI, CICYT TEC2008-06732-C02-02/TEC, CAM CONTEXTS (S2009/TIC-1485) and DPS2008-07029-C02-02.

References

1. Allchin, D.: "ErrorTypes". Perspectives on Science 9(1), 38–58 (2001)
2. Bashir, F.I., Khokhar, A.A., Schonfeld, D.: Segmented trajectory based indexing and retrieval of video data. In: Proceedings for the International Conference on Image Processing, ICIP (2003)
3. Kennedy, D., Gardner, A.B.: Tools for analysing the performance of ATC surveillance radars. IEE Colloquium (1998)
4. Famili, A., Shen, W.-M., Weber, R., Simoudis, E.: Data Preprocessing and Intelligent Data Analysis. Intelligent Data Analysis 1(1), 3–23 (1997)
5. Garcia, J., Perez, O., Molina, J.M., de Miguel, G.: Trajectory classification based on machine-learning techniques over tracking data. In: 9th International Conference on Information Fusion, Florence, Italy (2006)
6. Garcia, J., Molina, J.M., de Miguel, G., Besada, A.: Model-Based Trajectory Reconstruction using IMM Smoothing and Motion Pattern Identification. In: 10th International Conference on Information Fusion, Quebec, Canada (July 2007)
7. Guerrero, J.L., Garcia, J.: Domain Transformation for Uniform Motion Identification in Air Traffic Trajectories. In: International Symposium on Distributed Computing and Artificial Intelligence 2008 (DCAI). Springer, Heidelberg (2008)
8. Keogh, E., Chu, S., Hart, D., Pazzani, M.: Segmenting Time Series: A Survey and Novel Approach. In: Data Mining in Time Series Data Bases. Series in Machine Perception Artificial Intelligence, vol. 57, pp. 1–22
9. Mann, R., Jepson, A.D., El-Maraghi, T.: Trajectory segmentation using dynamic programming. In: Proceedings for the 16th International Conference on Pattern Recognition (2002)
10. Mazor, E., Averbuch, A., Bar-Shalom, Y., Dayan, J.: Interacting multiple model methods in target tracking: a survey. IEEE transactions in Aerospace and Electronic Systems (1998)
11. Meyer, P.: Introductory Probability and Statistical Applications, 2nd edn. Addison Wesley, Reading (1970)
12. Pérez, O., García, J., Molina, J.M.: Neuro-fuzzy Learning Applied to Improve the Trajectory Reconstruction Problem. In: International Conference on Computational Intelligence for Modelling, Control and Automation CIMCA 2006, Sydney, Australia (2006)

People Following Behaviour in an Industrial Enviroment Using Laser and Stereo Camera

J.M. Martínez-Otzeta, A. Ibarguren, A. Ansuategi, C. Tubío, and J. Aristondo

Fundación Tekniker, Av. Otaola 20, 20600 Eibar, Gipuzkoa, Spain
{jmmartinez,aibarguren,aansuategui,ctubio,jaristondo}@tekniker.es

Abstract. Mobile robots have a large application potential in industrial shop floors, improving the human action in this kind of environments. The productivity can be greatly increased while reducing cost, particularly for surface operations such as material transport, survey and sampling. In this paper a system able to follow a worker in an industrial environment based on information provided by a laser scan and a stereo camera is presented. In order to accomplish this goal, a probabilistic approach for human leg detection based on data provided by a laser scan is used, enhanced with an histogram based depth detector. The proposed approach also integrates tracking techniques as Kalman Filters to endow the system with an error recovering tool to be used in a real environment.

Keywords: Mobile robotics, sensor fusion, human-robot interaction.

1 Introduction

Mobile robots have a large application potential in industrial shop floors, improving the human action in this kind of environments. One of the main challenges in using mobile robots in industrial tasks is to find a good trade-off between completely remotely operated devices and full autonomy. The complexity of operations makes it difficult, if not impossible, to use fully autonomous devices. On the other hand, the amount of data and the drawbacks of limited communication possibilities make it undesirable if not unfeasible to put the full control of the robot into the hands of a human operator.

Human-robot collaboration has significant potential to improve industrial tasks, specifically by enabling humans and robots to work together in the field. The productivity can be greatly increased while reducing cost, particularly for surface operations such as material transport, survey, sampling, and in-situ site characterization. To achieve these goals, a person following behaviour is highly useful in most contexts.

There are several approaches in the literature that combine vision with other sensors (laser, sonar) to provide a reliable people following behaviour. Our approach is to build a backup system able to follow a person in an industrial environment based on information provided by a laser scan and a stereo camera. In order to accomplish the people following behaviour, this paper presents a probabilistic approach for human leg detection based on data provided by a laser

N. García-Pedrajas et al. (Eds.): IEA/AIE 2010, Part III, LNAI 6098, pp. 508–517, 2010.

scan and enhanced with an histogram based depth detector. Besides the theoretical aspects of the leg detection, the proposed approach integrates tracking techniques as Kalman Filters [1], to endow the system with an error recovering tool to be used in a real environment.

The paper is organized as follows. In Section 2 the related work is presented. Section 3 is devoted to the presented approach, while in Section 4 experimental setup and results are shown. Finally Section 5 presents the conclusions obtained and the future work to be done.

2   Related Work

People detection and tracking is a popular topic in the computer science community. Several approaches have been tested, most of them based in some kind of vision sensors. For example, color vision has been used [2], as well stereo [3] or infrarred cameras [4].

In [5] a person is detected and tracked in two different ways depending on the sensor: the vision sensor detects the face while a laser scan detects the legs. A fusion is made afterwards between these two modules. Though some papers deal only with leg detection with laser [6], without relying in other sensors, they are comparatively rare in the literature. More complex approaches have been also tested, using omnidireccional cameras [7], person models using color, edge and size information [8] or a particle filter built on cues such as color, depth, gradient and shape [9].

This paper describes a system for detecting legs and follow a person using laser readings and stereo camera images. To increase the reliability of the detector, a Kalman filter is implemented, as well as a procedure to recover when being stuck by a false detection.

3   Propossed Approach

In this paper an improvement over the work described in [10] is introduced. In that article, a laser-based person-following system was described. As the laser data do not provide enough information to reliably follow a person, a Kalman filter and a recovery procedure in case of getting stuck was introduced.

The approach presented here is based in the laser data too, but stereo camera readings are used to add reliability to the system. Several approaches combining laser with image data have been tested, but in the majority of them the image analysis procedure is computationally expensive, due to the use of face detection algorithms or similar. In our system, the stereo camera provides disparity calculations at a rate of 30 frames/second, and the on-robot computation involved is simple enough to not to become a bottleneck in the system.

The hardware used in this research has consisted of a robuLAB80 mobile robot, with dimensions of 772x590x475 mm and a weight of 125kg. This mobile robot, compatible with Microsoft Robotics Studio, is equipped with a Pentium 1.4 GHz, 512 MB RAM and multiple analog and digital inputs and outputs.

Besides the described hardware, the robuLAB80 has also been equiped with different sensors and actuators such as bumpers, Hokuyo laser scan and STOC stereo camera, security light and an ultrasound belt. The Hokuyo URG-04LX laser scan provides a measuring area of 240 angular degrees, from 60 to 4095 mm in depth and 625 readings per scan. The Videre STOC stereo camera provides mono (2D) and stereo (3D) monochrome images with a maximum resolution of 640H x 480V pixels and a frame rate up to 30Hz in stereo mode.

The system architecture comprises several modules: a leg detection unit, a stereo camera unit, a Kalman filter unit and a control unit that receives results from the other three modules and combines them to produce the final result. An scheme of the architecture is presented in Fig. 1.

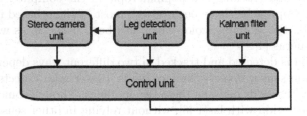

Fig. 1. System architecture

In the leg detection unit, a fuzzy leg pattern is defined from a sequence of maximums and minimums in the laser readings. The stereo camera unit analyzes the area above the detected pattern, calculates a distance, and this information is integrated with the laser readings to return a leg detection probability. A more detailed explanation is given in the following sections. To add reliability to the leg detection and tracking system, a Kalman filter has been implemented.

3.1 Leg Detection Unit

The proposed system has implemented a leg model as a sequence of $max \rightarrow min \rightarrow max \rightarrow min \rightarrow max$, given the laser readings, as in [5]. The main difference lies in the computation over those values. While in their work they implement rules of *all or nothing*, we have chosen a fuzzy approach, where the rules represent the likelihood of a characteristic of a leg. Therefore, to estimate the probability of a set of laser readings to be a leg, we have implemented several measures over the readings at P_a, P_b, P_c and P_d and P_e, as seen in Fig. 2.

Measures over the laser readings:

1. Likelihood of the distance between P_b and P_d supposed it is part of a leg (distance between feet)
2. Likelihood of the distance between P_b and P_c, and between P_c and P_d (distance between legs and the background between them)

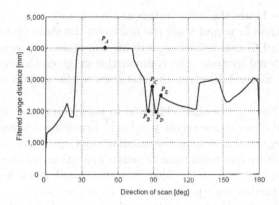

Fig. 2. Leg pattern as described in (Bellotto et al.)

3. Likelihood of the distance between P_a and P_b (distance between right foot and previous background)
4. Likelihood of the distance between P_d and P_e (distance between left foot and posterior background)

The function Φ introduced above has been implemented for every measure in the following way:

For measure 1: there is a value that is considered *optimum*, and a *minimum* and *maximum*, both of them defining the range length. Therefore,

$$\Phi(x) = \begin{cases} 0 & \text{if } x <= minimum \\ (x - minimum)/(optimum - minimum) & \text{if } x > minimum \wedge x < optimum \\ 1 & \text{if } x = optimum \\ (maximum - x)/(maximum - optimum) & \text{if } x > optimum \wedge x < maximum \\ 0 & \text{if } x >= maximum \end{cases}$$

For measure 2, 3 and 4: there is a *threshold* value, for which the values above it are asigned a maximum probability, and a *minimum* value, with the same meaning that in the previous measure.

$$\Phi(x) = \begin{cases} 0 & \text{if } x <= minimum \\ (x - minimum)/(threshold - minimum) & \text{if } x > minimum \wedge x < threshold \\ 1 & \text{if } x >= threshold \end{cases}$$

The overall probability of a leg is computed as a combination of these four measures, each of them ranging between 0 and 1. So far only an arithmetic average has been tested, taking into account that when one of the component values is zero, the probability of the resulting combination is zero too.

3.2 Kalman Filter Unit

The next equation shows the known Kalman filter formulas:

$$\mathbf{x(k)} = \mathbf{Ax(k-1)} + \mathbf{w(k-1)}, \quad \mathbf{y(k)} = \mathbf{Cx(k)} + \mathbf{v(k)}$$

where $\mathbf{x}(\mathbf{k})$, $\mathbf{x}(\mathbf{k}-\mathbf{1})$ are the state vectors at time k and $k-1$, $\mathbf{y}(\mathbf{k})$ is the observation vector at time k, $\mathbf{w}$ and $\mathbf{v}$ are the noises on the state and the observation respectively. $\mathbf{A}$ and $\mathbf{C}$ are matrices specifying the state and measurement models for the considered system. The Kalman theory gives the equations for the optimal estimate $\hat{\mathbf{x}}(\mathbf{k}+\mathbf{1}|\mathbf{k})$ given the statistics of the system and observation noises.

In the case of the leg tracking addressed in this paper, the next state vector $\mathbf{x} = [\,\alpha \;\; \omega\,]^{\mathbf{T}}$ and observation vector $\mathbf{y} = [\,\alpha\,]^{\mathbf{T}}$ are defined where α is the angle of the detected legs and ω defines the angular velocity of the leg position. The covariance of the state and measurement noises are estimated directly from data.

During leg tracking, a Kalman filter is instantiated when legs are detected and it is used to predict leg's position in the next time step. This Kalman filter is iteratively updated with the new leg position provided by the *Control unit*. On the other hand, when the *Leg detection unit* provides no output (legs are lost) the *Control unit* feeds the Kalman filter with its own (Kalman filter's) predictions to update it, allowing further predictions.

3.3 Stereo Camera Unit

To add reliability to the leg detection process, the following procedure has been implemented:

- Laser readings are extracted and analyzed searching for possible leg patterns; a probability is assigned to each of them.
- Stereo camera readings (disparity) in the area above the leg pattern are extracted.
- Concordance between laser and camera readings is computed.
- Leg patterns probabilities are updated.

The idea behind this procedure is that there should be an area (corresponding to the upper body) at similar distance above the leg pattern (according to laser data). Even though the distance could not be exactly the same due to the shape of the body and clothes. Another source of discrepance is the noise due to the nature of depth (more precisely, disparity) calculations from the stereo images. Unlike laser readings, whose accuracy depends on the physical nature of the analysed surface, stereo calculations depend on the difference between two images taken at a slightly different position. Due to this fact, different points lying in shirts with plain colors are difficult, if not impossible, to tell apart.

One of the crucial points in the previously explained procedure is to determine how to measure the *concordance between laser and camera readings*. First of all, it is necessary to asociate an image region to a leg pattern. As it is highly unlikely the person occupies the full height of the image (the person would have to be too close to the camera), only the lower half of the image is going to be analyzed. In the same way, points too much to the left or right of the tentative leg pattern could correspond to the background and not to the person. For these reasons, only a small rectangle centered in the medium point of the leg pattern has been considered, as show in Fig. 3(a).

(a) Monochrome image.   (b) Depth image.   (c) Histogram.

Fig. 3. Monochrome and depth image showing the analyzed rectangle and its histogram

Based on the area defined in the Fig. 3(a), the same region of the depth image (Fig. 3(b)), will be used to calculate the distance. To this end an histogram of this region will be extracted, as seen in Fig. 3(c). This histogram represents the different depths presented in the image. Once it is extracted, a natural approach would be to select its mode as the depth of the image, but this measure could be easily affected by noise. To avoid those noise effects, the use of a window structure is proposed to recalculate the histogram creating a new one with a lower number of bins, overcoming this way the noise effects. The idea is that once a window of size S is chosen, histogram H composed of B bins is recalculated creating a new histogram H' with $B - S$ bins where each bin contains the sum of S consecutive values of the previous histogram. Specifically, the frequency of each of the new bins is calculated as Eq. 1 and the distance asociated to this bin is calculated as Eq. 2, where i ranges from 0 to $B - S$. The H' bins group consecutive values of the original histogram H, reducing noise effects.

$$H'(i) = \sum_{j=i}^{i+S} H(j) \qquad (1) \quad distance(H', i) = \frac{\sum_{j=i}^{i+S} j*H(j)}{\sum_{j=i}^{i+S} H(j)} \qquad (2)$$

Once this new histogram H' is calculated its mode will be selected as the distance of the chosen depth. Even though, it is necessary to find a suitable size S of the window as a low value will not overcome the problem of the noise while a high value will cause a loss of precission.

In the same way it is also necessary to perform an analysis of the discrepance between the laser readings and the stereo camera readings, as the influence of noise in laser readings is much less than in the camera. To this end an analysis was performed to measure the discrepancies between both readings, taking as ground truth the laser readings. This discrepance can come from noise, erroneous leg detection by the laser, or different depth of the lower and upper body due to clothes, body size or gesture. The goal of this analysis is to measure if the discrepance lies between reasonable limits and for which window size is minimum. The measure of discrepance is the error, taken as the difference between laser and stereo camera readings, and the standard deviation of the error.

The result of one of those experiments (all of them follow a similar pattern) is shown in Fig. 4. In the horizontal axis is shown the window size (S) and in the vertical axis the error measured in cm. We have eliminated the values farther away of three standard deviations from the meanm to prevent outliers affect the

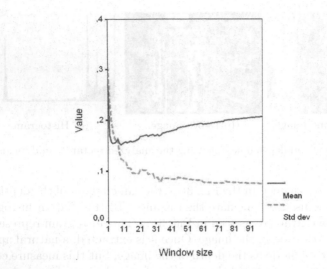

Fig. 4. Window size vs. mean and standard deviation of the stereo error (in m)

overall calculation. From the graph can be extracted that a good compromise between error mean and standard deviation is reached with a window size of around 20. In that point the error mean is still low (0.163 m) and the standard deviation has reached a fairly low value (0.095 m).

3.4   Control Unit

The output from the stereo camera unit is combined with the output of the leg detection unit, in such a way that stereo readings contribute positively or negatively to the probability of leg detection, according to how much they differ from laser readings. The combination of the data from the two sensors is made in the following fashion:

$$P(leg) = P(leg|laser) * (\lambda + f_N(abs(camera - laser))) \tag{1}$$

where the probability of detected leg is the product of the probability of a leg according to laser readings multiplied by the probability density function of the absolute value of the difference between laser readings and camera readings plus a positive constant λ. $f_N(abs(camera-laser))$ is the probability density function of a normal distribution with the mean and standard deviation calculated in the previous section. The constant λ is introduced to assure that a high value of $f_N(abs(camera - laser))$ will imply an increment of $P(leg|laser)$, and that very small values of $f_N(abs(camera - laser))$ will not make $P(leg|laser)$ almost zero.

Finally the *Control unit* combines the information provided by both the *Leg detection unit* and the *Kalman filter unit*. Initially it compares the difference between the detected leg position (α_{det}) and the Kalman filter's prediction (α_{Kalm}). If the difference is below a threshold K, the output from the *Leg detection unit* is accepted. On the other hand, if the difference is greater than the threshold K, the detected leg position is analysed. If the positions' confidence rate ($Conf_{det}$) is greater than threshold P, the detected leg position is accepted, otherwise the Kalman filter's prediction is the chosen position. A summary of the process is shown in equation (2).

$$\alpha_{returned} = \begin{cases} \alpha_{det} & if \; |\alpha_{det} - \alpha_{Kalm}| <= K \wedge Conf_{det} > P \\ \alpha_{Kalm} & otherwise \end{cases} \quad (2)$$

Apart from the previous information fusion, the *Control unit* also feeds and updates the *Kalman filter* when no leg is detected. For security reasons, if no leg is detected for a period of time (around 1-2 seconds) the *Control unit* stops updating and predicting by means of the Kalman filter and starts a new leg search process.

4   Experimental Set-Up and Results

To assess the performance of the built system, an experimental setup in a manufacturing scenario has been devised as it is shown in Fig. 5.

The manufacturing plant is a real manufacturing shop floor where machines and humans share the space in performing production activities. With regard to the exploration purposes the shop floor can be characterised as an industrial environment, with multiple machines, tools and materials in unpredictable arrangement. The experimental method comprises several runs along a path of about 30 meters with different ambient conditions (given by the daily changing activity), pace of walking and different people.

The laser readings have been restricted to the range between $-45°$ and $45°$, to avoid calculations over readings that are far away from the natural path of the robot. Denoting the definition of the Φ function (as defined in the previous section) corresponding to the measure number i as Φ_i, the following values have been taken in our experiments:

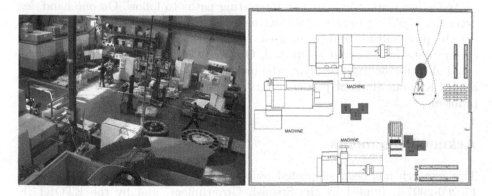

Fig. 5. Manufacturing plant and path covered in the experiments

- Φ_1: Optimum: 50 cm, Minimum: 5 cm, Maximum: 150 cm.
- Φ_2, Φ_3 and Φ_4: Threshold: 75 cm, Minimum: 5 cm.

The value of λ has been set to 0.3. With respect to the thresholds K and P defined in the *Control unit* section, a value of 5 angular degrees has been selected for K, and a confidence rate (probability of a leg) of 0.40 has been selected as value for threshold P.

Once a person (their legs) is detected, the robot moves in its direction, not approaching more than a predefined security distance. In these experiments, the distance has been of 100 cm.

Three people have taken part in the experiment, covering the path a number of five times. The system has shown to be robust, losing its track only in cases when the person walks so fast that the person disappears from its sight, or when the person walks close to glasses, which are difficult for the laser to deal with. Even in these adverse conditions, the system is able to recover itself pretty fast when the person locates in front of it again. The distance between the person and the robot, as measured by the laser readings, always lies over the minimum security distance, and even when the robot loses the person's track and the subject has to put him/herself in front of it, the robot is able to recover the track before colliding.

5   Conclusions and Future Work

In this paper a prototype of a robotic system able to show human-robot interaction capabilities in industrial environments has been presented. Specifically a leg detection architecture has been developed, including a tracking system to improve its reliability. Experiments have also been carried out to test the leg detection system, yielding good results.

A robotic mobile platform integrating this leg detection architecture has been developed, in which the robot movement will be directed by the user, through a person following behaviour. Current experiments show a good performance in a real industrial shop floor.

As further work, there are two interesting paths to follow. On one hand, leg detection could be improved adding new features to track as well as adjusting the probabilistic framework used. More sofisticated methods of laser and camera data fusion could be studied. On the other hand, the tracking system could also the modified, studying the use of other estimation algorithms as extended Kalman filters or particle filters to observe their efficiency in the posed problem.

Acknowledgements

This research has been supported by the PROFIT project ROBAUCO FIT-170200-2007-1, funded by the Spanish Government, and by the ETORTEK project TEReTRANS, funded by the Basque Government.

References

1. Kalman, R.E.: A new approach to linear filtering and prediction problems. Transactions of the ASME–Journal of Basic Engineering 82(Series D), 35–45 (1960)
2. Oren, M., Papageorgiou, C., Sinha, P., Osuna, E., Poggio, T.: Pedestrian detection using wavelet templates. In: CVPR '97, pp. 193–199 (1997)
3. Gavrila, D.M., Davis, L.S.: 3-D model-based tracking of humans in action: a multiview approach. In: CVPR '96, p. 73 (1996)
4. Dai, C., Zheng, Y., Li, X.: Pedestrian detection and tracking in infrared imagery using shape and appearance. Comput. Vis. Image Underst. 106(2-3), 288–299 (2007)
5. Bellotto, N., Hu, H.: Multisensor integration for human-robot interaction. The IEEE Journal of Intelligent Cybernetic Systems 1 (July 2005)
6. Xavier, J., Pacheco, M., Castro, D., Ruano, A., Nunes, U.: Fast line, arc/circle and leg detection from laser scan data in a Player driver. In: ICRA 2005, pp. 3930–3935 (2005)
7. Kobilarov, M., Sukhatme, G., Hyams, J., Batavia, P.: People tracking and following with mobile robot using an omnidirectional camera and a laser. In: ICRA 2006, pp. 557–562 (2006)
8. Dai, W., Cuhadar, A., Liu, P.: Robot tracking using vision and laser sensors. In: CASE 2008, pp. 169–174 (2008)
9. Kwolek, B.: Person following and mobile camera localization using particle filters. In: RoMoCo 2004, pp. 265–270 (2004)
10. Martínez-Otzeta, J.M., Ibarguren, A., Ansuategi, A., Susperregi, L.: Laser based people following behaviour in an emergency environment. In: Xie, M., Xiong, Y., Xiong, C., Liu, H., Hu, Z. (eds.) ICIRA 2009. LNCS (LNAI), vol. 5928, pp. 33–42. Springer, Heidelberg (2009)

A Type-2 Fuzzy Wavelet Neural Network for Time Series Prediction

Rahib H. Abiyev

Department of Computer Engineering, Near East University, P.O. Box 670,
Lefkosha, North Cyprus, Mersin-10, Turkey
Tel.: 0392 2236464 (383); Fax: 0392 223 66 22
rahib@neu.edu.tr

Abstract. This paper presents the development of novel type-2 wavelet neural network system for time series prediction. The structure of type-2 Fuzzy Wavelet Neural Network (FWNN) is proposed and its learning algorithm is derived. The proposed network is constructed on the base of a set of fuzzy rules that includes type-2 fuzzy sets in the antecedent part and a wavelet function in the consequent part of the rules. For generating the structure of prediction model a fuzzy clustering algorithm is implemented to generate the rules automatically and the gradient learning algorithm is used for parameter identification. Type-2 FWNN is used for modelling and prediction of exchange rate time series. Effectiveness of the proposed system is evaluated with the results obtained from the simulation of type-2 FWNN based systems and with the comparative simulation results of previous related models.

Keywords: Type-2 Fuzzy systems, Fuzzy Wavelet Neural Network, Time-series prediction.

1 Introduction

The prediction results of time-series can be applied to different areas, such as, business, engineering, economics, weather and stock market forecasting, inventory and production control, signal processing and many other fields. Exchange rates are amongst the most important economic indices in the international monetary markets and play an important role in controlling dynamics of exchange market. Exchange rates are affected by many economic, political and even psychological factors and are characterized by complexity, volatility and unpredictability. Accurate forecasting of exchange rate movements can result in substantial improvement in the firm's overall profitability and very important for the success of many business and fund managers. Numerous techniques have been developed to explore this nonlinearity and improve the accuracy of prediction of exchange rate. These are well-known Box-Jenkins method, autoregressive random variance (ARV) model, autoregressive conditional hetroscedasiticity(ARCH) and general autoregressive conditional heteroskedasticity (GARCH) models [1,2]. While these models may be good for a particular situation, they doesn't give satisfactory results for prediction of nonlinear time-series [2].

N. García-Pedrajas et al. (Eds.): IEA/AIE 2010, Part III, LNAI 6098, pp. 518–527, 2010.

Hence the idea of applying non-linear models, like softcomputing technologies, such as neural networks (NNs), fuzzy systems (FSs), genetic algorithms (GAs) has become important for time series prediction. These methods have shown clear advantages over the traditional statistical ones [2,3]. Recently neural networks [3], radial based networks [4], neuro-fuzzy networks [5] are widely used for time-series prediction.

During a day exchange rate are changed from morning to night. In this changeable traffic exchange market is usually described by four parameters: Open, High, Low, Close. These correspond to market opening price, high and low range of price volatility within a day and closing price. In this paper type-2 fuzzy logic is used in order to describe input exchange rate values of prediction system. Type-2 fuzzy variables with uncertain mean are used in order to describe opening and closing prises of exchange rate. The use of such approach allows to increase prediction accuracy for achieving the optimal solution, that will be demonstrated in simulation section.

The type-2 fuzzy sets is introduced as the extension of the type-1 fuzzy sets by Zadeh [6]. The theoretical background of type-2 fuzzy system and its design principles are given by Mendel and his co-authors in [7-10]. Type-2 fuzzy logic systems are find many diversified applications; such as for forecasting of time-series [9], classification of coded video streams [10], decision making [11], for control of speed of diesel engines [12], robot control [13], control of nonlinear dynamic systems [14,15] etc.

Traditionally, to develop a fuzzy system several approaches have been applied [6]. In this paper the integration of NN and wavelet function is considered. A wavelet neural network (WNN) uses localized basis functions in the hidden layer to achieve the desired input-output mapping. The integration of the localization properties of wavelets and the learning abilities of NN results in the advantages of WNN over NN for complex nonlinear system modeling [16-18].

A fuzzy wavelet neural network (FWNN) combines wavelet theory with fuzzy logic and neural networks. Several researchers [18-21] have used a combination of fuzzy technology and WNN for solving signal processing and control problems. In [18] the wavelet network model of a fuzzy inference system is proposed. The FWNN structure is used for approximating nonlinear functions [19], for the control of dynamic plants [20] and time-series prediction [21]. Wavelet transform has the ability to analyze non-stationary signals to discover their local details. NNs have self-learning characteristics that increases the accuracy of the model. Fuzzy logic allows to reduce the complexity of the data and to model uncertainty and imprecision. Their combination allows us to develop a system with fast learning capability that can describe nonlinear systems, characterized with uncertainties. In this paper these methodologies are combined to construct type-2 FWNN structure for time-series prediction, in particularly for prediction of exchange currency.

During design of FWNN system one of important problem is its learning and convergence. Recently a number of different approaches have been used for the design of fuzzy neural network systems. These are clustering techniques [23-28], the least-squares method (LSM) [5,24,30], gradient algorithms [5,19-21], genetic algorithms [5,21,22]. In this paper, the fuzzy clustering with the gradient algorithm is applied to design the FWNN prediction system.

The paper is organized as follows. In the following section, the structure of the type-2 FWNN proposed is presented. In section 3 parameter update rule is derived. In section 4, the simulation studies are presented for time-series prediction.

2 Structure of Type-2 Fuzzy Wavelet Neural System

The knowledge base of type-2 fuzzy systems is characterized by fuzzy IF-THEN rules, the parameters in the antecedent and/or the consequent parts of the rules include type-2 fuzzy values. In Gaussian type-2 fuzzy sets, uncertainties can be associated to the mean and the standard deviation (STD). In Figures 1.a and 1.b Gaussian type-2 fuzzy sets with uncertain STD and uncertain mean are shown. The mathematical expression for the membership function is given as

$$\tilde{\mu}(x) = \exp(-(x-c)^2 / 2\sigma^2) \qquad (1)$$

where c and σ are the centre and widths of membership function, x is the input vector with uncertain STD $\sigma \in [\sigma_1, \sigma_2]$ (Fig.1.a) and for uncertain mean $c \in [c_1, c_2]$ (Fig.1.b).

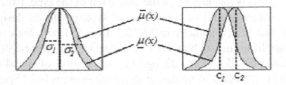

Fig. 1. Gaussian type-2 fuzzy set with uncertain STD (a) and uncertain mean (b)

In a type-2 fuzzy rule both sides, i.e. the antecedent and the consequent parts may be of type-2 or only one of the sides may be of type-2. In this paper, the design of type-2 TSK fuzzy system is considered, using a WNN structure. A type-2 FWNN integrates wavelet functions with type-2 fuzzy Takagi-Sugeno-Kang (TSK) fuzzy model. In [29], interval type-2 TSK fuzzy rules are classified into three types. This paper focuses on the second type of interval type-2 TSK rules described therein.

The consequent part of conventional TSK fuzzy systems are more often represented by either a constant or a linear function. These systems do not have localizability property, can model global features of the process. These TSK-type fuzzy networks do not provide full mapping capabilities, and, in the case of modelling of complex non-linear processes, these systems may require a high number of rules in order to achieve the desired accuracy. In this paper, the use of wavelet (rather than linear) functions are proposed to improve the computational power of the neuro-fuzzy system. The rules used thus have the following form:

$$\text{If } x_1 \text{ is } \tilde{A}_{j1} \text{ and } \dots \text{ and } x_m \text{ is } \tilde{A}_{jm} \text{ Then } y_j \text{ is } w_j \cdot \sum_{i=1}^{m} (1 - z_{ij}^2) e^{-\frac{z_{ij}^2}{2}} \qquad (2)$$

where, $z_{ij} = (x_i - b_{ij})/a_{ij}$ and a_{ij} and b_{ij} are dilation and translation parameters of the wavelet function between the i-th (i=1,..,m) input and the j-th output of (j=1,..,n), $x_1, x_2, \dots, x_m$ are the input variables, $y_1, y_2, \dots, y_n$ are the output variables, $\tilde{A}_{ji}$ is the type-2 membership function for j-th rule of the i-th input defined as a Gaussian function. The consequent parts of the rules contain Mexican Hat wavelet functions. The use of wavelets with different dilation and translation values allows us to capture different behaviors and the essential features of the nonlinear model under these fuzzy rules. The proper fuzzy model that is described by the set of IF-THEN rules can be obtained by learning the parameters of the wavelets in the conclusion parts and the parameters of the membership function of the premise parts.

The structure of the multi input-single output type-2 FWNN used in this paper is given in Fig. 2. In this structure, the input signals for the network are the external input signals X={x_1,...,x_n}. The type-2 FWNN is constructed using type-2 TSK fuzzy rules, given by (3). In the first layer of Fig. 2, the input signals are distributed. In the second layer each node corresponds to one linguistic term. This layer uses Gaussian membership functions with uncertain mean and fixed STD as in figure 1(b). Due to the antecedent uncertainties, the output of the type-2 fuzzy rules will have uncertainties. In this paper, the interval type-2 sets are used in the antecedents. Each membership function of the antecedent part is represented by an upper and a lower membership function. They are denoted as $\overline{\mu}(x)$ and $\underline{\mu}(x)$, or $\overline{A}(x)$ and $\underline{A}(x)$.

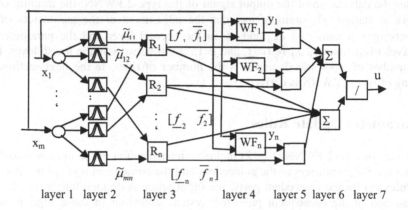

layer 1   layer 2   layer 3   layer 4   layer 5 layer 6 layer 7

Fig. 2. Structure of type-2 FWNN system

$$\mu_{\tilde{A}_k^i}(x_k) = [\underline{\mu}_{\tilde{A}_k^i}(x_k), \overline{\mu}_{\tilde{A}_k^i}(x_k)] = [\underline{\mu}^i, \overline{\mu}^i] \qquad (3)$$

In the second layer, for each input signal entering the system, the membership degrees $\underline{\mu}$ and $\overline{\mu}$ to which the input value belongs to a fuzzy set are determined.

The third layer realizes the inference engine. In this layer the t-norm prod operator is applied to calculate the membership degree of the given input signals for each rule.

$$\underline{f} = \underline{\mu}_{\tilde{A}_1}(x_1) * \underline{\mu}_{\tilde{A}_2}(x_2) * ... * \underline{\mu}_{\tilde{A}_n}(x_n); \quad \overline{f} = \overline{\mu}_{\tilde{A}_1}(x_1) * \overline{\mu}_{\tilde{A}_2}(x_2) * ... * \overline{\mu}_{\tilde{A}_n}(x_n) \quad (4)$$

where * is t-norm prod operator. The fourth layer determines the outputs of the Wavelet Functions (WFs) in the consequent part. In the fifth layer, the output signals of the third layer are multiplied by the output signals of the wavelet functions. The output of the j-th WFs is calculated as

$$y_j = w_j \Psi_j(z); \quad \Psi_j(z) = \sum_{i=1}^{m} \left| a_{ij} \right|^{-\frac{1}{2}} (1 - z_{ij}^2) e^{-\frac{z_{ij}^2}{2}} \qquad (5)$$

In this layer, the contribution of each wavelet to the output of the FWNN is determined. The sixth and the seventh layers perform the type reduction and the defuzzification operations. After determining the firing strengths of rules using (6), the defuzzified output of the type-2 FWNN system is determined. In this paper the inference engine given in [30] is used to determine the output of type-2 FWNN.

$$u = \left(q \sum_{j=1}^{N} \underline{f}_j y_j \right) \bigg/ \left(\sum_{j=1}^{N} \underline{f}_j \right) + \left((1-q) \sum_{j=1}^{N} \overline{f}_j y_j \right) \bigg/ \left(\sum_{j=1}^{N} \overline{f}_j \right) \tag{6}$$

where N is number of active rules, $\overline{f}_j$ and $\underline{f}_j$ are determined using (4), y_j is determined using (5), q is a design factor indicating the share of the lower and the upper values in the final output. The parameter q enables to adjust the lower or the upper portion depending on the level certainty of the system.

After the calculation of the output signal of the type-2 FWNN, the training of the network is started. The training includes the adjustment of the parameters of the membership functions $c1_{ij}$, $c2_{ij}$ and σ_{ij} in the second layer and the parameters of the wavelet functions w_j, a_{ij}, b_{ij} ($i=1,..,m$, $j=1,..,n$) of network in the fourth layer. Here m is number of input signals and n is the number of rules. In the next section, the learning of type-2 FWNN is derived.

3   Parameter Update Rules

The design of type-2 FWNN (Fig. 2) includes determination of the unknown parameters that are the parameters of the antecedent and the consequent parts of the fuzzy if-then rules (3). In the antecedent parts, the input space is divided into a set of fuzzy regions, and in the consequent parts the system behaviour in those regions is described. Recently, clustering [23-28], least-squares method (LSM) [5,24,30], gradient algorithms [5,19-21], genetic algorithms [5,21,22] have been used for designing fuzzy if-then rules. In this paper, the fuzzy clustering is applied to design the antecedent (premise) parts. The aim of clustering methods is to identify a certain group of data from a large data set, such that a concise representation of the behaviour of the system is produced. Each cluster centre can be translated into a fuzzy rule for identifying the class [24]. For type-2 fuzzy systems, subtractive clustering and fuzzy clustering have been developed recently [25-28]. Fuzzy c-means clustering (FCM) can efficiently be used for fuzzy systems [23] with simple structure and sufficient accuracy. However, it is well known that with many clustering algorithms, imprecise information may create imperfect representations of data sets. Therefore various types of uncertainties may have to be taken into account. To this end, the use of interval type-2 FCM is proposed for pattern recognition [25,26]. In this paper, type-2 FCM is used to select the cluster centres of the membership functions in the antecedent part of fuzzy rules of the type-2 FWNN using the input data set of the plant.

The fuzzy membership in type-1 FCM is determined by computing the relative distance among the data points and cluster prototypes [23]. The memberships and cluster centres are obtained as

$$u_j(x_i) = \left[\sum_{k=1}^{c} \left(\frac{d_{ji}}{d_{ki}} \right)^{2/(m-1)} \right]^{-1} ; \qquad c_j = \frac{\sum\limits_{i=1}^{I} x_i (u_j(x_i))^m}{\sum\limits_{i=1}^{I} (u_j(x_i))^m} \qquad (7)$$

Here i is the number of input patterns (data items), $u_j(x_i)$ is the membership value of pattern x_i for cluster j, d_{ji} (d_{ki}) denotes the distance between cluster prototypes $c_j(c_k)$ and data point x_i and m is fuzzifier that controls the amount of fuzziness in fuzzy classification.

Because of the imperfect information about the input data items, there exist uncertainties. The establishment of a maximum fuzzy region can result desirable clustering results. To overcome this problem, [25,26] propose the interval type-2 FCM, where the maximum fuzzy boundary is controlled by the two values of the fuzzifier m_1 and m_2. Consequently, the input data set is extended into interval type-2 fuzzy sets. For an input data point x_i, the highest and the lowest memberships are defined by using different fuzzy degrees m_1 and m_2 and the footprint of uncertainty is thus created. The primary memberships that extend data point x_i by interval type-2 fuzzy sets are determined [25,26] as

$$\bar{u}_j(x_i) = \begin{cases} \dfrac{1}{\sum\limits_{k=1}^{C} \left(\frac{d_{ji}}{d_{ki}} \right)^{\frac{2}{m_1-1}}}, & \text{if } \dfrac{1}{\sum\limits_{k=1}^{C} \left(\frac{d_{ji}}{d_{ki}} \right)^{\frac{2}{m_1-1}}} > \dfrac{1}{\sum\limits_{k=1}^{C} \left(\frac{d_{ji}}{d_{ki}} \right)^{\frac{2}{m_2-1}}} \\[4ex] \dfrac{1}{\sum\limits_{k=1}^{C} \left(\frac{d_{ji}}{d_{ki}} \right)^{\frac{2}{m_2-1}}}, & \text{otherwise} \end{cases} \qquad \underline{u}_j(x_i) = \begin{cases} \dfrac{1}{\sum\limits_{k=1}^{C} \left(\frac{d_{ji}}{d_{ki}} \right)^{\frac{2}{m_1-1}}}, & \text{if } \dfrac{1}{\sum\limits_{k=1}^{C} \left(\frac{d_{ji}}{d_{ki}} \right)^{\frac{2}{m_1-1}}} \leq \dfrac{1}{\sum\limits_{k=1}^{C} \left(\frac{d_{ji}}{d_{ki}} \right)^{\frac{2}{m_2-1}}} \\[4ex] \dfrac{1}{\sum\limits_{k=1}^{C} \left(\frac{d_{ji}}{d_{ki}} \right)^{\frac{2}{m_2-1}}}, & \text{otherwise} \end{cases}$$

$$(8)$$

Here d_{ji} (d_{ki}) denotes the distance between the cluster prototypes $c_j(c_k)$ and the data point x_i, C is the number of clusters and $\underline{u}_j(x_i)$ and $\bar{u}_j(x_i)$ are the lower and the upper memberships of the data point. Updating of the cluster centres are performed by the extension of interval type-2 fuzzy sets while executing fuzzy c-means algorithm.

The use of the fuzzifiers m_1 and m_2 result in two different objective functions to be minimized. Here $1 \leq m_1 \leq m_2 \leq \infty$.

$$J_{m_1} = \sum_{j=1}^{C} \sum_{i=1}^{I} u_{ji}^{m_1} d_{ji}^2, \quad \text{and } J_{m_2} = \sum_{j=1}^{C} \sum_{i=1}^{I} u_{ji}^{m_2} d_{ji}^2, \qquad (9)$$

Fuzzy clustering is carried out through an iterative optimization of the objective functions with the update of the memberships $u_j(x_i)$ and the cluster prototypes c_j. The procedure for updating of cluster prototypes in interval type-2 FCM requires type reduction and defuzzification operations.

The centroid of type-2 fuzzy set is determined by the extension principle. Since the secondary membership function of interval type-2 fuzzy set is equal to one, then employing fuzzy degree m in (10), the following can be obtained [25-27]

$$c_x = [c_L, c_R] = \sum_{u(x_1) \in J_{x_1}} \cdots \sum_{u(x_l) \in J_{x_l}} 1 \Bigg/ \frac{\sum_{i=1}^{l} x_i u(x_i)^m}{\sum_{i=1}^{l} u(x_i)^m} \tag{10}$$

The interval type-1 fuzzy set for the cluster centres can be represented as $c_j = 1/[c_L, c_R]$. Here $c_L \leq \forall c_j \leq c_R$. The crisp centre can be determined by defuzzification as $c_j = (c_L + c_R)/2$.

The iterative algorithm given in [25,26] is used to find the maximum c_R and minimum c_L value of centres. For the detailed analysis the reader can referee [25-27].

Taking into account the maximum of the centre c_R, and also the minimum of the centre c_L the cluster centres c_j are determined, where $c \leq \forall c_j \leq c_R$. In the simulation studies presented in the paper, we use type-2 membership functions with uncertain means for each input (see Fig.1(b)). The centres of these membership functions are obtained by spreading the cluster centres by $\pm \Delta c_j$, that is to say $c1 = c_j - \Delta c_j$ and $c2 = c_j + \Delta c_j$, where $c_L \leq c_j - \Delta c_j \leq c_j + \Delta c_j \leq c_R$. The widths of the membership functions are fixed using the distances between the membership function centres.

After the design of the antecedent parts by fuzzy clustering, the gradient descent algorithm is applied to design the consequent parts of the fuzzy rules (2), that is parameters of fourth layer type-2 FWNN. At first, the output error is calculated.

$$E = \frac{1}{2} \sum_{k=1}^{O} (u_k^d - u_k)^2 \tag{11}$$

Here O is number of output signals of the network (in the given case $O=1$), u_k^d and u_k are the desired and the current output values, respectively. The parameters w_j, a_{ij}, b_{ij} and $c1_{ij}$, $c2_{ij}$ and σ_{ij} $(i=1,..,m, \; j=1,..,n)$ are adjusted as

$$w_j(t+1) = w_j(t) - \gamma \frac{\partial E}{\partial w_j}; \quad a_{ij}(t+1) = a_{ij}(t) - \gamma \frac{\partial E}{\partial a_{ij}}; \quad b_{ij}(t+1) = b_{ij}(t) - \gamma \frac{\partial E}{\partial b_{ij}} \tag{12}$$

$$c1_{ij}(t+1) = c1_{ij}(t) - \gamma \frac{\partial E}{\partial c1_{ij}}; \quad c2_{ij}(t+1) = c2_{ij}(t) - \gamma \frac{\partial E}{\partial c2_{ij}}; \quad \sigma_{ij}(t+1) = \sigma_{ij}(t) - \gamma \frac{\partial E}{\partial \sigma_{ij}} \tag{13}$$

where γ is the learning rate. During learning the value of q in (6) is optimized from an initial value of 0.5 using $q(t+1) = q(t) - \gamma \cdot \partial E / \partial q$;

One important problem in learning algorithms is convergence. The convergence of the gradient descent method depends on the selection of the initial values of the learning rate. Usually, these values are selected in the interval [0-1]. A large value of the learning rate may lead to unstable learning, a small value of the learning rate results in a slow learning speed. In this paper, an adaptive approach is used for updating these parameters. That is, the learning of the type-2 FWNN parameters is started with a small value of the learning rate γ. During learning, γ is increased if the value of change of error $\Delta E = E(t) - E(t+1)$ is positive, and decreased if negative. This strategy ensures a stable learning for the type-2 FWNN, and speeds up the learning.

4 Simulation

The TYPE-2 FWNN system is applied for designing a prediction model of exchange rate USA/TL. Exchange rates play an important role in controlling dynamics of exchange market. Appropriate prediction of exchange rate is very important for the success of many business and fund managers. The type-2 FWNN structure is used to construct the prediction model of exchange rate. Four input data points [$x(t-6)$ $x(t-3)$ $x(t-1)$ $x(t)$] are used as input to the prediction model. The output training data corresponds to $x(t+3)$. In other words, since the exchange rates is considered daily, the value that is to be predicted will be after $pr=3$ day. The training input/output data for the prediction system will be a structure whose first component is the four dimension input vector, and the second component is the predicted output.

The type-2 FWNN structure is generated with four input and one output neurons. The learning of the FWNN parameters is accomplished by using fuzzy c-means clustering and the gradient descent algorithms. First, the type-2 fuzzy classification is applied to the input space in order to determine the cluster centres. These cluster centres are used in order to organize the premise parts of the fuzzy rules. Then the gradient algorithm is applied for the learning of the parameters in the consequent part. The initial values of wavelet's parameters a and b are selected randomly, in the interval [−1, 1]. Using the parameter update rules derived above, they are updated for the given input signals. The fuzzy rules are constructed using two clusters for each input variable and taking all possible combinations. In total 8 clusters will be derived for all inputs. Each cluster will represent the centre of Gaussian membership function. 16 fuzzy rules are constructed using different combination of these clusters for four inputs. After clustering input space gradient decent algorithm will be used for learning of consequent parts of the fuzzy rules, that is parameters of wavelet function.

For training of the system, the statistical data describing daily exchange rates from January 2007 to April 2009 is considered. The last 50 data are used for diagnostic testing. All input and output data are scaled in the interval [0, 1]. The training is carried out for 500 epochs. Fig. 3 demonstrate RMSE values obtained during learning. The values of the parameters of the type-2 FWNN system were determined at the conclusion of training. Once the type-2 FWNN has been successfully trained, it is then used for the prediction of the daily exchange rates. The training and test values of RMSE were 0.01508 and 0.01594 correspondingly.

In Figure 4, the output of the type-2 FWNN system for three-step ahead prediction of exchange rates for learning and generalization step is shown. Here the solid line is desired output, and the dotted line is the type-2 FWNN output. The plot of prediction error is shown in Figure 5. As shown in the figure, in generalization step (end part of error curve), the value of error increases. The result of the simulation of the type-2 FWNN prediction model is compared with result of simulation of the NN and FWNN (type-1) [20,21] based prediction model. To estimate the performance of the NN, FWNN and type-2 FWNN prediction systems, the RMSE values of errors between predicted and current output signal are compared. In Table 2, the comparative results of simulations for 3 and 6 step ahead predictions are given. As shown in the table the performance of type-2 FWNN prediction is better than the performance of the other models. The simulation results satisfy the efficiency of the application of type-2 FWNN in constructing a prediction model of exchange rates.

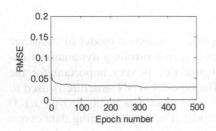

Fig. 3. RMSE value obtained during training

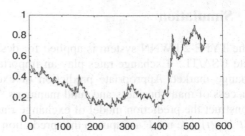

Fig. 4. Three step ahead prediction. Plot of output signals.

Fig. 5. Plot of prediction error

Table 4. Comparative results of simulation

Method	Predict.steps	Epochs	RMSE
NN	3	1000	0.019617
	6	1000	0.024186
FWNN	3	500	0.016490
[20,21]	6	500	0.022817
Type-2	3	500	0.015940
FWNN	6	500	0.019780

5 Conclusion

The time series prediction model is developed by integrating type-2 fuzzy logic, neural networks and wavelet technology. The wavelet networks are used to construct the fuzzy rules, and the functionality of the fuzzy system is realized by the neural network structure. The design of type-2 FWNN prediction model is performed using fuzzy clustering and gradient algorithm. The fuzzy clustering is applied in order to select the parameters antecedent part of fuzzy rules that is the parameters of second layer and gradient algorithm is used for consequent part- fourth layer of type-2 FWNN structure. The type-2 FWNN structure is applied for predicting future values of exchange rates. Using statistical data, the prediction model is constructed. The test results of the developed system are compared with these obtained from the feed-forward NN based system, and the first one has demonstrated better performance.

References

1. Box, G.E.P.: Time series analysis, forecasting and control, San Francisco, Holden Day (1970)
2. Maddala, G.S.: Introduction to econometrics. Prentice Hall, Englewood Cliffs (1996)
3. Kim, K.-J., Lee, W.B.: Stock market prediction using artificial neural networks with optimal feature transformation. Neural computing & applications 13(3), 255–260 (2004)
4. Górriz, J.M., Puntonet, C.G., Salmerón, M., de la Rosa, J.J.G.: A new model for time-series forecasting using radial basis functions and exogenous data. Neural computing & applications 13(2), 101–111 (2004)
5. Jang, J.-S.R., Sun, C.T., Mizutani, E.: Neuro-fuzzy and soft computing. ch 17. Prentice-Hall, New Jersey (1997)

6. Zadeh, L.A.: The concept of linguistic variable and its application to approximate reasoning. Information Sciences 8 (1975)
7. Mendel, J.M.: Uncertain Rule-Based Fuzzy Logic System: Introduction and New Directions. Prentice Hall, Upper Saddle River (2001)
8. Mendel, J.M., Robert, I.B.: Type-2 fuzzy sets made simple. IEEE Trans. Fuzzy Syst. 10, 117–127 (2002)
9. Karnik, N.N., Mendel, J.M.: Application of type-2 fuzzy logic systems to forecasting of time-series. Information Sciences 120, 89–111 (1999)
10. Liang, Q., Mendel, J.M.: MPEG VBR video traffic modeling and classification using fuzzy techniques. IEEE Trans. Fuzzy Syst. 9, 183–193 (2001)
11. Yager, R.R.: Fuzzy subsets of type-2 in decision. J. Cybern 10, 137–159 (1980)
12. Lynch, C., Hagras, H., Callaghan, V.: Embedded interval type-2 neuro-fuzzy speed controller for marine diesel engines. In: Proc. IPMU 2006, Paris, France, pp. 1340–1347 (2006)
13. Hagras, H.A.: A hierarchical type-2 fuzzy logic control architecture for autonomous mobile robots. IEEE Trans. on Fuzzy Syst. 12(4), 524–539 (2004)
14. Castillo, O., Melin, P.: Intelligent Systems with Interval Type-2 Fuzzy Logic. Int. Journal of Innovative Computing, Information and Control 4(2), 771–783 (2008)
15. Abiyev, R.H., Kaynak, O.: Type-2 Fuzzy Neural Structure for Identification and Control of Time-Varying Plants. IEEE Trans. on Industrial Electronics (2010), doi:10.1109/TIE.2010.2043036
16. Kugarajah, T., Zhang, Q.: Multidimensional Wavelet Frames. IEEE Trans. on Neural Networks 6, 1552–1556 (1995)
17. Zhang, Q., Benviste, A.: Wavelet Networks. IEEE Trans. on Neural Networks 3, 889–898 (1995)
18. Thuillard, M.: Wavelets in Softcomputing. World Scientific Press, Singapore (2001)
19. Ho, D.W.C., Zhang, P.-A., Xu, J.: Fuzzy Wavelet Networks for Function Learning. IEEE Trans. on Fuzzy Systems 9(1), 200–211 (2001)
20. Abiyev, R.H., Kaynak, O.: Fuzzy Wavelet Neural Networks for Identification and Control of Dynamic Plants – A Novel Structure and a Comparative Study. IEEE Trans. on Industrial Electronics 55(8), 3133–3140 (2008)
21. Abiyev, R.H.: Fuzzy Wavelet Neural Network for Prediction of Electricity Consumption. Artificial Intelligence for Engineering Design, Analysis and Manufacturing, vol. 23 (2008)
22. Nicolás, G.-P., Domingo, O.-B., César, H.-M.: An alternative approach for neural network evolution with a genetic algorithm: Crossover by combinatorial optimization. Neural Networks 19(4), 514–528 (2006)
23. Bezdek, J.C.: Pattern Recognition with Fuzzy Objective Function Algorithms. Plenum Press, New York (1981)
24. Kasabov, N.K.: DENFIS: Dynamic evolving neural-fuzzy inference system and its application for time-series. IEEE Transactions on Fuzzy Systems 10, 144–154 (2002)
25. Hwang, C., Rhee, F.C.-H.: Uncertain Fuzzy Clustering: Interval Type-2 Fuzzy Approach to C-Means. IEEE Trans. on Fuzzy Systems 15(1), 107–120 (2007)
26. Rhee, F.C.-H.: Uncertain Fuzzy Clustering: Insights and Recommendations. IEEE Computational Intelligence Magazine, 44–56 (February 2007)
27. Choi, B.-I., Rhee, F.C.-H.: Interval Type-2 Fuzzy Membership Generation Methods for Pattern Recognition. Information Sciences 179, 2102–2122 (2009)
28. Ren, Q., Baron, L., Balazinski, M.: Type-2 Takagi-Sugeno-Kanaga Fuzzy Logic Modelling using Subtractive Clustering. In: NAFIPS, Montreal, pp.120–125 (2006)
29. Liang, Q., Mendel, J.M.: An introduction to Type-2 TSK Fuzzy Logic Systems. In: IEEE International Fuzzy Systems Conference, Seul, Korea, pp. 1534–1539 (1999)
30. Begian, M.B., Melek, W.W., Mendel, J.M.: Parametric Design of Stable Type-2 TSK Fuzzy Systems. In: Proceedings of NAFIPS, pp. 1–6 (2008)

Pruning the Search Space for the Snake-in-the-Box Problem

J.D. Griffin and W.D. Potter

Institute for Artificial Intelligence
111 GSRC, University of Georgia
Athens, Georgia USA 30602-7415
joshua.d.griffin@gmail.com, potter@uga.edu

Abstract. This paper explores methods for reducing the search space when hunting for snakes using a Genetic Algorithm (GA). The first method attempts to reinterpret individuals in an effort to utilize the high degree of symmetry inherent in the problem and, thereby, make crossover more effective. The second method centers around removing snake blockers, which are sequences that prevent snakes, and the effects of snake blockers on the search space and GA effectiveness. Testing of these methods is limited to dimension 8; however, the concepts are applicable to all dimensions.

Keywords: Snake-In-The-Box, Genetic Algorithms, Hypercube, Snake Problem, Frequency-Based Transition Reassignment, FBTR, Tightness, Skin Density, Snake Blockers, Canonical Representation.

1 Background

The Snake-in-the-Box problem, referred to here as simply the snake problem, was first discussed by W. H. Kautz in 1958. Snakes were originally suggested as a solution to problems in analog-to-digital systems [1]. For their utility in real world applications, snakes are an important area of research and have applications in electrical engineering (analog-to-digital conversion), coding theory (data integrity checking), combination locking schemes, the simplification of disjunctive normal form, and computer network topologies (Kautz networks) [1, 2]. A snake, at its most basic level, is a sequence of integers and the snake problem centers on finding the longest possible snakes that can be created from a fixed set of integers, namely those that can be represented using a fixed number of bits.

A hypercube is a tool for conceptualizing how all of the numbers that can be expressed in a fixed number of bits relate to each other. The number of bits is called the dimension, and a hypercube for a given dimension, d, is called a d-dimensional hypercube. A d-dimensional hypercube consists of 2^d vertices, where each vertex is a numeral composed of binary digits, and $2^d \times \frac{d}{2}$ edges, where an edge connects each pair of vertices whose numerals differ by only one digit. The number of bits that are different between two binary numerals is referred to as their Hamming distance. The

N. García-Pedrajas et al. (Eds.): IEA/AIE 2010, Part III, LNAI 6098, pp. 528–537, 2010.

vertices of the hypercube that have a Hamming distance of one and, therefore, have an edge between them, are called neighbors.

A sequence of vertices is a snake if and only if, for each vertex v_i, $HammingDistance(v_i, v_{i-1})=1$ and $HammingDistance(v_i, v_{i+1})=1$, for $1 < i < m$ where m is the length of the sequence. And, for each vertex v_i, there does not exist v_j such that $HammingDistance(v_i, v_j) \leq 1$ for $j < i$-1 or $j > i$+1. Here $HammingDistance(v_i, v_j)$ returns the Hamming distance of the two vertices v_i and v_j, which is a reflexive operation. When applied to the hypercube, these rules dictate that the path cannot pass though a vertex that already neighbors another vertex on the path. The head of a snake is the vertex at the beginning of the sequence, and the tail of the snake is the last vertex of the sequence.

2 Previous Approaches

Searching for long snakes is a non-deterministically polynomial complete (NP-C) problem [3]. The hypercube, which serves as a representation of the available search space, doubles in number of vertices for every increment in dimension. As the size of the search space expands, finding long snakes becomes an increasingly difficult problem. In fact, the search space becomes so large that exhaustive search for dimensions higher than 7 is considered infeasible with current technology [4, 5].

The lengths of the longest snakes in dimensions 1 through 7 have been found using exhaustive search and can be found in Table 1 and the current records for dimensions 8 and higher are listed at http://www.ai.uga.edu/sib/records/index.php. Unfortunately, there exists no mathematical proof to confirm whether or not a snake of a particular length is the longest possible snake in a given dimension. Therefore, the only way to prove that there are no snakes larger than a given example is to do an exhaustive search. Current technology prohibits such a search in dimensions greater than 7, so the longest snake in dimensions 8 and greater will remain an open problem until technology is able to perform an exhaustive search on those dimensions or theory produces a method of proving that the known examples are the longest snakes possible.

Table 1. All of the known longest snakes for dimensions 1 through 7. These snakes were confirmed to be the longest snakes by iterative search of all possible snakes in each dimension.

Dimension	Longest Snake
1	1
2	2
3	4
4	7
5	13
6	26
7	50

Many different approaches have been used in an attempt to find long snakes. Theoretical approaches, based in mathematics, have been used as in [6]. The use of exhaustive search was successful in finding all snakes in dimensions less than 8, including the work done in dimension 7 in [4]. As iterative search methods fail, acceptance for heuristic-based approaches increases. In particular, evolutionary computation has been applied to the snake problem with significant success. In fact, applications have been developed to search for snakes using Genetic Algorithms, Ant Colony Optimization, and Stochastic Hill Climbing among others [5, 7, 8].

3 GA Representation

For the snake problem, two possible representations are vertex-based and transition-based. Vertex-based representations build a chromosome from vertices of the hypercube. Therefore, each candidate solution is a sequence of integers that correspond to the vertices of the hypercube.

In contrast, transition-based representations build a chromosome from the edges of the hypercube. Transition-based representations are also sequences of integers, but the integers correspond to the transitions in the hypercube. In other words, the numbers indicate which bit place changes between the previous vertex and the current vertex. The transition sequence representation is a generalized version of all snakes which follow the same sequence of transitions. Since there are 2^d vertices in a hypercube for dimension d, there can be 2^d valid heads for every transition sequence, making the transition based representation an expression for many different sequences of vertices. The head chosen for a transition sequence only affects where the sequence begins in the hypercube but, due to the symmetry of the hypercube, does not change whether the resulting vertex sequence is a snake or not. By taking advantage of this property of the hypercube, transition-based representations have a much smaller search space than vertex-based representations. This is because, for each unique candidate solution in a transition-based representation, there would exist 2^d candidate solutions in a vertex-based representation all starting at different vertices, where d is the number of dimensions. Considering that it is not necessary to represent each of these 2^d candidate solutions separately, the transition-based representation has fewer candidate solutions to consider.

Furthermore, in a transition-based representation, only valid transitions are being searched. A valid transition is a transition that corresponds to an edge in the hypercube. An invalid transition occurs whenever two consecutive vertices in a series are not neighbors. For example, vertex 0 and vertex 3 have a Hamming distance of 2. If these two vertices were to appear next to each other in a vertex-based representation, there could be no transition between them because they do not share an edge in the hypercube. A sequence of vertices cannot be a snake if it contains an invalid transition. In a vertex-based representation, invalid transitions are possible, whereas in transition-based representations only valid transitions are possible. Removing all candidate solutions with invalid transitions further reduces the search space for a transition-based representation versus a vertex-based representation.

Despite the advantages of a transition-based representation, the search space is still exceedingly large in dimensions 8 and higher. In an effort to reduce the search space and improve GA performance, this paper explores two techniques: Frequency-Based Transition Reassignment and the removal of snake blockers.

4 Frequency-Based Transition Reassignment

Transition reassignment is when all of the transitions from one transition class are swapped with the transitions of another transition class. When two individuals can be made to have the same transition sequence by performing one or more transition reassignments for the whole chromosome, they are said to be in the same equivalence class. For each snake using d transition classes, $d!$ snakes exist in the same equivalence class in dimension d [4]. Therefore, even with the utilization of a transition-based representation, there exist $d!$ equivalent individuals for each individual being analyzed, making it easy to waste time analyzing many equivalent versions of the same individual without making definitive progress.

In [4], the process of exhaustively searching dimension 7 is described. The work took over a month and was carried out on five SUN Microsystems SparcCenter 1000's, each having two processors. Only canonical solutions were considered. A canonical solution as starting at the vertex 0 with an initial transition of 0, with each subsequent transition class not yet represented in the chromosome being assigned to the next unused transition of least significance. In other words, each solution introduced the transitions in consecutive order: transition 0, 1, 2, 3, 4, 5, and, finally, 6 [4]. Searching only canonical solutions allowed the search space to be pruned significantly because it provided a meaningful baseline, in which transition classes were interpreted uniformly across all individuals. Therefore, it was only necessary to visit one individual from each equivalence class.

As an alternative to using the canonical representation presented in [4], this paper offers Frequency-Based Transition Reassignment (FBTR). As the name implies, FBTR performs transition reassignment on individuals based on the frequency with which the transition classes appear in the chromosome. In other words, the most frequently occurring transition class is mapped to 0, the second most frequently to 1, and so on until 7 for dimension 8. Two transition classes are considered to be conflicting when they occur with equal frequency. When conflicts are encountered, they are resolved by assigning the next available transition as the replacement for the transition class occurring in the leftmost position on the chromosome.

5 Snake Blockers

Snake blockers are transition patterns that act as barriers to block snakes. There are two types of simple snake blockers that are discussed here. The first is when a transition occurs twice in a row. The result of following the same transition twice is that the path doubles back on itself, which violates the rules for a snake. The second type of snake blocker is when the same transition occurs twice with only a single transition in between. This results in the path visiting a skin vertex, or a vertex that neighbors a vertex already on the path, which also violates the rules for a snake. Snake blockers can be introduced through the operators of the GA. Both reproduction operators and mutation operators are capable of producing snake blockers.

There are two primary reasons why snake blockers should be addressed. The first one is that they adversely affect the performance of the GA and are introduced very frequently by the GA operators. To illustrate, given two sequential transitions, t_i and t_{i+1}, which are the transitions immediately preceding the point of crossover after which two new transitions will be added, t_{i+2} and t_{i+3}, the probability that t_{i+2} or t_{i+3} will create a snake blocker is $\frac{2d+(d-2)}{d^2}$ for dimension d. This function is derived from the fact that there are d^2 possible value combinations for t_{i+2} and t_{i+3} and, when laid out in a square where the columns are values assumed by t_{i+2} and the rows are the values assumed by t_{i+3}, two columns and one row of these values will result in snake blockers. In dimension 8, crossover performed at a given point is likely to result in a snake blocker $\frac{2(8)+(8-2)}{8^2} = \frac{22}{64} = 34.375\%$ of the time. With snake blockers being introduced over one third of the time a crossover operation is performed in dimension 8, it seems unlikely that the GA will be able to sufficiently filter affected individuals.

The second reason to remove snake blockers is that it greatly reduces the search space. The number of transitions that would not generate a snake blocker at any given point in the path past the first two transitions is $d-2$, where d is the current dimension. At the first position, t_1, there are d potentially valid transitions. At the second position, t_2, there are $d-1$ valid transitions left to prevent two identical transitions in succession, $t_1 = t_2$. From the third position on, the previous two positions, t_1 and t_2, are occupied by transitions that must be avoided in the current position, leaving $d-2$ options, $t_k \neq t_{k-1}$ and $t_k \neq t_{k-2}$. Allowing snake blockers increases this back to d for every position because the preceding two positions are not taken into account, which changes the effective search space from $d(d-1)(d-2)^{(m-2)}$ to d^m, where m is the length of the individual.

Instead of allowing snake blockers, experiments done for this paper use a novel algorithm called the Snake Blocker Removal Algorithm (SBRA). The SBRA is designed to have no impact on the snakes in the chromosome. SBRA moves across the snake from left to right searching for snake blockers. When a snake blocker is located, it performs transition reassignment from the location of the snake blocker to the end of the chromosome. The result is that the portion of the snake before the snake blocker remains unchanged while the portion after the snake blocker is replaced with a sequence of transitions from the same equivalence class. Note that a snake blocker is more than one transition, but the location of the snake blocker is understood to mean the last transition in the snake blocker sequence. In other words, whether the sequence is (... $t1$, $t3$, $t1$ ...) or (... $t1$, $t1$ ...), the second $t1$ is considered to be the location of the snake blocker.

6 Setup

To test the relative merits of the different representations and the parameters that were being used in the GA, experimentation was performed by running a series of head-to-head competitions. The GA was designed to allow multiple, mutually exclusive populations to exist. Each population shared the same crossover, mutation, and selection settings for each run. Standard single point, double point, and triple point crossovers were used in the experiments. Two different mutation schemes were used: random mutation and XOR mutation. In random mutation, a gene in the individual is replaced with a randomly generated gene. XOR mutation takes advantage of the properties of the hypercube to introduce changes to the chromosome. There are two paths of length two between vertices of the hypercube having a Hamming distance of two. XOR mutation replaces one of these transition route with the other.

Fitness functions were the products of three factors: the length of the snake, tightness, and skin density. Tightness is the number of vertices that are left unoccupied by either the snake or the snake's skin. Skin density looks at the vertices that are part of the snake's skin and counts how many of their neighbors are part of the snake.

The GA was set to run until every population stopped making forward progress, measured in terms of maximum or average individual fitness, for ten consecutive generations. All populations were of size 500 and all used elitism, moving the top 10 individuals from each generation directly into the next generation.

When the GA halted, the results indicated which populations outperformed the others. Those individual configurations that consistently outperformed the others were taken to be superior. Additionally, this scheme ensured that each population was run for an equal number of generations, for a given set of parameters, thereby preventing bias against any population that had a slower convergence rate. Each population was given an equal chance to discover the longest snake for a run.

7 Representation Results

Initial testing was done to compare the use of FBTR to a standard transition-based representation. Ten populations were set up to use a transition-based representation and ten populations were set up to use FBTR. After 600 competitions, FBTR won 61.16% of the encounters. Furthermore, on average, populations using FBTR found significantly longer snakes. The maximum length snake found by populations using FBTR for these runs was 74 and the maximum length snake found by the populations using a transition-based representation was 76.

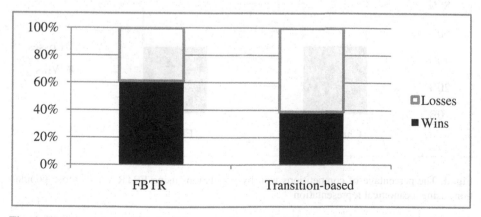

Fig. 1. The percentage of competitions won by populations using FBTR versus those populations using a transition-based representation

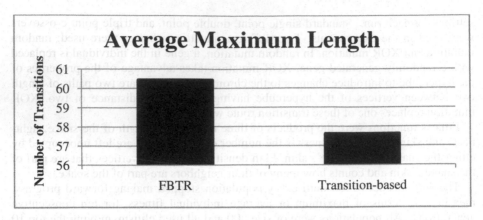

Fig. 2. The average maximum length snake found in competitions between populations using FBTR versus those populations using a transition-based representation

Subsequently, testing concentrated on comparing FBTR to the canonical representation. Ten populations were set up to use a canonical representation and ten populations were set up to use FBTR. After 1800 competitions, FBTR won 890 of the encounters and canonical representation won 910. The average performance of both representations was relatively comparable. FBTR generated slightly longer snakes on average and had a slightly larger total increase in the maximum snake length than canonical representation. The maximum length snake found by FBTR for these runs was 78 and the maximum length snake found by the populations using a canonical representation was 74.

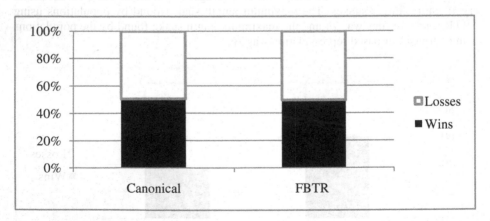

Fig. 3. The percentage of competitions won by populations using FBTR versus those populations using a canonical representation

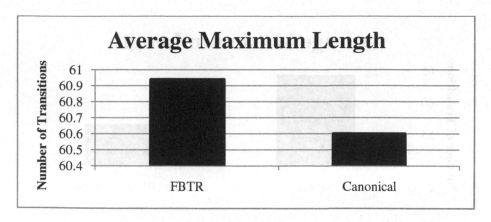

Fig. 4. The average maximum length snake found in competitions between populations using FBTR versus those populations using a canonical representation

8 Snake Blocker Results

In order to observe the effects of removing snake blockers, tests were run comparing populations in which snake blockers were allowed against populations where snake blockers were being removed using SBRA. Twelve populations were used; half allowed snake blockers and half removed them. After 54 competitions, all six of the populations using SBRA occupied the top six rankings. The maximum length snake found during this experiment was 73.

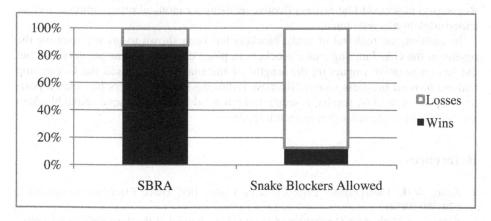

Fig. 5. The percentage of competitions won by populations using SBRA versus those populations allowing snake blockers

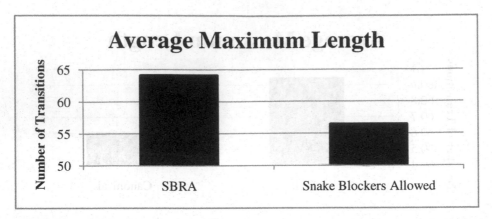

Fig. 6. The average maximum length snake found in competitions between populations using SBRA versus those populations allowing snake blockers

9 Conclusions

Frequency-Based Transition Reassignment has been proven to be more effective than a transition-based representation and appears to be effective at reducing the overall representation space associated with the problem. When compared to a transitional representation, Frequency-Based Transition Reassignment populations produced longer snakes. However, comparing Frequency-Based Transition Reassignment to a canonical representation is less clear cut. While using a canonical representation barely outperformed Frequency-Based Transition Reassignment, it did not improve the results enough to be truly significant. Given that using Frequency-Based Transition Reassignment seems to be just as effective as using a canonical representation, further experimentation is warranted.

In addition, the removal of snake blockers has been shown to greatly improve the results of the GA. Leaving snake blockers in place did not prevent convergence but did have a negative impact on the lengths of the snakes and caused the GA to stop making forward progress sooner. Because removing snake blockers has such a positive impact on the GA results, it seems to be a good tactic to remove snake blockers and benefit from the reduction in search space.

References

1. Kautz, W.H.: Unit-Distance Error-Checking Codes. IRE Trans. Electronic Computers 7, 179–180 (1958)
2. Klee, V.: A Method for Constructing Circuit Codes. Journal of the Association for Computing Machinery 14, 520–538 (1967)
3. Bitterman, D.S.: New Lower Bounds for the Snake-in-the-Box Problem. Master of Science Thesis, The University of Georgia (2004),
   http://getd.galib.uga.edu/public/bitterman_derrick_s_200412_ms/
   bitterman_derrick_s_200412_ms.pdf

4. Kochut, K.J.: Snake-in-the-Box Codes for Dimension 7. Journal of Combinatorial Mathematics and Combinatorial Computing 20, 175–185 (1996)
5. Casella, D.A., Potter, W.D.: Using Evolutionary Techniques to Hunt for Snakes and Coils. In: IEEE Congress on Evolutionary Computation (CEC 2005), vol. 3, pp. 2499–2504 (2005)
6. Rajan, D.S., Shende, A.M.: Maximal and Reversible Snakes in Hypercubes. In: 24th Annual Australasian Conference on Combinatorial Mathematics and Combinatorial Computing (1999)
7. Potter, W.D., Robinson, R.W., Miller, J.A., Kochut, K.J., Redys, D.Z.: Using the Genetic Algorithm to Find Snake-in-the-Box Codes. In: Industrial and Engineering Applications of Artificial Intelligence and Expert Systems - Proceedings of the Seventh International Conference, Austin, Texas, pp. 421–426 (1994)
8. Hardas, S.P.: An Ant Colony Approach to the Snake-in-the-Box Problem. Master of Science Thesis, The University of Georgia (2005),
   http://getd.galib.uga.edu/public/hardas_shilpa_p_200508_ms/
   hardas_shilpa_p_200508_ms.pdf

Percolating Swarm Dynamics

Manuel Graña, Carmen Hernández, Alicia D'Anjou, and Blanca Cases

Computational Intelligence Group, Universidad del Pais Vasco
www.ehu.es/ccwintco

Abstract. Swarm Intelligence has been a successful approach to solve some combinatorial problems through the metaphor of interacting evolving individuals of a a population P in a closed torus-like space S. Each individual usually perceives an space sorrounding it which can be generally modelled as disk of radius R. In this paper we discuss that Percolation conditions can be key to allow convergence to reach the optimal results of these kind of systems.

1 Introduction

In a physical sense, Percolation is the slow flow of fluids through a porous media, but in a mathematical setting it means the connectivity among random systems that can be layered over a spatial lattice. Basically, it deals with the thresholds on parameters that set conditions on the spatial connectivity and may allow or hinder complete connectivity [1,9,8]. Here we will look for such connectivity conditions in the framework of Swarm Intelligence (SI), trying to ascertain wether they may be the key to SI success and performance.

We find that there were three main approaches to apply Cellular Automata to evolutionary simulations. In the first approach, Cellular automata cells are the proccessing units, fixed in the nodes of a spatial lattice. In the second approach, the processing elements are agents that can move in the space without physical connections, Reynold's model of *Boids' steering behaviors* [11,12]. Particle Swarm Optimization approaches [7] showed that steering behaviors together with a memory of visited positions that maximize a local cost function are enough to solve combinatorial optimization problems. The third approach, inspired in the collective behavior of social insects are the so called *ant colonies* [3,5,6,4]. Ant colonies are strongly cohered by a kind of indirect communication called Stigmergy, that consists in leaving tracks of pheromone that subsequently atract other individuals in a positive feeback. The behaviour of Ant Colonies can be interpreted as intelligent, searching for optimal solutions to combinatorial optimization problems.

In a previous work [2] we found that a simple SI model based on *boid's steering behaviours*, with only the ability to distinguish friend from foe, is able, under the appropriate metaphorical interpretation, to solve efficiently the problem of coloring graphs[10]. Now the research question we address in this paper is wether the convergence can be affected through simple adjustments of the relationship between world size and individual boid perception spatial parameters.

N. García-Pedrajas et al. (Eds.): IEA/AIE 2010, Part III, LNAI 6098, pp. 538–545, 2010.

Our hypothesis is that the concept of Percolation, will give answers to this question and that these answers may give hints to its generalization to other spatial SI systems. We will apply the model of continumm disk Percolation to find the relation between the radius of vision of boids, the size of the world and the size of the population that ensures probabilistically the interaction of boid individuals within the flock. We show that there is a Percolation threshold for these parameters that affect convergence of the SI to optimal solutions of the metaphorical problem.

Section 2 gives some intuition and ideas about Percolation. Section 3 reviews the definition of a SI based on Boids steering behaviors. Section 4 gives computational solutions to the Percolation problem in the Boids system that is a necessary condition for convergence of the system to the optimal solution. Section 5 gives a final account of our conclussions.

2   Some Ideas about Percolation

The Percolation [1,8] concept comes from chemistry and refers to the way a liquid flows through a porous medium. A model of this phenomenon is the *bond Percolation*: given a square lattice in $\mathbb{Z}^2$, assume that we prune the link connecting a position(x, y) to an adjacent one (x', y') with probability $1 - p$, and we mainting it with probability p, defining in this way a random graph. The the critical value p_c that ensures the connectivity from one end of the lattice to the opposite for values $p \geq p_c$ is the Percolation threshold.

The concept of *site Percolation* puts emphasis on nodes and not in links. Imagine an electrical potential from one side to the opposite side of the grid. We started to cut the network nodes thereby preventing electrical current flow. What percentage of nodes should be maintained for the current to continue flowing?. The Percolation threshold p_c is the mean of that measure over all the possible grids.

At the Percolation threshold, the structure changes from a collection of many disconnected parts to a large aggregate. If the grid were infinite, an infinite cluster should be produced and this is the mathematical base of Percolation models. At the same time, the average size of clusters of finite size that are disconnected to the main cluster, decreases. Let p be the probability that a site or a link (depending on the model used) is open. The probability of a site or link belonging to the infinite cluster is:

$$\theta\left(p\right) \propto \left(p - p_c\right)^{\beta} \tag{1}$$

with $\beta = 5/36$ for 2D networks. Symbol $\propto$ denotes proportionality.

3   Boids SI Parameters

In Craig Reynold's Boids systme [11,12] the board is a continuous domain, and boids are agents that can change their positions in the world. Each individual boid exhibits a very simple behavior that is specified by a few simple rules that guide it to get along with the collective motion of the flock. The global behavior of the flock emerges from the individual boid decisions. The system parameters are:

Position and velocity: Given a set of n boids, the steering rules for i-th boid b_i, at time instant $t + 1$ are defined as a function of the position p_j and the velocity v_j of the neighboring boids at the previous instant t. Velocity vector $v_i = (x, y)$ has an angle γ_{v_i} relative to the horizontal axis.

Sensorial input: Each boid is aware of an spatial region around it, its neighborhood. The angle of vision, denoted ρ, comprises all the positions in the plane

$$p = p_i + v'$$ (2)

where

$$\gamma_{v_i} - \frac{\rho}{2} \leq \gamma_{v'} \leq \gamma_{v_i} + \frac{\rho}{2}.$$ (3)

In this article, the value $\rho = 360°$, meaning that individuals can even observe what happens behind their backs. Let R be the radius of vision: the spatial neighborhood is the disk sector of radius R and angle ρ around the boid. Let ∂_i denote the boids population in the spatial neighborhood. The set of boids lying inside the neighborhood of the i-th individual is denoted:

$$\partial_i = \partial(b_i) = \{b_j : \|p_i - p_j\| < R\}.$$ (4)

Effectors: The steering basic rules, used in our model, are the classical ones of the Reynolds model: alignment, separation, and cohesion. Combining these rules, the boids are able to flight co-coordinately avoiding collisions. The flocking rules for the boid b_i are formalized as follows:

- **Separation**: steer to avoid crowding local flockmates inside a private zone of radius z.

$$v_{s_i} = - \sum_{b_j \in \partial_i : d(b_j, b_i) < z} (p_j - p_i)$$ (5)

- **Cohesion**: steer to move toward the average position c_i of local flockmates

$$v_{c_i} = c_i - p_i \quad \text{where} \quad c_i = \frac{1}{|\partial_i|} \sum_{b_j \in \partial_i} p_j$$ (6)

- **Alignment**: steer in the direction of the average heading of local flockmates.

$$v_{a_i} = \frac{1}{|\partial_i|} \sum_{b_j \in \partial_i} v_j - v_i$$ (7)

- **Own velocity**: is the current velocity component, an inertia that has the effect of limiting the rotation angle of the object.

$$\alpha_o v_i$$ (8)

The motion model of flocking boids was a linear combination of separation, cohesion and alignment . Here $\|p\|$ denotes the norm of a position or vector p and f_{maxv}

is a non-negative parameter that limits the norm (the length in the Euclidean distance) of a vector and $\mathcal{N}(p) = \frac{p}{\|p\|}$ represents the normalized position or vector.

$$p_i(t+1) = p_i(t) + v_i(t+1) \qquad (9)$$

A basic flock model in a D-dimensional torus is a tuple $\mathcal{F} = \left(\mathcal{B}, \bar{\alpha}, \bar{\beta}, \bar{v}, \bar{v}(0), \bar{p}(0)\right)$ where:

- $\mathcal{B} = \{b_1, \ldots, b_P\}$ is the population of boids, of size $P \in \mathbb{N}$.
- $\bar{\alpha} = (\alpha_o, \alpha_s, \alpha_c, \alpha_a, \alpha_n)$ are the flock parameters.
- $\bar{\beta} = (S, R, \rho, z)$ where $S \in \mathbb{R}^+$ is the size of the world. The world is square, being the side S and the area S^2. It wraps horizontally and vertically forming a torus centered in the null position $\bar{0} \in \mathbb{R}^D$. The radius of vision is R and the angle of vision ρ. We denote the D-dimensional torus $\mathbb{T}^D$.
- The flock system that steers the boids in the in the world is given by the iteration:

$$v(t+1) = f_{\max v} \mathcal{N}\left(\alpha_o v(t) + \alpha_s v_s(t) + \alpha_c v_c(t) + \alpha_a v_a(t) + \alpha_n v_n\right) \quad (10)$$

where $v(t) \in \mathbb{T}^D$ $\alpha_o, \alpha_s, \alpha_c, \alpha_a \in [0,1]$ are global parameters for the *own*, *separation*, *coherence* and *alignment* velocities and the *noise* $\alpha_n v_{n_i}$ is the product of a random normalized vector v_n by a noise parameter α_n. Notation $v_i(t)$ and $v_{x_i}(t)$ with $x \in \{o, s, c, a, n\}$ represent the velocities of boid b_i at instant t.
- The initial conditions for $\bar{v}(0) = (v_1(0), \ldots, v_i(0), \ldots, v_P(0))$ gives the initial velocities to the boids and it is randomly generated for the extent of this work.
- The initial position is a tuple $\bar{p}(0) = (p_1(0), \ldots, p_i(0), \ldots, p_P(0))$.

4 Percolation Thresholds in Boids SI

Convergence of the Boid SI to some stable (and optimal state under some metaphorical interpretation of the system's configuration), needs that all the boids are connected through their sensory input. Here is where the notion of Percolation is relevant to the Swarm Dynamics. Percolation conditions must relate the size of the side of the world square with the boid's radius of vision R and the population of birds $\mathcal{P}$. Each bird has an area of vision (spatial neighborhood) $A = \pi R^2$. We want to ensure that a random initial distribution of the items will cross the world to the opposite side stepping only positions that are some boid spatial neighborhood. Figure 1 shows the spatial neighborhoods of boids put in random positions following an uniform probability. At a radius of vision $R=2$, the most of them are disconected. When radius is $R=5.9$, some large clusters are formed. Near the Percolation threshold, $R=11.9$, there is a single white cluster in the figure.

We want to determine the values of the parameters that ensure the mutual influence of individuals. For this purpose we consider the models of Percolation

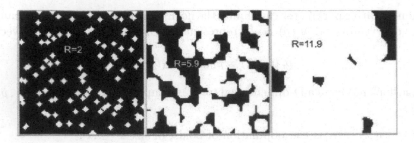

Fig. 1. Spatial neighborhoods of randomly positioned boids for various values of R. Largest radius ensures spatial connectivity.

of continuum systems [1] formed of overlapping $\mathcal{P}$ disks of radius R randomly placed following an uniform spatial distribution in the square world. This is the standard Gilbert disk model or equivalently the Boolean model $G_{R,\lambda}$, used to model an infinite communication network of transceivers that can communicate if they are at euclidean distance at most R. An algorithm to randomly generate such a graph $G_{R,\lambda}$, consists in generating a population of $\mathcal{P}$ disks of radius R whose centers (the nodes of G_R) are selected in the plane $\mathbb{R}^2$ by a two dimensional uniform distribution. After this, nodes at distance lower than R are linked by an undirected edge. The number of points $\mathcal{P}$ is a random variable generated from a Poisson distribution with mean λ that is approximated, for large values of λ by a normal distribution of mean λ and and standard deviation $\sqrt{\lambda}$ given by:

$$P_\lambda(n) = P(\mathcal{P} = n) = \frac{\lambda^n e^{-\lambda}}{n!} \tag{11}$$

An square world of side S is divided in S^2 patches of side 1 and a population of $\mathcal{P}$ individuals is distributed over it. Is the distribution randomly created?. Let $\lambda = \frac{\mathcal{P}}{S^2}$ be the mean number of individual per patch. The Poisson distribution predicts that the number of patches with n boids will be $S^2 P_\lambda(n)$ where $n = 0, 1, 2, \ldots, \mathcal{P}$. The problem of Percolation on Gilbert disk model consist in determining if an infinite graph $G_R = G_{R,\lambda}$ generated by a Poisson process is connected. Let $D_{R,\lambda} \subseteq \mathbb{R}^2$ be the set of points over the disks around the nodes of $G_{R,\lambda}$. It is well known that $G_{2R,\lambda}$ has an infinite connected component if an only if $D_{R,\lambda}$ is unbound. A few well-known results on disk Percolation:

– Let x be a node of $G_{R,\lambda}$. The degree of x has a Poisson distribution with mean:

$$a = \lambda A = \lambda \pi R^2 = \frac{\mathcal{P}}{S^2} \pi R^2, \tag{12}$$

therfore, in our problem the number of expected neighbors in the vision area per boid varies in the interval $\lambda \pi R^2 \pm R\sqrt{\lambda \pi}$. Usually, a is called the *degree* of graph $G_{R,\lambda}$, the *connected area* or simply the *area*. Imagine that the spatial neighborhood is filled with white while the background is black. Since $\mathcal{P}\pi R^2$ represents the sum of the areas of vision of all the boids, a is the fraction of white points per patch.

– Since $a > 1$ when $\mathcal{P}\pi R^2 > S^2$, function Φ represents the fraction of a normalized to interval $[0,1]$, $\Phi_{P,S}$ represents fraction f as a function of the radius R with a population parameter $\mathcal{P}$ and size parameter S. Figure 2 shows a as a function of R in comparison to $\Phi_{100,100}$; note that radius $R = \sqrt{\frac{S^2}{\pi P}} = \frac{10}{\sqrt{\pi}} = 5.642$ sets the limit when area $a = 1$ and white zone is large enough to cover the whole square. Increasing R from that Figure 3 shows $\Phi_{P,S}$ for population of $\mathcal{P} = 100$ boids in a square of side $S = 10,100$ and 1000 patches.

$$\Phi(a) = 1 - e^{-a} \tag{13}$$

$$\Phi_{P,S}(R) = 1 - e^{-\frac{P}{S^2}\pi R^2} \tag{14}$$

– Let $\mathcal{P}_\lambda$ be the set of centers of the disk, we can assume without loss of generality that point $\bar{0} = (0,0) \in \mathcal{P}_\lambda$. We denote $\theta(R,\lambda) = \theta(a)$ the probability that the connected component to which the origin beongs is infinite. Since $\theta(a)$ is an increasing function, $0 \le \theta(a) \le 1$, by the 0-1 law of Kolmogorov, there is a *critical area* a_c such that $\theta(a) = 0$ for $a < a_c$ and $\theta(a) > 0$ for $a > a_c$ and $\theta(a_c) = p_c$ is the Percolation probability threshold. To get bounds to approximate a_c, the easiest way is to compare to well known models based on regular lattices, such as the *face Percolation* (the face is the area of the polygon) on hexagonal lattice where a face is open with probability p and two faces are neighbors if they share an edge. In this way we know that the critical number of neighboring boids in a disk will be limited by:

$$2.184 \le a_c \le 10.588 \tag{15}$$

For a population of $\mathcal{P} = 100$ boids in a world of side $S = 100$, from equation 15 we may find bounds on the the radius of vision R using equation 15 as follows:

$$R(a) = \sqrt{\frac{aS^2}{\pi P}} \Rightarrow 8.338 \le R_c \le 18.358 \tag{16}$$

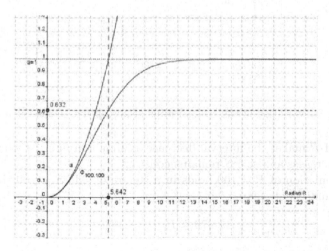

Fig. 2. Percolation: the connected area a as a function of R compared to $\Phi_{100,100}$

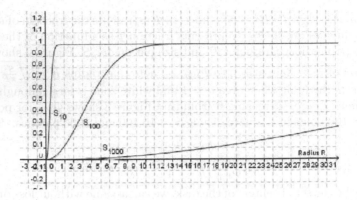

Fig. 3. $\Phi_{P,S}$ for population of $\mathcal{P} = 100$ boids in a square of side $S = 10, 100$ and 1000 patches

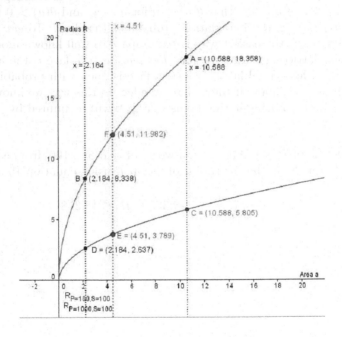

Fig. 4. Variation of the boid's radius of perception versus the area

The curve of R makes the interval decrease as shown in figure 4 when the population P increases and size S remains constant.

For a population of $P = 100$ boids in a square of side $S = 100$ the radius of vision is bounded between:

$$11.979 \leq R_c \leq 11.988 \tag{17}$$

5   Conclusions

Swarm Intelligence can provide good (close to optimal) responses to combinatorial optimization problems through the interpretation of the appropriate metaphor. However, we need also that this response is fast, if it can be of use for something close to practical aplications. In this paper we focus on flocking behaviors because we have shown in a previous paper [2] that this kind of Swarm Intelligence can be applied to find optimal solutions to the problem of graph coloring, improving over other heuristics given in the literature for this problem. Then we feel the strong need to study some convergence requirements. Convergence of the Boids SI needs at least that all the individual boids may somehow sense or be connected to all the other boids. Looking for simple relations among the system parameters that may influence convergence, we have related in this paper the notion of Percolation with the spatial connectivity of the boids provided through their sensing radius. We have provided computational results that show that the general theory of Percolation can actually be used to set the system parameters (sensing radius, space size depending on population size) so that convergence is guaranteed to the (near) optimal solution is minimized.

References

1. Bollobs, B., Riordan, O.: Percolation. Cambridge University Press, UK (2006)
2. Cases, B., Hernandez, C., Graña, M., D'anjou, A.: On the ability of swarms to compute the 3-coloring of graphs. In: Bullock, S., Noble, J., Watson, R., Bedau, M.A. (eds.) Artificial Life XI: Proceedings of the Eleventh International Conference on the Simulation and Synthesis of Living Systems, pp. 102–109. MIT Press, Cambridge (2008)
3. Deneubourg, J.L., Goss, S., Franks, N., Sendova-Franks, A., Detrain, C., Chrétien, L.: The dynamics of collective sorting robot-like ants and ant-like robots. In: Proceedings of the first international conference on simulation of adaptive behavior on From animals to animats, pp. 356–363. MIT Press, Cambridge (1990)
4. Dorigo, M., Blum, C.: Ant Colony Optimization theory: a survey. Theorical Computer Science 344, 243–278 (2005)
5. Dorigo, M., Di Caro, G.: Ant Colony Optimization: A New Meta-Heuristic. In: Angeline, P.J., Michalewicz, Z., Schoenauer, M., Yao, X., Zalzala, A. (eds.) Proceedings of Congress on Evolutionary Computation (CEC 1999), Washington DC, July 6-9. IEEE Press, Los Alamitos (1999)
6. Dorigo, M., Gambardella, L.M.: Ant Colonies for the Traveling Salesman Problem. BioSystems 43, 73–81 (1997)
7. Eberhart, R.C., Shi, Y., Kennedy, J.: Swarm Intelligence, 1st edn. Morgan Kaufmann, San Francisco (March 2001)
8. Grimmett, G.R.: Percolation, 2nd edn. Springer, Heidelberg (1999)
9. Kasteleyn, P.W., Fortuin, C.M.: Phase transitions in lattice systems with random local properties. Journal of the Physical Society of Japan 26(Suppl.), 11–14 (1969)
10. Mizuno, K., Nishihara, S.: Constructive generation of very hard 3-colorability instances. Discrete Applied Mathematics 156(2), 218–229 (2008)
11. Reynolds, C.W.: Flocks, herds, and schools: A distributed behavioral model. Computer Graphics 21 (1987)
12. Reynolds, C.W.: Steering Behaviors for Autonomous Characters (1999), http://www.red3d.com/cwr/papers/1999/gdc99steer.html

Using MOGA to Order Batches in a Real World Pipeline Network

L.V.R. Arruda, Flávio Neves-Jr., and Lia Yamamoto

Universidade Tecnoógica Federal do Paraná
Av. 7 de setembro, 3165,
80230-901 Curitiba-PR, Brazil
{lvrarruda,neves,lia}@uttpr.edu.br

Abstract. The scheduling of activities to distribute oil derivate products through a pipe network is a complex combinatorial problem that presents a hard computational solution. This problem could be decomposed on three sub problems according to the key elements of scheduling: assignment of resources, sequencing of activities, and determination of resource timing utilization by these activities. This work develops a model to the sequencing sub-problem. The main objective is to develop a multi-objective genetic algorithm to order oil derivate products batches input into the network. From the operational practice, the batches sequencing has great influence on the final scheduling result. The MOGA model provides a set of solutions that means different options of pipeline operations, in a small computational time. This work contributes to the development of a tool to aid the specialist to solve the batch sequencing problem, which reflects in a more efficient use of the pipeline network.

Keywords: scheduling, pipeline network, multi-objective genetic algorithm.

1 Introduction

Decision making problems arise in a variety of technical areas such as: logistics, finances, transportation, image processing, among others. In general these problems can be modeled as optimization problems with multiple objectives and constraints satisfaction and cannot be handled independently of the underlying optimizer. One approach to deal with these problems has been based on Integer/Linear Programming methods. An alternative approach to deal multi-objective optimization problems can be the use of metaheuristic methods, where the guaranty of finding optimal solutions is sacrificed for the sake of getting good solutions in a limited computational time [1]. Among the metaheuristic methods, the Genetic algorithms can be very robust and easy to be implemented [1]-[2].

In this context, this paper presents the development of an optimization model based on Multi-Objective Genetic Algorithm (MOGA) that helps scheduling activities of a pipeline network in the Brazilian oil industry. This network transports oil refined products and ethanol having high-aggregated value from refineries and harbors to

N. García-Pedrajas et al. (Eds.): IEA/AIE 2010, Part III, LNAI 6098, pp. 546–555, 2010.

distribution centers. The main goal is to support the decision-making process, which is particularly complex due to existence of many areas and pipes subject to particular operational constraints.

In a former paper, we have proposed a decomposition approach to address this scheduling problem [3]. This approach decomposes the problem into a hierarchy of sub-problems based on the three key elements of scheduling: assignment of resources, sequencing of activities and determination of timing for resources used by these activities [3]. Each problem can be solved separately by an appropriate technique. The assignment problem and the sequencing problem use constructive heuristics based on expert knowledge of network operation, and the timing solution is obtained with a Mixed Integer Linear Programming model [3]. However, the batches sequencing is a multi-objective problem, which includes the production and demand forecasts, the storage, and a list of transporting products priorities. The solution of this multi-objective problem is a very difficult task, due to conflicts between the objectives and the size of the network [4]. In general, the network scheduler cannot easily propose the several sequences of batches to transfer. They usually choose solutions (sequence) that solve the problem (transfer), without consider if there is a better or a cheaper alternative. Therefore it is proposed the use of multi-objective genetic algorithm to solve this multi-objective combinatorial optimization problem. The problem's complexity and the necessity of a tool which supports the specialist decisions makes this work have great influence on the operational scheduling result [4].

The remainder of the paper is organized as follows. The pipeline network and the batch sequencing sub-problem description are presented in section 2. The MOGA model to the sequencing problem is explained in section 3. Illustrative instances of a real-world scenario are given in section 4. The concluding remarks are presented in section 5.

2 Real Pipeline Network

The studied pipeline network is located at the southeast Brazil. Fig. 1 shows a schematic graph of this network which involves 9 areas (nodes) including 3 refineries (nodes N1, N3, and N7), 1 harbor (N9) which either receives or sends products, and 5 distribution centers. In addition, it includes 15 pipes, each one with a particular volume (e.g. pipe 1 has more than 42000 m3). The nodes are "connected" by various pipes (e.g. pipes 3, 4, and 5 connect nodes 2 and 3). A product can take many hours to reach the final destination. A batch can remain in a pipe until another batch pushes it. Pipes 5, 7, and 15 can have reversed their flow direction, according to operational procedures. Each product presents a specific tank farm within the considered node. More than 10 oil refined products and ethanol can be transported. For instance, a "typical operation" involves pumping a batch from N3 to N8, passing by N2, N5 and N7. In this case, product is pumped through pipes 4, 8, 12, and 14.

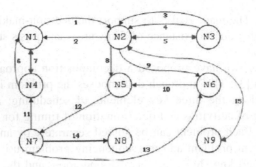

Fig. 1. The Southeast Brazilian pipeline network corresponding graph

The general guidelines used to model the pipeline network are summarized by items (1) to (9), described below:

1. The overall planning of production/consumption during a month for each product in each node is established in advance by the company. The total volume for each product has to be split into smaller volumes (batches), in order to be pumped.
2. Products can be pumped from different origin areas. For each area a set of pumping batches is computed and a list of all batches must be ordered (batch sequence) for the entire network. The generated sequence of batches is according to the scheduling horizon.
3. A route is a path of pipes connecting two network nodes. Note that a route can have only a pipe or several pipes connecting intermediary nodes, but it always links an origin area to a destination area. Due to operational practices, there are favourite routes for each product. These routes are set in a typical tuple composed by a product, an origin and a destination. Different routes can share the same pipe segments, thus the batches can compete to use these segments during the scheduling horizon.
4. For each product and/or route, there is a "typical flow rate value" (pumping rate) in each origin area. However, this pumping rate can be affected by the own products to be pumped.
5. Some network pipes can have reversed their flow direction according to operational convenience. Specific procedures are required to manage such operational condition. In order to implement a "flow reversion", an entire set of batches is pumped in one direction. Afterwards, it is necessary to insert an auxiliary batch of a non-miscible product with the same volume of the considered pipe to push out (finalize pumping) of batches in this flow direction. The pumping direction can then be reverted and a set of products can be pumped according to the new direction. The auxiliary batch that will be used to accomplish a flow reversion operation must be specified a priori in batch sequences.
6. A set of tanks in each area can store different products. Inventory level can increase or decrease according to the initial stored volume and pumping rate for each product. The inventory levels are also affected by local production and consumption market of areas. However, there are upper and lower limits to the overall product inventory in each node.

7. Due to product inventory constraints in each node, a specific batch has to be sent or received during a certain time interval (or time window). In order to avoid reaching inventory limits, the model determines time windows within batches should be sent or received.
8. There is no physical separation between successive products as they are pumped. Consequently, there is a contamination volume (interface) between miscible products. Some interfaces are not operationally recommended and a plug (a small volume of product) can be used to avoid them, even increasing the operational cost.
9. Pipes always operate fulfilled and some of them have a considerable volume. Thus, they can "store" different products during pumping procedures. These products can be pumped to tanks or routed to other pipes. Although a new product being pumped has a particular destination, previously "stored" products should be pushed out to their original destination.

Accurate interfaces detection and optimization of batch sizes, configuration and sequencing are important factors for reducing operational costs of pipeline transportation [3]-[4]. The pipeline operators take some actions for choosing batch configurations and sequences: They avoid interfacing products that are not miscible and group similar products sequentially. Moreover, they take care to order batch whose routes share the same pipe segments. A bad order can block the network during days. Other factors are also important for operational scheduling and they can influence a sequencing of batches: batch tracking and location throughout the entire pipe network, appropriated arrival time and expected delivering rate. These features are important for swapping of valves and pumps among products at each receiving node. In this paper, the batch sequencing problem consists of determining particular sequences of batches to be pumped at each origin area and following a given route, in order to minimize the overall operational cost. We propose a MOGA model for solving it.

2.1 The Sequencing Problem

As discussed in [3], the input data to the sequencing problem is a set of batches which must be ordered and inputted into the network subject to time constraints. Some other information about product transfers as route and typical flow rate must also be considered to generate the ordered list of batches. All information is shown in table 1. For example, if we look for batch #3 in this table, we can see that this batch must be sent from the refinery in node N7 to the destination node N5, by means of route #26. This is a batch composed by 10000 m^3 of product type 5 and it will be pumped with a typical flow rate of 350 m^3/h. Moreover, this batch must pump out refinery until 175h after the beginning of scheduling time (0h) and it must to attain the destination until 217h. These time limits are related to the inventory management. The lower time limit to pump (LTP) is given by the time when complete volume of product is available to be delivered. The upper time (UTP) establishes a time when there is no tank to store a product in a production node. Therefore, the batch should be delivered or the refinery campaign has to be stopped. In a destination node, the lower time limit (LTR) indicates when a tank farm has enough space to store a receiving batch. The upper time limit (UTR) occurs when the inventory level of a product fall down to the minimum allowed one.

Table 1. Example of input data to the sequencing problem

Batch (#)	Origin Node	Destination Node	Product (#)	Volume (m³)	Route (#)	Flow rate (m³/h)	LTP (h)	UTP (h)	LTR (h)	UTR (h)
1	N7	N4	5	15000	23	450	0	92	0	91
2	N3	N8	2	27000	18	1000	0	164	0	104
3	N7	N5	5	10000	26	350	0	175	0	217
4	N1	N9	6	25000	7	850	0	2000	0	104
5	N1	N4	3	5000	8	190	0	2000	0	134

The Sequencing MOGA model aims to put in order (reorganize) all batches in order to optimize batches sequencing to be pumped. This optimization problem must consider previously calculated time windows and network physical characteristics and inventory levels. The main goal is to provide one or more sequences of ordered batches which satisfy the different requirements for each area. The following performance indexes can be used to compare different sequences:

- Makespan – the total time needed to implement the scheduling.
- Interface – the total number of different products that have been alternated into all pipes. For example, three different batches B1, B2 and B3 must pass by the same pipe; the batches B1 and B2 are the same product and the batch B3 has a different product. If the sequence of batches in the pipe is B1, B2, B3 then only one interface is generated among B2 and B3, however if the sequence is B1, B3, B2 or B2,B3, B1, two interfaces are generated resulting in a bigger lost of products or a plug insertion.
- Time windows' violation: This index indicates the total number of batches delivered and/or received out of time windows discussed above. The index is related to inventory level violations, because the time windows were calculated based on consumption/production functions and the tank farm of the areas. There are four types of time violations:

For delivering terminals (refineries and harbors):

- Batch advanced time – a batch enters into the network in a time smaller than its "Lower time limit to pump". This situation may indicate a lack of product to compose the entire batch volume.
- Batch delayed time - a batch enters into the network in a time greater than its "Upper time limit to pump". This situation may indicate a lack of tank farm to store the product from the production line.

For receiving terminals (distribution centers and harbors):

- Batch advanced time – a batch arrives to a terminal in a time smaller than its "Lower time limit to receive". This situation may indicate a lack of tank farm to store the arriving product.
- Batch delayed time - a batch arrives to a terminal in a time greater than its "Upper time limit to receive". This situation may indicate a lack of product to supply the market demand. This constraint violation has a great impact in a real scenario (product shortage).

The concept of Pareto-optimality provides the potential to simultaneously address multiple objectives, such as time windows violation and interface counting. Considering an optimization problem with multiples objectives functions $f(x) = (f_1(x), f_2(x), $,

$f_n(x),)$, $i \in I = \{1,..., n\}$ and $n \geq 2$. We whish to determine from among the set of all solution x the particular $x*$ in which all the $f_i(x*)$, have a minimum in the feasible region F. The definition of Pareto-optimality establish that a point $x* \in F$ is Pareto optimal if there does not exist another $x \in F$ such that $f_i(x) \leq f_i(x^*)$ for all $i \in I$ and, $f_j(x) < f_j(x^*)$ for at least one j [2].

In words, this definition says that $x*$ is Pareto optimal if there exists no feasible solution x which would decrease some criterion without causing a simultaneous increase in at least one criterion. The Pareto optimum almost always gives not a single solution, but rather a set of solutions called non-dominated solutions [2].

3 MOGA Model

Metaheuristics and GA in particular, have proved to be suitable for solving scheduling problems in manufacturing industry. However, only a limited number of papers refer to a single pipeline or scheduling of a pipeline network based on a GA approach [4].Genetic Algorithms (GA's) are a technique of optimization and search proposed by Holland [5]. This technique is based on theory of biological evolution, using operators such as mutation and crossover to find good solutions for a broad range of problems [6].

The genetic search starts with a "population" of randomly generated solutions. The evaluation function and genetic operators of crossover and mutation are used to improve solutions, while searching for better solutions. There are two important issues in the evolution process of genetic search: population diversity and selective pressure [7]. Sampling mechanisms attempt to achieve balance between these two factors. The most used sampling mechanism, named elitism, enforces preserving the best individual in next generations.

One of the major difficulties of GA-based search in multi-criteria optimization regards middling points (points that are good but not excellent along any criterion). If the rationale of Pareto optimality is accepted, all locally non-dominated individuals should have the same reproductive potential. Although simple, this approach leads to the potential for bias against middling individuals. According to Goldberg [6], to maintain appropriate diversity, the non-dominated sorting procedure should be used in conjunction with the techniques of niche formation and speciation. One the most used technique is the fitness share that averages the fitness of individuals with the same rank, so that all of them are samples at the same rate. This procedure keeps the global population fitness constant while maintaining appropriate selective pressure. The MOGA algorithm with fitness share as proposed by [2] is a very simple, efficient and robust tool to solve multi-objective problem as the sequencing problem described above. In this paper we use the MOGA algorithm with fitness share as described in [8].

3.1 Individual Representation (Solution Codification)

Due to characteristics of the sequencing problem, a simple codification is to let the chromosome, i.e. the sequence of genes, represent the feed order in which the batches are "entered" into the network. Thus, each individual or chromosome in the population is formed by a permutation of the batches coded as an integer string. Each integer or gene corresponds to the number of the batch obtained from the initial list (batch #

column in table 1), generated by the assignment block. The position corresponds to the order of sequencing. Fig. 2 illustrates this encoding method in which the third batch entering in the network is the batch #5.

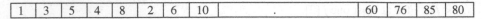

| 1 | 3 | 5 | 4 | 8 | 2 | 6 | 10 | . | 60 | 76 | 85 | 80 |

Fig. 2. Chromosome representation (solution)

3.2 Initialization

A set of "n" individuals are randomly generated from the initial list provided by the input data (batch # column in table 1). If any generated individual is infeasible, it is dismissed and replaced by a new one.

3.3 Fitness Assignment

Given an ordered list of batches, a set of computed time windows, and a network initial state, we use the MILP model described in [3] to determine the scheduling of operational activities during a programming horizon. This model compute to each sequence (individual in the population) the time duration of pumping and receiving operations (makespan), time duration of batch halts and delays or advance on delivering or receiving a batch at each node, according to time windows. This computation is used to rank the solution in accordance with the several criteria discussed above. The use of the MILP model to compute the performance indexes is a natural choice due to the decomposition approach used to solve the problem [3].

3.4 Crossover and Mutation Operators

The crossover operator uses two parents (two different solutions) to generate one or two offsprings (new solutions). In this paper, the uniform crossover is used. For each bit in the first offspring, it decides (with some probability p) which parent will contribute its value in that position. The second offspring would receive the bit from the other parent [7]. However, it is possible in a GA to obtain an unfeasible solution after applying genetic operators. A main issue is how to deal with such infeasible solutions. One option is to dismiss all infeasible solutions. Another common solution is to apply a repairing algorithm.

In this paper, an infeasible solution has a sequence of batches presenting an unrealistic time windows. For example, a batch is delivered before it is produced. In this case, a mutation operator is applied in order to repair the solution. The repair consists in to fix the batch times to the known limits of time windows (LTP and UTP for delivering nodes or LTR and UTR for receiving nodes). A mutation operator is also applied when crossover generates offsprings similar to individuals that are already present in population.

4 Simulated Results

A case study corresponding to a real scenario occurred in February, 2006 is used to validate the proposed model. The required demand of products for each node is given in Table 2. This demand must be scheduled during a month. The goal of the optimization is to reduce the time windows violations and the numbers of interfaces while minimizing the makespan. For this scenario the company planning has computed 74 batches and their associated route and time limits as shown in table 1. These batches were sequenced by our proposed MOGA model. The model is run for 2 different initial populations. The resultant non-dominated solutions for each execution are shown in table 3. For each experiment, these are the best obtained solution in the Pareto sense of optimality. Two possible scheduling (two selected solutions) to the studied scenario are illustrated through gantt charts in Fig. 3.

Table 2. Product demand (10^3 m^3) at each node to the studied scenario

	N1	N2	N3	N4	N5	N6	N7	N8	N9
Product 1	20	154							
Product 2								215	
Product 3	296		27	58	60		97		
Product 4									100
Product 5	30		39	68	52		86		
Product 6	694		80						200
Product 7	221		26						9

In the gantt charts, each batch has an identifying number, which remains the same as the batch passes through different pipelines (Pipe 1 is shown in top of gantt chart and pipe 15 is on the bottom). For example, in figure 3(a) batch 2 passes through pipes 2, 8, 12, and 14. The batches of the same product have the same color. By comparing both solutions, we can see that they are strongly different. For example, the sequence of batches passing through pipe 11 present 7 interfaces for solution 3(a) and only 4 interfaces for solution 3(b). Furthermore, the batch of blue product in pipe 1 is the 24rd batch to enter into the network for solution 3(a) and the same batch is the 14th in the solution 3(b).The solution 3(a) present a smaller makespan. Both solutions are feasible and the expert can choose one of them in accordance with his/her personal preferences.

Table 3. Non-dominated solutions for two experiments

Non-dominated solution		Makespan	Total number of interface	Number of batches sent out of time windows	Number of batches received out of time windows
Experiment	Solution				
1	1	717	35	10	12
	2	754	35	14	8
	3	734	27	12	13
	4	734	34	13	11
2	1	734	36	8	13
	2	774	30	9	11
	3	734	29	9	9
	4	734	35	10	8

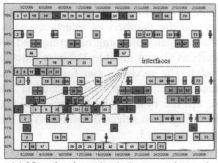

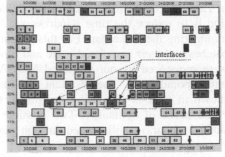

(a) Non-dominated solution experiment 1   (b) Non-dominated solution experiment 2

Fig. 3. Ordered sequences for 2 non-dominated solutions

In resume, the batch sequence entering into the pipeline network is a complex combinatorial problem and the proposed MOGA model has configured an efficient tool to support operational decisions of short-term scheduling in this real-world scenario.

5 Conclusions

We have developed a MOGA model for sequencing batches in a pipeline network scheduling problem. The proposed approach has been tested with real-world scenarios, which covering time horizons of a month and involves more than 70 batches. The several criteria used to order the batches consider operational characteristics of the network such as inventory constraints and production/demand profiles (associated to time windows), presence of interface among products, and others. Since the ordered sequence of pumped products has an important impact over the short-term scheduling, the activities ordering heuristic used by the expert can fail for particular cases. In general, the MOGA model allowed obtain satisfactory solutions with a reduction in the number of time windows violation. Furthermore, among the computed solutions, the network operator can choose the sequence which allows a better level of inventory during the time horizon or a reduced product interfaces. Finally, for future work over the sequencing model, a more detailed formulation would enable to obtain optimized sequences with other operational criteria. Also, an elitism strategy must be inserted into the MOGA model in order to select better solution over the entire Pareto frontier.

Acknowledgments. The authors acknowledge financial support from Brazilian Petroleum Agency (ANP/FINEP) grant PRH-ANP/MCT PRH10-UTFPR and Brazilian Research Council (CNPq) for grant 305188/2007-0.

References

1. Hertz, A., Widmer, M.: Guidelines for the use of meta-heuristics in combinatorial optimization. European Journal of Operational Research 151, 247–252 (2003)
2. Fonseca, C.M., Fleming, P.J.: Genetic algorithms for multi-objective optimization: formulation, discussion and generalization. In: Proceedings of the 5th international conference on genetic algorithms, pp. 416–423 (1993)

3. Neves Jr., F., Arruda, L.V.R., Magatão, L., Stebel, S.L., Boschetto, S.N., Felizari, L.C., Czaikowski, D.I., Rocha, R., Ribas, P.C.: An efficient approach to the operational scheduling of a real-world pipeline network. In: Proceedings of 17th European Symposium on Computer Aided Process Engineering (ESCAPE 17), Bucharest, pp. 697–702 (2007)
4. Yamamoto, L.: A metaheuristic based model to order batch in pipeline networks. Doctoral Dissertation, UTFPR, Brazil (2009) (in Portuguese)
5. Holland, J.H.: Adaptation in natural and artificial systems. University of Michigan Press, Ann Arbor (1975)
6. Goldberg, D.E.: Genetic algorithms in search, optimization, and machine learning. Addison-Wesley, Ann Arbor (1989)
7. Michalewicz, Z.: Genetic algorithms + data structures = evolution programs. Springer, Heidelberg (1996)
8. Konak, A., Coit, D.W., Smith, A.E.: Multi-objective optimization using genetics algorithms: a tutorial. Reliability Engineering and System Safety 91, 992–1007 (2006)

Temporal Bounded Planner Agent for Dynamic Industrial Environments

Juan F. De Paz[1], Martí Navarro[2], Sara Rodríguez[1], Vicente Julián[2], Javier Bajo[1], and Juan M. Corchado[1]

[1] Department of Computer Science and Automation, University of Salamanca Plaza de la Merced s/n, 37008, Salamanca, Spain
{fcofds,srg,jbajope,corchado}@dsic.upv.es
[2] Departamento de Sistemas Informáticos y Computación, Universidad Politécnica de Valencia Camino de Veras s/n, 46022, Valencia, España
{mnavarro,vinglada}@dsic.upv.es

Abstract. This paper presents a time bounded real-time agent, the core of a Multi-agent System aimed at managing the security in manufacturing environments, where time constraints are a key factor. The time bounded real-time agent integrates a novel case-based planning mechanism. The planning mechanism uses past experiences to generate new plans and focuses in optimizing the industrial and manufacturing processes, and more concretely the tasks performed by the available personnel focusing on the automatic temporal bounded reorganization of tasks. This study describes the new agent and presents a case study where the agent is applied to a real scenario.

Keywords: Multiagent Systems, Temporal Bounded reasoning.

1 Introduction

Multi-agent systems (MAS) [1] have been recently explored as supervision systems, with the flexibility to be implemented in a wide variety of devices and scenarios, including industrial and manufacturing environments. Most of the times MAS are used to monitor the workers´ activities. However, sometimes it is necessary to establish a temporal control of the actions that the system performs that allow the system to work in environments in real time.

This paper focuses on the problem of monitoring workers and task planning in manufacturing scenarios. It presents a MAS that incorporates a special type of intelligent real-time agent [2], characterized by an internal structure that integrates a mathematical model based on a symbolic computational model derived from the TB-CBP-BDI (Case-Based Planning) [3] [4] [5] (Beliefs, Desires, Intentions) [6] model. A typical real-time system is commonly known to be made up of a set of tasks characterized by a deadline, a period of time, a worst case execution time and an assigned priority. A TB-CBP is a specialization of a TB-CBR, which uses past experiences to resolve new problems with a temporal binding process, which is precisely one of the innovations of the paper. Moreover, the phases of the CBP system incorporate a subsymbolic BDI model, based on Artificial Neural Networks (ANN), for resolving the

N. García-Pedrajas et al. (Eds.): IEA/AIE 2010, Part III, LNAI 6098, pp. 556–565, 2010.

problems at a low level of detail. BDI agents use mental aptitudes as beliefs, desires and intentions to develop intentional processes.

The agent model proposed in this paper has been used to construct a MAS prototype initially designed to schedule and supervise routes for security guards working in manufacturing environments. The work presented in this paper is an extension of a previously existing system that aimed at monitoring workers, but did not take temporal constraints into account [7]. In this sense, we will focus on the temporal binding mechanism, which is capable of re-planning routes while complying with the temporal restrictions that inherent to real time agents, and how this mechanism can improve the performance of the overall system.

Section 2 explains the TB-CBP-BDI agent. Section 3 presents a case study in industrial scenarios, and finally, Section 4 reports the results and conclusions obtained.

2 Temporal Bounded Case-Based Planner Agent

CBR-BDI agents [3] use the CBR concept to gain autonomy and improve its problem-solving capabilities. CBP is a variation of CBR [8], which consists of the idea of planning as remembering [1]. In CBP, the solution proposed to solve a given problem is a plan, so this solution is generated by taking into account the plans applied to solve similar problems in the past. The problems and their corresponding plans are stored in a memory of plans. In practice, what is stored is not only a specific problem with a specific solution, but also additional information about how the plans have been derived.

To obtain a correct functioning of CBP in real-time environments it is necessary to redefine the classical CBR cycle as a TB-CBR. In the TB-CBP proposed in this paper it is possible to find two stages: the *learning stage*, which consists of the revise and retain phases of the classic CBR cycle, and the *deliberative stage*, which includes the retrieve and reuse phases. The execution of both phases will be time scheduled. Therefore, the real-time agent has the ability to choose between assigning more time to the deliberative stage or keeping more time for the learning stage (and thus, the design agents that are more sensitive to updates). These new stages must be designed as an anytime algorithm [9], where the process is iterative and each iteration is time-bounded and may improve the final response.

In this paper, we propose a novel model of CBP-BDI agent that integrates a TB-CBP engine to take temporal constraints into account. This makes it possible to integrate both the symbolic and sub-symbolic models so that the BDI-based agents can decide what action to take at any given moment according to their objectives. The terminology used for a BDI agent model [3][6] is as follows:

- The environment or world M and the changes that are produced within it, are represented as a set of variables that influence a problem faced by the agent

$$M = \{\tau_1, \tau_2, \cdots, \tau_s\} \text{ with } s < \infty \qquad (1)$$

- The beliefs are vectors of some (or all) of the attributes of the world using a set of concrete values

$$B = \{b_i / b_i = \{\tau_1^i, \tau_2^i, \cdots, \tau_n^i\}, n \le s \quad \forall i \in N\}_{i \in N} \subseteq M \tag{2}$$

- A state of the world $e_j \in E$ is represented for the agent by a set of beliefs that are true at a specific moment in time t. Let $E = \{e_j\}_{j \in N}$ set of status of the world. If we fix the value of t then

$$e_j^t = \{b_1^{jt}, b_2^{jt}, \cdots b_r^{jt}\}_{r \in N} \subseteq B \quad \forall j, t \tag{3}$$

- The desires are the applications between the state of the current world and another that it is trying to reach

$$d : E \quad \rightarrow \quad E \atop e_0 \quad \rightarrow \quad e_* \tag{4}$$

- Intentions are the way that the agent's knowledge is used in order to reach its objectives. A desire is attainable if the application i, defined through n beliefs exists:

$$i : \overset{n)}{BxBx \cdots xBxE} \quad \rightarrow \quad E \atop (b_1, b_2, \cdots\cdots\cdots, b_n, e_0) \quad \rightarrow \quad e_* \tag{5}$$

- We define an agent action as the mechanism that provokes changes in the world making it change the state,

$$a_j : E \quad \rightarrow \quad E \atop e_i \quad \rightarrow \quad a_j(e_i)=e_j \tag{6}$$

- Agent plan is the name we give to a sequence of actions that, from a current state e_0, define the path of states through which the agent passes in order to reach the other world state.

$$p_n : E \quad \rightarrow \quad E \atop e_0 \quad \rightarrow \quad p_n(e_0)=e_n \tag{7}$$

$$p_n(e_0) = e_n = a_n(e_{n-1}) = \cdots = (a_n \circ \cdots \circ a_1)(e_0) \quad p_n \equiv a_n \circ \cdots \circ a_1$$

The attributes that characterize the plans for a TB-CBP-BDI agent in the case base are presented below. These attributes allow us to relate the BDI model with the interest parameters within a TB-CBP. E is the environment, but it also represents the type of problem faced by the agent, characterized by $E = \{e_0, e_*\}$, where e_0 represents the starting point for the agent when it begins a plan, and $e*$ is the state or states that it is trying to attain. The calculation of the different actions that can reach the final state $e*$ is applied during the reuse phase, once the necessary cases have been recovered during the retrieve phase (both phases occur during the deliberative stage). The calculation is based on the application of different time sensitive techniques that are available for such situations $t_{deliberative}$. The methods used in both the recovery and the adaption phase should have a predictable execution time that can determine whether they can be executed within the period of time ($t_{retrieve}$, t_{reuse}).

The TB-CBP cycle starts at the learning stage, where it checks to see if there are previous cases waiting to be revised and possibly stored in the case-base. In our model, the plans provided at the end of the deliberative stage will be stored in a solution list while feedback about their utility is received. When each new TB-CBP cycle begins, this list is accessed. If there is enough time, the learning stage is implemented for those cases whose solution feedback has been recently received. If the list is empty, this process is omitted.

The next stage to be implemented is the deliberative stage. The retrieval algorithm is used to search the case-base and retrieve a case that is similar to the current case (i.e. one that characterizes the problem to be solved). Each time a similar case is found, it is sent to the reuse phase where it is transformed into a suitable plan for the current problem by using a *reuse* algorithm. Therefore, at the end of each iteration of the deliberative stage, the TB-CBP method is able to provide a plan for the problem at hand, although this plan can be improved in subsequent iterations if the deliberative stage has enough time to perform them.

Hence, the temporal cost of executing the *cognitive task* is greater than or equal to the sum of the execution times of the learning and deliberative stages (as shown in equation 1):

$$t_{cognitiveTask} \geq t_{learning} + t_{deliberative} \qquad (8)$$

$$t_{learning} \geq (t_{revise} + t_{retain}) * n$$

$$t_{deliberative} \geq (t_{retrieve} + t_{reuse}) * m$$

where $t_{cognitiveTask}$ is the maximum time available for the agent to provide a response, $t_{learning}$ and $t_{deliberative}$ are the total execution time of the learning and deliberative stages; t_x is the execution time of the phase x and n and m are the number of iterations of the learning and deliberative stages respectively.

The TB-CBP algorithm can be launched when the real-time agent considers it appropriate and there is enough time for it to be executed. The agent indicates to the TB-CBP the maximum time (t_{max}, where $t_{max} \geq t_{cognitiveTask}$) that it has available to complete its execution cycle. The time t_{max} must be divided between the learning and the deliberative stages to guarantee the execution of each stage. The $timeManager(t_{max})$ function is in charge of completing this task. Using this function, the designer must specify how the agent acts in the environment. The designer can assign more time to the learning stage if it desires an agent with a greater learning capacity. Otherwise, the function can allocate more time to the deliberation stage. Regardless of the type of agent, the $timeManager(t_{max})$ function should allow sufficient time for the deliberative stage to ensure a minimal answer.

The anytime behaviour of the TB-CBP is achieved through the use of two loop control sequences. The loop condition is built using the *enoughTime* function, which determines if a new iteration is possible according to the total time that the TB-CBR has to complete each stage.

The first phase of the algorithm executes the learning stage. This stage is executed only if the agent has the solutions from previous executions stored in the *solution-Queue*. The solutions are stored just after the end of the deliberative stage. The deliberative stage is only launched if the agent has a problem to solve in the *problem-Queue*. This configuration allows the agent to launch the TB-CBP in order to only learn (no solution is needed and the agent has enough time to reason previous decisions), only deliberate (there are no previous solutions to consider and there is a new problem to solve) or both.

3   Case Study: Multi-Agent System to Monitor Staff in a Industrial Environment

In order to evaluate the behaviour of the TB-CBP-BDI agents proposed in Section 2, a case study was developed in a industrial environment. The case study consisted of a multi-agent system aimed at providing control over the activities performed by the staff responsible for overseeing the manufacturing environments. The TB-CBP-BDI agents in the system calculate the surveillance routes for the security guards depending on the working shifts, the distance to be covered in the facilities and the security guards available. The system has the ability to re-plan the routes automatically according to the security personnel available. It is possible to track the workers′ activities (routes completion) using Radiofrequency Identification (RFID) [10]. The system structure is defined by five different kinds of agents:

- **Planner Agent.** Automatically generates the surveillance routes which are sent to the Manager Agent to distribute them among the security guards.
- **Guard Agent** is associated to each PDA. Manages the portable RFID readers to get the RFID tags information on every control point. Communicates with Controller Agents to check the completion of the assigned surveillance routes, to obtain new routes, and also to send the RFID tags information via Wi-Fi.
- **Manager Agent.** Controls the rest of agents in the system. Manages the connection and disconnection of Guard Agents to determine the number of security guards available. The information is sent to the Planner Agent to generate new surveillance routes.
- **Controller Agent.** Checks the control points to monitor security guards′ activities.
- **Advisor Agent.** Administers the communication with the supervisors (person). Receives an incident report from the Manager Agent and decides if it is sent to the supervisor. Incidents can be sent via Wi-Fi, SMS or GPRS.

The most important agent in the system is the Planner agent, which incorporates the TB-CBP-BDI model. The Planner agent is modeled as a real-time agent to ensure that the plans made by the TB-CBP-BDI reasoning model are carried out within the specified time. In order to adapt the TB-CBP-BDI model to the problem of security in manufacturing spaces, the environment equation (1) was defined through the following variables: security guards available, coordinates for every control point, initial time, start time, deadline and service time. The current state (3) is obtained through the number of available security guards and their corresponding control points at that moment and the time. The desires (4) are represented as the surveillance route that covers all the control points in the least amount of time given the temporal constraints. The intentions (5) are given for the neural networks that establish the sequence of states through which the system passes in order to reach the final state in which the surveillance routes have been successfully completed. The equations (10) (11) show the structure for a plan (7).

4   TB-CBP-BDI Planning Strategy

The planning is carried out by two methods: the first is a simple method that obtains very quick, albeit low quality, results; the second uses a neural network based on the Kohonen Network [11]. This method needs more time to obtain results which vary in quality according to the time spent calculating them. Next, each of the phases of the TB-CBP-BDI planner are explained in detail:

4.1   Learning Stage (Revise and Retain)

When the security guards complete their rounds they provide a report indicating whether the route was completed correctly. This information is stored in the *solution-Queue*. At the beginning of the Learning Stage, the system must confirm if there are solutions in the *solutionQueue*. If there is still time to continue carrying out this stage, the *analysisResult* function will be applied to every solution found in the *solution-Queue*. If this analysis indicates a positive assessment, then the complete plan is stored by the *retainResult* function. This plan contains the sequence of states and the corresponding belief value for each of them, i.e., the sequence of control points and their corresponding times. If the problem includes time restrictions, this information is added to the rest of the plan information. In this way, the plan will contain the following information:

$$\langle T = \{ \ x_i, a_i, s_i, e_i, t_i)/ x_i = (x_{i1}, x_{i2}), i = 1...n \}, g > \tag{9}$$

Where: x_i position (x, y) of every control point, a_i arrival Time, s_i initial time, e_i final time, t_i service time. Both the *analysisResult* and the *retainResult* functions have a fixed asintotic cost $O(1)$ and as a result, the execution time associated with each of the functions is predictable.

4.2   Retrieve Stage

In this phase the most similar plans resolved in the past, including all the control points indicated in the new problem, are recovered. The information from the plan is given by the following record.

$$< T =, t_i \} \ g > \ i = 1...n$$
$$t_i = (x_i, a_i)/ x_i = (x_{i1}, x_{i2}) \tag{10}$$

where x_i the control point i that will be visited, (x_{i1}, x_{i2}) the coordinates of point i and g the number of security guards, a_i arrival Time. The routes r_i is recovered following the equation (11) by means of *search* function.

$$R = \{r_i\}\, i = 1 \ldots g \text{ where } r_i \subseteq T, r_i \cap r_j = \phi \, \forall i \neq j \, j = 1 \ldots g \tag{11}$$

Where R is the variable case. The time that the search function allocates for recovering the cases is limited by its asintotic temporal cost O(n), where n is the number of cases stored in the database.

4.3 Reuse Stage

In this phase, the retrieved routes are represented as cases and adapted to the temporal restrictions stated in the problem description. In the first step, when no data has been retrieved in the recovery phase, uses the obtainSet function to generate a distribution of the control points that the security should visit. To do so, we use the k-means learning algorithm [12] to calculate the optimal routes and assign them to the available security guards. The inputs of the algorithm are $x_i \equiv (x_{i1}, x_{i2})$ $i = 1, \cdots N$ i the control point coordinates and N the number of control points in the route, w_{kj} is the position of the centroid k in the output layer that connects with the neuron j in the input layer. Once the input and output are established, the modified k-means algorithm is carried out to create a new allocation:

o   Establish the number k of initial groups.

o   Initiate the k initial patterns. $w_{ij} = x_{ij}$.

o   For each of the patterns, establish the nearest neuron of the output layer and associate the pattern with it. The Euclidean distance is used. Q_k represents the set of input patterns associated with the neuron of the output layer k.

$$Q_k = \{x_i / d(w_k, X_i) \leq d(w_r, X_i) \; \forall k \neq r\} \; d(w_r, X_i) = \|w_r - X_i\| \tag{12}$$

o   Calculate the new centroids of the neurons of the hidden layer as the average of the input associated patterns.

$$w_{kj} = \frac{1}{\#Q_k} \sum x_{sj} \text{ with } x_s \in Q_k \tag{13}$$

o   Repeat from step 3 until the modification of the centroids are less than α or until the maximum number of iterations is reached. It is necessary to establish a maximum number of iterations in order to shorten the maximum execution time.

$$\sum \Delta w_k = \sum \|w_k(t) - w_k(t-1)\| < \alpha \tag{14}$$

Once the points have been distributed among the different routes r_i has been made, the TB-CBP-BDI starts spreading the control points among the available security guards.

In order to obtain a solution within the specified time t_{reuse}, different procedures were used to generate the plan. The first procedure (lightPlanner) can generate a low quality, predictable solution in low execution time, while the second (heavyPlanner) uses a SOM [13] adapted to the AnyTime model to generate a priori solutions of superior quality (depending on the processing time of the method). Both systems employ automatic planning and select the best quality plan once the process is complete or the available time has expired. The quality is measured according to the final distance:

- o **lightPlanner.** The algorithm used to calculate the route is very basic. It simply puts the control points in order according to the arrival time and then selects each of the points that are closest to the last control point visited, much like the nearest neighbor algorithm. The algorithm has an asintotic cost of O(n log n) because the data must have already been put in order. As a result, the execution time can be reduced if the number of existing points is fixed.

- o **heavyPlanner.** is a modified SOM [13] that can calculate the routes that must satisfy certain temporal restrictions and must be calculated in a limited amount of time. The SOM has two layers: IN and OUT. The IN layer has two neurons, corresponding to the physical control points coordinates. The OUT layer has the same number of control points on each route [14]. Given $x_i \equiv (x_{i1}, x_{i2})$ $i = 1, \cdots . N$ the i control point coordinates and $n_i \equiv (n_{i1}, n_{i2})$ $i = 1, \cdots, N$ the i neuron coordinates on $\Re^2$, and N the number of control points in the route. The weight updating formula is defined by the following equation:

$$w_{ki}(t+1) = w_{ki}(t) + \eta(t) g(k,h,t)(x_i(t) - w_{ki}(t)). \tag{15}$$

Where w_{ki} is the weight that connects the IN layer i neuron with the OUT layer k neuron, t represents the interaction, $\eta(t)$ the learning rate; and $g(k,h,t)$ the neighborhood function, which depends on three parameters: the winning neuron, the current neuron and the interaction. A decreasing neighbourhood function is determined by the number of interactions and the winning neuron distance. To resolve optimization problems according to the temporal restrictions, it is necessary to modify the definition of the neighboring function. The restrictions that must be considered are: *service time* (the time a security guard needs to check a control point) and *initial time* and *final time,* which indicate the interval of time that the guard needs to arrive at the destination and check the control point. If the security guard arrives before start time then he will wait. The coordinates have been scaled so that the distance travelled is also a unit. This is because it is necessary for the units to be comparable to the input layer of the ANN. The information available to the input layer will be: Coordinates, start time, end time and Service.

5 Results and Conclusions

TB-CBP-BDI agents facilitate the development of temporal bounded multi-agent systems. Its model is based on a CBP approach, by incorporating a novel mechanism to take into account temporal constraints. The agent architecture proposes an alternative where agents are based on the BDI (*Belief, Desire, Intention*) model and act as planners of temporal bounded tasks. TB-CBP-BDI model exploits the agents' characteristics to provide a robust, flexible, modular and adaptable solution that can cover most requirements of a wide diversity of industrial environments. The intelligent agent presented in this paper was tested in the experimental scenario presented in Section 3. The tests included various simulations with varying configurations of the control points and a fixed number of security guards. This allowed us to compare the behavior of each of the algorithms and to estimate the execution time.

Table 1 shows the results obtained for the different configurations, with the case memory limited to 50 plans. Each of the different functions was executed 1000 times with the following results obtained, where n is the number of elements in the data base, m is the number of control points. All of the times are given in microseconds, except for those in the adaptSolution, which are milliseconds. For all of the tests performed, the real time agent was capable of finding a plan within the time limit assigned for the task. This time fluctuated within a range of values that included the minimum time required to execute the TB-CBP-BDI algorithm, in which the heavy-Planner function is not executed, and a value greater than what the heavyPlanner function allows. Lesser times are disregarded because the execution time would be greater than the imposed time restrictions.

Table 1. Execution times for the different system functions

Functions	Asintotic	20		30		40		50		60	
	Cost	$\bar{x}$	wcet	$\bar{x}$	wcet	$\bar{x}$	wcet	$\bar{x}$	wcet	$\bar{x}$	wcet
analysesResult	O(1)	>1	1	> 1	1	>1	1	>1	1	>1	1
retainResult	O(1)	201	307	224	307	217	307	232	307	224	307
search	O(n)	271	473	268	473	283	473	265	473	221	473
adaptSolution											
obtainSet	O(m)	0.006	0.02	0.008	0.02	0.010	0.03	0.011	0.03	0.013	0.03
lightPlanner	O(m log m)	0.001	0.1	0.002	0.01	0.003	0.01	0.003	0.015	0.004	0.015
heavyPlanner	---	1114		2416		4490		7322		11242	

The results obtained in the experiment are promising, since it is possible to determine the number of security guards needed to cover an entire area with routes, so the human resources are optimized. In addition, the system provides the supervisors with relevant information to monitor the workers´ activities, and to detect incidents in the surveillance routes automatically and in real-time. The system presented in this study can be easily adapted to other categories of workers and other scenarios with similar characteristics. That is our next challenge

Acknowledgements. This development was supported by the JCYL SA071A08 project.

References

[1] Wooldridge, M., Jennings, N.R.: Agent Theories, Architectures, and Languages: a Survey. In: Intelligent Agents, pp. 1–22. Springer, Heidelberg (1995)

[2] Julian, V., Botti, V.: Developing real-time multi-agent systems. Integrated Computer-Aided Engineering 11, 135–149 (2004)

[3] Corchado, J.M., Laza, R.: Constructing Deliberative Agents with Case-based Reasoning Technology. International Journal of Intelligent Systems 18(12), 1227–1241 (2003)

[4] Glez-Bedia, M., Corchado, J.M.: A planning strategy based on variational calculus for deliberative agents. Computing and Information Systems Journal 10(1), 2–14 (2002)

[5] Spalazzi, L.: A Survey on Case-Based Planning. Artificial Intelligence Review 16, 3–36 (2001)

[6] Bratman, M.: Intention, Plans and Practical Reason. Harvard University Press, Cambridge (1987)

[7] De Paz, J.F., Rodríguez, S., Bajo, J., Corchado, J.M.: Mathematical model for dynamic case based planning. International Journal of Computer Mathematics 86, 1719–1730 (2009)

[8] Kolodner, J.: Case-Based Reasoning. Morgan Kaufmann, San Francisco (1993)

[9] Dean, T., Boddy, M.: An analysis of time-dependent planning. In: Proceedings of the 7th National Conference on Artificial Intelligence, pp. 49–54 (1988)

[10] RFID Journal. RFID Journal LLC, The World's RFID Authority (2010), http://www.rfidjournal.com/

[11] Leung, K.S., Jin, H.D., Xu, Z.B.: An expanding Self-organizing Neural Network for the Traveling Salesman Problem. Neurocomputing 62, 267–292 (2004)

[12] Jennings, N., Wooldridge, M.: Applications of Intelligent Agents, Queen Mary & Westfield College, University of London (1998)

[13] Kohonen, T.: Self-Organising Maps. Springer, Heidelberg (2001)

[14] Martín, Q., Santos, M.T., De Paz, Y.: Operations research: Resolute problems and exercises, pp. 189–190. Pearson (2005)

Soft Computing, Genetic Algorithms and Engineering Problems: An Example of Application to Minimize a Cantilever Wall Cost

Fernando Torrecilla-Pinero[1], Jesús A. Torrecilla-Pinero[2],
Juan A. Gómez-Pulido[1], Miguel A. Vega-Rodríguez[1],
and Juan M. Sánchez-Pérez[1]

[1] Dep. of Technologies of Computers and Communications, University of
Extremadura, Spain
[2] Dep. of Building, University of Extremadura, Spain

Abstract. The present work offers an overview about the possibility of
using a genetic algorithm as an optimization tool for minimizing the cost
of a problem in the civil engineering area. Particularly, it goes into the
efficiency aspects of the method.

In the context of the used operators by applying the method, a new
cross-over type operator is set out, and its efficiency on its application
over a relatively simple problem is studied: cost minimization from a
cantilever wall of reinforced concrete.

Keywords: civil engineering, cantilever wall, genetic algorithms, soft-
computing, optimization.

1 Introduction

Optimization problems can generally be defined as the search of the minimum
value of a function, subject to several conditions. Although it can be considered, in an abstract form, from a strictly matematician pointview, its practical
consequences are obvius, in problems such us:

- Structural Optimization for the purpose of cost minimizing by changing
  the rigidity distribution of the elements which configure the structure. In
  structures of bars, three optimization types are usually treated as separated
  problems:
    - Topological Optimization, for obtaining the optimal position of the struc-
      tural knots.
    - Conectivity Optimization, whose purpose is, given the structural knots,
      to determine which nodes must be connected by a bar.
    - Sectional Optimization, whose purpose is, once the structural topology
      and connectivity are defined, to determine which sections are the optimal
      for the structure, that is, which sections make the global cost to be
      minimal.

N. García-Pedrajas et al. (Eds.): IEA/AIE 2010, Part III, LNAI 6098, pp. 566–575, 2010.

– Logistic Operations Optimization. In distribution or transport networks it is convenient, for the purpose of minimizing the global cost, to establish in which order must the passing nodes be connected to minimize the total number of transport unities (i.e. ton/km). In this class of problems it is also common to speak either about connectivity optimization problems, where there isn't still any transport network, or about network optimization problems, when existing it, it is tried to determine the order in which this network is covered.

At first, if the function to optimize may be expressed as $f(x)$, and it proves to be continuous and derivable, the problem could be raised in analytic form:

$$\frac{\partial f}{\partial x_i} = \mathbf{0}, i = 0, \ldots, n \tag{1}$$

Nevertheless, this approach is not usually applicable on most of the cases, among others, for the following reasons:

– The function is not usually defined $\forall x \in \Re^n$, but the possible values of the variables are limited to what we will name design space. So, in example, if we treat to optimize the section of a steel bar, the area is not a continuous function, but it is limited to the normalized profile.
– The function could not be expresable in explicit form, although its values can be calculated through an algorithm. This makes not to have neither an expression of the function, nor an analytic way to calculate its derivatives, but only approaches to them.
– Although each design variable could take any value, there could exist any design conditions that indirectly invalidate some determined variables combinations. In example, when calculating a L-wall, it could possible to have a 0.5 m toe (design variable) with a 2 m heel (another design variable), but that toe could not be compatible by wall stability reasons with another heel. So, both the heel and the cap can take any value, but only certain combinations of both variables are possible as a design.

Some simultenous procedures of analysis and optimization are, in fact, being developed, in which both processes are not differentiated as made in the classical approach [1].

2   Improved Operators Proposal

An operator quality is a messure of how much it improves the algorithm by using that operator instead of another one. Generally, in the genetic algorithms we have *hill climbing* type algorithms, that improve the solution monotonously from one generation to another, and *sampler* type algorithms, which try a huge number of solutions pseudorandomly searching the optimal.

When the possible number of designs is high, the *hill climbing* algorithms type beat the *sampler* type and, vice versa, if we have a very limited space of design, the procedures which search more systematically find a solution with a higher speed.

Given that a genetic algorithm is, by definition, iterative (it is neccessary to produce various generations-iterations to make the algorithm to begin converging), the operator that make the convergency in a minor number of iterations will be, generally, the best.

Furthermore, we can define, for the fixed population in a determined moment, two quality messures, one referred to the best design individual, which is a puntual stimation of what has been achieved with the algorithm application, and another one refered to the popultaion set, which will be given by a distributed probability function characterized by its average and its variance. If, for the number of the N-population elements, the density function gives a probability of $1/N$ to the best element to appear, both messures will be coherent, but if the probability will be lower than $1/N$, it would result that the first messure, the specific, could be deteriorated by random effects derivated from the evolution or by a specially lucky initial design.

2.1 General Approach to the Algorithm

The suggested algorithm is similar to a Genitor [8], given that two individuals from the population are going to be selected to produce a new element in the next generation. Furthermore, the algorithm is $(\mu + \lambda) - ES$-type, this is, the best elements will be selected among the ancestors and descendants to produce the new generation, and so the individual set with best value of the objective function survive through the iterations. This is so called *elitist behaviour*.

The Genitor like schema has been selected because it starts from the canonic one, it is the simplest to implement and easiest to establish the goodness of the raised algorithm.

Each one of the operators has been tuned up to, although a very strong stochastic content is present in the algorithm, maximize the probability of the descendants to inherits the ancestors aspects that make the objective function to take higher values.

2.2 Encoding-Decoding Operator

A binary alphabet has been selected, although, as commented previously in this work, binary alphabets contribute with a higher operator richness.

One 7-bit binary chain, one top value and one lower value have been stablished over each variable, so that the interval defined by [$valor_{min}$, $valor_{max}$] is divided into 128 parts. This *decision* is adopted arbitrariely, y could be selected a differnet decision for each one of the variables. In example, the wall batter, both the external and the internal, could be restricted to "constructive" values like $1/2$, $1/3$, $1/5$ and $1/10$, what would make that with only 3 bits, it will be enough for all the selected variety.

Nevertheless, this operator has been selected because it allows to change the object to optimize, since it has a coherent codification, in which each variable hold the same information quantity.

2.3   Crossing Operator

The selected crossing operator is an uniform operator in which, for each bit of descendant individual, the value corresponding to the ancestor 1 or the ancestor 2 is taken, with a probabilty proportional to the inverse of the cost function.

So, in example, if we have a wall with a cost of 100 and another one with a cost of 300, the result of their combination will have the same bits as the the first wall with a 75% probability and the same bits as the second wall with a 25% probability. This way, we can take the higher quantity of information from the best designs.

2.4   Mutation Operator

The individual obtained by crossing two ancestors is processed by the mutation operator, so, at the first, it is decided whether it is possible or not to have a mutation, with a probability inversely proportional to its cost function. For a design to be mutated, each one of its bits is changed with a prefixed probability.

That way, we reach two effects

- To have a certain selection within the mutation operator, so that the best designs are not changed by this operator.
- To change, in the worst designs, a few of their bits, so that there is a certain probability that what makes a bad design to change.

3   Improved Operator Application: An Example

A brief description of the problem and design condition imposition are exposed in this section.

3.1   Problem Description

The optimization of a reinforced concrete cantilever wall is set out. The parameters considered as design varibales in the optimization are shown in the fig. 1.

This optimization is set out from the point of view of the cost, by evaluating the following partial costs: footing excavation, concrete cost, passive steel cost and formwork cost.

The cost function is evaluated, for each design, as:

$$C(p_i) = \quad C_{ex} * Vol_{Zap} + C_h * Vol_{Muro} + C_s * \rho + \quad (2)$$
$$C_{en} * (2 * Canto_{Zap} + Long_{Intrados} + Long_{Trasdos})$$

The final design must carry out: overturning stability, slide stability, collapse stability, ultimate design limit of break for normal stress and ultimate design limit of break for shearing stress.

More design conditions could be added, but the ones set out allow an agile design of the simultaion and do not minimize generality to the problem approach.

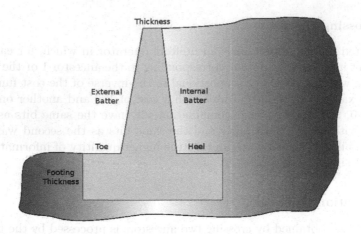

Fig. 1. Design variables used in the wall

3.2   Design Condition Imposition

The design conditions are imposed three way:

- Last design limit of break for shearing stress is imposed by restricting the space of design. Effectively, we have a design shearing stress at the beginning of the wall whose value is:

$$V_d = \frac{1}{2} \cdot K_a \cdot \gamma \cdot H^2 \cdot \gamma_f \tag{3}$$

being γ_f the coefficient of weighting actions.

The shearing stress which is able to support a section of concrete without web reinforcement, reinforced with the minimum longitudinal reinforcement in walls (0.9 per thousand as in 42.3.5 EHE[2]) is:

$$V_{u2}[0,12 \cdot \xi \cdot (100 \cdot \rho_l \cdot f_{ck})^{1/3} - 0,15\sigma_{cd}] \cdot b_0 \cdot d \tag{4}$$

Neglecting the effect of compression normal stress, and for a HA25-concrete we would have $V_{u2} = 157 \cdot dkN$. Equating $V_{u2} = V_d$ the value $d = \frac{K_a \cdot \gamma \cdot H^2 \cdot \gamma_f}{314,5}$ is obtained, and replacing the different parameters by their usual values, it is concluded $d = 0,00286 \cdot H^2$, what fixes the minimum value of d compatible with the ultimate limit state performance of shear rupture. Really, and as well known, it is not usually a limiting condition in L-walls (for 4 meters tall, in example, the minimum thickness returned by the previous function will be 5 cm), so this condition, on practical effects, is passive, since the ultimate limit state of shear rupture results more limiting and the constructive aspects that suggests a minimum thickness of 0,25 meters or H/10 to ensure proper disposal and vibrated.

- The condition of ultimate limit state of exhaustion for normal stresses is imposed through a posteriori determination of extrados vertical reinforcemente, once the thickness has been fixed. This reinforcement can, simply, be calculated from the applicant moment:

$$M_d = \frac{\gamma_f}{6} \cdot K_a H^3 \tag{5}$$

and the resisted moment for a rectangular concrete section:

$$M_r = 0,9 \cdot d \cdot A_s f_{yd} \tag{6}$$

from where we obtain

$$A_s = \frac{\frac{\gamma_f}{6} \cdot K_a H^3}{0,9 \cdot d \cdot f_{yd}} \tag{7}$$

, what take us to a simple expression of the neccessary reinforcement area:

$$A_s = 0,06264 \cdot \frac{H^3}{d} \tag{8}$$

– The conditions of overturning stability, slide and collapse have been imposed through a penalty function [5], by adding the expression

$$p \cdot \left(1 - \frac{1,5}{min(C_v, 1, 5)} \right) \tag{9}$$

to wall cost function for the overturning, the expression

$$p \cdot \left(1 - \frac{1,5}{min(C_d, 1, 5)} \right) \tag{10}$$

for the slide and the expression

$$p \cdot (min(0, \sigma_{media} - \sigma_{adm}) + min(0, \sigma_{max} - \sigma_{adm} * 1, 5)) \tag{11}$$

for the slide stability.

This way, the solutions out of the design space take higher values of the cost function the less they satisfy the conditions.

4   Results

In this section a brief exposition of the main results achieved is exposed.

4.1   Obtained Solution Speed: Sensibility to the Algotihm Parameters

As mentioned previously, there are some parameters within the genetic algorithm that strongly influence the algorithm evoultion, and therefore, the speed with which the solution can be obtained.

These parameters are, besides the selected operator type: the individuals number in the population, the generations number in which the algorithm can evolve, and the mutations rate performed in the algorithm.

To check the impact of each one of these parameters over the execution speed of the algorithm, some executions of the algorithm have been performed. Specifically, each one of the parameters has been changed to take different values, and 50 simulations with the corresponding genetic algorithm have been performed, so as we try to avoid random effects which could affect the conclussions.

We have studied the algorithm sensibility to the parameters variation with the values shown in the table 1:

Table 1. Algorithm Control Parameteres

Parameter	Minimum value	Maximum value
Specimens Number	10	30
Iterations	60	80
Mutations	0.0	0.1

The initial population has been randomly generated in each algorithm execution. We take the algorithm effectivity as:

$$\Delta = \frac{c_{min-final}}{c_{min-inicial}} \qquad (12)$$

this is, the cost function reduction in terms concerning to the best randomly generated individual.

The results obtained with the performed experiments are shown in fig. 2.

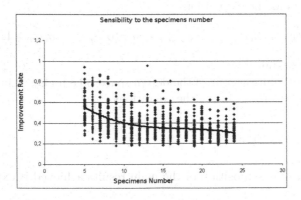

Fig. 2. Algorithm sensibility to the specimens number

As seen, increasing the specimens number makes the improvement achieved with the algorithm to increase, but from some value this improvement increase is very slow, until from 15 individuals no improvement is achieved practically in the results, although the execution time increases excessively.

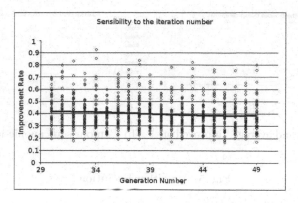

Fig. 3. Algorithm sensibility to the generations number

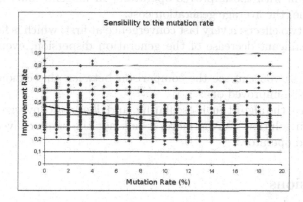

Fig. 4. Algorithm sensibility to the selected mutations rate

You can see a low algorithm sensibility to the iterations number. This can lead to misunderstandings. It is not that the iterations number is unimportant, but the convergence is very fast in the first iterations and then it is damped, so increasing that number does not notoriously improve the result.

Finally, and over the mutation rate, the result is that there is an optimum in that rate which can involve a method efficiency improvement of 20%.

4.2   Comparison with Other Algorithms

We selected the canonical genetic algorithm with an unique-point crossing operator to compare the goodness of the improved operators. The reason of selecting the canonic algorithm to make the comparison is that this is a very good reference to compare with other algorithms that could be implemented in future works. This way you could compare the improvement between algorithms comparing them to the canonic algorithm.

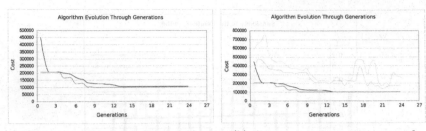

(a) Mininum and average. Improved operators

(b) Comparison canonic-improved

Fig. 5. Algorithm Evolution

In the fig. 5(a) it is shown the cost function evolution on the execution of the genetic algorithm with the improved operators. In magenta line, the minimum cost, in blue line, the average generation cost.

You observe two effects: a very fast convergence at first, which is fastly damped and a very significant decrease of the generation dispersion, even though the mutation rate.

In the fig. 5(b) you can see the comparison between this canonic algorithm execution and the improved one:

As you can see, the algorithm is oscillating, and does not converge monotonously to the optimum solution. Furthermore, it has not the same convergence speed as the improved operator.

5 Conclusions

The main conclusions of this work are:

- Heuristic techniques are not methods restricted in application scope to the optimization, but they offer some other applications, and can be applied to different engineering fields.
- In some cases, the genetic algorithms represent an advantageous alternative in terms of necessary computing power and obtained results compared with more traditional techiniques.
- The most important parameters when looking at the achieved improvement in the optimization are the individuals number and, overall, the mutation rate [1]. The efficiency variation with respect to the iterations number with the improved operators is irrelevant, since these operators makes a very high pressure that makes the most important improvements to be produced at the first iterations.

---

[1] This seems to point to some other investigators opinion, who say that the genetic algorithms can go wihtout the mutation operator to ensure convergence, what makes the crossing operator not to be necessary

Acknowledgements

This work was partially funded by the Spanish Ministry of Science and Innovation and ERDF (the European Regional Development Fund), under the contract TIN2008-06491-C04-04 (the MSTAR project).

References

1. Rahami, H., Kaveh, A.: Nonlinear analysis and optmial design of structures via force method and genetic algorithm. Computer and Structures 84(12), 770–778 (2006)
2. del Hormigón, C.P.: Instrucción Española de Hormigón Estructural (2008)
3. Eshelman, L.: The chc adaptive search algorithm. In: Rawlins, G.J.E. (ed.) Foundations of Genetic Algorithms, vol. I, pp. 265–283. Morgan Kauman, San Francisco (1991)
4. Goldberg, D., Deb, K.: A comparative analysis of selection schemes used in genetic algorithms. In: Foundations of Genetic Algorithms (1991)
5. Ibáñez, S.H.: Structural Optimum Design Methods. C.I.C.C.P, Coleccián SEINOR (1990)
6. Spears, W.M., De Jong, K.A.: An analysis of multi-point crossover. In: Rawlins, G.J.E. (ed.) Foundations of Genetic Algorithms, pp. 301–315. Morgan Kaufmann, San Francisco (1991)
7. Syswerda, G.: Schedule optimization using genetic algorithms. In: Davis, L. (ed.) Handbook of Genetic Algorithms, Van Nostrand Reinhold, pp. 332–349 (1991)
8. Whitley, D.: CUG369 — genitor. j-CUJ 10(11), 74 (1992)
9. Whitley, D.: A genetic algorithm tutorial (2005)

An Experimental Study of an Evolutionary Tool for Scheduling in Oil Wells

D. Pandolfi[1], A. Villagra[1], E. de San Pedro[1], M. Lasso[1], and G. Leguizamón[2]

[1] Laboratorio de Tecnologías Emergentes
Unidad Académica Caleta Olivia
Universidad Nacional de la Patagonia Austral
Caleta Olivia, Santa Cruz, Argentina
{dpandolfi,avillagra,edesanpedro,mlasso}@uaco.unpa.edu.ar
[2] Laboratorio de Investigación y Desarrollo en Inteligencia Computacional
Departamento de Informática
Facultad de Ciencias Físico Matemáticas y Naturales
Universidad Nacional de San Luis
San Luis, Argentina
legui@unsl.edu.ar

Abstract. The exploitation and the transport of oil are very important activities for the economic development of the industrial modern society. However, these activities are generating risks that are translated in accidental contaminations, or chronic contaminations, that directly affect the ecosystem. It is important that oil companies carry out a correct maintenance of their oil fields. In cases of scheduling maintenance of 200 or more oil wells, our so-called PAE, is a tool able to provide a maintenance visit schedule at the right moment. This tool was developed by LabTEm and uses an evolutionary algorithm to produce multiple solutions to this problem. In this work, we compare two approaches (Lamarckian versus Baldwinian) to a constrained scheduling in oil wells. Details of implementation, results, and benefits are presented.

1 Introduction

Oil is a natural resource of great importance for human development and technological employment. As an instrument of appropriation and transformation of natural resources, it has generated a significant and negative worldwide impacts due to their serious consequences for the environment.

In the last decade, Oil Companies engaged in exploitation, production, and transportation of this natural resource have seen the necessity of implementing preventive measures in order to avoid and/or to minimize the damages caused to the people, environment, and material goods. Accordingly, the best way to attack the problem of oil contamination is to prevent the incident.

Usually, problems occur due to equipment or material failure and human mistakes. Equipment or material failure can be corrected by means of periodic

N. García-Pedrajas et al. (Eds.): IEA/AIE 2010, Part III, LNAI 6098, pp. 576–585, 2010.

inspections and appropriate maintenance tasks; human failure can be corrected through a permanent training of personnel, especially those in charge of maintenance activities. For this reason, it is important for Oil Companies and for the environment surrounding them, to have a suitable maintenance of their fields.

Most problems of optimization include certain kinds of constrains that constitute big challenges to the resolution of optimization problems. The constraints are limits imposed to decision variables and in general the constraints are an integral part of the formulation of any problem [2].

The learning evolution influence can be easily understood inside the Darwinian environment since this it provides a mechanism through which the influence can be conducted. The inherited genotype is simultaneously the result of the evolution and learning. The learning is carried out as changes in the phenotypical individual, but these changes cannot be inherited (transmitted in the genetic sense). For the evolutionary biologist J. B. Lamarck the inheritance of the acquired characters was the main cause of the evolution, this hypothesis assumes that a bijective function exists between the genotypic structure and the phenotype. However, Weismann [11] discarded this idea where the acquired knowledge can be transmitted to the gametes.

The paleontologist Simpson called "Baldwin Effect" a new factor that was discovered in 1896 by Baldwin [1]. It proposed basically that: "If changes exist in the environment, the evolution tends to favor individuals with the capacity to learn how to adapt to the new environment accelerating genetic changes among similar individuals."

Apparently the Baldwin Effect has a similar consequence to the Lamarckian evolution. The last one required an inverse function from the phenotype and the environment to the genotype. This inverse function is biologically impossible. On the contrary, the Baldwin Effect is completely a darwinian process since it does not require this inverse function.

The Baldwin Effect acts on the selection and allows that those features or characters that favor adaptation from the organisms to its environment are genetically assimilated in later generations. Anything that the individual learns is transmitted to his offspring. However, the sufficiently fortunate individuals to be close, in the space of design, of a good learned behavior will tend to have more offspring that will also tend to be near that learning. However, this effect could not be observed if plasticity properties are not presented in the individuals. Thanks to this effect called Baldwin, the species with more plasticity will tend to evolve quicker than those that missed it.

Current trends in EAs make use of multirecombinative [3] and multiparent approaches [4]. For the resolution of diverse types of such problems of planning as scheduling or routing these approaches have turned out to be successful strategies. Particularly in scheduling problems, adding a new variant to the multirecombinative approach called MCMP-SRI (Stud and Random Immigrates) [7].

Our tool, called PAE [10] (Planificador basado en un Algoritmo Evolutivo, Evolutionary Algorithm for Planning), is a tool based in an evolutionary approach that aims to schedule the visits of a group of oil fields that: (a) minimize the total time of visits; that is to say, to find the schedule that visits the fields including the time of intervention in each one, in a shorter time; (b) re-schedule the visits, i.e., provide alternative schedules without significantly diminishing their quality, in case of the occurrence of some events that interrupt the execution of a maintenance schedule (dynamic features of the problem); and (c) obtain solutions that fulfil all problem constraints.

In a prototypical version, the application has been programmed in Pascal, and later on it was implemented in Java in order to achieve a more portable and improved version. Particularly, this work shows the obtained results that fulfil all the problem constrains.

The paper continues as follows. Section 2 shows the domain and problem description. Section 3 describes the evolutionary algorithm proposed to solve the problem. Section 4 shows experimental tests and results, and finally in Section 5, we give some conclusions and analyze future research directions.

2   Domain and Description of the Problem

Oil Companies carry out maintenance or prevention visits to each of their oil wells (producing wells, injectors, batteries, and collectors). An oil field is formed by blocks and this in turn of batteries. Each battery contains about 20 oil wells. Each oil well has different production levels known a priori and they vary in time. The well production defines the category and the number of times it shall be visited in a month. The oil wells can not be visited more than once in the same shift and depending on its type there are some tasks that shall be carried out. Each task has been given the necessary equipment, a frequency of realization and an approximate time for its duration. Currently the route carried out by the team in charge of maintenance visits is scheduled based on their experience. A work day begins in the morning and the oil wells are visited in two shifts of three hours. After a shift is concluded the team in charge should return to the base to carry out certain administrative activities and then continue with the following shift. The demanded time in each oil well will depend on its type. Occasionally, randomly contingencies may result in an unaccomplished shift maintenance schedule; that is to say, some oil wells may not be visited. When this event occurs, it affects the total scheduling and each person held responsible should redefine the new itinerary based on his experience.

2.1   Problem Formulation

The problem can be precisely stated as defined in [8]:

$$1|S_{jk}|C_{max}$$

It denotes a single-machine scheduling problem with n jobs subject to sequence-dependent setup times, where the jobs to be scheduled are the maintenance (or intervention) service in each of the oil fields. The objective is to minimize

Algorithm 1. EA-MCMP-SRI
1. $t = 0$ {current generation.}
2. initialize (Stud(t))
3. evaluate (Stud(t))
4. **while** not max_evaluations **do**
5.   mating_pool = Generate_Random_Immnmigrant $\cup$ Select (Stud(t))
6.   **while** not max_parents **do**
7.   **while** max_recombination **do**
8.   evolve (mating_pool){recombination and mutation.}
9.   **end while**
10.   **end while**
11.   evaluate (mating_pool)
12.   Studt+1 = select new population from mating_pool
13. $t = t + 1$
14. **end while**

the makespan (Cmax) subject to the dependent times of preparation of the sequence. It is well-known that this problem is equivalent to the so-called Traveling Salesman Problem (TSP). The makespan can be calculated as:

$$\sum_{k=1}^{n}(S_{jk} + t_k) \tag{1}$$

where S_{jk} represents the cost (in time) of going from oil field k to oil field j, and t_k the respective time of maintenance in location k.

3   PAE: The Evolutionary Tool

To solve this problem of scheduling the visits to the oil fields we used an evolutionary algorithm. The first step was developing an adequate encoding of the visits to the oil wells that represents a solution to the problem. A schedule of visits was encoded in a chromosome as a sequence of oil wells represented by natural numbers. Therefore, a chromosome will be a permutation $p = (p_1, p_2, \ldots, p_n)$ where n is the quantity of oil wells in the shift. Each element p_i represents an oil well i that shall be visited. The chromosome gives the sequence order to be followed in order to visit each oil well. The algorithm will devise the best possible permutation so that it finds an optimal schedule, which fulfills the objectives.

In Algorithm 1 we can see the structure of EA-MCMP-SRI used for solving our problem, which we will now explain. The algorithm creates an initial stud population Stud (0) of solutions to the schedule problem in a random way, and then these solutions are evaluated. After that, the stud population undergoes a multirecombined process where the algorithm creates a mating pool which contains the stud and random immigrants. The process for creating offspring is performed as follows. The stud mates with each of the parents, then couples undergo crossover and $2 \times n2$ ($n2$ *max_parents*) offspring are created. The best of this $2 \times n2$ offspring is stored in a temporary children pool. The crossover operation is repeated $n1$ times (*max_recombinations*), for different cut points each time, until the children pool is completed. Children may or may not be exposed to mutation. Finally, the best offspring created from $n2$ parents and $n1$ crossover is inserted in the new population.

The recombination operator used in this algorithm was PMX (Partial Mapped Crossover). This operator was proposed by Goldberg and Lingle [5]. It can be viewed as an extension of two-cut crossover for binary string to permutation representation. In the mutation operation used, named as Swapping Mutation (SM), we select two random positions and then swap their genes. The selection operator used for selecting an individual was a Proportional Selection.

Constraints handling in evolutionary algorithms can be approached from different techniques such as: Penalty Functions, Decoders, Repair Algorithms, Operators of preservation of constraints, among many others.

Penalty functions have been broadly discussed in the literature in the last decades [9]. Particularly, the penalty based techniques can be roughly divided as static, dynamic, adaptable, and mortal. On the other hand, those techniques based on repair algorithms transform infeasible solutions to became feasible by applying some specific process. The repair processes that genetically modify an infeasible solution are known as Lamarckians and the transformed infeasible solution, i.e., the feasible one, is that which is evolved by the algorithm. A less destructive approach of the infeasible solutions allows combine the learning and the evolution, it is well-known Baldwinian strategy. In this last approach the solutions are repaired only for their evaluation. Analytic and empiric studies indicate that this technique reduces the speed of convergence of the evolutionary algorithm and allows converging to global optimum [12].

In our evolutionary tool, a schedule of visits was encoded in a chromosome as a sequence of oil wells represented by natural numbers. Therefore, a chromosome will be a permutation $p = (p_1, p_2, \ldots, p_n)$ where n is the quantity of oil wells in the block. Each element p_i represents an oil well i that shall be visited. The chromosome gives the sequence order to be followed in order to visit each oil well. Also, one keeps in mind that exist oil wells that should be visited more than once which implies the incorporation of constraints to this problem. For these reason we define two problem constraints:

Hard constraint, the oil wells that should be visited more than once they cannot be scheduled in the same shift. A solution that does not fulfill this constraints is not considered feasible and therefore it should be repaired (see Figure 1).

Soft constraint, a schedules that includes two visits to an oil well in different shifts, but the time elapsed among both visits is longer than the previously established. Although a solution like this is considered feasible (i.e., it fulfills the hard constraint), it does not fulfill the difference of time between a visit and the other (soft constraint).

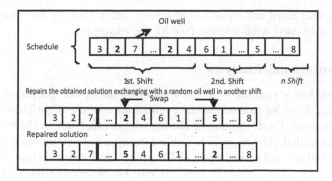

Fig. 1. Process for repairing an infeasible solution

When the Lamarckian approach is applied, an infeasible solution is replaced by the repaired solution, whereas in the Baldwinian approach it is only repaired in order to calculate its new fitness value.

In any of the above approaches, soft constraints are analyzed penalizing when necessary. The penalty value is calculated in the following way:

$$P_i = 2 \times S_{ik} \qquad (2)$$

where, S_{jk} represents the cost (in time) of going from oil well i to oil field k.

4   Experiments and Results

To solve the problem it was necessary to prepare the data since the original information about the distances among oil wells were not processed. The calculation of the distances among the oil wells based on the roads map and distribution of the oil field was carried out. It is known that the distance between two points that are in any place of the system of coordinated Cartesian, is determined by the relationship denominated Euclidean distance. Nevertheless, in this problem the distance between two points can be calculated, considering the existing routes connecting to the oil wells. For this reason, the oil field road map was used and the distances were scale down.

Let us discuss in this section the actual implementation to ensure that this work is replicable in the future. We performed 20 runs for each block and defined the following scenarios and problem contraints. We considered 110 oil wells belonging to a block of the exploitation region. The round speed was defined in 12 seconds every 100 meters and the time in the oil well making the maintenance was set in the same value (12 seconds). The population size for EA-MCMP-SRI is set to 15 individuals. The initial population was randomly generated. The maximum number of evaluations is 222. The recombination operator (PMX) is applied with a probability of 0.65, while the mutation operator (SW) was set with a probability of 0.05. The number $n1$ of recombination and $n2$ of parents were set, respectively, to 16 and 18. Parameters (population size, stop criterion, probabilities, etc) were not chosen at random, but rather by an examination of values previously used with success (see [6] for example).

4.1 Computational Analysis

In this subsection a summary of the results of using the proposed algorithm (PAE) is given. In order to analyze the performance of the algorithm, we worked on two experiments. First, to analyze the algorithm efficiency in the total number of oil wells scheduled (110 oil wells). Table 1 compares the summary of a specific schedule for 110 oil wells from the Oil Company and the schedule obtained by PAE for the same number of oil wells. It can be observed that PAE obtained a reduction of more than 50% of the shifts scheduled than the ones scheduled by the Oil Company. While the schedule performed by the Oil Company visited 18 oil wells PAE made a schedule on 27 oil wells. Thus, PAE uses fewer shifts to visit the same number of oil wells. It can also be observed that while the Oil Company schedules 3 days to visit 110 oil wells (6 shifts), PAE schedules the same number of oil wells in 2 days (4/5 shifts).

Generally, while the original schedule demands a total time of 18 hours and 24 minutes; PAE, in its best schedule, demands 11 hours and 57 minutes saving 6 hours and 27 minutes, more than 2 shifts from a total of 6.

Table 1. Comparison of the Oil Company and PAE schedule

Oil Company Schedule				PAE Schedule			
Day	Shift	Oil wells	Time	Day	Shift	Oil wells	Time
1	1	18	181	1	1	26	180
	2	16	178		2	26	181
2	3	18	184	2	3	28	184
	4	20	182		4	26	180
3	5	19	181	3	5	4	27
	6	19	198				
		110	1104			110	752

Second, when an external event happens, it could cause the non-fulfillment of the original schedule. In this case, the algorithm performance under two different repairing process is analyzed.

To study the algorithms' behavior, we considered a set of constraints randomly chosen. Table 2 shows six set of constraints that indicate the oil wells that should be visited twice.

Table 3 shows the results obtained for Best, Median, and Mean variables applied to the set of constraints. For Best variable, with the Lamarckian approach better minimum are obtained with 15, 19, and 20 constraints. While with the Baldwinian approach better results are obtained with 16, 17, and 18 constraints. For the Median variable, the Lamarckian approach obtained smaller medians in 5 of the 6 cases.

Table 2. Constraints used in the experiment

Constraints	Oil wells to visit twice
15	2, 104, 1342, 1275, 1154, 1269, 1213, 1147, 91, 1007, 1276, 1300, 1305, 1306, 1313
16	2,104, 1342, 1275, 1154, 1269, 1213, 1147, 91, 1007, 1276, 1300, 1305, 1306, 1313, 1327
17	2,104, 1342, 1275, 1154, 1269, 1213, 1147, 91, 1007, 1276, 1300, 1305, 1306, 1313, 1327, 1334
18	2,104, 1342, 1275, 1154, 1269, 1213, 1147, 91, 1007, 1276, 1300,1305, 1306, 1313, 1327, 1334, 1335
19	2,104, 1342, 1275, 1154, 1269, 1213, 1147, 91, 1007, 1276, 1300, 1305, 1306, 1313, 1327, 1334, 1335, 1339
20	2, 104, 1342, 1275, 1154, 1269, 1213, 1147, 91, 1007, 1276,1300, 1305, 1306, 1313, 1327, 1334, 1335, 1339, 1340

Table 3. Results for Best, Median, and Mean algorithms

Best

	15	16	17	18	19	20
Lamarckian	436.44	441.56	429.38	445.86	447.15	447.74
Baldwinian	443.72	440.40	421.74	444.38	449.44	451.80

Median

	15	16	17	18	19	20
Lamarckian	448.24	455.27	451.57	467.32	468.98	470.31
Baldwinian	448.73	449.17	460.2	467.92	479.32	474.00

Mean

	15	16	17	18	19	20
Lamarckian	452.14	457.32	457.24	468.23	468.14	474.40
Baldwinian	454.24	455.00	462.18	463.95	477.87	476.21

To analyze the computational effort of each algorithm it was used the performance variable Evals (number of thousands of evaluations made by each algorithm) for which 30 independent runs were executed.

Table 4 shows the median and mean values for the performance variable Evals. It can be observed that medians values are, while the means for the Lamarckian approach are 3% smaller than the Baldwinian approach. For a detailed

Table 4. Median and Mean for Evals

Evals	Median	Mean
Lamarckian	7995	7219
Baldwinian	7945	7443

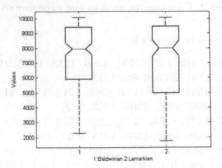

Fig. 2. Results distribution of Baldwinian and Lamarckian approaches

analysis of the Evals we show a boxplot graph (see Figure 2). It is observed that both algorithms have similar medians although, the Lamarckian approach has a distribution more elongated on the lower quartile.

5   Conclusions

PAE is an application built with the objective of providing an effective tool that facilitates the scheduling and re-scheduling of maintenance visits to oil fields. From the analysis and comparisons carried out with performed maintenance schedules, PAE provides the following comparative advantages:(a) EAs are stochastic algorithms that produce multiple solutions in different independent runs. Often a good quality solution (maintenance schedule) cannot be executed because of operative conditions, therefore it is necessary to seek another solution that may not be as good as the first one but it is feasible to be performed. (b) The performance obtained with the methods for handling constraints (Lamarckian and Baldwinian) for scheduling the visits to oil wells, preformed similarly. Therefore, it could not be affirmed that for the analyzed variables exists differences statistically significant between both methods. However, the Lamarckian approach has a distribution of the results that would imply runs that demand smaller computational effort.

Future works will include more precise processes of data verification, different types of constrains, and schedules based on multiple maintenance teams.

Acknowledgments. We acknowledge the cooperation of the project group of LabTEm for providing new ideas and constructive criticisms. Also to the Universidad Nacional de la Patagonia Austral from which we receive continuous support. The last author acknowledge the constant support afforded by the Universidad Nacional de San Luis and the ANPCYT that finances his current researches.

References

1. Baldwin, J.M.: A new factor in evolution. Americam Naturist (30), 441–451 (1896)
2. Dhar, V., Ranganathan, N.: Integer programming versus expert systems: An experimental comparison. Communications of the ACM 33, 323–336 (1990)
3. Eiben, A.E., Van Kemenade, C.H., Kok, J.N.: Orgy in the computer: Multi-parent reproduction in genetic algorithms. In: Morán, F., Merelo, J.J., Moreno, A., Chacon, P. (eds.) ECAL 1995. LNCS, vol. 929, pp. 934–945. Springer, Heidelberg (1995)
4. Esquivel, S., Leiva, H., Gallard, R.: Multiple crossovers between multiple parents to improve search in evolutionary algorithms. In: Congress on Evolutionary Computation (IEEE), pp. 1589–1594 (1999)
5. Goldberg, D., Lingle, R.: Alleles, loci and the traveling salesman problem. In: International Conference on Genetic Algorithms, pp. 154–159 (1987)
6. Lasso, M., Pandolfi, D., De San Pedro, M.E., Villagra, A., Gallard, R.: Solving dynamic tardiness problems in single machine environments. In: Congress on Evolutionary Computation, vol. 1, pp. 1143–1149 (2004)
7. Pandolfi, D., De San Pedro, M., Villagra, A., Vilanova, G., Gallard, R.: Studs mating immigrants in evolutionary algorithm to solve the earliness-tardiness scheduling problem. Cybernetics and Systems of Taylor and Francis, 391–400 (2002)
8. Pinedo, M.: Scheduling: Theory, Algorithms and System, 1st edn. Prentice-Hall, Englewood Cliffs (1995)
9. Smith, A., Coit, D.: Constraint Handling Techniques-Penalty Functions. In: Handbook of Evolutionary Computation, p. C 5.2. Oxford University Press and Institute of Physics (1997)
10. Villagra, A., de San Pedro, E., Lasso, M., Pandolfi, D.: Algoritmo multirecombinativo para la planificación dinámica del mantenimiento de locaciones petroleras. Revista Internacional INFORMACIÓN TECNOLÓGICA 19(4), 63–70 (2008)
11. Weismann, A.: Essays Upon Heredity and Kindred Biological Problems, vol. 1. Oxford Clarendon Press, Oxford (1889)
12. Whitley, D., Gordon, S., Mathias, K.: Lamarckian evolution, the baldwin effect and function optimization. In: Davidor, Y., Männer, R., Schwefel, H.-P. (eds.) PPSN 1994. LNCS, vol. 866. Springer, Heidelberg (1994)

Tackling Trust Issues in Virtual Organization Load Balancing

Víctor Sánchez-Anguix, Soledad Valero, and Ana García-Fornes

Grupo de Tecnología Informática - Inteligencia Artificial
Departamento de Sistemas Informáticos y Computación
Universidad Politécnica de Valencia
Camí de Vera s/n. 46022, Valencia, Spain
{sanguix,svalero,agarcia}@dsic.upv.es

Abstract. Agent-based Virtual Organizations are complex entities where dynamic collections of agents agree to share resources in order to accomplish a global goal. Virtual Organizations offer complex services that require of the cooperation of distributed agents. An important problem for the performance of the Virtual Organization is distributing the agents across the computational resources so that the system achieves a good load balancing. In this paper, a solution for the agent distribution across hosts in an agent-based Virtual Organization is proposed. The solution is based on a genetic algorithm that is meant to be applied just after the formation of the Virtual Organization. The developed genetic strategy uses an elitist crossover operator where one of the children inherits the most promising genetic material from the parents with higher probability. This proposal differs from current works since it takes into account load balancing, software requirements of the agents and trust issues. In order to validate the proposal, the designed genetic algorithm has been succesfully compared to different heuristic methods that solve the same addressed problem.

Keywords: Virtual Organizations, Genetic Algorithms, Multi-agent Systems.

1 Introduction

A Virtual Organization (VO) is a complex entity where dynamic collections of individuals and institutions agree to share resources (software services, computational resources, etc.). Some works have already stated that Multi-agent systems (MAS) and agent organizations are one of the possible technologies to implement VO's [1,2]. MAS are distributed systems where special software called *software agents* are executed [3].

Virtual Organizations may offer complex services that require the collaboration of several distributed and heterogeneous agents (different capabilities, designers, etc). The performance of the VO is one of the key factors in its success. Since the number of agents may be large and the number of computational resources are usually bounded, it is necessary to distribute the different agents across the computational resources in an intelligent way. Ideally, all of the resources should be employed with similar utility rates and none of them should be overloaded. The problem of distributing the load across computational resources is known in the literature as *load balancing*.

N. García-Pedrajas et al. (Eds.): IEA/AIE 2010, Part III, LNAI 6098, pp. 586–595, 2010.

In MAS, it is natural for agents to have different levels of confidence or untrust with their partners. It is also reasonable to assume that different agents have different software requirements (operating system, software libraries, etc.). Consequently, these requirements are interesting when tackling the problem of load balancing in agent-based VO's.

Thus, the problem of distribution in Virtual Organization consists of assigning computational resources (hosts) to agents. Due to the fact that the system may become large-scaled, the problem becomes a large combinatorial problem where the load balancing must be optimized. In this paper, a solution for the agent distribution across hosts in an agent-based VO is proposed. This approach is based on a Genetic Algorithm (GA) [4,5] that is meant to be applied just after the formation of the VO. The proposed GA takes into account trust issues, software requirements of the agents, and load balancing.

The remainder of this work is organized as follows. In Section 2, a formal definition of the problem is given. The design of the GA is thoroughly described in Section 3. In Section 4, experiments that were carried out to validate the proposed GA are detailed. It includes how the optimal parameters were found and a comparison with different heuristics that solve the same problem. Then, related work is described in Section 5. Finally, some lines of future work and conclusions are given.

2 Problem Definition

An agent-based VO is composed of a set of agents and hosts that belong to different entities. The problem of distribution in a VO consists of assigning agents to proper hosts for execution. However, agents cannot be executed in every host. Their software requirements, or more specifically software libraries, must be provided by the host in which they are to be executed. Furthermore, agents must be distributed in such a way that the hosts are not overloaded. Ideally, the load should be equal in all of the hosts that are part of the VO. Moreover, since agents represent different entities and hosts may be owned by different entities, there may be certain untrustness to share computational resources with other partners. Ideally, agents should be distributed in a way whereby they minimize the untrust generated. In this work, it is assumed that the load balancing solution is calculated by a trusted mediator who has profiles containing information about the different agents and hosts, and has an approximation to the trust among the different parties.

A Virtual Organization can be seen as a tuple $VO = (H, A, R, \Gamma, \Upsilon, \delta, \mu)$ where: H is the set of hosts resources that are shared; A is the set of agents that are part of the organization; R is the set of software requirements that the agents need in order to be executed; $\Gamma : HXA \rightarrow 0 \vee 1$ is a function that indicates if an agent is being executed in a node host; $\Upsilon : HXA \rightarrow x, x \in \Re \ \wedge \ x \in [0,1]$ is a function that measures the level of untrust regarding sharing the host resource with a specific agent; $\delta_h : H \rightarrow \Re$ represents the load the node host is capable of handling; $\delta_a : A \rightarrow \Re$ represents the load the agent generates; $\mu_h : H \rightarrow R' \ \wedge R' \subseteq R$ is the set of software requirements the node host offers and $\mu_a : H \rightarrow R' \ \wedge R' \subseteq R$ is the set of software requirements an agent needs in order to be executed. In this work, the load generated by an agent only concerns the use of the CPU (e.g. MFLOPS). This information can be provided by the owner of the agent. Additionally, more sophisticated profiling techniques like the ones presented in [6,7] can be used.

2.1 Constraints

When distributing agents across host resources, it is important to satisfy two different types of constraints. The first type is related to the load of the host. The maximum load provided by the host should not be surpassed by the total load generated by the executed agents. The formal definition of this constraint can be found in Equation 1.

$$\delta_h(h) \geq \sum_{a \in A} \Gamma(h, a) * \delta_a(a) . \tag{1}$$

The second type relates to the software requirements offered by the node hosts and the ones needed by the agents. One agent can be executed in an specific node host if its software requirements are provided by this host. The formalization of this constraint can be found in Equation 2.

$$\forall a, h \quad \Gamma(h, a) = 1 \rightarrow \mu_a(a) \subseteq \mu_h(h) . \tag{2}$$

2.2 Optimality Measures

In this case, there are two different measures that may describe the quality of a solution. First, it is appropiate that the utility rates of the hosts that are part of the system were balanced. Second, it is also important that the untrust generated in the VO is minimized. This is accomplished by distributing agents in hosts whose entities are more willing to share resources with them.

The global untrust level in a VO can be defined as a social welfare function that must be minimized in order to provide distributions where entities share resources with partners they are more confident with. It can be formally be defined as stated in Equation 3. This is the average of the untrust generated by the agents in their corresponding host.

$$\Theta = \frac{\sum_{a \in A} \sum_{h \in H} \Gamma(h, a) * \Upsilon(h, a)}{|A|} . \tag{3}$$

The other optimality measure relates to the load balance. The load x_h in a machine h can be defined as the sum of the loads generated by the agents divided by the load supported by the machine h.

$$x_h = \frac{\sum_{a \in A} \Gamma(h, a) * \delta_a(a)}{\delta_h(h)} . \tag{4}$$

The average load of the system $\bar{x}$ is defined as the average of the host loads that compose the system. We also define d as the standard deviation of this distribution.

$$\bar{x} = \frac{\sum_{h \in H} x_h}{|H|} . \qquad d = \sqrt{\frac{\sum_{h \in H} (\bar{x} - x_h)^2}{|H|}} . \tag{5}$$

Finally, the global load balance measure of the system is defined as $\beta = 1 - \frac{d}{\bar{x}}$. The best load balance is obtained when $\frac{d}{\bar{x}} = 0$ and consequently $\beta = 1$. The expression $\frac{d}{\bar{x}}$ is 0 when $d = 0$, therefore all of the hosts have the same level of load.

3 Genetic Algorithm Design

A Genetic Algorithm is proposed to solve the adressed problem. In this section, an explanation of its design is given. More specifically, some of the aspects explained are: chromosome and phenotype representation, initial population generation, fitness function, and genetic operators (crossover, mutation and selection).

3.1 Chromosome and Phenotype Representation

On the one hand, agents can be identified as integers that range from 1 to $|A|$, where $|A|$ is the total number of agents to be distributed. On the other hand, hosts are identified with integers that range from 1 to $|H|$, where $|H|$ is the total number of machines available. Each individual of the population is represented as an integer vector. Indexes of the vector represent the agent, whereas the content of a specific index position represents the host where the agent is assigned to be executed. A chromosome example of the proposed representation can be found in Fig. 1.

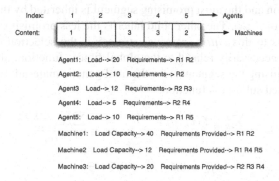

Fig. 1. This figure shows an example of agent distributions across the hosts of the VO. There are five different agents and three different hosts where agents can be assigned. The content of each chromosome position indicates a host where the agent, represented as a chromosome index, is to be executed. It must be highlighted that each host provides the software requirements needed by the agents that are planned to be exectuted in that specific host. Additionally, the load capacity of a specific host is not surpassed by the load generated by the agents that are to be executed there.

3.2 Initial Population Generation

Several initial populations of 512 individuals are generated in a random way. The most diverse population (higher population variance) is selected as the starting point for the GA. Furthermore, the solutions generated were assured to satisfy the constraints described in the previous section.

3.3 Fitness Function

The designed GA's goal is to reduce the untrust level and obtain the best possible load balancing. The best load balancing results are obtenied when $\beta = 1$. This is equivalent to minimizing the $\frac{d}{\bar{x}}$ term. The employed fitness function takes into account untrust and $\frac{d}{\bar{x}}$, trying to minimize the value of Equation 6.

$$f = 0.5 * \frac{d}{\bar{x}} + 0.5 * \Theta \ . \tag{6}$$

In this approach, untrust and load balacing are equally important. However, it is possible to adjust the weighting to give more importance to one specific goal.

3.4 Crossover

The developed crossover operator follows an *elitist crossover strategy*. The approximation is based on k-point crossover [8] with two parents and two children. A number of k+1 segments are determined by the k points selected in the chromosome. In classic k-point crossover, one child inherits the segment of one of his parents randomly, whereas the other child inherits the other parent's segment. However, the developed strategy assigns one of the children as the preferred one. The segments are evaluated by a subfitness function and the most promising segment is inherited by the preferred child with a probability of p_{good}. The other child inherits the less promising segment[1].

One of the keys to this *elitist crossover strategy* is the selection of the subfitness function. It is not necessarily related to the global fitness function, although it should measure how promising the segment is for the final genetic material. Equations 7 and 8 describe the selected subfitness function.

$$\Theta_v = \frac{\sum_{k=i}^{j} \Upsilon(v_k, a_k)}{|v|} \ . \qquad x_v = \frac{\sum_{k=i}^{j} \frac{\delta_a(a_k)}{\delta_h(v_k)}}{|v|} \ . \tag{7}$$

$$f_v = 0.5 * x_v + 0.5 * \Theta_v \ . \tag{8}$$

In equation 7, v denotes a segment of the phenotype. The Θ_v term relates to the average untrust of the segment, whereas x_v is the average load of the segment. Both values are weighted to 0.5 and combined linearly in the segment subfitness function f_v. It must also be remarked that parents and children are incorporated into the candidate solution pool for the next generation.

3.5 Mutation

The mutation is performed by randomly changing the assignation of an agent to a host [9]. The operation is governed by two different parameters: p_{mut} and $average_{mut}$. The first one relates to the probability of an individual being mutated, producing a new child. The $average_{mut}$ parameter is the average number of phenotypes to be mutated from an individual selected for mutation. The number of phenotypes mutated in an individual is lower or equal to $average_{mut}$ and is selected randomly. The original individual and the mutated child are added to the candidate solution pool for the next generation.

---

[1] If k is equal to the size of the vector and $p_{good} = 50\%$, then operator is similar to uniform crossover.

3.6 Selection

The selection operator is applied twice in our genetic approach. Firstly, it is employed in order to determine on which individuals the crossover operation is applied. Secondly, it is used in order to select which individuals are part of the next generation after the crossover and mutation phase. The selection method chosen is the ranking selection [10] which assigns an individual selection probability that is equal to

$$p_i = \frac{1}{N} \left(min + \frac{(max - min)(i - 1)}{N - 1} \right). \tag{9}$$

where N is the population size, i is the position in the ordered population and max and min are two parameters that determine how probable it is for the best and the worst individual to be selected. More specifically, the probability that the best individual is selected is $p_N = \frac{max}{N}$ and the probability that the worst individual is selected is $p_1 = \frac{min}{N}$. The number of individuals to be selected for crossover operation is governed by the parameter p_{select}, whereas the number of individuals to be selected as the next generation is equal to the maximum population P_{max}.

3.7 Stop Criteria

The proposed genetic algorithm continues its iterative process until one of the following two criteria has been fulfilled: (i) the best fitness has not improved in 10 generations; (ii) a total computation time of t_n seconds has been exceeded since the beginning of the GA.

4 Experiments and Results

In this section, the design of the experiments and their results are decribed. It must be highlighted that the experiments were designed to be carried out in a simulation environment where different problem instances can be generated. These instances are fed directly to the GA. Several experiments that aim to find the optimal values for different parameters of the GA were carried out (p_{mut}, $average_{mut}$, p_{select}, p_{good}, k, and P_{max}). After that, some experiments were necessary in order to compare the designed approach to other methods that solve the same problem.

Mutation Parameters. The first set of experiments were related to set the paremeters concerning the mutation operator. It was necessary to set the probability of an individual being mutated p_{mut} and the average number of attributes to be mutated $average_{mut}$. Values tested for p_{mut} were 2, 5, 8 and 10% whereas values tested for $average_{mut}$ were 3, 5 and 8%. The rest of pararametes was set to: $p_{good} = 50\%$, $p_{select} = 50\%$, $k = 500$, $P_{max} = 4096$, $t_n = 300$ seconds. The problem used as test during the parameter adjustment phase was a problem instance of 500 agents that need to be assigned to 70 different hosts. Each experimentation was repeated 10 times and information about the fitness of the best individual was gathered. The best configuration obtained was $p_{mut} = 10\%$ and $average_{mut} = 5\%$ with a fitness of [0.22-0.26] (confidence=95%).

Crossover Parameters. The parameters that affect the crossover operator are: the probability to be afected by the crossover operator (p_{select}); the number of crossover points (k); and the probability of the preferred child inheriting the best segment (p_{good}). Tests for finding the optimal values of p_{select} and k were performed first. Tested values were 40, 60, 80 and 100% for p_{select}; whereas 1, 10, 100, 200, 300, 400, and 500 for the parameter k. After those paremeters were stablished, different values for the p_{good} parameter were checked. In that test, the previous optimal values for p_{select}, k, and mutation parameters were mantained. The different checked configurations for p_{good} were 50, 60, 70, 80, 90 and 100%. Each experimentation was repeated 10 times and $t_n = 300$ seconds. Information about the fitness of the best individual was gathered. The best results obtained were k=500², p_{select}=60, and $p_{good} = 80\%$ with a fitness of [13.94-17.33] (confidence=95%). The value of the parameter p_{good} indicates that it is better to apply an elitist strategy where one of the children statistically inherist the best genetic material from both parents.

Population Control Parameters. The studied parameter that affects the population control is the maximum population (P_{max}). Values tested for P_{max} were 2048, 4096, and 8192. The same methodology and optimal values of the parameters found in previous experimentations were maintained. All the configurations performed similarly, thus additional time measures were taken into account. Finally a population of 2048 individuals was selected since it performed reasonably better in time with a fitness of [13.14-19.61] (confidence=95%).

Proposal Evaluation. Once the optimal parametrization for the GA was found, it was necessary to test the designed GA in several problem instances. Moreover, the implemented solution was also compared to several baselines. More specificially, it was compared to a grasp implementation, a GA that uses classic multicrossover³ (k=5 and k=$\frac{|V|}{2}$, $p_{good} = 50\%$), and other GA that employs uniform crossover (k=$|V|$, $p_{good} = 50\%$). The rest of parameters of the cited GA's are common, they only differ in the parameters concerning the crossover operator. Following, we describe the grasp implementation in more detail.

A grasp algorithm [11] is a metaheuristic method which consists of two different phases: construction phase and local search phase. In the construction phase, a random valid solution for the problem is built. The local search aims to look for better solutions (better fitness) in the neighborhood of the obtained solution. The solution vector obtained in the construction phase is analyzed in order. A change in the vector is made only if it does not violate problem constraints and it produces a better fitness than the actual state of the vector. Once the vector has been completely analyzed, if the solution is better than the best solution obtained until the current moment, then the best solution is updated with the recently produced solution. The grasp algorithm goes back to the construction phase and continues until a stop criteria is met. In this work, the grasp algorithm stops after t_n seconds.

In order to compare the different methods, two different sets of experiments were designed. In the first set of experiments, several instances of the problem were generated

---

² This indicates that the k parameter should be adjusted to the size of the chromosome.
³ $|V|$ is the size of the chromosome.

with different numbers of hosts and agents. The first test set was created with the number of agents ranging from 200 to 2000 and the number of hosts five times lower than the number of agents. Therefore, the problems increased their sized although they had similar characteristics. In the second set of experiments, the number of hosts remained static at 30 and the number of agents ranged from 200 to 600. Since the number of hosts was static and the number of agents gradually increased, the quality of the solution was expected to decrease. The goal of these experiments was to check that the designed GA outperformed the other methods in more complex problems. The proposed GA was configured with the best parametrization found in the previous experiments. Each experiment was repeated 10 times and the result was the fitness of the best individual (for all the methods). The maximum execution time for all of the methods was set to $t_n = \frac{|V|*48}{200}$ seconds, where $|V|$ is the size of the chromosome.

Fig. 2 shows the results achieved in the two sets of experiments. The left graphic shows the results for the first set, whereas the right graphic shows the result for the second set. More specifically, the average fitness reached in every tested method and its associated error bar are shown in both graphics. It can be observed that the proposed GA outperforms the other methods in both sets of experiments. Grasp is the only method that remains close to the proposed approach, although its performance is still worse than the proposed GA. It is also shown that results are not only better in average, but they are also statistically different. Therefore, it is possible to conclude that the developed GA is better than the other methods.

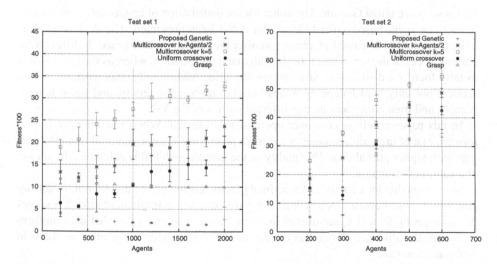

Fig. 2. The left figure shows the results for the first set of experiments, whereas the right figure shows the results for the second set of experiments

5 Related Work

To the best of our knowledge, the problem of VO distribution in Multi-agent Systems has not been addressed before. However, there are some works in Grid Computing that use GA in similar tasks.

Mello et al. [12] designed a GA to distribute tasks in a grid environment. Each application is divided into different tasks that are to be distributed between the machines of a neighborhood. Its main goal is to make a good initial distribution of the tasks throughout the neighborhood. The GA takes into account different performance measures such as CPU, memory usage, hard disk access and so forth. Nevertheless, it assumes that machines offer the same software requirements and trust issues are not studied.

Cao et al. [13] used a GA to schedule different tasks in a local grid environment. A local grid is a cluster of workstations. Therefore, the GA is only applied at a local level. This work also ignores trust and software requirements.

Di Martino [14] studied the use of a GA whose aim is task distribution in a Grid environment. In this work, it is assumed that different tasks have different constraints affecting where they can be executed. The GA takes these constraints into account and looks for a correct task allocation. However, trust issues are not taken into account by the GA.

The present work is different from related approaches in the sense that it applies the novel idea of resource distribution in agent-based VO's. Additionally, it takes into account software requirements of the agents and trust issues.

6 Conclusions and Future Work

In this work, an elitist Genetic Algorithm for the distribution of agents across the shared hosts in an agent-based Virtual Organization has been presented. The designed GA is to be perfomed by a trusted mediator just after the VO has been formed. It differs from current works in the sense that it deals with agent distribution, whereas the other works usually focus on distributing tasks across the grid. Additionally, this work takes into account not only load balancing issues but also resource diversity, and agent heterogeneity, and trust issues among the different parties of the VO.

In this paper an elitist crossover operator is presented. When this operator is performed, one of the children inherits the most promising genetic material from the parents with higher probability. The quality of the genetic material is calculated by means of a subfitness function.

Some tests that look for the GA's optimal parameters have been carried out. Additionally, the proposed elitist GA has been compared to a grasp implementation that solves the same problem, a GA that uses classic multicrossover, and a GA that uses uniform crossover. Results have shown that the designed GA outperforms the other methods in different scenarios.

Besides, this work focuses at the formation phase of a VO. However, the proposed approach could be applied when the performance of the VO decreses to a certain threshold. In the same way, it is also possible to dinamically adapt the calculated solution to new environmental conditions by other methods. This aspect is not covered in this work, being appointed as future lines of research.

Acknowledgments. This work is supported by TIN2008-04446, CSD2007-00022 and FPU grant AP2008-00600 of the Spanish government, and PROMETEO 2008/051 of the Generalitat Valenciana.

References

1. Argente, E., Julian, V., Botti, V.: MAS Modelling Based on Organizations. In: Luck, M., Gomez-Sanz, J.J. (eds.) Agent-Oriented Software Engineering IX. LNCS, vol. 5386, pp. 1–12. Springer, Heidelberg (2009)
2. Del Val, E., Criado, N., Rebollo, M., Argente, E., Julian, V.: Service-Oriented Framework for Virtual Organizations. In: The 2009 International Conference on Artificial Intelligence, pp. 108–114. CSREA Press, Las Vegas (2009)
3. Wooldridge, M.J.: Multi-agent Systems: An Introduction. Wiley & Sons, Chichester (2001)
4. Goldberg, D.E.: Genetic Algorithms in Search, Optimization and Machine Learning. Addison-Wesley, Boston (1989)
5. Holland, J.: Adaptation in Natural and Artificial Systems. MIT Press, Cambridge (1992)
6. Harchol-Balter, M., Downey, A.B.: Exploiting Process Lifetimes Distributions for Dynamic Load Balancing. ACM Transactions on Computer Systems 15, 253–285 (1997)
7. Senger, L.J., Santana, M.J., Santana, R.H.C.: An Instance-Based Learning Approach for Predicting Execution Times of Parallel Applications. In: The 3rd International Information and Telecommunication Technologies Symposium, pp. 9–15. Sao Carlos (2005)
8. Eshelman, L.J., Caruana, R.A., Schaffer, J.D.: Biases in the Crossover Landscape. In: The 3rd International Conference on Genetic Algorithms, pp. 10–19. Morgan Kaufmann, San Francisco (1989)
9. Michalewicz, Z.: Genetic Algorithms + Data Structures = Evolution Programs. Springer, New York (1994)
10. Baker, J.E.: Adaptive Selection Methods for Genetic Algorithms. In: Proceedings of the 1st International Conference on Genetic Algorithms, pp. 101–111. L. Erlbaum Associates, Hillsdale (1985)
11. Feo, T.A., Resende, M.G.C.: A Probabilistic Heuristic for a Computationally Difficult Set Covering Problem. Operations Research Letters 8, 67–71 (1989)
12. de Mello, R.F., Filho, J.A.A., Senger, L.J., Yang, L.T.: RouteGA: A Grid Load Balancing Algorithm with Genetic Support. In: The 21st International Conference on Advanced Networking and Applications, pp. 885–892. IEEE Computer Society, Washington (2007)
13. Cao, J., Spooner, D.P., Jarvis, S.A., Nudd, G.R.: Grid Load Balancing Using Intelligent Agents. Future Gener. Comput. Syst. 21, 135–149 (2005)
14. Di Martino, V., Mililotti, M.: Sub Optimal Scheduling in a Grid Using Genetic Algorithms. Parallel Computing 30, 553–565 (2004)

An Intelligent Memory Model for Short-Term Prediction: An Application to Global Solar Radiation Data

Llanos Mora-Lopez[1], Juan Mora[2],
Michel Piliougine[3], and Mariano Sidrach-de-Cardona[3]

[1] Dpto. Lenguajes y Computación. ETSI Informática. Univ. Málaga
[2] Dpto. Fund. de Análisis Económico. Univ. Alicante
[3] Dpto Física Aplicada II. Univ. Málaga
Campus de Teatinos. 29071 Málaga, Spain
llanos@lcc.uma.es, juan@merlin.fae.ua.es, {michel,msidrach}@ctima.uma.es

Abstract. This paper presents a machine learning model for short-term prediction. The proposed procedure is based on regression techniques and on the use of a special type of probabilistic finite automata. The model is built in two stages. In the first stage, the most significant independent variable is detected, then observations are classified according to the value of this variable and regressions are re-run separately for each Group. The significant independent variables in each group are then discretized. The PFA is built with all this information. In the second stage, the next value of the dependent variable is predicted using an algorithm for short term forecasting which is based on the information stored in the PFA. An empirical application for global solar radiation data is also presented. The predictive performance of the procedure is compared to that of classical dynamic regression and a substantial improvement is achieved with our procedure.

Keywords: Machine Learning, Modelling Data, Time Series.

1 Introduction

Short-term prediction with time sequences has been performed using both statistical models and machine learning models. Many of these methods aim to find models which are able both to reproduce the statistical and sequential characteristics of the sequence, and to forecast short and long term values. The traditional statistical approach can be found in [1]. In this approach, a previous selection of the models must be performed and, once these models have been identified and their parameters have been estimated, it is assumed that the relationship between the parameters is constant over time. Several statistical methods have been developed to circumvent these problems, [2], [3].

Other models not only use statistical methods but also methods and techniques from the machine learning area. For example, machine learning models

N. García-Pedrajas et al. (Eds.): IEA/AIE 2010, Part III, LNAI 6098, pp. 596–605, 2010.

have been used to model different types of sequences, [4], [5], [6], [7], [8], [9], [10], [11].

In the case of a univariate time sequence for some climatic parameters, such as temperature and solar radiation, the models based on the use of probabilistic finite automata have proven to be very powerful, see [12]. However, the problem with these models is that when they "decide" to forget, they forget everything -all the information included in the sequence up to the order of the model- and when they "decide" to learn, they learn the whole sequence for an order. It would at times be very useful if the model could forget recent unimportant values (or facts), but remember distant-in-time important values. We propose a model that is capable of learning the important information. This model is based on the use of a general framework described in the second section. In that section, a procedure to select what must be remembered (and how) is also presented. In the third section, an example of the use of the model for a real time sequence is presented.

2 Description of the Procedure

2.1 Foundations

This paper seeks to propose a model for short-term prediction of a univariate dependent variable given a set of independent variables, which may include lags of the dependent variable. The model is built in two stages, but feedback is allowed so that information can be exchanged from one stage to the other.

In the first stage, statistical techniques are used to determine the most significant information to predict the dependent variable. This most significant information typically comes from the past values of the dependent variable, but many other sources of information may be included. Among the independent variables, the one that is globally most significant (typically, the first lag of the dependent variable) plays a key role, since it is used to classify the observations into groups. The independent variables that are significant for each group are then selected. It is important to group the observations because our aim is to apply this procedure to situations where the relationship between the dependent variable and the independent ones may differ substantially, depending on the value taken on by the most significant independent variable. Data sets with this type of behaviour can be found in Finance (interest rates, stock prices, etc.) and Climatology (values of available energy at the earth's surface, clearness indices, etc.), among many other disciplines. For instance, a high recent value in a sequence of clearness index (e.g. no clouds) is very likely to be followed by another high value. Consequently, only a few independent variables (one or two lags of the dependent variable) in this case contain all the relevant information for prediction. However, a low recent value (e.g. patchy cloud) is usually related to higher volatility, and an accurate prediction typically requires the use of many dependent variables (not only lags of the dependent variable, but also other types of information, such as season, temperature, wind speed, and so on).

The final step in the first stage is based on the use of a certain type of probabilistic finite automata (PFA), which have been developed in the field of machine learning. These PFA can only be applied to data described by discrete numerical or nominal attributes (features); thus, when attributes are continuous, a discretization algorithm which transforms them into discrete ones must be applied. In our procedure, this discretization process is performed at the end of the selection of significant variables, using those continuous variables that are significant at each group. The discretization process requires threshold values as input values that determine how many values (and which ones) the discretized variable takes on.

The PFA is built using the information stored in the significant variables. It works in an iterative fashion: a maximum admissible error, which is fixed in advance by the researcher, is considered, and the procedure only finishes if the in-sample prediction error (as defined below) is lower than the maximum admissible error. Otherwise, an alternative discretization process is performed (assuming that not all the possible discretization processes have already been performed). In order to ensure that this iterative procedure ends, the possible discretization processes that can be performed, which in principle could be infinite, are restricted as follows: the distance between two threshold values of a discretization process is not allowed to be lower than a certain fixed-in-advance value; for example, when a continuous variable which takes values in the interval $(0,1)$ is discretized, one can start with eleven threshold values ($j/10$ for $j = 0, 1, ..., 10$), then allow for twenty-one threshold values ($j/20$ for $j = 0, 1, ..., 20$), and continue until, say, one hundred and one threshold values are allowed ($j/100$ for $j = 0, 1, ..., 100$), if it has been assumed that the minimum distance allowen between two threshold values is 0.01. If the iterative process has to perform all possible discretization processes, and the in-sample prediction error is always greater than the maximum admissible error, then the discretization process which yields the minimum in-sample prediction error is selected. Note that with this iterative process not only can one decide in advance how accurate the prediction should be, but also computation time may be saved since it is not necessary to explore all possible possible ways to discretize the continuous variables. In Figure 1 the description of this first stage is shown.

It also needs to be emphasized that the researcher here also decides when an independent variable is considered as significant in each of the regressions that are performed in the first stage. In fact, this decision could also be incorporated in the iterative process, together with the decision about how the discretization processes are performed. However, promising results are obtained in our application even when fixing the value that determines when a variable is considered as significant. Hence, we do not consider this as a variable in the description of the procedure. In the second stage, the PFA that is built at the end of the first stage is used for the short-term prediction of the dependent variable, as it is described in next section.

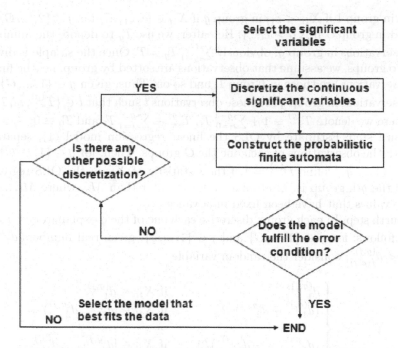

Fig. 1. Description of the first stage in the proposed procedure

2.2   Steps in the Prediction Procedure

Assume that observations $\{(Y_t, X_t)\}_{t=1}^T$ are available, where Y_t is a univariate random variable, X_t is a q-dimensional random vector and t denotes time. We are interested in building a PFA for the prediction of Y_{T+1} when X_{T+1} is known. We propose a two-stage procedure. In the first stage, regression analysis based on the observations $t \in \{1, ..., T\}$ is used to determine the information that may be relevant for the prediction. In the second stage, the information stored after the first stage, together with the value X_{T+1}, is used to propose a prediction of Y_{T+1}.

The first stage uses the ordinary least squares (OLS) estimation of regression models and discretization techniques to select the information that must be stored for the second stage. More specifically, this first stage consists of the following steps:

– First step: Estimate by OLS a linear regression model, i.e. the model:

$$Y_t = \beta_0 + \beta_1 X_{1t} + ... + \beta_q X_{qt} + \text{Error} \qquad (1)$$

Hereafter, we assume that the components of the random vector X_t are sorted in such way that the first one, i.e. X_{1t}, is the one with greatest t-statistic, in absolute value, in this OLS regression.

– Second step: Split the sample into G groups, depending on the value of X_{1t}, i.e. given real numbers $c_1 < ... < c_{G-1}$, the tth observation is considered to be in group 1 if $X_{1t} < c_1$, in group g if $X_{1t} \in [c_{g-1}, c_g)$ for $g \in \{2, ..., G-1\}$, and in group G if $X_{1t} \geq c_{G-1}$. Hereafter, we use T_g to denote the number of observations in group g; obviously $\sum_{g=1}^{G} T_g = T$. Once the sample is divided into groups, we assume that observations are sorted by group, i.e. the first T_1 observations are those in Group 1, and so on. Thus, given $g \in \{1, ..., G\}$, the observations in group g are those observations t such that $t \in \{T_*^{(g)}, ..., T_{**}^{(g)}\}$, where we denote $T_*^{(g)} \equiv 1 + \sum_{i=0}^{g-1} T_i$, $T_{**}^{(g)} \equiv \sum_{i=1}^{g} T_i$ and $T_0 \equiv 0$.

- Third step: Estimate by OLS the linear regression model (1), separately with the observations of each one the G groups. Then, for $g \in \{1, ..., G\}$ and $j \in \{1, ..., q\}$ define $D_j^{(g)} = 1$ if the t-statistic of X_{jt} in the OLS regression for the gth group is, in absolute value, greater than M_g, where $M_1, ..., M_G$ are values that have been fixed in advance.

- Fourth step: In each group, discretize each one of the q explanatory variables as follows: for $g \in \{1, ..., G\}$ and $j \in \{1, ..., q\}$, given real numbers $d_1^{(g,j)} < ... < d_{I(g,j)}^{(g,j)}$, consider the random variable

$$
X_{jt}^{(g)*} := \begin{cases}
d_1^{(g,j)} & \text{if } X_{jt} < d_1^{(g,j)} \\
(d_1^{(g,j)} + d_2^{(g,j)})/2 & \text{if } X_{jt} \in [d_1^{(g,j)}, d_2^{(g,j)}) \\
... & ... \\
(d_{I(g,j)-1}^{(g,j)} + d_{I(g,j)}^{(g,j)})/2 & \text{if } X_{jt} \in [d_{I(g,j)-1}^{(g,j)}, d_{I(g,j)}^{(g,j)}) \\
d_{I(g,j)} & \text{if } X_{jt} \geq d_{I(g,j)}^{(g,j)}
\end{cases}
\tag{2}
$$

And, given real numbers $d_1^{(g,0)} < ... < d_{I(g,0)}^{(g,0)}$, discretize also the dependent variable in a similar way, and thus derive the random variable $Y_t^{(g)*}$.

- Fifth step: For each $g \in \{1, ..., G\}$, build a PFA with the the information $D_1^{(g)}, ..., D_q^{(g)}$ and $\{Y_t^{(g)*}, X_{1t}^{(g)*}, ..., X_{qt}^{(g)*}\}_{t=T_*^{(t)}}^{t=T_{**}^{(t)}}$, using the procedure that is described in [13].

Note that at the end of this first stage, the stored information is qualitative, since only discrete variables are used. Thus, the cost of storing this information is extremely low. In the second stage, once X_{T+1} is observed, the procedure to predict Y_{T+1} is the following:

- First step: Depending on the value of $X_{1,T+1}$, find the group g where the new observation must be placed.

- Second step: Discretize X_{T+1} as in the fourth step of the first stage, taking into account the group g to which these observation belongs. As a result, $(X_{1,T+1}^{(g)*}, ..., X_{q,T+1}^{(g)*})$ is obtained.

- Third step: Using the PFA for the group g obtained at the end of the first stage, derive the observations in the gth group that satisfy $X_{jt}^{(g)*} D_j^{(g)} = X_{j,T+1}^{(g)*} D_j^{(g)}$ for all $j \in \{1, .., q\}$, using the procedure described in [13]; the set of subscripts t in $\{T_*^{(g)}, ..., T_{**}^{(g)}\}$ for which the tth observation satisfies this condition will be denoted by $\mathcal{S}$.

- Fourth step: Use Y_{T+1}^* to denote the median of $\{Y_t^{(g)*}\}_{t \in \mathcal{S}}$. Then, the prediction interval for Y_{T+1} is defined as the interval $[d_k^{(g,0)}, d_{k+1}^{(g,0)})$ which contains Y_{T+1}^*, where $d_1^{(g,0)} < ... < d_{I(g,0)}^{(g,0)}$ are the values that were used to discretize the dependent variable in the fourth step of the first stage. (The mean or the mode of $\{Y_t^{(g)*}\}_{t \in \mathcal{S}}$ could also be used instead of the median, depending on the kind of error function that one wants to minimize).

Before performing the second stage of the procedure, the accuracy of the PFA that is built at the end of the first stage is checked as follows: apply the procedure to predict the value of all the observations in the sample, i.e. construct Y_t^* for $t = 1, ..., T$, and then derive the proportional in-sample mean square prediction error, i.e.

$$\text{MSPE} = \frac{1}{T} \sum_{i=1}^{T} \frac{(Y_t^* - Y_t)^2}{Y_t^2} \qquad (3)$$

If this value is greater than a fixed-in-advance maximum admissible error ε, then the first stage must be performed using different values in the discretization process that is performed in the fourth step. This iterative process continues until the condition MSPE$\leq \varepsilon$ is met, or until all possible discretization processes have been performed, in which case the discretization process that is finally considered is the one which yields lower MSPE.

2.3   Selection of Input Data

In practice, the proposed prediction procedure requires to fix various input data, which should be chosen by the researcher in advance. Specifically, this is the list of input data that are required, together with hints about how this input data should be selected.

1. The values $c_1, ..., c_{G-1}$ determine the G initial groups taking into account the most significant variable. They should be decided after examining how the relationship between $X_{1,t}$ and Y_t behaves at different intervals.
2. The values $M_1, ..., M_G$ determine whether a variable is considered significant or not in each one of the G regressions. In principle, all of them could be fixed to 1.96, which amounts to saying that a 0.05 significance level is used to determine whether a variable is significant or not. However, this value could be related to the sample size, in order to avoid an excess of fit that may worsen the predictive power of the procedure.
3. The values $d_1^{(g,j)}, ..., d_{I(g,j)}^{(g,j)}$ describe the discretization of the jth explanatory variable in the gth group. The problem of how to choose the thresholds that must be used to discretize a continuous variable has been widely used in contexts similar to these (see e.g. [14], [15] and [16]), since many algorithms used in supervised machine learning are restricted to discrete data.
4. The maximum admissible error ε for the prediction model. This value should depend on the sample size and on the kind of data set. It may not be sensible to propose a method to select this value which could be used in all contexts.

5. The parameters for building the PFA, according to the procedure proposed in [13], i.e. the probability threshold and the order (length or memory) of the PFA; the former is used to decide when a node is added to the PFA, depending on the minimum number of observations that will have each node. It should depend on the number of observations and it is used to avoid the problem of overfitting (in our empirical application, the criterion proposed in [12] is used).

In any case, experience and knowledge about the behaviour of the dependent variable play arguably the most important role when selecting these input data. It is also important to emphasize that, once these input data are decided, the procedure works in an automatic way.

3   A Practical Case

The proposed model has been used to forecast the next value of an hourly sequence of a climatic parameter called the clearness index k_h. This variable is very useful to establish the performance of all the systems that use solar radiation as an energy source, such as thermal and photovoltaic systems. The sequence of hourly clearness index are obtained from the hourly global solar radiation sequence G_h as follows:

$$k_h = \frac{G_h}{G_{0,h}} \tag{4}$$

where $G_{0,h}$ is the hourly extraterrestrial solar radiation, which is introduced in order to remove the yearly trend of the hourly global radiation sequence. The season at which each observation is taken is used as an additional information; it has been incorporated using three dummy variables in the regression model (an intercept is included, hence no dummy variable is included for winter to avoid multicollinearity). We have used 6 values from the hourly sequence of clearness index of each day (from 9 to 15 hours), because the values of k_h are zero at night, and very low in the early and last hours of the day. Moreover, we have only used 6 values for each day because the useful values of these parameters, in most applications (e.g. in the prediction of the energy generated by many solar systems) are those centered around the middle of the day.

We have grouped the different subsequences of the time sequence using the value of the sequence in period $t-1$ as this is the most significant variable in the first-step regression analysis. We have used the following 9 intervals: $[(j-1)/10, j/10]$ for $j = 1, ..., 8$, and $[0.8, 1.0]$ as ninth interval (the last interval is greater because there are only a few values greater than 0.85).

In order to check the accuracy of the procedure, the analysis is performed by dividing all the available observations in two sets: the training set, which is used to apply the model such as it is described in the previous section, and the test set that has been used for checking the out-of-sample predictive performance of the procedure. We have divided the observations in a random way, selecting

Table 1. Results of the dynamic regression (*significance level=0.05*) in each group of observations for the training set

Independent Var	All	0-0.1	0.1-0.2	0.2-0.3	0.3-0.4	0.4-0.5	0.5-0.6	0.6-0.7	0.7-0.8	0.8-1
Intercept	24.744	2.613	3.523	-0.009	2.996	2.802	2.904	4.432	6.951	3.045
$k_{h-1.d}$	225.602	11.624	12.907	12.831	8.865	9.681	13.315	29.905	28.618	0.131
$k_{h-2.d}$	2.757	0.108	0.361	1.459	0.390	-1.786	-1.011	-1.008	8.910	6.156
$k_{h-3.d}$	12.458	3.676	5.001	3.469	3.806	4.152	3.951	4.934	3.158	1.422
$k_{h.d-1}$	16.232	-0.550	0.805	2.985	2.551	3.520	6.850	13.747	12.913	2.738
$k_{h.d-2}$	7.605	1.383	-1.349	1.877	0.919	0.734	1.734	7.036	8.864	2.105
$k_{h.d-3}$	9.697	0.382	2.240	2.565	2.272	2.719	2.705	5.607	7.078	2.461
S_1	0.062	-0.733	-0.947	-0.138	-0.023	-0.143	-1.161	3.104	3.860	-1.794
S_2	1.431	-1.879	0.973	-0.194	1.110	-1.706	-1.180	2.920	7.173	-0.599
S_3	5.362	1.180	1.459	1.663	0.754	0.149	-0.505	5.270	8.435	-0.062

Table 2. Selected variables for each interval (*significance level=0.05*)

Interval	Selected var
0-0.1	$k_{h-1,d}$, $k_{h-3,d}$
0.1-0.2	$k_{h-1,d}$, $k_{h-3,d}$
0.2-0.3	$k_{h-1,d}$, $k_{h-3,d}$, $k_{h,d-3}$
0.3-0.4	$k_{h-1,d}$, $k_{h-3,d}$, $k_{h,d-1}$, $k_{h,d-3}$
0.4-0.5	$k_{h-1,d}$, $k_{h-3,d}$ $k_{h,d-1}$, $k_{h,d-3}$
0.5-0.6	$k_{h-1,d}$, $k_{h,d-1}$, $k_{h-3,d}$, $k_{h,d-3}$
0.6-0.7	$k_{h-1,d}$, $k_{h,d-1}$, $k_{h,d-2}$, $k_{h,d-3}$, S_3, $k_{h-3,d}$, S_1, S_2
0.7-0.8	$k_{h-1,d}$, $k_{h,d-1}$, $k_{h-2,d}$, $k_{h,d-2}$, S_3, S_2, $k_{h,d-3}$, S_1, $k_{h-3,d}$
0.8-1	$k_{h-2,d}$, $k_{h,d-1}$, $k_{h,d-3}$, $k_{h,d-2}$

the 90 percent of the observations for the training set and the 10 percent for the test set. When applying our procedure, we have considered four different discretization processes for each continuous variable.

Monthly sequences of hourly global solar radiation from 10 Spanish locations are the data set used. The total period of time used depends on the location; the total number of available monthly time sequence is 745.

Our dependent variable is $k_{h,d}$, and the independent variables are the intercept and $k_{h-1,d}$, $k_{h-2,d}$, $k_{h-3,d}$, $k_{h,d-1}$, $k_{h,d-2}$, $k_{h,d-3}$, S_{1d}, S_{2d}, S_{3d}, where h is the hour, d is the day and S_{jd}, for $j = 1, 2, 3, 4$, are the seasonal dummy variables corresponding to day d. As expected, the most significant variable in this empirical application proves to be $k_{h-1,d}$. In Table 1 we report the results that have been obtained when performing the first and the third step in the first stage of our estimation procedure; in Table 2 we report the variables that are selected as significant for each group, using 0.05 as a significance level.

The iterative process which is described in Figure 2.1 is used to construct the model. The algorithm always starts performing the discretization process that leads to a lower number of intervals (i.e. intervals with greater length), and continues until a model with in-sample prediction error below 5% is found, or until all possible discretization processes have been performed.

Table 3. Mean square errors of the short-term forecast using the proposed model and the estimated dynamic regression for the training set and the test set

	MSE Training set		MSE Test set	
Interval	proposed model	dynamic regression	proposed model	dynamic regression
0-0.1	0.336	2.836	0.364	2.402
0.1-0.2	0.386	1.048	0.305	0.887
0.1-0.2	0.388	1.048	0.357	0.887
0.2-0.3	0.298	0.588	0.395	0.465
0.3-0.4	0.32	0.587	0.368	0.456
0.4-0.5	0.43	0.684	0.297	0.301
0.5-0.6	0.198	0.218	0.187	0.196
0.6-0.7	0.068	0.081	0.045	0.048
0.7-0.8	0.042	0.045	0.03	0.03
0.8-1	0.034	0.092	0.069	0.076

Finally, the in-sample mean squared prediction error (i.e., the MSPE for the training set) and the out-of-sample mean squared prediction error (i.e., the MSPE for the test set) are found. These values are reported in Table 3, together with the corresponding values that are obtained when the prediction is performed with a standard dynamic regression using $k_{h,d}$ as a dependent variable, and $k_{h-1,d}$, $k_{h-2,d}$, $k_{h-3,d}$, $k_{h,d-1}$, $k_{h,d-2}$, $k_{h,d-3}$, S_{1d}, S_{2d}, S_{3d}, as independent variables. These results show that our short-term forecasting procedure yields a remarkable improvement in prediction (both in-sample and out-sample), with respect to classical dynamic regression analysis.

4   Conclusions

This paper proposes a procedure for short-term prediction that combines regression techniques and the use of probabilistic finite automata. The procedure may be particularly useful in situations where the number of significant independent variables, and the type of relationship between the dependent variable and the independent variables, crucially depends on the interval to which the observation belongs. Some input values have to be decided by the researcher, but the selection of these values can also be incorporated within the iterative algorithm performed for prediction. Thus the method is flexible enough to perform well in a wide variety of situations. We present an application with solar global radiation data. Our empirical results show that our procedure leads to a remarkable improvement with respect to classical dynamic regression. How is this improvement achieved? One possible explanation is that our procedure is capable of selecting only the important information for the prediction, and forgetting (not considering) the unimportant information, in contrast to the dynamic regression model, which uses all the information in a less selective way. Further research is required to analyze the extent to which this improvement is also found in other empirical applications.

Acknowledgments. This work has been partially supported by the projects TIN2008-06582-C03-03, ECO2008-05721/ECON and ENE07-67248 of the Spanish Ministry of Science and Innovation (MICINN).

References

1. Box, G.E.P., Jenkins, G.M.: Time Series Analysis forecasting and control. Prentice Hall, USA (1976)
2. Tong, H.: Non-linear time series. A dynamical system approach. Oxford University Press, Oxford (1990)
3. TeRäsvirta, T., Lin, F., Granger, C.W.J.: Power of the neural network linearity test. Journal of time series analysis 14 (1993)
4. Nadas, A.: Estimation of probabilities in the language model of the IBM speech recognition system. IEEE Trans. on ASSP 32(4) (1984)
5. Rabiner, L.R.: A tutorial on Hidden Markov Models and Selected Applications in Speech Recognition. In: Proceedings of the Seventh Annual Workshop on Computational Learning Theory (1994)
6. Ron, D., Singer, Y., Tishby, N.: On the Learnability and Usage of Acyclic Probabilistic Finite Automata. Journal of Computer and System Sciences 56 (1998)
7. Zhang, G., Peter, Q.I., QI, M.: Neural network forecasting for seasonal and trend time series. European Journal of Operational Research 160 (2005)
8. Vidal, E., Thollard, F., Higuera, C., Casacuberta, F., Carrasco, R.C.: Probabilistic Finite-State Machines-Part I. IEEE Transactions on Pattern Analysis and Machine Intelligence 27(7), 1013–1025 (2005)
9. Palmer, N., Goldberg, P.W.: PAC-learnability of probabilistic deterministic finite state automata in terms of variation distance. Theoretical Computer Science 387(1), 18–31 (2007)
10. Ingsrisawang, L., Ingsriswang, S., Somchit, S., Aungsuratana, P., Khantiyanan, W.: Machine Learning Techniques for Short-Term Rain Forecasting System in the Northeastern Part of Thailand. Proceedings of World Academy of Science, Engineering and Technology 31 (2008)
11. Wang, C.H., Hsu, L.C.: Constructing and applying an improved fuzzy time series model: Taking the tourism industry for example. Expert Systems with Applications 34 (2008)
12. Mora-López, L., Mora, J., Sidrach-de-Cardona, M., Morales-Bueno, R.: Modelling time series of climatic parameters with probabilistic finite automata. Environmental modelling and software 20(6) (2004)
13. Ron, D., Singer, Y., Tishby, N.: Learning Probabilistic Automata with Variable Memory Length. In: Proceedings of the Seventh Annual ACM Conference on Computational Learning Theory (1994)
14. Dougherty, J., Kohavi, R., Sahami, M.: Supervised and Unsupervised Discretization of Continuous Features. In: Proceedings of the Twelf International Conference on Machine Learning, Los Altos, CA, pp. 194–202. Morgan Kaufmann, San Francisco (1995)
15. Lui, H., Hussain, F., Lim Tan, C., Dash, M.: Discretization: An enabling Technique. Data Mining and Knowledge Discovery 6, 393–423 (2002)
16. Perner, P., Trautzsch, S.: Multi-interval Discretization Methods for Decision Tree Learning. In: SSPR/SPR, pp. 475–482 (1998)

Binding Machine Learning Models and OPC Technology for Evaluating Solar Energy Systems

Ildefonso Martinez-Marchena[1], Llanos Mora-Lopez[1],
Pedro J. Sanchez[2], and Mariano Sidrach-de-Cardona[2]

[1] Dpto. Lenguajes y C.Computacion
[2] Dpto Física Aplicada II
University of Malaga. Campus de Teatinos. 29071 Málaga, Spain
{ilde,llanos}@lcc.uma.es, {pjsanchez,msidrach}@ctima.uma.es

Abstract. This paper describes a framework to develop software to monitor and evaluate solar installations using machine-learning models and OPC technology. The proposed framework solves both the problem of monitoring solar installations when there are devices from different manufacturers and the problem of evaluating solar installations whose operation changes throughout the plant operation period. Moreover, the evaluation programs can be integrated with the monitoring problems. The proposed solution is based on the use of machine-learning models to evaluate the plants and on the use of OPC technology to integrate the monitoring program with the evaluation program. This framework has been used for monitoring and evaluating several real photovoltaic solar plants.

Keywords: OPC technology, machine learning models, evaluation of solar energy systems.

1 Introduction

The monitoring and evaluation of solar energy systems is usually performed as two separate processes, particularly for small and medium size plants, as the evaluation is carried out using physical or statistical models that cannot be easily integrated in the monitoring programs. Moreover, these evaluation models have been fitted in a general way without taking into account the characteristics of each installation and they are the same throughout the plant operation period. However, it would be very important to adjust these models for considering the real performance of each installation and for including the possible operation changes along the time. Some of the problems that can have a different impact on different installations are, for example, dust losses, shading effects or wiring losses, that can produce significant differences in the performance of the installation. Therefore, programs that could learn from the behaviour of the plant and that could be fitted according to how the plant operation evolves would be very useful. Keep in mind that a proper solar plant operation assessment can help to achieve better performance and early detection of problems (shading, degradation, dust,...).

N. García-Pedrajas et al. (Eds.): IEA/AIE 2010, Part III, LNAI 6098, pp. 606–615, 2010.

The main purpose of a monitoring and evaluating process in solar energy installations is to reveal the performance of the system. There is no general framework to develop systems to monitor and evaluate this type of systems. Consequently, the generation of these types of programs does not use previously developed programs and the existing programs have no possibility of connecting different systems and applications, particularly n the case of solar plants subsystems. Components that make connectivity of subsystems easier, [1], [2] both for monitoring and for evaluation are therefore important. That is, the lack of application-level interface standards makes it difficult to interconnect the different applications. Object distribution models, [3] are developed to meet the need to distribute object-oriented functionality and to encapsulate it with well-defined application programming interfaces.

This paper presents a framework that allows the monitoring and evaluation of solar systems to be integrated. The evaluation can be done by using machine-learning models, such as neural networks or probabilistic finite automata. This integration is possible thanks to the use of OPC technology (OLE for Process Control). In the proposed framework, OPC XML-DA is used both to model monitoring systems and to evaluate the performance of solar energy installations. We propose the use of OPC technology to solve the interconnection problem both when monitoring and evaluating solar energy systems. OPC is based on OLE/COM technology (Object Linking and Embedding/ Component Model from Microsoft), [4], [5]. Originally named "OLE for Process Control" after Microsofts Object Linking and Embedding technology, it is now known simply as "OPC," which stands for Open Process Control or Open Connectivity, [6], [7]. This technology enables software components developed by experts in one sector to be used by applications in any other sector. The OPC interface design supports distributed architectures. Access to remote OPC servers is made by using the Distributed Component Object Model (DCOM) technology from Microsoft, [8].

We have used OPC technology to integrate the algorithm for evaluating the solar installations with the monitoring algorithm. This technology allows us to develop flexible, consistent rules and formats to work with plant floor data using XML.

The second section describes the proposed framework to monitor and evaluate solar energy installations. The third section explains how the evaluation of solar plant is integrated into the framework and which models are used for the plant assessment. The fourth section gives some examples of monitoring and evaluation systems developed with the proposed framework. Finally, the conclusions are presented in the last section.

2   The Proposed Framework for System Modelling

The proposed framework has different levels of definitions: measures, devices and system. Each installation is modelled using a set of generic description rules and the XML language [9] to describe the elements that make up the system and to implement interoperation between different object distribution models. The powerful XML description capacity enables us to extend the modelling possibilities to any installation if more parameters have to be described. A complex system can therefore be described by using easy rules that will have different characteristics and devices in each case.

The minimum usable unit by the framework is the *measure*. A *measure* is a representation of one channel from any device that supplies any type of information about the system. A *measure* can also be one attribute of one device (that we will treat as a constant or calculated value). A *measure* has several attributes, such as the name, a description, the associated data and the minimum or maximum value. A *device* is any physical or abstract element in the installation. In general, the *devices* have some measures and attributes such as the name, device class and others. A *device* can also consist of a set of devices, each of them with its own attributes. Figure 1 shows the modelling of a *device*. A *device* will be modelled as an element with several measures that can simultaneously have a list of elements. In this way, it is possible to model a device that comprises several devices and one abstract element can even be created from a set of devices; the measurements of this abstract element could be the calculated value from any of its channels. This type of abstract element is used to store the machine-learning models used to evaluate the installation.

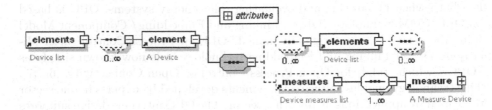

Fig. 1. Proposed framework based on the use of OPC technology

It is easy to build a database of the most-used devices as a device can be modelled using XML labels.

Finally, the *system* represents an installation with its devices, its attributes and the associated channels. This is the only information that the framework needs. The framework uses the specifications included in the XML document to generate a structure in runtime that connects to the installation and updates the measurements using the current data of the different devices and that evaluates the performance of an installation. When the framework is started, communications are begun and there is then one-to-one mapping between each measure attribute and the corresponding value of the real device channel. In this way, the device channels of the installation are always represented.

3   Evaluation of Solar Plants Using Multilayer Artificial Neural Networks

The evaluation process of a solar installation in the proposed framework builds on the development of automatic learning models using the data from the same installation being evaluated. The model for each installation is therefore learned using different data sources.

When a learning model on a data set is developed, we usually do so in a controlled environment where the data source is often unique. However, when these models are integrated in different settings, the problem of how to integrate the entire set of elements (models and data) needs to be solved .

We propose a solution to address this problem that is based on OPC technology that is already used for integrating both industrial systems and monitoring systems, and where its versatility has been proven with thousands of successful cases. OPC technology can separate source and data types by developing and calculating evaluation models to enable the abstraction. In this case, our evaluation model can be treated as one element of a system and integrated using this technology. Figure 2 shows a generic scheme of an architecture that integrates the use of data-learned evaluation models with a general monitoring system.

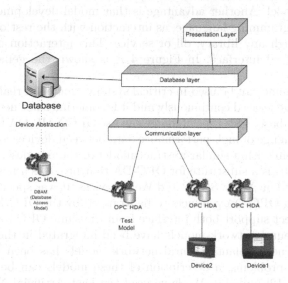

Fig. 2. Integration of evaluation models with OPC technology

This scheme shows the communication layer that enables data to be extracted from devices using HDA (OPC Historical Data Access) OPC technology. New devices can be included by replacing OPC servers with appropriate add-on devices Once the downloaded information is stored in the database, it is characterized in an abstract way. A direct correspondence between data and devices is established. The decision to incorporate assessment models arises as a new device is included that will generate the necessary data using the information for each device in the database.

The container used for the model behaves as an OPC client that can access all data in the database as if it were any device connecting to the Model Database access through OPC technology. Furthermore, the container behaves as an OPC server that enables it to be easily integrated into the system, see Figure 3.

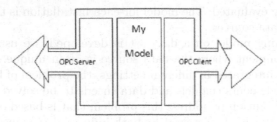

Fig. 3. OPC server

The change in the model only affects the OPC server that implements it and does not require any changes to be made to the architecture of the system. This configuration allows the model to rely on input from different devices and different sources can also be used just by changing the OPC server that contains the model. Another advantage is that model development is independent of any programming language, as interaction with the rest of the system is not made through any library, dll or service. This interaction occurs through the OPC standard interface. In Figure 4 it is shown the general framework developed.

The same scheme can be used in critical systems (included real time systems) where data are generated continuously and it is sometimes not necessary to store them in the database. This type of model can use OPC XML-DA technology that enables the exchange of high-performance data between devices and components of a single system with a similar abstract model to the one described above.

OPC XML-DA is a substitute for OPC-DA that provides a new form of communication based on XML, SOAP and Web Services. It was specifically designed to allow existing OPC-DA products to be wrapped by the OPC XML-DA interfaces and in effect support both interface from the same OPC Server [10].

Multilayer neural network models have been integrated in the framework to evaluate solar energy plants. Neural network models has been widely used in many practical problems, a description of these models can be found, for instance, in [11], [12] and [13]. We have used the Fast Artificial Neural Network Library (FANN) described in [14]. FANN is a free open source neural network library, which implements multilayer artificial neural networks in C with support for both fully connected and sparsely connected networks. It includes a framework that allows training data sets to be easily handled. The FANN features are as follows:

1. Multilayer Artificial Neural Network Library in C
2. Backpropagation training (RPROP, Quickprop, Batch, Incremental)
3. Evolving topology training which dynamically builds and trains the ANN (Cascade2).

For evaluating the performance of solar photovoltaic plants we have used an artificial neural network with one hidden layer using backpropagation learning algorithm, which is performed 50 epochs. As transference function we choose the

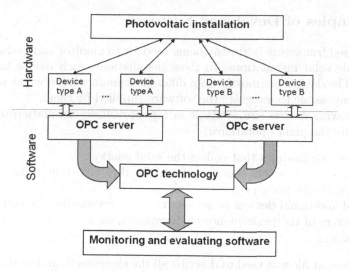

Fig. 4. Developed framework

well-known sigmoid function, $\sigma(x)$, for the hidden and output layer and identity function for the input layer:

$$\sigma(x) = \frac{1}{1 + e^{-x}}$$

Since sigmoid function returns values in the interval $(0, 1)$, input and output data are normalized within their minimum and maximum values in order to let the network operate within the interval $[0, 1]$ for input and output variables. For integrating the evaluation model, we have developed the OPC server the implement the model and that exchange information with the whole system. The used input data are the solar global radiation and the temperature. With these two values, the energy that the plant should have generated is estimated. Figure 5 shows the scheme of the artificial neural network used.

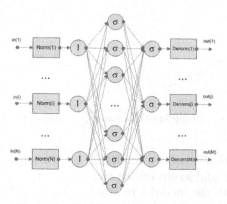

Fig. 5. Artificial neural network used

4   Examples of Developed Systems

The proposed framework is already being used for to monitor and evaluate many photovoltaic solar installations. In these installations, each device has several channels. The devices are mostly from different manufacturers, which sometimes makes it impossible to integrate the software supplied by them.

The following devices are available in a photovoltaic installation to monitor and evaluate the plant operations:

1. Photovoltaic modules that collect the solar energy
2. One or more inverters that transform the direct current collected by the modules in alternating current
3. Several additional devices or sensors that are responsible for collecting the parameters of the performance of the system, such as the temperature, radiation, etc.

An XML format file was used to describe all the elements in an installation. The modelling of some of the most-common devices is already included in a XML label data base. Therefore, the building of the final system is done by copying the labels of the system devices and by adding them to the original XML. So, we have described the attributes for each inverter, its channels and the necessary virtual channels to allow the system and the relationship among them to be evaluated. Finally, the different elements with the OPC items responsible for the communications will be linked the framework responsible for all other tasks.

Figure 6 shows an example of the process for building the monitoring and the evaluation program (only a piece of the framework is shown).

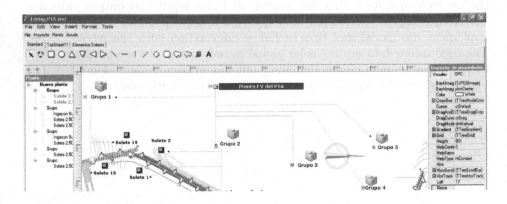

Fig. 6. Process of building the monitoring and evaluation program

Once the installation has been modelled, all the graphic elements, such as labels, charts, shapes, and so on, will be included in the system and the channels will be connected with the modules to evaluate the installation. Figure 7 shows one program to monitor and evaluate a real installation when it is running.

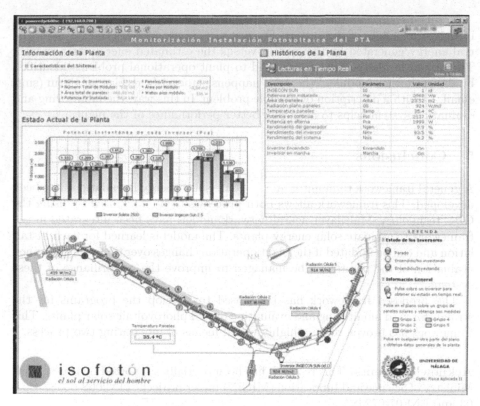

Fig. 7. Program for the monitoring and the evaluation of a real installation

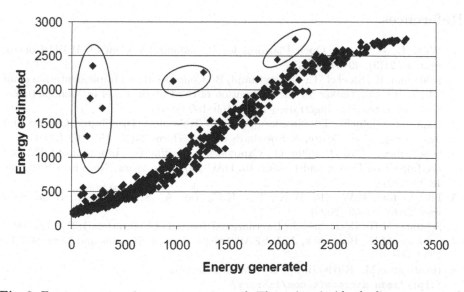

Fig. 8. Energy generated vs energy estimated. The points inside the lines correspond to plant operational problems identified by the framework.

In this installation, the evaluation module has detected several possible faults in the performance of the system. For instance, figure 8 shows the values of the real energy generated by the system versus the estimated energy for a month. The points inside the lines correspond to plant operational problems identified by the evaluation module. When this happens, supervisor receive an alarm (sms, email,...) with a description of possible problem. In this way, the monitoring and evaluating system helps to achieve a better performance of the plant.

5   Conclusions

A general framework to monitor and evaluate solar energy installations has been developed. This framework allows both processes to be integrated by using the OPC technology. Multilayer neural network models have been integrated in the framework to evaluate solar energy plants. The model is learned for each installation and can be updated if the plant operation changes over time. The obtained evaluation of the plants can be managed to improve the performance of these systems.

The proposed framework has been used to develop the programs for the straightforward monitoring and evaluation of real photovoltaic solar plants. This framework has proven to be a highly useful means of integrating two process.

Acknowledgments. This research has been partially supported by the Spanish Ministry of Science and Innovation (MICIN) under projects TIN2008-06582-C03-03 and ENE07-67248.

References

1. Wills, L., et al.: An Open Platform for Reconfigurable Control. IEEE Control Systems 21(3), 49–64 (2001)
2. Feldmann, K., Stockel, T., Gaberstumpf, B.: Conception and Implementation of an Object Request Broker for the Integration of the Process Level in Manufacturing Systems. J. Systems Ingetration 10(2), 169–180 (2001)
3. Raptis, D., Spinellis, D., Katsikas, S.: Multi-Technology Distributed Objects and Their Integration. Computer Standards and Interfaces 23(3), 157–168 (2001)
4. Schellenberg, F.M., Toublan, O., Capodieci, L., Socha, B.: Adoption of OPC and the Impact on Design and Layout. In: DAC 2001, Las Vegas, Nevada, USA, June 18-22 (2001)
5. Liu, J., Lim, K.W., Ho, W.K., Tan, K.C., Tay, A., Srinivasan, R.: IEEE Software 22(6), 54–59 (2005)
6. Schwarz, M.H., Boercsoek, J.: International Journal of Computers 1(4), 245 (2007)
7. Schwarz, M.H., Boercsoek, J.: WSEAS Transactions on Systems and Control 3(3), 195 (2008)
8. Horstmann, M., Kirtland, M.: DCOM Architecture,
   http://msdn.microsoft.com/library/
9. The World Wide Web Consortium (W3C) XML Specifications:
   http://www.w3.org/XML/

10. Tan, V.V., Yoo, D.S., Yi, M.J., Modern, M.J.: Proceedings 14th European Photovoltaic Solar Energy Conference, vol. 115 (2007)
11. Anderson, J.A.: An Introduction to Neural Networks. The MIT Press, Cambridge (1995)
12. Hassoun, M.H.: Fundamentals of Artificial Neural Networks. The MIT Press, Cambridge (1995)
13. Hertz, J., Krogh, A., Palmer, R.G.: Introduction to The Theory of Neural Computing. Addison-Wesley Publishing Company, Reading (1991)
14. Nissen, S.: Implementation of a Fast Artificial Neural Network Library (fann), Graduate project, Department of Computer Science. University of Copenhagen, DIKU (October 2003)

Processing of Crisp and Fuzzy Measures in the Fuzzy Data Warehouse for Global Natural Resources[*]

Bożena Małysiak-Mrozek, Dariusz Mrozek, and Stanisław Kozielski

Institute of Informatics, Silesian University of Technology
Akademicka 16, 44-100 Gliwice, Poland
{Bozena.Malysiak,Dariusz.Mrozek,Stanislaw.Kozielski}@polsl.pl

Abstract. Fuzzy Data Warehouse (FDW) is a data repository, which contains fuzzy data and allows fuzzy processing of the data. Incorporation of fuzziness into data warehouse systems gives the opportunity to process data at higher level of abstraction and improves the analysis of imprecise data. It also gives the possibility to express business indicators in natural language using terms, like: *high, low, about 10, almost all*, etc., represented by appropriate membership functions. Fuzzy processing in data warehouses can affect many operations, like data selection, filtering, aggregation, and grouping. In the paper, we concentrate on various cases of data aggregation in our recently implemented fuzzy data warehouse storing consumption and requirement for global natural resources represented as crisp and fuzzy measures. We show several examples of data aggregation and filtering using the extended syntax of the SQL SELECT statement.

Keywords: fuzzy data warehouse, data aggregation, fuzzy sets, membership function, query language, natural resources, decision support.

1 Introduction

Data warehouses are special purpose repositories that collect huge volumes of data usually for reporting and querying. These kinds of systems support fast and complex data analysis and constitute a foundation for decision support systems. Data warehouses are optimized for fast data retrieval. The goal is often achieved through the denormalization of the data warehouse schema towards so called star schema or snowflake schema [1]. This minimizes the number of join operations during the querying process. In data warehouse systems, fact data are organized in central fact table, which stores numerical values of some business indicators. These facts can be analyzed along different dimensions, like time or geography, which are represented by dimension tables. In order to guarantee the fast data retrieval from data warehouse systems, data are usually pre-aggregated at different levels of attribute hierarchies in particular dimensions [2].

---

[*] The research presented here were done as a part of research and development project no. O R00 0068 07 and have been supported by Ministry of Science and Higher Education funds in the years 2009-2011.

N. García-Pedrajas et al. (Eds.): IEA/AIE 2010, Part III, LNAI 6098, pp. 616–625, 2010.
© Springer-Verlag Berlin Heidelberg 2010

Analysis of the consumption and requirement for global natural resources is very important for the long-term management of these resources. It delivers useful information for ecologists, giving them an insight into the politics of natural resource use in particular countries and how it affects the natural environment. It is also one of the key indicators for the Ministry of Economy in every country providing the information about the current exploitation and exhaustion of the resources deposits. Furthermore, it allows to predict the future exploitation capabilities and therefore, has a vast influence on the economic safety and independence of the country. In the analysis of global natural resources some facts cannot be represented by crisp measures. E.g. if we consider requirement for particular resources and the cost of the requirement, these values can be merely estimated. For this reason, it seems desirable to include some fuzziness into the data warehouse storing this kind of facts. Furthermore, processing crisp measures with the use of fuzzy techniques gives huge latitude in the formulation of analysis criteria. Therefore, we define the Fuzzy Data Warehouse (FDW) as the data repository, which contains fuzzy data and allows the fuzzy processing of the data. This approach to data analysis and processing gives several advantages. One of the advantages is the possibility to analyze data in more general manner, e.g. users can search the information based on imprecise terms [3-5]. Moreover, the use of fuzzy techniques makes it easy to concentrate similar data using appropriate criteria [6]. Finally, it is natural to use fuzzy techniques, when we collect inaccurate data, e.g. measures coming from test systems or estimated facts, and we need to explore them with a bit of tolerance. Having fuzzy measures (measures defined on columns that store fuzzy data), we must implement the arithmetic of fuzzy numbers in order to aggregate fuzzy data. The following works [7-9] present successful implementations of fuzzy methods in processing data in data warehouse systems. However, they usually concentrate on fuzzy processing of crisp values.

In the paper, we show different methods and cases of data aggregation for crisp and fuzzy measures stored in the fuzzy data warehouse for global natural resources.

2 Theoretical Background

A fuzzy number is of L-R type, if there exist reference functions L (left), R (right) and scalars $\alpha > 0$, $\beta > 0$ and m – called modal value. The scalars α, β are called left and right spreads, appropriately [10].

Symbolically, the L-R fuzzy number is represented by the triple (m, α, β). Generally, we can say the L-R fuzzy number is a fuzzy set A, for which the membership function is described by the expression (1).

$$\mu_A = \begin{cases} L\left(\dfrac{m-x}{\alpha}\right) & for\ x < m \\ 1 & for\ x = m, \\ R\left(\dfrac{x-m}{\beta}\right) & for\ x > m \end{cases} \quad where\ m,\ \alpha,\ \beta \in R \tag{1}$$

A fuzzy interval is of L-R type, if there exist reference functions L, R and left and right spreads $\alpha > 0$, $\beta > 0$ and m, n, where $m < n$, and (m, n) is the interval of modal values. The L-R fuzzy interval is denoted by the four (m, n, α, β) [10].

Generally, we can say that the L-R fuzzy interval is a fuzzy set A, for which the membership function is described by the expression (2).

$$\mu_A = \begin{cases} L\left(\dfrac{m-x}{\alpha}\right) & for \ x < m \\ 1 & for \ m \leq x \leq n, \\ R\left(\dfrac{x-n}{\beta}\right) & for \ x > n \end{cases} \quad where \ m, n, \alpha, \beta \in R \tag{2}$$

Data aggregation is a key element for the analytical processing in all OLAP (On-Line Analytical Processing) systems [1], [2]. During the OLAP processing, we usually want to perform a sum or an average of values for the particular range of rows, and sometimes we need to know the minimal or maximal value of some attributes in a group of records. While aggregating fuzzy data, sum and average aggregates can be implemented according to the arithmetic of fuzzy numbers, the other two aggregates, min and max, can be applied thanks to the fuzzy logic. The fifth important operation allows to count the number of rows or values in a group of records. This operation does not require any special implementation and can be used regardless of the type of data that we operate on – crisp or fuzzy.

Addition of L-R fuzzy numbers
In order to implement the sum aggregate (FSUM) for fuzzy data, we have to define the addition of L-R fuzzy numbers. If we assume that fuzzy numbers A_1 and A_2 are represented by triples:

$$A_1 = (m_{A1}, \alpha_{A1}, \beta_{A1}), \ and \ A_2 = (m_{A2}, \alpha_{A2}, \beta_{A2}), \tag{3}$$

the sum of them has the following form [11]:

$$A_1 + A_2 = (m_{A1+A2}, \alpha_{A1+A2}, \beta_{A1+A2}) = (m_{A1} + m_{A2}, \alpha_{A1} + \alpha_{A2}, \beta_{A1} + \beta_{A2}) \tag{4}$$

Addition of two L-R fuzzy numbers is presented in Fig. 1.

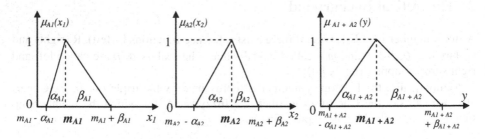

Fig. 1. Addition of two L-R fuzzy numbers A_1 and A_2

Division of L-R fuzzy number by a crisp value
In the work, we use the division of the L-R fuzzy number by a crisp value in order to calculate the average aggregate function FAVG, which operates on fuzzy data. In this case, we adopt dependencies that are defined for the division of two L-R fuzzy numbers. Crisp value is a special instance of the L-R fuzzy number, which has not left and right spreads ($\alpha_B = 0$, $\beta_B = 0$). In the situation, the following dependencies occur [11]:

$$m_{A/B} = m_A/m_B$$
$$m_{A/B} + \beta_{A/B} = (m_A + \beta_A)/m_B \qquad (5)$$
$$m_{A/B} - \alpha_{A/B} = (m_A - \alpha_A)/m_B$$

Both operations (addition and division) can be also applied to L-R fuzzy intervals. For example, for two L-R fuzzy intervals A_1 and A_2 represented by four parameters:

$$A_1 = (m_{A1}, n_{A1}, \alpha_{A1}, \beta_{A1}), \text{ and } A_2 = (m_{A2}, n_{A2}, \alpha_{A2}, \beta_{A2}), \qquad (6)$$

the sum of these L-R fuzzy intervals is determined by the expression (7).

$$A_1 + A_2 = (m_{A1}, n_{A1}, \alpha_{A1}, \beta_{A1}) + (m_{A2}, n_{A2}, \alpha_{A2}, \beta_{A2}) =$$
$$= (m_{A1} + m_{A2}, n_{A1} + n_{A2}, \alpha_{A1} + \alpha_{A2}, \beta_{A1} + \beta_{A2}). \qquad (7)$$

Logical operators
We have to define the majority and minority operators for fuzzy numbers in order to compare and sort fuzzy data, and also to implement the maximum (FMAX) and minimum (FMIN) aggregate functions.

For given fuzzy numbers the majority relation is defined on the basis of comparison of appropriate parameters of their membership functions. In our approach, we first compare the modal values and check, which of them is greater. If they are equal, we check right spreads, and if they are equal, we check left spreads.

The minority relation is calculated in the same way, but if the modal values are equal, we first check left spreads and if they are equal, we then check right spreads.

Linguistic Quantifiers
Linguistic quantifiers are special terms introduced by Zadeh and taken from the natural language. They are expressed by terms, like: *almost all, most, at least half, several, at least 20%* [10]. Since these terms include the information about proportions, Zadeh suggested they can be represented as fuzzy subsets of the unit interval [0,1]. Linguistic quantifiers express the cardinality of the group of aggregated data. With the use of linguistic quantifiers we can also specify filtering conditions on groups of data. In the syntax of the SQL SELECT statement the fuzzy linguistic quantifiers occupy the place of aggregate functions. For these reasons, they are sometimes called linguistic aggregate functions.

3 Example of a Fuzzy Data Warehouse

In data warehouses, we store business or other types of facts in so called fact table. These facts are described by means of measures – calculable attributes in the fact table. Since some facts can be provided with a bit of approximation, some measures must have the fuzzy representation. Therefore in our work, in order to gather and analyze fuzzy values, we have defined the new data type LR and methods that operate on the LR data in the data warehouse management system.

In section 4, we show different cases of data aggregation in the data warehouse containing fuzzy measures. We present extensions of the SELECT statements regarding aggregation of fuzzy data and filtering groups. In given examples, we base on our last implementation of the *Resources* fuzzy data warehouse storing consumption and requirement for global natural resources.

In the simplified schema of the *Resources* data warehouse presented in Fig. 2, we can distinguish the following elements of the multidimensional model:
- Dimensions
  - *Geography*, with the hierarchy of attributes: *Continent→Country*
  - *Time*, with the hierarchy of attributes: *Year→Quarter→Month*
  - *Resource*, with the hierarchy of attributes: *Category→Resource*
- Facts – *Requirements*, with measures:
  - *ConsumptionAmount* – resource consumption, crisp data
  - *ConsumptionCost* – cost of the resource consumption, crisp data
  - *RequirementAmount* – requirement for a resource, **L-R fuzzy number**
  - *RequirementCost* – cost of the requirement for a resource, **L-R fuzzy number**

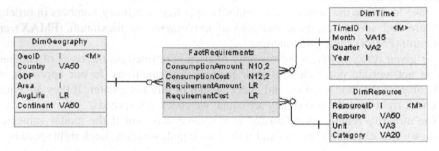

Fig. 2. Structure of the *Resources* data warehouse

Fuzzy data stored in the *Resources* data warehouse can be presented in two forms:
- as the four *(l, m, n, p)*, where: *(m, n)* is the interval of modal values, $l=m-\alpha$, $p=n+\beta$; and $\alpha>0$, $\beta>0$ are left and right spreads, respectively. The four *(l, m, n, p)* determines the trapezoidal membership function for a fuzzy number. The triangular membership function is a special case of the trapezoidal function, where $m=n$.
- as linguistic value *approx. x*, where x is a mean of m and n values.

Sample values of the *RequirementAmount* fuzzy measure in both presentation forms are shown below.

```
RequirementAmount          RequirementAmount
-------------------------   --------------------
(2416;2517;2617;2717)       approx.2567
(976;1017;1017;1057)        approx.1017
(1571;1637;1697;1762)       approx.1667
```

The *Resources* data warehouse is stored in the ROLAP technology, where data and aggregates are maintained by the relational database engine. The data warehouse was populated with data from bulletin boards, press news and electronic papers.

4   Data Aggregation and Filtering Groups in FDW

Data warehouse systems are generally oriented on querying and aggregating data. If a data warehouse consists of fuzzy measures, we need to extend the standard syntax of the SQL SELECT statement, which is commonly used while retrieving data. This implicates not only the implementation of fuzzy aggregates, like: FSUM, FAVG, FMIN, FMAX, but also extensions to the HAVING clause, which is applied to filter groups of records during data analysis. In the section, we present several examples of aggregation of fuzzy measures incorporated in the extended SQL language. In our analysis of the global resources requirements, we have identified the following cases, which differ from each other with the processing procedure:

1. aggregation of fuzzy data,
2. aggregation of crisp data with a fuzzy condition in the HAVING clause,
3. aggregation of fuzzy data with a crisp condition in the HAVING clause,
4. aggregation of fuzzy data with a fuzzy condition in the HAVING clause,
5. usage of fuzzy quantifiers that operate on the selected group of rows.

Example 1: In the example, we present the aggregation of fuzzy values for the *RequirementCost* measure.

We want to generate the ranking of 10 countries, which GDP per capita exceeds 30 000$ and bear the highest expenses of the required coal resource in the 2010.

The query in our extended SQL language has the following form:

```
SELECT TOP 10 g.Country, FSUM(RequirementCost) AS TotalCost
FROM  DimGeography g JOIN FactRequirements rf ON g.GeoId=rf.GeoId
     JOIN DimTime t ON rf.TimeId=t.TimeId
     JOIN DimResource r ON rf.ResId=r.ResId
WHERE r.Resource='coal' AND g.GDP > 30000 AND t.Year=2010
GROUP BY g.Country ORDER BY TotalCost DESC;
```

In the presented query, the FSUM aggregate function operates on fuzzy numbers stored in the *RequirementCost* column. Results of the SELECT statement are shown below. Aggregated value of the *RequirementCost* measure is presented with the use of linguistic value. In the result set we present sample data.

```
Country          TotalReqCost
--------------   ----------------
USA              approx. 1863
Japan            approx. 1632
France           approx. 1629
Australia        approx. 1534
...
```

Example 2: In this example, we show the use of standard average aggregate function (AVG) operating on crisp data. In the case, the AVG function appears also in the HAVING clause of the SELECT statement. In this statement, we construct the fuzzy filtering condition for particular groups of data.

Display average month consumption of the oil resource in particular years and countries, which area exceeds 120000 km². In the final result display only these countries, which consumption is high with the compatibility degree greater than 0.7.

The query in the extended SQL language has the following form:

```
SELECT g.Country, t.Year, r.Resource,
     AVG(ConsumptionAmount) AS AverageMonthConsumption
FROM  DimGeography g JOIN FactRequirements rf ON g.GeoID=rf.GeoID
     JOIN DimTime t ON rf.TimeID=t.TimeID
     JOIN DimResource r ON rf.ResID=r.ResID
```

```
WHERE g.Area > 120000 AND r.Resource = 'oil'
GROUP BY r.Resource, g.Country, t.Year
HAVING ( AVG(ConsumptionAmount) ~= high() ) > 0.7;
```

In the fuzzy filtering condition of the HAVING clause the result of the AVG function (crisp value) is compared to the L-R fuzzy number (*high consumption*) represented by the trapezoidal membership function (Fig. 3) defined earlier by the domain specialist. The result of the comparison is the compatibility degree between crisp value and fuzzy number. The compatibility degree (CD) should be greater than 0.7.

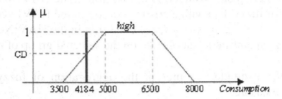

Fig. 3. Comparison of the crisp value (4184) and fuzzy number (*high consumption*)

In order to compare the crisp value of the AVG aggregate function with the fuzzy number, we had to develop the new equality operator (~=). This operator returns the value of the compatibility degree from the set [0,1]. Returned compatibility degree is compared to the given threshold 0.7, determining whether the row is displayed in the result set, or not. The result of the sample SQL query is presented below.

```
Country   Year     Resource  AverageMonthConsumption
--------  ------   --------  -----------------------
China     2009     oil       5773
Russia    2007     oil       5142
USA       1998     oil       4184
```

Example 3: In this example, we show the use of the average aggregate function (FAVG) operating on fuzzy data. The FAVG function appears in the fuzzy filtering condition in the HAVING clause. The result of the aggregation (fuzzy number) is compared to the given crisp value.

Generate report showing average costs of requirements for particular resource categories in particular countries and continents in the year 2010. Show only these countries, where costs of requirements are about US$ 150mln with the compatibility degree greater than or equal to 0.5.

The query in the extended SQL language has the following form:

```
SELECT g.Continent, g.Country, r.Category,
       FAVG(RequirementCost) AS AverageReqCost
FROM  DimGeography g JOIN FactRequirements rf ON g.GeoID=rf.GeoID
      JOIN DimTime t ON rf.TimeID=t.TimeID
      JOIN DimResource r ON rf.ResID=r.ResID
WHERE t.Year = 2010 GROUP BY g.Continent, g.Country, r.Category
HAVING ( FAVG(RequirementCost) ~= 150 ) >= 0.5;
```

Processing of the fuzzy filtering condition is similar to the previous example (comparison of the crisp value and fuzzy number, Fig. 3). Results of the query look as follows (sample data):

Continent	Country	Category	AverageReqCost
Asia	China	non-renewable	approx. 146
Asia	Saudi Arabia	non-renewable	approx. 148
Europe	France	non-renewable	approx. 150
Europe	Italy	renewable	approx. 146
North America	USA	non-renewable	approx. 153

Example 4: In the example, we present the use of the sum aggregate function (FSUM) operating on fuzzy data. We also show the fuzzy filtering condition in the HAVING clause, which consists of two fuzzy numbers.

Display total requirements for resources in particular continents. Show these continents, where total requirement is low, with a compatibility degree greater than 0.8.

The query in the extended SQL language has the following form:

```
SELECT g.Continent, r.Resource, r.Unit,
    FSUM(RequirementAmount) AS TotalRequirement
FROM  DimGeography g JOIN FactRequirements rf ON g.GeoID=rf.GeoID
    JOIN DimTime t ON rf.TimeID=t.TimeID
    JOIN DimResource r ON rf.ResID=r.ResID
GROUP BY g.Continent, r.Resource, r.Unit
HAVING ( FSUM(RequirementAmount) ~= low() ) > 0.8;
```

The result of the FSUM function (in the HAVING clause), which is a fuzzy number, is compared to the fuzzy value *low requirement*. The comparison is realized by the ~= equality operator, which returns the compatibility degree between two fuzzy numbers (Fig. 4). In the final result we obtain rows having the degree grater than 0.8.

Continent	Resource	Unit	TotalRequirement
Australia & Oceania	gas	ton	approx. 315491
Australia & Oceania	tea	kg	approx. 316487
Australia & Oceania	water	m3	approx. 301659
South America	coffee	kg	approx. 318204
South America	grain	ton	approx. 307051
South America	oil	ton	approx. 316282

In Fig. 4 we can observe different possible cases of the comparison of two fuzzy numbers represented by trapezoidal membership functions. If two fuzzy numbers have only one common point (Fig. 4a), this point determines the compatibility degree of these two fuzzy numbers. If there is more than one common point (Fig. 4b) and we obtain more compatibility degrees, we choose the highest one.

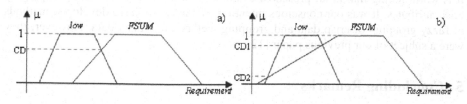

Fig. 4. Comparison of two fuzzy numbers: a) one common point, b) many common points

Example 5: In the last example, we use the *almost_all* fuzzy linguistic quantifier in order to determine the proportion of data in the group, for which the FSUM aggregate function is calculated. The proportion is determined based on the given condition.

Show these countries, for which almost whole requirement for the coal took place in the 3rd quarter of the 2009. Show only these cases, for which the compatibility degree is greater than 0.7.

The query in the extended SQL language looks as follows:

```
SELECT g.Country, FSUM(RequirementAmount) AS TotalRequirement
FROM  DimGeography g JOIN FactRequirements rf ON g.GeoID=rf.GeoID
      JOIN DimTime t ON rf.TimeID=t.TimeID
      JOIN DimResource r ON rf.ResID=r.ResID
WHERE t.Year = 2009 AND r.Resource = 'coal' GROUP BY g.Country
HAVING allmost_all( t.Quarter = 'Q3' ) > 0.7;
```

We treat the *almost all* linguistic quantifier as a fuzzy subset of the unit interval [0,1]. This quantifier is defined by the membership function presented in Fig. 5a. For each group of rows (for each country) we calculate the percentage of rows, which fulfil the specified condition (t.Quarter = 'Q3'). Afterwards, we determine the compatibility degree between the percentage and the *almost_all* quantifier (Fig. 5b).

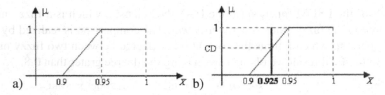

Fig. 5. Membership function for the *almost_all* linguistic quantifier (a). Calculation of the compatibility degree between sample percentage (0.925) and the *almost_all* quantifier (b).

In the result set, we want to show only these countries, which have the compatibility degree is greater than the given threshold 0.7 (we present sample data):

```
Country          TotalRequirement
---------------  ----------------------
China            approx. 30661
France           approx. 25783
Germany          approx. 26836
Japan            approx. 23773
```

It is worth noting that in all presented examples, we used only classical grouping by crisp attributes. It was our conscious intention. Actually, we have developed methods of fuzzy grouping of crisp data and grouping methods for fuzzy data. However, they were a subject of our previous paper [12].

5 Concluding Remarks

Exploring the consumption and requirement for global natural resources needs soft computing methods in order to extend the spectrum of the analysis. Implementation of the L-R fuzzy type in a data warehouse allows to store and analyze imprecise data and study data, which have similar characteristics. Especially, in huge data repositories, this leads to the rough and fast data analysis and filtering. Therefore, it makes the general improvement of the investigation possibilities, which is sometimes difficult to achieve in standard data warehouses.

If we decide to include fuzzy measures (e.g. numerical values of some estimated facts), we have to use elements of arithmetic of fuzzy numbers or fuzzy logic during data aggregation. This may lead to the increase of the response time. However, our research on the effectiveness of presented queries shows the response time rises about 10% in comparison to corresponding queries implemented with the use of the standard SQL language. Such a good efficiency of our solution was achieved through the implementation of presented methods as a part of a database management system, where the fuzzy data warehouse resided.

Data aggregation is one of the basic operations performed in data warehouses and methods presented in the paper have a general purpose. Recently, we have been developing a fuzzy data warehouse for forensic and criminalistic analysis as a part of the project O R00 0068 07.

References

1. Kimball, R., Reeves, L., Margy, R., Thornthwaite, W.: The Data Warehouse Lifecycle Toolkit. John Wiley & Sons, Chichester (1998)
2. Ponniah, P.: Data Warehousing Fundamentals. A Comprehensive Guide for IT Professionals. John Wiley & Sons, Chichester (2001)
3. Bosc, P., Pivert, O.: SQLf: A Relational Database Language for Fuzzy Querying. IEEE Transactions on Fuzzy Systems 3(1), 1–17 (1995)
4. Kacprzyk, J., Zadrozny, S.: SQLf and FQUERY for Access. In: IFSA World Congress and 20th NAFIPS International Conference, pp. 2464–2469 (2001)
5. Małysiak, B., Mrozek, D., Kozielski, S.: Processing Fuzzy SQL Queries with Flat, Context-Dependent and Multidimensional Membership Functions. In: 4th IASTED International Conference on Computational Intelligence, pp. 36–41. ACTA Press, Calgary (2005)
6. Chaudhuri, S., Ganjam, K., Ganti, V., Motwani, R.: Robust and Efficient Fuzzy Match for Online Data Cleaning. In: 2003 ACM SIGMOD International Conference on Management of Data, San Diego, California, pp. 313–324 (2003)
7. Lin, H.-Y., Hsu, P.-Y., Sheen, G.-J.: A Fuzzy-based Decision-Making Procedure for Data Warehouse System Selection. Journal of Expert Systems with Applications, 939–953 (2007)
8. Perez, D., Somodevilla, M.J., Pineda, I.H.: Fuzzy Spatial Data Warehouse: A Multidimensional Model. In: 8th Mexican International Conference on Current Trends in Computer Science, pp. 3–9. IEEE, Los Alamitos (2007)
9. Fasel, D., Zumstein, D.: A Fuzzy Data Warehouse Approach for Web Analytics. In: Lytras, M.D., Damiani, E., Carroll, J.M., Tennyson, R.D., Avison, D., Naeve, A., Dale, A., Lefrere, P., Tan, F., Sipior, J., Vossen, G. (eds.) WSKS 2009. LNCS, vol. 5736, pp. 276–285. Springer, Heidelberg (2009)
10. Bouchon-Meunier, B., Yager, R.R., Zadeh, L.A.: Fuzzy Logic and Soft Computing. Advances in Fuzzy Systems, Application and Theory 4 (1995)
11. Dubois, D., Prade, H.: Fundamentals of Fuzzy Sets. Kluwer Academic Publishers, Dordrecht (2000)
12. Małysiak-Mrozek, B., Mrozek, D., Kozielski, S.: Data Grouping Process in Extended SQL Language Containing Fuzzy Elements. In: AISC, vol. 59, pp. 247–256. Springer, Heidelberg (2009)

Stochastic Chaotic Simulated Annealing Using Neural Network for Minimizing Interference in Mobile Hierarchical Ad Hoc and Sensor Networks

Jerzy Martyna

Institute of Computer Science,
Jagiellonian University, ul. Prof. S. Lojasiewicza 6, 30-348 Cracow

Abstract. In this paper, stochastic chaotic simulated annealing for minimizing interference in mobile ad hoc and sensor networks is studied. Following a general formulation of the channel assignment problem (CAP), the demand constraints for energy function of this problem are determined. The CAP problem for these networks was solved with the help of the neural network. Our simulation results indicate that by selecting a set of parameters we can obtain interference minimization in these networks. An extension of this technique allows us to use it in the dynamic CAP to solve more sophisticated optimization problems.

1 Introduction

The forthcoming wireless multi-hop networks such as ad hoc and sensor networks will allow nodes to communicate directly each other using wireless transceivers without the need for a fixed infrastructure. Moreover, in these networks the nodes can communicate without base stations, such as the wired radio antennae. Ad hoc networks are built by exploiting wireless technology and various portable devices (laptops, cellular phones, etc.) and the fixed equipment (wireless Internet access points, etc.) which can be connected together.

Wireless sensor networks are a particular type of ad hoc networks in which the nodes are so-called 'sensors' with advanced sensing functionalities (thermal, pressure, acoustic, etc.), a processor and a short-range wireless transceiver. These networks can gather data from the environment and send them to a data-sink to build a global view of the monitored region, which is accessible to the external users through one or more gateway node(s).

Mobile ad hoc and sensor networks are additionally equipped with moving devices, such as PDA, laptops or data gathering nodes. These devices allow one to communicate with the immobile nodes, first of all with the clusterhead nodes, if the network is two- or more layered. The presence of clusterhead nodes impose a hierarchy of nodes onto the networks. These networks can act as a so-called hierarchical ad hoc and sensor networks to enable the communication between clusters.

N. García-Pedrajas et al. (Eds.): IEA/AIE 2010, Part III, LNAI 6098, pp. 626–635, 2010.

The building of wireless networks is associated with the radio *channel assignment problem* (CAP). According to the classification of the CAP [11] we can formulate two categories, i.e., CAP1 and CAP2. The former is associated with the minimization of the span of channels subject to demand and interference-free constraints. The CAP2 is used to minimize interference subject to demand constraints. In addition to this, in practical cases the one more useful is the CAP2 due to, among others, the high demand in mobile communications and the often used topology control protocols.

In both types of wireless networks interference belongs to the undesirable phenomena. Informally, node a may interfere with another node b if a's interference range covers b. The amount of interference that b posseses is the number of such nodes as a. The ad hoc and sensor networks are additionally exposed the interference. For these networks the small interference helps in reducing the coding overhead. It means that the energy of battery-driven devices can be saved up. Thus, the minimizing interference may increase the network lifetime.

The upper bounds of some of the interference problems have been obtained in a different context. Among others, the problem of reducing the *total amount of energy* spent by the nodes in wireless ad hoc networks with connectivity requirements was given by G. Calinescu [3]. The positive aspect of this approach was prolongation of the lifetime of the ad hoc network.

The problem of reducing interference in ad hoc and sensor networks was studied by T. Moscibroda and R. Wattenhofer in the paper [9], in which a greedy algorithm for approximation to the interference with connectivity requirements was given. In recent papers presented by von Rickenbach [10], the problem of minimizing the maximum interference was studied. An $O\sqrt[4]{n}$ approximation algorithm to evaluate the interference was given.

The method of artificial intelligence was also used to minimize interference in wireless networks. Among others, minimizing the severity of interferences in the cellular radio was given by Kunz [8]. The author solved channel assignment problem by minimizing the energy or the cost function representing interference and channel assignment constraints. The same problem was resolved by K. Smith and M. Palaniswami [11] by means of the simulated annealing, a modified Hopfield neural network, and a self-organizing neural network. In a paper by L. Wang et al. [12], the authors studied the proposed stochastic chaotic simulated annealing (SCSA) to solve the traveling salesman problem and the channel assignment problem (CA) for cellular mobile communications.

In this paper, we propose a stochastic simmulated annealing to minimize interference in mobile hierarchical ad hoc and sensor networks. We formulate this problem regarding the demand constraints for these networks by the total interference in the mobile network. Then, we define the computational energy and derive the dynamics of the SCSA for the CAP problem in these networks. Simulation studies bring out the effectiveness of the proposed method.

The rest of the paper is organized as follows. The SCSA method is described in Section 2. Section 3 presents the proposed solution. The simulation results of the proposed method are given in section 4. Section 5 concludes the paper.

2 Stochastic Chaotic Simulated Annealing

The stochastic chaotic simulated annealing related to the CAP problem was described by L. Chen and K. Aihara [4], [5], [6] as the following equation, namely

$$x_{ik}(t+1) = \frac{1}{1 + e^{-y_{ik}(t)/\epsilon}} \tag{1}$$

$$y_{ik}(t+1) = k \cdot y_{ik}(t) + \alpha \left(\sum_{i=1,i\neq j}^{N} \sum_{l=1,l\neq k}^{M} w_{ikjl} x_{1k}(t) + I_{ik} \right) - z(t)(x_{ik}(t) - I_0) \tag{2}$$

$$z(t+1) = (1 - \beta_1)z(t) \tag{3}$$

$$A[n(t+1)] = (1 - \beta_2)A[n(t)] \tag{4}$$

where the variables are:

N - number of call nodes;
M - number of channels;
x_{ik} - output of neuron ik;
y_{ik} - internal state of neuron ik;
I_{ik} - input bias of neuron ik;
α - positive scaling parameter for the inputs;
$z(t)$ - self-feedback neuronal connection height or refractory stremgth
        $(z(t) \geq 0)$;
β_1, β_2 - damping factors for the time-dependent neuronal self coupling
        and the added random noise $(0 \leq \beta_1 \leq 1, 0 \leq \beta_2 \leq 1)$;
I_0 - positive parameter;
ϵ - steepness parameter of the neuronal output function $(\epsilon > 0)$;
$n(t)$ - random noise injected into the neurons, with its actual value being
        in the range $[-A, A]$ and with a uniform distribution, $A[n]$ is the
        noise amplitude;
w_{ikjl} - connection weight from neuron ik to neuron jl, with $w_{ikjl} = w_{jlik}$
        and $w_{ikik} = 0$.

The connection weights can be obtained from

$$\sum_{j=1,i\neq j}^{N} \sum_{l=1,l\neq k}^{M} w_{ikjl} x_{ik} + I_{jl} = -\frac{\partial E}{\partial x_{ik}} \tag{5}$$

where E is the energy function of the network or the cost function to be minimized in the formulated combinatorial optimization problem. In the absence of noise $n(t) = 0$ for all t the problem is reduced to the mentioned above solution of the CSA given by Chen and Aihara [4], [5], [6].

In the absence of noise and damping of the self-neural coupling (i.e. $n(t) = 0$ for all t and $\beta_1 = 0$), the Eq. (1) - (5) of the above given equation become the Aihara-Takaba-Toyoda chaotic neural network [1]. This network possesses several dynamic behaviours. Among others, this network can have static fixed points, periodic oscillations, and chaos depending on the value of the network parameters.

3   Minimizing Interference Using Stochastic Chaotic Simulated Annealing

In this section, we introduce a stochastic chaotic simulated annealing for minimizing interference in mobile ad hoc and sensor networks formulated as the CAP2 problem.

We assume that a hierarchical mobile ad hoc or sensor network has I immobile and J mobile nodes. The total number of the available channels is equal to M. The channel requirements for the transmission inside and outside the cluster i are give by D_i and D_n $(i = 1, \ldots, \phi_n, n = 1, \ldots, \Phi)$, respectively. Each element d_i in D_i or D^n represents the number of frequencies to be assigned to a call. The minimum distance in the frequency domain by which two nodes are separated in such a way that an acceptable low signal/interference ratio in each cluster must be guaranteed. It is called a *compatibility matrix* $\mathbf{C}$ [7], where c_{ij} is the frequency separation between a call of node i and a call of node j without interferences with each other. Each nondiagonal element c_{ij} in $\mathbf{C}$ represents the minimum separation distance in the frequency domain between the frequency assigned to call of node i and the frequency assigned to call of node j. The cochannel constraint is represented by $c_{ij} = 1$, and the adjacent channel constraint is represented by $c_{ij} = 2$. $c_{ij} = 0$ indicates that calls of node i and j are allowed to use the same frequency. We recall that the CAP problem is formulated as finding a conflict-free frequency assignment with the minimum number of total frequencies, where the matrices $\mathbf{C}$ and $\mathbf{D}$ are given.

The CAP2 problem can be formulated here by means of using a neural network with $N \times M$ neurons [11]. Thus, the output of each neuron x_{jk} is follows:

$$x_{jk} = \begin{cases} 1, & \text{if node } j \text{ is assigned to channel } k \\ 0, & \text{otherwise} \end{cases} \tag{6}$$

To measure the degree of interference between nodes j and i cost tensor $P_{ji(m-1)}$ [11] is used, where $m = \mid k - l \mid$ is the distance in the frequency domain between channels k and l. The cost tensor P is defined as follows

$$P_{ji(m+1)} = \max(0, P_{jim} - 1), \quad \text{for } m = 1, \ldots, M+1 \tag{7}$$

$$P_{ji1} = c_{ji}, \quad \forall j, i \neq j \tag{8}$$

$$P_{jj1} = 0, \quad \forall j \tag{9}$$

The minimization interference regarding the demand constraints for wireless ad hoc/sensor networks can be defined by the following cost

$$F(x) = \sum_{j=I+1}^{I+J} \sum_{j=1}^{I} \sum_{k=1}^{M} x_{jk} \sum_{i=I+1}^{I+J} \sum_{i=1}^{I} \sum_{l=1}^{M} P_{ji}(\mid k - l \mid +1)x_{il} \tag{10}$$

subject to

$$\sum_{k=1}^{M} x_{jk} = D_j, \quad \forall j = 1, \ldots, I + J, \tag{11}$$

$$\sum_{n=1}^{\phi_n} x_{jn} = D^n, \quad \forall j = 1, \ldots, \Phi \tag{12}$$

where $F(x)$ is the total inference in the mobile network.

The computational energy function E can be defined as a sum of the interferences and constraints

$$E = \frac{W_1}{2} \sum_{j=I+1}^{I+J} \sum_{j=1}^{I} (\sum_{k=1}^{M} x_{jk} - D_j)^2 + \frac{W_2}{2} \sum_{n=1}^{\phi_n} (\sum_{k=1}^{M} x_{jk} - D^n)^2 \tag{13}$$

$$+ \frac{W_3}{2} \sum_{j=I+1}^{I+J} \sum_{j=1}^{I} \sum_{k=1}^{M} x_{jk} \sum_{j=I+1}^{I+J} \sum_{i=1}^{I} \sum_{l=1}^{M} P_{ji(|k-l|+1)} x_{il}$$

where W_1, W_2, W_3 are the weight coefficients corresponding to the constraints and interference, respectively.

Next, we derive the dynamics of the SCSA for the CAP problem in wireless ad hoc and sensor networks as follows, namely

$$y_{ik}(t+1) = k y_{ik}(t) - z(t)(x_{ik}(t) - I_0) \tag{14}$$

$$+ \alpha \{ -W_1 \sum_{h \neq j}^{\phi_n} \sum_{k=1}^{M} x_{ih}(t) - W_2 \sum_{f \neq j}^{\phi_n} \sum_{k=1}^{M} x_{fj}(t) \tag{15}$$

$$+ W_1 - W_2 \sum_{f \neq i}^{\phi_n} \sum_{k=1}^{M} (x_{fj+1}(t) + x_{fj-1}(t)) d_{if} \} \tag{16}$$

$$+ n(t) \tag{17}$$

4   Simulation Results

In this section, we consider an experiments for assessing the effectiveness of our proposed method. The experiment involves the immobile and mobile nodes of the ad hoc/sensor network.

In the experiment we take into considerations the static location of two clusters with the clusterheads and eight immobile and one mobile nodes. In the experiment, we take into consideration the scenario with the single node which is harvesting the data from the network through the connection with the clusterhead node in the cluster. In our approach, only the transmission between the mobile node and the clusterhead node is possible. We have considered three moments in the movement of mobile node, namely: outside the cluster (Fig. 1), inside the cluster (Fig. 2), and outside the handoff zone (Fig. 3).

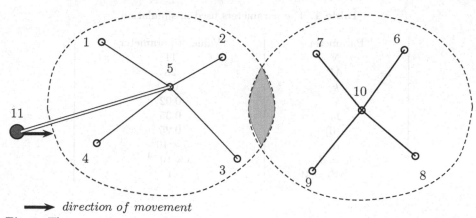

→ *direction of movement*

Fig. 1. The event corresponds to the scenario at time $t = 1$ where just one mobile node, labeled 11, outside the cluster communicates with the first clusterhead node

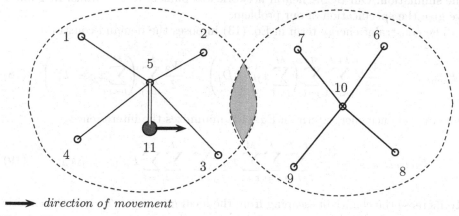

→ *direction of movement*

Fig. 2. The event corresponds to the scenario at time $t = 2$ where a mobile node inside the cluster communicates with the first clusterhead node

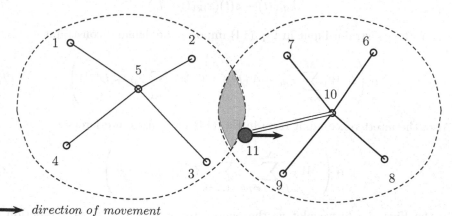

→ *direction of movement*

Fig. 3. The event corresponds to the scenario at time $t = 3$ where a mobile node outside the handoff zone communicates with the second clusterhead node

Table 1. The parameters used in simulation

Parameter	Value of parameter
N	11
M	28
k	0.8
ϵ	0.02
I_0	0.35
$z(0)$	0.25
α	5×10^2
$\beta_1 = \beta_2$	5×10^{-3}
$W_1 = W_2 = W_3$	1

The number of required frequencies for all the nodes was determined before the simulation. Our SCSA neural network was built of 312 neurons. In Table 1 we give the specification of our problem.

The constraint energy term in Eq. (13) imposes the demand constraint:

$$E_{constraits} = \frac{W_1}{2} \sum_{j=I+1}^{I+J} \sum_{j=1}^{I} \left(\sum_{k=1}^{M} x_{jk} - D_j \right)^2 + \frac{W_2}{2} \sum_{n=1}^{\phi_n} \left(\sum_{k=1}^{M} x_{jk} - D^n \right)^2 \quad (18)$$

The interference energy term in Eq. (13) minimizes the interference

$$E_{interference} = \frac{W_3}{2} \sum_{j=I+1}^{I+J} \sum_{j=1}^{I} \sum_{k=1}^{M} x_{jk} \sum_{j=I+1}^{I+J} \sum_{i=1}^{I} \sum_{l=1}^{M} P_{ji(|k-l|+1)} x_{il} \quad (19)$$

To increase the chance of escaping from the local minima we include the chaotic dynamics in the single-neuron input term, namely

$$k y_{ik}(t) - z(t)(x_{ik}(t) - I_0) \quad (20)$$

Then, the constraint input in Eq. (14) imposes the demand constraint

$$\alpha \left((-W_1 \sum_{h \neq k}^{M} x_{jh} + W_1 D_j) + (-W_2 \sum_{h \neq k}^{M} x_{jh} + D^{(n)}) \right) \quad (21)$$

Also, the interference input term in Eq. (14) minimizes interference

$$\alpha \left(-W_3 \sum_{f=1, f \neq j}^{N} \sum_{h=1, h \neq k}^{M} P_{ji(|k-h|+1)}^{M} x_{fh} \right) \quad (22)$$

In the Figs. 4 - 6, we plot as the energy terms in Eq. (13) as a function of iteration steps in SCSA: a) the total energy, b) the constraints term, and b) the optimization term.

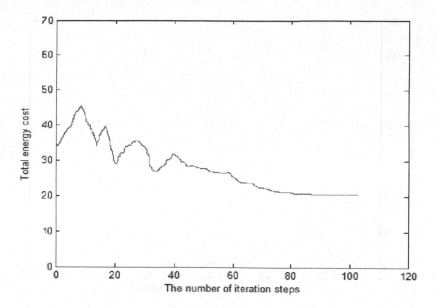

Fig. 4. The total energy in Eq. (13) as a function of iteration steps in SCSA

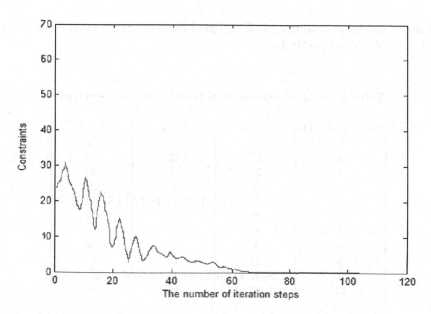

Fig. 5. The constraints energy in Eq. (13) as a function of iteration steps in SCSA

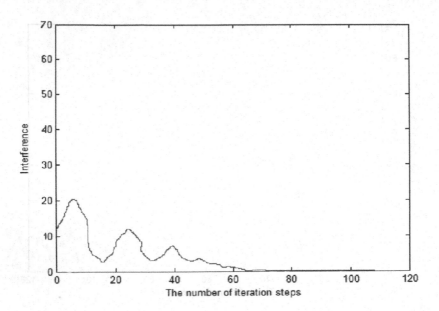

Fig. 6. The interference energy in Eq. (13) as a function of iteration steps in SCSA

Table 2 shows an example of all assigned frequencies for each node at time $t = 1, t = 2, t = 3$, respectively.

Table 2. Assigned frequencies at time $t = 1, 2, 3$, respectively

Number of node	$t = 1$	$t = 2$	$t = 3$
1	38	27	52
2	17	12	16
3	23	9	43
4	5	3	22
5	1 8 11 47 53	24 33 39 48 42	13 31 34 37 49
6	29	21	10
7	35	15	1
8	8	6	40
9	41	18	55
10	14 26 32 44 50	30 36 45 51 54	7 19 25 28 46
11	20	56	4

5   Conclusions

We have presented an experimental analysis of minimizing the severity of interference, subject to the demand constraints. Our solution based on the chaotic simulated annealing was able to make dynamic change of node locations and for themselve to take into consideration the movement of some nodes. The three constraints are considered, namely: the constraint energy inside the cluster, the constraint energy outside the cluster, and the interference energy term. In the simulation results, the assigned frequencies for the defined situations are shown.

   In the future research, we will exploit the more sophisticated topologies of our network and also experiment with the mobility models.

References

[1] Aihara, K., Takabe, T., Toyoda, M.: Chaotic Neural Networks. Phys. Lett. A 144(6, 7), 333–340 (1990)

[2] Burkhart, M., von Rickenbach, P., Wattenhofer, R., Zollinger, A.: Does Topology Control Reduce Interference. In: Proceedings of the 5th ACM Int. Symposium on Mobile Ad Hoc Networking and Computing, MobiHoc (2004)

[3] Calinescu, G., Kaspoor, S., Olshevsky, A., Zelikovsky, A.: Network Lifetime and Power Assignment in Ad Hoc Wireless Networks. In: Di Battista, G., Zwick, U. (eds.) ESA 2003. LNCS, vol. 2832, pp. 114–126. Springer, Heidelberg (2003)

[4] Chen, L., Aihara, K.: Transient Chaotic Neural Network Model as a Globally Coupled Map. In: Yamguti, M. (ed.) Toward the Harnessing of Chaos, and Sequence Processing, pp. 347–352. Elsevier Science, Amsterdam (1994)

[5] Chen, L., Aihara, K.: Chaotic Simulated Annealing by a Neural Network Model with Transient Chaos. Neural Networks 8(6), 915–930 (1995)

[6] Chen, L., Aihara, K.: Global Searching Ability of Chaotic Neural Networks. IEEE Trans. Circuits Syst. I 46, 978–981 (1999)

[7] Gamst, A., Rave, W.: On Frequency Assignment in Mobile Automatic Telephone Systems. In: Proc. GLOBECOM '82, pp. 309–315 (1982)

[8] Kunz, D.: Channel Assignment for Cellular Radio Using Neural Networks. IEEE Trans. on Vehicular Technology (40), 188–193 (1991)

[9] Moscibroda, T., Wattenhofer, R.: Minimizing Interference in Ad Hoc and Sensor Networks. In: Proc. DIALM-POMC '05, September 2, pp. 24–33 (2005)

[10] von Rickenbach, P., Schmid, S., Wattenhofer, R., Zollinger, A.: Robust Interference Model for Wireless Ad Hoc Networks. In: Proc. 5th IEEE Int. Workshop on Algorithms for Wireless, Mobile, Ad Hoc and Sensor Networks, WMAN (2005)

[11] Smith, K., Palaniswami, M.: Static and Dynamic Channel Assignment Using Neural Network. IEEE Journal on Selected Areas in Communications 15, 238–249 (1997)

[12] Wang, L., Li, S., Tian, F., Fu, X.: A Noisy Chaotic Neural Network for Solving Combinatorial Optimization Problems: Stochastic Chaotic Simulated Annealing. IEEE Trans. on Systems, Man, and Cybernetics 14(5), 2119–2125 (2004)

Modelling of Heat Flux in Building Using Soft-Computing Techniques

Javier Sedano[1], José Ramón Villar[2], Leticia Curiel[3], Enrique de la Cal[2], and Emilio Corchado[4]

[1] Department of Electromechanical Engineering. University of Burgos, Burgos, Spain
[2] Department of Computer Science, University of Oviedo, Spain
[3] Department of Civil Engineering, University of Burgos, Burgos, Spain
[4] Department of Computer Science and Automation,
University of Salamanca, Salamanca, Spain
jsedano@ubu.es, villarjose@uniovi.es, lcuriel@ubu.es,
delacal@uniovi.es, escorchado@usal.es

Abstract. Improving the detection of thermal insulation failures in buildings includes the development of models for heating process and fabric gain -heat flux through exterior walls in the building-. Thermal insulation standards are now contractual obligations in new buildings, the energy efficiency in the case of buildings constructed before the regulations adopted is still an open issue, and the assumption is that it will be based on heat flux and conductivity measurement. A three-step procedure is proposed in this study that begins by considering the local building and heating system regulations as well as the specific features of the climate zone. Firstly, the dynamic thermal performance of different variables is specifically modeled. Secondly, an exploratory projection pursuit method called Cooperative Maximum-Likelihood Hebbian Learning is used to extract the relevant features. Finally, a supervised neural model and identification techniques are applied, in order to detect the heat flux through exterior walls in the building. The reliability of the proposed method is validated for a winter zone, associated to several cities in Spain.

Keywords: Computational Intelligence, Soft computing Systems, Identification Systems, Artificial Neural Networks, Non-linear Systems.

1 Introduction

The identification of thermal insulation failures (TIF) could significantly increase building energy efficiency and substantially contribute to reductions in energy consumption and in the carbon footprints of domestic heating systems. Conventional methods can be greatly improved through the application of learning techniques to detect the TIF when a building is in operation through heat flux model - heat flux through exterior walls in the building-.

N. García-Pedrajas et al. (Eds.): IEA/AIE 2010, Part III, LNAI 6098, pp. 636–645, 2010.
© Springer-Verlag Berlin Heidelberg 2010

Nevertheless, predicting the thermal dynamics of a building is a complex task. The dynamic thermal performance of a building has mainly been used to estimate its power requirements. As an example, the difficulties of obtaining a black-box model for a generic building are documented in [1]. Furthermore, [2] cites examples of the errors associated with different kinds of techniques while providing possible solutions. Also, in order to determine the thermal insulation failures local building regulations need to be analysed in order to profile the premises and the legal specifications for the physical parameters.

This research represents a step forward in the development of techniques to improve dynamic thermal efficiency in existing buildings through a modelling of heat flux in the building. Although this may appear simple at first sight, noise due to occupancy and lighting profiles can introduce distortions and complicate detection. A three-step procedure for testing and validating the model is proposed: firstly, the dynamic thermal behaviour of a specific configuration is calculated using HTB2 software [3]. The outcome of the HTB2 should then be post-processed to obtain a suitable dataset. Subsequently, the dataset is analysed using an exploratory projection pursuit (EPP) [4, 5] called Cooperative Maximum-Likelihood Hebbian Learning (CMLHL) [6, 7], extract the dataset structure and key relationships between the variables. A model is then produced, at the modelling stage, to estimate the heat flux through exterior walls in the building at a specific configuration.

This paper is organised as follows. The following Sub-Section 1.1 details the problem description. Section 2 introduces the unsupervised connectionist techniques for analysing the datasets in order to extract their relevant internal structures. Section 3 deals with classical identification techniques used in the system modelling. Section 4 describes the case of study details and the multi-step procedure. Section 5 describes the results obtained and finally, the conclusions are set out and comments are made on future lines of work.

1.1 Spanish Regulations and the Problem Description

In 2007, several regulations on buildings and construction were approved in Spain. Firstly, the minimum pre-requisites for energy efficiency with which buildings must comply are given in the European Directive 2002/91/CE [8]. Project and specifications, the constructing conditions and the basic requirements in Spain are specified in the CTE (Código Técnico de Edificación [Building Regulations]) [9]. One of the basic requirements is document HE1 that considers the energy consumption limitation in buildings [9] and its updates.

The local regulations shall be analysed to extract the minimum requirements and parameters for heating systems and thermal comfort, and the energy efficiency certifying procedure as well. In Spain, the energy efficiency is calculated as the ratio of combustible consumption needed to satisfy the energy demand of the building. The energy efficiency in the case of buildings constructed before the CTE approval is still an open issue, and the assumption is that it will be based on heat flux and conductivity measurement.

2 Analysis of the Internal Structure of the Data Set

2.1 Principal Component Analisis

Principal Component Analysis (PCA) originated in work by Pearson [10], and independently by Hotelling [11] describing multivariate data set variations in terms of uncorrelated variables, each of which is a linear combination of the original variables. Its main goal is to derive new variables, in decreasing order of importance, which are linear combinations of the original variables and are uncorrelated with each other.

2.2 A Neural Implementation of Exploratory Projection Pursuit

The standard statistical method of EPP [4, 5], provides a linear projection of a data set, but it projects the data onto a set of basic vectors which best reveal the interesting structure in data; interestingness is usually defined in terms of how far the distribution is from the Gaussian distribution [12].

One neural implementation of EPP is Maximum Likelihood Hebbian Learning (MLHL) [5, 13]. It identifies interestingness by maximising the probability of the residuals under specific probability density functions that are non-Gaussian.

An extended version of this model is the Cooperative Maximum Likelihood Hebbian Learning (CMLHL) [6] model. CMLHL is based on MLHL [5, 13] adding lateral connections [14, 6], which have been derived from the Rectified Gaussian Distribution [12]. The resultant net can find the independent factors of a data set but does so in a way that captures some type of global ordering in the data set.

Considering an N-dimensional input vector (x), and an M-dimensional output vector (y), with W_{ij} being the weight (linking input j to output i), then CMLHL can be expressed [14, 13] as:

1. Feed-forward step:

$$y_i = \sum_{j=1}^{N} W_{ij} x_j, \forall i \ .$$ (1)

2. Lateral activation passing:

$$y_i(t+1) = [y_i(t) + \tau(b - Ay)]^+ \ .$$ (2)

3. Feedback step:

$$e_j = x_j - \sum_{i=1}^{M} W_{ij} y_i, \forall j \ .$$ (3)

4. Weight change:

$$\Delta W_{ij} = \eta . y_i . sign(e_j) |e_j|^{p-1} \ .$$ (4)

Where: η is the learning rate, [ ]+ is necessary to ensure that the y-values remain within the positive quadrant, τ is the "strength" of the lateral connections, b the bias parameter, p a parameter related to the energy function [5, 6, 13] and A the symmetric matrix used to modify the response to the data [6]. The effect of this matrix is based on the relation between the distances separating the output neurons.

3 System Modelling Using Identification Algorithms

System identification (SI) aims to obtain mathematic models to estimate one or more behaviours from a physical process whose dynamic equations are unknowns. Classic SI refers to the parametrical literature [15], which has its origin from the linear system analysis.

The SI procedure includes several steps [15]: the selection of the models and their structure, the learning methods, the identification and optimization criteria and the validation method. The validation ensures that the selected model meets the necessary conditions for estimation and prediction. Typically, validation is carried out using three different methods: the residual analysis $\varepsilon(t, \hat{\theta}(t))$ -by means of a correlation test between inputs, their residuals and their combinations-; the final prediction error (FPE) estimated as explained by Akaike [16] and finally a graphical comparison between desired outputs and the outcome of the models through simulation, with one (or k) steps ahead.

3.1 The ANN in the Identification Process

The use of ANN in the process of identification requires the selection of several parameters: the number of layers, the number of neurons per layer and the activation functions. The methods by which the parameters are set up are fully documented in the literature [17]. It was found that ANNs with two layers using non-linear functions in the hidden layer are universal approximators or predictors.

The number of neurons per layer is also a relevant design parameter. It should be analyzed in order to avoid over fitting. Each algorithm will introduce some restrictions in the weight matrix. The most widely used training algorithms in system identification are the Levenberg-Marquardt method, recursive Gauss-Newton method, the batch and recursive versions of the back-propagation algorithm.

Several well-known model structures are used when merging system identification with ANN. If the ARX (Autoregressive with external input) model is used as the regression vector θ, the model structure is called NNARX (neural network for ARX model), as can be seen in Eq. (5). Likewise, NNFIR for neural network FIR (Finite Impulse Response) Eq. (6), NNARMAX for neural network ARMAX (Autoregressive Moving Average with external input) Eq. (7) and NNOE for neural network OE (Output Error) Eq. (8), are also extensively used. In the same way, it is possible to use an estimator for the one-step ahead prediction of the output $\hat{y}_1(t \mid \theta)$, i.e., the NNARX and the NNFIR –using Eq. (9)–, or the NNARMAX and the NNOE –using Eq. (10)–. The polynomial degree values $-n_a$, n_b, n_c, n_d, n_f and n_k- are given as parameters.

$$\varphi(t) = \left[y(t-1) \ldots y(t-n_a) u(t-n_k) \ldots u(t-n_b-n_k+1) \right]^T . \tag{5}$$

$$\varphi(t) = \left[u(t-n_k) \ldots u(t-n_b-n_k+1) \right]^T . \tag{6}$$

$$\varphi(t) = \left[y(t-1) \ldots y(t-n_a) u(t-n_k) \ldots u(t-n_b-n_k+1) e(t-1) \ldots e(t-n_c) \right]^T . \tag{7}$$

$$\varphi(t) = \left[\hat{y}(t-1 \mid \theta) \ldots \hat{y}(t-n_a \mid \theta) u(t-n_k) \ldots u(t-n_b-n_k+1) \right]^T . \tag{8}$$

$$\hat{y}(t \mid \theta) = \hat{y}(t \mid t-1, \theta) = g(\varphi(t), \theta) . \tag{9}$$

$$\hat{y}(t \mid \theta) = g(\varphi(t), \theta) . \tag{10}$$

4 A Multi-step Method for Modelling of Heat Flux in Buildings

A novel three-step method is proposed to detect the heat flux through exterior walls in the building. Firstly, the building is parameterised and its dynamic thermal performance in normal operation is obtained by means of simulation. Then, the data gathered is processed using CMLHL as a dimensionality reduction technique to choose the most relevant features in order to determine the heat flux. The second step outcome is a data set which is finally used to train and validate the heat flux model.

4.1 Thermal Dynamics Data Gathering by Means of Simulation

In order to simulate the thermal behaviour of a building, the following variables and data sets should be gathered: building topology; climate zone according to the specific regulations; building materials that comply with local regulations for the chosen climate zone; meteorological data for the climate zone and the simulated time period: such as solar radiation, outdoor temperature, wind speed, etc., and realistic profiles for heating, lighting, small power devices, occupancy and ventilation.

In this study, the country where the system is applied is Spain. The Spanish regulations establish five winter/summer zones, from E1 (more severe climate zones) to A3 (gentler climate zone).

Having defined and/or gathered these data sets, then the chosen simulation tool is applied to obtain the output data. In our case, the simulation software used is HTB2 [3]. The typical values that each variable could take for an E winter climate zone of maximum severity in Spain -i.e. the cities of León, Burgos or Soria among others- are shown in Table 1.

Table 1. Typical values of each variable in a E winter climate zone city in Spain

Variable (Units)	Range of values	Transmittance level (W/m^{2}K)
Fabric gain -heat flux- (w), $y_1(t)$.	0 to -7,100	-External cavity wall: 0.54 -Double glazing: 2.90 -Floor/ceiling: 1.96 -Party wall between buildings: 0.96 -Others party wall: 1.05 -Internal partition: 2.57
Heater gain (W), $u_1(t)$.	0 to 4,500	
Occasional gain –small power, occupancy and lighting gain- (W), $u_2(t)$.	0 to 5,500	
Ventilation gain (w), $u_3(t)$.	0 to -5,500	
Exterior air temperature in February (°C), $u_4(t)$.	1 to 7	
Air temperature of the house (°C), $u_5(t)$.	14 to 24	

4.2 Selection of the Relevant Features

As detailed in Section 2, PCA (Fig. 1.a.) and CMLHL (Fig. 1.b.), which were both applied to this real-life problem, are instrumental in identifying the internal structure of the data. In this procedure, the data set gathered in the previous step is analysed. The objective is to find the relationships between the input variables with respect to the heat flux. CMLHL (Fig. 1.b.) allows to detect the relations of dependence and to choose the more relevant features. The outcome of this step is a new data set with the features for which a relationship with the heat flux is found.

4.3 System Identification Applied to Model Normal Building Operation

Once the relevant variables and their transformations have been extracted from the thermal dynamics data, then a model to fit the normal building operation should be obtained in order to identify bias in the heat flux through exterior walls in the building. The different model learning methods used in this study were implemented in Matlab© [18]. The experiment followed the identification procedure detailed in Section 3: the model structures were analyzed in order to obtain the models that best suited the dataset. The Akaike Information Criterion (AIC) is used to obtain the best degree of the model and its delay for each model structure. A total of seventy techniques were carried out to obtain the models, among which are the following: the frequency response analysis; the finite impulse response method (FIR); Black-box techniques: up to 31 different combinations of model structure and optimization techniques are considered -such as the least-squares method and QR factorization of ARX models [15]. The nonlinear model structures synthesis: up to thirty four different combinations of model structures and optimization techniques are considered -such as the Levenberg-Marquardt method and the recursive Gauss-Newton method for the NNARX, NNFIR, NNARMAX and NNOE models [15].

Three different residual analyses based on cross correlation are carried out: residual analysis between the residual $\hat{R}_\varepsilon^N(\tau)$, between the residual and the input $\hat{R}_{\varepsilon u}^N(\tau)$ and the non-linear residual correlation $\hat{R}_{\varepsilon^2 u^2}^N(\tau)$.

The heating process exhibits nonlinear behaviour between output and inputs. Due to this reason, the linear modelling techniques do not behave properly except in the linear behaviour zones of the process. Consequently, the heating process has been modelled using soft-computing techniques, specifically an ANN.

5 Experimentation and Results

In order to validate the proposal some realistic situations have been considered. A building in the E winter zone, in the city of Avila city is used as the actual building. This building was parameterised and the HTB2 simulation tool was used to gather the data set. This initial data set has been analysed in order to select the features that best described the relationships with the heat flux. As may be seen in Fig. 1, PCA (Fig. 1.a) and CMLHL (Fig. 1.b), both methods have identified the occasional gain as the most relevant variable but in the CMLHL projections (Fig. 1.b.) can be noticed more structured clusters than in the PCA projections.

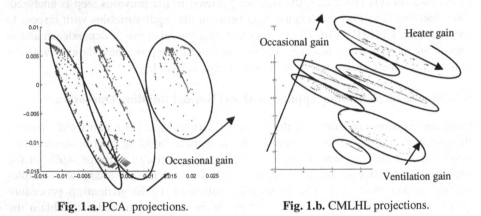

Fig. 1.a. PCA projections.   Fig. 1.b. CMLHL projections.

Fig. 1. PCA projections (Fig. 1.a.) and CMLHL projection (Fig. 1.b.) after 20000 iterations using a learning rate of 0.05, 3 output neurons p=0.3 and τ=0.3

Having analysed the results obtained with the CMLHL model (Fig. 1.b.) it is concluded that CMLHL has identified four relevant variables and seven clusters order by occasional gain. Inside each cluster there are further classifications by the heater gain, the ventilation gain and to a lesser degree the exterior air temperature. Then, the heat flux and the dataset may be said to have an interesting internal structure. When the dataset is considered sufficiently informative, the third step in the process begins. This step performs an accurate and efficient optimization of the heating system model to detect heat flux model in the building, through the application of several conventional modelling systems.

Thus, an ANN was used to monitor the thermal dynamics of the building. The objective was to find the best suite of polynomial model orders [n_a n_{b1} n_{b2} n_{b3} n_{b4} n_c n_d n_f

$n_{k1}\ n_{k2}\ n_{k3}\ n_{k4}$]. Using the data set from the previous stage and the Optimal Brain Surgeon (OBS) network pruning strategy to remove superfluous weights, the best suite model was found from the residual analysis. Fig. 2 shows the time responses of the heat flux - $y_1(t)$ - and of the estimated heat flux - $\hat{y}_1(t\,|\,m)$ - for the NNARX model described in Eq. (5). The x-axis shows the number of samples used in the estimation and validation of the model and the y-axis represents the normalized output variable range: which is the normalized heat flux of the house. The estimation and validation data sets include 2000 and 1126 samples, respectively, and have a sampling rate of 1 sample/minute. Fig. 3 indicates the final neural network structure chosen for modelling the heat flux.

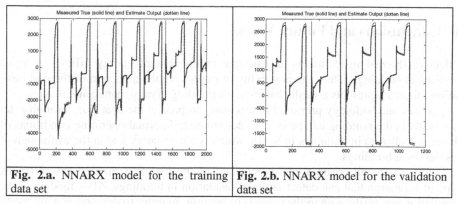

Fig. 2.a. NNARX model for the training data set | **Fig. 2.b.** NNARX model for the validation data set

Fig. 2. Output response of NNARX model: The actual output (solid line) is graphically presented with one-step-ahead prediction (dotted line). In Fig. 2.a. the real measure can be compared with the estimated data, while in Fig. 2.b. the real measure is compared with the validation data.

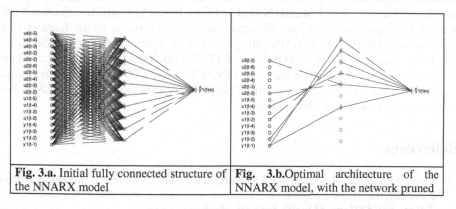

Fig. 3.a. Initial fully connected structure of the NNARX model | **Fig. 3.b.** Optimal architecture of the NNARX model, with the network pruned

Fig. 3. Optimal architecture of the NNARX model, with the network pruned, for the heat flux through exterior walls in the building -output $y_1(t)$- (Fig. 3.b.). Positive weights are represented in solid lines, while a dashed line represents a negative weight. A vertical line through the neuron represents a bias. The initial fully connected structure is shown in the Fig. 3.a.

From Fig. 2, it can be concluded that the pruned network NNARX model is able to simulate and predict the behaviour of the heat flux through exterior walls in the building –as a consequence of the heating process- and it is capable of modelling more than 91,4% of the actual measurements. The model thus obtained is ANN model, NNARX regressor, the order of the polynomials of the initial fully connected structure are $n_a=4$, $n_{b1}=4$, $n_{b2}=5$, $n_{b3}=1$, $n_{b4}=4$, $n_{k1}=2$, $n_{k2}=2$, $n_{k3}=2$, $n_{k4}=2$. The model was obtained using the regularized criterion. This model was optimised by CMLHL analysis, residual analysis and the pruned network, using OBS. The model structure has 10 hidden hyperbolic tangent units and 1 linear output unit. The network is estimated using the Levenberg-Marquardt method, and the model order is decided on the basis of the best AIC criterion of the ARX model.

6 Conclusions and Future Work

Effective thermal insulation is an essential component of energy efficient heating systems in buildings. Thus, the possibility of improving the detection of thermal insulation failures represents a fresh challenge for building energy management.

The new methodology proposed in this study to predict the heat flux through exterior walls in the building can be used to determine the normal operating conditions of thermal insulation in buildings in Spain, which is a mandatory test in the evaluation of insulation in buildings.

Future work will create a quality standard of the heat flux process, based on the type of insulation that can detect faults of insulation in buildings. Also, modelling the ventilation and infiltration in the process of heating, in order to develop generic methods, so that it can allow adequate ventilation in intelligent buildings, but efficiently, that is at the lowest possible cost.

Acknowledgments. We would like to extend our thanks to Phd. Magnus Nørgaard for his freeware version of Matlab Neural Network Based System Identification Toolbox. This research has been partially supported through projects of the Junta of Castilla and León (JCyL): [BU006A08], the project of the Spanish Ministry of Education and Innovation [CIT-020000-2008-2] and CIT-020000-2009-12, the project of Spanish Ministry of Science and Technology [TIN2008-06681-C06-04] and Grupo Antolin Ingenieria, S.A., within the framework of project MAGNO2008 - 1028.- CENIT also funded by the same Government Ministry.

References

1. Villar, J.R., de la Cal, E., Sedano, J.: Minimizing energy consumption in heating systems under uncertainty. In: Corchado, E., Abraham, A., Pedrycz, W. (eds.) HAIS 2008. LNCS (LNAI), vol. 5271, pp. 583–590. Springer, Heidelberg (2008)
2. de la Cal, E., Villar, J.R., Sedano, J.: A thermodynamical model study for an energy saving algorithm. In: Corchado, E., Wu, X., Oja, E., Herrero, Á., Baruque, B. (eds.) HAIS 2009. LNCS (LNAI), vol. 5572, pp. 384–390. Springer, Heidelberg (2009)
3. Lewis, P.T., Alexander, P.K.: A flexible model for dynamic building simulation: HTB2. Building and Environment 1, 7–16 (1990)

4. Freedman, J.H., Tukey, J.W.: Projection pursuit algorithm for exploratory data-analysis. IEEE Transactions on Computers 23(9), 881–890 (1974)
5. Corchado, E., MacDonald, D., Fyfe, C.: Maximum and minimum likelihood Hebbian Learning for Exploratory Projection Pursuit. Data Mining and Knowledge Discovery 8(3), 203–225 (2004)
6. Corchado, E., Fyfe, C.: Connectionist techniques for the identification and suppression of interfering underlying factors. International Journal of Pattern Recognition and Artificial Intelligence 17(8), 1447–1466 (2003)
7. Corchado, E., Fyfe, C.: Orientation selection using Maximum Likelihood Hebbian learning. International Journal of Knowledge-Based Intelligent Engineering 7(2) (2003)
8. Directive 2002/91/CE of the European Parliament and the Council of 16 December 2002 on the energy performance of buildings. Official Journal of the European Community (2003)
9. Real Decreto 314/2006, de 17 de Marzo. BOE núm 74, Reino de España (2006)
10. Pearson, K.: On lines and planes of closest fit to systems of points in space. Philosophical Magazine 2(6), 559–572 (1901)
11. Hotelling, H.: Analysis of a complex of statistical variables into principal components. Journal of Education Psychology 24, 417–444 (1933)
12. Seung, H.S., Socci, N.D., Lee, D.: The rectified Gaussian distribution. Advances in Neural Information Processing Systems 10, 350–356 (1998)
13. Fyfe, C., Corchado, E.: Maximum likelihood Hebbian rules. In: Proceedings of the 10th European Symposium on Artificial Neural Networks (ESANN 2002), pp. 143–148. D-side Publishers, Bruges (2002)
14. Corchado, E., Han, Y., Fyfe, C.: Structuring global responses of local filters using lateral connections. Journal of Experimental & Theoretical Artificial Intelligence 15(4), 473–487 (2003)
15. Ljung, L.: System Identification. Theory for the User, 2nd edn. Prentice-Hall, Upper Saddle River (1999)
16. Akaike, H.: Fitting autoregressive models for prediction. Ann. Inst. Stat. Math. 20, 425–439 (1969)
17. Bekiros, S.D., Georgoutsos, D.A.: Evaluating direction-of-change forecasting: Neurofuzzy models versus neural networks. Mathematical and Computer Modelling 46, 38–46 (2007)
18. Nørgaard. M.: Neural network based system identification toolbox. Technical Report 00-E-891, Dept. of Automation, Technical University of Denmark (2000)

Hybrid Pareto Differential Evolutionary Artificial Neural Networks to Determined Growth Multi-classes in Predictive Microbiology

M. Cruz-Ramírez*, J. Sánchez-Monedero, F. Fernández-Navarro,
J.C. Fernández, and C. Hervás-Martínez

Department of Computer Science and Numerical Analysis, University of Córdoba,
Rabanales Campus, Albert Einstein building 3° floor, 14071, Córdoba, Spain

Abstract. The main objective of this work is to automatically design artificial neural network, ANN, models with sigmoid basis units for multiclassification tasks in predictive microbiology. The classifiers obtained achieve a double objective: high classification level in the dataset and high classification level for each class. For learning, the structure and weights of the ANN we present an Hybrid Pareto Differential Evolution Neural Network (HPDENN), a Differential Evolutionary approach based on the PDE multiobjective evolutionary algorithm . The PDE algorithm is augmented with a local search using the improved Resilient Backpropagation with backtraking–$IRprop^+$ algorithm. To analyze the robustness of this methodology, we have applied it to two complex problems of classification in predictive microbiology (*Staphylococcus Aureus* and *Shigella Flexneri*). The results obtained in Correct Classification Rate (C) and Minimum Sensitivity (S) for each class show that the generalization ability and the classification rate in each class can be more efficiently improved within this multiobjective algorithm.

Keywords: Neural Networks; Multiobjective; Accuracy; Sensitivity; Multiclassification; Memetic Algorithms; Differential Evolution; Predictive Microbiology.

1 Introduction

Growth/No Growth models have been arisen in the predictive microbiology field as an approach to determine the ability of growth of microorganisms. At this respect, many works have been published in recent years for both spoilage and pathogenic microorganisms. This fact is mainly due to the necessity of gaining knowledge, by using mathematical models, about the microbial behaviour in limiting conditions that prevent growth. Consequently, these mathematical models may lead to more realistic estimations of food safety risks and can provide

* Corresponding author at: E-mail address: i42crram@uco.es Phone: +34-957218349
  This work has been partially subsidized by TIN 2008-06681-C06-03 (MICYT),
  FEDER funds and the P08-TIC-3745 project of the "Junta de Andalucía" (Spain).

N. García-Pedrajas et al. (Eds.): IEA/AIE 2010, Part III, LNAI 6098, pp. 646–655, 2010.
© Springer-Verlag Berlin Heidelberg 2010

useful quantitative data for the development of processes which allow production of safer food products [1].

The main problems in modelling microbial interface are related to the abrupt transition, i.e. the large change in the value of growth probability (p) at a very narrow range of environmental factors, that is encountered between growth and no growth conditions. Then, to define more properly the interface, growth and no growth should only be considered if all replicas (or at least a very high percentage of them) grow and do not grow, respectively. Indeed, in this paper four observed microbial responses are obtained based in the probability of growth for a microorganism, ($p = 1$ (growth), G; $0.5 \leq p < 1$ (growth high probability), GHP; $0 < p < 0.5$ (growth low probability), GLP, and $p = 0$ (no growth), NG).

The importance of the use of ANNs in predictive microbiology as an alternative to regression techniques was stated by Basheer and Hajmeer [2] due to their flexibility and high degree of accuracy to fit to experimental data. In this work, we discuss learning and generalization improvement of classifiers designed using a Multi-Objective Evolutionary learning Algorithm (MOEA) [3] for the determination of growth limits for two pathogenic *Staphylococcus Aureus* and *Shigella Flexneri*. We specifically investigate the generation of neural network classifiers that achieve high classification level for each class. The methodology is based on two measures: the Correct Classification Rate, C, and the Sensitivity, S, as the minimum of the sensitivities of all classes.

The basic structure of our MOEA has been modified by introducing an additional step, where some individuals in the population have been enhanced by a local search method. For this purpose, a Hybrid Pareto Differential Evolution Neural Network (HPDENN) algorithm has been developed.

The rest of the paper is organized as follows. In section 2 an explanation of Accuracy and Sensitivity is shown. Section 3 describes the HPDENN algorithm, followed by the experimental design in Section 4. Section 5 shows the obtained results and finally, the conclusions are drawn in Section 6.

2 Related Works

2.1 Accuracy and Sensitivity

In this section we present two measures to evaluate a classifier: the Correct Classification Rate or Accuracy, C, and the Sensitivity, S. To evaluate a classifier, the machine learning community has traditionally used C to measure its default performance. Actually, we simply have to realize that accuracy cannot capture all the different behavioural aspects found in two different classifiers in multiclassification problems. For that problems we consider two performance measures; the traditionally-used accuracy, $C = \frac{1}{N} \sum_{j=1}^{Q} n_{jj}$ (where Q is the number of classes, N is the number of patterns in training or testing and n_{jj} is the number of patterns from class j-th that are correctly classified), and the minimum of the sensitivities of all classes, S, that is, the lowest percentage of examples correctly predicted as belonging to each class, S_i, with respect to the total number of examples in the corresponding class, $S = \min\{S_i\}$. The Sensitivity versus

Accuracy pair (S, C) expresses two features associated with a classifier: global performance (C) and the rate of the worst classified class (S). The selection of S as a complementary measure of C can be justified upon considering that C is the weighted average of the sensitivities of each class.

One point in (S, C) space *dominates* another if it is above and to the right, i.e. it has more Accuracy and greater Sensitivity. Let C and S be respectively the accuracy and the sensitivity associated with a classifier g, then $S \leq C \leq 1 - (1 - S)p^*$, where p^* is the minimum of the estimated prior probabilities. Therefore, each classifier will be represented as a point in the shaded region in Fig. 1, hence the area outside of the triangle is marked as unfeasible.

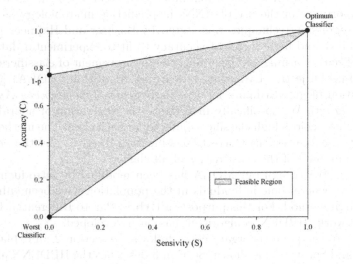

Fig. 1. Feasible region in the two dimensional (S, C) space

The area inside the triangle in Fig. 1 may be feasible (attainable), or may not be, depending upon the classifier and the difficulty of the problem. *A priori*, we can think that S and C objectives can be positively correlated, but while this may be true for small values of S and C, it is not for values close to 1 on both S and C. In this way competitive objectives are at the top right corner of the shaded region. This fact justifies the use of a MOEA.

3   Learning Methodology

At the beginning of this section describes the neural networks employed. Then, the proposed algorithm is shown and concludes with a description of the local search algorithm used.

3.1   Base Classifier Framework

In this paper we use the Base Classifier Framework described in [4].

3.2 Memetic Pareto Algorithm

We construct a MOEA with a local search algorithm, named as Hybrid Pareto Differential Evolutionary Neural Network (HPDENN), that tries to move the classifier population towards the optimum classifier located at the $(1, 1)$ point in the (S, C) space. The MOEA proposed is based on the PDE [5] and the local search algorithm is the Improved Resilient Backpropagation–$IRprop^+$ [6].

The Memetic Multiobjective Evolutionary Neural Network algorithm used in this work considers a fully specified ANN as an individual and it evolves architectures and connection weights simultaneously. The ANNs are represented using an object-oriented approach and the algorithm deals directly with the ANN phenotype. Each connection is specified by a binary value, which indicates whether the connection exists, and a real value representing its weight.

The HPDENN is based on the algorithm described in [4]. In HPDENN, local search does not apply to all childs to be added to the population. Instead, the childs most representative of the population are optimized in some generations. The pseudocode shown in Fig. 2.

```
 1: Create a random initial population
 2: while Stop condition is not met do
 3:     Evaluate population
 4:     Adjust the size of the population
 5:     while The population is not complete do
 6:         Select parents
 7:         Cross parents
 8:         Mutate the child
 9:         Evaluate the child
10:         Add the child in the population according to dominance relationships with the main parent
11:     end while
12:     if k mod(LS) = 0 then
13:         if Number of individuals of the first Pareto front of P_k < num then
14:             Apply iRprop+ to the individuals of the first Pareto front
15:         else
16:             Generate num cluster in the first Pareto front using K-means
17:             Apply iRprop+ to the num centers
18:         end if
19:     end if
20: end while
```

Fig. 2. HPDENN algorithm pseudocode

The algorithm starts generating a random population P_0 of size M. The population is sorted according to the non-domination concept explained in Section 2.1. Dominated individuals are removed from the population. Then the population is adjusted until its size is between 3 and half the maximum size by adding dominated individuals or deleting individuals according to their distance from the nearest neighbour respectively. After that, the population is completed with news child generated from three randomly selected individuals of the population. The child is generated by crossing the three parents. The resultant child is a perturbation of the main parent. This perturbation occurs with a probability P_c for each neuron. This perturbation may be structural, according to the expression (1), with which neurons are removed or added to the hidden layer;

or parametric, according to the expression (2) (for de hidden layer) or (3) (for the output layer), with which weight of the main parent is modified with the difference of the weights of secondary parents.

$$\rho_h^{child} \leftarrow \begin{cases} 1 \; if \; (\rho_h^{\alpha_1} +) \, N\,(0,1)\,(\rho_h^{\alpha_2} - \rho_h^{\alpha_3}) \geq 0.5 \\ 0 \; otherwise \end{cases} \tag{1}$$

$$w_{ih}^{child} \leftarrow w_{ih}^{\alpha_1} + N\,(0,1)\,(w_{ih}^{\alpha_2} - w_{ih}^{\alpha_3}) \tag{2}$$

$$w_{ho}^{child} \leftarrow w_{ho}^{\alpha_1} + N\,(0,1)\,(w_{ho}^{\alpha_2} - w_{ho}^{\alpha_3}) \tag{3}$$

Afterwards, the mutation operator is applied on the child. The mutation operator consists on adding or deleting neurons in the hidden layer depending on a P_m probability for each them. Taking into account the maximum number of hidden neurons that may exist in an individual in a specific problem, the probability will be used as many times as number of neuron has the classifier. If the neuron exists, is deleted, but if it does not exist, then it is created and the weights are established randomly, according to the expression (4).

$$\rho_h^{child} \leftarrow \begin{cases} 1 \; if \, \rho_h^{child} = 0 \\ 0 \; otherwise \end{cases} \tag{4}$$

Finally, the child is added to the population according to dominance relationships with the main parent. In some generations, depending on the size of the first Pareto front, local search is applied to all individuals in the first Pareto front or the most representative individuals in this front (obtained by the K-means algorithm [7]).

3.3   Local Search Algorithm

The combination of Evolutionary Algorithms, EA, and local procedures, EAs would carry out a global search inside the space of solutions, locating ANNs near the global optimum and the local procedure would arrive quick and efficiently to the best solution. This type of algorithms receives the name of Memetic or Hybrid Algorithms [8].

Many MOEAs use local optimizers to fine tune the ANNs weights. This is called "lifetime learning" and it consists in updating each individual regarding the approximation error. In addition, the weights modified during the lifetime learning are encoded back to the chromosome, which is known as the Lamarckian type of inheritance. This procedure has a high computational cost, something that we wanted to avoid. For this reason we propose the following.

For reducing the runtime, local search is applied only in three generations of evolution, the first to start the second half and the third at the end.

The local search algorithm is applied once the population is completed. Thus, local search is not applied to those children who are rejected. Local search does not apply to all individuals, but to the most representative. The process for selecting these individuals is as follows: If the number of individuals in the first

Pareto front is less than or equal to the desired number of clusters (num), local search is carried out without necessity of applying the K-means [7]. Instead, if the number of individuals of the first front is greater than num, the K-means is applied to the first front to get the most representative num individuals to which local search will be applied.

This local search will improve the obtained Pareto front in only one objective, specifically in the direction of the objective that tries to minimize the classification error.

As far as we are concerned, *Rprop* (resilient Backpropagation) algorithm [9] is used to be one of the best techniques in terms of convergence speed, accuracy and robustness.

4   Experiments

To analyze the robustness of the proposed methodology, in the experimental design we consider two complex problems on predictive microbiology for describing the behavior of pathogen and spoilage micro-organism under a given set of environmental conditions. The objective is to determine the conditions under which these microorganisms can be classified as G/GHP/GLP/NG, and to create a neural classifier for this purpose. Specifically, we have considered as problems the pathogen growth limits of *Staphylococcus Aureus* and *Shigella Flexneri*.

In all experiment, the population size for HPDENN is established to $M = 25$. The crossover probability is 0.8 and the mutation probability is 0.1. For IRprop$^+$, the adopted parameters are $\eta^+ = 1.2$, $\eta^- = 0.5$, $\Delta_0 = 0.0125$ (the initial value of the Δ_{ij}), $\Delta_{min} = 0$, $\Delta_{max} = 50$ and $Epochs = 25$, see [9] for IRprop$^+$ parameters description. The optimization process is applied 3 times during the execution (each 33.33% of generations, $LS = 33.33$) and use $num = 5$ cluster in the clustering algorithm. To start processing data, each one of the input variables was scaled in the ranks $[-1.0, 1.0]$ to avoid the saturation of the signal.

In Table 1 we can see the features for each dataset. For each database we had used the fractional factorial design present in different papers [10] for *Staphylococcus Aureus* and [11] for *Shighella Flexneri*) in order to find out the growth limits of each microorganism.

During the experiment, we train models using Entropy (E) and Sensitivity (S) as objective functions, but when validated using Accuracy (C) and Sensitivity (S). E is used instead of C in training because C is a discontinuous function, which makes convergence vary difficult in neural network optimization.

Once the Pareto front is built, two methodologies are considered in order to build a neural network model with the information of the models on it. These

Table 1. Characteristics for Datasets

Dataset	#Patterns	#Training patterns	#Test patterns	#Input variables	#Classes	#Patterns per class	p^*
S. Aureus	287	146	141	3	4	$(117, 45, 12, 113)$	0.0418
S. Flexneri	123	76	47	5	4	$(39, 8, 7, 69)$	0.0569

are called HPDENN-E and HPDENN-S. These methodologies provide us single models that can be compared with other classification methods existing in the literature. The process followed in these methodologies is the next one: once the first Pareto front is calculated using the patterns of the training set, the best individual belonging to the Pareto front on Entropy (EI) is chosen for HPDENN-E, and the best individual in terms of sensitivity (SI) is selected for HPDENN-S. Once this is done, the values of C and S are obtained by testing the EI and SI individuals. Therefore we will have an individual $EI_{testing} = (C_{testing}, S_{testing})$ and an individual $SI_{testing} = (C_{testing}, S_{testing})$. This is repeated 30 times and then the average and standard deviation obtained from the individuals is estimated, $\overline{EI}_{testing} = (\overline{C}_{testing}, \overline{S}_{testing})$ and $\overline{SI}_{testing} = (\overline{C}_{testing}, \overline{S}_{testing})$. The first expression is the average obtained taking entropy into account as the primary objective, and the second one is obtained by taking sensitivity into account as the primary objective. So, the opposite extremes of the Pareto front are taken in each of the executions. Hence, the first procedure is called HPDENN-E (Entropy) and the second HPDENN-S (Sensitivity).

5   Results

In Table 2 we present the values of the average and the standard deviation for C, S and runtime in 30 runs of all experiments performed. It can be seen that de HPDENN algorithm produces good results with respect to C, S and runtime. In fact, from a purely descriptive point of view, HPDENN algorithm obtains the best result in C in a dataset (equal that MPANN), the best result in S in *Staphylococcus Aureus* and the best result in runtime in *Shighella Flexneri* (with times well below those of MPANN).

In Fig. 3, we can see the graphical results obtained for HPDENN algorithm for the datasets *Staphylococcus Aureus* and *Shigella Flexneri* in the training (S, E) and the test (S, C) spaces. For the (S, E) space we select the Pareto front for one specific run output of the 30 realized for each dataset, concretely the execution that presents the best individual on Entropy in training, where Entropy and Sensitivity are the objectives that guide HPDENN. On the (S, C)

Table 2. Statistical Resuls for PDE, MPANN and HPDENN

Dataset	Method	$C(\%)$	$S(\%)$	runtime(s)
S. Aureus	PDE-E	$71,27 \pm 2,50$	0 ± 0	$49,34 \pm 5,24$
	PDE-S	$53,52 \pm 6,57$	$20,59 \pm 10,98$	$49,34 \pm 5,24$
	MPANN-E	$74,44 \pm 1,41$	0 ± 0	$309,14 \pm 11,51$
	MPANN-S	$66,71 \pm 8,87$	$9,36 \pm 10,82$	$309,14 \pm 11,51$
	HPDENN-E	$73,00 \pm 1,59$	0 ± 0	$48,72 \pm 3,70$
	HPDENN-S	$53,64 \pm 7,24$	$21,81 \pm 14,02$	$48,72 \pm 3,70$
S. Flexneri	PDE-E	$83,75 \pm 1,04$	0 ± 0	$234,90 \pm 17,93$
	PDE-S	$84,04 \pm 3,77$	$9,77 \pm 14,82$	$234,90 \pm 17,93$
	MPANN-E	$87,02 \pm 0,85$	0 ± 0	$1956,93 \pm 45,28$
	MPANN-S	$87,02 \pm 0,85$	0 ± 0	$1956,93 \pm 45,28$
	HPDENN-E	$87,02 \pm 1,16$	0 ± 0	$249,12 \pm 13,99$
	HPDENN-S	$86,59 \pm 2,80$	$2,22 \pm 8,45$	$249,12 \pm 13,99$

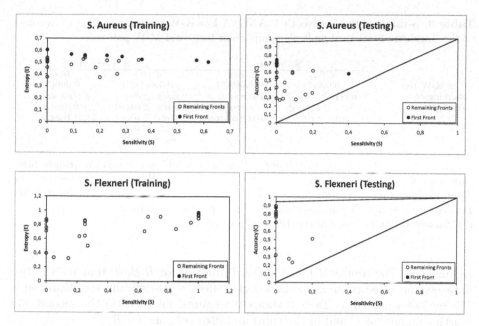

Fig. 3. Pareto front in training (S, E) and (S, C) associated values in testing in one specific run of the 30 runs carried out

testing graphics we show the S (Sensitivity) and C (Accuracy) values over the testing set for the individuals who are reflected in the (S, E) training graphics. Observe that the (S, C) values do not form Pareto fronts in testing, and the individuals that in the training graphics were in the first Pareto front, now can be located within space in a worst region. In general the structure of a Pareto front in training is not maintained in testing. Sometimes it is very difficult to obtain classifiers with a high percentage of classification and a high percentage of sensitivity, for this reason some fronts have few individuals.

In order to determine the best methodology for training MLP neural networks (in the sense of its influence on the Accuracy, C, and Sensitivity, S, in the test dataset), and minimum runtime, R, in the training procedure; an ANalysis Of the VAriance of one factor (ANOVA I) statistical method and the non parametric Kruskal-Wallis (K-W) tests were used. The tests were used, depending on the satisfaction of the normality hypothesis of C and R values. The factor F_i analyzes the effect over C (or S or R) of the i-th level of this factor, where F_i represents the different methodologies used in the algorithm, with levels: $i = 1$ to 6, (PDE-E (PE), PDE-S (PS), MPANN-E (ME), MPANN-S (MS), HPDENN-E (HE) and HPDENN-S (HS)). It is not possible to perform these test for S, because some methodologies in the two data sets present cero values. For R, the resuls are the same for -E and -S, and then there only exist three populations. The results of the ANOVA I analysis for test C values show that for the two datasets the six training methodologies effect is statistically significant at a 5% level of

Table 3. p-values of the Snedecor's F ANOVA I or K-W test and ranking of averages of the Tamhane Statistical multiple comparison tests and M-W pair test

	S. Aureus		S. Flexneri	
	$C(\%)$	$R(s)$	$C(\%)$	$R(s)$
F or K-W test	0.000(*)	0.000(*)	0.000(*)(°)	0.000(*)
Ranking of averages	$\mu_{ME} \geq \mu_{HE} \geq$ $\mu_{PE} \geq \mu_{MS} \geq$ $\mu_{HS} > \mu_{PS}$	$\mu_{MPANN} >$ $\mu_{PDE} \geq$ μ_{HPDENN}	$\mu_{HE} \geq \mu_{MS};$ $\mu_{HE} \geq \mu_{ME};$ $\mu_{HE} \geq \mu_{HS};$ $\mu_{HE} > \mu_{PS};$ $\mu_{HE} > \mu_{PE}$	$\mu_{MPANN} >$ μ_{HPDENN} $\geq \mu_{PDE}$

(*)*The average difference is significant with p-value=0.05, $\mu_A \geq \mu_B$: the fitness function A yields better results in mean than the fitness function B, but the difference are not significant; and $\mu_A > \mu_B$: the fitness function A yields better results in mean than the fitness function B with significant differences. The binary relation $\geq$ is not transitive.* (°)*Kruskal-Walis Test and Mann-Whitney pairs test.*

significance. The results of the ANOVA I analysis for R show that for the two datasets the three training methodologies effect is statistically significant at a 5% level of significance. Table 3 shows the results obtained (in the second and fourth columns for C and in the third and fifth columns for R).

Because there exists a significant difference in mean for C and R using the Snedecor's F or the K-W test; we perform, in the first case, under the normality hypothesis, a post hoc multiple comparison test of the mean of C and R obtained with the different levels of each factor. We perform a Tamhane test under normality and a pair-wise Mann-Whitney test in other case. Table 3 shows the results obtained (in the second and fourth columns for C and in the third and fifth columns for R). If we analyze the test results for Accuracy C, we can observe that HPDENN-E methodology obtains results that are, in mean, similar to the obtained with MPANN-E (the second best methodology) in the two datasets, but with a statistical significant less runtime. On the other hand, the results of average Sensitivity S show that the HPDENN-S methodology obtains a performance that is better than the rest of methodologies for S in $S.$ *Aureus* database and the second best for $S.$ *Flexneri*. It can be noticed than the -E methodologies classify the two databases but they leave a class with no well classified pattern.

6   Conclusions

In this paper we study the application of a memetic algorithm based on differential evolution in the resolution of multiclass classification problems in redictive microbiology. With this algorithm, we intend to obtain good results in Sensitivity and Accuracy (S, C), but also decrease the computational cost to reduce the runtime. We have proposed to apply local search to the most representative individuals of the population, selected through clustering techniques, to optimize the most promising individuals. This memetic algorithm has obtained similar results in C and better in S with respect to MPANN. In addition, HPDENN runs much faster. That's why we recommend using those HPDENN to address multiclass problems in which good results are desired in a reduced runtime.

References

1. Garcia, D., Ramos, A.J., Sanchis, V., Marin, S.: Predicting mycotoxins in foods: A review. Food Microbiology 26, 757–769 (2009)
2. Basheer, I.A., Hajmeer, M.N.: Artificial neural networks: fundamentals, computation, design and application. Journal of Microbiological Methods 43, 3–31 (2000)
3. Coello, C.A., Lamont, G.B., Veldhuizen, D.A.V.: Evolutionary Algorithms for Solving Multi-Objective Problems. Springer, Heidelberg (2007)
4. Fernández, J.C., Hervás-Martínez, C., Martínez-Estudillo, F.J., Gutiérrez, P.A., Cruz-Ramírez, M.: Memetic Pareto Differential Evolution for designing Artificial Neural Networks in Multiclassification Problems using Cross-Entropy versus Sensitivity. In: 10th International Work-Conference on Artificial Neural Networks (IWANN 2009), Salamanca, Spain, pp. 433–441 (2009)
5. Abbass, H.A.: A Memetic Pareto Evolutionary Approach to Artificial Neural Networks. In: Stumptner, M., Corbett, D.R., Brooks, M. (eds.) Canadian AI 2001. LNCS (LNAI), vol. 2256, pp. 1–12. Springer, Heidelberg (2001)
6. Igel, C., Hüsken, M.: Improving the Rprop Learning Algorithm. In: Proc. Proceedings of the Second International ICSC Symposium on Neural Computation (NC 2000), pp. 115–121. ICSC Academic Press (2000)
7. MacQueen, J.B.: Some Methods for classification and Analysis of Multivariate Observations. In: Proceedings of 5th Berkeley Symposium on Mathematical Statistics and Probability, vol. 1, pp. 281–297. University of California Press, Berkeley (1967)
8. Cotta, C., Moscato, P.: A Gentle Introduction To Memetic Algorithms. In: Glover, F., Kochenberger, G.A. (eds.) Handbook on Metaheuristics. Kluwer Academics, Dordrecht (2001)
9. Igel, C., Hüsken, M.: Empirical evaluation of the improved Rprop learning algorithms. Neurocomputing 50(6), 105–123 (2003)
10. Valero, A., Pérez-Rodríguez, F., Carrasco, E., Fuentes-Alventosa, J.M., García-Gimeno, R.M., Zurera, G.: Modelling the growth boundaries of Staphylococcus aureus: Effect of temperature, pH and water activity. International Journal Food Microbiology 133, 186–194 (2009)
11. Zaika, L.L., Moulden, E., Weimer, L., Phillips, J.G., Buchanan, R.L.: Model for the combined effects of temperature, initial pH, sodium chloride and sodium nitrite concentrations on anaerobic growth of Shigella Flexneri. International Journal of Food Microbiology 23, 345–358 (1994)

A Multiobjective GRASP for the 1/3 Variant of the Time and Space Assembly Line Balancing Problem

M. Chica[1], O. Cordón[1], S. Damas[1], and J. Bautista[2,3,*]

[1] European Centre for Soft Computing, Mieres (Asturias), Spain
{manuel.chica,oscar.cordon,sergio.damas}@softcomputing.es
[2] Universitat Politècnica de Catalunya, Barcelona, Spain
{joaquin.bautista}@upc.edu
[3] Nissan Chair
http://www.nissanchair.com

Abstract. Time and space assembly line balancing considers realistic multiobjective versions of the classical assembly line balancing industrial problems, involving the joint optimisation of conflicting criteria such as the cycle time, the number of stations, and/or the area of these stations. The aim of this contribution is to present a new algorithm, based on the GRASP methodology, for the 1/3 variant of this family of industrial problems. This variant involves the joint minimisation of the number and the area of the stations, given a fixed cycle time limit. The good behaviour of our proposal is demonstrated by means of performance indicators in four problem instances and a real one from a Nissan factory.

1 Introduction

An assembly line is made up of a number of workstations, arranged either in series or in parallel. Since the manufacturing of a production item is divided into a set of tasks, a usual and difficult problem is to determine how these tasks can be assigned to the stations fulfilling certain restrictions. Consequently, the aim is to get an optimal assignment of subsets of tasks to the stations of the plant. Moreover, each task requires an operation time for its execution.

A family of academic problems –referred to as simple assembly line balancing problems (SALBP)– was proposed to model this situation [1]. Taking this family as a base and adding spatial information to enrich it, Bautista and Pereira recently proposed a more realistic framework: the time and space assembly line balancing problem (TSALBP) [2]. This framework considers an additional space constraint to become a simplified version of real-world problems. The new space constraint emerged due to the study of the specific characteristics of the Nissan plant in Barcelona (Spain).

As many real-world problems, TSALBP formulations have a multicriteria nature because they contain three conflicting objectives to be minimised: the cycle time of the assembly line, the number of the stations, and the area of these stations. In this

* This work is supported by the UPC Nissan Chair and the Spanish Ministerio de Educación y Ciencia under project DPI2007-63026 and by the Spanish Ministerio de Ciencia e Innovación under project TIN2009-07727, both including EDRF fundings.

N. García-Pedrajas et al. (Eds.): IEA/AIE 2010, Part III, LNAI 6098, pp. 656–665, 2010.

paper we deal with the TSALBP-1/3 variant which tries to minimise the number of stations and their area for a given product cycle time. TSALBP-1/3 has an important set of hard constraints like precedences or cycle time limits for each station. Thus, the use of constructive approaches is more convenient than others like local or global search procedures [3]. In [4,5], we successfully tackled the TSALBP-1/3 by means of a specific procedure based on the Multiple Ant Colony System (MACS) algorithm [6], that approach is the state-of-the-art of TSALBP-1/3.

In addition, we proposed a multiobjective randomised greedy algorithm [4]. Although the performance of the MACS algorithm was better, the randomised greedy algorithm showed a good behaviour in some problems instances.

In this paper, we propose a multiobjective greedy randomised adaptive search procedure (GRASP) [7]. Its first stage corresponds to the randomised greedy construction presented in [4]. The second stage is based on a multiobjective local search with two improvement methods, one per objective. We consider two different GRASP approaches: the typical GRASP scheme and an alternative one, characterised by a random plus greedy construction. An experimentation is carried out in five problem instances, including a real-world one from the Nissan industry plant of Barcelona, Spain. Multi-objective performance indicators are used to analyse the behaviour of the algorithms.

The paper is structured as follows. In Section 2, the problem formulation is explained. Then, our new GRASP proposal to solve the problem is described in Section 3. The experimentation setup as well as the analysis of results are presented in Section 4. Finally, some concluding remarks and future research are discussed in Section 5.

2 The Time and Space Assembly Line Balancing Problem

The manufacturing of a production item is divided into a set V of n tasks. Each task j requires an operation time for its execution $t_j > 0$ that is determined as a function of the manufacturing technologies and the employed resources. Each station k is assigned to a subset of tasks S_k ($S_k \subseteq V$), called workload. A task j is assigned to a station k.

Each task j has a set of direct predecessors, P_j, which must be accomplished before starting it. These constraints are normally represented by means of an acyclic precedence graph, whose vertices stand for the tasks and where a directed arc (i, j) indicates that task i must be finished before starting task j on the production line. Thus, if $i \in S_h$ and $j \in S_k$, then $h \leq k$ must be fulfilled. Each station k presents a station workload time $t(S_k)$ that is equal to the sum of the tasks' lengths assigned to the station k. SALBP [1] focuses on grouping tasks in workstations by an efficient and coherent way.

The need of introducing space constraints in the assembly lines' design is based on two main reasons: (a) the length of the workstation is limited in the majority of the situations, and (b) the required tools and components to be assembled should be distributed along the sides of the line. Hence, an area constraint may be considered by associating a required area a_j to each task j and an available area A_k to each station k that, for the sake of simplicity, we shall assume it to be identical for every station and equal to $A : A = max_{\forall k \in \{1..n\}}\{A_k\}$. Thus, each station k requires a station area $a(S_k)$ that is equal to the sum of areas required by the tasks assigned to station k.

This leads us to a new family of problems called TSALBP in [2]. It may be stated as: given a set of n tasks with their temporal t_j and spatial a_j attributes ($1 \leq j \leq n$) and a precedence graph, each task must be assigned to a single station such that: (i) every precedence constraint is satisfied, (ii) no station workload time ($t(S_k)$) is greater than the cycle time (c), and (iii) no area required by any station ($a(S_k)$) is greater than the available area per station (A).

TSALBP presents eight variants depending on three optimisation criteria: m (the number of stations), c (the cycle time) and A (the area of the stations). Within these variants there are four multiobjective problems and we will tackle one of them, the TSALBP-1/3. It consists of minimising the number of stations m and the station area A, given a fixed value of the cycle time c, mathematically formulated as follows:

$$f^0(x) = m = \sum_{k=1}^{UB_m} \max_{j=1,2,\ldots,n} x_{jk} \qquad f^1(x) = A = \max_{k=1,2,\ldots,UB_m} \sum_{j=1}^{n} a_j x_{jk} \qquad (1)$$

where UB_m is the upper bound for the number of stations m, a_j is the area information for task j, x_{jk} is a decision variable taking value 1 if task j is assigned to station k, and n is the number of tasks.

We chose this variant because it is realistic in the automotive industry since the annual production of an industrial plant (and therefore, the cycle time c) is usually set by some market objectives. For more information we refer the interested reader to [4].

The specialised literature includes a large variety of exact and heuristic problem-solving procedures as well as metaheuristics for solving the SALBP [8]. However, there are not many proposals for solving the multiobjective 1/3 variant of the TSALBP. The MACS algorithm is the state-of-the-art for TSALBP-1/3 and was presented in [4], where its performance was compared against a multiobjective extension of the SALBP genetic algorithm and a multiobjective randomised greedy algorithm.

3   Our Multiobjective GRASP Proposal

In this section, our multiobjective proposal, based on the GRASP methodology, is described. Following a GRASP approach, a solution is generated at each iteration. As our problem is multiobjective, the solution will be included in a multiobjective archive if it is not dominated. The algorithm finishes with a set of non-dominated solutions generated during all the iterations. Section 3.1 explains the generation of the greedy solutions. The multiobjective local search applied to those solutions is detailed in Section 3.2.

3.1   First Stage: Generation of Randomised Greedy Solutions

In the creation of greedy solutions during GRASP we introduce randomness in two processes. On the one hand, we allow the random selection of the next task among the best candidates. It will be assigned to the current station. This process starts by creating a candidate list of unassigned tasks. For each candidate task j, we compute its heuristic value η_j. It measures the preference of assigning it to the current opened station. η_j is proportional to the processing time and area ratio of that task (normalised with the upper bounds given by the time cycle, c, and the sum of all tasks' areas, respectively). In addition, η_j is also proportional to the ratio between the number of successors of task j and the maximum number of successors of any eligible task.

Then, we sort all the candidate tasks according to their heuristic values and we set a quality threshold for them given by $q = max_{\eta_j} - \gamma \cdot (max_{\eta_j} - min_{\eta_j})$. All the candidate tasks with a heuristic value η_j greater or equal than q are selected to be in the restricted candidate list (RCL). In the former expression, γ is the diversification-intensification trade-off control parameter. When $\gamma = 1$ we find a completely random choice inducing the maximum possible diversification. In contrast, if $\gamma = 0$ the choice is close to a pure greedy decision, with a low diversification. Proceeding in this way, the RCL size is adaptive and variable, thus achieving a good diversification-intensification trade-off. Finally at the current construction step, we randomly select a task among the elements of the RCL. The construction procedure finishes when all the tasks have been allocated in the needed stations.

We have also considered an alternative construction procedure, introduced in [9] as random plus greedy construction. We will call it GRASP RCL2. It first chooses candidates randomly. Then it evaluates each candidate according to a greedy function to make the greedy choice. GRASP RCL2 first constructs the restricted candidate list (RCL2) with a fraction β ($0 \leq \beta \leq 1$) of the elements, selected at random. Then, it evaluates all the elements in RCL2, computing the heuristic value η_j. The iteration of the algorithm finishes selecting the best one, i.e. the element j having the highest η_j value. After a preliminary study, we found that $\beta = 0.5$ was the best value for this parameter.

On the other hand, we also introduce randomness in the decision of closing the current station according to a probability distribution given by the filling rate of the station:
$$p\,(closing\ k) = \frac{\sum_{i \in s_k} t_i}{c}.$$
The filling thresholds approach is also used to achieve a diverse enough Pareto front. A different threshold is selected in isolation at each iteration of the multiobjective randomised greedy algorithm, i.e., the construction procedure of each solution considers a different threshold.

The algorithm is run a number of iterations to generate different solutions. The final output consists of a Pareto set approximation composed of the non-dominated solutions.

3.2 Second Stage: Multiobjective Local Search

The second phase of the GRASP methodology consists of the improvement of each constructed solution considering a local search procedure. Mainly there are two stochastic local search approaches to multiobjective combinatorial optimisation problems [10]. The first one uses an acceptance criterion based on the weak component-wise ordering of the objective value vectors of neighbouring solutions. In addition, it maintains an unbounded archive of non-dominated solutions found during the search process [11]. The second class is based on different scalarizations of the objective function vector [12]. We will use the second approach for our GRASP proposal. A weighted sum scalarization of the two objectives of our problem, A and m, are calculated by the following formula: $Min\ (\lambda^1 A + \lambda^2 m)$.

This will be the function to be optimised by the local search. The weight vector $\lambda = (\lambda^1, \lambda^2)$ is created at random for each greedy solution constructed in the first phase of the GRASP.

In addition, we will consider two different local search methods, one per objective. The algorithm will apply them to the greedy solution depending on the weight vector λ. If $\lambda^1 > \lambda^2$, the local search method for minimising the A objective will be followed. Otherwise, the local search method for m will be considered. If the selected local search method does not succeed minimising the weighted sum scalarization, the other method is then applied.

The local improvement procedures for balancing problems are based on moves [11]. Our local search methods are based on such moves of the tasks. To explain this procedure, it is necessary to define for each task j the first, ES_j, and last, LP_j, station where a task may be assigned according to the assignment of its immediate predecessors and successors. In general, a move (j, k_1, k_2) describes the movement of the task j from station k_1 to station k_2, where $k1 \neq k2$ and $k2 \in [ES_j, LP_j]$. The description of the two local search methods for objectives A and m follows:

- **Local search method for objective A.** The pseudo-code of the method is described in Algorithm 1. In this method, the neighbourhood of the solution is built by means of the explained task moves. The goal is to reduce the area occupied by the station with the highest area by moving tasks to other stations. This process of selecting the station with the highest area and removing tasks from it is repeated $MAX\_ITERATIONS$ times. After a preliminary study, $MAX\_ITERATIONS = 20$ was considered.

- **Local search method for objective m.** In this case, the objective is reducing the number of stations m. From the initial greedy solution, a neighbour is created by moving all the tasks from the station with the lowest number of tasks to other stations, keeping a feasible solution. The loop of the method is shown in Algorithm 2. Given a station to be removed, the algorithm uses a branch & bound function (BB function in the pseudo-code) to search for a feasible solution having the tasks reallocated in other stations.

  The local search is also run $MAX\_ITERATIONS = 20$ times. In addition, we have to specify a maximum number of stations ($MAX\_STATIONS$) to limit the computational time of the local search.

4 Experiments

We explain the instances, parameters and performance indicators used for the experimentation. Then, we analyse the results of the different algorithms.

4.1 Problem Instances and Parameter Values

Five problem instances with different features have been selected for the experimentation: arc111 with cycle time limits of $c = 5755$ and $c = 7520$ (P1 and P2), lutz2

Algorithm 1. The pseudo-code of the local search method for the A objective.

```
1  while Iterations ≤ MAX_ITERATIONS do
2      Target_Station ← Find the station with the highest area;
3      Tasks ← Descending_Sort(tasks of Target_Station);
4      while no scalarization improvement AND Tasks ≠ ∅ do
5          Task ← First element of Set_Of_Tasks ;
6          Find First_Station and Last_Station of Task;
7          while no scalarization improvement do
8              Possible_Station ← station with the lowest area
                   ∈ [First_Station,Last_Station];
9              Move Task from Target_Station to Possible_Station;
10             if scalarization improvement then
11                 │ Make the movement permanent;
12             end
13         end
14         Remove Task from Set_Of_Tasks;
15     end
16     if Target_Station = ∅ then
17         │ Remove Target_Station;
18     end
19     Iterations ← Iterations +1;
20 end
21 return true if scalarization is improved;
```

Algorithm 2. The pseudo-code of the local search method for the m objective.

```
1  while Iterations ≤ MAX_ITERATIONS do
2      Stations ← Ascending sort with respect no. of tasks;
3      i ← 1;
4      while i ≤ MAX_STATIONS AND no scalarization improvement do
5          Target_Station ← i-th element of Set_Of_Stations;
6          Set_Of_Tasks ← Descending_Sort(tasks of Target_Station);
7          for all elements of Set_Of_Tasks do
8              │ Find First_Station and Last_Station;
9          end
10         BB(First element of Set_Of_Tasks, Set_Of_Tasks);
11         if no scalarization improvement then
12             │ i ← i + 1;
13         end
14     end
15     Iterations ← Iterations +1;
16 end
17 return true if scalarization is improved;
```

(P3), mukherje (P4), and nissan (P5). Originally, these instances but nissan were SALBP-1 instances[1] only having time information. However, we have created their area information by reverting the task graph to make them bi-objective (as done in [2]). In addition, we have considered a real-world problem instance (P5) corresponding to the assembly process of the Nissan Pathfinder engine, assembled at the Nissan industrial plant in Barcelona (Spain) [2]. The five TSALBP-1/3 instances considered are publicly available at http://www.nissanchair.com/TSALBP.

We run each algorithm 10 times with different random seeds, setting the time as stopping criteria (900 seconds). All the algorithms were launched in the same computer: Intel Pentium^{TM} D with two CPUs at 2.80GHz, and CentOS Linux 4.0. GRASP and GRASP RCL2 were launched with $\alpha = 0.3$ and $\beta = 0.5$ respectively. For the multiobjective local search, 20 as the maximum number of iterations and $MAX\_STATIONS = 20$. On the other hand, for the MACS algorithm, we consider 10 different ants, $\beta = 2$, an evaporation rate $\rho = 0.2$, and a value of 0.2 for the transition rule parameter q_0. The MACS algorithm also uses two ants for each of the five ants' thresholds considered $\{0.2, 0.4, 0.6, 0.7, 0.9\}$ to make the algorithm multicolony.

4.2 Multiobjective Performance Indicators

We will consider two different multiobjective performance indicators [13] to evaluate the quality of the new GRASP proposal with respect to the TSALBP-1/3 state-of-the-art, the MACS algorithm.

On the one hand, we selected one unary performance indicator: the hypervolume ratio (HVR). On the other hand, we have also considered a binary performance indicator, the set coverage indicator C. We have used boxplots based on the C indicator that calculates the dominance degree of the approximate Pareto sets of every pair of algorithms (see Figure 1). Each rectangle contains five boxplots representing the distribution of the C values for a certain ordered pair of algorithms in the five problem instances (P1 to P5). Each box refers to algorithm A in the corresponding row and algorithm B in the corresponding column and gives the fraction of B covered by A ($C(A, B)$).

In addition, in Figure 2 we show an example of the aggregated Pareto front approximation for instance P1 to allow a visual analysis of the results.

4.3 Analysis of Results

The experimental results obtained by the two multiobjective GRASP variants, i.e. GRASP and GRASP RCL2, and the MACS algorithm can be seen in the C performance indicator boxplots of Figure 1, the HVR values in Table 1, and the attainment surfaces of Figure 2.

Considering the C boxplots and only the first four problem instances, from P1 to P4, we can draw the following conclusions:

---

[1] Available at http://www.assembly-line-balancing.de

- If we compare MACS with GRASP, our new multiobjective proposal outperforms the state-of-the-art algorithm. Boxplots are clear and GRASP obtains better[2] Pareto sets than MACS in all the instances but P5 (nissan). As the last problem instance is different from the rest, it will be discussed later.
- The behaviour of GRASP RCL2 with respect to MACS is not as clear as the previous comparison. GRASP RCL2 dominates MACS in two instances, P1 and P4. However, the Pareto sets obtained by the MACS algorithm are better in the P2 and P3 instances. Therefore, both algorithms behave similarly and we cannot say which one is better just taking in mind the C performance indicator.
- Comparing both versions of GRASP in the C boxplots (Figure 1), it can be observed that the original one is significantly "better" than GRASP RCL2. This behaviour is common in all the problem instances.

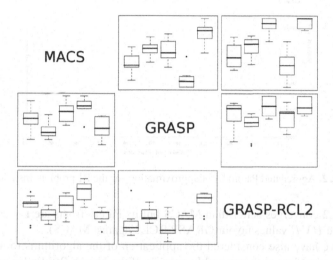

Fig. 1. C metric values represented by boxplots comparing MACS vs. the new GRASP proposals

Hence, according to the binary performance indicator C, the approach followed up by GRASP is useful to tackle the TSALBP-1/3. Nevertheless, the greedy construction phase is important for the problem solving since the difference between GRASP and GRASP RCL2 is high. Thus, selecting one task at random after restricting the candidate list is better than selecting the best task according to the greedy value after the random selection of the candidate tasks.

We can draw similar conclusions analysing the HVR values (see Table 1). The HVR values of GRASP are always the highest in all the problem instances but P5 (nissan). In contrast, if we compare the values of GRASP RCL2 and MACS, we can see how GRASP RCL2 is always better or equal than MACS. This means that generally

---

[2] When we refer to the best or better performance comparing the C performance indicator values of two algorithms we mean that the Pareto set derived from one algorithm significantly dominates that one achieved by the other. Likewise, the latter algorithm does not dominate the former one to a high degree.

Table 1. Mean and standard deviation values (in brackets) of the HVR metric

	P1	P2	P3	P4	P5
MACS	0.925 (0.006)	0.914 (0.012)	0.877 (0.024)	0.886 (0.012)	**0.939 (0.009)**
GRASP	**0.969 (0.005)**	**0.935 (0.008)**	**0.889 (0.034)**	**0.944 (0.013)**	0.925 (0.027)
GRASP RCL2	0.948 (0.007)	0.919 (0.007)	0.827 (0.037)	0.909 (0.008)	0.896 (0.008)

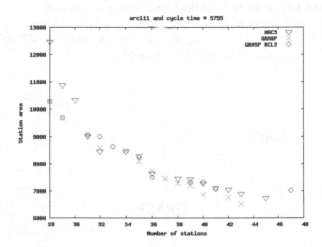

Fig. 2. Aggregated Pareto front approximation for the P1 problem instance

GRASP RCL2 converges better than MACS but its Pareto fronts are not as diverse as in MACS (the HVR values favour GRASP RCL2 against MACS).

As said, we have also considered the application of the algorithms to a real-world problem corresponding to the assembly process of the Nissan Pathfinder engine at the plant of Barcelona (Spain). The assembly of these engines is divided into 378 operation tasks, although we have grouped these operations into 140 different tasks. The Nissan instance data is also available at *http://www.nissanchair.com/TSALBP*.

With this instance, P5, results are different. If we analyse the C performance indicator (fifth column of the boxplots in Figure 1), MACS is better than both versions of GRASP. The corresponding values for the HVR performance indicator, Table 1, show the same behaviour, i.e. the MACS algorithm obtains Pareto sets of better quality.

Figure 2 graphically shows the aggregated Pareto fronts corresponding to P1 and P5. The same conclusions arise. GRASP is the best algorithm considering all instances but P5 (second Pareto front of the figure). However, MACS is more suitable for the Nissan problem instance, P5.

The P5 instance has some features making it different from the rest of the instances. As explained, it is the real case of the Nissan industry plant placed in Barcelona. The main difference of this problem instance with respect to the remainder is the area of the tasks to be allocated. Almost all the tasks have a very low area (less than one unit of area). Even more than 25 tasks have no area assigned. This particular characteristic makes the MACS algorithm more competitive to solve this instance, making the Pareto set approximations spread out in a better way.

5   Concluding Remarks and Future Works

In this contribution, we have successfully applied a new algorithm based on the GRASP methodology to solve the TSALBP-1/3. The new algorithm is multiobjective to tackle the industrial problem and makes use of a multiobjective local search procedure with two problem-specific local improvement methods, one per objective.

Good results were achieved in the majority of the problem instances, obtaining even better results than the state-of-the-art algorithm, MACS. Nevertheless, the MACS algorithm still outperforms our multiobjective GRASP in the real-world Nissan instance. Therefore, we aim to explore in future works the application of the local search to the MACS algorithm as well as multiobjective memetic algorithms to increase the quality of the Pareto fronts.

References

1. Scholl, A.: Balancing and Sequencing of Assembly Lines, 2nd edn. Physica-Verlag, Heidelberg (1999)
2. Bautista, J., Pereira, J.: Ant algorithms for a time and space constrained assembly line balancing problem. European Journal of Operational Research 177, 2016–2032 (2007)
3. Glover, F., Kochenberger, G.A. (eds.): Handbook of Metaheuristics. Kluwer Academic, Dordrecht (2003)
4. Chica, M., Cordón, O., Damas, S., Bautista, J.: Multi-objective, constructive heuristics for the 1/3 variant of the time and space assembly line balancing problem: ACO and randomised greedy. Technical Report AFE-09-01, European Centre for Soft Computing, Asturias, Spain (2009) (submitted to Information Sciences)
5. Chica, M., Cordón, O., Damas, S., Bautista, J.: Adding diversity to a multiobjective ant colony algorithm for time and space assembly line balancing. In: 2009 IEEE International Symposium on Assembly and Manufacturing (ISAM 2009), Suwon, Korea, pp. 364–379 (2009)
6. Barán, B., Schaerer, M.: A multiobjective ant colony system for vehicle routing problem with time windows. In: 21st IASTED Conference, Innsbruck, Germany, pp. 97–102 (2003)
7. Feo, T.A., Resende, M.G.C.: Greedy randomized adaptive search procedures. Journal of Global Optimization 6, 109–133 (1995)
8. Scholl, A., Becker, C.: State-of-the-art exact and heuristic solution procedures for simple assembly line balancing. European Journal of Operational Research 168(3), 666–693 (2006)
9. Resende, M.G.C., Werneck, R.F.: A hybrid heuristic for the p-median problem. Journal of Heuristics 10, 59–88 (2004)
10. Teghem, J., Jaszkiewicz, A.: Multiple objective metaheuristics for combinatorial optimization: A tutorial. In: 4th Metaheuristic International Conference (MIC 2003), Kyoto, Japan, pp. 25–28 (2003)
11. Rachamadugu, R., Talbot, B.: Improving the equality of workload assignments in assembly lines. International Journal of Production Research 29, 619–633 (1991)
12. Jaszkiewicz, A.: Genetic local search for multiple objective combinatorial optimization. European Journal of Operational Research 137(1), 50–71 (2002)
13. Coello, C.A., Lamont, G.B., Van Veldhuizen, D.A.: Evolutionary Algorithms for Solving Multi-objective Problems, 2nd edn. Springer, Heidelberg (2007)

Author Index

672   Author Index